D1154644

# Philosophy of Religion

*edited by*

## GEORGE L. ABERNETHY
DAVIDSON COLLEGE

*and*

## THOMAS A. LANGFORD
DUKE UNIVERSITY

# PHILOSOPHY

## OF

# RELIGION

*A Book of Readings*

## SECOND EDITION

THE MACMILLAN COMPANY

COLLIER-MACMILLAN LIMITED
London

© Copyright, The Macmillan Company, 1968

All rights reserved. No part of this book may be reproduced or transmitted in any form or by any means, electronic or mechanical, including
photocopying, recording or by any information storage and retrieval
system, without permission in writing from the Publisher.

Second Printing, 1969

Earlier edition © 1962 by The Macmillan Company.

Library of Congress catalog card number: 68–10237

THE MACMILLAN COMPANY
COLLIER-MACMILLAN CANADA, LTD., TORONTO, ONTARIO

Printed in the United States of America

*for Helen and Ann Marie*

# Preface to
# the Second Edition

The favorable reception of the first edition of *Philosophy of Religion* and the growing list of adoptions have encouraged the publisher and the editors to bring out a second edition. Our experience has confirmed the hopes and principles expressed in the original preface. We trust that this second edition will be a stronger and more useful book.

In preparing this edition a number of changes have been made. We have deleted nine selections from the former edition. In an effort to be more representative we have included material from Alfred North Whitehead and Rudolf Otto in our opening chapter. The increasing interest in the ontological argument has encouraged us to add substantial essays by Norman Malcolm, J. N. Findlay, Charles Hartshorne. Several contemporary writers not previously included are now represented: Paul van Buren provides insight into the claims of the death-of-God theologians; Kai Nielsen discusses the problem of verification in theology; and Ninian Smart adds a new dimension to probing the problem of evil. A short selection from Ludwig Wittgenstein on death has been added to Chapter VII, and Charles Hartshorne is represented a second time in an essay on the way God may be known. In addition, the selection from Schleiermacher has been changed; we have used a portion from the second speech *On Religion,* which we think is more understandable for the student than our previous selection. The material from Feuerbach has been enlarged and several selections have been repositioned in the book to provide more natural complementarity.

One of the advantages of this second edition is that the total number of pages has been increased. This has provided the opportunity for longer, often more adequate, selections. Finally, the Suggested Additional Readings have been enlarged and brought up to date to provide the instructor with more alternatives for supplementary assignments.

Special thanks are due to a number of teachers. Suggestions and comments have come from many who have used the first edition—some in letters to the editors, some in conversations at professional gatherings, and some in comments offered to the representatives of the publisher. We wish to record again our gratitude to John Dennis Moore and members of his staff at Macmillan for their assistance in the preparation of this second edition.

G. L. A.

T. A. L.

# Preface to
# the First Edition

We believe that serious study and discussion of philosophical issues in religion are on the rise. Among scholars in the fields of philosophy and theology there is more interest in the work being done in each other's discipline and more of an effort to take seriously each other's interests than at any time for several decades. Philosophers and theologians are beginning to talk to each other, even if hesitantly and intermittently. Among students also there appears to be increased interest, and even so superficial a criterion as the phenomenal sale in college communities of paperbacks in the fields of philosophy and religion seems to support this contention. Philosophy of religion should be the bridge discipline which facilitates this kind of communication. We hope our book of readings will sustain such a dialogue.

The contemporary focus of our volume is deliberate. We believe that much recent work in this area is significant and should be better known. The distinctive contributions and claims of both contemporary theologians and philosophers have moved far beyond the positions of the early nineteen hundreds. For instance, in Britain philosophers trained in linguistic analysis have been seriously turning to the problems of religious language. Although it is still too early to predict the full significance of that development, thoughtful students should be made aware of this growing field. In Europe and America existentialism has become prominent. We believe that something of this orientation should also be presented to the student.

At the same time, we have included important historical and traditional material. These selections furnish indispensable background for the new developments and deserve to be carefully studied. However, we have omitted readings from Plato and Aristotle, in spite of their significant contributions to the origins of the philosophy of religion, because their writings are already easily obtainable. Rather we have included source material less likely to be found in the average college library or, if found, not available in multiple copies. The lists of suggested readings at the end of each section of our book include references to works of these two philosophers and of other writers whom we acknowledge are important. These lists should, therefore, be regarded as integral to each section and not merely adventitious.

Since philosophy of religion is a serious discipline that demands careful, purposeful study, students of the subject should be required to do systematic and rigorous work. Accordingly, we have avoided selections that "write down" to students and have attempted instead to provide selections with sufficient vitality to draw students into the lively experience of philosophizing. Further, we have chosen deliberately to confine the book to the Western tradition of philosophy and theology. The soundness of a course in philosophy of religion depends in part upon a careful delimitation of objectives and materials. In addition, most of our American students come with some experience, however minimal, of Judaism and Christianity. A sound liberal education, it seems to us, ought to make them aware of the basic philosophical issues and positions prominent in that heritage.

Some teachers have suggested we include materials from Eastern religions. We agree that materials from the Eastern religious and philosophical tradition are interesting and unquestionably significant, but to evaluate them solely in Western terms is to falsify them. The Eastern tradition, too, deserves systematic and rigorous study if it is to be understood, and six or seven selections from that tradition included in our book would not have served to represent it adequately. The teacher who is competent to interpret the Eastern literature and who is fortunate enough to have students with prior study of world religions will find the necessary materials already collected for him. Professor William Theodore de Bary and his associates have brilliantly assembled the central materials in a three-volume *Introduction to Oriental Civilizations: Sources of Indian Tradition, Sources of the Japanese Tradition, Sources of Chinese Tradition.* S. Radhakrishnan and C. A. Moore have edited a useful book, *A Sourcebook in Indian Philosophy.* Heinrich R. Zimmer's *Philosophies of India,* a first-rate work of scholarship, is available in paperback. Among older works Paul Deussen's *The Philosophy of the Vedanta* and *The Philosophy of the Upanishads* contain useful selections and commentary. In the Mentor series of paperbacks, the instructor will find Professor E. A. Burtt's anthology *The Teachings of the Compassionate Buddha,* as well as the Bhagavad Gita and the Upanishads (without commentary) in fresh translation. Students of the philosophy of religion who have first become familiar with their own tradition will be in a better position to study these important Eastern materials.

Our object is to provide a useful collection of sources, without claim that we have been able to include all that a student should read in a semester. Individual teachers have different orientations and will prefer different materials. Although we too have our own perspectives, we have tried to be fair to various points of view and thus to philosophy of religion as a whole. If we have succeeded in this and in assembling writings that provoke the thought and interest of students, we shall be pleased.

This book has brought together a person from philosophy and one from theology in an effort of common concern. The experience has proved to be stimulating and rewarding. We covet such interdisciplinary opportunity for others. Our appreciation should be expressed to more people than we can name. We especially acknowledge the generous cooperation of many authors and publishers without which this volume would not have been possible. Many friends and colleagues have made suggestions to us; for their criticisms and encouragement we are indebted. The manuscript has been read, in whole or in part, by Professor Horace L. Friess of Columbia University, Professor John A. Hutchison of Claremont Graduate School, Professor Michael Wyschogrod of Hunter College, Mr. J. P. Fell, Professor Henry LeRoy Finch of Sarah Lawrence College, and Professor William A. Gerhard of Brooklyn College. We are grateful for their searching criticism and friendly advice. Finally a word of thanks to Messrs. Roger Howley and John Dennis Moore, of Macmillan, for their competent help in the completion of this book.

G. L. A.

T. A. L.

# Contents

[xiii]

# III.

## The Problem of the
## Existence of God

## IV.

## How Is God Known?

## —Some Contemporary Answers                        249

## V.

## Religious Language                                 331

# VI.

## The Problem of Evil                                           425

# VII.

## Immortality and Eschatology                                  495

# I.   What Is Religion?

R ELIGION IS A pervasive and almost universal phenomenon in human societies. Yet one of the striking facts about the word *religion* is that, although we use it without hesitation, we find it very difficult to tell others what we mean by it. The most casual analysis of definitions of religion will often reveal that the authors treat some significant aspect of religion as though it were the whole or offer a definition so general as to be of little help in distinguishing religion from other phenomena. The lack of agreement among students of religion as to the nature of the subject is an inevitable consequence of wide differences in intellectual orientation and basic assumptions. Perhaps the most common orientations are rooted in the assumption that religion either has a truly objective referent or is merely a subjective experience. Theories of religion, then, often involve working out or modifying one of these assumptions, or attempting to combine them.

It may be debated whether any one religion is completely unique or whether all religions are basically the same with only trivial differences. But it is obvious that different religions do attempt, to some extent, to give different answers to human questions. Definitions and theories of religion reflect these differences. The philosophy of religion is, among other things, an attempt to think critically and comprehensively about these religious beliefs and claims. Clarity of statements, consistency of claims, adequacy of evidence, validity of argument and comprehensiveness of generalization are matters of primary concern for the philosophy of religion as it seeks to examine the definitions and theories of religion.

The selections which follow bring together representative thought from major western traditions on the understanding of

the nature of religion. The selections form a series of contrasts
ranging from mysticism, which claims direct intuitive awareness
of ultimate reality and therefore considers itself supra-rational,
to rationalism which includes the attempt to define religion
within the limits of reason alone. Definitions will be found
which view religion primarily in terms of supra-naturalism, that
is, in terms of a power beyond the visible, observable world,
and those which eschew all supra-natural reference. There are
also contrasts between views of religion as essentially a personal
or subjective reality and of religion as primarily a social concern.

These selections are further representative of writers from
different academic disciplines: e.g., philosophy, theology, psychoanalysis and sociology. While the types of interpretations included are not exhaustive, they should be adequate to provide
significant background for the discussion of the nature of religion. The writings are arranged in what is generally a chronological order, but this should not be taken to imply that the
positions they present are limited in their influence to specific
historical eras; many of them have had lively champions in several centuries.

The first selection, from the writings of Plotinus, represents
the mystical tradition. Plotinus is one of the major philosophical
figures of the first centuries of the Christian era and his type of
mystical religious experience has influenced the thinking of
many subsequent thinkers.

Friedrich Schleiermacher and Søren Kierkegaard represent
two different positions from within the Christian tradition.
Schleiermacher found God and religion at the deepest level of
every man's experience, in the natural and universal "feeling of
absolute dependence." Kierkegaard, on the other hand, felt that
every man in his natural experience is alien to God and separated from Him by an infinite gulf, so that every religion arising
out of man's experience is necessarily false. True religion, he
claims, comes into being only when the infinite gulf is bridged
by a revelation which is appropriated in "a leap of faith" that
defies the experience of alienation and affirms the encounter
with the true God as revealed in Jesus Christ. A contemporary
of these men who represents a position which is opposed to
Christianity is Ludwig Feuerbach. Feuerbach, like his contemporaries, is concerned with the subjective basis of religion. But,
unlike them, he pushes his analysis to the point of questioning
the reality of the object of religious faith. Feuerbach insists that

the gods are only the product of human imagination and thereby he reduces the religious realm to man and man's inner life. The psychological analyses of religion by these men constitute a fundamental contribution in the long line of investigations in this field.

Both John Dewey and William James, American philosophers in the first decades of this century, attempt to enlarge the province of religion: Dewey by broadening the social inclusiveness of religion and James by broadening the dimensions of the individual self. Dewey argues for the reality of a religious attitude which he finds compatible with a naturalistic and humanistic view of life. In other words, Dewey denies that reality has a supranatural significance although he insists that there is a basis for a strong sense of obligation to one's fellowman in a rational assessment of life. In Dewey's thought interest in the social implications of religion is central. William James concludes his famous study, *The Varieties of Religious Experience,* with his own interpretation of religion as the "subconscious continuation of the conscious life." James is one of the important figures responsible for our century's developing interest in man's subconscious life. Because of this dimension of life, James claims that man knows himself to be continuous with a wider, subconscious self in terms of which he can find a religious meaning.

Continuing with interpreters from the present century, we have selections from widely divergent perspectives. Alfred North Whitehead, from the vantage point of his organismic philosophy, delineates the various aspects of religion as it is embodied in external expressions, beliefs, and intellectual interpretations. Rudolf Otto examines the phenomena of common and ordinary forms of religious experience in order to reveal the basic character of religious awareness, an awareness which underlies the various forms of interpretation, rite, moral activity and worship in all religions. W. T. Stace represents a modern philosophical mysticism. Stace understands religion as the desire to break completely away from existence and to get beyond immediate reality "into that nothingness where the great light is." God remains a mystery, but a mystery in which man can find his true being. Finally, Erich Fromm, a contemporary psychoanalyst, looks at religion from the perspective of psychoanalytic theory. Fromm argues that in humane religion, which he espouses, "God is the image of man's higher self, a symbol of what man potentially is or ought to become." Thus the problem of religion is not the problem of God, but the problem of man. It is the unique nature of man's religious experience which Fromm wants to delineate and assess.

A critical examination of each of these points of view will lead one to an awareness of the varieties of religious experience and will form a background against which comparative judgments can be made.

# PLOTINUS

*Plotinus* (204–270), a Neo-Platonic philosopher, taught at Rome and became one of the germinal influences in Western mysticism. His book *The Enneads* contains his most important philosophical and religious writings.

## The Enneads

7. Therefore we must ascend again towards the Good, the desired of every Soul. Anyone that has seen This, knows what I intend when I say that it is beautiful. Even the desire of it is to be desired as a Good. To attain it is for those that will take the upward path, who will set all their forces towards it, who will divest themselves of all that we have put on in our descent: so, to those that approach the Holy Celebrations of the Mysteries, there are appointed purifications and the laying aside of the garments worn before, and the entry in nakedness—until, passing, on the upward way, all that is other than the God, each in the solitude of himself shall behold that solitary-dwelling Existence, the Apart, the Unmingled, the Pure, that from Which all things depend, for Which all look and live and act and know, the Source of Life and of Intellection and of Being.

And one that shall know this vision—with what passion of love shall he not be seized, with what pang of desire, what longing to be molten into one with This, what wondering delight! If he that has never seen this Being must hunger for It as for all his welfare, he that has known must love and reverence It as the very Beauty; he will be flooded with awe and gladness, stricken by a salutary terror; he loves with a veritable love, with sharp desire; all other loves than this he must despise, and disdain all that once seemed fair.

This, indeed, is the mood even of those who, having witnessed the manifestation of Gods or Supernals, can never again feel the old delight in the comeliness of material forms: what then are we to think of one that contemplates Absolute Beauty in Its essential integrity, no accumulation of flesh and matter, no dweller on earth or in the heavens—so perfect Its purity—

From Plotinus, *The Enneads,* trans. Stephen McKenna, revised by B. S. Page, pp. 61–64. Copyright, 1956, by Faber and Faber. Used by permission of Faber and Faber, Ltd., and Pantheon Books, Inc.

far above all such things in that they are non-essential, composite, not primal but descending from This?

Beholding this Being—the Choragus of all Existence, the Self-Intent that ever gives forth and never takes—resting, rapt, in the vision and possession of so lofty a loveliness, growing to Its likeness, what Beauty can the Soul yet lack? For This, the Beauty supreme, the absolute, and the primal, fashions Its lovers to Beauty and makes them also worthy of love.

And for This, the sternest and the uttermost combat is set before the Souls; all our labour is for This, lest we be left without part in this noblest vision, which to attain is to be blessed in the blissful sight, which to fail of is to fail utterly.

For not he that has failed of the joy that is in colour or in visible forms, not he that has failed of power or of honours or of kingdom has failed, but only he that has failed of only This, for Whose winning he should renounce kingdoms and command over earth and ocean and sky, if only, spurning the world of sense from beneath his feet, and straining to This, he may see.

8. But what must we do? How lies the path? How come to vision of the inaccessible Beauty, dwelling as if in consecrated precincts, apart from the common ways where all may see, even the profane?

He that has the strength, let him arise and withdraw into himself, foregoing all that is known by the eyes, turning away for ever from the material beauty that once made his joy. When he perceives those shapes of grace that show in body, let him not pursue: he must know them for copies, vestiges, shadows, and hasten away towards That they tell of. For if anyone follow what is like a beautiful shape playing over water—is there not a myth telling in symbol of such a dupe, how he sank into the depths of the current and was swept away to nothingness? So too, one that is held by material beauty and will not break free shall be precipitated, not in body but in Soul, down to the dark depths loathed of the Intellective-Being, where, blind even in the Lower-World, he shall have commerce only with shadows, there as here.

"Let us flee then to the beloved Fatherland": this is the soundest counsel. But what is this flight? How are we to gain the open sea? For Odysseus is surely a parable to us when he commands the flight from the sorceries of Circe or Calypso—not content to linger for all the pleasure offered to his eyes and all the delight of sense filling his days.

The Fatherland to us is There whence we have come, and There is The Father.

What then is our course, what the manner of our flight? This is not a journey for the feet; the feet bring us only from land to land; nor need you think of coach or ship to carry you away; all this order of things you must set aside and refuse to see: you must close the eyes and call instead upon another vision which is to be waked within you, a vision, the birth-right of all, which few turn to use.

9. And this inner vision, what is its operation?

Newly awakened it is all too feeble to bear the ultimate splendour. There-fore the Soul must be trained—to the habit of remarking, first, all noble pursuits, then the works of beauty produced not by the labour of the arts but by the virtue of men known for their goodness: lastly, you must search the souls of those that have shaped these beautiful forms.

But how are you to see into a virtuous Soul and know its loveliness?

Withdraw into yourself and look. And if you do not find yourself beau-tiful yet, act as does the creator of a statue that is to be made beautiful: he cuts away here, he smoothes there, he makes this line lighter, this other purer, until a lovely face has grown upon his work. So do you also: cut away all that is excessive, straighten all that is crooked, bring light to all that is overcast, labour to make all one glow of beauty and never cease chiselling your statue, until there shall shine out on you from it the godlike splendour of virtue, until you shall see the perfect goodness surely estab-lished in the stainless shrine.

When you know that you have become this perfect work, when you are self-gathered in the purity of your being, nothing now remaining that can shatter that inner unity, nothing from without clinging to the authentic man, when you find yourself wholly true to your essential nature, wholly that only veritable Light which is not measured by space, not narrowed to any circumscribed form nor again diffused as a thing void of term, but ever unmeasurable as something greater than all measure and more than all quantity—when you perceive that you have grown to this, you are now become very vision: now call up all your confidence, strike forward yet a step—you need a guide no longer—strain, and see.

This is the only eye that sees the mighty Beauty. If the eye that adven-tures the vision be dimmed by vice, impure, or weak, and unable in its cowardly blenching to see the uttermost brightness, then it sees nothing even though another point to what lies plain to sight before it. To any vision must be brought an eye adapted to what is to be seen, and having some likeness to it. Never did eye see the sun unless it had first become sunlike, and never can the Soul have vision of the First Beauty unless itself be beautiful.

Therefore, first let each become godlike and each beautiful who cares to see God and Beauty. So, mounting, the Soul will come first to the Intel-lectual-Principle and survey all the beautiful Ideas in the Supreme and will avow that this is Beauty, that the Ideas are Beauty. For by their efficacy comes all Beauty else, by the offspring and essence of the Intellectual-Being. What is beyond the Intellectual-Principle we affirm to be the nature of Good radiating Beauty before it. So that, treating the Intellectual-Cosmos as one, the first is the Beautiful: if we make distinction there, the Realm of Ideas constitutes the Beauty of the Intellectual Sphere; and The Good, which lies beyond, is the Fountain at once and Principle of Beauty: the Primal Good and the Primal Beauty have the one dwelling-place and, thus, always, Beauty's seat is There.

# FRIEDRICH SCHLEIERMACHER

*Friedrich Schleiermacher* (1768–1834) was a German theologian who came out of Moravian pietism and German romanticism to become the systematizer of Protestant liberal theology. He was the most important Protestant theologian of the nineteenth century.

## The Nature of Religion

In order to make quite clear to you what is the original and characteristic possession of religion, it resigns, at once, all claims on anything that belongs either to science or morality. Whether it has been borrowed or bestowed it is now returned. What then does your science of being, your natural science, all your theoretical philosophy, in so far as it has to do with the actual world, have for its aim? To know things, I suppose, as they really are; to show the peculiar relations by which each is what it is; to determine for each its place in the Whole, and to distinguish it rightly from all else; to present the whole real world in its mutually conditioned necessity; and to exhibit the oneness of all phenomena with their eternal laws. This is truly beautiful and excellent, and I am not disposed to deprecate. Rather, if this description of mine, so slightly sketched, does not suffice, I will grant the highest and most exhaustive you are able to give.

And yet, however high you go; though you pass from the laws to the Universal Lawgiver, in whom is the unity of all things; though you allege that nature cannot be comprehended without God, I would still maintain that religion has nothing to do with this knowledge, and that, quite apart from it, its nature can be known. Quantity of knowledge is not quantity

From Friedrich Schleiermacher, *On Religion, Speeches to Its Cultural Despisers,* trans. John Oman. Reprinted by permission of Routledge & Kegan Paul.

of piety. Piety can gloriously display itself, both with originality and individuality, in those to whom this kind of knowledge is not original. They may only know it as everybody does, as isolated results known in connection with other things. The pious man must, in a sense, be a wise man, but he will readily admit, even though you somewhat proudly look down upon him, that, in so far as he is pious, he does not hold his knowledge in the same way as you.

Let me interpret in clear words what most pious persons only guess at and never know how to express. Were you to set God as the apex of your science as the foundation of all knowing as well as of all knowledge, they would accord praise and honour, but it would not be their way of having and knowing God. From their way, as they would readily grant, and as is easy enough to see, knowledge and science do not proceed.

It is true that religion is essentially contemplative. You would never call anyone pious who went about in impervious stupidity, whose sense is not open for the life of the world. But this contemplation is not turned, as your knowledge of nature is, to the existence of a finite thing, combined with and opposed to another finite thing. It has not even, like your knowledge of God—if for once I might use an old expression—to do with the nature of the first cause, in itself and in its relation to every other cause and operation. The contemplation of the pious is the immediate consciousness of the universal existence of all finite things, in and through the Infinite, and of all temporal things in and through the Eternal. Religion is to seek this and find it in all that lives and moves, in all growth and change, in all doing and suffering. It is to have life and to know life in immediate feeling, only as such an existence in the Infinite and Eternal. Where this is found religion is satisfied, where it hides itself there is for her unrest and anguish, extremity and death. Wherefore it is a life in the infinite nature of the Whole, in the One and in the All, in God, having and possessing all things in God, and God in all. Yet religion is not knowledge and science, either of the world or of God. Without being knowledge, it recognizes knowledge and science. In itself it is an affection, a revelation of the Infinite in the finite, God being seen in it and it in God.

Similarly, what is the object of your ethics, of your science of action? Does it not seek to distinguish precisely each part of human doing and producing, and at the same time to combine them into a whole, according to actual relations? But the pious man confesses that, as pious, he knows nothing about it. He does, indeed, contemplate human action, but it is not the kind of contemplation from which an ethical system takes its rise. Only one thing he seeks out and detects, action from God, God's activity among men. If your ethics are right, and his piety as well, he will not, it is true, acknowledge any action as excellent which is not embraced in your system. But to know and to construct this system is your business, ye learned, not his. If you will not believe, regard the case of women. You ascribe to them religion, not only as an adornment, but you demand of them the finest feeling for distinguishing the things that excel: do you equally expect them to know your ethics as a science?

It is the same, let me say at once, with action itself. The artist fashions what is given him to fashion, by virtue of his special talent. These talents are so different that the one he possesses another lacks; unless someone, against heaven's will, would possess all. But when anyone is praised to you as pious, you are not accustomed to ask which of these gifts dwell in him by virtue of his piety. The citizen—taking the word in the sense of the ancients, not in its present meagre significance—regulates, leads, and influences in virtue of his morality. But this is something different from piety. Piety has also a passive side. While morality always shows itself as manipulating, as self-controlling, piety appears as a surrender, a submission to be moved by the Whole that stands over against man. Morality depends, therefore, entirely on the consciousness of freedom, within the sphere of which all that it produces falls. Piety, on the contrary, is not at all bound to this side of life. In the opposite sphere of necessity, where there is no properly individual action, it is quite as active. Wherefore the two are different. Piety does, indeed, linger with satisfaction on every action that is from God, and every activity that reveals the Infinite in the finite, and yet it is not itself this activity. Only by keeping quite outside the range both of science and of practice can it maintain its proper sphere and character. Only when piety takes its place alongside of science and practice, as a necessary, an indispensable third, as their natural counterpart, not less in worth and splendour than either, will the common field be altogether occupied and human nature on this side complete.

But pray understand me fairly. I do not mean that one could exist without the other, that, for example, a man might have religion and be pious, and at the same time be immoral. That is impossible. But, in my opinion, it is just as impossible to be moral or scientific without being religious. But have I not said that religion can be had without science? Wherefore, I have myself begun the separation. But remember, I only said piety is not the measure of science. Just as one cannot be truly scientific without being pious, the pious man may not know at all, but he cannot know falsely. His proper nature is not of that subordinate kind, which, according to the old adage that like is only known to like, knows nothing except semblance of reality.

His nature is reality which knows reality, and where it encounters nothing it does not suppose it sees something. And what a precious jewel of science, in my view, is ignorance for those who are captive to semblance. If you have not learned it from my Speeches or discovered it for yourselves, go and learn it from your Socrates. Grant me consistency at least. With ignorance your knowledge will ever be mixed, but the true and proper opposite of knowledge is presumption of knowledge. By piety this presumption is most certainly removed, for with it piety cannot exist.

Such a separation of knowledge and piety, and of action and piety, do not accuse me of making. You are only ascribing to me, without my deserving it, your own view and the very confusion, as common as it is unavoidable, which it has been my chief endeavour to show you in the mirror of my Speech. Just because you do not acknowledge religion as the third, knowledge and action are so much apart that you can discover no unity, but believe that right knowing can be had without right acting, and *vice versa*. I hold that is it only in contemplation that there is division. There, where it is necessary, you despise it, and instead transfer it to life, as if in life itself objects could be found independent one of the other. Consequently you have no living insight into any of these activities. Each is for you a part, a fragment. Because you do not deal with life in a living way, your conception bears the stamp of perishableness, and is altogether meagre. True science is complete vision; true practice is culture and art self-produced; true religion is sense and taste for the Infinite. To wish to have true science or true practice without religion, or to imagine it is possessed, is obstinate, arrogant delusion, and culpable error. It issues from the unholy sense that would rather have a show of possession by cowardly purloining than have secure possession by demanding and waiting. What can man accomplish that is worth speaking of, either in life or in art, that does not arise in his own self from the influence of this sense for the Infinite? Without it, how can anyone wish to comprehend the world scientifically, or if, in some distinct talent, the knowledge is thrust upon him, how should he wish to exercise it? What is all science, if not the existence of things in you, in your reason? what is all art and culture if not your existence in the things to which you give measure, form and order? And how can both come to life in you except in so far as there lives immediately in you the eternal unity of Reason and Nature, the universal existence of all finite things in the Infinite?

Wherefore, you will find every truly learned man devout and pious. Where you see science without religion, be sure it is transferred, learned up from another. It is sickly, if indeed it is not that empty appearance which serves necessity and is no knowledge at all. And what else do you take this deduction and weaving together of ideas to be, which neither live nor correspond to any living thing? Or in ethics, what else is this wretched uniformity that thinks it can grasp the highest human life in a single dead formula? The former arises because there is no fundamental feeling of that living nature which everywhere presents variety and individuality, and the latter because the sense fails to give infinity to the finite by determining its nature and boundaries only from the Infinite. Hence the dominion of the mere notion; hence the mechanical erections of your systems instead of an organic structure; hence the vain juggling with analytical formulas, in which, whether categorical or hypothetical, life will not be fettered. Science is not your calling, if you despise religion and fear to surrender yourself to reverence and aspiration for the primordial. Either science must become as low as your life, or it must be separated and stand alone, a division that precludes success. If man is not one with the Eternal in the unity of intuition and feeling which is immediate, he remains, in the unity of consciousness which is derived, for ever apart.

What, then, shall become of the highest utterance of the speculation of our days, complete rounded idealism, if it do not again sink itself in this unity, if the humility of religion do not suggest to its pride another realism than that which it so boldly and with such perfect right, subordinates to itself? It annihilates the Universe, while it seems to aim at constructing it. It would degrade it to a mere allegory, to a mere phantom of the one-sided limitation of its own empty consciousness. Offer with me reverently a tribute to the manes of the holy, rejected Spinoza. The high World-Spirit pervaded him; the Infinite was his beginning and his end; the Universe was his only and his everlasting love. In holy innocence and in deep humility he beheld himself mirrored in the eternal world, and perceived how he also was its most worthy mirror. He was full of religion, full of the Holy Spirit. Wherefore, he stands there alone and unequalled; master in his art, yet without disciples and without citizenship, sublime above the profane tribe.

Why should I need to show that the same applies to art? Because, from the same causes, you have here also a thousand phantoms, delusions, and mistakes. In place of all else I would point to another example which should be as well known to you all. I would point in silence—for pain that is new and deep has no words. It is that superb youth, who has too early fallen asleep, with whom everything his spirit touched became art. His whole contemplation of the world was forthwith a great poem. Though he had scarce more than struck the first chords, you must associate him with the most opulent poets, with those select spirits who are as profound as they are clear and vivacious. See in him the power of the enthusiasm and the caution of a pious spirit, and acknowledge that when the philosophers shall become religious and seek God like Spinoza, and the artists be pious and love Christ like Novalis, the great resurrection shall be celebrated for both worlds.

But, in order that you may understand what I mean by this unity and difference of religion, science and art, we shall endeavour to descend into the inmost sanctuary of life. There, perhaps, we may find ourselves agreed. There alone you discover the original relation of intuition and feeling from which alone this identity and difference is to be understood. But I must direct you to your own selves. You must apprehend a living movement. You must know how to listen to yourselves before your own consciousness. At least you must be able to reconstruct from your consciousness your own state. What you are to notice is the rise of your consciousness and not to reflect upon something already there. Your thought can only embrace what is sundered. Wherefore as soon as you have made any given definite activity of your soul an object of communication or of contemplation, you have already begun to separate. It is impossible, therefore, to adduce any definite example, for, as soon as anything is an example, what I wish to indicate is already past. Only the faintest trace of the original unity could then be shown. Such as it is, however, I will not despise it, as a preliminary.

Consider how you delineate an object. Is there not both a stimulation and a determination by the object, at one and the same time, which for one particular moment forms your existence? The more definite your image, the more, in this way, you become the object, and the more you lose yourselves. But just because you can trace the growing preponderance of one side over the other, both must have been one and equal in the first, the original moment that has escaped you. Or sunk in yourselves, you find all that you formerly regarded as a disconnected manifold compacted now indivisibly into the one peculiar content of your being. Yet when you give heed, can you not see as it disappears, the image of an object, from whose influence, from whose magical contact this definite consciousness has proceeded? The more your own state sways you the paler and more unrecognizable your image becomes. The greater your emotion, the more you are absorbed in it, the more your whole nature is concerned to retain for the memory an imperishable trace of what is necessarily fleeting, to carry over to what you may engage in, its colour and impress, and so unite two moments into a duration, the less you observe the object that caused it. But just because it grows pale and vanishes, it must before have been nearer and clearer. Originally it must have been one and the same with your feeling. But, as was said, these are mere traces. Unless you will go back on the first beginning of this consciousness, you can scarcely understand them.

And suppose you cannot? Then say, weighing it quite generally and originally, what is every act of your life in itself and without distinction from other acts. What is it merely as act, as movement? Is it not the coming into being of something for itself, and at the same time in the Whole? It is an endeavour to return into the Whole, and to exist for oneself at the same time. These are the links from which the whole chain is made. Your whole life is such an existence for self in the Whole. How now are you in the Whole? By your senses. And how are you for yourselves? By the unity of your self-consciousness, which is given chiefly in the possibility of comparing the varying degrees of sensation. How both can only rise together, if both together fashion every act of life, is easy to see. You become sense and the Whole becomes object. Sense and object mingle and unite, then each returns to its place, and the object rent from sense is a perception, and you rent from the object are for yourselves, a feeling. It is this earlier moment I mean, which you always experience yet never experience. The phenomenon of your life is just the result of its constant departure and return. It is scarcely in time at all, so swiftly it passes; it can scarcely be described, so little does it properly exist. Would that I could hold it fast and refer to it your commonest as well as your highest activities.

Did I venture to compare it, seeing I cannot describe it, I would say it is fleeting and transparent as the vapour which the dew breathes on blossom and fruit, it is bashful and tender as a maiden's kiss, it is holy and fruitful as a bridal embrace. Nor is it merely like, it is all this. It is the first contact of the universal life with an individual. It fills no time and fashions nothing palpable. It is the holy wedlock of the Universe with the incarnated Reason for a creative, productive embrace. It is immediate, raised above all error and misunderstanding. You lie directly on the bosom of the infinite world. In that moment, you are its soul. Through one part of your nature you feel, as your own, all its powers and its endless life. In that moment it is your body, you pervade, as your own, its muscles and members and your thinking and forecasting set its inmost nerves in motion. In this way every living, original movement in your life is first received. Among the rest it is the source of every religious emotion. But it is not, as I said, even a moment. The incoming of existence to us, by this immediate union, at once stops as soon as it reaches consciousness. Either the intuition displays itself more vividly and clearly, like the figure of the vanishing mistress to the eyes of her lover; or feeling issues from your heart and overspreads your whole being, as the blush of shame and love over the face of the maiden. At length your consciousness is finally determined as one or other, as intuition or feeling. Then, even though you have not quite surrendered to this division and lost consciousness of your life as a unity, there remains nothing but the knowledge that they were originally one, that they issued simultaneously from the fundamental relation of your nature. Wherefore, it is in this sense true what an ancient sage has taught you, that all knowledge is recollection. It is recollection of what is outside of all time, and is therefore justly to be placed at the head of all temporal things.

And, as it is with intuition and feeling on the one hand, so it is with knowledge which includes both and with activity on the other. Through the constant play and mutual influence of these opposites, your life expands and has its place in time. Both knowledge and activity are a desire to be identified with the Universe through an object. If the power of the objects preponderates, if, as intuition or feeling, it enters and seeks to draw you into the circle of their existence, it is always a knowledge. If the preponderating power is on your side, so that you give the impress and reflect yourselves in the objects, it is activity in the narrower sense, external working. Yet it is only as you are stimulated and determined that you can communicate yourselves to things. In founding or establishing anything in the world you are only giving back what that original act of fellowship has wrought in you, and similarly everything the world fashions in you must be by the same act. One must mutually stimulate the other. Only in an interchange of knowing and activity can your life consist. A peaceful existence, wherein one side did not stimulate the other, would not be your life. It would be that from which it first developed, and into which it will again disappear.

There then you have the three things about which my Speech has so far turned—perception, feeling and activity, and you now understand what I mean when I say they are not identical and yet are inseparable. Take what belongs to each class and consider it by itself. You will find that those moments in which you exercise power over things and impress yourselves upon them, form what you call your practical, or, in the narrower sense, your moral life; again the contemplative moments, be they few or many, in which things produce themselves in you as intuition, you will doubtless call your scientific life. Now can either series alone form a human life? Would it not be death? If each activity were not stimulated and renewed by the other, would it not be self-consumed? Yet they are not identical. If you would understand your life and speak comprehensibly of it, they must be distinguished. As it stands with these two in respect of one another, it must stand with the third in respect of both. How then are you to name this third, which is the series of feeling? What life will it form? The religious as I think, and as you will not be able to deny, when you have considered it more closely.

The chief point in my Speech is now uttered. This is the peculiar sphere which I would assign to religion—the whole of it, and nothing more. Unless you grant it, you must either prefer the old confusion to clear analysis, or produce something else, I know not what, new and quite wonderful. Your feeling is piety, in so far as it expresses, in the manner described, the being and life common to you and to the All. Your feeling is piety in so far as it is the result of the operation of God in you by means of the operation of the world upon you. This series is not made up either of perceptions or of objects of perception, either of works or operations or of different spheres of operation, but purely of sensations and the influence of all that lives and moves around, which accompanies them and conditions them. These feelings are exclusively the elements of religion, and none are excluded. There is no sensation that is not pious, except it indicate some diseased and impaired state of the life, the influence of which will not be confined to religion. Wherefore, it follows that ideas and principles are all foreign to religion. This truth we here come upon for the second time. If ideas and principles are to be anything, they must belong to knowledge which is a different department of life from religion.

# SØREN KIERKEGAARD

*Søren Kierkegaard* (1813–1855), Danish Protestant lay theologian, reacted against the philosophy of Hegel. He was sharply critical of the identification of Christianity with culture, demanded radical faith, and was the key figure in the development of modern religious existentialism.

## What It Is to Become a Christian

*Objectively, What It Is to Become or to Be a Christian*
*Is Defined in the Following Way:*

1. A Christian is one who accepts the doctrine of Christianity. But if it is the doctrine which is to decide in the last resort whether one is a Christian, then instantly attention is directed outward, in order to learn to know in the minutest detail what the doctrine of Christianity is, because this indeed is to decide, not what Christianity is, but whether I am a Christian. That same instant begins the erudite, the anxious, the timorous effort at approximation. Approximation can be protracted as long as you please, and in the end the decision whereby one becomes a Christian is relegated to oblivion.

This incongruity has been remedied by the assumption that everyone in Christendom is a Christian, we are all of us what one in a way calls Christians. With this assumption things go better with the objective theories. We are all Christians. The Bible-theory has now to investigate quite objectively what Christianity is (and yet we are in fact Christians, and the objective information is assumed to make us Christians, the objective information which we who are Christians shall now for the first time learn to know— for if we are not Christians, the road here taken will never lead us to become such). The Church theory assumes that we are Christians, but now

From Søren Kierkegaard, *Concluding Unscientific Postscript.* trans. David F. Swenson and Walter Lowrie, pp. 537–544. Copyright, 1941, Princeton University Press. Reprinted by permission of Princeton University Press. [Several footnotes omitted, Eds.]

we have to be assured in a purely objective way what Christianity is, in order that we may defend ourselves against the Turk and the Russian and the Roman yoke, and gallantly fight out the battle of Christianity so that we may make our age, as it were, a bridge to the peerless future which already is glimpsed. This is sheer aesthetics. Christianity is an existence-communication, the task is to become a Christian and continue to be such, and the most dangerous of all illusions is to be so sure of being such that one has to defend the whole of Christendom against the Turk—instead of being alert to defend our own faith against the illusion about the Turk.

2. One says, No, not every acceptance of the Christian doctrine makes one a Christian; what it principally depends upon is appropriation, that one appropriates and holds fast this doctrine quite differently from anything else, that one is ready to live in it and to die in it, to venture one's life for it, etc.

This seems as if it were something. However, the category "quite differently" is a mediocre category, and the whole formula, which makes an attempt to define more subjectively what it is to be a Christian, is neither one thing nor the other, in a way it avoids the difficulty involved in the distraction and deceit of approximation, but it lacks categorical definition. The pathos of approximation which is talked of here is that of immanence; one can just as well say that an enthusiastic lover is so related to his love: he holds fast to it and appropriates it quite differently from anything else, he is ready to live in it and die in it, he will venture everything for it. To this extent there is no difference between a lover and a Christian with respect to inwardness, and one must again recur to the *what,* which is the doctrine—and with that we again come under No. 1.

The pathos of appropriation needs to be so defined that it cannot be confused with any other pathos. The more subjective interpretation is right in insisting that it is appropriation which decides the matter, but it is wrong in its definition of appropriation, which does not distinguish it from every other immediate pathos.

Neither is this distinction made when one defines appropriation as faith, but at once imparts to faith headway and direction towards reaching an understanding, so that faith becomes a provisional function whereby one holds what essentially is to be an object for understanding, a provisional function wherewith poor people and stupid men have to be content, whereas *Privatdocents* and clever heads go further. The mark of being a Christian (i.e., faith) is appropriated, but in such a way that it is not specifically different from other intellectual appropriation where a preliminary assumption serves as a provisional function looking forward to understanding. Faith is not in this case the specific mark of the relationship to Christianity, and again it will be the *what* of faith which decides whether one is a Christian or not. But therewith the thing is again brought back under No. 1.

That is to say, the appropriation by which a Christian is a Christian must be so specific that it cannot be confused with anything else.

3. One defines the thing of becoming and being a Christian, not objectively by the *what* of the doctrine, nor subjectively by appropriation, not by what has gone on in the individual, but by what the individual has undergone: that he was baptized. Though one adjoins to baptism the assumption of a confession of faith, nothing decisive will be gained, but the definition will waver between accentuating the *what* (the path of approximation) and talking indefinitely about acceptance and acceptance and appropriation, etc., without any specific determination.

If being baptized is to be the definition, attention will instantly turn outward towards the reflection, whether I have really been baptized. Then begins the approximation with respect to a historical fact.

If, on the other hand, one were to say that he did indeed receive the Spirit in baptism and by the witness it bears together with his spirit, he knows that he was baptized—then the inference is inverted, he argues from the witness of the Spirit within him to the fact that he was baptized, not from the fact of being baptized to the possession of the Spirit. But if the inference is to be drawn in this way, baptism is quite rightly not regarded as the mark of the Christian, but inwardness is, and so here in turn there is needed a specific definition of inwardness and appropriation whereby the witness of the Spirit in the individual is distinguished from all other (universally defined) activity of spirit in man.

It is noteworthy moreover that the orthodoxy which especially has made baptism the decisive mark is continually complaining that among the baptized there are so few Christians, that almost all, except for an immortal little band, are spiritless baptized pagans—which seems to indicate that baptism cannot be the decisive factor with respect to becoming a Christian, not even according to the latter view of those who in the first form insist upon it as decisive with respect to becoming a Christian.

## *Subjectively, What It Is to Become a Christian Is Defined Thus:*

The decision lies in the subject. The appropriation is the paradoxical inwardness which is specifically different from all other inwardness. The thing of being a Christian is not determined by the *what* of Christianity but by the *how* of the Christian. This *how* can only correspond with one thing, the absolute paradox. There is therefore no vague talk to the effect that being a Christian is to accept, and to accept, and to accept quite differently, to appropriate, to believe, to appropriate by faith quite differently (all of them purely rhetorical and fictitious definitions); but *to believe* is specifically different from all other appropriation and inwardness. Faith is the objective uncertainty due to the repulsion of the absurd held fast by the passion of inwardness, which in this instance is intensified to the utmost degree. This formula fits only the believer, no one else, not a lover, not an enthusiast, not a thinker, but simply and solely the believer who is related to the absolute paradox.

Faith therefore cannot be any sort of provisional function. He who from the vantage point of a higher knowledge would know his faith as a factor resolved in a higher idea has *eo ipso* ceased to believe. Faith *must* not *rest content* with unintelligibility; for precisely the relation to or the repulsion from the unintelligible, the absurd, is the expression for the passion of faith.

This definition of what it is to be a Christian prevents the erudite or anxious deliberation of approximation from enticing the individual into byways so that he becomes erudite instead of becoming a Christian, and in most cases a smatterer instead of becoming a Christian; for the decision lies in the subject. But inwardness has again found its specific mark whereby it is differentiated from all other inwardness and is not disposed of by the chatty category "quite differently" which fits the case of every passion at the moment of passion.

The psychologist generally regards it as a sure sign that a man is beginning to give up a passion when he wishes to treat the object of it objectively. Passion and reflection are generally exclusive of one another. Becoming objective in this way is always retrogression, for passion is man's perdition, but it is his exaltation as well. In case dialectic and reflection are not used to intensify passion, it is a retrogression to become objective; and even he who is lost through passion has not lost so much as he who lost passion, for the former had the possibility.

Thus it is that people in our age have wanted to become objective with relation to Christianity; the passion by which every man is a Christian has become too small a thing for them, and by becoming objective we all of us have the prospect of becoming . . . *a Privatdocent*. . . .

Precisely because people in our age and in the Christendom of our time do not appear to be sufficiently aware of the dialectic of inward appropriation, or of the fact that the "how" of the individual is an expression just as precise and more decisive for what he has, than is the "what" to which he appeals—precisely for this reason there crop up the strangest and (if one is in the humor and has time for it) the most laughable confusions, more comic than even the confusions of paganism, because in them there was not so much at stake, and because the contradictions were not so strident. . . .

An orthodox champion fights in defense of Christianity with the most frightful passion, he protests with the sweat of his brow and with the most concerned demeanor that he accepts Christianity pure and simple, he will live and die in it—and he forgets that such acceptance is an all too general expression for the relation to Christianity. He does everything in Jesus' name and uses Christ's name on every occasion as a sure sign that he is a

Christian and is called to fight in defense of Christendom in our age—and he has no inkling of the little ironical secret that a man merely by describing the "how" of his inwardness can show indirectly that he is a Christian without mentioning God's name.[1] A man becomes converted New Year's Eve precisely at six o'clock. With that he is fully prepared. Fantastically decked out with the fact of conversion, he now must run out and proclaim Christianity . . . in a Christian land. Well, of course, even though we are all baptized, every man may well need to become a Christian in another sense. But here is the distinction: there is no lack of information in a Christian land, something else is lacking, and this is a something which the one man cannot directly communicate to the other. And in such fantastic categories would a converted man work for Christianity; and yet he proves (just in proportion as he is the more busy in spreading and spreading) that he himself is not a Christian. For to be a Christian is something so deeply reflected that it does not admit of the aesthetical dialectic which allows one man to be for others something he is not for himself. On the other hand, a scoffer attacks Christianity and at the same time expounds it so reliably that it is a pleasure to read him, and one who is in perplexity about finding it distinctly set forth may almost have recourse to him.

All ironical observations depend upon paying attention to the "how," whereas the gentleman with whom the ironist has the honor to converse is attentive only to "what." A man protests loudly and solemnly, "This is my opinion." However, he does not confine himself to delivering this formula verbatim, he explains himself further, he ventures to vary the expressions. Yes, for it is not so easy to vary as one thinks it is. More than one student would have got *laudabilis* for style if he had not varied his expressions, and a great multitude of men possess the talent which Socrates so much admired in Polos: they never say the same thing—about the same. The ironist then is on the watch, he of course is not looking out for what is printed in large letters or for that which by the speaker's diction betrays itself as a formula (our gentleman's "what"), but he is looking out for a little subordinate clause which escapes the gentleman's haughty attention, a little beckoning predicate, etc., and now he beholds with astonishment (glad of the variation—*in variatione voluptas*) that the gentleman *has not* that opinion—not that he is a hypocrite, God forbid! that is too serious a matter for an ironist

---

[1] In relation to love (by which I would illustrate again the same thing) it does not hold good in the same sense that a man merely by defining his "how" indicates what or whom it is he loves. All lovers have the "how" of love in common, the particular person must supply the name of his beloved. But with respect to believing (*sensu strictissimo*) it holds good that this "how" is appropriate only to one as its object. If anybody would say, "Yes, but then one can also learn the 'how' of faith by rote and patter"; to this one must reply that it cannot be done, for he who declares it directly contradicts himself, because the content of the assertion must constantly be reduplicated in the form of expression, and the isolation contained in the definition must reduplicate itself in the form.

—but that the good man has concentrated his force in bawling it out instead of possessing it within him. To that extent the gentleman may be right in asserting that he has that opinion which with all his vital force he persuades himself he has, he may do everything for it in the quality of talebearer, he may risk his life for it, in very much troubled times he may carry the thing so far as to lose his life for this opinion—with that, how the deuce can I doubt that the man had this opinion; and yet there may have been living contemporaneously with him an ironist who even in the hour when the unfortunate gentleman is executed cannot resist laughing, because he knows by the circumstantial evidence he has gathered that the man had never been clear about the thing himself. Laughable it is, nor is it disheartening that such a thing can occur; for he who with quiet introspection is honest before God and concerned for himself, the Deity saves from being in error, though he be never so simple, him the Deity leads by the suffering of inwardness to the truth. But meddlesomeness and noise is the sign of error, the sign of an abnormal condition, like wind in the stomach, and this thing of stumbling by chance upon getting executed in a tumultous turn of affairs is not the sort of suffering which essentially characterizes inwardness.

It is said to have chanced in England that a man was attacked on the highway by a robber who had made himself unrecognizable by wearing a big wig. He falls upon the traveller, seizes him by the throat and shouts, "Your purse!" He gets the purse and keeps it, but the wig he throws away. A poor man comes along the same road, puts it on and arrives at the next town where the traveller had already denounced the crime, he is arrested, is recognized by the traveller, who takes his oath that he is the man. By chance, the robber is present in court-room, sees the misunderstanding, turns to the judge and says, "It seems to me that the traveller has regard rather to the wig than to the man," and he asks permission to make a trial. He puts on the wig, seizes the traveller by the throat, crying, "Your purse!"—and the traveller recognizes the robber and offers to swear to it—the only trouble is that already he has taken an oath. So it is, in one way or another, with every man who has a "what" and is not attentive to the "how": he swears, he takes his oath, he runs errands, he ventures life and blood, he is executed—all on account of the wig. . . .

# LUDWIG FEUERBACH

*Ludwig Feuerbach* (1804–1872) was a German philosopher who belonged to the left-wing Hegelian school. He taught that religion is a prejection of human imagination and an expression of human need. His book *The Essence of Christianity* has long been recognized as a provocative interpretation of religious belief.

## The Essence of Religion

Religion has its basis in the essential difference between man and the brute—the brutes have no religion. It is true that the old uncritical writers on natural history attributed to the elephant, among other laudable qualities, the virtue of religiousness; but the religion of elephants belongs to the realm of fable. Cuvier, one of the greatest authorities on the animal kingdom, assigns, on the strength of his personal observations, no higher grade of intelligence to the elephant than to the dog.

But what is this essential difference between man and the brute? The most simple, general, and also the most popular answer to this question is—consciousness—but consciousness in the strict sense; for the consciousness implied in the feeling of self as an individual, in discrimination by the senses, in the perception and even judgment of outward things according to definite sensible signs, cannot be denied to the brutes. Consciousness in the strictest sense is present only in a being to whom his species, his essential nature, is an object of thought. The brute is indeed conscious of himself as an individual—and he has accordingly the feeling of self as the common centre of successive sensations—but not as a species: hence, he is without that consciousness which in its nature, as in its name, is akin to science. Where there is this higher consciousness there is a capability of science. Science is the cognisance of species. In practical life we have to do with individuals; in science, with species. But only a being to whom his own species, his own nature, is an object of thought, can make the essential nature of other things or beings an object of thought.

Hence the brute has only a simple, man a twofold life: in the brute, the

From Ludwig Feuerbach, *The Essence of Christianity,* trans. George Eliot, pp. 1–3, 12–14. 29–32. Published, 1957, Harper & Row (Torchbook Series). In the public domain. [Several footnotes omitted, Eds.]

[22]

inner life is one with the outer; man has both an inner and an outer life. The inner life of man is the life which has relation to his species, to his general, as distinguished from his individual, nature. Man thinks—that is, he converses with himself. The brute can exercise no function which has relation to its species without another individual external to itself; but man can perform the functions of thought and speech, which strictly imply such a relation, apart from another individual. Man is himself at once I and thou; he can put himself in the place of another, for this reason, that to him his species, his essential nature, and not merely his individuality, is an object of thought.

Religion, being identical with the distinctive characteristic of man, is then identical with self-consciousness—with the consciousness which man has of his nature. But religion, expressed generally, is consciousness of the infinite; thus it is and can be nothing else than the consciousness which man has of his own—not finite and limited, but infinite nature. A really finite being has not even the faintest adumbration, still less consciousness, of an infinite being, for the limit of the nature is also the limit of the consciousness. The consciousness of the caterpillar, whose life is confined to a particular species of plant, does not extend itself beyond this narrow domain. It does, indeed, discriminate betweeen this plant and other plants, but more it knows not. A consciousness so limited, but on account of that very limitation so infallible, we do not call consciousness, but instinct. Consciousness, in the strict or proper sense, is identical with consciousness of the infinite; a limited consciousness is no consciousness; consciousness is essentially infinite in its nature. The consciousness of the infinite is nothing else than the consciousness of the infinity of the consciousness; or, in the consciousness of the infinite, the conscious subject has for his object the infinity of his own nature. . . .

What we have hitherto been maintaining generally, even with regard to sensational impressions, of the relation between subject and object, applies especially to the relation between the subject and the religious object.

In the perceptions of the senses consciousness of the object is distinguishable from consciousness of self; but in religion, consciousness of the object and self-consciousness coincide. The object of the senses is out of man, the religious object is within him, and therefore as little forsakes him as his self-consciousness or his conscience; it is the intimate, the closest object. "God," says Augustine, for example, "is nearer, more related to us, and therefore more easily known by us, than sensible, corporeal things." The object of the senses is in itself indifferent—independent of the disposition or of the judgment; but the object of religion is a selected object; the most excellent, the first, the supreme being; it essentially presupposes a critical judgment, a discrimination between the divine and the non-divine, between that which is worthy of adoration and that which is not worthy. And here may be applied, without any limitation, the proposition: the object of any subject is nothing else than the subject's own nature taken objectively. Such as are a man's thoughts and dispositions, such is his God; so much worth as a man has, so much and no more has his God. Consciousness of God is self-consciousness, knowledge of God is self-knowledge. By his God thou knowest the man, and by the man his God; the two are identical. Whatever is God to a man, that is his heart and soul; and conversely, God is the manifested inward nature, the expressed self of a man—religion the solemn unveiling of a man's hidden treasures, the revelation of his intimate thoughts, the open confession of his love-secrets.

But when religion—consciousness of God—is designated as the self-consciousness of man, this is not to be understood as affirming that the religious man is directly aware of this identity; for, on the contrary, ignorance of it is fundamental to the peculiar nature of religion. To preclude this misconception, it is better to say, religion is man's earliest and also indirect form of self-knowledge. Hence, religion everywhere precedes philosophy, as in the history of the race, so also in that of the individual. Man first of all sees his nature as if *out of* himself, before he finds it in himself. His own nature is in the first instance contemplated by him as that of another being. Religion is the childlike condition of humanity; but the child sees his nature —man—out of himself; in childhood a man is an object to himself, under the form of another man. Hence the historical progress of religion consists in this: that what by an earlier religion was regarded as objective, is now recognised as subjective; that is, what was formerly contemplated and worshipped as God is now perceived to be something *human*. What was at first religion becomes at a later period idolatry; man is seen to have adored his own nature. Man has given objectivity to himself, but has not recognised the object as his own nature: a later religion takes this forward step; every advance in religion is therefore a deeper self-knowledge. But every particular religion, while it pronounces its predecessors idolatrous, excepts itself—and necessarily so, otherwise it would no longer be religion—from the fate, the common nature of all religions: it imputes only to other religions what is the fault, if fault it be, of religion in general. Because it has a different object, a different tenor, because it has transcended the ideas of preceding religions, it erroneously supposes itself exalted above the necessary eternal laws which constitute the essence of religion—it fancies its object, its ideas, to be superhuman. But the essence of religion, thus hidden from the religious, is evident to the thinker, by whom religion is viewed objectively, which it cannot be by its votaries. And it is our task to show that the antithesis of divine and human is altogether illusory, that it is nothing else than the antithesis between the human nature in general and the human individual; that, consequently, the object and contents of the Christian religion are altogether human.

Religion, at least the Christian, is the relation of man to himself, or more correctly to his own nature i.e., his subjective nature); but a relation to it, viewed as a nature apart from his own. The divine being is nothing else than the human being, or, rather, the human nature purified, freed from the limits of the individual man, made objective—i.e., contemplated and revered as another, a distinct being. All the attributes of the divine nature are, therefore, attributes of the human nature. . . .

Man—this is the mystery of religion—projects his being into objectivity, and then again makes himself an object to this projected image of himself thus converted into a subject; he thinks of himself as an object to himself, but as the object of an object, of another being than himself. Thus here. Man is an object to God. That man is good or evil is not indifferent to God; no! He has a lively, profound interest in man's being good; he wills that man should be good, happy—for without goodness there is no happiness. Thus the religious man virtually retracts the nothingness of human activity, by making his dispositions and actions an object to God, by making man the end of God—for that which is an object to the mind is an end in action; by making the divine activity a means of human salvation. God acts, that man may be good and happy. Thus man, while he is apparently humiliated to the lowest degree, is in truth exalted to the highest. Thus, in and through God, man has in view himself alone. It is true that man places the aim of his action in God, but God has no other aim of action than the moral and eternal salvation of man: thus man has in fact no other aim than himself. The divine activity is not distinct from the human.

How could the divine activity work on me as its object, nay, work in me, if it were essentially different from me; how could it have a human aim, the aim of ameliorating and blessing man, if it were not itself human? Does not the purpose determine the nature of the act? When man makes his moral improvement an aim to himself, he has divine resolutions, divine projects; but also, when God seeks the salvation of man, he has human ends and a human mode of activity corresponding to these ends. Thus in God man has only his own activity as an object. But for the very reason that he regards his own activity as objective, goodness only as an object, he necessarily receives the impulse, the motive not from himself, but from this object. He contemplates his nature as external to himself, and this nature as goodness; thus it is self-evident, it is mere tautology to say that the impulse to good comes only from thence where he places the good.

God is the highest subjectivity of man abstracted from himself; hence man can do nothing of himself, all goodness comes from God. The more subjective God is, the more completely does man divest himself of his subjectivity, because God is, *per se,* his relinquished self, the possession of which he however again vindicates to himself. As the action of the arteries drives the blood into the extremities, and the action of the veins brings it back again, as life in general consists in a perpetual systole and diastole; so is it in religion. In the religious systole man propels his own nature from himself, he throws himself outward; in the religious diastole he receives the rejected nature into his heart again. God alone is the being who acts of himself,—this is the force of repulsion in religion; God is the being who acts in me, with me, through me, upon me, for me, is the principle of my salvation, of my good dispositions and actions, consequently my own good principle and nature,—this is the force of attraction in religion.

The course of religious development which has been generally indicated consists specifically in this, that man abstracts more and more from God, and attributes more and more to himself. This is especially apparent in the belief in revelation. That which to a later age or a cultured people is given by nature or reason, is to an earlier age, or to a yet uncultured people, given by God. Every tendency of man, however natural—even the impulse to cleanliness, was conceived by the Israelites as a positive divine ordinance. From this example we again see that God is lowered, is conceived more entirely on the type of ordinary humanity, in proportion as man detracts from himself. How can the self-humiliation of man go further than when he disclaims the capability of fulfilling spontaneously the requirements of common decency? The Christian religion, on the other hand, distinguished the impulses and passions of man according to their quality, their character; it represented only good emotions, good dispositions, good thoughts, as revelations, operations—that is, as dispositions, feelings, thoughts,—of God; for what God reveals is a quality of God himself: that of which the heart is full overflows the lips; as is the effect such is the cause; as the revelation, such the being who reveals himself. A God who reveals himself in good dispositions is a God whose essential attribute is only moral perfection. The Christian religion distinguishes inward moral purity from external physical purity; the Israelites identified the two. In relation to the Israelitish religion, the Christian religion is one of criticism and freedom. The Israelite trusted himself to do nothing except what was commanded by God; he was without will even in external things; the authority of religion extended itself even to his food. The Christian religion, on the other hand, in all these external things made man dependent on himself, i.e., placed in man what the Israelite placed out of himself in God. Israel is the most complete presentation of Positivism in religion. In relation to the Israelite, the Christian is an *esprit fort,* a free-thinker. Thus do things change. What yesterday was still religion is no longer such to-day; and what to-day is atheism, to-morrow will be religion.

# JOHN DEWEY

*John Dewey* (1859–1952), longtime professor at Columbia University, was the most influential American philosopher of this century. His chief effort was to apply a form of pragmatism to all of the important areas of philosophy and to many political, social, and educational problems in American life.

## Religion Versus the Religious

Never before in history has mankind been so much of two minds, so divided into two camps, as it is today. Religions have traditionally been allied with ideas of the supernatural, and often have been based upon explicit beliefs about it. Today there are many who hold that nothing worthy of being called religious is possible apart from the supernatural. Those who hold this belief differ in many respects. They range from those who accept the dogmas and sacraments of the Greek and Roman Catholic church as the only sure means of access to the supernatural to the theist or mild deist. Between them are the many Protestant denominations who think the Scriptures, aided by a pure conscience, are adequate avenues to supernatural truth and power. But they agree in one point: the necessity for a Supernatural Being and for an immortality that is beyond the power of nature.

The opposed group consists of those who think the advance of culture and science has completely discredited the supernatural and with it all religions that were allied with belief in it. But they go beyond this point. The extremists in this group believe that with elimination of the supernatural not only must historic religions be dismissed but with them everything of a religious nature. When historical knowledge has discredited the claims made for the supernatural character of the persons said to have founded historic religions; when the supernatural inspiration attributed to literatures held sacred has been riddled, and when anthropological and psychological knowledge has disclosed the all-too-human source from which religious beliefs and practices have sprung, everything religious must, they say, also go.

There is one idea held in common by these two opposite groups: identification of the religious with the supernatural. The question I shall raise in

From John Dewey, *A Common Faith*, pp. 1–28. Copyright, 1934, by Yale University Press. Used by permission of Yale University Press.

these chapters concerns the ground for and the consequences of this identification: its reasons and its value. In the discussion I shall develop another conception of the nature of the religious phase of experience, one that separates it from the supernatural and the things that have grown up about it. I shall try to show that these derivations are encumbrances and that what is genuinely religious will undergo an emancipation when it is relieved from them: that then, for the first time, the religious aspect of experience will be free to develop freely on its own account.

This view is exposed to attack from both the other camps. It goes contrary to traditional religions, including those that have the greatest hold upon the religiously minded today. The view announced will seem to them to cut the vital nerve of the religious element itself in taking away the basis upon which traditional religions and institutions have been founded. From the other side, the position I am taking seems like a timid halfway position, a concession and compromise unworthy of thought that is thoroughgoing. It is regarded as a view entertained from mere tendermindedness, as an emotional hangover from childhood indoctrination, or even as a manifestation of a desire to avoid disapproval and curry favor.

The heart of my point, as far as I shall develop it in this first section, is that there is a difference between religion, *a* religion, and the religious; between anything that may be denoted by a noun substantive and the quality of experience that is designated by an adjective. It is not easy to find a definition of religion in the substantive sense that wins general acceptance. However, in the *Oxford Dictionary* I find the following: "Recognition on the part of man of some unseen higher power as having control of his destiny and as being entitled to obedience, reverence and worship."

This particular definition is less explicit in assertion of the supernatural character of the higher unseen power than are others that might be cited. It is, however, surcharged with implications having their source in ideas connected with the belief in the supernatural, characteristic of historic religions. Let us suppose that one familiar with the history of religions, including those called primitive, compares the definition with the variety of known facts and by means of the comparison sets out to determine just what the definition means. I think he will be struck by three facts that reduce the terms of the definition to such a low common denominator that little meaning is left.

He will note that the "unseen powers" referred to have been conceived in a multitude of incompatible ways. Eliminating the differences, nothing is left beyond the bare reference to something unseen and powerful. This has been conceived as the vague and undefined Mana of the Melanesians; the Kami of primitive Shintoism; the fetish of the Africans; spirits, having some human properties, that pervade natural places and animate natural forces; the ultimate and impersonal principle of Buddhism; the unmoved mover of Greek thought; the gods and semi-divine heroes of the Greek and Roman Pantheons; the personal and loving Providence of Christianity, omnipotent, and limited by a corresponding evil power; the arbitrary Will of Moslemism; the supreme legislator and judge of deism. And these are but a few of the outstanding varieties of ways in which the invisible power has been conceived.

There is no greater similarity in the ways in which obedience and reverence have been expressed. There has been worship of animals, of ghosts, of ancestors, phallic worship, as well as of a Being of dread power and of love and wisdom. Reverence has been expressed in the human sacrifices of the Peruvians and Aztecs; the sexual orgies of some Oriental religions; exorcisms and ablutions; the offering of the humble and contrite mind of the Hebrew prophet, the elaborate rituals of the Greek and Roman Churches. Not even sacrifice has been uniform; it is highly sublimated in Protestant denominations and in Moslemism. Where it has existed it has taken all kinds of forms and been directed to a great variety of powers and spirits. It has been used for expiation, for propitiation and for buying special favors. There is no conceivable purpose for which rites have not been employed.

Finally, there is no discernible unity in the moral motivations appealed to and utilized. They have been as far apart as fear of lasting torture, hope of enduring bliss in which sexual enjoyment has sometimes been a conspicuous element; mortification of the flesh and extreme asceticism; prostitution and chastity; wars to extirpate the unbeliever; persecution to convert or punish the unbeliever, and philanthropic zeal; servile acceptance of imposed dogma, along with brotherly love and aspiration for a reign of justice among men.

I have, of course, mentioned only a sparse number of the facts which fill volumes in any well-stocked library. It may be asked by those who do not like to look upon the darker side of the history of religions why the darker facts should be brought up. We all know that civilized man has a background of bestiality and superstition and that these elements are still with us. Indeed, have not some religions, including the most influential forms of Christianity, taught that the heart of man is totally corrupt? How could the course of religion in its entire sweep not be marked by practices that are shameful in their cruelty and lustfulness, and by beliefs that are degraded and intellectually incredible? What else than what we find could be expected, in the case of people having little knowledge and no secure method of knowing; with primitive institutions, and with so little control of natural forces that they lived in a constant state of fear?

I gladly admit that historic religions have been relative to the conditions of social culture in which peoples lived. Indeed, what I am concerned with is to press home the logic of this method of disposal of outgrown traits of past religions. Beliefs and practices in a religion that now prevails are by this logic relative to the present state of culture. If so much flexibility has obtained in the past regarding an unseen power, the way it affects human destiny, and the attitudes we are to take toward it, why should it be assumed that change in conception and action has now come to an end? The logic involved in getting rid of inconvenient aspects of past religions compels us to inquire how much in religions now accepted are survivals from outgrown cultures. It compels us to ask what conception of unseen powers and our relations to them would be consonant with the best achievements and aspirations of the present. It demands that in imagination we wipe the slate clean and start afresh by asking what would be the idea of the unseen, of the manner of its control over us and the ways in which reverence and obedience would be manifested, if whatever is basically religious in experience had the opportunity to express itself free from all historic encumbrances.

So we return to the elements of the definition that has been given. What boots it to accept, in defense of the universality of religion, a definition that applies equally to the most savage and degraded beliefs and practices that have related to unseen powers and to noble ideals of a religion having the greatest share of moral content? There are two points involved. One of them is that there is nothing left worth preserving in the notions of unseen powers, controlling human destiny to which obedience, reverence and worship are due, if we glide silently over the nature that has been attributed to the powers, the radically diverse ways in which they have been supposed to control human destiny, and in which submission and awe have been manifested. The other point is that when we begin to select, to choose, and say that some present ways of thinking about the unseen powers are better than others; that the reverence shown by a free and self-respecting human being is better than the servile obedience rendered to an arbitrary power by frightened men; that we should believe that control of human destiny is exercised by a wise and loving spirit rather than by madcap ghosts or sheer force—when I say, we begin to choose, we have entered upon a road that has not yet come to an end. We have reached a point that invites us to proceed farther.

For we are forced to acknowledge that concretely there is no such thing as religion in the singular. There is only a multitude of religions. "Religion" is a strictly collective term and the collection it stands for is not even of the kind illustrated in textbooks of logic. It has not the unity of a regiment or assembly but that of any miscellaneous aggregate. Attempts to prove the universality prove too much or too little. It is probable that religions have been universal in the sense that all the peoples we know anything about have had *a* religion. But the differences among them are so great and so shocking that any common element that can be extracted is meaningless. The idea that religion is universal proves too little in that the older apologists for Christianity seem to have been better advised than some modern ones in condemning every religion but one as an imposter, as at bottom some kind of demon worship or at any rate a superstitious figment. Choice among religions is imperative, and the necessity for choice leaves nothing of any force in the argument from universality. Moreover, when once we enter upon the road of choice, there is at once presented a possibility not yet generally realized.

For the historic increase of the ethical and ideal content of religions suggests that the process of purification may be carried further. It indicates that further choice is imminent in which certain values and functions in experience may be selected. This possibility is what I had in mind in speaking of the difference between the religious and a religion. I am not proposing a religion, but rather the emancipation of elements and outlooks that may be called religious. For the moment we have a religion, whether that of the Sioux Indian or of Judaism or of Christianity, that moment the ideal factors in experience that may be called religious take on a load that is not inherent in them, a load of current beliefs and of institutional practices that are irrelevant to them.

I can illustrate what I mean by a common phenomenon in contemporary life. It is widely supposed that a person who does not accept any religion is thereby shown to be a non-religious person. Yet it is conceivable that the present depression in religion is closely connected with the fact that religions now prevent, because of their weight of historic encumbrances, the religious quality of experience from coming to consciousness and finding the expression that is appropriate to present conditions, intellectual and moral. I believe that such is the case. I believe that many persons are so repelled from what exists as a religion by its intellectual and moral implications, that they are not even aware of attitudes in themselves that if they came to fruition would be genuinely religious. I hope that this remark may help make clear what I mean by the distinction between "religion" as a noun substantive and "religious" as adjectival.

To be somewhat more explicit, a religion (and as I have just said there is no such thing as religion in general) always signifies a special body of beliefs and practices having some kind of institutional organization, loose or tight. In contrast, the adjective "religious" denotes nothing in the way of a specifiable entity, either institutional or as a system of beliefs. It does not denote anything to which one can specifically point as one can point to this and that historic religion or existing church. For it does not denote anything that can exist by itself or that can be organized into a particular and distinctive form of existence. It denotes attitudes that may be taken toward every object and every proposed end or ideal.

Before, however, I develop my suggestion that realization of the distinction just made would operate to emancipate the religious quality from encumbrances that now smother or limit it, I must refer to a position that in some respects is similar in words to the position I have taken, but that in fact is a whole world removed from it. I have several times used the phrase "religious elements of experience." Now at present there is much talk, especially in liberal circles, of religious experience as vouching for the authenticity of certain beliefs and the desirability of certain practices, such as particular forms of prayer and worship. It is even asserted that religious experience is the ultimate basis of religion itself. The gulf between this position and that which I have taken is what I am now concerned to point out.

Those who hold to the notion that there is a definite kind of experience which is itself religious, by that very fact make out of it something specific, as a kind of experience that is marked off from experience as aesthetic, scientific, moral, political; from experience as companionship and friendship. But "religious" as a quality of experience signifies something that may belong to all these experiences. It is the polar opposite of some type of experience that can exist by itself. The distinction comes out clearly when it is noted that the concept of this distinct kind of experience is used to validate a belief in some special kind of object and also to justify some special kind of practice.

For there are many religionists who are now dissatisfied with the older "proofs" of the existence of God, those that go by the name of ontological, cosmological and teleological. The cause of the dissatisfaction is perhaps not so much the arguments that Kant used to show the insufficiency of these alleged proofs, as it is the growing feeling that they are too formal to offer any support to religion in action. Anyway, the dissatisfaction exists. Moreover, these religionists are moved by the rise of the experimental method in other fields. What is more natural and proper, accordingly, than that they should affirm they are just as good empiricists as anybody else— indeed, as good as the scientists themselves? As the latter rely upon certain kinds of experience to prove the existence of certain kinds of objects, so the religionists rely upon a certain kind of experience to prove the existence of the object of religion, especially the supreme object, God.

The discussion may be made more definite by introducing, at this point, a particular illustration of this type of reasoning. A writer says: "I broke down from overwork and soon came to the verge of nervous prostration. One morning after a long and sleepless night . . . I resolved to stop drawing upon myself so continuously and begin drawing upon God. I determined to set apart a quiet time every day in which I could relate my life to its ultimate source, regain the consciousness that in God I live, move and have my being. That was thirty years ago. Since then I have had literally not one hour of darkness or despair."

This is an impressive record. I do not doubt its authenticity nor that of the experience related. It illustrates a religious aspect of experience. But it illustrates also the use of that quality to carry a superimposed load of a particular religion. For having been brought up in the Christian religion, its subject interprets it in the terms of the personal God characteristic of that religion. Taoists, Buddhists, Moslems, persons of no religion including those who reject all supernatural influence and power, have had experiences similar in their effect. Yet another author commenting upon the passage says: "The religious expert can be more sure that this God exists than he can of either the cosmological God of speculative surmise or the Christlike God involved in the validity of moral optimism," and goes on to add that such experiences "mean that God the savior, the power that gives victory over sin on certain conditions that man can fulfill, is an existent, accessible and scientifically knowable reality." It should be clear that this inference is sound only if the conditions, of whatever sort, that produce the effect are called "God." But most readers will take the inference to mean that the existence of a particular Being, of the type called "God" in the Christian religion, is proved by a method akin to that of experimental science.

In reality, the only thing that can be said to be "proved" is the existence of some complex of conditions that have operated to effect an adjustment in life, an orientation, that brings with it a sense of security and peace. The particular interpretation given to this complex of conditions is not inherent in the experience itself. It is derived from the culture with which a particular person has been imbued. A fatalist will give one name to it; a Christian Scientist another, and the one who rejects all supernatural being still another. The determining factor in the interpretation of the experience is the particular doctrinal apparatus into which a person has been inducted. The emotional deposit connected with prior teaching floods the whole situation. It may readily confer upon the experience such a peculiarly sacred preciousness that all inquiry into its causation is barred. The stable outcome is so invaluable that the cause to which it is referred is usually nothing but a reduplication of the thing that has occurred, plus some name that has acquired a deeply emotional quality.

The intent of this discussion is not to deny the genuineness of the result nor its importance in life. It is not, save incidentally, to point out the possibility of a purely naturalistic explanation of the event. My purpose is to indicate what happens when religious experience is already set aside as something *sui generis*. The actual religious quality in the experience described is the *effect* produced, the better adjustment in life and its conditions, not the manner and cause of its production. The way in which the experience operated, its function, determines its religious value. If the reorientation actually occurs, it, and the sense of security and stability accompanying it, are forces on their own account. It takes place in different persons in a multitude of ways. It is sometimes brought about by devotion to a cause; sometimes by a passage of poetry that opens a new perspective; sometimes as was the case with Spinoza—deemed an atheist in his day—through philosophical reflection.

The difference between an experience having a religious force because of what it does in and to the processes of living and religious experience as a separate kind of thing gives me occasion to refer to a previous remark. If this function were rescued through emancipation from dependence upon specific types of beliefs and practices, from those elements that constitute a religion, many individuals would find that experiences having the force of bringing about a better, deeper and enduring adjustment in life are not so rare and infrequent as they are commonly supposed to be. They occur frequently in connection with many significant moments of living. The idea of invisible powers would take on the meaning of all the conditions of nature and human association that support and deepen the sense of values which carry one through periods of darkness and despair to such an extent that they lose their usual depressive character.

I do not suppose for many minds the dislocation of the religious from a religion is easy to effect. Tradition and custom, especially when emotionally charged, are a part of the habits that have become one with our very being. But the possibility of the transfer is demonstrated by its actuality. Let us then for the moment drop the term "religious," and ask what are the attitudes that lend deep and enduring support to the processes of living. I have, for example, used the words "adjustment" and "orientation." What do they signify?

While the words "accommodation," "adaptation," and "adjustment" are frequently employed as synonyms, attitudes exist that are so different that for the sake of clear thought they should be discriminated. There are conditions we meet that cannot be changed. If they are particular and limited, we modify our own particular attitudes in accordance with them. Thus we accommodate ourselves to changes in weather, to alterations in income when we have no other recourse. When the external conditions are lasting we become inured, habituated, or, as the process is now often called, conditioned. The two main traits of this attitude, which I should like to call accommodation, are that it affects *particular* modes of conduct, not the entire self, and that the process is mainly *passive*. It may, however, become general and then it becomes fatalistic resignation or submission. There are other attitudes toward the environment that are also particular but that are more active. We re-act against conditions and endeavor to change them to meet our wants and demands. Plays in a foreign language are "adapted" to meet the needs of an American audience. A house is rebuilt to suit changed conditions of the household; the telephone is invented to serve the demand for speedy communication at a distance; dry soils are irrigated so that they may bear abundant crops. Instead of accommodating ourselves to conditions, we modify conditions so that they will be accommodated to our wants and purposes. This process may be called adaptation.

Now both of these processes are often called by the more general name of adjustment. But there are also changes in ourselves in relation to the world in which we live that are much more inclusive and deep seated. They relate not to this and that want in relation to this and that condition of our surroundings, but pertain to our being in its entirety. Because of their scope, this modification of ourselves is enduring. It lasts through any amount of vicissitude of circumstances, internal and external. There is a composing and harmonizing of the various elements of our being such that, in spite of changes in the special conditions that surround us, these conditions are also arranged, settled, in relation to us. This attitude includes a note of submission. But it is voluntary, not externally imposed; and as voluntary it is something more than a mere Stoical resolution to endure unperturbed throughout the buffetings of fortune. It is more outgoing, more ready and glad, than the latter attitude, and it is more active than the former. And in calling it voluntary, it is not meant that it depends upon a particular resolve or volition. It is a change *of* will conceived as the organic plenitude of our being, rather than any special change *in* will.

It is the claim of religions that they effect this generic and enduring change in attitude. I should like to turn the statement around and say that whenever this change takes place there is a definitely religious attitude. It is not *a* religion that brings it about, but when it occurs, from whatever cause and by whatever means, there is a religious outlook and function. As I have said before, the doctrinal or intellectual apparatus and the institutional accretions that grow up are, in a strict sense, adventitious to the intrinsic quality of such experiences. For they are affairs of the traditions of the culture with which individuals are inoculated. Mr. Santayana has connected the religious quality of experience with the imaginative, as that is expressed in poetry. "Religion and poetry," he says, "are identical in essence, and differ merely in the way in which they are attached to practical affairs. Poetry is called religion when it intervenes in life, and religion, when it merely supervenes upon life, is seen to be nothing but poetry." The difference between intervening *in* and supervening *upon* is as important as is the identity set forth. Imagination may play upon life or it may enter profoundly into it. As Mr. Santayana puts it, "poetry has a universal and a moral function," for "its highest power lies in its relevance to the ideals and purposes of life." Except as it intervenes, "all observation is observation of brute fact, all discipline is mere repression, until these facts digested and this discipline embodied in humane impulses become the starting point for a creative movement of the imagination, the firm basis for ideal constructions in society, religion, and art."

If I may make a comment upon this penetrating insight of Mr. Santayana,

I would say that the difference between imagination that only supervenes and imagination that intervenes is the difference between one that completely interpenetrates all the elements of our being and one that is interwoven with only special and partial factors. There actually occurs extremely little observation of brute facts merely for the sake of the facts, just as there is little discipline that is repression and nothing but repression. Facts are usually observed with reference to some practical end and purpose, and that end is presented only imaginatively. The most repressive discipline has some end in view to which there is at least imputed an ideal quality; otherwise it is purely sadistic. But in such cases of observation and discipline imagination is limited and partial. It does not extend far; it does not permeate deeply and widely.

The connection between imagination and the harmonizing of the self is closer than is usually thought. The idea of a whole, whether of the whole personal being or of the world, is an imaginative, not a literal, idea. The limited world of our observation and reflection becomes the Universe only through imaginative extension. It cannot be apprehended in knowledge nor realized in reflection. Neither observation, thought, nor practical activity can attain that complete unification of the self which is called a whole. The *whole* self is an ideal, an imaginative projection. Hence the idea of a thoroughgoing and deepseated harmonizing of the self with the Universe (as a name for the totality of conditions with which the self is connected) operates only through imagination—which is one reason why this composing of the self is not voluntary in the sense of an act of special volition or resolution. An "adjustment" possesses the will rather than is its express product. Religionists have been right in thinking of it as an influx from sources beyond conscious deliberation and purpose—a fact that helps explain, psychologically, why it has so generally been attributed to a supernatural source and that, perhaps, throws some light upon the reference of it by William James to unconscious factors. And it is pertinent to note that the unification of the self throughout the ceaseless flux of what it does, suffers, and achieves, cannot be attained in terms of itself. The self is always directed toward something beyond itself and so its own unification depends upon the idea of the integration of the shifting scenes of the world into the imaginative totality we call the Universe.

The intimate connection of imagination with ideal elements in experience is generally recognized. Such is not the case with respect to its connection with faith. The latter has been regarded as a substitute for knowledge, for sight. It is defined, in the Christian religion, as *evidence* of things not seen. The implication is that faith is a kind of anticipatory vision of things that are now invisible because of the limitations of our finite and erring nature. Because it is a substitute for knowledge, its material and object are intellectual in quality. As John Locke summed up the matter, faith is "assent to a proposition . . . on the credit of its proposer." Religious faith is then given to a body of propositions as true on the credit of their supernatural author, reason coming in to demonstrate the reasonableness of giving such credit. Of necessity there results the development of theologies, or bodies of systematic propositions, to make explicit in organized form the content of the propositions to which belief is attached and assent given. Given the point of view, those who hold that religion necessarily implies a theology are correct.

But belief or faith has also a moral and practical import. Even devils, according to the older theologians, believe—and tremble. A distinction was made, therefore, between "speculative" or intellectual belief and an act called "justifying" faith. Apart from any theological context, there is a difference between belief that is a conviction that some end should be supreme over conduct, and belief that some object or being exists as a truth for the intellect. Conviction in the moral sense signifies being conquered, vanquished, in our active nature by an ideal end; it signifies acknowledgment of its rightful claim over our desires and purposes. Such acknowledgment is practical, not primarily intellectual. It goes beyond evidence that can be presented to *any* possible observer. Reflection, often long and arduous, may be involved in arriving at the conviction, but the import of thought is not exhausted in discovery of evidence that can justify intellectual assent. The authority of an ideal over choice and conduct is the authority of an ideal, not of a fact, of a truth guaranteed to intellect, not of the status of the one who propounds the truth.

Such moral faith is not easy. It was questioned of old whether the Son of Man should find faith on the earth in his coming. Moral faith has been bolstered by all sorts of arguments intended to prove that its object is not ideal and that its claim upon us is not primarily moral or practical, since the ideal in question is already embedded in the existent frame of things. It is argued that the ideal is already the final reality at the heart of things that exist, and that only our senses or the corruption of our natures prevent us from apprehending its prior existential being. Starting, say, from such an idea as that justice is more than a moral ideal because it is embedded in the very make-up of the actually existent world, men have gone on to build up vast intellectual schemes, philosophies, and theologies, to prove that ideals are real not as ideals but as antecedently existing actualities. They have failed to see that in converting moral realities into matters of intellectual assent they have evinced lack of *moral* faith. Faith that something should be in existence as far as lies in our power is changed into the intellectual belief that it is already in existence. When physical existence does not bear out the assertion, the physical is subtly changed into the metaphysical. In this way, moral faith has been inextricably tied up with intellectual beliefs about the supernatural.

The tendency to convert ends of moral faith and action into articles of an intellectual creed has been furthered by a tendency of which psychologists are well aware. What we ardently desire to have thus and so, we tend to believe is already so. Desire has a powerful influence upon intellectual beliefs. Moreover, when conditions are adverse to realization of the objects of our desire—and in the case of significant ideals they are extremely adverse—it is an easy way out to assume that after all they are already embodied in the ultimate structure of what is, and that appearances to the contrary are *merely* appearances. Imagination then merely supervenes and is freed from the responsibility for intervening. Weak natures take to reverie as a refuge as strong ones do to fanaticism. Those who dissent are mourned over by the first class and converted through the use of force by the second.

What has been said does not imply that all moral faith in ideal ends is by virtue of that fact religious in quality. The religious is "morality touched by emotion" only when the ends of moral conviction arouse emotions that are not only intense but are actuated and supported by ends so inclusive that they unify the self. The inclusiveness of the end in relation to both self and the "universe" to which an inclusive self is related is indispensable. According to the best authorities, "religion" comes from a root that means being bound or tied. Originally, it meant being bound by vows to a particular way of life—as *les religieux* were monks and nuns who had assumed certain vows. The religious attitude signifies something that is bound through imagination to a *general* attitude. This comprehensive attitude, moreover, is much broader than anything indicated by "moral" in its usual sense. The quality of attitude is displayed in art, science and good citizenship.

If we apply the conception set forth to the terms of the definition earlier quoted, these terms take on a new significance. An unseen power controlling our destiny becomes the power of an ideal. All possibilities, as possibilities, are ideal in character. The artist, scientist, citizen, parent, as far as they are actuated by the spirit of their callings, are controlled by the unseen. For all endeavor for the better is moved by faith in what is possible, not by adherence to the actual. Nor does this faith depend for its moving power upon intellectual assurance or belief that the things worked for must surely prevail and come into embodied existence. For the authority of the object to determine our attitude and conduct, the right that is given it to claim our allegiance and devotion is based on the intrinsic nature of the ideal. The outcome, given our best endeavor, is not with us. The inherent vice of all intellectual schemes of idealism is that they convert the idealism of action into a system of beliefs about antecedent reality. The character assigned this reality is so different from that which observation and reflection lead to and support that these schemes inevitably glide into alliance with the supernatural.

All religions, marked by elevated ideal quality, have dwelt upon the power of religion to introduce perspective into the piecemeal and shifting episodes of existence. Here too we need to reverse the ordinary statement and say that whatever introduces genuine perspective is religious, not that religion is something that introduces it. There can be no doubt (referring to the second element of the definition) of our dependence upon forces beyond our control. Primitive man was so impotent in the face of these forces that, especially in an unfavorable natural environment, fear became a dominant attitude, and, as the old saying goes, fear created the gods.

*With* increase of mechanisms of control, the element of fear has, relatively speaking, subsided. Some optimistic souls have even concluded that the forces about us are on the whole essentially benign. But every crisis, whether of the individual or of the community, reminds man of the precarious and partial nature of the control he exercises. When man, individually and collectively, has done his uttermost, conditions that at different times and places have given rise to the ideas of Fate and Fortune, of Chance and Providence, remain. It is the part of manliness to insist upon the capacity of mankind to strive to direct natural and social forces to humane ends. But unqualified absolutistic statements about the omnipotence of such endeavors reflect egoism rather than intelligent courage.

The fact that human destiny is so interwoven with forces beyond human control renders it unnecessary to suppose that dependence and the humility that accompanies it have to find the particular channel that is prescribed by traditional doctrines. What is especially significant is rather the form which the sense of dependence takes. Fear never gave stable perspective in the life of anyone. It is dispersive and withdrawing. Most religions have in fact added rites of communion to those of expiation and propitiation. For our dependence is manifested in those relations to the environment that support our undertakings and aspiration as much as it is in the defeats inflicted upon us. The essentially unreligious attitude is that which attributes human achievement and purpose to man in isolation from the world of physical nature and his fellows. Our successes are dependent upon the cooperation of nature. The sense of the dignity of human nature is as religious as is the sense of awe and reverence when it rests upon a sense of human nature as a cooperating part of a larger whole. Natural piety is not of necessity either a fatalistic acquiescence in natural happenings or a romantic idealization of the world. It may rest upon a just sense of nature as the whole of which we are parts, while it also recognizes that we are parts that are marked by intelligence and purpose, having the capacity to strive by their aid to bring conditions into greater consonance with what is humanly desirable. Such piety is an inherent constituent of a just perspective in life.

Understanding and knowledge also enter into a perspective that is religious in quality. Faith in the continued disclosing of truth through directed cooperative human endeavor is more religious in quality than is any faith in a completed revelation. It is of course now usual to hold that revelation is not completed in the sense of being ended. But religions hold that the essential framework is settled in its significant moral features at least, and that new elements that are offered must be judged by conformity to this framework. Some fixed doctrinal apparatus is necessary for *a* religion. But faith in the possibilities of continued and rigorous inquiry does not limit access to truth to any channel or scheme of things. It does not first say that truth is universal and then add there is but one road to it. It does not depend for assurance upon subjection to any dogma or item of doctrine. It trusts that the natural interactions between man and his environment will breed more intelligence and generate more knowledge provided the scientific methods that define intelligence in operation are pushed further into the mysteries of the world, being themselves promoted and improved in the operation. There is such a thing as faith in intelligence becoming religious in quality—a fact that perhaps explains the efforts of some religionists to disparage the possibilities of intelligence as a force. They properly feel such faith to be a dangerous rival.

Lives that are consciously inspired by loyalty to such ideals as have been mentioned are still comparatively infrequent to the extent of that comprehensiveness and intensity which arouse an ardor religious in function. But before we infer the incompetency of such ideals and of the actions they inspire, we should at least ask ourselves how much of the existing situation is due to the fact that the religious factors of experience have been drafted into supernatural channels and thereby loaded with irrelevant encumbrances. A body of beliefs and practices that are apart from the common and natural relations of mankind must, in the degree in which it is influential, weaken and sap the force of the possibilities inherent in such relations. Here lies one aspect of the emancipation of the religious from religion.

Any activity pursued in behalf of an ideal end against obstacles and in spite of threats of personal loss because of conviction of its general and enduring value is religious in quality. Many a person, inquirer, artist, philanthropist, citizen, men and women in the humblest walks of life, have achieved, without presumption and without display, such unification of themselves and of their relations to the conditions of existence. It remains to extend their spirit and inspiration to ever wider numbers. If I have said anything about religions and religion that seems harsh, I have said those things because of a firm belief that the claim on the part of religions to possess a monopoly of ideals and of the supernatural means by which alone, it is alleged, they can be furthered, stands in the way of the realization of distinctively religious values inherent in natural experience. For that reason, if for no other, I should be sorry if any were misled by the frequency with which I have employed the adjective "religious" to conceive of what

I have said as a disguised apology for what have passed as religions. The opposition between religious values as I conceive them and religions is not to be bridged. Just because the release of these values is so important, their identification with the creeds and cults of religions must be dissolved.

# WILLIAM JAMES

*William James* (1842–1910) was professor at Harvard College and a distinguished American philosopher and psychologist. He attempted to use the pragmatic theory of truth to reconcile the basic claims of religion with an empiricist theory of knowledge. His book *The Varieties of Religious Experience* is a classic work.

## The Varieties of Religious Experience

### Conclusions

The material of our study of human nature is now spread before us; and in this parting hour, set free from the duty of description, we can draw our theoretical and practical conclusions. In my first lecture, defending the empirical method, I foretold that whatever conclusions we might come to could be reached by spiritual judgments only, appreciations of the significance for life of religion, taken "on the whole." Our conclusions cannot be as sharp as dogmatic conclusions would be, but I will formulate them, when the time comes, as sharply as I can.

Summing up in the broadest possible way the characteristics of the religious life, as we have found them, it includes the following beliefs:—

(1) That the visible world is part of a more spiritual universe from which it draws its chief significance;

(2) That union or harmonious relation with that higher universe is our true end;

(3) That prayer or inner communion with the spirit thereof—be that spirit "God" or "law"—is a process wherein work is really done,

From William James, *The Varieties of Religious Experience,* pp. 485–501, 512–515. Copyright, 1902, Longmans, Green and Co. In the public domain. [Footnotes omitted, Eds.]

and spiritual energy flows in and produces effects, psychological or material, within the phenomenal world.

Religion includes also the following psychological characteristics:—

(4) A new zest which adds itself like a gift to life, and takes the form either of lyrical enchantment or of appeal to earnestness and heroism.

(5) An assurance of safety and a temper of peace, and, in relation to others, a preponderance of loving affections.

In illustrating these characteristics by documents, we have been literally bathed in sentiment. In re-reading my manuscript, I am almost appalled at the amount of emotionality which I find in it. After so much of this, we can afford to be dryer and less sympathetic in the rest of the work that lies before us.

The sentimentality of many of my documents is a consequence of the fact that I sought them among the extravagances of the subject. If any of you are enemies of what our ancestors used to brand as enthusiasm, and are, nevertheless, still listening to me now, you have probably felt my selection to have been sometimes almost perverse, and have wished I might have stuck to soberer examples. I reply that I took these extremer examples as yielding the profounder information. To learn the secrets of any science, we go to expert specialists, even though they may be eccentric persons, and not to commonplace pupils. We combine what they tell us with the rest of our wisdom and form our final judgment independently. Even so with religion. We who have pursued such radical expressions of it may now be sure that we know its secrets as authentically as any one can know them who learns them from another; and we have next to answer, each of us for himself, the practical question: what are the dangers in this element of life? and in what proportion may it need to be restrained by other elements, to give the proper balance?

But this question suggests another one which I will answer immediately and get it out of the way, for it has more than once already vexed us. Ought it to be assumed that in all men the mixture of religion with other elements should be identical? Ought it, indeed, to be assumed that the lives of all men should show identical religious elements? In other words, is the existence of so many religious types and sects and creeds regrettable?

To these questions I answer "No" emphatically. And my reason is that I do not see how it is possible that creatures in such different positions and with such different powers as human individuals are, should have exactly the same functions and the same duties. No two of us have identical difficulties, nor should we be expected to work out identical solutions. Each, from his peculiar angle of observation, takes in a certain sphere of fact and trouble, which each must deal with in a unique manner. One of us must soften himself, another must harden himself; one must yield a point, another must stand firm—in order the better to defend the position assigned him. If an Emerson were forced to be a Wesley, or a Moody forced to be a Whitman, the total human consciousness of the divine would suffer. The divine can mean no single quality, it must mean a group of qualities, by being champions of which in alternation, different men may all find worthy missions. Each attitude being a syllable in human nature's total message, it takes the whole of us to spell the meaning out completely. So a "god of battles" must be allowed to be the god for one kind of person, a god of peace and heaven and home, the god for another. We must frankly recognize the fact that we live in partial systems, and that parts are not interchangeable in the spiritual life. If we are peevish and jealous, destruction of the self must be an element of our religion; why need it be one if we are good and sympathetic from the outset? If we are sick souls, we require a religion of deliverance; but why think so much of deliverance, if we are healthy-minded? Unquestionably, some men have the completer experience and the higher vocation, here just as in the social world; but for each man to stay in his own experience, whate'er it be, and for others to tolerate him there, is surely best.

But, you may now ask, would not this one-sidedness be cured if we should all espouse the science of religion as our own religion? In answering this question I must open again the general relations of the theoretic to the active life.

Knowledge about a thing is not the thing itself. You remember what Al-Ghazzali told us in the Lecture on Mysticism,—that to understand the causes of drunkenness, as a physician understands them, is not to be drunk. A science might come to understand everything about the causes and elements of religion, and might even decide which elements were qualified, by their general harmony with other branches of knowledge, to be considered true; and yet the best man at this science might be the man who found it hardest to be personally devout. *Tout savoir c'est tout pardonner.* The name of Renan would doubtless occur to many persons as an example of the way in which breadth of knowledge may make one only a dilettante in possibilities, and blunt the acuteness of one's living faith. If religion be a function by which either God's cause or man's cause is to be really advanced, then he who lives the life of it, however narrowly, is a better servant than he who merely knows about it, however much. Knowledge about life is one thing; effective occupation of a place in life, with its dynamic currents passing through your being, is another.

For this reason, the science of religions may not be an equivalent for living religion; and if we turn to the inner difficulties of such a science, we see that a point comes when she must drop the purely theoretic attitude, and either let her knots remain uncut, or have them cut by active faith. To see this, suppose that we have our science of religions constituted as a matter of fact. Suppose that she has assimilated all the necessary historical material and distilled out of it as its essence the same conclusions which I myself a few moments ago pronounced. Suppose that she agrees that religion, wherever it is an active thing, involves a belief in ideal presences, and a belief that in our prayerful communion with them, work is done, and something real comes to pass. She has now to exert her critical activity, and to decide how far, in the light of other sciences and in that of general philosophy, such beliefs can be considered *true*.

Dogmatically to decide this is an impossible task. Not only are the other sciences and the philosophy still far from being completed, but in their present state we find them full of conflicts. The sciences of nature know nothing of spiritual presences, and on the whole hold no practical commerce whatever with the idealistic conceptions towards which general philosophy inclines. The scientist, so-called, is, during his scientific hours at least, so materialistic that one may well say that on the whole the influence of science goes against the notion that religion should be recognized at all. And this antipathy to religion finds an echo within the very science of religions itself. The cultivator of this science has to become acquainted with so many groveling and horrible superstitions that a presumption easily arises in his mind that any belief that is religious probably is false. In the "prayerful communion" of savages with such mumbo-jumbos of deities as they acknowledge, it is hard for us to see what genuine spiritual work—even though it were work relative only to their dark savage obligations—can possibly be done.

The consequence is that the conclusions of the science of religions are as likely to be adverse as they are to be favorable to the claim that the essence of religion is true. There is a notion in the air about us that religion is probably only an anachronism, a case of "survival," an atavistic relapse into a mode of thought which humanity in its more enlightened examples has outgrown; and this notion our religious anthropologists at present do little to counteract.

This view is so widespread at the present day that I must consider it with some explicitness before I pass to my own conclusions. Let me call it the "Survival theory," for brevity's sake.

The pivot round which the religious life, as we have traced it, revolves, is the interest of the individual in his private personal destiny. Religion, in short, is a monumental chapter in the history of human egotism. The gods believed in—whether by crude savages or by men disciplined intellectually —agree with each other in recognizing personal calls. Religious thought is carried on in terms of personality, this being, in the world of religion, the one fundamental fact. To-day, quite as much as at any previous age, the religious individual tells you that the divine meets him on the basis of his personal concerns.

Science, on the other hand, has ended by utterly repudiating the personal point of view. She catalogues her elements and records her laws indifferent as to what purpose may be shown forth by them, and constructs her theories quite careless of their bearing on human anxieties and fates. Though the scientist may individually nourish a religion, and be a theist in his irresponsible hours, the days are over when it could be said that for Science herself the heavens declare the glory of God and the firmament showeth his handiwork. Our solar system, with its harmonies, is seen now as but one passing case of a certain sort of moving equilibrium in the heavens, realized by a local accident in an appalling wilderness of worlds where no life can exist. In a span of time which as a cosmic interval will count but as an hour, it will have ceased to be. The Darwinian notion of chance production, and subsequent destruction, speedy or deferred, applies to the largest as well as to the smallest facts. It is impossible, in the present temper of the scientific imagination, to find in the driftings of the cosmic atoms, whether they work on the universal or on the particular scale, anything but a kind of aimless weather, doing and undoing, achieving no proper history, and leaving no result. Nature has no one distinguishable ultimate tendency with which it is possible to feel a sympathy. In the vast rhythm of her processes, as the scientific mind now follows them, she appears to cancel herself. The books of natural theology which satisfied the intellects of our grandfathers seem to us quite grotesque, representing as they did, a God who conformed the largest things of nature to the paltriest of our private wants. The God whom science recognizes must be a God of universal laws exclusively, a God who does a wholesale, not a retail business. He cannot accommodate his processes to the convenience of individuals. The bubbles on the foam which coats a stormy sea are floating episodes, made and unmade by the forces of the wind and water. Our private selves are like those bubbles—epiphenomena, as Clifford, I believe, ingeniously called them; their destinies weigh nothing and determine nothing in the world's irremediable currents of events.

You see how natural it is, from this point of view, to treat religion as a mere survival, for religion does in fact perpetuate the traditions of the most primeval thought. To coerce the spiritual powers, or to square them and get them on our side, was, during enormous tracts of time, the one great object in our dealings with the natural world. For our ancestors, dreams, hallucinations, revelations, and cock-and-bull stories were inextricably mixed with facts. Up to comparatively recent date such distinctions as those between what has been verified and what is only conjectured, between the impersonal and the personal aspects of existence, were hardly suspected or conceived. Whatever you imagined in a lively manner, whatever you thought fit to be true, you affirmed confidently; and whatever you affirmed, your comrades believed. Truth was what had not yet been contradicted, most things were taken into the mind from the point of view of their human suggestiveness, and the attention confined itself exclusively to the aesthetic and dramatic aspects of events.

How indeed could it be otherwise? The extraordinary value, for explanation and prevision, of those mathematical and mechanical modes of conception which science uses, was a result that could not possibly have been expected in advance. Weight, movement, velocity, direction, position, what thin, pallid, uninteresting ideas! How could the richer animistic aspects of Nature, the peculiarities and oddities that make phenomena picturesquely striking or expressive, fail to have been first singled out and followed by philosophy as the more promising avenue to the knowledge of Nature's life? Well, it is still in these richer animistic and dramatic aspects that religion delights to dwell. It is the terror and beauty of phenomena, the "promise" of the dawn and of the rainbow, the "voice" of the thunder, the "gentleness" of the summer rain, the "sublimity" of the stars, and not the physical laws which these things follow, by which the religious mind still continues to be most impressed; and just as of yore, the devout man tells you that in the solitude of his room or of the fields he still feels the divine presence, that inflowings of help come in reply to his prayers, and that sacrifices to this unseen reality fill him with security and peace.

Pure anachronism! says the survival-theory—anachronism for which deanthropomorphization of the imagination is the remedy required. The less we mix the private with the cosmic, the more we dwell in universal and impersonal terms, the truer heirs of Science we become.

In spite of the appeal which this impersonality of the scientific attitude makes to a certain magnanimity of temper, I believe it to be shallow, and I can now state my reason in comparatively few words. That reason is that, so long as we deal with the cosmic and the general, we deal only with the symbols of reality, but *as soon as we deal with private and personal phenomena as such, we deal with realities in the completest sense of the term.* I think I can easily make clear what I mean by these words.

The world of our experience consists at all times of two parts, an objective and a subjective part, of which the former may be incalculaby more extensive than the latter, yet the latter can never be omitted or suppressed. The objective part is the sum total of whatsoever at any given time we may be thinking of, the subjective part is the inner "state" in which the thinking comes to pass. What we think of may be enormous—the cosmic times and spaces, for example—whereas the inner state may be the most fugitive and paltry activity of mind. Yet the cosmic objects, so far as the experience yields them, are but ideal pictures of something whose existence we do not inwardly possess but only point at outwardly, while the inner state is our very experience itself; its reality and that of our experience are one. A conscious field *plus* its object as felt or thought of *plus* an attitude towards the object *plus* the sense of a self to whom the attitude belongs—such a concrete bit of personal experience may be a small bit, but it is a solid bit as long as it lasts; not hollow, not a mere abstract element of experience, such as the "object" is when taken all alone. It is a *full* fact, even though it be an insignificant fact; it is of the *kind* to which all realities whatsoever must belong; the motor currents of the world run through the like of it; it is on the line connecting real events with real events. That unsharable feeling which each of us has of the pinch of his individual destiny as he privately feels it rolling out on fortune's wheel may be disparaged for its egotism, may be sneered at as unscientific, but it is the one thing that fills up the measure of our concrete actuality, and any would-be existent that should lack such a feeling, or its analogue, would be a piece of reality only half made up.

If this be true, it is absurd for science to say that the egotistic elements of experience should be suppressed. The axis of reality runs solely through the egotistic places—they are strung upon it like so many beads. To describe the world with all the various feelings of the individual pinch of destiny, all the various spiritual attitudes, left out from the description—they being as describable as anything else—would be something like offering a printed bill of fare as the equivalent for a solid meal. Religion makes no such blunder. The individual's religion may be egotistic, and those private realities which it keeps in touch with may be narrow enough; but at any rate it always remains infinitely less hollow and abstract, as far as it goes, than a science which prides itself on taking no account of anything private at all.

A bill of fare with one real raisin on it instead of the word "raisin," with one real egg instead of the word "egg," might be an inadequate meal, but it would at least be a commencement of reality. The contention of the survival-theory that we ought to stick to non-personal elements exclusively seems like saying that we ought to be satisfied forever with reading the naked bill of fare. I think, therefore, that however particular questions connected with our individual destinies may be answered, it is only by acknowledging them as genuine questions, and living in the sphere of thought which they open up, that we become profound. But to live thus is to be religious; so I unhesitatingly repudiate the survival-theory of religion, as being founded on an egregious mistake. It does not follow, because our ancestors made so many errors of fact and mixed them with their religion, that we should therefore leave off being religious at all. But being religious we establish ourselves in possession of ultimate reality at the only points at which reality is given us to guard. Our responsible concern is with our private destiny, after all. . . .

Let me then propose, as an hypothesis, that whatever it may be on its *farther* side, the "more" with which in religious experience we feel ourselves connected is on its *hither* side the subconscious continuation of our conscious life. Starting thus with a recognized psychological fact as our basis, we seem to preserve a contact with "science" which the ordinary theologian lacks. At the same time the theologian's contention that the religious man is moved by an external power is vindicated, for it is one of the peculiarities of invasions from the subconscious region to take on objective appearances, and to suggest to the Subject an external control. In the religious life the control is felt as "higher"; but since on our hypothesis it is primarily the higher faculties of our own hidden mind which are controlling, the sense of union with the power beyond us is a sense of something, not merely apparently, but literally true.

This doorway into the subject seems to me the best one for a science of religions, for it mediates between a number of different points of view. Yet it is only a doorway, and difficulties present themselves as soon as we step through it, and ask how far our transmarginal consciousness carries us if we follow it on its remoter side. Here the over-beliefs begin: here mysticism and the conversion-rapture and Vedantism and transcendental idealism bring in their monistic interpretations and tell us that the finite self rejoins the absolute self, for it was always one with God and identical with the soul of the world. Here the prophets of all the different religions come with their visions, voices, raptures, and other openings, supposed by each to authenticate his own peculiar faith.

Those of us who are not personally favored with such specific revelations must stand outside of them altogether and, for the present at least, decide that, since they corroborate incompatible theological doctrines, they neutralize one another and leave no fixed result. If we follow any one of them, or if we follow philosophical theory and embrace monistic pantheism on non-mystical grounds, we do so in the exercise of our individual freedom, and build out our religion in the way most congruous with our personal susceptibilities. Among these susceptibilities intellectual ones play a decisive part. Although the religious question is primarily a question of life, of living or not living in the higher union which opens itself to us as a gift, yet the spiritual excitement in which the gift appears a real one will often fail to be aroused in an individual until certain particular intellectual beliefs or ideas which, as we say, come home to him, are touched. These ideas will thus be essential to that individual's religion—which is as much as to say that over-beliefs in various directions are absolutely indispensable, and that we should treat them with tenderness and tolerance so long as they are not intolerant themselves. As I have elsewhere written, the most interesting and valuable things about a man are usually his over-beliefs.

Disregarding the over-beliefs, and confining ourselves to what is common and generic, we have in *the fact that the conscious person is continuous with a wider self through which saving experiences come,* a positive content of religious experience which, it seems to me, *is literally and objectively true as far as it goes.*

# ALFRED NORTH WHITEHEAD

*Alfred North Whitehead* (1861–1947), British philosopher, mathematician, and influential scholar, who became professor of philosophy at Harvard University in 1924, was the author of *Process and Reality,* one of the most significant works in philosophy produced in this century.

## Religion in the Making

### I. Religion Defined

It is my purpose in the four lectures of this course to consider the type of justification which is available for belief in doctrines of religion. This is a question which in some new form challenges each generation. It is the peculiarity of religion that humanity is always shifting its attitude towards it.

The contrast between religion and the elementary truths of arithmetic makes my meaning clear. Ages ago the simple arithmetical doctrines dawned on the human mind, and throughout history the unquestioned dogma that two and three make five reigned whenever it has been relevant. We all know what this doctrine means, and its history is of no importance for its elucidation.

But we have the gravest doubt as to what religion means so far as doctrine is concerned. There is no agreement as to the definition of religion in its most general sense, including true and false religion; nor is there any agreement as to the valid religious beliefs, nor even as to what we mean by the truth of religion. It is for this reason that some consideration of religion as an unquestioned factor throughout the long stretch of human history is necessary to secure the relevance of any discussion of its general principles.

Reprinted with permission of The Macmillan Company and Cambridge University Press from *Religion in the Making* by Alfred North Whitehead. Copyright 1926 by The Macmillan Company, renewed 1954 by Evelyn Whitehead.

There is yet another contrast. What is generally disputed is doubtful, and what is doubtful is relatively unimportant—other things being equal. I am speaking of general truths. We avoid guiding our actions by general principles which are entirely unsettled. If we do not know what number is the product of 69 and 67, we defer any action pre-supposing the answer, till we have found out. This little arithmetical puzzle can be put aside till it is settled, and it is capable of definite settlement with adequate trouble.

But as between religion and arithmetic, other things are not equal. You *use* arithmetic, but you *are* religious. Arithmetic of course enters into your nature, so far as that nature involves a multiplicity of things. But it is there as a necessary condition, and not as a transforming agency. No one is invariably "justified" by his faith in the multiplication table. But in some sense or other, justification is the basis of all religion. Your character is developed according to your faith. This is the primary religious truth from which no one can escape. Religion is force of belief cleansing the inward parts. For this reason the primary religious virtue is sincerity, a penetrating sincerity.

A religion, on its doctrinal side, can thus be defined as a system of general truths which have the effect of transforming character when they are sincerely held and vividly apprehended.

In the long run your character and your conduct of life depend upon your intimate convictions. Life is an internal fact for its own sake, before it is an external fact relating itself to others. The conduct of external life is conditioned by environment, but it receives its final quality, on which its worth depends, from the internal life which is the self-realization of existence. Religion is the art and the theory of the internal life of man, so far as it depends on the man himself and on what is permanent in the nature of things.

This doctrine is the direct negation of the theory that religion is primarily a social fact. Social facts are of great importance to religion, because there is no such thing as absolutely independent existence. You cannot abstract society from man; most psychology is herd-psychology. But all collective emotions leave untouched the awful ultimate fact, which is the human being, consciously alone with itself, for its own sake.

Religion is what the individual does with his own solitariness. It runs through three stages, if it evolves to its final satisfaction. It is the transition from God the void to God the enemy, and from God the enemy to God the companion.

Thus religion is solitariness; and if you are never solitary, you are never religious. Collective enthusiasms, revivals, institutions, churches, rituals, bibles, codes of behaviour, are the trappings of religion, its passing forms. They may be useful, or harmful; they may be authoritatively ordained, or merely temporary expedients. But the end of religion is beyond all this.

Accordingly, what should emerge from religion is individual worth of character. But worth is positive or negative, good or bad. Religion is by no means necessarily good. It may be very evil. The fact of evil, interwoven with the texture of the world, shows that in the nature of things there remains effectiveness for degradation. In your religious experience the God with whom you have made terms may be the God of destruction, the God who leaves in his wake the loss of the greater reality.

In considering religion, we should not be obsessed by the idea of its necessary goodness. This is a dangerous delusion. The point to notice is its transcendent importance; and the fact of this importance is abundantly made evident by the appeal to history.

## II. *The Emergence of Religion*

Religion, so far as it receives external expression in human history, exhibits four factors or sides of itself. These factors are ritual, emotion, belief, rationalization. There is definite organized procedure, which is ritual: there are definite types of emotional expression: there are definitely expressed beliefs: and there is the adjustment of these beliefs into a system, internally coherent and coherent with other beliefs.

But all these four factors are not of equal influence throughout all historical epochs. The religious idea emerged gradually into human life, at first barely disengaged from other human interests. The order of the emergence of these factors was in the inverse order of the depth of their religious importance: first ritual, then emotion, then belief, then rationalization.

The dawn of these religious stages is gradual. It consists in an increase of emphasis. Perhaps it is untrue to affirm that the later factors are ever wholly absent. But certainly, when we go far enough back, belief and rationalization are completely negligible, and emotion is merely a secondary result of ritual. Then emotion takes the lead, and the ritual is for the emotion which it generates. Belief then makes its appearance as explanatory of the complex of ritual and emotion, and in this appearance of belief we may discern the germ of rationalization.

It is not until belief and rationalization are well established that solitariness is discernible as constituting the heart of religious importance. The great religious conceptions which haunt the imaginations of civilized mankind are scenes of solitariness: Prometheus chained to his rock, Mahomet brooding in the desert, the meditations of the Buddha, the solitary Man on the Cross. It belongs to the depth of the religious spirit to have felt forsaken, even by God.

## III. *Ritual and Emotion*

Ritual goes back beyond the dawn of history. It can be discerned in the animals, in their individual habits and still more in their collective evolutions. Ritual may be defined as the habitual performance of definite actions which have no direct relevance to the preservation of the physical organisms of the actors.

Flocks of birds perform their ritual evolutions in the sky. In Europe rooks and starlings are notable examples of this fact. Ritual is the primitive outcome of superfluous energy and leisure. It exemplifies the tendency of living bodies to repeat their own actions. Thus the actions necessary in hunting for food, or in other useful pursuits, are repeated for their own sakes; and their repetition also repeats the joy of exercise and the emotion of success.

In this way emotion waits upon ritual; and then ritual is repeated and elaborated for the sake of its attendant emotions. Mankind became artists in ritual. It was a tremendous discovery—how to excite emotions for their own sake, apart from some imperious biological necessity. But emotions sensitize the organism. Thus the unintended effect was produced of sensitizing the human organism in a variety of ways diverse from what would have been produced by the necessary work of life.

Mankind was started upon its adventures of curiosity and of feeling.

It is evident that, according to this account, religion and play have the same origin in ritual. This is because ritual is the stimulus to emotion, and an habitual ritual may diverge into religion or into play, according to the quality of the emotion excited. Even in comparatively modern times, among the Greeks of the fifth century before Christ, the Olympic Games were tinged with religion, and the Dionysiac festival in Attica ended with a comic drama. Also in the modern world, a holy day and a holiday are kindred notions.

Ritual is not the only way of artificially stimulating emotion. Drugs are equally effective. Luckily the range of drugs at the command of primitive races was limited. But there is ample evidence of the religious use of drugs in conjunction with the religious use of ritual. For example Athenaeus tells us that among the Persians it was the religious duty of the King, once a year, at some stated festival in honour of Mithras, to appear in the temple intoxicated.[1] A relic of the religious awe at intoxication is the use of wine in the Communion service. It is an example of the upward trend of ritual by which a widespread association of thought is elevated into a great symbolism, divested of its primitive grossness.

In this primitive phase of religion, dominated by ritual and emotion, we are dealing with essentially social phenomena. Ritual is more impressive, and emotion more active, when a whole society is concerned in the same ritual and the same emotion. Accordingly, a collective ritual and a collective emotion take their places as one of the binding forces of savage tribes. They represent the first faint glimmerings of the life of the spirit raised beyond

---

[1] Cf. *The Deipnosophistae of Athenaeus*, Book X. I am indebted to my friend Professor J. H. Woods for this reference.

concentration upon the task of supplying animal necessities. Conversely, religion in its decay sinks back into sociability.

## IV. Belief

Mere ritual and emotion cannot maintain themselves untouched by intellectuality. Also the abstract idea of maintaining the ritual for the sake of the emotion, though it may express the truth about the subconscious psychology of primitive races, is far too abstract to enter into their conscious thoughts. A myth satisfies the demands of incipient rationality. Men found themselves practising various rituals, and found the rituals generating emotions. The myth explains the purpose both of the ritual and of the emotion. It is the product of the vivid fancy of primitive men in an unfathomed world.

To primitive man, and to ourselves on our primitive side, the universe is not so much unfathomable as unfathomed—by this I mean undiscriminated, unanalyzed. It is not a complex of definite unexplained happenings, but a dim background shot across by isolated vivid effects charged with emotional excitements. The very presuppositions of a coherent rationalism are absent. Such a rationalism presupposes a complex of definite facts whose interconnections are sought. But the prior stage is a background of indefiniteness relieved by vivid acts of definition, inherently isolated. One exception must be made in favour of the routine of tribal necessities which are taken for granted. But what lies beyond the routine of life is in general void of definition; and when it is vivid, it is disconnected.

The myth which meets the ritual is some exceptional vivid fancy, or recollection of some actual vivid fact—probably distorted in remembrance— which appears not only as explanatory both of ritual and emotion, but also as generative of emotion when conjoined with the ritual. Thus the myth not only explains but reinforces the hidden purpose of the ritual, which is emotion.

Then rituals and emotions and myths reciprocally interact; and the myths have various grades of relationship to actual fact, and have various grades of symbolic truth as being representative of large ideas only to be apprehended in some parable. Also in some cases the myth precedes the ritual. But there is the general fact that ritualism precedes mythology. For we can observe ritualism even among animals, and presumably they are destitute of a mythology.

A myth will involve special attention to some persons or to some things, real or imaginary. Thus in a sense, the ritual, as performed in conjunction with the explanatory purpose of the myth, is the primitive worship of the hero-person or the hero-thing. But there can be very little disinterested worship among primitive folk—even less than now, if possible. Accordingly, the belief in the myth will involve the belief that something is to be got out of him or it, or that something is to be averted in respect to the evil to be feared from him or it. Thus incantation, prayer, praise, and ritual absorption of the hero deity emerge.

If the hero be a person, we call the ritual, with its myth, "religion"; if the hero be a thing, we call it "magic." In religion we induce, in magic we compel. The important difference between magic and religion is that magic is unprogressive and religion sometimes is progressive; except in so far as science can be traced back to the progress of magic.

Religion, in this stage of belief, marks a new formative agent in the ascent of man. For just as ritual encouraged *emotion* beyond the mere response to practical necessities, so religion in this further stage begets *thoughts* divorced from the mere battling with the pressure of circumstances. Imagination secured in it a machinery for its development; thought has been thereby led beyond the immediate objects in sight. Its concepts may in these early stages be crude and horrible; but they have the supreme virtue of being concepts of objects beyond immediate sense and perception.

This is the stage of uncoördinated beliefs. So far as this is the dominant phase there can be a curious tolerance, in that one cult does not war upon another cult. Since there is a minimum of coördination, there is room for all. But religion is still a thoroughly social phenomenon. The cult includes the tribe, or at least it includes some well-defined body of persons within the social organism. You may not desert your own cults, but there need be no clash between cults. In the higher stages of such a religion there are tribal gods, or many gods within a tribe, with the loosest coördination of cults and myths.

Though religion can be a source of progress, it need not be so, especially when its dominant feature is this stage of uncriticized belief. It is easy for a tribe to stabilize its ritual and its myths, and there need be no external spur to progress. In fact, this is the stage of religious evolution in which the masses of semi-civilized humanity have halted—the stage of satisfactory ritual and of satisfied belief without impulse towards higher things. Such religion satisfies the pragmatic test: It works, and thereby claims that it be awarded the prize for truth.

## V. Rationalism

The age of martyrs dawns with the coming of rationalism. The antecedent phases of religion had been essentially sociable. Many were called, and all were chosen. The final phase introduces the not of solitariness: "Strait is the gate, and narrow is the way, . . . and few there be that find it." When a modern religion forgets this saying, it is suffering from an atavistic relapse into primitive barbarism. It is appealing to the psychology of the herd, away from the intuitions of the few.

The religious epoch which we are now considering is very modern. Its past duration is of the order of six thousand years. Of course exact dates do not count; you can extend the epoch further back into the past in order to include some faint anticipatory movement, or you can contract its duration so as to exclude flourishing survivals of the earlier phase. The movement has extended over all the civilized races of Asia and Europe. In the past Asia has proved the most fertile in ideas, but within the last two thousand years Europe has given the movement a new aspect. It is to be noted that the two most perfect examples of rationalistic religions have flourished chiefly in countries foreign to the races among which they had their origin.

The Bible is by far the most complete account of the coming of rationalism into religion, based on the earliest documents available. Viewed as such an account, it is only relevant to the region between the Tigris and the Nile. It exhibits the note of progressive solitariness in the religious idea: first, types of thought generally prevalent; then protesting prophets, isolated figures of denunciation and exhortation stirring the Jewish nation; then one man, with twelve disciples, who met with almost complete national rejection; then the adaptation for popular survival of this latter doctrine by another man who, very significantly, had no first-hand contact with the original teaching. In his hands, something was added and something was lost; but fortunately the Gospels also survive.

It is evident that I have drawn attention to the span of six thousand years because, in addition to being reasonable when we have regard to all the evidence, it corresponds to the chronology of the Bible. We—in Europe and America—are the heirs of the religious movements depicted in that collection of books. Discussion on the methods of religion and their justification must, in order to be relevant, base itself upon the Bible for illustration. We must remember, however, that Buddhism and Mahometanism, among others, must also be included in the scope of general statements, even if they are not explictly referred to.

Rational religion is religion whose beliefs and rituals have been reorganized with the aim of making it the central element in a coherent ordering of life—an ordering which shall be coherent both in respect to the elucidation of thought, and in respect to the direction of conduct towards a unified purpose commanding ethical approval.

The peculiar position of religion is that it stands between abstract metaphysics and the particular principles applying to only some among the experiences of life. The relevance of its concepts can only be distinctly discerned in moments of insight, and then, for many of us, only after suggestion from without. Hence religion bases itself primarily upon a small selection from the common experiences of the race. On this side, religion ranges itself as one among other specialized interests of mankind whose truths are of limited validity. But on its other side, religion claims that its concepts, though derived primarily from special experiences, are yet of universal validity, to be applied by faith to the ordering of all experience.

Rational religion appeals to the direct intuition of special occasions, and to the elucidatory power of its concepts for all occasions. It arises from that which is special, but it extends to what is general. The doctrines of rational religion aim at being that metaphysics which can be derived from the supernormal experience of mankind in its moments of finest insight. Theoretically, rational religion could have arisen in complete independence of the antecedent social religions of ritual and mythical belief. Before the historical sense had established itself, that was the way in which the apologetic theologians tended to exhibit the origins of their respective religions. But the general history of religion, and in particular that portion of its history contained in the Bible, decisively negatives that view. Rational religion emerged as a gradual transformation of the preëxisting religious forms. Finally, the old forms could no longer contain the new ideas, and the modern religions of civilization are traceable to definite crises in this process of development. But the development was not then ended; it had only acquired more suitable forms for self-expression.

The emergence of rational religion was strictly conditioned by the general progress of the races in which it arose. It had to wait for the development in human consciousness of the relevant general ideas and of the relevant ethical intuitions. It required that such ideas should not merely be casually entertained by isolated individuals, but that they should be stabilized in recognizable forms of expression, so as to be recalled and communicated. You can only speak of mercy among a people who, in some respects, are already merciful.

A language is not a universal mode of expressing all ideas whatsoever. It is a limited mode of expressing such ideas as have been frequently entertained, and urgently needed, by the group of human beings who developed that mode of speech. It is only during a comparatively short period of human history that there has existed any language with an adequate stock of general terms. Such general terms require a permanent literature to define them by their mode of employment.

The result is that the free handling of general ideas is a late acquirement. I am not maintaining that the brains of men were inadequate for the task. The point is that it took ages for them to develop first the appliances and then the habits which made generality of thought possible and prevalent. For ages, existing languages must have been ready for development. If men had been in contact with a superior race, either personally or by a survival of their literature, a process which requires scores or even hundreds of generations might have been antedated, so as to have been effected almost at once. Such, in fact, was the later history of the development of the races of Northern Europe. Again, a social system which encourages developments of thought can procure the advent. This is the way in which the result was first obtained. Society and language grew together.

The influence of the antecedent type of religion, ceremonial, mythical, and sociable, has been great; and the estimates as to its value diverse. During the thousand years preceding the Christian era, there was a peculiarly intense struggle on the part of rationalism to transform the more primitive type. The issue was a new synthesis which, in the forms of the various great religions, has lasted to the present day. A rational generality was introduced into the religious ideas; and the myth, when retained, was reorganized with the intention of making it an account of verifiable historical circumstances which exemplified the general ideas with adequate perfection.

Thus rational criticism was admitted in principle. The appeal was from the tribal custom to the direct individual intuition, ethical, metaphysical, or logical: "For I desired mercy, and not sacrifice; and the knowledge of God more than burnt offerings," are words which Hosea ascribes to Jehovah; and he thereby employs the principles of individual criticism of tribal custom, and bases it upon direct ethical intuition.

In this way the religions evolved towards more individualistic forms, shedding their exclusively communal aspect. The individual became the religious unit in the place of the community; the tribal dance lost its importance compared to the individual prayer; and, for the few, the individual prayer merged into justification through individual insight.

So to-day it is not France which goes to heaven, but individual Frenchmen; and it is not China which attains nirvana, but Chinamen.

During this epoch of struggle—as in most religious struggles—the judgments passed by the innovators on the less-developed religious forms were very severe. The condemnation of idolatry pervades the Bible; and there are traces of a recoil which go further: "I hate, I despise your feast days," writes Amos, speaking in the name of Jehovah.

Such criticism is wanted. Indeed history, down to the present day, is a melancholy record of the horrors which can attend religion: human sacrifice, and in particular the slaughter of children, cannibalism, sensual orgies, abject superstition, hatred as between races, the maintenance of degrading customs, hysteria, bigotry, can all be laid at its charge. Religion is the last refuge of human savagery. The uncritical association of religion with goodness is directly negatived by plain facts. Religion can be, and has been, the main instrument for progress. But if we survey the whole race, we must pronounce that generally it has not been so: "Many are called, but few are chosen."

# RUDOLF OTTO

*Rudolf Otto* (1869–1937), German Protestant theologian and philosopher
of religion, is famous for his analysis of the unique religious sense of the
numinous in his classic work *The Idea of the Holy.*

## The Idea of the Holy

### The Elements in the *"Numinous"*

CREATURE-FEELING. The reader is invited to direct his mind to a moment
of deeply-felt religious experience, as little as possible qualified by other
forms of consciousness. Whoever cannot do this, whoever knows no such
moments in his experience, is requested to read no farther; for it is not easy
to discuss questions of religious psychology with one who can recollect the
emotions of his adolescence, the discomforts of indigestion, or, say, social
feelings, but cannot recall any intrinsically religious feelings. We do not
blame such an one, when he tries for himself to advance as far as he can
with the help of such principles of explanation as he knows, interpreting
"aesthetics" in terms of sensuous pleasure, and "religion" as a function of
the gregarious instinct and social standards, or as something more primitive
still. But the artist, who for his part has an intimate personal knowledge of
the distinctive element in the aesthetic experience, will decline his theories
with thanks, and the religious man will reject them even more uncompro-
misingly.

Next, in the probing and analysis of such states of the soul as that of
solemn worship, it will be well if regard be paid to what is unique in them
rather than to what they have in common with other similar states. To be
*rapt* in worship is one thing; to be morally *uplifted* by the contemplation of
a good deed is another; and it is not to their common features, but to those
elements of emotional content peculiar to the first that we would have attention directed as precisely as possible. As Christians we undoubtedly here first
meet with feelings familiar enough in a weaker form in other departments
of experience, such as feelings of gratitude, trust, love, reliance, humble

From Rudolf Otto, *The Idea of the Holy,* trans. John Harvey, pp. 8–34. Copyright
1923, Oxford University Press. Reprinted by permission.

submission, and dedication. But this does not by any means exhaust the content of religious worship. Not in any of these have we got the special features of the quite unique and incomparable experience of solemn worship. In what does this consist?

Schleiermacher has the credit of isolating a very important element in such an experience. This is the "feeling of dependence." But this important discovery of Schleiermacher is open to criticism in more than one respect.

In the first place, the feeling or emotion which he really has in mind in this phrase is in its specific quality not a "feeling of dependence" in the "natural" sense of the word. As such, other domains of life and other regions of experience than the religious occasion the feeling, as a sense of personal insufficiency and impotence, a consciousness of being determined by circumstances and environment. The feeling of which Schleiermacher wrote has an undeniable analogy with these states of mind: they serve as an indication to it, and its nature may be elucidated by them, so that, by following the direction in which they point, the feeling itself may be spontaneously felt. But the feeling is at the same time also qualitatively different from such analogous states of mind. Schleiermacher himself, in a way, recognizes this by distinguishing the feeling of pious or religious dependence from all other feelings of dependence. His mistake is in making the distinction merely that between "absolute" and "relative" dependence, and therefore a difference of degree and not of intrinsic quality. What he overlooks is that, in giving the feeling the name "feeling of dependence" at all, we are really employing what is no more than a very close analogy. Anyone who compares and contrasts the two states of mind introspectively will find out, I think, what I mean. It cannot be expressed by means of anything else, just because it is so primary and elementary a datum in our psychical life, and therefore only definable through itself. It may perhaps help him if I cite a well-known example, in which the precise "moment" or element of religious feeling of which we are speaking is most actively present. When Abraham ventures to plead with God for the men of Sodom, he says (Gen. xviii. 27) : "Behold now, I have taken upon me to speak unto the Lord, which am but dust and ashes." There you have a self-confessed "feeling of dependence," which is yet at the same time far more than, and something other than, *merely* a feeling of dependence. Desiring to give it a name of its own, I propose to call it "creature-consciousness" or creature-feeling. It is the emotion of a creature, submerged and overwhelmed by its own nothingness in contrast to that which is supreme above all creatures.

It is easily seen that, once again, this phrase, whatever it is, is not a *conceptual* explanation of the matter. All that this new term, "creature-feeling," can express, is the note of submergence into nothingness before an overpowering, absolute might of some kind; whereas everything turns upon the *character* of this overpowering might, a character which cannot be expressed verbally, and can only be suggested indirectly through the tone and content of a man's feeling-response to it. And this response must be directly experienced in oneself to be understood.

We have now to note a second defect in the formulation of Schleiermacher's principle. The religious category discovered by him, by whose means he professes to determine the real content of the religious emotion, is merely a category of *self*-valuation, in the sense of self-depreciation. According to him the religious emotion would be directly and primarily a sort of *self*-consciousness, a feeling concerning oneself in a special, determined relation, viz. one's dependence. Thus, according to Schleiermacher, I can only come upon the very fact of God as the result of an inference, that is, by reasoning to a cause beyond myself to account for my "feeling of dependence." But this is entirely opposed to the psychological facts of the case. Rather, the "creature-feeling" is itself a first subjective concomitant and effect of another feeling-element, which casts it like a shadow, but which in itself indubitably has immediate and primary reference to an object outside the self.[1]

Now this object is just what we have already spoken of as "the numinous." For the "creature-feeling" and the sense of dependence to arise in the mind the "numen" must be experienced as present, a *numen praesens,* as is in the case of Abraham. There must be felt a something "numinous," something bearing the character of a "numen," to which the mind turns spontaneously; or (which is the same thing in other words) these feelings can only arise in the mind as accompanying emotions when the category of "the numinous" is called into play.

The numinous is thus felt as objective and outside the self. We have now to inquire more closely into its nature and the modes of its manifestation.

---

[1] This is so manifestly borne out by experience that it must be about the first thing to force itself upon the notice of psychologists analysing the facts of religion. There is a certain naïveté in the following passage from William James's *Varieties of Religious Experience* (p. 58), where, alluding to the origin of the Grecian representations of the gods, he says: "As regards the origin of the Greek gods, we need not at present seek an opinion. But the whole array of our instances leads to a conclusion something like this: It is as if there were in the human consciousness *a sense of reality, a feeling of objective presence,* a *perception* of what we may call *'something there,'* more deep and more general than any of the special and particular 'senses' by which the current psychology supposes existent realities to be originally revealed." (The italics are James's own.) James is debarred by his empiricist and pragmatist standpoint from coming to a recognition of faculties of knowledge and potentialities of thought in the spirit itself, and he is therefore obliged to have recourse to somewhat singular and mysterious hypotheses to explain this fact. But he grasps the fact itself clearly enough and is sufficient of a realist not to explain it away. But this "feeling of reality," the feeling of a "numinous" *object* objectively given, must be posited as a primary immediate datum of consciousness, and the "feeling of dependence" is then a consequence, following very closely upon it, viz. a depreciation of the *subject* in his own eyes. The latter presupposes the former.

## *"Mysterium Tremendum"*

THE ANALYSIS OF "TREMENDUM." We said above that the nature of the numinous can only be suggested by means of the special way in which it is reflected in the mind in terms of feeling. "Its nature is such that it grips or stirs the human mind with this and that determinate affective state." We have now to attempt to give a further indication of these determinate states. We must once again endeavour, by adducing feelings akin to them for the purpose of analogy or contrast, and by the use of metaphor and symbolic expressions, to make the states of mind we are investigating ring out, as it were, of themselves.

Let us consider the deepest and most fundamental element in all strong and sincerely felt religious emotion. Faith unto salvation, trust, love—all these are there. But over and above these is an element which may also on occasion, quite apart from them, profoundly affect us and occupy the mind with a wellnigh bewildering strength. Let us follow it up with every effort of sympathy and imaginative intuition wherever it is to be found, in the lives of those around us, in sudden, strong ebullitions of personal piety and the frames of mind such ebullitions evince, in the fixed and ordered solemnities of rites and liturgies, and again in the atmosphere that clings to old religious monuments and buildings, to temples and to churches. If we do so we shall find we are dealing with something for which there is only one appropriate expression, *"mysterium tremendum."* (The feeling of it may at times come sweeping like a gentle tide, pervading the mind with a tranquil mood of deepest worship. It may pass over into a more set and lasting attitude of the soul, continuing, as it were, thrillingly vibrant and resonant, until at last it dies away and the soul resumes its "profane," non-religious mood of everyday experience. It may burst in sudden eruption up from the depths of the soul with spasms and convulsions, or lead to the strangest excitements, to intoxicated frenzy, to transport, and to ecstasy. It has its wild and demonic forms and can sink to an almost grisly horror and shuddering. It has its crude, barbaric antecedents and early manifestations, and again it may be developed into something beautiful and pure and glorious. It may become the hushed, trembling, and speechless humility of the creature in the presence of—whom or what? In the presence of that which is a *mystery* inexpressible and above all creatures.)

It is again evident at once that here too our attempted formulation by means of a concept is once more a merely negative one. Conceptually *mysterium* denotes merely that which is hidden and esoteric, that which is beyond conception or understanding, extraordinary and unfamiliar. The term does not define the object more positively in its qualitative character.

But though what is enunciated in the word is negative, what is meant is something absolutely and intensely positive. This pure positive we can experience in feelings, feelings which our discussion can help to make clear to us, in so far as it arouses them actually in our hearts.

1. THE ELEMENT OF AWEFULNESS. To get light upon the positive *"quale"* of the object of these feelings, we must analyse more closely our phrase *mysterium tremendum,* and we will begin first with the adjective.

*Tremor* is in itself merely the perfectly familiar and "natural" emotion of *fear*. But here the term is taken, aptly enough but still only by analogy, to denote a quite specific kind of emotional response, wholly distinct from that of being afraid, though it so far resembles it that the analogy of fear may be used to throw light upon its nature. There are in some languages special expressions which denote, either exclusively or in the first instance, this "fear" that is more than fear proper. The Hebrew *hiqdīsh* (hallow) is an example. To "keep a thing holy in the heart" means to mark it off by a feeling of peculiar dread, not to be mistaken for any ordinary dread, that is, to appraise it by the category of the numinous. But the Old Testament throughout is rich in parallel expressions for this feeling. Specially noticeable is the *'ēmāh* of Yahweh ("fear of God"), which Yahweh can pour forth, dispatching almost like a daemon, and which seizes upon a man with paralysing effect. It is closely related to the δεῖμα πανικόν of the Greeks. Compare Exod. xxiii. 27: "I will send my fear before thee, and will destroy all the people to whom thou shalt come . . ."; also Job ix. 34; xiii. 21 ("let not his fear terrify me"; "let not thy dread make me afraid"). Here we have a terror fraught with an inward shuddering such as not even the most menacing and overpowering created thing can instil. It has something spectral in it.

In the Greek language we have a corresponding term in σεβαστός. The early Christians could clearly feel that the title σεβαστός (*augustus*) was one that could not fittingly be given to any creature, not even to the emperor. They felt that to call a man σεβαστός was to give a human being a name proper only to the *numen,* to rank him by the category proper only to the *numen,* and that it therefore amounted to a kind of idolatry. Of modern languages English has the words "awe," "aweful," which in their deeper and most special sense approximate closely to our meaning. The phrase, "he stood aghast," is also suggestive in this connexion. On the other hand, German has no native-grown expression of its own for the higher and riper form of the emotion we are considering, unless it be in a word like *erschauern,* which does suggest it fairly well. It is far otherwise with its cruder and more debased phases, where such terms as *grausen* and *Schauer,* and the more popular and telling *gruseln* ("grue"), *gräsen,* and *grässlich* ("grisly"), very clearly designate the numinous element. In my examination of Wundt's Animism I suggested the term *Scheu* (dread); but the special "numinous" quality (making it "awe" rather than "dread" in the ordinary sense) would then, of course, have to be denoted by inverted commas. "Religious dread" (or "awe") would perhaps be a better designation. Its antecedent stage is "daemonic dread" (cf. the horror of Pan) with its queer perversion, a sort of abortive offshoot, the "dread of ghosts." It first begins to stir in the feeling of "something uncanny," "eerie," or "weird." It is this feeling which, emerging in the mind of primeval man, forms the starting-point for the entire religious development in history. "Daemons" and "gods" alike spring from this root, and all the products of "mythological apperception" or "fantasy" are nothing but different modes in which it has been objectified. And all ostensible explanations of the origin of religion in terms of animism or magic or folk-psychology are doomed from the outset to wander astray and miss the real goal of their inquiry, unless they recognize this fact of our nature—primary, unique, underivable from anything else—to be the basic factor and the basic impulse underlying the entire process of religious evolution.[2]

Not only is the saying of Luther, that the natural man cannot fear God perfectly, correct from the standpoint of psychology, but we ought to go farther and add that the natural man is quite unable even to "shudder" (*grauen*) or feel horror in the real sense of the word. For "shuddering" is something more than "natural," ordinary fear. It implies that the mysterious is already beginning to loom before the mind, to touch the feelings. It implies the first application of a category of valuation which has no place in the everyday natural world of ordinary experience, and is only possible to a being in whom has been awakened a mental predisposition, unique in kind and different in a definite way from any "natural" faculty. And this newly-revealed capacity, even in the crude and violent manifestations which are all it at first evinces, bears witness to a completely new function of experience and standard of valuation, only belonging to the spirit of man.

Before going on to consider the elements which unfold as the *"tremendum"* develops, let us give a little further consideration to the first crude, primitive forms in which this "numinous dread" or *awe* shows itself. It is the mark which really characterizes the so-called "religion of primitive man," and there it appears as "daemonic dread." This crudely naïve and

---

[2] Cf. my papers in *Theologische Rundschau,* 1910, vol. i., on "Myth and Religion in Wundt's *Völkerpsychologie,*" and in *Deutsche Literaturzeitung,* 1910, No. 38. I find in more recent investigations, especially those of R. R. Marett and N. Söderblom, a very welcome confirmation of the positions I there maintained. It is true that neither of them calls attention quite as precisely as, in this matter, psychologists need to do, to the unique character of the religious "awe" and its qualitative distinction from all "natural" feelings. But Marett more particularly comes within a hair's breadth of what I take to be the truth about the matter. Cf. his *Threshold of Religion* (London, 1909), and N. Söderblom's *Das Werden des Gottesglaubens* (Leipzig, 1915), also my review of the latter in *Theol. Literaturzeitung,* Jan. 1915.

primordial emotional disturbance, and the fantastic images to which it gives rise, are later overborne and ousted by more highly developed forms of the numinous emotion, with all its mysteriously impelling power. But even when this has long attained its higher and purer mode of expression it is possible for the primitive types of excitation that were formerly a part of it to break out in the soul in all their original naïveté and so to be experienced afresh. That this is so is shown by the potent attraction again and again exercised by the element of horror and "shudder" in ghost stories, even among persons of high all-round education. It is a remarkable fact that the physical reaction to which this unique "dread" of the uncanny gives rise is also unique, and is not found in the case of any "natural" fear or terror. We say: "my blood ran icy cold," and "my flesh crept." The "cold blood" feeling may be a symptom of ordinary, natural fear, but there is something non-natural or supernatural about the symptom of "creeping flesh." And any one who is capable of more precise introspection must recognize that the distinction between such a "dread" and natural fear is not simply one of degree and intensity. The awe or "dread" *may* indeed be so overwhelmingly great that it seems to penetrate to the very marrow, making the man's hair bristle and his limbs quake. But it may also steal upon him almost unobserved as the gentlest of agitations, a mere fleeting shadow passing across his mood. It has therefore nothing to do with intensity, and no natural fear passes over into it merely by being intensified. I may be beyond all measure afraid and terrified without there being even a trace of the feeling of uncanniness in my emotion.

We should see the facts more clearly if psychology in general would make a more decisive endeavour to examine and classify the feelings and emotions according to their qualitative differences. But the far too rough division of elementary feelings in general into pleasures and pains is still an obstacle to this. In point of fact "pleasures" no more than other feelings are differentiated merely by degrees of intensity: they show very definite and specific differences. It makes a specific difference to the condition of mind whether the soul is merely in a state of pleasure, or joy, or aesthetic rapture, or moral exaltation, or finally in the religious bliss that may come in worship. Such states certainly show resemblances one to another, and on that account can legitimately be brought under a common class-concept ("pleasure"), which serves to cut them off from other psychical functions, generically different. But this class-concept, so far from turning the various subordinate species into merely different degrees of the same thing, can do nothing at all to throw light upon the essence of each several state of mind which it includes.

Though the numinous emotion in its completest development shows a world of difference from the mere "daemonic dread," yet not even at the highest level does it belie its pedigree or kindred. Even when the worship of "daemons" has long since reached the higher level of worship of "gods," these gods still retain as *numina* something of the "ghost" in the impress they make on the feelings of the worshipper, viz. the peculiar quality of the "uncanny" and "aweful," which survives with the quality of exaltedness and sublimity or is symbolized by means of it. And this element, softened though it is, does not disappear even on the highest level of all, where the worship of God is at its purest. Its disappearance would be indeed an essential loss. The "shudder" reappears in a form ennobled beyond measure where the soul, held speechless, trembles inwardly to the farthest fibre of its being. It invades the mind mightily in Christian worship with the words: "Holy, holy, holy"; it breaks forth from the hymn of Tersteegen:

> God Himself is present:
> Heart, be stilled before Him:
> Prostrate inwardly adore Him.

The "shudder" has here lost its crazy and bewildering note, but not the ineffable something that holds the mind. It has become a mystical awe, and sets free as its accompaniment, reflected in self-consciousness, that "creature-feeling" that has already been described as the feeling of personal nothingness and submergence before the awe-inspiring object directly experienced.

The referring of this feeling numinous *tremor* to its object in the numen brings into relief a property of the latter which plays an important part in our Holy Scriptures, and which has been the occasion of many difficulties, both to commentators and to theologians, from its puzzling and baffling nature. This is the ὀργή (*orgé*), the Wrath of Yahweh, which recurs in the New Testament as ὀργή θεοῦ, and which is clearly analogous to the idea occurring in many religions of a mysterious *ira deorum*. To pass through the Indian Pantheon of gods is to find deities who seem to be made up altogether out of such an ὀργή; and even the higher Indian gods of grace and pardon have frequently, beside their merciful, their "wrath" form. But as regards the "wrath of Yahweh," the strange features about it have for long been a matter for constant remark. In the first place, it is patent from many passages of the Old Testament that this "wrath" has no concern whatever with moral qualities. There is something very baffling in the way in which it "is kindled" and manifested. It is, as has been well said, "like a hidden force of nature," like stored-up electricity, discharging itself upon anyone who comes too near. It is "incalculable" and "arbitrary." Anyone who is accustomed to think of deity only by its rational attributes must see in this "wrath" mere caprice and wilful passion. But such a view would have been emphatically rejected by the religious men of the Old Covenant, for to them the Wrath of God, so far from being a diminution of His Godhead, appears as a natural expression of it, an element of "holiness" itself, and a quite indispensable one. And in this they are entirely right. This ὀργή is nothing but the *tremendum* itself, apprehended and expressed by the aid of a naïve analogy from the domain of natural experience, in this case from the ordinary passional life of men. But naïve as it may be, the analogy is most disconcertingly apt and striking; so much so that it will always retain its value and for us no less than for the men of old be an inevitable way of expressing one element in the religious emotion. It cannot be doubted that, despite the protest of Schleiermacher and Ritschl, Christianity also has something to teach of the "wrath of God."

It will be again at once apparent that in the use of this word we are not concerned with a genuine intellectual "concept," but only with a sort of illustrative substitute for a concept. "Wrath" here is the "ideogram" of a unique emotional moment in religious experience, a moment whose singularly *daunting* and awe-inspiring character must be gravely disturbing to those persons who will recognize nothing in the divine nature but goodness, gentleness, love, and a sort of confidential intimacy, in a word, only those aspects of God which turn towards the world of men.

This ὀργή is thus quite wrongly spoken of as "natural" wrath: rather it is an entirely non- or super-natural, i.e., numinous, quality. The rationalization process takes place when it begins to be filled in with elements derived from the moral reason: righteousness in requital, and punishment for moral transgression. But it should be noted that the idea of the wrath of God in the Bible is always a synthesis, in which the original is combined with the later meaning that has come to fill it in. Something supra-rational throbs and gleams, palpable and visible, in the "wrath of God," prompting to a sense of "terror" that no "natural" anger can arouse.

Beside the "wrath" or "anger" of Yahweh stands the related expression "jealousy of Yahweh." The state of mind denoted by the phrase "being jealous *for* Yahweh" is also a numinous state of mind, in which features of the *tremendum* pass over into the man who has experience of it.

2. THE ELEMENT OF "OVERPOWERINGNESS" ("MAJESTAS"). We have been attempting to unfold the implications of that aspect of the *mysterium tremendum* indicated by the adjective, and the result so far may be summarized in two words, constituting, as before, what may be called an "ideogram," rather than a concept proper, viz. "absolute unapproachability."

It will be felt at once that there is yet a further element which must be added, that, namely, of "might," "power," "absolute overpoweringness." We will take to represent this the term *majestas,* majesty—the more readily because anyone with a feeling for language must detect a last faint trace of the numinous still clinging to the word. The *tremendum* may then be rendered more adequately *tremenda majestas,* or "aweful majesty." This second element of majesty may continue to be vividly preserved, where the first, that of unapproachability, recedes and dies away, as may be seen, for example, in mysticism. It is especially in relation to this element of majesty or absolute overpoweringness that the creature-consciousness, of which we have already spoken, comes upon the scene, as a sort of shadow or subjective reflection of it. Thus, in contrast to "the overpowering" of which we are conscious as an object over against the self, there is the feeling of one's own submergence, of being but "dust and ashes" and nothingness. And this forms the numinous raw material for the feeling of religious humility.[1]

Here we must revert once again to Schleiermacher's expression for what we call "creature-feeling," viz. the "feeling of dependence." We found fault with this phrase before on the ground that Schleiermacher thereby takes as basis and point of departure what is merely a secondary effect; that he sets out to teach a consciousness of the religious *object* only by way of an inference from the shadow it casts upon *self*-consciousness. We have now a further criticism to bring against it, and it is this. By "feeling of dependence" Schleiermacher means consciousness of *being conditioned* (as effect by cause), and so he develops the implications of this logically enough in his sections upon Creation and Preservation. On the side of the deity the correlate to "dependence" would thus be "causality," i.e., God's character as all-causing and all-conditioning. But a sense of this does not enter at all into that immediate and first-hand religious emotion which we have in the moment of worship, and which we can recover in a measure for analysis; it belongs on the contrary decidedly to the *rational* side of the idea of God; its implications admit of precise conceptual determination; and it springs from quite a distinct source. The difference between the "feeling of dependence" of Schleiermacher and that which finds typical utterance in the words of Abraham already cited might be expressed as that between the consciousness of *createdness* [2] and the consciousness of *creaturehood*.[3] In the one case you have the creature as the work of the divine creative act; in the other, impotence and general nothingness as against overpowering might, dust and ashes as against "majesty." In the one case you have the fact of having been created; in the other, the status of the creature. And as soon as speculative thought has come to concern itself with this latter type of consciousness—as soon as it has come to analyse this "majesty"—we are introduced to a set of ideas quite different from those of creation or preservation. We come upon the ideas, first, of the annihilation of self, and then, as its complement, of the transcendent as the sole and entire reality. These are the characteristic notes of mysticism in all its forms, however otherwise various in content. For one of the

---

[1] Cf. R. R. Marett, "The Birth of Humility," in *The Threshold of Religion,* 2nd ed., 1914. [Tr.]

[2] *Geschaffenheit.*

[3] *Geschöpflichkeit.*

chiefest and most general features of mysticism is just this *self-depreciation* (so plainly parallel to the case of Abraham), the estimation of the self, of the personal "I," as something not perfectly or essentially real, or even as mere nullity, a self-depreciation which comes to demand its own fulfilment in practice in rejecting the delusion of selfhood, and so makes for the annihilation of the self. And on the other hand mysticism leads to a valuation of the transcendent object of its reference as that which through plenitude of being stands supreme and absolute, so that the finite self contrasted with it becomes conscious even in its nullity that "I am naught, Thou art all." There is no thought in this of any causal relation between God, the creator, and the self, the creature. The point from which speculation starts is not a "consciousness of absolute dependence"—of myself as result and effect of a divine cause—for that would in point of fact lead to insistence upon the reality of the self; it starts from a consciousness of the absolute superiority or supremacy of a power other than myself, and it is only as it falls back upon ontological terms to achieve its end—terms generally borrowed from natural science—that that element of the *tremendum,* originally apprehended as "plenitude of power," becomes transmuted into "plenitude of being."

This leads again to the mention of mysticism. No mere inquiry into the genesis of a thing can throw any light upon its essential nature, and it is hence immaterial to us how mysticism historically arose. But essentially mysticism is the stressing to a very high degree, indeed the overstressing, of the non-rational or supra-rational elements in religion; and it is only intelligible when so understood. The various phases and factors of the non-rational may receive varying emphasis, and the type of mysticism will differ according as some or others fall into the background. What we have been analysing, however, is a feature that recurs in all forms of mysticism everywhere, and it is nothing but the "creature-consciousness" stressed to the utmost and to excess, the expression meaning, if we may repeat the contrast already made, not "feeling of our createdness" but "feeling of our creaturehood," that is, the consciousness of the littleness of every creature in face of that which is above all creatures.

A characteristic common to all types of mysticism is the *Identification,* in different degrees of completeness, of the personal self with the transcendent Reality. This identification has a source of its own, with which we are not here concerned, and springs from "moments" of religious experience which would require separate treatment. "Identification" alone, however, is not enough for mysticism; it must be Identification with the Something that is at once absolutely supreme in power and reality and wholly non-rational. And it is among the mystics that we most encounter this element of religious consciousness. Récéjac has noticed this in his *Essai sur les fondements de la connaissance mystique* (Paris, 1897). He writes (p. 90):

Le mysticisme commence par la crainte, par le sentiment d'une *domination universelle, invincible,* et devient plus tard un désir d'union avec ce qui domine ainsi.

And some very clear examples of this taken from the religious experience of the present day are to be found in W. James (*op. cit.,* p. 66):

The perfect stillness of the night was thrilled by a more solemn silence. The darkness held a presence that was all the more felt because it was not seen. I could not any more have doubted that *He* was there than that I was. Indeed, I felt myself to be, if possible, the less real of the two.

This example is particularly instructive as to the relation of mysticism to the "feelings of identification," for the experience here recounted was on the point of passing into it.[5]

3. THE ELEMENT OF "ENERGY" OR URGENCY. There is, finally, a third element comprised in those of *tremendum* and *majestas,* awefulness and majesty, and this I venture to call the "urgency" or "energy" of the numinous object. It is particularly vividly perceptible in the ὀργή or "wrath"; and it everywhere clothes itself in symbolical expressions—vitality, passion, emotional temper, will, force, movement,[6] excitement, activity, impetus. These features are typical and recur again and again from the daemonic level up to the idea of the "living" God. We have here the factor that has everywhere more than any other prompted the fiercest opposition to the "philosophic" God of mere rational speculation, who can be put into a definition. And for their part the philosophers have condemned these expressions of the energy of the numen, whenever they are brought on to the scene, as sheer anthropomorphism. In so far as their opponents have for the most part themselves failed to recognize that the terms they have borrowed from the sphere of human conative and affective life have merely value as analogies, the philosophers are right to condemn them. But they are wrong, in so far as, this error notwithstanding, these terms stood for a genuine aspect of the divine nature—its non-rational aspect—a due consciousness of which served to protect religion itself from being "rationalized" away.

For wherever men have been contending for the "living" God or for voluntarism, there, we may be sure, have been non-rationalists fighting rationalists and rationalism. It was so with Luther in his controversy with Erasmus; and Luther's *omnipotentia Dei* in his *De Servo Arbitrio* is nothing

---

[5] Compare too the experience on p. 70: ". . . What I felt on these occasions was a temporary loss of my own identity."
[6] The "mobilitas Dei" of Lactantius.

but the union of "majesty"—in the sense of absolute supremacy—with this "energy," in the sense of a force that knows not stint nor stay, which is urgent, active, compelling, and alive. In mysticism, too, this element of "energy" is a very living and vigorous factor, at any rate in the "voluntaristic" mysticism, the mysticism of love, where it is very forcibly seen in that "consuming fire" of love whose burning strength the mystic can hardly bear, but begs that the heat that has scorched him may be mitigated, lest he be himself destroyed by it. And in this urgency and pressure the mystic's "love" claims a perceptible kinship with the ὀργή itself, the scorching and consuming wrath of God; it is the same "energy," only differently directed. "Love," says one of the mystics, "is nothing else than quenched wrath."

The element of "energy" reappears in Fichte's speculations on the Absolute as the gigantic, never-resting, active world-stress, and in Schopenhauer's daemonic "Will." At the same time both these writers are guilty of the same error that is already found in myth; they transfer "natural" attributes, which ought only to be used as "ideograms" for what is itself properly beyond utterance, to the non-rational as real qualifications of it, and they mistake symbolic expressions of feelings for adequate concepts upon which a "scientific" structure of knowledge may be based.

In Goethe, as we shall see later, the same element of energy is emphasized in a quite unique way in his strange descriptions of the experience he calls "daemonic."

# The Analysis of "Mysterium"

*Ein begriffener Gott ist kein Gott.*
"A God comprehended is no God."
(TERSTEEGEN.)

We gave to the object to which the numinous consciousness is directed the name *mysterium tremendum,* and we then set ourselves first to determine the meaning of the adjective *tremendum*—which we found to be itself only justified by analogy—because it is more easily analysed than the substantive idea *mysterium.* We have now to turn to this, and try, as best we may, by hint and suggestion, to get to a clearer apprehension of what it implies.

4. THE "WHOLLY OTHER." It might be thought that the adjective itself gives an explanation of the substantive; but this is not so. It is not merely analytical; it is a synthetic attribute to it; i.e., *tremendum* adds something

not necessarily inherent in *mysterium*. It is true that the reactions in consciousness that correspond to the one readily and spontaneously overflow into those that correspond to the other; in fact, anyone sensitive to the use of words would commonly feel that the idea of "mystery" (*mysterium*) is so closely bound up with its synthetic qualifying attribute "aweful" (*tremendum*) that one can hardly say the former without catching an echo of the latter, "mystery" almost of itself becoming "awful mystery" to us. But the passage from the one idea to the other need not by any means be always so easy. The elements of meaning implied in "awefulness" and "mysteriousness" are in themselves definitely different. The latter may so far preponderate in the religious consciousness, may stand out so vividly, that in comparison with it the former almost sinks out of sight; a case which again could be clearly exemplified from some forms of mysticism. Occasionally, on the other hand, the reverse happens, and the *tremendum* may in turn occupy the mind without the *mysterium*.

This latter, then, needs special consideration on its own account. We need an expression for the mental reaction peculiar to it; and here, too, only one word seems appropriate, though, as it is strictly applicable only to a "natural" state of mind, it has here meaning only by analogy: it is the word "stupor." *Stupor* is plainly a different thing from *tremor;* it signifies blank wonder, an astonishment that strikes us dumb, amazement absolute.[7] Taken, indeed, in its purely natural sense, *mysterium* would first mean merely a secret or a mystery in the sense of that which is alien to us, uncomprehended and unexplained; and so far *mysterium* is itself merely an ideogram, an analogical notion taken from the natural sphere, illustrating, but incapable of exhaustively rendering, our real meaning. Taken in the religious sense, that which is "mysterious" is—to give it perhaps the most striking expression—the "wholly other" ($\theta\acute{a}\tau\epsilon\rho\sigma\nu$, *anyad, alienum*), that which is quite beyond the sphere of the usual, the intelligible, and the familiar, which therefore falls quite outside the limits of the "canny," and is contrasted with it, filling the mind with blank wonder and astonishment.

This is already to be observed on the lowest and earliest level of the religion of primitive man, where the numinous consciousness is but an inchoate stirring of the feelings. What is really characteristic of this stage is *not*—as the theory of Animism would have us believe—that men are here concerned with curious entities, called "souls" or "spirits," which hap-

---

[7] Compare also *obstupefacere*. Still more exact equivalents are the Greek $\theta\alpha\mu\beta\sigma\varsigma$ and $\theta\alpha\mu\beta\epsilon\iota\nu$. The sound $\theta\ \alpha\ \mu\ \beta$ (*thamb*) excellently depicts this state of mind of blank, staring wonder. And the difference between the moments of *stupor* and *tremor* is very finely suggested by the passage, Mark x. 32 (cf. *infra*, p. 158). On the other hand, what was said above of the facility and rapidity with which the two moments merge and blend is also markedly true of $\theta\alpha\mu\beta\sigma\varsigma$, which then becomes a classical term for the (ennobled) awe of the numinous in general. So Mark xvi. 5 is rightly translated by Luther "und sie entsetzten sich," and by the English Authorized Version "and they were affrighted."

pen to be invisible. Representations of spirits and similar conceptions are rather one and all early modes of "rationalizing" a precedent experience, to which they are subsidiary. They are attempts in some way or other, it little matters how, to guess the riddle it propounds, and their effect is at the same time always to weaken and deaden the experience itself. They are the source from which springs, not religion, but the rationalization of religion, which often ends by constructing such a massive structure of theory and such a plausible fabric of interpretation, that the "mystery" is frankly excluded.[8] Both imaginative "myth," when developed into a system, and intellectualist Scholasticism, when worked out to its completion, are methods by which the fundamental fact of religious experience is, as it were, simply rolled out so thin and flat as to be finally eliminated altogether.

Even on the lowest level of religious development the essential characteristic is therefore to be sought elsewhere than in the appearance of "spirit" representations. It lies rather, we repeat, in a peculiar "moment" of consciousness, to wit, the *stupor* before something "wholly other," whether such an other be named "spirit" or "daemon" or "deva," or be left without any name. Nor does it make any difference in this respect whether, to interpret and preserve their apprehension of this "other," men coin original imagery of their own or adapt imaginations drawn from the world of legend, the fabrications of fancy apart from and prior to any stirrings of daemonic dread.

In accordance with laws of which we shall have to speak again later, this feeling or consciousness of the "wholly other" will attach itself to, or sometimes be indirectly aroused by means of, objects which are already puzzling upon the "natural" plane, or are of a surprising or astounding character; such as extraordinary phenomena or astonishing occurrences or things in inanimate nature, in the animal world, or among men. But here once more we are dealing with a case of association between things specifically different—the "numinous" and the "natural" moments of consciousness—and not merely with the gradual enhancement of one of them —the "natural"—till it becomes the other. As in the case of "natural fear" and "daemonic dread" already considered, so here the transition from natural to daemonic amazement is not a mere matter of degree. But it is only with the latter that the complementary expression *mysterium* perfectly harmonizes, as will be felt perhaps more clearly in the case of the adjectival form "mysterious." No one says, strictly and in earnest, of a piece of clockwork that is beyond his grasp, or of a science that he cannot understand: "That is 'mysterious' to me."

---

[8] A spirit or soul that has been conceived and comprehended no longer prompts to "shuddering," as is proved by Spiritualism. But it thereby ceases to be of interest for the psychology of religion.

It might be objected that the mysterious is something which is and re-mains absolutely and invariably beyond our understanding, whereas that which merely eludes our understanding for a time but is perfectly in-telligible in principle should be called, not a "mystery," but merely a "prob-lem." But this is by no means an adequate account of the matter. The truly "mysterious" object is beyond our apprehension and comprehension, not only because our knowledge has certain irremovable limits, but because in it we come upon something inherently "wholly other," whose kind and character are incommensurable with our own, and before which we there-fore recoil in a wonder that strikes us chill and numb.[9]

This may be made still clearer by a consideration of that degraded off-shoot and travesty of the genuine "numinous" dread or awe, the fear of ghosts. Let us try to analyse this experience. We have already specified the peculiar feeling-element of "dread" aroused by the ghost as that of "grue," grisly horror.[10] Now this "grue" obviously contributes something to the attraction which ghost-stories exercise, in so far, namely, as the relaxation of tension ensuing upon our release from it relieves the mind in a pleasant and agreeable way. So far, however, it is not really the ghost itself that gives us pleasure, but the fact that we are rid of it. But obviously this is quite insufficient to explain the ensnaring attraction of the ghost-story. The ghost's real attraction rather consists in this, that of itself and in an uncom-mon degree it entices the imagination, awakening strong interest and curiosity; it is the weird thing itself that allures the fancy. But it does this, not because it is "something long and white" (as someone once defined a ghost), nor yet through any of the positive and conceptual attributes which fancies about ghosts have invented, but because it is a thing that "doesn't really exist at all," the "wholly other," something which has no place in our scheme of reality but belongs to an absolutely different one, and which at the same time arouses an irrepressible interest in the mind.

But that which is perceptibly true in the fear of ghosts, which is, after all, only a caricature of the genuine thing, is in a far stronger sense true of the "daemonic" experience itself, of which the fear of ghosts is a mere off-shoot. And while, following this main line of development, this element in the numinous consciousness, the feeling of the "wholly other," is height-ened and clarified, its higher modes of manifestation come into being,

---

[9] In *Confessions,* ii. 9. I, Augustine very strikingly suggests this stiffening, benumbing element of the "wholly other" and its contrast to the rational aspect of the numen; the *dissimile* and the *simile:*

"Quid est illud, quod interlucet mihi et percutit cor meum sine laesione? Et inhorresco et inardesco. *Inhorresco,* in quantum *dissimilis* ei sum. Inardesco, in quantum similis ei sum."

("What is that which gleams through me and smites my heart without wounding it? I am both a-shudder and a-glow. A-shudder, in so far as I am unlike it, a-glow in so far as I am like it.")

[10] *gruseln, gräsen.*

which set the numinous object in contrast not only to everything wonted and familiar (i.e., in the end, to nature in general), thereby turning it into the "supernatural," but finally to the world itself, and thereby exalt it to the "supramundane," that which is above the whole world-order.

In mysticism we have in the "beyond" (ἐπέκεινα) again the strongest stressing and over-stressing of those non-rational elements which are already inherent in all religion. Mysticism continues to its extreme point this contrasting of the numinous object (the numen), as the "wholly other," with ordinary experience. Not content with contrasting it with all that is of nature or this world, mysticism concludes by contrasting it with Being itself and all that "is," and finally actually calls it "that which is nothing." By this "nothing" is meant not only that of which nothing can be predicated, but that which is absolutely and intrinsically other than and opposite of everything that is and can be thought. But while exaggerating to the point of paradox this *negation* and contrast—the only means open to conceptual thought to apprehend the *mysterium*—mysticism at the same time retains the *positive quality* of the "wholly other" as a very living factor in its overbrimming religious emotion.

But what is true of the strange "nothingness" of our mystics holds good equally of the *sūnyam* and the *sūnyatā,* the "void" and "emptiness" of the Buddhist mystics. This aspiration for the "void" and for becoming void, no less than the aspiration of our western mystics for "nothing" and for becoming nothing, must seem a kind of lunacy to anyone who has no inner sympathy for the esoteric language and ideograms of mysticism, and lacks the matrix from which these come necessarily to birth. To such an one Buddhism itself will be simply a morbid sort of pessimism. But in fact the "void" of the eastern, like the "nothing" of the western, mystic is a numinous ideogram of the "wholly other."

These terms "supernatural" and "transcendent" [11] give the appearance of positive attributes, and, as applied to the mysterious, they appear to divest the *mysterium* of its originally negative meaning and to turn it into an affirmation. On the side of conceptual thought this is nothing more than appearance, for it is obvious that the two terms in question are merely negative and exclusive attributes with reference to "nature" and the world or cosmos respectively. But on the side of the feeling-content it is otherwise; that *is* in very truth positive in the highest degree, though here too, as before, it cannot be rendered explicit in conceptual terms. It is through this positive feeling-content that the concepts of the "transcendent" and "supernatural" become forthwith designations for a unique "wholly other" reality and quality, something of whose special character we can *feel,* without being able to give it clear conceptual expression.

---

[11] Literally, supramundane: *überweltlich.*

# The Element of Fascination

The qualitative *content* of the numinous experience, to which "the mysterious" stands as *form,* is in one of its aspects the element of daunting "awefulness" and "majesty," which has already been dealt with in detail; but it is clear that it has at the same time another aspect, in which it shows itself as something uniquely attractive and *fascinating.*

These two qualities, the daunting and the fascinating, now combine in a strange harmony of contrasts, and the resultant dual character of the numinous consciousness, to which the entire religious development bears witness, at any rate from the level of the "daemonic dread" onwards, is at once the strangest and most noteworthy phenomenon in the whole history of religion. The daemonic-divine object may appear to the mind an object of horror and dread, but at the same time it is no less something that allures with a potent charm, and the creature, who trembles before it, utterly cowed and cast down, has always at the same time the impulse to turn to it, nay even to make it somehow his own. The "mystery" is for him not merely something to be wondered at but something that entrances him; and beside that in it which bewilders and confounds, he feels a something that captivates and transports him with a strange ravishment, rising often enough to the pitch of dizzy intoxication; it is the Dionysiac-element in the numen.

The ideas and concepts which are the parallels or "schemata" on the rational side of this non-rational element of "fascination" are love, mercy, pity, comfort; these are all "natural" elements of the common psychical life, only they are here thought as absolute and in completeness. But important as these are for the experience of religious bliss or felicity, they do not by any means exhaust it. It is just the same as with the opposite experience of religious infelicity—the experience of the ὀργή or "wrath" of God—both alike contain fundamentally non-rational elements. Bliss or beatitude is more, far more, than the mere natural feeling of being comforted, of reliance, of the joy of love, however these may be heightened and enhanced. Just as "wrath," taken in a purely rational or a purely ethical sense, does not exhaust that profound element of *awefulness* which is locked in the mystery of deity, so neither does "graciousness" exhaust the profound element of *wonderfulness* and rapture which lies in the mysterious beatific experience of deity. The term "grace" may indeed be taken as its aptest designation, but then only in the sense in which it is really applied in the language of the mystics, and in which not only the "gracious intent" but "something more" is meant by the word. This "something more" has its antecedent phases very far back in the history of religions.

It may well be possible, it is even probable, that in the first stage of its development the religious consciousness started with only one of its poles —the "daunting" aspect of the numen—and so at first took shape only as "daemonic dread." But if this did not point to something beyond itself, if it were not but one "moment" of a completer experience, pressing up gradually into consciousness, then no transition would be possible to the feelings of positive self-surrender to the numen. The only type of worship that could result from this "dread" alone would be that of ἀπαιτεῖσθαι and ἀποτρέπειν, taking the form of expiation and propitiation, the averting or the appeasement of the "wrath" of the numen. It can never explain how it is that "the numinous" is the object of search and desire and yearning, and that too for its own sake and not only for the sake of the aid and backing that men expect from it in the natural sphere. It can never explain how this takes place, not only in the forms of "rational" religious worship, but in those queer "sacramental" observances and rituals and procedures of communion in which the human being seeks to get the numen into his possession.

Religious practice may manifest itself in those normal and easily intelligible forms which occupy so prominent a place in the history of religion, such forms as propitiation, petition, sacrifice, thanksgiving, &c. But besides these there is a series of strange proceedings which are constantly attracting greater and greater attention, and in which it is claimed that we may recognize, besides mere religion in general, the particular roots of mysticism. I refer to those numerous curious modes of behaviour and fantastic forms of mediation, by means of which the primitive religious man attempts to master "the mysterious," and to fill himself and even to identify himself with it. These modes of behaviour fall apart into two classes. On the one hand the "magical" identification of the self with the numen proceeds by means of various transactions, at once magical and devotional in character —by formula, ordination, adjuration, consecration, exorcism, &c.: on the other hand are the "shamanistic" ways of procedure, possession, indwelling, self-fulfilment in exaltation and ecstasy. All these have, indeed, their starting-points simply in magic, and their intention at first was certainly simply to appropriate the prodigious force of the numen for the natural ends of man. But the process does not rest there. Possession of and by the numen becomes an end in itself; it begins to be sought for its own sake; and the wildest and most artificial methods of asceticism are put into practice to attain it. In a word, the *vita religiosa* begins; and to remain in these strange and bizarre states of numinous possession becomes a good in itself, even a way of salvation, wholly different from the profane goods pursued by means of magic. Here, too, commences the process of development by which the experience is matured and purified, till finally it reaches its consummation in the sublimest and purest states of the "life within the Spirit" and in the noblest mysticism. Widely various as these states are in themselves, yet they have this element in common, that in them the *mysterium* is experienced in its essential, positive, and specific character, as something that bestows upon man a beatitude beyond compare, but one whose real nature he can neither proclaim in speech nor conceive in thought, but may know only by a direct and living experience. It is a bliss which embraces all those blessings that are indicated or suggested in positive fashion by any "doctrine of salvation," and it quickens all of them through and through; but these do not exhaust it. Rather by its all-pervading, penetrating glow it makes of these very blessings more than the intellect can conceive in them or affirm of them. It gives the peace that passes understanding, and of which the tongue can only stammer brokenly. Only from afar, by metaphors and analogies, do we come to apprehend what it is in itself, and even so our notion is but inadequate and confused.

# WALTER T. STACE

*Walter T. Stace* (1886–      ), emeritus professor of philosophy at Princeton, is a close student of mysticism and Eastern religions. He calls himself an empiricist but is not closely associated with any particular school. He has written on Greek philosophy, Hegel, theory of knowledge, morals, and religion.

## What Religion Is

"Religion," says Whitehead, "is the vision of something which stands beyond, behind, and within, the passing flux of immediate things; something which is real, and yet waiting to be realized; something which is a remote possibility, and yet the greatest of present facts; something which gives meaning to all that passes, and yet eludes apprehension; something whose possession is the final good, and yet is beyond all reach; something which is the ultimate ideal, and the hopeless quest." [1]

These words evidently express a direct intuition of the writer. They well

From Walter T. Stace, *Time and Eternity*, pp. 3–8. Copyright, 1952, by Princeton University Press. Reprinted by permission of Princeton University Press.
[1] A. N. Whitehead, *Science and the Modern World*, Chapter 12.

up from his own personal religious experience and therefore stir the depths in us who read. What he says is not a faded copy of what someone else has felt or thought or seen, as the majority of pious utterances are—hackneyed and worn-out clichés, debased by parrot-like repetition, although they too, poor dead things, once issued fresh-minted from a living human soul. Here and there amid the arid hills of human experience are well-springs and fountain-heads of religious intuition. They are the original sources of all religion. They need not always be of great grandeur. They may be humble rivulets of feeling. Or they may give rise to great rivers of refreshment flowing through the centuries. But always, great or small, they bear upon themselves the stamp of their own authenticity. They need no external proof or justification. Indeed they are incapable of any. We know them because the God in us cries out, hearing the voice of the God in the other, answering back. The deep calls to the deep.

Whitehead's words are of this kind.

Note first their paradoxical character. To the "something" of which they speak are attributed opposite characters which barely avoid, if they do avoid, the clash of flat contradiction. Each clause is a balance of such contradicting predicates. The meaning cannot be less than that paradox and contradiction are of the very essence of that "something" itself.

Note, too, the final words. That something which man seeks as his ultimate ideal is the "hopeless quest." This is not a careless expression, an exaggeration, a loose use of words. It is not rhetoric. If this phrase had come at the beginning of the passage, it might have been toned down in the succeeding sentences. But it strikes the final note. It is the last word.

And one can see why. For religion is the hunger of the soul for the impossible, the unattainable, the inconceivable. This is not something which it merely happens to be, an unfortunate accident or disaster which befalls it in the world. This is its essence, and this is its glory. This is what religion *means*. The religious impulse in men *is* the hunger for the impossible, the unattainable, the inconceivable—or at least for that which is these things in the world of time. And anything which is less than this is not religion—though it may be some very admirable thing such as morality. Let it not be said that this makes religion a foolish thing, fit only for madmen—although indeed from the world's point of view the religious man *is* a madman. For, mad or not, this impulse lies deep down in every human heart. It is of the essence of man, quite as much as is his reason.

Religion seeks the infinite. And the infinite by definition is impossible, unattainable. It is by definition that which can never be reached.

Religion seeks the light. But it is not a light which can be found at any place or time. It is not somewhere. It is the light which is nowhere. It is "the light which never was on sea or land." Never was. Never will be, even in the infinite stretches of future time. The light is non-existent, as the poet himself says. Yet it is the great light which lightens the world. And this, too, the poet implies.

Religion is the desire to break away from being and existence altogether, to get beyond existence into that nothingness where the great light is. It is the desire to be utterly free from the fetters of being. For every being is a fetter. Existence is a fetter. To be is to be tied to what you are. Religion is the hunger for the non-being which yet is.

In music sometimes a man will feel that he comes to the edge of breaking out from the prison bars of existence, breaking out from the universe altogether. There is a sense that the goal is at hand, that the boundary wall of the universe is crumbling and will be breached at the next moment, when the soul will pass out free into the infinite. But the goal is not reached. For it is the unspeakable, the impossible, the inconceivable, the unattainable. There is only the sense of falling backward into time. The goal is only glimpsed, sensed, and then lost.

One thing is better than another thing. Gold is perhaps better than clay, poetry than push-pin. One place is pleasanter than another place. One time is happier than another time. In all being there is a scale of better and worse. But just because of this relativity, no being, no time, no place, satisfies the ultimate hunger. For all beings are infected by the same disease, the disease of existence. If owning a marble leaves your metaphysical and religious thirst unquenced, so will owning all the planets. If living on the earth for three-score years and ten leaves it unsatisfied, neither will living in a fabled Heaven for endless ages satisfy it. For how do you attain your end by making things bigger, or longer, or wider, or thicker, or more this or more that? For they will still be *this* or *that*. And it is being this or that which is the disease of things.

So long as there is light in your life, the light has not yet dawned. There is in your life much darkness—that much you will admit. But you think that though this thing, this place, this time, this experience is dark, yet that thing, that place, that time, that experience is, or will be, bright. But this is the great illusion. You must see that all things, all places, all times, all experiences are equally dark. You must see that all stars are black. Only out of the *total* darkness will the light dawn.

Religion is that hunger which no existence, past, present, or future, no actual existence and no possible existence, in this world or in any other world, on the earth or above the clouds and stars, material or mental or spiritual, can ever satisfy. For whatever is or could be will have the curse on it of thisness or thatness.

This is no new thought. It is only what religious men have always said. To the saint Narada the Supreme Being offered whatsoever boon his heart could imagine—abundance of life, riches, health, pleasure, heroic sons. "That," said Narada "and precisely that is what I desire to be rid of and pass beyond." It is true that the things here spoken of—health, riches, even heroic sons—are what we call worldly, even material, things. But they are symbolic only. They stand for all things of any kind, whether material or non-material—for all things, at least, which could have an existence in the order of time, whether in the time before death or in the time after.

It is true that simple-minded religious men have conceived their goal as a state of continued existence beyond the grave filled with all happy things and experiences. But plainly such happy things and experiences were no more than symbolic, and the happy heavens containing such things have the character of myth. To the human mind, fast fettered by the limits of its poor imagination, they stand for and represent the goal. One cannot conceive the inconceivable. So in place of it one puts whatever one can imagine of delight; wine and houris if one's imagination is limited to these; love, kindness, sweetness of spiritual living if one is of a less materialistic temper. But were these existences and delights, material or spiritual, to be actually found and enjoyed as present, they would be condemned by the saint along with all earthly joys. For they would have upon them the curse, the darkness, the disease, of all existent things, of all that is this or that. This is why we cannot conceive of any particular pleasure, happiness, joy, which would not *cloy*, which—to be quite frank—would not in the end be boring.

"In the Infinite only is bliss. In the finite there is no bliss," says the ancient Upanishad.[2] And we are apt to imagine that this is a piece of rhetoric, or at least an exaggeration. For surely it is not strictly speaking true that in the finite there is no happiness at all. No doubt the saint or the moralist is right to speak disparagingly of the mere pleasures of sense. But is there, then, no joy of living? What of the love of man and woman, of parent and child? What of the sweetness of flowers, the blue of the sky, the sunlight? Is it not quite false that there is no bliss in these? And yet they are finite. So we say. But we fail to see that the author of the verse is speaking of something quite different from what we have in mind, namely of that ultimate bliss in God which is the final satisfaction of the religious hunger. And we think that this ultimate blessedness differs only *in degree* from the happy and joyful experiences of our lives. Whereas the truth is that it differs *in kind*. The joys, not only of the earth, but of any conceivable heaven— which we can conceive only as some fortunate and happy prolongation of our lives in time—are not of the same order as that ultimate blessedness. We imagine any joyful, even ecstatic, experience we please. We suppose that the blessedness of salvation is something like this, only more joyful. Perhaps if it were multiplied a million times. . . . But all this is of no avail. Though we pile mountain of earthly joy upon mountain of earthly joy, we reach no nearer to the bliss which is the end. For these things be-

---

[2]Chandogya Upanishad.

long to different orders; the one, however great, to the order of time; the other to the order of eternity. Therefore all the temporal joys which we pile upon one another to help our imaginations, are no more than symbolic, and the accounts of possible heavens mere myths.

Hence the religious soul must leave behind all things and beings, including itself. From being it must pass into Nothing. But in this nothing it must still be. Therefore also what it seeks is the being which is non-being. And God, who is the only food which will appease its hunger, is this Being which is Non-Being. Is this a contradiction? Yes. But men have always found that, in their search for the Ultimate, contradiction and paradox lie all around them. Did we not see that the words of Whitehead, with which we opened this chapter, must mean at least that contradiction and paradox lie at the heart of things? And is there any more contradiction here than we find—to give the most obvious example from traditional theology—in the doctrine of the Trinity? That, too, proclaims in unmistakable terms that there is contradiction in the Ultimate. The rationalizing intellect, of course, will not have it so. It will attempt to explain away the final Mystery, to logicize it, to reduce it to the categories of "this" and "that." At least it will attempt to water it down till it looks something like "common sense," and can be swallowed without too much discomfort! But the great theologians knew better. In the self-contradictory doctrine of the Trinity they threw the Mystery of God uncomprisingly in men's faces. And we shall see that all attempts to make religion a purely rational, logical, thing are not only shallow but would, if they could succeed, destroy religion. Either God is a Mystery or He is nothing at all.

# ERICH FROMM

*Erich Fromm* (1900–    ), well-known psychoanalyst, has been interested
in the phenomenon of religion in both individual and social life. He
received his doctorate at the University of Heidelberg, came to America in
1934, and has taught at Columbia, Yale, Bennington, and various psychi-
atric institutes.

## What Is Humanistic Religion?

It would far transcend the scope of this chapter to attempt a review of
all types of religion. Even to discuss only those types which are relevant
from the psychological standpoint cannot be undertaken here. I shall therefore deal with only one distinction, but one which in my opinion is the most
important, and which cuts across nontheistic and theistic religions: that
between *authoritarian* and *humanistic* religions.

What is the principle of authoritarian religion? The definition of religion
given in the *Oxford Dictionary,* while attempting to define religion as such,
is a rather accurate definition of authoritarian religion. It reads: "[Religion
is] recognition on the part of man of some higher unseen power as having
control of his destiny, and as being entitled to obedience, reverence, and
worship."

Here the emphasis is on the recognition that man is controlled by a
higher power outside of himself. But this alone does not constitute authoritarian religion. What makes it so is the idea that this power, because of the
control it exercises, is *entitled* to "obedience, reverence and worship." I
italicize the word "entitled" because it shows that the reason for worship,
obedience, and reverence lies not in the moral qualities of the deity, not in
love or justice, but in the fact that it has control, that is, has power over
man. Furthermore it shows that the higher power has a right to force man
to worship him and that lack of reverence and obedience constitutes sin.

The essential element in authoritarian religion and in the authoritarian
religious experience is the surrender to a power transcending man. The
main virtue of this type of religion is obedience, its cardinal sin is dis-

From Erich Fromm, *Psychoanalysis and Religion,* pp. 34–38, 40–47, 48–55, 113–114.
Copyright, 1950, by Erich Fromm. Reprinted by permission of Yale University Press.

obedience. Just as the deity is conceived as omnipotent or omniscient, man is conceived as being powerless and insignificant. Only as he can gain grace or help from the deity by complete surrender can he feel strength. Submission to a powerful authority is one of the avenues by which man escapes from his feeling of aloneness and limitation. In the act of surrender he loses his independence and integrity as an individual but he gains the feeling of being protected by an awe-inspiring power of which, as it were, he becomes a part.

In Calvin's theology we find a vivid picture of authoritarian, theistic thinking. "For I do not call it humility," says Calvin, "if you suppose that we have anything left. . . . We cannot think of ourselves as we ought to think without utterly despising everything that may be supposed an excellence in us. This humility is unfeigned submission of a mind overwhelmed with a weighty sense of its own misery and poverty; for such is the uniform description of it in the word of God." [1]

The experience which Calvin describes here, that of despising everything in oneself, of the submission of the mind overwhelmed by its own poverty, is the very essence of all authoritarian religions whether they are couched in secular or in theological language.[2] In authoritarian religion God is a symbol of power and force, He is supreme because He has supreme power, and man in juxtaposition is utterly powerless.

Authoritarian secular religion follows the same principle. Here the Führer or the beloved "Father of His People" or the State or the Race or the Socialist Fatherland becomes the object of worship; the life of the individual becomes insignificant and man's worth consists in the very denial of his worth and strength. Frequently authoritarian religion postulates an ideal which is so abstract and so distant that it has hardly any connection with the real life of real people. To such ideals as "life after death" or "the future of mankind" the life and happiness of persons living here and now may be sacrificed; the alleged ends justify every means and become symbols in the names of which religious or secular "elites" control the lives of their fellow men.

Humanistic religion, on the contrary, is centered around man and his strength. Man must develop his power of reason in order to understand himself, his relationship to his fellow men and his position in the universe. He must recognize the truth, both with regard to his limitations and his potentialities. He must develop his powers of love for others as well as for himself and experience the solidarity of all living beings. He must have principles and norms to guide him in this aim. Religious experience in this

---

[1] Johannes Calvin, *Institutes of the Christian Religion* (Presbyterian Board of Christian Education, 1928), p. 681.

[2] See Erich Fromm, *Escape from Freedom* (Farrar & Rinehart, 1941), pp. 141 ff. This attitude toward authority is described there in detail.

kind of religion is the experience of oneness with the All, based on one's relatedness to the world as it is grasped with thought and with love. Man's aim in humanistic religion is to achieve the greatest strength, not the greatest powerlessness; virtue is self-realization, not obedience. Faith is certainty of conviction based on one's experience of thought and feeling, not assent to propositions on credit of the proposer. The prevailing mood is that of joy, while the prevailing mood in authoritarian religion is that of sorrow and of guilt.

Inasmuch as humanistic religions are theistic, God is a symbol of *man's own powers* which he tries to realize in his life, and is not a symbol of force and domination, having *power over man*.

Illustrations of humanistic religions are early Buddhism, Taoism, the teachings of Isaiah, Jesus, Socrates, Spinoza, certain trends in the Jewish and Christian religions (particularly mysticism), the religion of Reason of the French Revolution. It is evident from these that the distinction between authoritarian and humanistic religion cuts across the distinction between theistic and nontheistic, and between religions in the narrow sense of the word and philosophical systems of religious character. What matters in all such systems is not the thought system as such but the human attitude underlying their doctrines.

One of the best examples of humanistic religions is early Buddhism. The Buddha is a great teacher, he is the "awakened one" who recognizes the truth about human existence. He does not speak in the name of a super-natural power but in the name of reason. He calls upon every man to make use of his own reason and to see the truth which he was only the first to find. Once man takes the first step in seeing the truth, he must apply his efforts to live in such a way that he develops his powers of reason and of love for all human creatures. Only to the degree to which he succeeds in this can he free himself from the bondage of irrational passions. While man must recognize his limitations according to Buddhistic teaching, he must also become aware of the powers in himself. The concept of Nirvana as the state of mind the fully awakened one can achieve is not one of man's helplessness and submission but on the contrary one of the development of the highest powers man possesses. . . .

Zen-Buddhism, a later sect within Buddhism, is expressive of an even more radical anti-authoritarian attitude. Zen proposes that no knowledge is of any value unless it grows out of ourselves; no authority, no teacher can really teach us anything except to arouse doubts in us; words and thought systems are dangerous because they easily turn into authorities whom we worship. Life itself must be grasped and experienced as it flows, and in this lies virtue. . . .

Another illustration of a humanistic religious system is to be found in Spinoza's religious thinking. While his language is that of medieval theology, his concept of God has no trace of authoritarianism. God could not have created the world different from what it is. He cannot change anything; in fact, God is identical with the totality of the universe. Man must see his own limitations and recognize that he is dependent on the totality of forces outside himself over which he has no control. Yet his are the powers of love and of reason. He can develop them and attain an optimum of freedom and of inner strength.

The distinction between authoritarian and humanistic religion not only cuts across various religions, it can exist within the same religion. Our own religious tradition is one of the best illustrations of this point. Since it is of fundamental importance to understand fully the distinction between authoritarian and humanistic religion I shall illustrate it further from a source with which every reader is more or less familiar, the Old Testament.

The beginning of the Old Testament [3] is written in the spirit of authoritarian religion. The picture of God is that of the absolute ruler of a patriarchal clan, who has created man at his pleasure and can destroy him at will. He has forbidden him to eat from the tree of knowledge of good and evil and has threatened him with death if he transgresses this order. But the serpent, "more clever than any animal," tells Eve, "Ye shall not surely die: For God doth know that in the day ye eat thereof, then your eyes shall be opened, and ye shall be as gods, knowing good and evil." [4] God proves the serpent to be right. When Adam and Eve have transgressed he punished them by proclaiming enmity between man and nature, between man and the soil and animals, and between men and women. But man is not to die. However, "the man has become as one of us, to know good and evil: and now, lest he put forth his hand, and take also of the tree of life, and eat, and live for ever," [5] God expels Adam and Eve from the garden of Eden and puts an angel with a flaming sword at the east "to keep the way of the tree of life."

The text makes very clear what man's sin is: it is rebellion against God's command; it is disobedience and not any inherent sinfulness in the act of eating from the tree of knowledge. On the contrary, further religious development has made the knowledge of good and evil the cardinal virtue to which man may aspire. The text also makes it plain what God's motive is: it is concern with his own superior role, the jealous fear of man's claim to become his equal.

A decisive turning point in the relationship between God and man is to be seen in the story of the Flood. When God saw "that the wickedness of

---

[3] The historical fact that the beginning of the Bible may not be its oldest part does not need to be considered here since we use the text as an illustration of two principles and not to establish a historical sequence.

[4] Genesis 3:4–5.

[5] *Ibid.* 3:22.

man was great on the earth . . . it repented the Lord that he had made man and the earth, and it grieved him at his heart. And the Lord said, I will destroy man whom I have created from the face of the earth; both man, and beast, and the creeping thing, and the fowls of the air; for it repenteth me that I have made them." [6]

There is no question here but that God has the right to destroy his own creatures; he has created them and they are his property. The text defines their wickedness as "violence," but the decision to destroy not only man but animals and plants as well shows that we are not dealing here with a sentence commensurate with some specific crime but with God's angry regret over his own action which did not turn out well. "But Noah found grace in the eyes of the Lord," and he, together with his family and a representative of each animal species, is saved from the Flood. Thus far the destruction of man and the salvation of Noah are arbitrary acts of God. He could do as he pleased, as can any powerful tribal chief. But after the Flood the relationship between God and man changes fundamentally. A covenant is concluded between God and man in which God promises that "neither shall all flesh be cut off any more by the waters of a flood; neither shall there any more be a flood to destroy the earth." [7] God obligates himself never to destroy all life on earth, and man is bound to the first and most fundamental command of the Bible, not to kill: "At the hand of every man's brother will I require the life of man." [8] From this point on the relationship between God and man undergoes a profound change. God is no longer an absolute ruler who can act at his pleasure but is bound by a constitution to which both he and man must adhere; he is bound by a principle which he cannot violate, the principle of respect for life. God can punish man if he violates this principle, but man can also challenge God if he is guilty of its violation.

The new relationship between God and man appears clearly in Abraham's plea for Sodom and Gomorrah. When God considers destroying the cities because of their wickedness, Abraham criticizes God for violating his own principles. "That be far from thee to do after this manner, to slay the righteous with the wicked: and that the righteous should be as the wicked, that be far from thee. Shall not the Judge of all the earth do right?" [9]

The difference between the story of the Fall and this argument is great indeed. There man is forbidden to know good and evil and his position toward God is that of submission—or sinful disobedience. Here man uses his knowledge of good and evil, criticizes God in the name of justice, and God has to yield.

---

[6] *Ibid.* 6:5 ff.
[7] *Ibid.* 9:11.
[8] *Ibid.* 9:5.
[9] *Ibid.* 18:25.

Even this brief analysis of the authoritarian element in the biblical story shows that at the root of the Judaeo-Christian religion both principles, the authoritarian and the humanistic, are present. In the development of Judaism as well as of Christianity both principles have been preserved and their respective preponderance marks different trends in the two religions.

The following story from the Talmud expresses the unauthoritarian, humanistic side of Judaism as we find it in the first centuries of the Christian era.

A number of other famous rabbinical scholars disagreed with Rabbi Eliezar's views in regard to a point of ritual law. "Rabbi Eliezar said to them: 'If the law is as I think it is then this tree shall let us know.' Whereupon the tree jumped from its place a hundred yards (others say four hundred yards). His colleagues said to him, 'One does not prove anything from a tree.' He said, 'If I am right then this brook shall let us know.' Whereupon the brook ran upstream. His colleagues said to him, 'One does not prove anything from a brook.' He continued and said, 'If the law is as I think then the walls of the house will tell.' Whereupon the walls began to fall. But Rabbi Joshua shouted at the walls and said, 'If scholars argue a point of law, what business have you to fall?' So the walls fell no further out of respect for Rabbi Joshua but out of respect for Rabbi Eliezar did not straighten up. And that is the way they still are. Rabbi Eliezar took up the argument again and said, 'If the law is as I think, they shall tell us from heaven.' Whereupon a voice from heaven said, 'What have you against Rabbi Eliezar, because the law is as he says.' Whereupon Rabbi Joshua got up and said, 'It is written in the Bible: The law is not in heaven. What does this mean? According to Rabbi Jirmijahu it means since the Torah has been given on Mount Sinai we no longer pay attention to voices from heaven because it is written: You make your decision according to the majority opinion.' It then happened that Rabbi Nathan [one of the participants in the discussion] met the Prophet Elijah [who had taken a stroll on earth] and he asked the Prophet, 'What did God himself say when we had this discussion?' The Prophet answered, 'God smiled and said, My children have won, my children have won.' " [10]

This story is hardly in need of comment. It emphasizes the autonomy of man's reason with which even the supernatural voices from heaven cannot interfere. God smiles, man has done what God wanted him to do, he has become his own master, capable and resolved to make his decisions by himself according to rational, democratic methods. . . .

That early Christianity is humanistic and not authoritarian is evident from the spirit and text of all Jesus' teachings. Jesus' precept that "the kingdom of God is within you" is the simple and clear expression of non-

---

[10] Talmud, Baba Meziah, 59, b. (My translation.)

authoritarian thinking. But only a few hundred years later, after Christianity had ceased to be the religion of the poor and humble peasants, artisans, and slaves (the *Am haarez*) and had become the religion of those ruling the Roman Empire, the authoritarian trend in Christianity became dominant. Even so, the conflict between the authoritarian and humanistic principles in Christianity never ceased. It was the conflict between Augustine and Pelagius, between the Catholic Church and the many "heretic" groups and between various sects within Protestantism. The humanistic, democratic element was never subdued in Christian or in Jewish history, and this element found one of its most potent expressions in the mystic thinking within both religions. The mystics have been deeply imbued with the experience of man's strength, his likeness to God, and with the idea that God needs man as much as man needs God; they have understood the sentence that man is created in the image of God to mean the fundamental identity of God and man. Not fear and submission but love and the assertion of one's own powers are the basis of mystical experience. *God is not a symbol of power over man but of man's own powers*.

Thus far we have dealt with the distinctive features of authoritarian and humanistic religions mainly in descriptive terms. But the psychoanalyst must proceed from the description of attitudes to the analysis of their dynamics, and it is here that he can contribute to our discussion from an area not accessible to other fields of inquiry. The full understanding of an attitude requires an appreciation of those conscious and, in particular, unconscious processes occurring in the individual which provide the necessity for and the conditions of its development.

While in humanistic religion God is the image of man's higher self, a symbol of what man potentially is or ought to become, in authoritarian religion God becomes the sole possessor of what was originally man's: of his reason and his love. The more perfect God becomes, the more imperfect becomes man. He *projects* the best he has onto God and thus impoverishes himself. Now God has all love, all wisdom, all justice—and man is deprived of these qualities, he is empty and poor. He had begun with the feeling of smallness, but he now has become completely powerless and without strength; all his powers have been projected onto God. This mechanism of projection is the very same which can be observed in interpersonal relationships of a masochistic, submissive character, where one person is awed by another and attributes his own powers and aspirations to the other person. It is the same mechanism that makes people endow the leaders of even the most inhuman systems with qualities of superwisdom and kindness.[11]

When man has thus projected his own most valuable powers onto God, what of his relationship to his own powers? They have become separated

---

[11] Cf. the discussion about symbiotic relationship in *Escape from Freedom*, pp. 158 ff.

from him and in this process he has become *alienated* from himself. Everything he has is now God's and nothing is left in him. *His only access to himself is through God*. In worshipping God he tries to get in touch with that part of himself which he has lost through projection. After having given God all he has, he begs God to return to him some of what originally was his own. But having lost his own he is completely at God's mercy. He necessarily feels like a "sinner" since he has deprived himself of everything that is good, and it is only through God's mercy or grace that he can regain that which alone makes him human. And in order to persuade God to give him some of his love, he must prove to him how utterly deprived he is of love; in order to persuade God to guide him by his superior wisdom he must prove to him how deprived he is of wisdom when he is left to himself.

But this alienation from his own powers not only makes man feel slavishly dependent on God, it makes him bad too. He becomes a man without faith in his fellow men or in himself, without the experience of his own love, of his own power of reason. As a result the separation between the "holy" and the "secular" occurs. In his wordly activities man acts without love, in that sector of his life which is reserved to religion he feels himself to be a sinner (which he actually is, since to live without love is to live in sin) and tries to recover some of his lost humanity by being in touch with God. Simultaneously, he tries to win forgiveness by emphasizing his own helplessness and worthlessness. Thus the attempt to obtain forgiveness results in the activation of the very attitude from which his sins stem. He is caught in a painful dilemma. The more he praises God, the emptier he becomes. The emptier he becomes, the more sinful he feels. The more sinful he feels, the more he praises his God—and the less able is he to regain himself.

Analysis of religion must not stop at uncovering those psychological processes within man which underly his religious experience; it must proceed to discover the conditions which make for the development of authoritarian and humanistic character structures, respectively, from which different kinds of religious experience stem. Such a sociopsychological analysis goes far beyond the context of these chapters. However, the principal point can be made briefly. What people think and feel is rooted in their character and their character is molded by the total configuration of their practice of life —more precisely, by the socio-economic and political structure of their society. In societies ruled by a powerful minority which holds the masses in subjection, the individual will be so imbued with fear, so incapable of feeling strong or independent, that his religious experience will be authoritarian. Whether he worships a punishing, awesome God or a similarly conceived leader makes little difference. On the other hand, where the individual feels free and responsible for his own fate, or among minorities striving for freedom and independence, humanistic religious experience develops. The history of religion gives ample evidence of this correlation between social structure and kinds of religious experience. Early Christianity was a religion of the poor and downtrodden; the history of religious sects fighting against authoritarian political pressure shows the same principle again and again. Judaism, in which a strong anti-authoritarian tradition could grow up because secular authority never had much of a chance to govern and to build up a legend of its wisdom, therefore developed the humanistic aspect of religion to a remarkable degree. Whenever, on the other hand, religion allied itself with secular power, the religion had by necessity to become authoritarian. The real fall of man is his alienation from himself, his submission to power, his turning against himself even though under the guise of his worship of God.

From the spirit of authoritarian religion stem two fallacies of reasoning which have been used again and again as arguments for theistic religion. One argument runs as follows: How can you criticize the emphasis on dependence on a power transcending man; is not man dependent on forces outside himself which he cannot understand, much less control?

Indeed, man is dependent; he remains subject to death, age, illness, and even if he were to control nature and to make it wholly serviceable to him, he and his earth remain tiny specks in the universe. But it is one thing to recognize one's dependence and limitations, and it is something entirely different to indulge in this dependence, to worship the forces on which one depends. To understand realistically and soberly how limited our power is is an essential part of wisdom and of maturity; to worship it is masochistic and self-destructive. The one is humility, the other self-humiliation.

We can study the difference between the realistic recognition of our limitations and the indulgence in the experience of submission and power-lessness in the clinical examination of masochistic character traits. We find people who have a tendency to incur sickness, accidents, humiliating situations, who belittle and weaken themselves. They believe that they get into such situations against their will and intention, but a study of their unconscious motives shows that actually they are driven by one of the most irrational tendencies to be found in man, namely, by an unconscious desire to be weak and powerless; they tend to shift the center of their life to powers over which they feel no control, thus escaping from freedom and from personal responsibility. We find furthermore that this masochistic tendency is usually accompanied by its very opposite, the tendency to rule and to dominate others, and that the masochistic and the dominating tendencies form the two sides of the authoritarian character structure.[12] Such masochistic tendencies are not always unconscious. We find them overtly in the sexual masochistic perversion where the fulfillment of the

---

[12] See *Escape from Freedom,* pp. 141 ff.

wish to be hurt or humiliated is the condition for sexual excitement and satisfaction. We find it also in the relationship to the leader and the state in all authoritarian secular religions. Here the explicit aim is to give up one's own will and to experience submission under the leader or the state as profoundly rewarding.

Another fallacy of theological thinking is closely related to the one concerning dependence. I mean here the argument that there must be a power or being outside of man because we find that man has an ineradicable longing to relate himself to something beyond himself. Indeed, any sane human being has a need to relate himself to others; a person who has lost that capacity completely is insane. No wonder that man has created figures outside of himself to which he relates himself, which he loves and cherishes because they are not subject to the vacillations and inconsistencies of human objects. That God is a symbol of man's need to love is simple enough to understand. But does it follow from the existence and intensity of this human need that there exists an outer being who corresponds to this need? Obviously that follows as little as our strongest desire to love someone proves that there is a person with whom we are in love. All it proves is our need and perhaps our capacity. . . .

The underlying theme of the preceding chapters is the conviction that the problem of religion is not the problem of God but the problem of man; religious formulations and religious symbols are attempts to give expression to certain kinds of human experience. What matters is the nature of these experiences. The symbol system is only the cue from which we can infer the underlying human reality. Unfortunately the discussion centered around religion since the days of the Enlightenment has been largely concerned with the affirmation or negation of a belief in God rather than with the affirmation or negation of certain human attitudes. "Do you believe in the existence of God?" has been made the crucial question of religionists and the denial of God has been the position chosen by those fighting the church. It is easy to see that many who profess the belief in God are in their human attitude idol worshipers or men without faith, while some of the most ardent "atheists," devoting their lives to the betterment of mankind, to deeds of brotherliness and love, have exhibited faith and a profoundly religious attitude. Centering the religious discussion on the acceptance or denial of the symbol God blocks the understanding of the religious problem as a human problem and prevents the development of that human attitude which can be called religious in a humanistic sense.

Many attempts have been made to retain the symbol God but to give it a meaning different from the one which it has in the monotheistic tradition. One of the outstanding illustrations is Spinoza's theology. Using strictly theological language he gives a definition of God which amounts to saying there is no God in the sense of the Judaeo-Christian tradition.

He was still so close to the spiritual atmosphere in which the symbol God seemed indispensable that he was not aware of the fact that he was negating the existence of God in the terms of his new definition.

In the writings of a number of theologians and philosophers in the nineteenth century and at present one can detect similar attempts to retain the word God but to give it a meaning fundamentally different from that which it had for the Prophets of the Bible or for the Christian and Jewish theologians of the Middle Ages. There need be no quarrel with those who retain the symbol God although it is questionable whether it is not a forced attempt to retain a symbol whose significance is essentially historical. However this may be, one thing is certain. [The real conflict is not between belief in God and "atheism" but between a humanistic, religious attitude and an attitude which is equivalent to idolatry regardless of how this attitude is expressed—or disguised—in conscious thought.]

## Suggested Additional Readings

WHAT IS RELIGION?

Bergson, Henri L. *The Two Sources of Morality and Religion.* Trans., R. Ashley Andra (and others). New York: Holt, Rinehart, & Winston, Inc., 1935. (Also published in paperback by Doubleday and Co., Anchor Series.) A French philosopher contrasts static and dynamic religion and challenges the reader with his arguments for dynamic religion.

Bonaventura. *The Mind's Road to God.* Trans., George Boas. New York: Liberal Arts Press, 1953. (This is a paperback edition.) A medieval theologian of the Platonic tradition writes on the experience and knowledge of God.

Brightman, Edgar S. *A Philosophy of Religion.* Englewood Cliffs, N.J.: Prentice-Hall, 1940. See especially pp. 16 f. The nature of religion is explored by a twentieth-century American philosopher who represents personal idealism.

Durkheim, Emil. *Elementary Forms of the Religious Life.* Trans., J. W. Swain. New York: The Macmillan Company, n.d. See especially Book I, Chapter 1. Religion, in the most general sense, is analyzed by a noted French sociologist in terms of its origins and meaning.

Freud, Sigmund. *The Future of an Illusion.* Trans., W. D. Robson-Scott. New York: Liveright Publishing Corporation, 1949. (Also published in paperback by Doubleday and Co., Anchor Series.) A book in which Freud describes religion in terms of the projection of human needs and desires.

Hocking, William E. *The Meaning of God in Human Experience.* New Haven: Yale University Press, 1934. An American philosopher evaluates the place and importance in human life of belief in God.

Hook, Sydney, editor. *Religious Experience and Truth.* New York: New York University Press, 1961. This symposium contains among other things two papers by Tillich on symbolism and a critique by William Alston of Tillich's conception of symbols.

Kierkegaard, Søren. *Fear and Trembling*. Trans., Walter Lowrie. Princeton: Princeton University Press, 1941. (Also published in paperback by Doubleday and Co., Anchor Series.) A matchless meditation on the philosophical, ethical and religious problems presented by the story of the temptation of Abraham to sacrifice Isaac.

Lessa, William A., and Evon Z. Vogt. *Reader in Comparative Religion*. New York: Harper & Row, 1958. A source book that brings together valuable anthropological materials.

Meister Eckhart. "The Aristocrat," *Meister Eckhart*. Trans., Richand B. Blakney. New York: Harper & Row, 1941, pp. 74f. A representative selection from the works of a medieval German mystic whose writings are among the most philosophically oriented of those in the mystical tradition.

Niebuhr, Richard R. *Schleiermacher on Christ and Religion*. New York: Charles Scribner's Sons, Inc., 1965. A solid, sharply focused study of Schleiermacher's intellectual development.

Oman, John. "The Sphere of Religion," *Science, Religion and Reality*. Edited by Joseph Neeedham. New York: The Macmillan Company, 1925. A helpful analysis of various interpretations of religion and their value by a recent British theologian.

Smith, W. C. *Meaning and End of Religion*. New York: The Macmillan Company, 1962. An approach to the meaning and function of religion by a Harvard professor of comparative religion, by way of tradition and personal faith.

Underhill, Evelyn. *Mysticism*. London: Methuen Publishing Company, 1949. (Published also in paperback by Meridian Books.) A basic study of the nature of mystical experience by an outstanding authority in the field.

Wach, Joachim. *The Sociology of Religion*. Chicago: The University of Chicago Press, 1944. (Also published in paperback by University of Chicago Press, Phoenix Books.) An important contribution in its field and valuable to anyone studying the nature of religion.

Yinger, J. Milton. *Religion, Society and the Individual*. New York: The Macmillan Company, 1957. A functional sociological analysis of religion.

# The Relation
# II.  of Philosophy
# to Religion

EVERY DISCIPLINE MUST attempt to make clear its place in the intellectual enterprise. This is especially difficult when a discipline is a "border" or "bridge" discipline, such as philosophy of religion, and it is rendered even more troublesome when those standing on each end of the bridge speak from a commitment to a "way of life." Nonetheless, the student of philosophy of religion needs to understand how adjudication of the claims of philosophy and of religion has been attempted, and thus what the major types of relationship are between the two.

In the history of the reciprocal influence of theology and philosophy in the Western tradition, a number of views of the relationship between these two areas have been expressed. Some philosophers and theologians have tended to deny that any connection is possible, each claiming that the other's discipline is either irrelevant to his own or without any validity whatsoever. In such cases the possibility of philosophy of religion is denied.

At the other extreme there have been attempts to fuse the two disciplines completely. Here the view is that no disparity exists between reason and revelation, for they are two sides of the same coin: reason seeks and can find what revelation would make evident. Proponents of this position feel that the best rational structuring of the universe is the best theology, for revelation is reason exercising its inherent power.

The majority of writers stand between these two polar positions and represent a number of alternative positions. One of these "middle" ways is to attempt to define a complementary relationship between theology and philosophy so that each discipline has a province of its own which completes the other. This approach finds its most important expression in the thought

[95]

of Thomas Aquinas. Although theology was of primary importance for Thomas, he had, methodologically, a distinctive place for
philosophy also. Another approach within this "middle ground"
asserts that both philosophy and theology have validity in their
own realms, but each realm remains in tension and in an unsettled relation with the other. The theologian feels that theology
is based on revelation which relates to the most essential dimensions of human life, such as man's capacity for finding ultimate
value and meaning; whereas philosophy is primarily concerned
with life at the level of sensory experience and logical analysis.
Because man dwells in both realms, both are necessary and must
be held together, even though such a correlation is tenuous. The
philosopher who accepts this position may simply maintain that
man lives in several dimensions—the religious and the scientific,
for example—each of which represents one phase of an individual's manifold experience.

Another of the mediating ways may be characterized as theology's attempt to transform philosophy. In this approach the
power of man's natural reason is taken to be of prime importance.
Reason is not considered incompetent, but simply misguided.
Theology does not impart "new" knowledge so much as it gives
light and new direction to reason, a motive and goal by which
it may more fully realize its inherent power. It is also possible
for philosophy to attempt to transform theology. Here the effort
is to make theological ideas an integral part of the total philosophical system, and thereby to make evident the truth of the
theological statements in light of the entire philosophical structure.

In the foregoing discussion a broad background is provided
against which the following selections may be more easily approached and assessed. None of these tendencies is to be taken
as a complete delimitation of any single thinker's approach nor
as exhaustive of all of the possibilities, but they provide a framework within which individual selections may be evaluated.

Immanuel Kant's discussion of religion within the limits of
reason is an influential effort to explore the nature of religion
from within the confines of scientific and moral rationality.
Emphasizing his interest in religion as "naturally" understood,
Kant assesses the interplay of reason and religion upon one another. In Wallace's essay on Hegel a position is depicted which
represents the fusion of philosophy and theology. Hegel argues
that the Absolute Mind, or Spirit of the Universe, becomes conscious of itself in human reason, and that therefore the laws
of reason are the laws of the universe. In the exercise of reason

the spirit of man participates in the Spirit of the Absolute, and thereby reveals the truth of the nature of the Absolute.

The articles by Thomas Aquinas and Samuel Thompson illustrate attempts to bring theology and philosophy together in a complementary way. Both Aquinas, a medieval Roman Catholic theologian, and Thompson, a contemporary American Protestant philosopher, are concerned with the same task—that of showing how philosophy provides the fundamental groundwork upon which theology can build and add its own distinctive truth.

The selections from Emil Brunner and Karl Jaspers display views of a theologian and a philosopher who look rather askance at each other's discipline. Brunner questions the validity of a positive relationship between philosophy and theology on the grounds that any such unity implies bringing together two disparate types of knowledge. For this reason Brunner disparages the possibility of finding common ground between the two disciplines. Jaspers, for his part, raises some questions about theologians, especially in regard to attitudes which he thinks lack flexibility, and as a result questions the possibility of genuine relationship.

The writings of Paul Tillich and William Temple, however, affirm that connection between philosophy and theology is not only possible but necessary. From two different perspectives these philosophical theologians attempt to make their case for a recognition of the coinvolvement of the two disciplines. Temple acknowledges that both philosophy and theology have their proper spheres and that each is quite distinct from the other. Tension is inevitable when two disparate ways of reaching the same object—in this case God, or the spiritual realm—are employed. But the tension can be creative in the sense that the two disciplines can help each other to understand themselves more adequately, and even to find some common grounds for agreement. Tillich argues that philosophy analyzes the structures of life and meaning, and by so doing raises questions about the purpose and significance of man's life. Theology, says Tillich, takes on its importance at this point. The task of theology is to explicate the answers that religion offers in response to these questions. In the case of each man, relation between philosophy and theology is understood as one of coinvolvement and of mutual help.

In the assessment of these possibilities the student should come to a clearer understanding of what the province of philosophy of religion is and how the initial starting points of men who work in the area affect their methods and conclusions.

# IMMANUEL KANT

*Immanuel Kant* (1724–1804) was professor at Koenigsberg, Germany, and one of the great philosophers. His writings stimulated much subsequent discussion of theory of knowledge, metaphysics, ethics, and religion. The most significant among his many works are *The Critique of Pure Reason* and *The Critique of Practical Reason.*

## Religion Within the Limits of Reason Alone

### Concerning the Service of God in Religion in General

Religion is (subjectively regarded) the recognition of all duties as divine commands.[1] That religion in which I must know in advance that something is a divine command in order to recognize it as my duty, is the *revealed*

---

From Immanuel Kant, *Religion Within the Limits of Reason Alone,* trans. T. M. Greene and H. H. Hudson, pp. 142–151. Copyright, 1934, by Open Court Publishing Company. Used by permission of the Open Court Publishing Company.

[1] By means of this definition many an erroneous interpretation of the concept of a religion in general is obviated. *First,* in religion, as regards the theoretical apprehension and avowal of belief, no assertorial knowledge is required (even of God's existence), since, with our lack of insight into supersensible objects, such avowal might well be dissembled; rather is it merely a *problematical* assumption (hypothesis) regarding the highest cause of things that is presupposed speculatively, yet with an eye to the object toward which our morally legislative reason bids us strive—an *assertorial* faith, practical and therefore free, and giving promise of the realization of this its ultimate aim. This faith needs merely *the idea of God,* to which all morally earnest (and therefore confident) endeavor for the good must inevitably lead; it need not presume that it can certify the objective reality of this idea through theoretical apprehension. Indeed, the *minimum* of knowledge (it is possible that there may be a God) must suffice, subjectively, for whatever can be made the duty of every man. *Second,* this definition of a religion in general obviates the erroneous representation of religion as an aggregate of *special* duties having reference directly to God; thus it prevents our taking on (as men are otherwise very much inclined to do) *courtly obligations* over and above the ethico-civil duties of humanity (of man to man) and our seeking, perchance, even to make good the deficiency of the latter by means of the former. There are no special duties to God in a universal religion, for God can receive nothing from us; we cannot act for Him, nor yet upon Him. To wish to transform a guilty awe of Him into a duty of the sort described is to forget that awe is not a special act of religion but rather the religious temper in all our actions done in conformity with duty. And when it is said: "We ought to obey God rather than men,"† this means only that when statutory com-

† *Cf.* Acts V, 29.

religion (or the one standing in need of a revelation); in contrast, that religion in which I must first know that something is my duty before I can accept it as a divine injunction is the *natural* religion. He who interprets the natural religion alone as morally necessary, i.e., as duty, can be called the *rationalist* (in matters of belief); if he denies the reality of all supernatural divine revelation he is called a *naturalist;* if he recognizes revelation, but asserts that to know and accept it as real is not a necessary requisite to religion, he could be named a *pure rationalist;* but if he holds that belief in it is necessary to universal religion, he could be named the pure *supernaturalist* in matters of faith.

The rationalist, by virtue of his very title, must of his own accord restrict himself within the limits of human insight. Hence he will never, as a naturalist, dogmatize, and will never contest either the inner possibility of revelation in general or the necessity of a revelation as a divine means for the introduction of true religion; for these matters no man can determine through reason. Hence the question at issue can concern only the reciprocal claims of the pure rationalist and the supernaturalist in matters of faith, namely, what the one or the other holds as necessary and sufficient, or as merely incidental, to the unique true religion.

When religion is classified not with reference to its first origin and its inner possibility (here it is divided into natural and revealed religion) but with respect to its characteristics which makes it *capable of being shared widely with others,* it can be of two kinds: either the *natural* religion, of which (once it has arisen) everyone can be convinced through his own reason, or a *learned* religion, of which one can convince others only through the agency of learning (in and through which they must be guided). This distinction is very important: for no inference regarding a religion's qualification or disqualification to be the universal religion of mankind can be drawn merely from its origin, whereas such an inference is possible from its capacity or incapacity for general dissemination, and it is this capacity which constitutes the essential character of that religion which ought to be binding upon every man.

Such a religion, accordingly, can be *natural,* and at the same time *revealed,* when it is so constituted that men *could and ought to have discovered it*

---

mands, regarding which men can be legislators and judges, come into conflict with duties which reason prescribes unconditionally, concerning whose observance or transgression God alone can be the judge, the former must yield precedence to the latter. But were we willing to regard the statutory commands, which are given out by a church as coming from God, as constituting that wherein God must be obeyed more than man, such a principle might easily become the war-cry, often heard, of hypocritical and ambitious clerics in revolt against their civil superiors. For that which is permissible, *i.e.,* which the civil authorities command, is *certainly* duty; but whether something which is indeed permissible in itself, but cognizable by us only through divine revelation, is really commanded by God—that is (at least for the most part) highly uncertain.

of themselves merely through the use of their reason, although they *would* not have come upon it so early, or over so wide an area, as is required. Hence a revelation thereof at a given time and in a given place might well be wise and very advantageous to the human race, in that, when once the religion thus introduced is here, and has been made known publicly, everyone can henceforth by himself and with his own reason convince himself of its truth. In this event the religion is *objectively* a natural religion, though *subjectively* one that has been revealed; hence it is really entitled to the former name. For, indeed, the occurrence of such a supernatural revelation might subsequently be entirely forgotten without the slightest loss to that religion either of comprehensibility, or of certainty, or of power over human hearts. It is different with that religion which, on account of its inner nature, can be regarded only as revealed. Were it not preserved in a completely secure tradition or in holy books, as records, it would disappear from the world, and there must needs transpire a supernatural revelation, either publicly repeated from time to time or else enduring continuously within each individual, for without it the spread and propagation of such a faith would be impossible.

Yet in part at least every religion, even if revealed, must contain certain principles of the natural religion. For only through reason can thought add revelation to the concept of a *religion,* since this very concept, as though deduced from an obligation to the will of a *moral* legislator, is a pure concept of reason. Therefore we shall be able to look upon even a revealed religion on the one hand as a *natural,* on the other as a *learned* religion, and thus to test it and decide what and how much has come to it from one or the other source.

If we intend to talk about a revealed religion (at least one so regarded) we cannot do so without selecting some specimen or other from history, for we must devise instances as examples in order to be intelligible, and unless we take these from history their possibility might be disputed. We cannot do better than to adopt, as the medium for the elucidation of our idea of revealed religion in general, some book or other which contains such examples, especially one which is closely interwoven with doctrines that are ethical and consequently related to reason. We can then examine it, as one of a variety of books which deal with religion and virtue on the credit of a revelation, thus exemplifying the procedure, useful in itself, of searching out whatever in it may be for us a pure and therefore a universal religion of reason. Yet we do not wish thereby to encroach upon the business of those to whom is entrusted the exegesis of this book, regarded as the summary of positive doctrines of revelation, or to contest their interpretation based upon scholarship. Rather is it advantageous to scholarship, since scholars and philosophers aim at one and the same goal, to wit, the morally good, to bring scholarship, through its own rational principles, to the very point which it already expects to reach by another road. Here the New Testament, considered as the source of the Christian doctrine, can be the book chosen. In accordance with our intention we shall now offer our demonstration in two sections, first, the Christian religion as a natural religion, and, second, as a learned religion, with reference to its content and to the principles which are found in it.

## The Christian Religion as a Natural Religion

Natural religion, as morality (in its relation to the freedom of the agent) united with the concept of that which can make actual its final end (with the concept of *God* as moral Creator of the world), and referred to a continuance of man which is suited to this end in its completeness (to immortality), is a pure practical idea of reason which, despite its inexhaustible fruitfulness, presupposes so very little capacity for theoretical reason that one can convince every man of it sufficiently for practical purposes and can at least require of all men as a duty that which is its effect. This religion possesses the prime essential of the true church, namely, the qualification for universality, so far as one understands by that a validity for everyone (*universitas vel omnitudo distributiva*), i.e., universal unanimity. To spread it, in this sense, as a world religion, and to maintain it, there is needed, no doubt, a body of servants (*ministerium*) of the invisible church, but not officials (*officiales*), in other words, teachers but not dignitaries, because in the rational religion of every individual there does not yet exist a church as a universal *union* (*omnitudo collectiva*), nor is this really contemplated in the above idea.

Yet such unanimity could not be maintained of itself and hence could not, unless it became a visible church, be propagated in its universality; rather is this possible only when a collective unanimity, in other words a union of believers in a (visible) church under the principles of a pure religion of reason, is added; though this church does not automatically arise out of that unanimity nor, indeed, were it already established, would it be brought by its free adherents (as were shown above) to a permanent status as a *community* of the faithful (because in such a religion none of those who has seen the light believes himself to require, for his religious sentiments, fellowship with others). Therefore it follows that unless there are added to the natural laws, apprehensible through unassisted reason, certain statutory ordinances attended by legislative prestige (authority), that will still be lacking which constitutes a special duty of men, and a means to their highest end, namely, their enduring union into a universal visible church; and the authority mentioned above, in order to be a founder of such a church, presupposes a realm of fact[2] and not merely the pure concepts of reason.

Let us suppose there was a teacher of whom an historical record (or, at least, a widespread belief which is not basically disputable) reports that he was the first to expound publicly a pure and searching religion, comprehensible to the whole world (and thus natural). His teachings, as preserved to us, we can in this case test for ourselves. Suppose that all he did was done even in the face of a dominant ecclesiastical faith which was onerous and not conducive to moral ends (a faith whose perfunctory worship can serve as a type of all the other faiths, at bottom merely statutory, which were current in the world at the time). Suppose, further, we find that he had made this universal religion of reason the highest and indispensable condition of every religious faith whatsoever, and then had added to it certain statutes which provided forms and observances designed to serve as means of bringing into existence a church founded upon those principles. Now, in spite of the adventitiousness of his ordinances directed to this end, and the elements of arbitrariness in them, and though we can deny the name of true universal church to these, we cannot deny to him himself the prestige due the one who called men to union in this church; and this without further adding to this faith burdensome new ordinances or wishing to transform acts which he had initiated into peculiar holy practices, required in themselves as being constituent elements of religion.

After this description one will not fail to recognize the person who can be reverenced, not indeed as the *founder* of the *religion* which, free from every dogma, is engraved in all men's hearts (for it does not have its origin in an arbitrary will), but as the founder of the first true *church*. For attestation of his dignity as of divine mission we shall adduce several of his teachings as indubitable evidence of religion in general, let historical records be what they may (since in the idea itself is present adequate ground for its acceptance); these teachings, to be sure, can be no other than those of pure reason, for such alone carry their own proof, and hence upon them must chiefly depend the attestation of the others.

First, he claims that not the observance of outer civil or statutory churchly duties but the pure moral disposition of the heart alone can make man well-pleasing to God (Matthew V, 20–48); that sins in thought are regarded, in the eyes of God, as tantamount to action (V, 28) and that, in general, holiness is the goal toward which man should strive (V, 48); that, for example, to hate in one's heart is equivalent to killing (V, 22); that injury done one's neighbor can be repaired only through satisfaction rendered to the neighbor himself, not through acts of divine worship (V, 24), and that, on the point of truthfulness, the civil device for extorting it, by

---

[2] [*ein Factum*]

oath,[3] does violence to respect for truth itself (V, 34–37); that the natural but evil propensity of the human heart is to be completely reversed, that the sweet sense of revenge must be transformed into tolerance (V, 39, 40) and the hatred of one's enemies into charity (V, 44). Thus, he says, does he intend to do full justice to the Jewish law (V, 17); whence it is obvious that not scriptural scholarship but the pure religion of reason must be the law's interpreter, for taken according to the letter, it allowed the very opposite of all this. Furthermore, he does not leave unnoticed, in his designations of the strait gate and the narrow way, the misconstruction of the law which men allow themselves in order to evade their true moral duty and, holding themselves immune through having fulfilled their churchly duty (VII, 13).[4] He further requires of these pure dispositions that they manifest themselves also in *works* (VII, 16) and, on the other hand, denies the insidious hope of those who imagine that, through invocation and praise of the Supreme Lawgiver in the person of His envoy, they will make up for their lack of good works and ingratiate themselves into favor (VII, 21). Regarding these works he declares that they ought to be performed publicly, as an example for imitation (V, 16); and in a cheerful mood, not as actions extorted from slaves (VI, 16); and that thus, from a small beginning in the sharing and spreading of such dispositions, religion, like a grain of seed in good soil, or a ferment of goodness, would gradually, through its inner power, grow into a kingdom of God (XIII, 31–33). Finally, he combines all duties (1) in one *universal* rule (which includes within itself both the inner and the outer moral relations of men), namely: Perform your duty for no motive [5] other than unconditioned esteem for duty itself, i.e., love God (the Legislator of all duties) above all else; and (2) in a *particular* rule that, namely, which

---

[3] It is hard to understand why this clear prohibition against this method of forcing confession before a civil tribunal of religious teachers—a method based upon mere superstition, not upon conscientiousness—is held as so unimportant. For that it is superstition whose efficacy is here most relied on is evident from the fact that the man whom one does not trust to tell the truth in a solemn statement, on the truthfulness of which depends a decision concerning the rights of a human being (a holy thing, so far as this world goes), is yet expected to be persuaded to speak truly, by the use of a formula through which, over and above that statement, he simply calls down upon himself divine punishments (which, in any event, with such a lie, he cannot escape), just as though it rested with him whether or not to render account to this supreme tribunal. In the passage of Scripture cited above, the mode of confirmation by oath is represented as an *absurd* presumption, the attempt to make actual, as though with magical words, what is really not in our power. But it is clearly evident that the wise Teacher who here says that whatever goes beyond Yea, Yea, and Nay, Nay, in the asseveration of truth comes of evil, had in view the bad effect which oaths bring in their train—namely, that the greater importance attached to them almost lends a sanction to the common lie.
[4] The *strait gate* and the narrow way, which leads to life, is that of good life-conduct; the *wide gate* and the broad way, found by many, is the *church*. Not that the church and its doctrines are responsible for men being lost, but that the *entrance* into it and the knowledge of its statutes or celebration of its rites are regarded as the manner in which God really wishes to be served.
[5] [*Triebfeder*]

concerns man's external relation to other men as universal duty: Love every one as yourself, i.e., further his welfare from good-will that is immediate and not derived from motives of self-advantage. These commands are not mere laws of virtue but precepts of *holiness* which we ought to pursue, and the very pursuit of them is called *virtue*.

Accordingly he destroys the hope of all who intend to wait upon this moral goodness quite passively, with their hands in their laps, as though it were a heavenly gift which descends from on high. He who leaves unused the natural predisposition to goodness which lies in human nature (like a talent entrusted to him) in lazy confidence that a higher moral influence will no doubt supply the moral character and completeness which he lacks, is confronted with the threat that even the good which, by virtue of his natural predisposition, he may have done, will not be allowed to stand him in stead because of this neglect (XXV, 29).

As regards men's very natural expectation of an allotment of happiness proportional to a man's moral conduct, especially in view of the many sacrifices of the former which must be undergone for the sake of the latter, he promises (V, 11, 12) a reward for these sacrifices in a future world, but one in accordance with the differences of disposition in this conduct between those who did their duty *for the sake of the reward* (or for release from deserved punishment) and the better men who performed it merely for its own sake; the latter will be dealt with in a different manner. When the man governed by self-interest, the god of this world, does not renounce it but merely refines it by the use of reason and extends it beyond the con-stricting boundary of the present, he is represented (Luke XVI, 3–9) as one who, in his very person [as servant], defrauds his master [self-interest] and wins from him sacrifices in behalf of "duty." For when he comes to realize that sometime, perhaps soon, the world must be forsaken, and that he can take along into the other world nothing of what he here possessed, he may well resolve to strike off from the account what he or his master, self-interest, has a legal right to exact from the indigent, and, as it were, thereby to acquire for himself bills of exchange, payable in another world. Herein he acts, no doubt, *cleverly* rather than *morally,* as regards the mo-tives of such charitable actions, and yet in conformity with the moral law, at least according to the letter of that law; and he can hope that for this too he may not stand unrequited in the future.[6] Compare with this what

---

[6] We know nothing of the future, and we ought not to seek to know more than what is rationally bound up with the incentives of morality and their end. Here belongs the belief that there are no good actions which will not, in the next world, have their good conse-quences for him who performs them; that, therefore, however reprehensible a man may find himself at the end of his life, he must not on that account refrain from doing at least *one* more good deed which is in his power, and that, in so doing, he has reason to hope that, in proportion as he possesses in this action a purely good intent, the act will be of greater worth than those actionless absolutions which are supposed to compensate for the deficiency of good deeds without providing anything for the lessening of the guilt.

is said of charity toward the needy from sheer motives of duty (Matthew XXV, 35–40), where those, who gave succor to the needy without the idea even entering their minds that such action was worthy of a reward or that they thereby obligated heaven, as it were, to recompense them, are, for this very reason, because they acted thus without attention to reward, declared by the Judge of the world to be those really chosen for His kingdom, and it becomes evident that when the Teacher of the Gospel spoke of rewards in the world to come he wished to make them thereby not an incentive to action but merely (as a soul-elevating representation of the consummation of the divine benevolence and wisdom in the guidance of the human race) an object of the purest respect and of the greatest moral approval when reason reviews human destiny in its entirety.

Here then is a complete religion, which can be presented to all men comprehensibly and convincingly through their own reason; while the possibility and even the necessity of its being an archetype for us to imitate (so far as men are capable of that imitation) have, be it noted, been made evident by means of an example without either the truth of those teachings nor the authority and the worth of the Teacher requiring any external certification (for which scholarship or miracles, which are not matters for everyone, would be required). When appeals are here made to older (Mosaic) legislation and prefiguration, as though these were to serve the Teacher as means of confirmation, they are presented not in support of the truth of his teachings but merely for the introduction of these among people who clung wholly, and blindly, to the old. This introduction, among men whose heads, filled with statutory dogmas, have been almost entirely unfitted for the religion of reason, must always be more difficult than when this religion is to be brought to the reason of people uninstructed but also unspoiled. For this reason no one should be astonished to find an exposition, that adapted itself to the prejudices of those times, now puzzling and in need of pains-taking exegesis; though indeed it everywhere permits a religious doctrine to shine forth and, in addition, frequently points explicitly to that which must be comprehensible and, without any expenditure of learning, convincing to all men.

# WILLIAM WALLACE

William Wallace (1844–1897) was Whyte Professor of Moral Philosophy at Oxford and translator of Hegel's *Logic* and *Philosophy of Mind*. His discussion of Hegel's philosophy of religion constitutes a part of his introduction to Hegel's *Philosophy of Mind*.

George W. F. Hegel (1770–1831), nineteenth-century German philosopher, is a major representative of absolute idealism.

## Hegel's Philosophy of Mind

### Religion and Philosophy

It may be well at this point to guard against a misconception of this serial order of exposition. As stage is seen to follow stage, the historical imagination, which governs our ordinary current of ideas, turns the logical dependence into a time-sequence. But it is of course not meant that the later stage follows the earlier in history. The later is the more real, and therefore the more fundamental. But we can only understand by abstracting and then transcending our abstractions, or rather by showing how the abstraction implies relations which force us to go further and beyond our arbitrary arrest. Each stage therefore either stands to that preceding it as an antithesis, which inevitably dogs its steps as an accusing spirit, or it is the conjunction of the original thesis with the antithesis, in a union which should not be called synthesis because it is a closer fusion and true marriage of minds. A truth and reality, though fundamental, is only appreciated at its true value and seen in all its force where it appears as the reconciliation and reunion of partial and opposing points of view. Thus, e.g., the full significance of the State does not emerge so long as we view it in isolation as a supposed single state, but only as it is seen in the conflict of history, in its actual "energy" as a world-power among powers, always pointing beyond itself to a something universal which it fain would be, and yet cannot be. Or, again, there never was a civil or economic society which existed save under the wing of a state, or in one-sided assumption of state powers to itself: and a family is

From William Wallace, *Hegel's Philosophy of Mind*, Tr. from *The Encyclopaedia of the Philosophical Sciences* by William Wallace, pp. xxxv–xlix. Published, 1894, by The Clarendon Press. In the public domain.

no isolated and independent unit belonging to a supposed patriarchal age, but was always mixed up with, and in manifold dependence upon, political and civil combinations. The true family, indeed, far from preceding the state in time, presupposes the political power to give it its precise sphere and its social stability: as is well illustrated by that typical form of it presented in the Roman state.

So, again, religion does not supervene upon an already existing political and moral system and invest it with an additional sanction. The true order would be better described as the reverse. The real basis of social life, and even of intelligence, is religion. As some thinkers quaintly put it, the known rests and lives on the bosom of the Unknowable. But when we say that, we must at once guard against a misconception. There are religions of all sorts; and some of them which are most heard of in the modern world only exist or survive in the shape of a traditional name and venerated creed which has lost its power. Nor is a religion necessarily committed to a definite conception of a supernatural—of a personal power outside the order of Nature. But in all cases, religion is a faith and a theory which gives unity to the facts of life, and gives it, not because the unity is in detail proved or detected, but because life and experience in their deepest reality inexorably demand and evince such a unity to the heart. The religion of a time is not its nominal creed, but its dominant conviction of the meaning of reality, the principle which animates all its being and all its striving, the faith it has in the laws of nature and the purpose of life. Dimly or clearly felt and perceived, religion has for its principle (one cannot well say, its object) not the unknowable, but the inner unity of life and knowledge, of act and consciousness, a unity which is certified in its every knowledge, but is never fully demonstrable by the summation of all its ascertained items. As such a felt and believed synthesis of the world and life, religion is the unity which gives stability and harmony to the social sphere; just as morality in its turn gives a partial and practical realisation to the ideal of religion. But religion does not merely establish and sanction morality; it also frees it from a certain narrowness it always has, as of the earth. Or, otherwise put, morality has to the keener inspection something in it which is more than the mere moral injunction at first indicates. Beyond the moral, in its stricter sense, as the obligatory duty and the obedience to law, rises and expands the beautiful and the good: a beautiful which is disinterestedly loved, and a goodness which has thrown off all utilitarian relativity, and become a free self-enhancing joy. The true spirit of religion sees in the divine judgment not a mere final sanction to human morality which has failed of its earthly close, not the re-adjustment of social and political judgments in accordance with our more conscientious inner standards, but a certain, though, for our part-by-part vision, incalculable proportion between what is done and suffered. And in this liberation of the moral from its restrictions, Art renders no slight aid. Thus in different ways, religion presupposes morality to fill up its vacant form, and morality presupposes religion to give its laws an ultimate sanction, which at the same time points beyond their limitations.

But art, religion, and philosophy still rest on the national culture and on the individual mind. However much they rise in the heights of the ideal world, they never leave the reality of life and circumstance behind, and float in the free empyrean. Yet there are degrees of universality, degrees in which they reach what they promised. As the various psychical *nuclei* of an individual consciousness tend through the course of experience to gather round a central idea and by fusion and assimilation form a complete mental organisation; so, through the march of history, there grows up a complication and a fusion of national ideas and aspirations which, though still retaining the individuality and restriction of a concrete national life, ultimately present an organisation social, aesthetic, and religious which is a type of humanity in its universality and completeness. Always moving in the measure and on the lines of the real development of its social organisation, the art and religion of a nation tend to give expression to what social and political actuality at its best but imperfectly sets in existence. They come more and more to be, not mere competing fragments as set side by side with those of others, but comparatively equal and complete representations of the many-sided and many-voiced reality of man and the world. Yet always they live and flourish in reciprocity with the fullness of practical institutions and individual character. An abstractly universal art and religion is a delusion—until all diversities of geography and climate, of language and temperament, have been made to disappear. If these energies are in power and reality and not merely in name, they cannot be applied like a panacea or put on like a suit of ready-made clothes. If alive, they grow with individualised type out of the social situation: and they can only attain a vulgar and visible universality, so far as they attach themselves to some simple and uniform aspects—a part tolerably identical everywhere—in human nature in all times and races.

Art, according to Hegel's account, is the first of the three expressions of Absolute Mind. But the key-note to the whole is to be found in Religion: for Religion is the generic description of that phase of mind which has found rest in the fullness of attainment and is no longer a struggle and a warfare, but a fruition. "It is the conviction of all nations," he says, "that in the religious consciousness they hold their truth; and they have always regarded religion as their dignity and as the Sunday of their life. Whatever excites our doubts and alarms, all grief and all anxiety, all that the petty fields of finitude can offer to attract us, we leave behind on the shoals of time: and as the traveller on the highest peak of a mountain range, removed from every distinct view of the earth's surface, quietly lets his vision neglect all the restrictions of the landscape and the world; so in this pure region of faith man, lifted above the hard and inflexible reality, sees it with his mind's eye reflected in the rays of the mental sun to an image where its discords, its lights and shades, are softened to eternal calm. In this region of mind flow the waters of forgetfulness, from which Psyche drinks, and in which she drowns all her pain: and the darknesses of this life are here softened to a dream-image, and transfigured into a mere setting for the splendours of the Eternal.''

If we take Religion, in this extended sense, we find it is the sense, the vision, the faith, the certainty of the eternal in the changeable, of the infinite in the finite, of the reality in appearance, of the truth in error. It is freedom from the distractions and pre-occupations of the particular details of life; it is the sense of permanence, repose, certainty, rounding off, toning down and absorbing the vicissitude, the restlessness, the doubts of actual life. Such a victory over palpable reality has no doubt its origin—its embryology—in phases of mind which have been already discussed in the first section. Religion will vary enormously according to the grade of national mood of mind and social development in which it emerges. But whatever be the peculiarities of its original swaddling-clothes, its cardinal note will be a sense of dependence on, and independence in, something more permanent, more august, more of a surety and stay than visible and variable nature and man— something also which whether God or devil, or both in one, holds the keys of life and death, of weal and woe, and holds them from some safe vantage-ground above the lower realms of change. By this central being the outward and the inward, past and present and to come, are made one. And as already indicated, Religion, emerging, as it does, from social man, from mind ethical, will retain traces of the two *foci* in society: the individual subjectivity and the objective community. Retain them however only as traces, which still show in the actually envisaged reconciliation. For that is what religion does to morality. It carries a step higher the unity or rather combination gained in the State: it is the fuller harmony of the individual and the collectivity. The moral conscience rests in certainty and fixity on the religious.

But Religion (thus widely understood as the faith in sempiternal and all-explaining reality) at first appears under a guise of Art. The poem and the pyramid, the temple-image and the painting, the drama and the fairy legend, these are religion: but they are, perhaps, religion as Art. And that means that they present the eternal under sensible representations, the work of an artist, and in a perishable material of limited range. Yet even the carvers of a long-past day whose works have been disinterred from the plateaux of Auvergne knew that they gave to the perishable life around them a quasi-immortality: and the myth-teller of a savage tribe elevated the incident of a season into a perennial power of love and fear. The cynic may remind us that from the finest picture of the artist, readily

> "We turn
> To yonder girl that fords the burn."

And yet it may be said in reply to the cynic that, had it not been for the deep-imprinted lesson of the artist, it would have been but a brutal instinct that would have drawn our eyes. The artist, the poet, the musician, reveal the meaning, the truth, the reality of the world: they teach us, they help us, backward younger brothers, to see, to hear, to feel what our rude senses had failed to detect. They enact the miracle of the loaves and fishes, again and again: out of the common limited things of every day they produce a bread of life in which the generations continue to find nourishment.

But if Art embodies for us the unseen and the eternal, it embodies it in the stone, the colour, the tone, and the word: and these are by themselves only dead matter. To the untutored eye and taste the finest picture-gallery is only a weariness: when the national life has drifted away, the sacred book and the image are but idols and enigmas. "The statues are now corpses from which the vivifying soul has fled, and the hymns are words whence faith has departed: the tables of the Gods are without spiritual meat and drink, and games and feasts no longer afford the mind its joyful union with the being of being. The works of the Muse lack that intellectual force which knew itself strong and real by crushing gods and men in its winepress. They are now (in this iron age) what they are for us—fair fruits broken from the tree, and handed to us by a kindly destiny. But the gift is like the fruits which the girl in the picture presents: she does not give the real life of their existence, not the tree which bore them, not the earth and the elements which entered into their substance, nor the climate which formed their quality, nor the change of seasons which governed the process of their growth. Like her, Destiny in giving us the works of ancient art does not give us their world, not the spring and summer of the ethical life in which they blossomed and ripened, but solely a memory and a suggestion of this actuality. Our act in enjoying them, therefore, is not a Divine service: were it so, our mind would achieve its perfect and satisfying truth. All that we do is a mere externalism, which from these fruits wipes off some rain-drop, some speck of dust, and which, in place of the inward elements of moral actuality that created and inspired them, tries from the dead elements of their external reality, such as language and historical allusion, to set up a tedious mass of scaffolding, not in order to live ourselves into them, but only to form a picture of them in our minds. But as the girl who proffers the plucked fruits is more and nobler than the natural element with all its details of tree, air, light, etc., which first yielded them, because she gathers all this together, in a nobler way, into the glance of the conscious eye and the gesture which proffers them; so the spirit of destiny which offers us those works of art is more than the ethical life and actuality of the ancient people: for it is the inwardising of that mind which in them was still self-estranged and self-dispossessed—it is the spirit of tragic destiny, the destiny which collects all those individualised gods and attributes of substance into the one

Pantheon. And that temple of all the gods is Mind conscious of itself as mind."

Religion enters into its more adequate form when it ceases to appear in the guise of Art and realises that the kingdom of God is within, that the truth must be *felt,* the eternal *inwardly* revealed, the holy one apprehended by *faith,* not by outward vision. Eye hath not seen, nor ear heard, the things of God. They cannot be presented, or delineated: they come only in the witness of the spirit. The human soul itself is the only worthy temple of the Most High, whom heaven, and the heaven of heavens, cannot contain. Here in truth God has come down to dwell with men; and the Son of Man, caught up in the effusion of the Spirit, can in all assurance and all humility claim that he is divinified. Here apparently Absolute Mind is reached: the soul knows no limitation, no struggle: in time it is already eternal. Yet, there is, according to Hegel, a flaw—not in the essence and the matter, but in the manner and mode in which the ordinary religious consciousness represents to itself, or pictures that unification which it feels and experiences.

"In religion then this unification of ultimate Being with the Self is implicitly reached. But the religious consciousness, if it has this symbolic idea of its reconciliation, still has it as a mere symbol or representation. It attains the satisfaction by tacking on to its pure negativity, and that externally, the positive signification of its unity with the ultimate Being: its satisfaction remains therefore tainted by the antithesis of another world. Its own reconciliation, therefore, is presented to its consciousness as something far away, something far away in the future: just as the reconciliation which the other Self accomplished appears as a far-away thing in the past. The one Divine Man had but an implicit father and only an actual mother; conversely the universal divine man, the community, has its own deed and knowledge for its father, but for its mother only the eternal Love, which it only *feels,* but does not *behold* in its consciousness as an actual immediate object. Its reconciliation therefore is in its heart, but still at variance with its consciousness, and its actuality still has a flaw. In its field of consciousness the place of implicit reality or side of pure mediation is taken by the reconciliation that lies far away behind: the place of the actually present, or the side of immediacy and existence, is filled by the world which has still to wait for its transfiguration to glory. Implicitly no doubt the world is reconciled with the eternal Being; and that Being, it is well known, no longer looks upon the object as alien to it, but in its love sees it as like itself. But for self-consciousness this immediate presence is not yet set in the full light of mind. In its immediate consciousness accordingly the spirit of the community is parted from its religious: for while the religious consciousness declares that they are implicitly not parted, this implicitness is not raised to reality and not yet grown to absolute self-certainty."

Religion therefore, which as it first appeared in art-worship had yet to realise its essential inwardness or spirituality, so has now to overcome the antithesis in which its (the religious) consciousness stands to the secular. For the peculiarly religious type of mind is distinguished by an indifference and even hostility, more or less veiled, to art, to morality and the civil state, to science and to nature. Strong in the certainty of faith, or of its implicit rest in God, it resents too curious inquiry into the central mystery of its union, and in its distincter consciousness sets the foundation of faith on the evidence of a fact, which, however, it in the same breath declares to be unique and miraculous, the central event of the ages, pointing back in its reference to the first days of humanity, and forward in the future to the winding-up of the business of terrestrial life. Philosophy, according to Hegel's conception of it, does but draw the conclusion supplied by the premisses of religion: it supplements and rounds off into coherence the religious implications. The unique events in Judea nearly nineteen centuries ago are for it also the first step in a new revelation of man's relationship to God: but while it acknowledges the transcendent interest of that age, it lays main stress on the permanent truth then revealed, and it insists on the duty of carrying out the principle there awakened to all the depth and breadth of its explication. Its task—its supreme task—is to *explicate religion.* But to do so is to show that religion is no exotic, and no *mere* revelation from an external source. It is to show that religion is the truth, the complete reality, of the mind that lived in Art, that founded the state and sought to be dutiful and upright: the truth, the crowning fruit of all scientific knowledge, of all human affections, of all secular consciousness. Its lesson ultimately is that there is nothing essentially common or unclean: that the holy is not parted off from the true and the good and the beautiful.

Religion thus expanded descends from its abstract or "intelligible" world, to which it had retired from art and science, and the affairs of ordinary life. Its God—as a true God—is not of the dead alone, but also of the living: not a far-off supreme and ultimate Being, but also a man among men. Philosophy thus has to break down the middle partition-wall of life, the fence between secular and sacred. It is but religion come to its maturity, made at home in the world, and no longer a stranger and a wonder. Religion has pronounced in its inmost heart and faith of faith, that the earth is the Lord's, and that day unto day shows forth the divine handiwork. But the heart of unbelief, of little faith, has hardly uttered the word, than it forgets its assurance and leans to the conviction that the prince of this world is the Spirit of Evil. The mood of Théodicée is also—but with a difference—the mood of philosophy. It asserts the ways of Providence: but its providence is not the God of the Moralist, or the ideal of the Artist, or rather is not these only, but also the Law of Nature, and more than that. Its aim is the Unity of History. The words have sometimes been lightly used to mean that events run on in one continuous flow, and that there are no abrupt, no ultimate beginnings, parting age from age. But the Unity of History in its full sense is beyond history: it is history "reduced" from the expanses of time to the eternal present: its thousand years made one day—made even the glance of a moment. The theme of the Unity of History—in the full depth of unity and the full expanse of history—is the theme of Hegelian philosophy. It traces the process in which Mind has to be all-inclusive, self-upholding, one with the Eternal reality.

"That process of the mind's self-realisation," says Hegel in the close of his *Phenomenology*, "exhibits a lingering movement and succession of minds, a gallery of images, each of which, equipped with the complete wealth of mind, only seems to linger because the Self has to penetrate and to digest this wealth of its Substance. As its perfection consists in coming completely to *know* what it *is* (its substance), this knowledge is its self-involution in which it deserts its outward existence and surrenders its shape to recollection. Thus self-involved, it is sunk in the night of its self-consciousness: but in that night its vanished being is preserved, and that being, thus in idea preserved—old, but now new-born of the spirit—is the new sphere of being, a new world, a new phase of mind. In this new phase it has again to begin afresh and from the beginning, and again nurture itself to maturity from its own resources, as if for it all that preceded were lost, and it had learned nothing from the experience of the earlier minds. Yet is that recollection a preservation of experience: it is the quintessence, and in fact a higher form, of the substance. If therefore this new mind appears only to count on its own resources, and to start quite fresh and blank, it is at the same time on a higher grade that it starts. The intellectual and spiritual realm, which is thus constructed in actuality, forms a succession in time, where one mind relieved another of its watch, and each took over the kingdom of the world from the preceding. The purpose of that succession is to reveal the depth, and that depth is the absolute comprehension of mind: this revelation is therefore to uplift its depth, to spread it out in breadth, so negativing this self-involved Ego, wherein it is self-dispossessed or reduced to substance. But it is also its time: the course of time shows this dispossession itself dispossessed, and thus in its extension it is no less in its depth, the self. The way to that goal—absolute self-certainty—or the mind knowing itself as mind—is the inwardising of the minds, as they severally are in themselves, and as they accomplish the organisation of their realm. Their conservation—regarded on the side of its free and apparently contingent succession of fact—is history: on the side of their comprehended organisation, again, it is the science of mental phenomenology: the two together, comprehended history, form at once the recollection and the grave-yard of the absolute Mind, the actuality, truth, and certitude of his throne, apart from which he were lifeless and alone."

Such in brief outline—lingering most on the points where Hegel has here been briefest—is the range of the Philosophy of Mind. Its aim is to comprehend, not to explain: to put together in intelligent unity, not to analyse into a series of elements. For it psychology is not an analysis or description of mental phenomena, of laws of association, of the growth of certain powers and ideas, but a "comprehended history" of the formation of subjective mind, of the intelligent, feeling, willing self or ego. For it Ethics is part and only part of the great scheme or system of self-development; but continuing into greater concreteness the normal endowment of the individual mind, and but preparing the ground on which religion may be most effectively cultivated. And finally Religion itself, released from its isolation and other world sacro-sanctity, is shown to be only the crown of life, the ripest growth of actuality, and shown to be so by philosophy, whilst it is made clear that religion is the basis of philosophy, or that a philosophy can only go as far as the religious stand-point allows. The hierarchy, if so it be called, of the spiritual forces is one where none can stand alone, or claim an abstract and independent supremacy. The truth of egoism is the truth of altruism: the truly moral is the truly religious: and each is not what it professes to be unless it anticipate the later, or include the earlier.

# ST. THOMAS AQUINAS

*Thomas Aquinas* (c. 1226–1274), Dominican Friar and the greatest of the medieval philosophers, produced a synthesis of Christian faith and Aristotle's metaphysics which became the official theology of the Roman Catholic Church. His chief works are *Summa Theologica* and *Summa Contra Gentiles.*

## The Summa Contra Gentiles

*Chapter VII*
*That the Truth of Reason Is Not in Opposition to the*
*Truth of the Christian Faith*

Now though the aforesaid truth of the Christian faith surpasses the ability of human reason, nevertheless those things which are naturally instilled in human reason cannot be opposed to this truth. For it is clear that those

From Thomas Aquinas, *The Summa Contra Gentiles,* trans. the English Dominican Fathers, I, Chapters VII–XII, pp. 14–23. Published, 1924, Burns, Oates & Washbourne Ltd. Used by permission of Burns & Oates Limited.

things which are implanted in reason by nature, are most true, so much so that it is impossible to think them to be false. Nor is it lawful to deem false that which is held by faith, since it is so evidently confirmed by God. Seeing then that the false alone is opposed to the true, as evidently appears if we examine their definitions, it is impossible for the aforesaid truth of faith to be contrary to those principles which reason knows naturally.

Again. The same thing which the disciple's mind received from its teacher is contained in the knowledge of the teacher, unless he teach insincerely, which it were wicked to say of God. Now the knowledge of naturally known principles is instilled into us by God, since God Himself is the author of our nature. Therefore the divine Wisdom also contains these principles. Consequently whatever is contrary to these principles, is contrary to the divine Wisdom; wherefore it cannot be from God. Therefore those things which are received by faith from divine revelation cannot be contrary to our natural knowledge.

Moreover. Our intellect is stayed by contrary arguments, so that it cannot advance to the knowledge of truth. Wherefore if conflicting knowledges were instilled into us by God, our intellect would thereby be hindered from knowing the truth. And this cannot be ascribed to God.

Furthermore. Things that are natural are unchangeable so long as nature remains. Now contrary opinions cannot be together in the same subject. Therefore God does not instill into man any opinion or belief contrary to natural knowledge.

Hence the Apostle says (Rom. x. 8): *The word is nigh thee even in thy heart and in thy mouth. This is the word of faith which we preach.* Yet because it surpasses reason some look upon it as though it were contrary thereto; which is impossible.

This is confirmed also by the authority of Augustine who says (*Gen. ad lit.* ii): *That which truth shall make known can nowise be in opposition to the holy books whether of the Old or of the New Testament.*

From this we may evidently conclude that whatever arguments are alleged against the teachings of faith, they do not rightly proceed from the first self-evident principles instilled by nature. Wherefore they lack the force of demonstration, and are either probable or sophistical arguments, and consequently it is possible to solve them.

## Chapter VIII
### In What Relation Human Reason Stands to the Truth of Faith

It would also seem well to observe that sensible things from which human reason derives the source of its knowledge, retain a certain trace of likeness to God, but so imperfect that it proves altogether inadequate to manifest the substance itself of God. For effects resemble their causes according to their own mode, since like action proceeds from like agent; and yet the effect does not always reach to a perfect likeness to the agent. Accordingly human reason is adapted to the knowledge of the truth of faith, which can be known in the highest degree only by those who see the divine substance, in so far as it is able to put together certain probable arguments in support thereof, which nevertheless are insufficient to enable us to understand the aforesaid truth as though it were demonstrated to us or understood by us in itself. And yet however weak these arguments may be, it is useful for the human mind to be practised therein, so long as it does not pride itself on having comprehended or demonstrated: since although our view of the sublimest things is limited and weak, it is most pleasant to be able to catch but a glimpse of them, as appears from what has been said.

The authority of Hilary is in agreement with this statement: for he says (*De Trin.*) while speaking of this same truth: *Begin by believing these things, advance and persevere; and though I know thou wilt not arrive, I shall rejoice at thy advance. For he who devoutly follows in pursuit of the infinite, though he never come up with it, will always advance by setting forth. Yet pry not into that secret, and meddle not in the mystery of the birth of the infinite, nor presume to grasp that which is the summit of understanding: but understand that there are things thou canst not grasp.*

## Chapter IX
### Of the Order and Mode of Procedure in This Work

Accordingly, from what we have been saying it is evident that the intention of the wise man must be directed to the twofold truth of divine things and to the refutation of contrary errors: and that the research of reason is able to reach to one of these, while the other surpasses every effort of reason. And I speak of a twofold truth of divine things, not on the part of God Himself Who is Truth one and simple, but on the part of our knowledge, the relation of which to the knowledge of divine things varies.

Wherefore in order to deduce the first kind of truth we must proceed by demonstrative arguments whereby we can convince our adversaries. But since such arguments are not available in support of the second kind of truth, our intention must be not to convince our opponent by our arguments, but to solve the arguments which he brings against the truth, because, as shown above, natural reason cannot be opposed to the truth of faith. In a special way may the opponent of this kind of truth be convinced by the authority of Scripture confirmed by God with miracles: since we believe not what is above human reason save because God has revealed it. In support, however, of this kind of truth, certain probable arguments must be adduced for the practice and help of the faithful, but not for the conviction of our opponents, because the very insufficiency of these arguments would rather confirm them in their error, if they thought that we assented to the truth of faith on account of such weak reasonings.

With the intention then of proceeding in the manner laid down, we shall first of all endeavour to declare that truth which is the object of faith's confession and of reason's researches, by adducing arguments both demonstrative and probable, some of which we have gathered from the writings of the philosophers and of holy men, so as thereby to confirm the truth and convince our opponents. After this, so as to proceed from the more to the less manifest, we shall with God's help proceed to declare that truth which surpasses reason, by refuting the arguments of our opponents, and by setting forth the truth of faith by means of probable arguments and authority.

Seeing then that we intend by the way of reason to pursue those things about God which human reason is able to investigate, the first object that offers itself to our consideration consists in those things which pertain to God in Himself; the second will be the procession of creatures from Him; and the third the relation of creatures to Him as their end. Of those things which we need to consider about God in Himself, we must give the first place (this being the necessary foundation of the whole of this work), to the question of demonstrating that there is a God: for unless this be established, all questions about divine things are out of court.

## Chapter X
## Of the Opinion of Those Who Aver That It Cannot
## Be Demonstrated That There Is a God,
## Since This Is Self-Evident

Possibly it will seem to some that it is useless to endeavour to show that there is a God: they say that it is self-evident that God is, so that it is impossible to think the contrary, and thus it cannot be demonstrated that there is a God. The reasons for this view are as follow. Those things are said to be self-evident which are known as soon as the terms are known: thus as soon as it is known what is a whole, and what is a part, it is known that the whole is greater than its part. Now such is the statement *God is.* For by this word *God* we understand a thing a greater than which cannot be thought of: this is what a man conceives in his mind when he hears and understands this word *God:* so that God must already be at least in his mind. Nor can He be in the mind alone, for that which is both in the mind and in reality is greater than that which is in the mind only. And the very signification of the word shows that nothing is greater than God. Wherefore it follows that it is self-evident that God is, since it is made clear from the very signification of the word.

Again. It is possible to think that there is a thing which cannot be thought not to exist: and such a thing is evidently greater than that which can be thought not to exist. Therefore if God can be thought not to exist, it follows that something can be thought greater than God: and this is contrary to the signification of the term. Therefore it remains that it is self-evident that God is.

Further. Those propositions are most evident in which the selfsame thing is predicated of itself, for instance: *Man is man;* or wherein the predicate is included in the definition of the subject, for instance: *Man is an animal.* Now, as we shall show further on, in God alone do we find that His being is His essence, as though the same were the answer to the question, *What is He?* as to the question, *Is He?* Accordingly when we say, *God is,* the predicate is either identified with the subject, or *at least* is included in the definition of the subject. And thus it will be self-evident that God is.

Moreover. Things that are known naturally are self-evident, for it is not by a process of research that they become evident. Now it is naturally known that God is, since man's desire tends naturally to God as his last end, as we shall show further on. Therefore it is self-evident that God is.

Again. That whereby all things are known must needs be self-evident. Now such is God. For just as the light of the sun is the principle of all visual perception, so the divine light is the principle of all intellectual knowledge, because it is therein that first and foremost intellectual light is to be found. Therefore it must needs be self-evident that God is.

On account of these and like arguments some are of opinion that it is so self-evident that God is, that it is impossible for the mind to think the contrary.

## Chapter XI
### Refutation of the Foregoing Opinion and Solution of the Aforesaid Arguments

The foregoing opinion arose from their being accustomed from the beginning to hear and call upon the name of God. Now custom, especially if it date from our childhood, acquires the force of nature, the result being that the mind holds those things with which it was imbued from childhood as firmly as though they were self-evident. It is also a result of failing to distinguish between what is self-evident simply, and that which is self-evident to us. For it is simply self-evident that God is, because the selfsame thing which God is, is His existence. But since we are unable to conceive mentally the selfsame thing which is God, that thing remains unknown in regard to us. Thus it is self-evident simply that every whole is greater than its part, but to one who fails to conceive mentally the meaning of a whole, it must needs be unknown. Hence it is that those things which are most evident of all are to the intellect what the sun is to the eye of an owl, as stated in *Metaph. ii.*

Nor does it follow, as the first argument alleged, that as soon as the meaning of the word *God* is understood, it is known that God is. First, because it is not known to all, even to those who grant that there is a God, that God is that thing than which no greater can be thought of, since many of the ancients asserted that this world is God. Nor can any such conclusion be gathered from the significations which Damascene assigns to this word *God*. Secondly because, granted that everyone understands this word *God* to signify something than which a greater cannot be thought of, it does not follow that something than which a greater cannot be thought of exists in reality. For we must needs allege a thing in the same way as we allege the signification of its name. Now from the fact that we conceive mentally that which the word *God* is intended to convey, it does not follow that God is otherwise than in the mind. Wherefore neither will it follow that the thing than which a greater cannot be thought of is otherwise than in the mind. And thence it does not follow that there exists in reality something than which a greater cannot be thought of. Hence this is no argument against those who assert that there is no God, since whatever be granted to exist, whether in reality or in the mind, there is nothing to prevent a person from thinking of something greater, unless he grants that there is in reality something than which a greater cannot be thought of.

Again it does not follow, as the second argument pretended, that if it is possible to think that God is not, it is possible to think of something greater than God. For that it be possible to think that He is not, is not on account of the imperfection of His being or the uncertainty thereof, since in itself His being is supremely manifest, but is the result of the weakness of our mind which is able to see Him, not in Himself but in His effects, so that it is led by reasoning to know that He is.

Wherefore the third argument also is solved. For just as it is self-evident to us that a whole is greater than its part, so is it most evident to those who see the very essence of God that God exists, since His essence is His existence. But because we are unable to see His essence, we come to know His existence not in Himself but in His effects.

The solution to the fourth argument is also clear. For man knows God naturally in the same way as he desires Him naturally. Now man desires Him naturally in so far as he naturally desires happiness, which is a likeness of the divine goodness. Hence it does not follow that God considered in Himself is naturally known to man, but that His likeness is. Wherefore man must needs come by reasoning to know God in the likenesses to Him which he discovers in God's effects.

It is also easy to reply to the fifth argument. For God is that in which all things are known, not so that other things be unknown except He be known, as happens in self-evident principles, but because all knowledge is caused in us by His outpouring.

*Chapter XII*
*Of the Opinion of Those Who Say That the Existence of God*
*Cannot Be Proved, and That It Is Held by Faith Alone*

The position that we have taken is also assailed by the opinion of certain others, whereby the efforts of those who endeavour to prove that there is a God would again be rendered futile. For they say that it is impossible by means of the reason to discover that God exists, and that this knowledge is acquired solely by means of faith and revelation.

In making this assertion some were moved by the weakness of the arguments which certain people employed to prove the existence of God.

Possibly, however, this error might falsely seek support from the statements of certain philosophers, who show that in God essence and existence are the same, namely that which answers to the question, *What is He?* and that which answers to the question, *Is He?* Now it is impossible by the process of reason to acquire the knowledge of what God is. Wherefore seemingly neither is it possible to prove by reason whether God is.

Again. If, as required by the system of the Philosopher, in order to prove whether a thing is we must take as principle the signification of its name, and since according to the Philosopher (4 *Metaph.*) *the signification of a name is its definition:* there will remain no means of proving the existence of God, seeing that we lack knowledge of the divine essence or quiddity.

Again. If the principles of demonstration become known to us originally through the senses, as is proved in the *Posterior Analytics,* those things which transcend all sense and sensible objects are seeemingly indemonstrable. Now such is the existence of God. Therefore it cannot be demonstrated.

The falseness of this opinion is shown to us first by the art of demonstration, which teaches us to conclude causes from effects. Secondly, by the order itself of sciences: for if no substance above sensible substance can be an object of science, there will be no science above Physics, as stated in 4 *Metaph.* Thirdly, by the efforts of the philosophers who have endeavoured to prove the existence of God. Fourthly, by the apostolic truth which asserts (Rom. i. 20) that the *invisible things of God are clearly seen, being understood by the things that are made.*

Nor should we be moved by the consideration that in God essence and existence are the same, as the first argument contended. For this is to be understood of the existence by which God subsists in Himself, of which we are ignorant as to what kind of a thing it is, even as we are ignorant of His essence. But it is not to be understood of that existence which is signified by the composition of the mind. For in this way it is possible to prove the existence of God, when our mind is led by demonstrative arguments to form a proposition stating that God is.

Moreover. In those arguments whereby we prove the existence of God, it is not necessary that the divine essence or quiddity be employed as the middle term, as the second argument supposed: but instead of the quiddity we take His effects as middle term, as in the case in *a posteriori* reasoning: and from these effects we take the signification of this word *God*. For all the divine names are taken either from the remoteness of God's effects from Himself, or from some relationship between God and His effects.

It is also evident from the fact that, although God transcends all sensibles and senses, His effects from which we take the proof that God exists, are sensible objects. Hence our knowledge, even of things which transcend the senses, originates from the senses.

# SAMUEL M. THOMPSON

*Samuel M. Thompson* (1902–    ), Professor of Philosophy at Monmouth College, Illinois, is a Protestant who has attempted to restate some traditional emphases in contemporary terms. His book, *A Modern Philosophy of Religion*, develops these views.

## The Philosophy of Religion

### Can Religion Establish Its Own Truth?

The question of whether a religion is true or false is not likely to arise directly from religious experience and practice. It is in our reflective moments, when we look back upon the religious attitudes and actions of ourselves and others, that the question comes. We discover that different people have different religious practices and ideas and that they seem as sincere and as sure they are right as we do ourselves.

Doubts of the truth of religion come also from the seeming conflicts between what we have been taught in the name of religion and what we learn from other sources about ourselves and our world. The whole range of modern culture in the western world has been marked in recent centuries by a persistent conflict between science and religion. There are conflicts also between religion and politics, religion and education, and between certain religious conceptions of man and the uses which modern industry makes of

From Samuel M. Thompson, *A Modern Philosophy of Religion,* pp. 24–40. Copyright, 1955, by Henry Regnery Company. Used by permission of the publishers.

him. We could extend our catalogue to cover the whole range of modern life. For modern life, in those of its aspects which are distinctively modern, is fundamentally secular. Rather than something which permeates life and society and their institutions, religion in the modern world tends to be only one compartment among many. It is expected to keep its proper place and not to intrude beyond its established boundary lines. As Professor Allport says, some people "take over the ancestral religion much as they take over the family jewels. It would be awkward to bring it into too close a relationship with science, with suffering, and with criticism." [1]

It is quite possible that the question of the truth of religion, as it appears in modern thought, is not so much a question of truth in its specific philosophical or logical sense as it is an expression of conflicting loyalties. For where a life is divided into different compartments there is bound to be some degree of rivalry among the various interests involved. Each attempts to capture more of the self and, in so far as the self is a divided self, the more the self is taken by one interest the less is left for the others. We have carried this so far in modern life that we live by the clock and divide ourselves into parts which we measure by hours, minutes, and even by seconds.

If religion is, as we have suggested, an expression of basic evaluations and ultimate loyalties then to try to confine religion to a separate compartment of life as one activity among many is simply incompatible with its nature. As the human self is single and indivisible so the basic attitudes and values of a life must be all of one piece. A man cannot adopt one policy for one part of his activity and another and incompatible policy for another area of activity without destroying his own integrity. For when he is engaged in the one he must at times be aware of the other, and of the fact that the other is his; and so he must in some way or another be perplexed as to which man he is, whether he is one who follows now a policy of kindness and consideration or whether he is a man of ruthless selfishness and cruelty and disregard for the concerns of other people. He may think up excuses for his inconsistencies, or he may not permit himself to think of the matter at all; but he cannot remain in a condition of actual internal, or spiritual, disruption, whether it is conscious or unconscious, and find any real peace and satisfaction. For what brings peace to one part of him will be at odds with the other part. So long as he is aware of himself as the same self which thinks and acts at different times he remains one single self, and he cannot act fully as a self unless the principles on which he acts are compatible with each other. This is the real conflict between the religious and secular aspects of modern life.

Although religious doubt may express a conflict of loyalties yet once it

---

[1] *The Individual and His Religion* by Gordon W. Allport (New York: The Macmillan Company, 1930), p. 52. . . .

comes out into the open it is a challenge to religion's claim to be true. It makes little difference what is responsible for raising the question, once the truth of a religion is challenged that religion can meet the challenge only by justifying its claim to truth. I may be accused of lying or of dishonesty by someone whose only motive is malice or jealousy and who has no ground for his charge. But I cannot meet the charge by attacking his sincerity or his motives. To attempt to do so is to commit a logical fallacy, the fallacy of argument *ad hominem*. My only defense *against the charge,* if I feel it necessary to defend myself against it, is to show that it is false.

Charles A. Bennett insists that the

metaphysical pretensions of religion [by which he means its claim to be true] are the most important thing about it. We cannot reduce the drama of the religious life to a mere record of mental conflict, to so much natural history of the mind. Unless the issues of destiny are at stake, there is no genuine conflict and no drama. Thus I reject all attempts to hand over religion and its problems to anthropology or sociology or psychology, as though these sciences, separately or together, could provide us with a sufficient explanation or interpretation. The problems of religion are philosophical, and there is no substitute for a philosophy of religion.[2]

It is one thing to understand how it happens that we raise the question of the truth of religion; it is quite another thing to determine how that question is to be answered. Once it is raised, however, either we must find some way of answering it or find some way in which we can live with the question without destroying the basis of our life.

When we look at the question directly it seems quite evident that a religion cannot examine its own truth. If it tries to do this in its own terms, as a part of the expression of the attitudes and practices of which it is composed, it would of course beg the question. It would be trying to answer a question in terms of what has itself been brought into question.

This is the reason religious dispute is so seldom convincing. To be convinced by an argument, in so far as the conviction is to be a logical one, we must accept the argument's premises. If the argument is about the truth of a religion then the premises themselves are in question. To argue from these premises in favor of them can convince only those who are unaware of what is happening. When we concern ourselves with the doctrines of a religion, and deal with them from the standpoint of that religion itself, then those doctrines are simply accepted. A religion proclaims what it takes to be true, and the hearer accepts or rejects. He is convinced or he is not convinced. To try to justify or establish the truth of what a religion proclaims it is necessary to go beyond what it contains within itself.

---

[2] *The Dilemma of Religious Knowledge,* by Charles A. Bennett (New Haven: Yale University Press, 1930), p. 120.

*Can Theology Establish the Truth of Religion?* — no

One of the facts of life today is that few except theologians take theology seriously. It is not true, at least to the same extent, that only scientists take science seriously or that only artists take art seriously or that only philosophers take philosophy seriously. Even philosophy and science, areas of thought we should expect to find somewhat interested in its truth or falsity, pay little attention to theology. They do not listen to theology; at most they notice only that she has spoken and reply to her only to silence her.

Some explanation of the present-day indifference to theology may be found in the tendency for modern interests to separate themselves from each other, and in the relation of this tendency to certain distinctive features of theology itself. A theology is in one respect a rational system and in another respect it is not; its internal structure of ideas is a rational structure but its foundation is faith. It is composed of a set of doctrines concerning God, man, the world, history, and destiny. These doctrines may be organized in a thoroughly logical order. So far as this is the case a theology is a rational system. But the more complete is its logical order the more evident is the dependence of the whole system upon its basic premises. This is true of any logical system, but it is of special importance in the case of theology because theology admittedly obtains its premises from faith. So although theology is a rational system in its inner structure it is a system which rests on faith, and it neither questions nor inquires into the truth of its premises.

As was pointed out before, with his tendency to divide up life into separate compartments the modern man is unlikely to have any single set of basic principles. Jumping from one set to another as he moves from one activity to another, he feels no need to reconcile his various policies with each other in terms of something fundamental to them all. Even a system of philosophy may be built out of a cluster of hypotheses and inferences which have sprung from a thinker's preoccupation with some technical problem of quite limited scope. Whole philosophies have come out of attempts to deal with such problems as the nature of perception, the status of colors and sounds in the physical world, or the nature of verification and of symbolic utterance. Sometimes we find the philosophizing so quaintly naive that the resulting philosophy describes the kind of a world in which the process of constructing a world view could not possibly take place. It is not surprising that schizophrenia, the splitting up of a mind, is today one of the commonest and most characteristic mental disorders.

Modern inquiry and thinking is so specialized it has become provincial, not in a geographic sense but with respect to its subject matter. There are advantages in this, as there are advantages in many other kinds of specializations; but the disadvantages are precisely those which interfere with the achievement of a unified and integrated point of view.

Each specialized interest has its own assumptions which it does not examine, and the less contact there is between these different areas the easier it is to forget the fact that assumptions are made. So some of the attitudes typical of thought today contain the bland assumption that no assumptions are being made. This is one important reason why other fields of inquiry pay no attention to theology, for theology is a field which never ignores its assumptions; or, if it does now and then ignore some of its assumptions, it never ignores the fact that it makes assumptions. Its very admission that it rests upon faith makes theology seem out of step with the rest of modern thought, and so it is left out of the picture.

When theology does try to ignore its assumptions it gives up its claim to be true, and some theologians have been willing to pay even this price in order to feel at home in our splintered society. These theologians, as Arnold S. Nash points out, "vainly seek to make theology 'scientific' by cutting it free from metaphysics and history and resting it on religious experience. Theology then becomes thinking about our nice feelings rather than thinking about God and His relation to man and the world." [3] President Nathan M. Pusey, of Harvard University, reminds us of the consequences of the neglect of metaphysics when he says "it has now become frighteningly clear that if you try to ignore metaphysical considerations (I would say considerations of ultimate things) or cover them up in bursts of energy, they will rise up in perverted and distorted forms to mock one's thus too-circumscribed efforts." [4]

It is not reason, however, which opens the door to theology, it is faith; and unless the door is opened we cannot enter the structure. Some have insisted, in opposition to this, that a person might become an expert in theology without accepting the truth of its principal tenets, even as an anthropologist might become an expert on some primitive system of magic without himself believing in the effectiveness of the magic he studies. It is true we may come to know a great deal about a theology without a belief in its truth, but there is serious question whether we could think ourselves into it and grasp the full meaning of its doctrines without actually entering through the door of faith. The chief importance of theology, to a greater extent perhaps than in any other field of inquiry, lies in the truth or falsity of its premises. Its premises are of such a nature that adequate understanding of what they mean may require a belief in their truth, just as adequate

---

[3] *The University and the Modern World* by Arnold S. Nash (New York: The Macmillan Company, 1944), p. 290.

[4] "A Religion for Now," by Nathan M. Pusey, in *Harper's* for December 1953 (New York: Harper & Row), pp. 20–21.

understanding of another's expression of love may depend upon belief in the truth of the expression. Tremendous consequences hinge upon the truth or falsity of the premises of theology, consequences which completely overshadow its merely historical or cultural or psychological significance. The issues are the issues of man's destiny.

Thus far we have found that theology is important if true, and we have found some of the reasons why it is ignored by other fields of inquiry. Our question now is whether theology itself is competent to determine its own truth or falsity. It is likely that a theology originates in the attempt to defend a religious doctrine which has been challenged. But its defense is confined to showing that the doctrine is implied by the basic beliefs of the religion concerned. In other words theology originates in connection with challenges and objections which arise from within a religion; it is not concerned with attacks which come from outside the religion, except in so far as it may serve to protect from heresy those who would reject heresy solely because it is heresy.

As a religion comes into closer contact with ideas and influences alien or antagonistic to itself, more and more questions arise concerning its basic doctrines. As an answer to these questions theology finds itself inadequate. This, however, has not always prevented theologians from making the attempt, and in making the attempt they are not always clear as to their own purpose and function. They sometimes attempt to defend their theological premises by an appeal to theology. From such confusion was born the discipline known as "apologetics." The fate which the various systems of apologetics have met is the appropriate consequence of the confusion upon which they rest. Apologetics is an illegitimate discipline; for if it assumes its premises it is special pleading or else a mere restatement of the theology it purports to defend, while if it examines its premises it is philosophy and so can plead no case but that of truth itself. Apologetics can disguise its dilemma only by a sleight of hand substitution of rationalizing for reason. ✳ Theology is important, but its importance is in the service it renders to those who accept the religious position to which it gives logical and systematic expression. It is important to him who professes a faith to know what is and what is not consistent with his profession. A little theology quickly cools the overheated religious imagination.

Theology helps prevent extravagance and inconsistency; and it uncovers the less obvious consequences of religious belief. As soon as a religious idea becomes definite enough to pass for a concept it is subject to examination by theology. Thus reason is brought to bear upon it, and only an enemy of reason would venture to say that the long run results of the work of reason can be anything but good.

When we have gone as far as truth will take us in emphasizing the importance of theology we find still echoing in our minds the statement of its limitations. A theology assumes the truth of its own premises; it obtains them from faith and for it their truth is not in question. When question is raised concerning their truth theology has nothing to say. If it is a mistake for other fields of inquiry to ignore theology, it is every bit as serious an error for theology to ignore other fields. This is what happens when theology attempts to assume a position independent of science and philosophy, and attempts to find within itself the warrant of its own truth. In every attempt it may make to insulate itself from other fields, and protect itself from the implications of their discoveries, theology by its own act accepts the very separation from the rest of life and thought to which the modern temper has condemned it. Theology has life in itself only as it permeates all life.

## The Unique Position of Philosophy as a Mode of Inquiry

In one important respect philosophy differs from all other methods of seeking knowledge. This difference does not necessarily denote superiority, except with respect to matters to which it is relevant. Nor is philosophy warranted, because of this difference between it and other modes of inquiry, in making any claim of infallibility. Its unique position does not protect philosophy from error.

The distinguishing character of philosophy, to which it owes its special position, is found in the fact that it accepts no assumptions as inaccessible to examination. In this respect philosophy differs from theology; for, as we have seen, theology does not subject its basic premises to rational examination. A theology is constructed because of a conviction that certain primary religious beliefs are true and because it seems important to discover what these beliefs imply and what is inconsistent with their truth.

The difference we have mentioned not only distinguishes philosophy from theology, it also marks it off clearly from the natural sciences, from history, and from the social studies. No science can use its own methods to examine the soundness of those methods. When a scientist finds it necessary to appraise the methods of his science he must shift his position, at least temporarily, from the field of his science to the fields of logic and epistemology, both of which belong to philosophy. Nor can a science examine the truth of its basic assumptions about the objects of its inquiry. It assumes, for example, that knowledge is possible, that there is a world of objects to be known, that the acquisition of knowledge is of value, and that the world it inquires into is a rational order to which the laws of logic and mathematics apply. Similar assumptions are made by history and the social studies, with additional assumptions which apply more directly to their special fields.

To point this out is not to suggest that these assumptions are false. On the contrary we have exceedingly strong reasons to consider them true. The point rather is simply that these modes of inquiry do make assumptions which they themselves are incapable of examining, and if it becomes necessary to attack or to defend any of these assumptions the methods used cannot be the methods of the field of inquiry in which the assumption is made. To pretend to avoid metaphysical assumptions is only to confess failure to recognize them.

Why, then, is not philosophy in the same predicament? How is it possible to justify the assumptions of philosophy except from a standpoint outside philosophy itself? This may seem, at first thought, to rest philosophy on dogma or on arbitrary assertion. But such is not the case. The special position of philosophy results from the special character of its assumptions. The key to the puzzle is the fact that philosophy itself is synonymous with the assertion that in its final nature all actual and possible existence is intelligible.

To deny that existence is intelligible cuts us off from any knowledge of it. Such a denial is the assertion of philosophical skepticism, the assertion that real existence cannot be known. But how can we make such an assertion, and pretend that it is known to be true? As Professor DeWolf says, "It has often been pointed out by the critics of complete philosophical skepticism that to establish skepticism a man would have to be omniscient. How can a thinker know that nothing can ever be known, unless he knows so much about everything there is as to be sure that all is of such a character as to be unknowable?" [5]

But suppose, it may be proposed, that someone questions the intelligibility of existence. How can philosophy assume that which is brought into question and at the same time justify what it assumes? The answer is that the question itself assumes the very thing it questions, and the role of philosophy in such a dispute is simply to point out that fact. Try as we may to bring reason into question it is only by the use of reason that we can do so. To one who says he rejects reason philosophy's only reply is that the objection cannot be stated without resting the statement upon the very thing it attempts to reject. The act of stating the rejection of reason is one which requires the validity of reason to give it meaning. With the rejection of reason meaning disappears. Existence makes sense, or else it makes sense to say that existence does not make sense; therefore, in not making sense existence does make sense. The intelligibility of existence is the condition which makes it possible for us to make meaningful statements about it.

This becomes clear as soon as we recognize that any statement which claims truth is a statement which rests its claim on such principles of reason as identity and non-contradiction. Unless we admit that what we talk about

---

[5] *The Religious Revolt against Reason* by L. Harold DeWolf (New York: Harper & Row, 1949), p. 145.

is what it is, and is not what it is not, our attempt to talk fails. It fails to mean anything. If, then, I try to say that "the rational is false" either I mean it is true that the rational is false, and it is false that the rational is not false, or else my statement means nothing at all. Whatever else it means it has to mean this; and it has to mean this or it means nothing. But the relations by which this minimum meaning operates are logical and rational relationships. So I rest my claim that my denial of reason is true and meaningful upon a relation of reason. If I am at the same time both denying and asserting the same thing, anyone is entitled to ask which I mean. If I answer that I mean both together even though the two are mutually incompatible, then the only remaining course is to reject the statement as meaningless—or perhaps to call in a psychiatrist. With one who attempts to deny the validity of reason we are in the same position we should be with someone who said, "I am going to tell you something important and true but don't believe anything I say." We cannot refute a theory that does not make sense; we can only expose it. But a theory that does not make sense does us this great service, *it* exposes those who think it may be true.

In order that an assertion shall mean any one thing definitely it has to exclude from itself other meanings. Suppose I should utter the sounds appropriate to, "Bladso gellux infism." When I am asked what this means suppose I reply, "Oh, it means everything; there is nothing at all that it does not mean." It would be shorter, and as revealing, simply to say, "It is meaningless; I am merely making up sound combinations." Every meaningful affirmation is also a negation, and every meaningful negation is also an affirmation. Even my assertion that " 'Bladso gellux infism' means everything" is itself meaningless unless this assertion involves the denial that "Bladso gellux infism" has a restricted meaning which excludes other meanings. If, when I say "grass is green," I do not mean "grass is not that which is not green" then I mean nothing at all. But the relation between the two is a logical relation, apprehended by reason, and the one involves the other by virtue of this relation.

Every inquiry has its own assumptions, assumptions bound up with the distinctive methods. Philosophy differs from other inquiries in the fact that its assumptions are the assumptions of any inquiry whatsoever. You accept them or you do not inquire; you do not even inquire about whether you can inquire. Either you accept these assumptions or you do not speak; you accept them or you do not even think, and that includes thinking about not accepting them.

We have here a fundamental principle of our inquiry, and we shall return to this frequently. It is the principle of intelligibility—that whatever is presupposed by the possibility of knowledge cannot itself be brought into question. The furthest we can go is to question the contention that this or that proposition is presupposed by the possibility of knowledge. In so far as the presuppositions of inquiry itself are the presuppositions of philosophy then it follows that no attempt to discredit philosophy as such can be successful. For the attempt to discredit philosophy *is* philosophy in so far as it claims to be true and rests its case on reason and fact; in so far as it does not claim to be true, or does not rest its case on reason and fact, it is senseless and deserves only to be ignored or to have its senselessness pointed out. As Professor Urban says, "Philosophy not only buries its undertakers; it also, by its own inherent logic or dialectic, refutes and reduces to futility those forms of philosophizing which violate the conditions of philosophical intelligibility as such." [6]

## The Aim of a Philosophy of Religion

The aim of philosophy is understanding, the discovery of truth, the satisfaction of reason. In the philosophy of religion this aim is directed toward religion. It may be interpreted in two ways, not in conflict with each other but supplementing each other.

There is first the attempt to understand religion, to discover what it is and to uncover the rational meanings which belong to its ideas. Religious ideas are to some degree conceptual; they have logical significance, and by this we mean that it makes sense to raise the question of whether they are true or false. In this aspect of the philosophy of religion we seek to find the rational truth which is contained in religion. This does not mean that all the truth in religion is contained in the rational content we discover, nor does it mean even that we make our chief contact with religious truth by the use of reason. The philosophy of religion is an effort to discover so far as we can what there is in religion which is accessible to our reason.

There is another aspect of the philosophy of religion not adequately expressed in what has been said so far. All knowledge must, in the end, be of a single piece because truth has unity. So far as our knowledge is incomplete the unity of truth may escape us; but when we do not see the unity of truth it is because our knowledge is incomplete, it is not because of any final disruption of any part of truth from any other part. We are like one who has been a short way through a few of the entrances to an enormously complex building. He may know that all the parts he has seen belong to the same building but he may not have gone far enough to see how they fit together.

So far as religion adds to our rational understanding of anything it contributes something to our grasp of the whole pattern of truth. Religion

---

[6] *Beyond Realism and Idealism* by Wilbur Marshall Urban (London: George Allen and Unwin, 1949; New York: The Macmillan Company), p. 246. See also pp. 134–135. The same problem is discussed in *The Intelligible World* and in *Language and Reality,* both by the same author.

throws light not only on its own objects but on the whole realm of existence, for the objects of religion are related to other things and these relations make a difference to our understanding of the other things. So far as religion has any truth accessible to human reason the philosophy of religion is an essential part of any comprehensive philosophical view. It may well be that religion provides contacts with reality which thought itself cannot give, which are more intimate and more immediate than reason provides. Although we cannot achieve these contacts in philosophy yet a philosophy of religion may help us understand what they are and help us recognize them for what they are. Whatever direct contact with reality religion may provide a comprehensive philosophy must reckon with it, just as a philosophy must take account of our perceptual and aesthetic experience.

When we say that the aim of a philosophy of religion is to try to reach a rational understanding of the truth which religion contains, we do not mean we are primarily concerned with understanding the origins and varieties of religion, and the phases of its development. Those are matters for historians, anthropologists, and psychologists. The kind of understanding which the philosophy of religion seeks is the discovery of what rational grounds there may be for considering its beliefs to be true or false.

Although philosophy is concerned with the rational aspect of religious ideas and beliefs this does not mean that the rational content which philosophy is able to discover is the only content, or even that it is the most important. Nor are we entitled to assume that the only justification of a religious belief is to show rationally that it is true. There may be other and possibly even superior ways of justifying the claim of religious beliefs to be true. Even this, however, does not put religion out of contact with philosophy. For if there is any other than a rational justification of the truth claim of a religious belief the contention that this kind of justification is itself sound must be subjected to rational examination. Otherwise the claim is sheer assertion.[7]

I may be warranted in believing that my sense perception is a reliable guide in my attempt to discover some of the characteristics of physical objects. It is also quite clear that sense perception is not wholly an act of reason, for it includes sensation as well. Yet my claim that perception provides reliable information is itself subject to rational examination. So even though there may be in religion processes beyond our rational acts and though these may bring us into contact with something real in a way which is not the way of rational thought, yet the claim that these processes are effective needs rational justification.

There are religions and religious sects which attempt to deny all contact between religious faith and reason. Even if they were right they could not

---

[7] See the discussion of revelation and reason in Chapter XXIV, "The Revelation of God."

consistently give any reasons why they were right. So far as they reject reason they renounce any claim of truth which is entitled to the respect of anyone else. If they should happen to have any truth it is an entirely private truth for which they can make no case.

## The Difference Between Philosophy and Religion

Philosophy seeks a rational understanding of things and events, of relationships and patterns, in terms of the most general concepts which pertain to knowledge and being. Lack of philosophy is absence of understanding; to lack philosophy is to be naive and provincially minded, to be guillible with respect to current fads of thought, and to be the victim of random associations of ideas and of suggestions planted by those who wish to control the thought of others. It is a kind of ignorance, but it is a special kind of ignorance. It is not like ignorance of chemistry, for example; for although ignorance of chemistry may be a misfortune and on occasion may even have serious consequences, it is not the kind of ignorance which infects the whole outlook and basic judgments of a mind. "No man can live without any basis of philosophy, however primitive, naive, childish or unconscious," Berdyaev tells us. "Every man thinks and speaks, makes use of notions, categories, symbols, myths, and gives vent to appreciations. There is always a childish philosophy at the foundation of a childish faith." [8]

Religion has a certain underlying similarity with philosophy in spite of the very important differences between them. It is similar in the fact that it colors a person's whole outlook. So far as it is genuine it is reflected to some degree in a man's every act and every judgment. It is not one compartment of a self, but rather the design of the whole.

Religion, however, is quite different from philosophy; it is a different kind of activity. There is philosophy of religion but there is no such thing as religious philosophy. Where philosophy's activity is rational inquiry and understanding, religion is an appreciation and appropriation of values by means of contact with the ultimate ground of existence. In philosophy we think about things in terms of concepts; in religion we feel ourselves into a scheme of life and perform the acts which express our devotion to its object. Religion does not explain, or perhaps we should say that its explanations are not conceptual explanations; it does not minister primarily to the needs of reason. Quite the contrary, religion claims to put us in touch with existence in a special way; and in so far as religion's claim is just, philosophy can no more take religion's place than it can take the place of eating and loving. [9]

---

[8] *Solitude and Society* by Nicolas Berdyaev (London: Geoffrey Bles, 1938), p. 18.
[9] See Chapter VIII, "Religious Truth," and Chapter IX, "The Test of Religious Truth."

Even though philosophy cannot take the place of religion it is still not necessary for philosophy to depart in order to permit religion to enter. For the contact with existence which religion provides is one of those matters which philosophy most desires to understand. Where religion is the living out of a value scheme, philosophy is the examination and analysis of it. "In the conflict between religion and philosophy, truth is on the side of religion when philosophy claims to replace it in the sphere of salvation and eternal life; but truth is on the side of philosophy when it claims to attain a higher degree of knowledge than that allowed by the elements of naive knowledge incorporated in religion." [10]

Nothing we have said about the difference between philosophy and religion is intended to deny that understanding, as an activity and as a goal, has its own value. But the value of understanding, the highest of all the intellectual virtues, is not a substitute for religion. The value of religion in its highest forms lies in something which understanding alone does not give, it lies in the special contact with reality which it provides and in the transformation of the self which that contact brings about. It may well be that we are all the better for understanding this work of religion as adequately as we can, but it is something which does not need to be understood in order that it shall take place. Still, the greater the importance we see in religion the more intensely we desire to understand it as well as to experience it. It is this desire that the philosophy of religion attempts to satisfy.

In philosophy, so far as it is true, we come to know and understand reality, but in religion we make contact with it. If reality is the kind which answers our needs and rewards our search for fulfilment, then it is only in *contact* with it that we can find these supports. "And surely," says Professor Bennett, "the most striking historic function of religion has been to lift men from doubt and perplexity to a region of assurance and serenity. If there is any anchorage for human emotions, any one goal for human ambition, any solid foundation for courage to build on, it is religion that has supplied these things. If anywhere we break through from illusion into reality it is in religion that we do so, and any interpretation of faith which ignores or denies this is frankly preposterous." [11]

---

[10] Berdyaev, *op. cit.,* p. 20.
[11] Bennett, *op. cit.,* p. 17.

# EMIL BRUNNER

*Emil Brunner* (1889–1965), Swiss Protestant theologian, who revolted, with Karl Barth, against Protestant liberalism and attempted to restate classic Protestant doctrines in contemporary terms. He has written extensively in the field of Christian theology.

## The Meaning of Philosophy of Religion for Protestantism

Philosophy consists in reflection on the connection between all particular facts, and the means it employs to this end is thought investigating the way in which the facts are intellectually founded. But we shall need first to supply the ground for the inquiry into connection by showing that the latter has intelligible meaning. Hence we must define the problem of philosophy more closely and say that it inquires how far a mental ground is discoverable for the connection between particular facts. By this means we shall become convinced of the necessity, and therefore of the justification, of the inquiry in itself irrespective of its subject matter. Such an inquiry, again, will include that into the meaning of all science, all civilization and indeed human life in general. But when any school of philosophy surveys the more significant expressions of human life, it will discover among them a form of life which on the one hand is in the closest connection with the set of problems peculiar to philosophy, while on the other it has characteristic differences from every school of philosophy, or is even actually opposed to philosophy. This form of life is religion. The kinship between the two rests on the fact that religion as well as philosophy has in view the whole of existence and life; the opposition between them consists in the fact that religion itself claims to supply an answer to the crucial question about reality. It gives this answer in the shape of revelation, and not as the result of the methodical reflection of the intellect, i.e., of an activity within the bounds of reason. Thus philosophy is brought face to face with a most difficult problem, that of showing the meaning and justification of religion

From Emil Brunner, *The Philosophy of Religion*, trans. A. J. D. Farrer and Bertram Lee Woolf, pp. 11–21. Published, 1937, Charles Scribner's Sons. Used by permission of Emil Brunner and James Clarke & Co., Ltd.

[134]

within the mental ground known to philosophy. In this way philosophy of religion arises as a part, and perhaps indeed as the culminating point, of philosophy in general.

Provided, however, that the philosopher is serious in his concern about the truth of religion, he cannot avoid listening in the first place to the affirmations of religion about itself—and this always means the affirmations of some specific form of religion. It might of course be the case that religion will have to reject altogether any such classification under philosophy on the plea that it would involve a misinterpretation of religion. In that case the relation between the two would have to be determined conversely, i.e., by starting from religion. Then religion would not have its basis assigned within the bounds of philosophy, but conversely, viz. philosophy, being a special department of man's activity as a reasonable creature, would take its place within the bounds of revealed truth. If such an assertion is not meant to forego every connection with the mind of science, civilization, and philosophy, we must of course make several requirements: that religion should find in her own presuppositions the grounds for thus inverting the relationship between ground and consequence; that it should also report on its mode of supplying these grounds; and once more, that, on the second presupposition, it should make plain the possibility of science, civilization, and philosophy. That would be the way in which, starting from the side of religion, the discussion would have to be carried on with a philosophy originating in the general cultural consciousness. But such an undertaking could be called philosophy of religion only in a secondary sense, and the name as just defined could merely serve to designate the sphere of the discussion.

The state of the case only becomes really clear when, as is incumbent upon us, we look from the stand-point of general possibilities at the special situation that faces us. There are two reasons why we can speak only in a secondary sense of a Christian, and more particularly of a Protestant, philosophy of religion. First, Christian faith, especially in the particular form given to it in Protestant theology, is a fundamentally different thing from every philosophy. To philosophize is to reflect on the mental grounds, with the assumption that ultimate validity belongs to the complex of grounds and consequences developed by natural reason. Christian faith on the other hand involves recognizing that this complex has been broken into by revelation. It is on this revelation that the affirmations of Christian faith are grounded. Theology, which is Christian faith in scientific form, could only lay claim to a scientific character provided it gave clear and exact expression to the fact that its complex of grounds and consequences differs from that of all other sciences as to the final authority it recognizes; provided further that it developed all affirmations purely out of its own presuppositions and thus founded them on that complex; and provided finally, that on this basis it investigated the relations, whether positive or negative, between revealed faith and rational knowledge. Thus theology is on common ground with philosophy in showing the existence of an intelligible connection embracing all things; but this is not, as it is for philosophy, the logos of the natural reasoning process, but the logos of revelation. Hence Christian theology can never be required to make faith rational by giving it scientific form; on the contrary, it has to keep revelation and religion duly apart by means of clearly defined concepts.

> It would be to weaken, or rather to do away with, the opposition were we to equate the relation between reason and revelation with that betweeen rational and irrational. Revelation in the Christian sense stands in the same two-fold relation to the irrational as it does to the rational. The irrational (feeling, intuition, etc.) has not more but, on the contrary, less to do with the paradox of revelation than has the logos of reason. In the modern irrationalist philosophies of religion, the irrational is in every case grafted on a rational system (e.g., in the case of Otto and Scholz on an idealistic, and in that of James, on a naturalistic rationalism).

✳ Neither can there be philosophy of religion in the strict sense of the term in the realm of Christian theology, for the further reason that theology has to do not with religion but with revelation. Whatever else religion may be, it is a mode of human life, whereas revelation is a self-disclosure of God. While the philosopher of religion is concerned with historical phenomena, i.e., with the historical religions and their "nature," the theologian is concerned with the ground of all phenomena.

To the philosopher as to the theologian, religion is not the ultimate fact but something that roots in the ultimate. In the former case it is reason that supplies the ultimate ground, while in the latter it is revelation. The aim of theology is thus something quite different from religion, and at bottom is no more closely related to religion than it is to any other department of human life. This conclusion, moreover, follows directly from the fundamental presupposition of theology: its ground, its content, and its standard alike are found not in any consciousness of man's, but in God's self-disclosure.

Christian faith, to which theology gives the form of scientific conceptions, is the knowledge and acknowledgment of God's self-revelation in Jesus Christ. He, the incarnate logos, is the ground, content, and standard of all the affirmations of faith. That is where faith differs from every religion as well as from every philosophy. By Christian faith is meant, not some universal truth, nor yet some universal religious experience, but a definite fact which as such is opposed to every universal, be it religion or philosophy. Not that it denies the existence of a certain universal knowledge of God, religious as well as philosophical: rather it presupposes this. But it does deny that the personal and living God can be generally known from possibilities that lie either in the world or in man's spirit as such. It contends that the living and personal God can be known only by a personal meeting, through His personal word, through that special event to which the Bible, and the Bible alone, bears witness, and the content of which is Jesus Christ. Hence this definite fact is not to be understood merely as an illustration, or an embodiment, or even a symbol; where such language is used concerning this matter it is not Christian faith with which we have to do. On the contrary, the definite fact of revelation takes the place of what is universal, of truth in general, or of the final criterion of valid assertions; the incarnate logos here occupies the position otherwise held by the logos of reason, the essential idea of truth. This is the case because the personal God, who is the ground of all truth, cannot be known as personal by means of idea, but only by personal, concrete revelation; only when He no longer hides Himself, but issues forth and discloses Himself as the ground of all being, all values, and all thought.

This particular fact, this miracle of divine revelation, which by its very particularity is a stumbling block to thinking in universals, is the presupposition of Christian theology. Christian faith consists precisely in taking this peculiar view of ultimate truth. It would cease to be faith, it would indeed give the lie to its own affirmation, if it wanted to ground the truth of this affirmation on a universal truth. Either revelation supplies its own grounds or else it is not revelation. The only man who can look for some other foundation beside the *Deus dixit* is the man who withholds belief from the *Deus dixit* and wants secretly to replace revelation by symbol. Hence theology cannot substantiate its scientific character by such a change in the class of ground and consequent as falsifies faith, but on the contrary, only by giving a logically exact expression to this special, non-universal quality in all its uniqueness. But this means that theology is not a free science void of presuppositions, but one that is closely tied. It is tied to the definite fact of the revelation of God in Jesus Christ. How tied it is appears most clearly in the fact that theology is only possible within the borders of the Christian community or church, and has its definite content and its definite standard in the Bible. Only by perceiving in Scripture the utterance of God does a man become a believer; and only as such, i.e., as a member of the community of believers, is the thinker in a position to think theologically. Theology is in place only in the church, just as in the same way its ground and content are to be found only in the Scriptural revelation.

This again is the starting point for a Protestant philosophy of religion, using this term now in the modified or secondary sense. Such a philosophy must come from theology and, further back still, from faith. It is not the case that it leads towards faith. It is a part of Christian theology as such,

i.e., that part in which it carries on the discussion with the common consciousness of truth, i.e., with philosophy; it is that chapter of Christian
theology whose business is to start from definitely Christian presuppositions,
and give a well-founded description of the relations between revelation and
rational knowledge on the one hand, and between revelation and religion
on the other. Hence it is not a universal science, of which Christian theology
would form a subdivision as being the doctrine of a particular religion.
This erroneous view was largely followed in the nineteenth century. The
very nature of revealed faith involves reversing the classification of universal and special in this case, because here a particular, viz. revelation, is
regarded as ranking above every universal.

Despite the fact then that for us philosophy of religion can be only a
branch of theology in general, we have good reason for separating it as a
special science from theology; the reason lies in the need of the times,
which demands very special attention to this problem; and the need of the
times always has determined and always should determine the perspective
of theology. Unlike the rest of theology, philosophy of religion is concerned with the formal and general problems of Christian faith, i.e., specifically with the complex of grounds and consequences set forth in the
affirmations of faith as distinct from all other affirmations, in other words,
with the problem of revelation. Nowhere, however, is it less possible than
here to keep form and content apart: what is to be the Christian conception of revelation can only be made clear in connection with the content
of that revelation. But it is at least possible to distinguish between form
and content. On this distinction will depend the possibilities of discussing
the problems of philosophy of religion apart from those of theology proper.
Such separation involves the further condition that, to a greater extent than
in theology as such, philosophy of religion must have its being in the realm
of abstract concepts, despite the fact that the conceptions have here just the
same wholly concrete and personal basis as they have in the simplest confession of faith ever made by an unlettered man. At bottom, the philosopher
of religion knows no more than any plain Christian: he merely knows it
in the more exact form of abstract conceptions and in connection with the
rational knowledge of his age. The reverse side of this advantage is that
the abstract nature of his knowledge imperils the personal character of
his faith—which ought to penetrate the said knowledge—even more than
does the abstract nature of theology in general.

> There is no fundamental difference between a theological and a nontheolog-
> ical expression of Christian faith. All utterance about God, no matter how much
> of personal earnestness it may have, has always the abstractness of theology.
> Even the parables of Jesus are theology. And conversely, the very earnestness
> of a personal, vital faith may lead it in certain circumstances, e.g., in its dis-
> cussion and contention with the thought of one's age, to avail itself of the most

abstract forms conceivable. Yet the primary interest of Christianity is not systematic knowledge, but the relation of a personal faith to revelation. Hence of course faith is constantly directed towards overcoming abstract concepts as completely as possible; and therefore the philosophy of religion must be judged as lying at best on the edge of Christian doctrine and never at its centre.

Revelation meets and fits human consciousness. It is not a matter of indifference that this consciousness should be defined as human, although on the other hand it is not essential to know in what more specific way it is so defined. Faith is indeed bound up with humanity but not with any particular grade of humanity. Of course it presupposes man as man, but not a particular type of humanity, nor yet any particular feature in man. It takes man in his totality, not in some special locus that can be fixed by psychology. The locus in which revelation and the spirit of man meet each other cannot be assigned positively but only negatively: it consists in receptivity. If in place of this we would rather put a particular form of consciousness, we might say that it is "inquiry" when this has assumed the form of a vital need. But although this is a presupposition for faith, it does not designate a particular psychological quality, but, on the contrary, what is universally human. In fact, we can indicate the locus yet more definitely without thereby abandoning what is universally human: the negative point of contact is a consciousness of vital need which is at the same time a consciousness of guilt. Therefore we might fittingly express our meaning as follows: any account of the faith evoked by revelation should be preceded by another account giving the results of man's investigation of universal mental characteristics, which investigation would lead up to the afore-mentioned point of contact. Lack of space obliges us to omit such an account. Ultimately, however, this makes no difference because in every case faith appropriate to revelation must be understood entirely by itself and not by means of any common consciousness of man's. Faith appropriate to revelation can be understood only by revelation, just in the same way as any rational thought can only be understood by its ground in reason, or a sensation of light only by the light-stimulus. Therefore it is necessary to start from revelation as known to faith; in doing so we have only to bear in mind that revelation is always the answer to a question on man's part. But whether man's question, and indeed humanity itself, have their ground in revelation, and only in it can attain their proper meaning; and therefore whether man's question has not its *prius* in God's address to him—these are matters that can be discussed only in connection with the knowledge appropriate to revelation. At all events faith is certain that revelation alone enables us rightly to apprehend that need, that vital incapacity, which is the presupposition of faith; and that thereby revelation itself begets its own presupposition in the crucial sense.

# KARL JASPERS

*Karl Jaspers* (1883–      ), after receiving a medical education, became a
psychologist and then a professor of philosophy at the University of
Heidelberg in Germany. As an existentialist he is concerned with man's
immediate existence—especially the experiences of failure, guilt, and
death—rather than with the construction of a philosophical system.

## Philosophy and Religion

Throughout the millennia philosophy and religion have stood in alliance
with, or in hostility to one another.

They go hand in hand, originally in the myths and cosmologies, later in
theology—for philosophy has appeared in the cloak of theology, just as at
other times it has worn the dress of poetry and, most frequently, of science.

But, then, as the two separate, religion becomes for philosophy the great
mystery that it cannot understand. The cult, the claim to revelation, the
claim to power of a community founded on religion, of its organization and
politics, and the interpretation that religion confers upon itself, become
objects of philosophical inquiry.

In this attitude of inquiry lies the germ of the struggle. For philosophy,
the struggle can only take the form of a striving for truth by exclusively
intellectual means.

Neither religion nor philosophy is a clearly defined entity; we cannot take
them as fixed points from which to start on our comparative investigation.
They are both involved in historical transformation, but both conceive of
themselves at all times as vehicles of eternal truth, whose historical garb at
once conceals and transmits the truth. I cannot speak of the one eternal religious truth. Philosophical truth is the *philosophia perennis* to which no one
can lay claim, but with which everyone engaged in philosophical thought is
concerned, and which is present wherever there are true philosophers.

There is no standpoint outside the opposition of philosophy and religion.
Each one of us stands at one of the poles and speaks of some crucial aspect

From Karl Jaspers, *The Perennial Scope of Philosophy,* trans. Ralph Manheim, pp. 75–84,
105–107, 109–112. Copyright, 1949, by Philosophical Library. Used by permission of Karl
Jaspers.

[140]

of the other, without personal experience. Consequently you can expect me too to be blind in certain points and to misunderstand. I hesitate and yet I must speak. To speak of religion, without being personally involved in it, is questionable, but it is indispensable as a means of expressing one's own clear deficiency, as a means of seeking after the truth, and also of testing religious faith by the questions that thus arise. Religion is no enemy of philosophy, but something that essentially concerns it and troubles it.

But today we are in a situation that I shall illustrate by a personal reference. Because religion is of such prime importance, awareness of my deficiency made me eager to hear what was being said in religious circles. It is among the sorrows of my life spent in the search for truth, that discussion with theologians always dries up at crucial points; they fall silent, state an incomprehensible proposition, speak of something else, make some categoric statement, engage in amiable talk, without really taking cognizance of what one has said—and in the last analysis they are not really interested. For on the one hand they are certain of their truth, terrifyingly certain; and on the other hand they do not regard it as worth while to bother about people like us, who strike them as merely stubborn. And communication requires listening and real answers, forbids silence or the evasion of questions; it demands above all that all statements of faith (which are after all made in human language and directed toward objects, and which constitute an attempt to get one's bearings in the world) should continue to be questioned and tested, not only outwardly, but inwardly as well. No one who is in definitive possession of the truth, can speak properly with someone else—he breaks off authentic communication in favor of the belief he holds.

I can touch on this great problem only from certain angles and only inadequately, I am concerned in this discussion with throwing light on the original philosophical faith.

Religion, contrasted with philosophy, reveals the following characteristics:

Religion has its cult, is bound up with a peculiar community of men, arising from the cult, and it is inseparable from the myth. Religion always embodies man's practical relation to the transcendent, in the shape of something holy in the world, as delimited from the profane or unholy. Where this is no longer present, or is rejected, the peculiar character of religion has vanished. Almost the whole of mankind, as far as historical memory extends, has lived religiously, and this is an indication that can scarcely be ignored, of the truth and central importance of religion.

Philosophy proper, on the other hand, knows no cult, no community led by a priesthood, no existent invested with a sacred character and set apart from other existents in the world. What religion localizes in a specific place, can for philosophy be present everywhere and always. Philosophy is a product of the individual's freedom, not of socially determined conditions, and it does not carry the sanction of a collectivity. Philosophy has no rites, no roots in a primitive mythology. Men take it from a free tradition and transform it as they make it their own. Although pertaining to man as man, it remains the concern of individuals.

Religion is intent upon embodying its truth in tangible symbols, philosophy pursues only effective subjective certainty.—To religion the God of the philosophers seems threadbare, pale, empty; it disparagingly calls the philosophical state of mind "deism"; to philosophy the tangible symbols of religion seem like deceptive veils and misleading simplifications.—Religion denounces the God of philosophy as a mere abstraction, philosophy distrusts the religious images of God as seductive idols, magnificent as they may be.

Yet, though the manifestations of philosophy and religion seem to clash, there is a contact, and even a convergence in their contents, as may be illustrated by the ideas of God, prayer, revelation.

THE IDEA OF GOD. In the West, the idea of the one God arose in Greek philosophy and in the Old Testament. In both cases, a stupendous work of abstraction was effected, but in entirely different ways.

In Greek philosophy monotheism arose as an idea, it was postulated from ethical considerations, it imposed itself on the mind in an atmosphere of philosophic serenity. It did not set its imprint upon masses of men, but upon individuals. Its results were individuals of a high human type and a free philosophy. It was not an effective civilizing agent.

In the Old Testament, on the other hand, monotheism grew up in the passion of battle for the pure, the true, the one God. The abstraction was not accomplished by logic but by a reaction against the images and embodiments of the deity, which veil God more than they reveal him, and a revolt against the seductions of the cult, against Dionysian rites, and against belief in the efficacy of sacrifice. This cult of the one, living God was won in battle against the Baals, against immanent religion with its shallow optimism, its festivals and orgies, its self-complacency and moral indifference.

This true God suffers no image and likeness, sets no store by cult and sacrifice, by temple and rites and laws, but only by righteous actions and love of our fellowmen (Micah, Isaiah, Jeremiah).—The monotheistic abstraction, like nihilism, negates all worldly existence, but actually springs from the spiritual fullness of a mind to which the supra-mundane creator-God with his ethical laws has revealed himself.—This abstraction is not based upon the development of an idea, but upon the word of God, upon God himself, who was experienced in the word which the prophet imparted as the word of God. The force of God's reality refracted in such a prophetic mind, and not the power of an idea, brought forth this monotheism. Hence the miraculous part of it is that in thought content the monotheism of the Greeks and of the Old Testament should coincide, though they differ radically as to the mode of God's presence. The difference is that between philosophy and religion. Consequently it is also the difference between divinity and God—between transcendence as an intellectual idea, and the living God; the One of philosophy is not the One of the Bible.

But if philosophical clarity prevails, the question arises whether the incomparable faith of the prophets, that moves us so deeply even today, was possible only because they were still intellectually naive, still unaffected by philosophical thought, and accordingly failed to notice that the "word," spoken immediately by God, still embodied a remnant of sensible reality— of the image and likeness which they combated.

Greek and Old Testament monotheism have together dominated the Western idea of God. They interpreted each other. That was possible because the faith of the prophets effected an abstraction that is analogous to philosophical abstraction. The prophetic faith is more powerful than the philosophical idea, because it arises from the direct experience of God. But in intellectual clarity it is inferior to philosophy; hence it was lost in subsequent religious development, even in the Bible.

PRAYER. The cult is the act of the community, prayer is an act of the individual in his solitude. The cult exists everywhere, while prayer is discernible here and there in history; in the Bible it becomes distinct only with Jeremiah. The liturgy, in which the cult is embodied, contains a number of texts that are called prayers, because they serve to invoke, praise, and supplicate the godhead. But their salient feature is that they originated in the remotest past, that although they once grew and changed over a period of generations, they have since then retained rigid, immutable forms and are experienced as something permanent. Parts of them have long since become incomprehensible, they either play the role of a mystery or have been endowed with a new, transformed meaning. In contradistinction to this, prayer is individual, existentially present. As a subordinate element of the cult, it is performed by the individual in a fixed form, and then he remains entirely within the sphere of religion. But when it is really personal and primal, prayer stands at the frontier of philosophy, and it becomes philosophy in the moment when it is divested of any pragmatic relation to the godhead or desire to influence the godhead for practical ends. It marks a break with the concreteness of a personal relation to a personal God, which is one of the sources of religion, and a movement toward abstract philosophical contemplation; at first it expresses only devotion and gratitude to God, but later it becomes progressively internalized and man finds in it a firm ground on which to stand. The aim of this contemplation is no longer to achieve practical mundane results, but inward transfiguration. Where such speculative spiritualization developed into genuine contemplation, it was like one continuous prayer. While this contemplation was a part of the whole that is embodied in religion, today it has become separate from religious activity and possible by itself.

REVELATION. Religions are based on revelation; this is clearly and consciously the case with the Indian and Biblical religions. Revelation is the immediate utterance of God, localized in time and valid for all men, through word, commandments, action, event. God issues his commandments, he institutes the congregation, founds the cult. Thus the cult of the Christians is founded as an act of God, who instituted the Lord's Supper. Since the content of a religion derives originally from revelation, this content is not valid in itself, but only within a community—the people, the congregation, the church—which is its actual authority and guaranty.

With reference to the efforts to arrive at a philosophical concept of God, these efforts in which each step seems to cancel out the preceding,—we often hear it said that any attempt to arrive at God by thought is vain, and that man knows God and can know God only through revelation. God gave the law, God sent the prophets, He himself descended in the form of his servant, to redeem us on the Cross.

But revelation that is communicated as such, must have a mundane form. Once it is stated, it deteriorates into finiteness, and even into trivial rationality. In speech, its meaning is perverted. The word of man is not the word of God. That part of revelation that concerns man as man, becomes a content of philosophy and as such is valid without revelation. Have we to do with an attenuation of religion, a loss of its substance?—then we call the process secularization. Or have we to do with a purification, a deepening, a distillation or even realization of its primal essence? Both processes would seem to exist. The danger of an emptying by rationalization is coupled with the possibility that man may realize an authentic truth. . . .

CLARIFICATION AND ENHANCEMENT OF THE ETERNAL TRUTH. By our experience of the tensions, the dialectic and the contradictions striving toward a decision, we can positively apprehend what words can express only abstractly—the truth that we outlined in formulating the basic characteristics of Biblical religion. Let us restate the elements of this truth, which constitutes philosophical faith. They are:

the idea of the one God;
the realization of the absolute nature of the decision between good and evil in finite man;
love as the fundamental actualization of the eternal in man;
the act—both inward and external—as the test of man;
types of moral world order which are always historically absolute, although none of their manifestations is absolute or exclusive;

the incompleteness of the created world, the fact that it does not stand
by itself, the inapplicability of all types of order to borderline cases, the
experience of the extreme;
the idea that the ultimate and only refuge is with God.

How pale does all we have said seem beside the religious reality. As soon
as we set out to discuss the question, we enter upon the plane of philosophical faith. We are thus led automatically to interpret renewal of religious
faith as a return to the primal source, as a renewal of the philosophical faith
that is implicit in the religious, as a transformation of religion into philosophy (or philosophical religion). But this, though perhaps it will be the
road of a minority, will certainly not be that of mankind.

The philosopher cannot possibly tell the theologians and the churches
what to do. The philosopher can only hope to help create the preliminary
requirements. He would like to help prepare the ground and to help produce awareness of the intellectual situation necessary for the growth of what
he himself cannot create.

What more and more people have been saying for half a century continues
to be quickly forgotten, though nearly everyone has been saying it: a new
era is arising, in which man, down to the very last individual, is subject to
a process of transformation more radical than ever before in history. But
since the transformation in our objective living conditions goes so deep, the
transformation in our forms of religious belief must go correspondingly
deeper in order to mould the new, to fructify and spiritualize it. A change
is to be expected in what we have called the matter, the dress, the manifestation, the language of faith, a change as far-reaching as all the other changes
that have taken place in our era—or else the eternal truth of Biblical religion
will recede beyond the horizon of man; he will no longer experience this
truth, and it is impossible to say what might take its place. Hence it is in
order, that we do everything in our power to restore the eternal truth; we
must plumb its very depths and, unconcerned over what is transient and
historical, utter this truth in a new language. . . .

Philosophy, whether it affirms or combats religion, withdraws from religion in fact, and yet is constantly concerned with it.

(a) Philosophy takes up the cause of Biblical religion: Western philosophy cannot hide from itself the fact that none of its great philosophers up
to and including Nietzsche approached philosophical thought without a
thorough knowledge of the Bible. This is no accident. We repeat:

First: Philosophy cannot give man the same thing as religion. Hence it
at least leaves the field open for religion. It does not force itself on mankind
as the whole and exclusive truth for all men.

Second: Philosophy can scarcely hold its position in the world if the
human collectivity does not live in the people through religious faith. Philo-

sophical communication in thought has no compelling force, but only clarifies for the individual man, what arises from within himself. Philosophy would be dispersed among fewer and fewer individuals and finally disappear, if the human collectivity did not live by what becomes clear in philosophical faith. Philosophy cannot realize the sociologically effective transmission of the contents indispensable to man, which occurs solely through religious tradition assimilated from early childhood, thus becoming the vehicle also of philosophy.

Third: The contents of the Bible can be replaced for us by no other book.

(b)  Philosophy goes beyond Biblical religion: The development of communications, which has brought all the things ever produced on earth into contact with one another, and which has created a need for ever closer understanding among men, has in addition to the Bible revealed to us two other great religious areas: India with the Upanishads and Buddhism, China with Confucius and Laotse. The soul of the thoughtful man cannot remain closed to the depth of the truth emanating from these sources. The soul strives to extend its horizons without end.

Here an error is likely to crop up. The Enlightenment sought to find the true religion by assembling the best from all religions. The result however was not the authentic truth, purified of historical accident, but a collection of abstractions watered down by rationalism. The source of this universal faith was in fact only a critical, measuring intelligence. The profound meaning, the poignancy was lost. Trivial generalizations remained.

Since all faith is historical, its truth does not lie in a sum of articles of faith, but in a primal source that is historically manifested in various forms. True, the many religions lead to the one truth, but this truth cannot be attained at one stroke, but only along the roads that were really traveled, roads which cannot be traveled all at once and in the same way.

Hence no rational critique can apprehend this truth. On the contrary, man must, in the context of his own destiny, let the truth be revealed to him as it is uttered through tradition, i.e. he must make it his own. In sounding the depths of the past, one can accomplish this only by being given to oneself through inner action.

With regard to religion, philosophy will in practice approve the following propositions: In order to participate in Biblical religion, one must grow up in the tradition of a definite denomination. Every denomination is good to the extent that the people living in it take possession of the Biblical religion as a whole in spite of the special and finite historical degenerations of the particular historical form. Loyalty and historical consciousness bind me to the denomination in which I awakened. A change of religion is difficult without a breach in the soul. But though in every denominational form of Biblical religion the fixation of faith is determined by the specific time in which it occurs, in individual believers the presence of the full Biblical religion is possible and real. The community of the pious cuts across all denominational lines. And the endless struggles, schisms, and condemnations that have occurred in this field can, in Melanchthon's words, be designated as *rabies theologorum.*

# WILLIAM TEMPLE

*William Temple* (1881–1944), the Archbishop of Canterbury, was the best-known Anglican theologian of the first half of the twentieth century. He was also a prominent leader in the ecumenical movement in the Christian churches and was keenly interested in the application of Christian doctrine to contemporary problems.

## The Tension Between
## Philosophy and Religion

The main type of that tension, then, which we have now to consider, is not caused by particular doctrines either of Religion or of Philosophy, but consists in a sharp difference in mental habit and outlook with reference to the same objects of attention. This may be briefly expressed by saying that *the primary assurances of Religion are the ultimate questions of Philosophy.* Religion finds its fullest expression in absolute surrender to the Object of its worship. But the very existence of that Object is a main theme of philosophical disputation. It is not possible to surrender one's self to what is felt to be an unverified hypothesis; it is not possible to discuss impartially the existence of a Being to whom one is utterly self-surrendered. How then can a religious person be a true philosopher? Or how can a philosopher who has not yet solved the problems of existence permit himself the exercise of religion? And if he do not permit himself this exercise, how can he know Religion from within in such a fashion as to qualify himself to pronounce upon its validity and to place it rightly within, or exclude it justly from, his ultimate construction?

That these are grave questions no one who has seriously attempted to

From William Temple, *Nature, Man and God,* pp. 34–39, 44–45, 51–56. Copyright, 1934, Macmillan & Co., Ltd. Reprinted by permission of Mrs. Temple, St. Martin's Press, Inc., and Macmillan & Co., Ltd.

combine the two activities is likely to deny. Yet the difficulties are not insuperable in principle, and it seems to be the special duty of some persons at least to engage in the hazardous enterprise of overcoming them.

The divergence of view is specially evident in relation to three central convictions of Religion in its higher forms. These are perhaps different expressions of one truth, but as expressions of it they differ, and it is well to state them separately:

First is the conviction that Spirit is a true source of initiation of processes— a real ἀρχή, a *vera causa;*
Second is the conviction that all existence finds its source (ἀρχή, *vera causa*) in a Supreme Reality of which the nature is Spirit;
Third is the conviction that between that Spirit and ourselves there can be, and to some extent already is, true fellowship, at least such as is involved in our conscious dependence on that Spirit.

The first of these convictions is, as stated, little more than the denial of materialism; but this denial carries positive implications of momentous import. The true nature of spiritual freedom must occupy our attention later; but some aspects of it concern us now. If it were true that by inspection of the Nebula, from which our solar system formed itself, an intelligence of sufficient scope could have predicted all the acts of moral choice that would ever be made by human beings living on this planet, then the whole aspiration and endeavour of Religion would be dismissible as part of the phantasmagoria of a consciousness which emerged only to take note of, never to direct, the process in which it was a transient and ineffectual episode.

Now the sense of the inherent determinism of the physical system, including our bodily organisms, is so strong that some great religions have to a certain extent made terms with it. The Hindu doctrine of Maya is such a compromise. It expresses despair of the spiritual domination of matter; but in order to safeguard both the reality and the supremacy of spirit, it dismisses the material as illusory; the great aim of life which it proposes, is to be delivered from the Wheel of Change (the figure of materialistic Determinism) so that the spiritual reality may exist in its own freedom. This attempt altogether to exclude matter from reality issues in a curiously uncontrolled empire of matter, so that Hinduism, which finds expression in some of the loftiest spiritual philosophy of the world, also makes room for obscenity in connexion with worship itself. You cannot regulate what you do not recognise. If matter is so unreal that spirit, which is real, has neither need for it nor control of it, then in its own sphere it will make havoc. The way to be spiritually effective is not to ignore matter but to use it.

Yet to deny the reality of matter in order to assert that of spirit is less disastrous to Religion than to let the spiritual be swallowed up in the material, as the West is always liable to do. The assertion of the reality and independence of Spirit in the Universe and in Man is a primary necessity for Religion. In the case of Man we may, for the moment, put this at the very lowest and be content to say that the causal process, as it affects human conduct, passes through consciousness and is modified by this passage. If preferred, the same thought may be expressed by saying that, attention having been attracted to the causal process, volition intervenes as an additional determinant of the result. The main point is that consciousness does affect the result, but this does not make the process leading to it other than causal, so that human beings act differently because they are conscious and self-conscious from the way in which they (or rather their bodies) would act if they had no consciousness and self-consciousness.

But while this alone is enough to break the chain of sheer materialistic Determinism, much more is required for the assertion that the Ultimate Ground of the Universe and all things in it is spiritual. This is a claim, not only for the independence of Spirit, but for the universal supremacy of Spirit. It is the claim that Spirit is not only *a* source of initiation, one ἀρχή among others, but is the only ultimate source of the whole World-process. All the more developed religions, which do not deny the reality of matter, have advanced this claim. It is the doctrine of Creation. It is not of direct importance to Religion to assert a date for the act of Creation, or even to assert that it is an act having any date at all; it may be a never-beginning and never-ending activity. But it is of vital importance to Religion to assert that the existence of the world is due to the Will of God. This is the essential notion of Creation, and Religion dare not let it go, unless it is prepared to deny the real existence of the material world. For the only remaining alternative is the acceptance of limitation in the conception of the Supreme Spirit, not only in the sense of an actual finitude which none the less includes or controls all existence, but in the sense of leaving some part of existence outside its control. Such a dualism would be repudiated by Philosophy, which cannot rest in a multiplicity or duality of ultimate principles; and it is entirely fatal to Religion, because to a limited authority only a limited allegiance is due, and absoluteness of allegiance is the very life-breath of Religion.[1]

But this claim to absolute allegiance is one which Philosophy must investigate. Enquiry must be made into its precise meaning, and then into the relation of the claim so interpreted to the facts of common experience. If, for example, it is meant that all things exist only in dependence upon the Will of a Spiritual Being who is good and wise in the ordinary sense of those words, then there is a great deal of experience which cannot be treated

---

[1] Of course this does not mean that no one may properly be called religious who has not in practice attained to this absoluteness of allegiance; but it is essential to Religion in all its higher phases that the worshipper should regard his Deity as entitled to such allegiance and himself as under obligation to render it.

as unreal and yet is very hard to appreciate as illustrating the goodness and wisdom of its Author. This is, of course, the familiar problem of Evil, which becomes acute in exact correspondence with the moral sensitiveness of the mind reflecting on it. A mind of low moral sensitiveness may be little troubled by this problem, for it will have a less exalted conception of the divine goodness, and will also be less afflicted by the evil elements in experience. As sensitiveness to moral issues develops, bewilderment before the problem of Evil deepens. It has found no more passionate expression than that given to it in many of the Hebrew Psalms.

That fact alone is sufficient evidence that this problem is not the creation of an alien criticism, but arises out of the heart of religious faith itself. Yet it is inevitable that when rationalising criticism sets to work, it should intensify the perplexity of religious people by seeming to exploit it in a hostile manner. For the aim of the religious person is to stabilise and deepen his faith; the aim of the philosopher is to understand, to "follow the argument wherever it leads," and to regard nothing as assured which is not supported by sufficient evidence. Between these two there is manifest tension; but no one is so intimately aware of that tension as a person who tries wholeheartedly to play both rôles at once. . . .

This reflection leads to a new consideration. The difference between Religion and scientific Philosophy [2] in relation to the Object of attention is not only one of temper but also one of method. The latter results from the former. In temper the attitude of Religion is that of assurance; the attitude of Philosophy is that of enquiry. It is hard enough to combine these, and probably it can only be done by deliberate alternation. But to combine the resultant methods is harder still. Religion, of which the essence is assurance of fellowship with, or at least of dependence on, the Supreme Spirit, and therefore also of the existence of that Supreme Spirit, necessarily makes its start from that point, and, so far as it enters on the field of Philosophy, seeks to offer explanations of the facts of experience by reference to the character of the Supreme Spirit. This is Theological Philosophy, and I had better here confess my belief that it is in the end the only Philosophy which has any hope of being altogether satisfactory. But it is also most hazardous, and is certain to lead the mind that follows it into all manner of fantasies unless it is constantly checked by a purely critical Philosophy which makes its approach from the other end. In the Middle Ages the course was clear for Theological Philosophy, and the wonder is that it avoided the fantastic as

---

[2] By the phrase "scientific Philosophy" I mean any philosophy which takes its start from the departmental sciences, ranging from Physics to Epistemology or Ethics, as distinct from a philosophy which takes its start from the deliverances of religious experience as formulated by Theology. Wherever I speak of "Philosophy" without any epithet it is to be understood as "scientific Philosophy" in this sense. Of course Theological Philosophy is no less scientific than this in its own procedure.

much as it did; yet that element is present in it in sufficient quantity to show the danger.

Theology, which is the science of Religion, starts from the Supreme Spirit and explains the world by reference to Him. Philosophy starts from the detailed experience of men, and seeks to build up its understanding of that experience by reference to that experience alone. Its inevitable and wholesome kinship to Science inclines it to account for everything by the "lowest" category that will in fact account for it; Theology begins with the "highest" category of all and fits in the "lower" categories in the most orderly hierarchy that it can devise in subordination to that "highest" principle. And this difference is inevitable, though it has been exaggerated by the dominant tendencies of European thought from the time of Descartes onwards. With that exaggeration, its causes, and the way to correct it, we shall be concerned in later lectures. Our present concern is with the difference itself, which would still exist if there were no exaggeration at all. The source of the method of Theological Philosophy in the nature of Religion itself has already been made clear. But the method of critical Philosophy is equally inevitable. . . .

The inevitability of tension between Religion and Science or the Philosophy which is in line with the scientific impulse is now clear. The method of Natural Theology no doubt requires ideally that the validity of Religion itself should be established before we consider, even cursorily, how this tension may be relieved. For if one of the two parties to it has no real right to exist, the tension is only to be properly relieved by the abolition of that party. Yet for purposes of exposition it is convenient to deal with this whole question of tension together, and the principles to be observed with a view to reconciliation are easily stated, though their detailed application is difficult enough.

First, then, the adherents of Religion must be ready to distinguish between the elements or expression of their faith which are of real spiritual importance, and those which have come to have sentimental value through association with the former. They will not be agreed among themselves about this distinction with regard to any point which is newly called in question. Some will be specially eager to say the point does not matter, so as to avoid the spiritual loss always involved in the tension between Religion and Science; these will be called Latitudinarians or Modernists, according to the fashion of the day; they will usually have intellectual clarity but little spiritual *élan*. Others will hold on till the last possible minute to every questioned phrase, lest what is lost be not only of sentimental but also of spiritual value. These will be called Traditionalists or Obscurantists; they will often have great spiritual force, and often, too, great learning, but as a rule, little intellectual enterprise. Between these two there will be others representing every possible gradation. But all may be loyal to the principle just stated, and may fulfil various necessary parts in winning for it a justly discriminating application. What must be excluded, and is very hard to exclude, is the element of purely personal sentiment. To cling to some belief, when it appears to have no inherent spiritual value and to be discredited by scientific advance, on the ground that it is bound up with what has spiritual value by ties of mere association, is a form of self-assertion which must be condemned by Science and Religion alike. But the nature of spiritual value is such that it is very hard to distinguish between it and personal attachment so that great sympathy is due to those who are perplexed by the need of making such a distinction at all.

The requirements to be made of scientific enquirers are different, though these too are largely various forms of the demand to avoid all self-assertion. Two are perhaps the most important. First it is to be remembered that Science, in following its method of using the "lowest" category applicable, is not entitled to deny the applicability of "higher" categories but is only seeing how far it can go without them. Even if it can cover all the facts and hold them together by means of "lower," as for instance mechanical, categories, it does not necessarily follow that the "higher" categories, such as purpose, have no rightful application at all. Indeed, while an actual machine is an entity of which the unifying principle is mechanical, the natural inference from its existence is that a living intelligence designed and constructed it.[3] And if that is true of a steam-engine, it is hard to see why it should not be true of the stellar system or of the cosmos generally. It would be hard to refute the argument which urges that the more perfect the universe is in itself as mechanism, the more forcibly does it suggest an intelligent Creator as its cause. But this carries us past the main point, which is that the positive work of Science, in giving an account of observable facts by its own method, never justifies Science in proceeding to negative inferences concerning other methods of interpretation, provided that these in their turn do not exclude the method of Science.

Secondly, it is to be remembered that there are spheres in which the most characteristic methods of Science are inapplicable. This is true in varying degrees of Ethics and of Art. Our appreciation of Right and Good is independent of argument and experiment. These may certainly affect our estimate of various actions or relationships; we may be persuaded that an action or a social order which we had thought good was in truth bad. But this never touches the ultimate objects of moral judgment. If a man tells me that he finds indulgence in cruelty one of the best things in life, I may try

---

[3] I.e., "living" when it so designed and constructed. All arguments of this type are open to Hume's devastating suggestions in the *Dialogue* of which the following may be quoted: "This world, for aught (any man) knows, is very faulty and imperfect compared to a superior standard; and was only the first rude essay of some infant deity, who afterwards abandoned it, ashamed of his lame performance."

to make him contradict himself, as Socrates did with Callicles in a similar connexion,[4] and so show that he did not really mean what he was saying; or I may try to have him shut up in a prison or an asylum; but I cannot directly attack his proposition by argument. "Our sense of value, and in the end for every man his own sense of value, is ultimate and final." [5]

The realm of Art offers an illustration as clear as that of Ethics. In these days when our minds are chiefly influenced by scientific activity people are often inclined to say that they cannot believe where they have no proof; or at least they demand a balance of probability calculated by formulable laws of evidence. Yet they will without hesitation affirm and even passionately insist on (say) the superiority of Schubert to Mendelssohn, though it would puzzle them to prove it or show it to be manifestly probable.

But it is in personal relationships that the inadequacy of Science is most manifest. We should not recommend a pair of lovers to test the advisability of marriage by making each a psychological analysis of the other. We even use the word "understand" with a different sense in relation to other persons from that which it bears in relation to impersonal objects. To "understand" a person is to have that insight into his character and motives which is another aspect of what is also called sympathy. A wise scientist does not follow only scientific methods, as these are commonly understood, in choosing his wife or expressing his affection for his children.

The heart of Religion is not an opinion about God, such as Philosophy might reach as the conclusion of its argument; it is a personal relationship with God. Its closest analogy is not found in our study of astronomy or any other science, but in our relation to a person whom we trust and love. If Science is not the best of aids in helping the child to determine his relation to his father, no more is it—still less is it—the best of aids in determining the relation of a man to his God.

We have seen that tension between Philosophy and Religion is inevitable; and as both are here assumed to have a rightful place in life, this tension must even be regarded as good. We have seen ways in which it may be alleviated, through the recollection by the adherents of each, what is the real nature and concern of that activity to which they are committed. We may reasonably hope to find here the grounds for an ultimate reconciliation in principle; but that can only be when each is perfect in its own kind. Till then the tension will remain, to the special bewilderment of those who are conscious of an obligation to be loyal to both at once. Yet these may hope that through their travail the progress towards ultimate reconciliation is being made.

Prof. A. Wolf ends his admirable chapter on "Recent and Contemporary

[4] Plato, *Gorgias,* 494–495.
[5] F. H. Bradley, *Essays on Truth and Reality,* p. 132.

Philosophy" in *An Outline of Modern Knowledge* with a warning against the dangers involved in "the unusually friendly relationship which is loudly proclaimed to exist now between science and the Churches"; and he adds this paragraph:

> Contemporary philosophy likewise seems to stand in need of an analogous warning. Considering the fact that so many philosophers were formerly students of theology, the relations between philosophy and theology are naturally expected to be friendly. Among British philosophers, indeed, the number of defenders of the faith seems to be abnormally large. It may be that academic conditions, and institutions like the Gifford Trust, either encourage this tendency or give undue prominence to those who follow it. But philosophy will be in a healthier condition when it has entirely ceased to be a handmaid to theology, and pursues its cosmic problems as independently as possible of vested interests.[6]

Prof. Wolf is more concerned with the welfare of Philosophy; I am, no doubt, more concerned with the welfare of Religion. Consequently my phraseology would differ from his. Yet I agree with him in substance. There not only is, but there ought to be, a tension between Philosophy and Religion. That tension is only relaxed when one of the two assimilates itself excessively to the other. The present atmosphere of friendliness may blunt the edge of philosophic criticism because there is an unwillingness to wound the feelings of religious people; it may also lead Religion to tone down its note of Authority because it does not wish to antagonise its philosophic friends. But the tension is not to be regretted; it is right in principle and stimulating in effect. And it can be delivered from the danger of doing harm if both parties respect the principle of Justice—τὸ τὰ αὐτοῦ πράττειν. But let no one suppose that this principle is as easy to practice as it is to enunciate.

---

[6] *Op. cit.*, p. 592.

# PAUL TILLICH

*Paul Tillich* (1886–1965) was a German philosophical theologian who taught for three decades in American universities. His system reflects a wide-ranging interest in the fields of classical Greek thought, German philosophy, art, history, psychoanalysis and existentialism. *Systematic Theology* is his major work.

## Theology and Philosophy: A Question

Theology claims that it constitutes a special realm of knowledge, that it deals with a special object and employs a special method. This claim places the theologian under the obligation of giving an account of the way in which he relates theology to other forms of knowledge. He must answer two questions: What is the relationship of theology to the special sciences (*Wissenschaften*) and what is its relationship to philosophy? The first question has been answered implicitly by the preceding statement of the formal criteria of theology. If nothing is an object of theology which does not concern us ultimately, theology is unconcerned about scientific procedures and results and vice versa. Theology has no right and no obligation to prejudice a physical or historical, sociological or psychological, inquiry. And no result of such an inquiry can be directly productive or disastrous for theology. The point of contact between scientific research and theology lies in the philosophical element of both, the sciences and theology. Therefore, the question of the relation of theology to the special sciences merges into the question of the relation between theology and philosophy.

The difficulty of this question lies partly in the fact that there is no generally accepted definition of philosophy. Every philosophy proposes a definition which agrees with the interest, purpose, and method of the philosopher. Under these circumstances the theologian can only suggest a definition of philosophy which is broad enough to cover most of the important philosophies which have appeared in what usually is called the history of philos-

Reprinted from *Systematic Theology,* Vol. I, pp. 18–28, by Paul Tillich, by permission of The University of Chicago Press. Copyright, 1951, by The University of Chicago Press.

ophy. The suggestion made here is to call philosophy *that cognitive approach to reality in which reality as such is the object.* Reality as such, or reality as a whole, is not the whole of reality; it is the structure which makes reality a whole and therefore a potential object of knowledge. Inquiring into the nature of reality as such means inquiring into those structures, categories, and concepts which are presupposed in the cognitive encounter with every realm of reality. From this point of view philosophy is by definition critical. It separates the multifarious materials of experience from those structures which make experience possible. There is no difference in this respect between constructive idealism and empirical realism. The question regarding the character of the general structures that make experience possible is always the same. It is *the* philosophical question.

The critical definition of philosophy is more modest than those philosophical enterprises which try to present a complete system of reality, including the results of all the special sciences as well as the general structures of prescientific experience. Such an attempt can be made from "above" or from "below." Hegel worked from "above" when he filled the categorical forms, developed in his *Logic,* with the available material of the scientific knowledge of his time and adjusted the material to the categories. Wundt worked from "below" when he abstracted general and metaphysical principles from the available scientific material of his time, with the help of which the entire sum of empirical knowledge could be organized. Aristotle worked from both "above" and "below" when he carried through metaphysical and scientific studies in interdependence. This also was the ideal of Leibniz when he sketched a universal calculus capable of subjecting all of reality to mathematical analysis and synthesis. But in all these cases the limits of the human mind, the finitude which prevents it from grasping the whole, became visible. No sooner was the system finished than scientific research trespassed its boundaries and disrupted it in all directions. Only the general principles were left, always discussed, questioned, changed, but never destroyed, shining through the centuries, reinterpreted by every generation, inexhaustible, never antiquated or obsolete. These principles are the material of philosophy.

This understanding of philosophy is, on the other hand, less modest than the attempt to reduce philosophy to epistemology and ethics, which was the goal of the Neo-Kantian and related schools in the nineteenth century, and less modest also than the attempt to reduce it to logical calculus, which has been the goal of logical positivism and related schools in the twentieth century. Both attempts to avoid the ontological question have been unsuccessful. The later adherents of the Neo-Kantian philosophy recognised that every epistemology contains an implicit ontology. It cannot be otherwise. Since knowing is an act which participates in being or, more precisely, in an "ontic relation," every analysis of the act of knowing must refer to an interpretation of being (cf. Nicolai Hartmann). At the same time the problem of values pointed toward an ontological foundation of the validity of value-judgments. If values have no *fundamentum in re* (cf. Plato's identification of the good with the essential structures, the ideas of being), they float in the air of a transcendent validity, or else they are subjected to pragmatic tests which are arbitrary and accidental unless they introduce an ontology of essences surreptitiously. It is not necessary to discuss the pragmatic-naturalistic line of philosophical thought, for, in spite of the anti-metaphysical statements of some of its adherents, it has expressed itself in definite ontological terms such as life, growth, process, experience, being (understood in an all-embracing sense), etc. But it is necessary to compare the ontological definition of philosophy, suggested above, with the radical attempts to reduce philosophy to scientific logic. The question is whether the elimination of almost all traditional philosophical problems by logical positivism is a successful escape from ontology. One's first reaction is the feeling that such an attitude pays too high a price, namely, the price of making philosophy irrelevant. But, beyond this impression, the following argument can be put forward. If the restriction of philosophy to the logic of the sciences is a matter of taste, it need not be taken seriously. If it is based on an analysis of the limits of human knowledge, it is based, like every epistemology, on ontological assumptions. There is always at least one problem about which logical positivism, like all semantic philosophies, must make a decision. What is the relation of signs, symbols, or logical operations to reality? Every answer to this question says something about the structure of being. It is ontological. And a philosophy which is so radically critical of all other philosophies should be sufficiently self-critical to see and to reveal its own ontological assumptions.

Philosophy asks the question of reality as a whole; it asks the question of the structure of being. And it answers in terms of categories, structural laws, and universal concepts. It must answer in ontological terms. Ontology is not a speculative-fantastic attempt to establish a world behind the world; it is analysis of those structures of being which we encounter in every meeting with reality. This was also the original meaning of metaphysics; but the preposition *meta* now has the irremediable connotation of pointing to a duplication of this world by a transcendent realm of beings. Therefore, it is perhaps less misleading to speak of ontology instead of metaphysics.

Philosophy necessarily asks the question of reality as a whole, the question of the structure of being. Theology necessarily asks the same question, for that which concerns us ultimately must belong to reality as a whole; it must belong to being. Otherwise we could not encounter it, and it could not concern us. Of course, it cannot be one being among others; then it would not concern us infinitely. It must be the ground of our being, that which determines our being or not-being, the ultimate and unconditional power of being. But the power of being, its infinite ground or "being-itself," expresses itself in and through the structure of being. Therefore, we can encounter it, be grasped by it, know it, and act toward it. Theology, when dealing with our ultimate concern, presupposes in every sentence the structure of being, its categories, laws, and concepts. Theology, therefore, cannot escape the question of being any more easily than can philosophy. The attempt of biblicism to avoid nonbiblical, ontological terms is doomed to failure as surely as are the corresponding philosophical attempts. The Bible itself always uses the categories and concepts which describe the structure of experience. On every page of every religious or theological text these concepts appear: time, space, cause, thing, subject, nature, movement, freedom, necessity, life, value, knowledge, experience, being and not-being. Biblicism may try to preserve their popular meaning, but then it ceases to be theology. It must neglect the fact that a philosophical understanding of these categories has influenced ordinary language for many centuries. It is surprising how casually theological biblicists use a term like "history" when speaking of Christianity as a historical religion or of God as the "Lord of history." They forget that the meaning they connect with the word "history" has been formed by thousands of years of historiography and philosophy of history. They forget that historical being is one kind of being in addition to others and that, in order to distinguish it from the word "nature," for instance, a general vision of the structure of being is presupposed. They forget that the problem of history is tied up with the problems of time, freedom, accident, purpose, etc., and that each of these concepts has had a development similar to the concept of history. The theologian must take seriously the meaning of the terms he uses. They must be known to him in the whole depth and breadth of their meaning. Therefore, the systematic theologian must be a philosopher in critical understanding even if not in creative power.

The structure of being and the categories and concepts describing this structure are an implicit or explicit concern of every philosopher and of every theologian. Neither of them can avoid the ontological question. Attempts from both sides to avoid it have proved abortive. If this is the situation, the question becomes the more urgent: What is the relation between the ontological question asked by the philosopher and the ontological question asked by the theologian?

## Theology and Philosophy: An Answer

Philosophy and theology ask the question of being. But they ask it from different perspectives. Philosophy deals with the structure of being in itself; theology deals with the meaning of being for us. From this difference convergent and divergent trends emerge in the relation of theology and philosophy.

The first point of divergence is a difference in the cognitive attitude of the philosopher and the theologian. Although driven by the philosophical *erōs,* the philosopher tries to maintain a detached objectivity toward being and its structures. He tries to exclude the personal, social, and historical conditions which might distort an objective vision of reality. His passion is the passion for a truth which is open to general approach, subject to general criticism, changeable in accordance with every new insight, open and communicable. In all these respects he feels no different from the scientist, historian, psychologist, etc. He collaborates with them. The material for his critical analysis is largely supplied by empirical research. Just as all sciences have their origin in philosophy, so they contribute in turn to philosophy by giving to the philosopher new and exactly defined material far beyond anything he could get from a pre-scientific approach to reality. Of course, the philosopher, as a philosopher, neither criticises nor augments the knowledge provided by the sciences. This knowledge forms the basis of his description of the categories, structural laws, and concepts which constitute the structure of being. In this respect the philosopher is as dependent on the scientist as he is dependent on his own pre-scientific observation of reality—often more dependent. This relation to the sciences (in the broad sense of *Wissenschaften*) strengthens the detached, objective attitude of the philosopher. Even in the intuitive-synthetic side of his procedure he tries to exclude influences which are not purely determined by his object.

The theologian, quite differently, is not detached from his object but is involved in it. He looks at his object (which transcends the character of being an object) with passion, fear, and love. This is not the *erōs* of the philosopher or his passion for objective truth; it is the love which accepts saving, and therefore personal, truth. The basic attitude of the theologian is commitment to the content he expounds. Detachment would be a denial of the very nature of this content. The attitude of the theologian is "existential." He is involved—with the whole of his existence, with his finitude and his anxiety, with his self-contradictions and his despair, with the healing forces in him and in his social situation. Every theological statement derives its seriousness from these elements of existence. The theologian, in short, is determined by his faith. Every theology presupposes that the theologian is in the theological circle. This contradicts the open, infinite, and changeable character of philosophical truth. It also differs from the way in which the philosopher is dependent on scientific research. The theologian has no direct relation to the scientist (including the historian, sociologist, psychologist). He deals with him only in so far as philosophical implications are at stake. If he abandons the existential attitude, as some of the "empirical" theologians have done, he is driven to statements the reality of which will not be acknowledged by anybody who does not share the existential presuppositions of the assumedly empirical theologian. Theology is necessarily existential, and no theology can escape the theological circle.

The second point of divergence between the theologian and the philosopher is the difference in their sources. The philosopher looks at the whole of reality to discover within it the structure of reality as a whole. He tries to penetrate into structures of being by means of the power of his cognitive function and its structures. He assumes—and science continuously confirms this assumption—that there is an identity, or at least an analogy, between objective and subjective reason, between the *logos* of reality as a whole and the *logos* working in him. Therefore, this *logos is* common; every reasonable being participates in it, uses it in asking questions and criticising the answers received. There is no particular place to discover the structure of being; there is no particular place to stand to discover the categories of experience. The place to look is all places; the place to stand is no place at all; it is pure reason.

The theologian, on the other hand, must look where that which concerns him ultimately is manifest, and he must stand where its manifestation reaches and grasps him. The source of his knowledge is not the universal *logos* but the Logos "who became flesh," that is, the *logos* manifesting itself in a particular historical event. And the medium through which he receives the manifestation of the *logos* is not common rationality but the church, its traditions, and its present reality. He speaks in the church about the foundation of the church. And he speaks because he is grasped by the power of this foundation and by the community built upon it. The concrete *logos* which he sees is received through believing commitment and not, like the universal *logos* at which the philosopher looks, through rational detachment.

The third point of divergence between philosophy and theology is the difference in their content. Even when they speak about the same object they speak about something different. The philosopher deals with the categories of being in relation to the material which is structured by them. He deals with causality as it appears in physics or psychology; he analyses biological or historical time; he discusses astronomical as well as microcosmic space. He describes the epistemological subject and the relation of person and community. He presents the characteristics of life and spirit in their dependence on, and independence of, each other. He defines nature and history in their mutual limits and tries to penetrate into ontology and logic of being and nonbeing. Innumerable other examples could be given. They all reflect the cosmological structure of the philosophical assertions. The theologian, on the other hand, relates the same categories and concepts to the quest for a "new being." His assertions have a soteriological character. He discusses causality in relation to a *prima causa,* the ground of the whole series of causes and effects; he deals with time in relation to eternity, with space in relation to man's existential homelessness. He speaks of the self-estrangement of the subject, about the spiritual center of personal life, and about community as a possible embodiment of the "New Being." He relates the structures of life to the creative ground of life and the structures of spirit to the divine Spirit. He speaks of the participation of nature in the "history of salvation," about the victory of being over nonbeing. Here also the examples could be increased indefinitely; they show the sharp divergence of theology from philosophy with respect to their content.

The divergence between philosophy and theology is counterbalanced by an equally obvious convergence. From both sides converging trends are at work. The philosopher, like the theologian, "exists," and he cannot jump over the concreteness of his existence and his implicit theology. He is conditioned by his psychological, sociological, and historical situation. And, like every human being, he exists in the power of an ultimate concern, whether or not he is fully conscious of it, whether or not he admits it to himself and to others. There is no reason why even the most scientific philosopher should not admit it, for without an ultimate concern his philosophy would be lacking in passion, seriousness and creativity. Wherever we look in the history of philosophy, we find ideas and systems which claim to be ultimately relevant for human existence. Occasionally the philosophy of religion openly expresses the ultimate concern behind a system. More often it is the character of the ontological principles, or a special section of a system, such as epistemology, philosophy of nature, politics and ethics, philosophy of history, etc., which is most revealing for the discovery of the ultimate concern and the hidden theology within it. Every creative philosopher is a hidden theologian (sometimes even a declared theologian). He is a theologian in the degree to which his existential situation and his ultimate concern shape his philosophical vision. He is a theologian in the degree to which his intuition of the universal *logos* of the structure of reality as a whole is formed by a particular *logos* which appears to him on his particular place and reveals to him the meaning of the whole. And he is a theologian in the degree to which the particular *logos* is a matter of active commitment within a special community. There is hardly a historically significant philosopher who does not show these marks of a theologian. But the philosopher does not intend to be a theologian. He wants to serve the universal *logos*. He tries to turn away from his existential situation, including his ultimate concern, toward a place above all particular places, toward pure reality. The conflict between the intention of becoming universal and the destiny of remaining particular characterizes every philosophical existence. It is its burden and its greatness.

The theologian carries an analogous burden. Instead of turning away from his existential situation, including his ultimate concern, he turns toward it. He turns toward it, not in order to make a confession of it, but in order to make clear the universal validity, the *logos* structure, of what concerns him ultimately. And he can do this only in an attitude of detachment from his existential situation and in obedience to the universal *logos*. This obliges him to be critical of every special expression of his ultimate concern. He cannot affirm any tradition and any authority except through a "No" and a "Yes." And it is always possible that he may not be able to go all of the way from the "No" to the "Yes." He cannot join the chorus of those who live in unbroken assertions. He must take the risk of being driven beyond the boundary line of the theological circle. Therefore, the pious and powerful in the church are suspicious of him, although they live in dependence upon the work of the former theologians who were in the same situation. Theology, since it serves not only the concrete but also the universal *logos,* can become a stumbling block for the church and a demonic temptation for the theologian. The detachment required in honest theological work can destroy the necessary involvement of faith. This tension is the burden and the greatness of every theological work.

The duality of divergence and convergence in the relation between theology and philosophy leads to the double question: Is there a necessary conflict between the two and is there a possible synthesis between them? Both questions must be answered negatively. Neither is a conflict between theology and philosophy necessary, nor is a synthesis between them possible.

A conflict presupposes a common basis on which to fight. But there is no common basis between theology and philosophy. If the theologian and the philosopher fight, they do so either on a philosophical or on a theological basis. The philosophical basis is the ontological analysis of the structure of being. If the theologian needs this analysis, either he must take it from a philosopher or he must himself become a philosopher. Usually he does both. If he enters the philosophical arena, conflicts as well as alliances with other philosophers are unavoidable. But all this happens on the philosophical level. The theologian has no right whatsoever to argue for a philosophical opinion in the name of his ultimate concern or on the basis of the theological circle. He is obliged to argue for a philosophical decision in the name of the universal *logos* and from the place which is no place: pure reason. It is a disgrace for the theologian and intolerable for the philosopher if in a philosophical discussion the thologian suddenly claims an authority other than pure reason. Conflicts on the philosophical level are conflicts between two philosophers, one of whom happens to be a theologian, but they are not conflicts between theology and philosophy.

Often, however, the conflict is fought on the theological level. The hidden theologian in the philosopher fights with the professed theologian. This situation is more frequent than most philosophers realise. Since they have developed their concepts with the honest intention of obeying the universal *logos,* they are reluctant to recognise the existentially conditioned elements in their systems. They feel that such elements, while they give colour and direction to their creative work, diminish its truth value. In such a situation the theologian must break the resistance of the philosopher against a theological analysis of his ideas. He can do this by pointing to the history of philosophy, which discloses that in every significant philosopher existential passion (ultimate concern) and rational power (obedience to the universal *logos*) are united and that the truth value of a philosophy is dependent on the amalgamation of these two elements in every concept. The insight into this situation is, at the same time, an insight into the fact that two philosophers, one of whom happens to be a theologian, can fight with each other, and that two theologians, one of whom happens to be a philosopher, can fight with each other; but there is no possible conflict between theology and philosophy because there is no common basis for such a conflict. The philosopher may or may not convince the philosopher-theologian. And the theologian may or may not convert the theologian-philosopher. In no case does the theologian as such stand against the philosopher as such and vice versa.

Thus there is no conflict between theology and philosophy, and there is no synthesis either—for exactly the same reason which ensures that there will be no conflict. A common basis is lacking. The idea of a synthesis between theology and philosophy has led to the dream of a "Christian philosophy." The term is ambiguous. It can mean a philosophy whose existential basis is historical Christianity. In this sense all modern philosophy is Christian, even if it is humanistic, atheistic, and intentionally anti-Christian. No philosopher living within Western Christian culture can deny his dependence on it, as no Greek philosopher could have hidden his dependence on an Apollonian-Dionysian culture, even if he was a radical critic of the gods of Homer. The modern vision of reality and its philosophical analysis is different from that of pre-Christian times, whether one is or is not existentially determined by the God of Mount Zion and the Christ of Mount Golgotha. Reality is encountered differently; experience has other dimensions and directions than in the cultural climate of Greece. No one is able to jump out of this "magic" circle. Nietzsche, who tried to do so, announced the coming of the Anti-Christ. But the Anti-Christ is dependent on the Christ against whom he arises. The early Greeks, for whose culture Nietzsche was longing, did not have to fight the Christ; indeed, they unconsciously prepared for his coming by elaborating the questions to which he gave the answer and the categories in which the answer could be expressed. Modern philosophy is not pagan. Atheism and anti-Christianity are not pagan. They are anti-Christian in Christian terms. The scars of the Christian tradition cannot be erased; they are a *character in-delebilis*. Even the paganism of Nazism was not really a relapse to paganism (just as bestiality is not a relapse to the beast).

But the term "Christian philosophy" is often meant in a different sense. It is used to denote a philosophy which does not look at the universal *logos* but at the assumed or actual demands of a Christian theology. This can be done in two ways: either the church authorities or its theological interpreters nominate one of the past philosophers to be their "philosophical saint" or they demand that contemporary philosophers should develop a philosophy under special conditions and with a special aim. In both cases the philosophical *erōs* is killed. If Thomas Aquinas is officially named *the* philosopher of the Roman Catholic church, he has ceased to be for Catholic philosophers a genuine partner in the philosophical dialogue which goes on through the centuries. And if present-day Protestant philosophers are asked to accept the idea of personality as their highest ontological principle because it is the principle most congenial to the spirit of the Reformation, the work of these philosophers is mutilated. There is nothing in heaven and earth, or beyond them, to which the philosopher must subject himself except the universal *logos* of being as it gives itself to him in experience. Therefore, the idea of a "Christian philosophy" in the narrower sense of a philosophy which is intentionally Christian must be rejected. The fact that every modern philosophy has grown on Christian soil and shows traces of the Christian culture in which it lives has nothing to do with the self-contradicting ideal of a "Christian philosophy."

Christianity does not need a "Christian philosophy" in the narrower sense of the word. The Christian claim that the *logos* who has become concrete in Jesus as the Christ is at the same time the universal *logos* includes the claim that wherever the *logos* is at work it agrees with the Christian message. No philosophy which is obedient to the universal *logos* can contradict the concrete *logos,* the Logos "who became flesh."

## Suggested Additional Readings

### THE RELATION OF PHILOSOPHY TO RELIGION

Adams, James Luther. *Paul Tillich's Philosophy of Culture, Science and Religion.* New York: Harper & Row, 1966. A valuable doctoral dissertation which confines its attention to Tillich's writings prior to 1945. For advanced students.

Berdyaev, Nicolai A. *Truth and Revelation.* Trans., R. M. French. London: Geoffrey Bles, 1953. An important existentialist compares the meaning of truth as it is used in philosophy with its meaning in the context of religious faith.

Bochenski, Joseph M. *The Logic of Religion.* New York: New York University

Press, 1965. A pioneering attempt to use modern, mathematical logic to establish a general logic of religion for ascertaining the validity and structure of religious assertions.

Calvin, John. *Institutes of the Christian Religion,* two volumes. Trans., John Allen. Philadelphia: Presbyterian Board of Christian Education, n.d. See especially the first seven books of Volume I. A classic statement of the truth which theology affirms and its relation to philosophy as seen by a founder of the Reformed tradition in Protestantism.

Christian, William A. *Meaning and Truth in Religion.* Princeton, N.J.: Princeton University Press, 1964. A significant attempt to provide a theory of religious inquiry and principles of judgment for the evaluation of religious beliefs.

Cobb, John B. *Living Options in Protestant Theology.* Philadelphia: Westminster, 1962. A careful and critical survey of the methodologies of recent Protestant theology.

Collins, James. *God in Modern Philosophy.* Chicago: Henry Regnery Company, 1959. A balanced and careful exposition of the work of many important modern philosophers.

Frank, Erich. *Philosophical Understanding and Religious Truth.* Oxford: Oxford University Press, 1945. A perceptive and sensitive approach to the problem of reconciling philosophy and theology.

Hartshorne, Charles and William L. Reese. *Philosophers Speak of God.* Chicago: University of Chicago Press, 1953. A good source book with critical comment on the work of figures important in the history of philosophy, some of whom are not represented in our selections.

Hick, John, editor. *Faith and the Philosophers.* New York: St. Martin's Press, 1964. Papers and critical comments by philosophers and theologians at a symposium held at Princeton Theological Seminary.

Kaufman, Gordon. "Philosophy of Religion and Christian Theology," *The Journal of Religion* (October, 1957), XXXVII, pp. 233–242. A contemporary American theologian gives expression to one of the widely held views of the relation between philosophy and theology and indicates possible future relationships between the two disciplines.

Lewis, H. D. *Philosophy of Religion.* London: English Universities Press, 1965. A brief, lucid introduction for beginning students in philosophy.

MacQuarrie, John. *Twentieth Century Thought: The Frontiers of Philosophy and Theology.* New York: Harper & Row, 1963. A very useful, broad survey of contemporary thinkers and problems.

Niebuhr, H. Richard. *The Meaning of Revelation.* New York: The Macmillan Company (Macmillan Paperback series). A book useful for understanding the foundations of an influential Protestant attitude toward revelation and reason. See especially Chapter 1.

Randall, John H., Jr. *The Role of Knowledge in Western Religion.* Boston: Starr King Press, 1958. A brief historical sketch of the chief solutions proposed by Western philosophers and theologians for defining the relation of knowledge to faith.

Thomas, George F. *Religious Philosophies of the West.* New York: Charles Scribner's Sons, 1965. (Available in paperback.) Contains an exposition and limited criticism of important religious philosophers and philosophical theologians from Plato to Tillich.

Tillich, Paul. "Two Types of Philosophy of Religion," *Theology of Culture.* Edited by Robert C. Kimball. New York: Oxford University Press, 1959. An incisive analysis of Augustinian and Thomistic types of philosophy of religion.

Zuurdeeg, Willem F. *An Analytical Philosophy of Religion.* New York: Abingdon Press, 1958. See especially pp. 139f. An independent analytical statement of the relation of philosophy to theology by a contemporary philosopher of religion.

# The Problem of
# III.    the Existence
# of God

ARGUMENTS FOR THE existence of God have been undertaken for diverse reasons. Some have undertaken them believing that such arguments will remove unnecessary obstacles to belief, that in the process of constructing a careful argument they may somehow discover a God they can worship. Others rely on arguments for the existence of God to provide the foundation upon which belief in God must be based. Rather than simply creating the possibility of God's existence, such arguments prove it and thereby make belief in God mandatory, insofar as the person engaged in the argument is willing to be "rational."

Still others argue that probably few people, if any, initially become theists because of an argument for the existence of God. They contend that the procedure is usually quite the reverse —a person believes that there is a God and then looks for arguments to justify his belief. Arguments, in this case, answer one's desire to have rational clarification of what he already takes to be of ultimate significance. Evidently there is a certain ambiguity in this point of view, for one believes and yet desires support for his belief. Consequently, this argument demands unusually careful examination.

For whatever reason a person approaches the question of the existence of God, it is a significant question. The importance of the problem can be no better illustrated than by pointing to the number of philosophers and theologians who have undertaken to struggle with it. Selections included in this section of readings not only indicate the vigor with which this task has been attacked and the great variety of ways devised to answer the question of the existence of God either positively or negatively, but they also provide statements of some major positive positions and of important critiques of these arguments.

The ontological argument, as developed by St. Anselm, provides our beginning point. This argument predicates the necessity of God's existence upon the fact that man is able to conceive of "a being than which nothing greater can be conceived," and that such a perfect being must necessarily exist, or else a still greater, i.e., one who does exist, could be conceived. This argument is not necessarily the oldest or the most important, but it does represent a position that grows out of the Platonic philosophical tradition and that is reflected in the thought of men ranging from Augustine to such modern philosophers as Hegel. With the selection from Anselem we have included a dialogue he carried on with an opponent, Gaunilon. In addition, there is included an argument against this proof by Immanuel Kant, the significant eighteenth-century German philosopher. Although Kant's criticism was not accepted by Hegel, it has been considered crucial by many subsequent philosophers and theologians.

In Thomas Aquinas we have the classical statement of the cosmological arguments for the existence of God. This type of argument begins with the assumption that the existence of things in the ordinary realm of experience calls for an explanation. Is there anything that exists "necessarily," i.e., in and of itself, and that can provide the principle by which all other existence can be explained? The cosmological argument answers this question in the affirmative and attempts to prove the existence of the first cause of all consequent existence. Aquinas holds the belief that these arguments are decisive in providing the foundation for theism. Aquinas' faith in reason and his belief that these arguments can be persuasive for any man willing to approach the matter with an open mind underlies a position derived from Aristotle and one that is of continuing importance, especially in the Roman Catholic tradition. In contrast to this position, David Hume voices his questions, which remain among the most difficult for a traditional Christian to answer, and Immanuel Kant, in the second selection from his works reprinted in this section, presents his reasons for doubting the legitimacy of the cosmological method of argumentation.

W. R. Sorley presents an argument for God proceeding from his belief in the existence of moral values; these he considers to be ultimately a structure of a Supreme Mind. Charles Sanders Peirce presents an argument beginning with the experience of man in his instinctual awareness of the reality of God in the psychophysical universe.

Discussion of the ontological argument has recently been revived. In the last decade a number of significant reassessments have been made and, from among these, we have chosen three important philosophical discussions. J. N. Findlay's article opens the question from a negative position; juxtaposed to this position is Norman Malcolm's careful restatement of the two types of argument which Anselm presents. The third selection is from Charles Hartshorne, one of the vigorous contemporary exponents of this argument. These three selections provide a good introduction to the present state of this problem.

# ST. ANSELM

*Saint Anselm* (1033–1109) was Archbishop of Canterbury and the fore-most theologian of the eleventh century. His formulation of the ontological argument has become classic. For a time he served as Abbot of the Monastery at Bec in Normandy, which was in his day the greatest center of learning in Europe.

## The Ontological Argument

. . . I began to ask myself whether there might be found a single argument which would require no other for its proof than itself alone; and alone would suffice to demonstrate that God truly exists, and that there is a supreme good requiring nothing else, which all other things require for their existence and well-being; and whatever we believe regarding the divine Being.

Although I often and earnestly directed my thought to this end, and at some times that which I sought seemed to be just within my reach, while again it wholly evaded my mental vision, at last in despair I was about to cease, as if from the search for a thing which could not be found. But when I wished to exclude this thought altogether, lest, by busying my mind to no purpose, it should keep me from other thoughts, in which I might be successful; then more and more, though I was unwilling and shunned it, it began to force itself upon me, with a kind of importunity. So, one day, when I was exceedingly wearied with resisting its importunity, in the very conflict of my thoughts, the proof of which I had despaired offered itself, so that I eagerly embraced the thoughts which I was strenuously repelling.

. . . I do not endeavor, O Lord, to penetrate thy sublimity, for in no wise do I compare my understanding with that; but I long to understand in some degree thy truth, which my heart believes and loves. For I do not seek to understand that I may believe, but I believe in order to understand. For this also I believe—that unless I believed, I should not understand.

From St. Anselm, *Proslogium,* trans. Sidney Norton Deane, pp. 1–2, 6–9, 149–151, 158–159. Copyright, 1903, Open Court Publishing Company. Reprinted with permission of The Open Court Publishing Company.

## Chapter II

And so, Lord, do thou, who dost give understanding to faith, give me, so far as thou knowest it to be profitable, to understand that thou art as we believe; and that thou art that which we believe. And, indeed, we believe that thou art a being than which nothing greater can be conceived. Or is there no such nature, since the fool hath said in his heart, there is no God? (Psalms xiv. 1) But, at any rate, this very fool, when he hears of this being of which I speak—a being than which nothing greater can be conceived—understands what he hears, and what he understands is in his understanding; although he does not understand it to exist.

For, it is one thing for an object to be in the understanding, and another to understand that the object exists. When a painter first conceives of what he will afterwards perform, he has it in his understanding, but he does not yet understand it to be, because he has not yet performed it. But after he has made the painting, he both has it in his understanding, and he understands that it exists, because he has made it.

Hence, even the fool is convinced that something exists in the understanding, at least, than which nothing greater can be conceived. For, when he hears of this, he understands it. And whatever is understood, exists in the understanding. And assuredly that, than which nothing greater can be conceived, cannot exist in the understanding alone. For, suppose it exists in the understanding alone: then it can be conceived to exist in reality; which is greater.

Therefore, if that, than which nothing greater can be conceived, exists in the understanding alone, the very being, than which nothing greater can be conceived, is one, than which a greater can be conceived. But obviously this is impossible. Hence, there is no doubt that there exists a being, than which nothing greater can be conceived, and it exists both in the understanding and in reality.

## Chapter III

And it assuredly exists so truly, that it cannot be conceived not to exist. For, it is possible to conceive of a being which cannot be conceived not to exist, and this is greater than one which can be conceived not to exist. Hence, if that, than which nothing greater can be conceived, can be conceived not to exist, it is not that, than which nothing greater can be conceived. But this is an irreconcilable contradiction. There is, then, so truly a being than which nothing greater can be conceived to exist, that it cannot even be conceived not to exist; and this being thou art, O Lord, our God.

So truly, therefore, dost thou exist, O Lord, my God, that thou canst not be conceived not to exist; and rightly. For, if a mind could conceive of a being better than thee, the creature would rise above the Creator; and this is most absurd. And, indeed, whatever else there is, except thee alone, can be conceived not to exist. To thee alone, therefore, it belongs to exist more truly than all other beings, and hence in a higher degree than all others. For, whatever else exists does not exist so truly, and hence in a less degree it belongs to it to exist. Why, then, has the fool said in his heart, there is no God, . . . , since it is so evident, to a rational mind, that thou dost exist in the highest degree of all? Why, except that he is dull and a fool? . . .

## In Behalf of the Fool
## An Answer to the Argument of Anselm in the Proslogium
## by Gaunilon, a Monk of Marmoutier

5. . . . if it should be said that a being which cannot be even conceived in terms of any fact, is in the understanding, I do not deny that this being is, accordingly, in my understanding. But since through this fact it can in no wise attain to real existence also, I do not yet concede to it that existence at all, until some certain proof of it shall be given.

For he who says that this being exists, because otherwise the being which is greater than all will not be greater than all, does not attend strictly enough to what he is saying. For I do not yet say, no, I even deny or doubt that this being is greater than any real object. Nor do I concede to it any other existence than this (if it should be called existence) which it has when the mind, according to a word merely heard, tries to form the image of an object absolutely unknown to it.

How, then, is the veritable existence of that being proved to me from the assumption, by hypothesis, that it is greater than all other beings? For I should still deny this, or doubt your demonstration of it, to this extent, that I should not admit that this being is in my understanding and concept even in the way in which many objects whose real existence is uncertain and doubtful, are in my understanding and concept. For it should be proved first that this being itself really exists somewhere; and then, from the fact that it is greater than all, we shall not hesitate to infer that it also subsists in itself.

6. For example: it is said that somewhere in the ocean is an island, which, because of the difficulty, or rather the impossibility, of discovering what does not exist, is called the lost island. And they say that this island has an inestimable wealth of all manner of riches and delicacies in greater abundance than is told of the Islands of the Blest; and that having no owner or inhabitant, it is more excellent than all other countries, which are inhabited by mankind, in the abundance with which it is stored.

Now if someone should tell me that there is such an island, I should easily understand his words, in which there is no difficulty. But suppose that he went on to say, as if by a logical inference: "You can no longer doubt that this island which is more excellent than all lands exists somewhere, since you have no doubt that it is in your understanding. And since it is more excellent not to be in the understanding alone, but to exist both in the understanding and in reality, for this reason it must exist. For if it does not exist, any land which really exists will be more excellent than it; and so the island already understood by you to be more excellent will not be more excellent."

If a man should try to prove to me by such reasoning that this island truly exists, and that its existence should no longer be doubted, either I should believe that he was jesting, or I know not which I ought to regard as the greater fool: myself, supposing that I should allow this proof; or him, if he should suppose that he had established with any certainty the existence of this island. For he ought to show first that the hypothetical excellence of this island exists as a real and indubitable fact, and in no wise as any unreal object, or one whose existence is uncertain, in my understanding.

## Chapter III
### Anselm's Apologetic
### In Reply to Gaunilon's Answer in Behalf of the Fool

But, you say, it is as if one should suppose an island in the ocean, which surpasses all lands in its fertility, and which, because of the difficulty, or rather the impossibility, of discovering what does not exist, is called a lost island; and should say that there can be no doubt that this island truly exists in reality, for this reason, that one who hears it described easily understands what he hears.

Now I promise confidently that if any man shall devise anything existing either in reality or in concept alone (except that than which a greater cannot be conceived) to which he can adapt the sequence of my reasoning, I will discover that thing, and will give him his lost island, not to be lost again.

But it now appears that this being than which a greater is inconceivable cannot be conceived not to be, because it exists on so assured a ground of truth; for otherwise it would not exist at all.

Hence, if any one says that he conceives this being not to exist, I say that at the time when he conceives of this either he conceives of a being than which a greater is inconceivable, or he does not conceive at all. If he does not conceive, he does not conceive of the non-existence of that of which he does not conceive. But if he does conceive, he certainly conceives of a being which cannot be even conceived not to exist. For if it could be conceived not to exist, it could be conceived to have a beginning and an end. But this is impossible.

He, then, who conceives of this being conceives of a being which cannot be even conceived not to exist; but he who conceives of this being does not conceive that it does not exist; else he conceives what is inconceivable. The non-existence, then, of that than which a greater cannot be conceived is inconceivable.

# IMMANUEL KANT

*Immanuel Kant* (1724–1804) was professor of philosophy at Koenigsberg, Germany, and one of the great philosophers. His writings stimulated much subsequent discussion of theory of knowledge, metaphysics, ethics and religion. The most significant among his many works are *The Critique of Pure Reason* and *The Critique of Practical Reason*.

## Sec. IV—Of the Impossibility of an Ontological Proof of the Existence of God

It is evident from what has been said, that the conception of an absolutely necessary being is a mere idea, the objective reality of which is far from being established by the mere fact that it is a need of reason. On the contrary, this idea serves merely to indicate a certain unattainable perfection, and rather limits the operations than, by the presentation of new objects, extends the sphere of the understanding. But a strange anomaly meets us at the very threshold; for the inference from a given existence in general to an absolutely necessary existence, seems to be correct and unavoidable, while the conditions of the *understanding* refuse to aid us in forming any conception of such a being.

Philosophers have always talked of an *absolutely necessary* being, and have nevertheless declined to take the trouble of conceiving, whether—and how—a being of this nature is even cogitable, not to mention that its exist-

From Immanuel Kant, *Critique of Pure Reason*, trans. J. M. D. Meiklejohn, pp. 331–337. Published, 1943, Willey Book Company. In the public domain. [Footnote omitted, Eds.]

ence is actually demonstrable. A verbal definition of the conception is certainly easy enough; it is something, the non-existence of which is impossible. But does this definition throw any light upon the conditions which render it impossible to cogitate the non-existence of a thing—conditions which we wish to ascertain, that we may discover whether we think anything in the conception of such a being or not? For the mere fact that I throw away, by means of the word *Unconditioned,* all the conditions which the understanding habitually requires in order to regard anything as necessary, is very far from making clear whether by means of the conception of the unconditionally necessary I think of something, or really of nothing at all.

Nay, more, this chance-conception, now become so current, many have endeavored to explain by examples, which seemed to render any inquiries regarding its intelligibility quite needless. Every geometrical proposition—a triangle has three angles—it was said, is absolutely necessary; and thus people talked of an object which lay out of the sphere of our understanding as if it were perfectly plain what the conception of such a being meant.

All the examples adduced have been drawn, without exception, from *judgments,* and not from *things.* But the unconditioned necessity of a judgment does not form the absolute necessity of a thing. On the contrary, the absolute necessity of a judgment is only a conditioned necessity of a thing, or of the predicate in a judgment. The proposition above-mentioned, does not enounce that three angles necessarily exist, but, upon condition that a triangle exists, three angles must necessarily exist—in it. And thus this logical necessity has been the source of the greatest delusions. Having formed an *a priori* conception of a thing, the content of which was made to embrace existence, we believed ourselves safe in concluding that, because existence belongs necessarily to the object of the conception (that is, under the condition of my positing this thing as given), the existence of the thing is also posited necessarily, and that it is therefore absolutely necessary—merely because its existence has been cogitated in the conception.

If, in an identical judgment, I annihilate the predicate in thought, and retain the subject, a contradiction is the result; and hence I say, the former belongs necessarily to the latter. But if I suppress both subject and predicate in thought, no contradiction arises; for there is *nothing* at all, and therefore no means of forming a contradiction. To suppose the existence of a triangle and not that of its three angles, is self-contradictory; but to suppose the non-existence of both triangle and angles is perfectly admissible. And so is it with the conception of an absolutely necessary being. Annihilate its existence in thought, and you annihilate the thing itself with all its predicates; how then can there be any room for contradiction? Externally, there is nothing to give rise to a contradiction, for a thing cannot be necessary externally; nor internally, for, by the annihilation or suppression of the thing itself, its internal properties are also annihilated. God is omnipotent

—that is a necessary judgment. His omnipotence cannot be denied, if the existence of a Deity is posited—the existence, that is, of an infinite being, the two conceptions being identical. But when you say, God *does not exist,* neither omnipotence nor any other predicate is affirmed; they must all disappear with the subject, and in this judgment there cannot exist the least self-contradiction.

You have thus seen, that when the predicate of a judgment is annihilated in thought along with the subject, no internal contradiction can arise, be the predicate what it may. There is no possibility of evading the conclusion —you find yourselves compelled to declare: There are certain subjects which cannot be annihilated in thought. But this is nothing more than saying: There exist subjects which are absolutely necessary—the very hypothesis which you are called upon to establish. For I find myself unable to form the slightest conception of a thing which, when annihilated in thought with all its predicates, leave behind a contradiction; and contradiction is the only criterion of impossibility, in the sphere of pure *a priori* conceptions.

Against these general considerations, the justice of which no one can dispute, one argument is adduced, which is regarded as furnishing a satisfactory demonstration from the fact. It is affirmed, that there is one and only one conception, in which the non-being or annihilation of the object is self-contradictory, and this is the conception of an *ens realissimum*. It possesses, you say, all reality, and you feel yourselves justified in admitting the possibility of such a being. (This I am willing to grant for the present, although the existence of a conception which is not self-contradictory, is far from being sufficient to prove the possibility of an object.) Now the notion of all reality embraces in it that of existence; the notion of existence lies, therefore, in the conception of this possible thing. If this thing is annihilated in thought, the internal possibility of the thing is also annihilated, which is self-contradictory.

I answer: It is absurd to introduce—under whatever term disguised— into the conception of a thing, which is to be cogitated solely in reference to its possibility, the conception of its existence. If this is admitted, you will have apparently gained the day, but in reality have enounced nothing but a mere tautology. I ask, is the proposition, *this or that thing* (which I am admitting to be possible) *exists,* an analytical or a synthetical proposition? If the former, there is no addition made to the subject of your thought by the affirmation of its existence; but then the conception in your minds is identical with the thing itself, or you have supposed the existence of a thing to be possible, and then inferred its existence from its internal possibility—which is but a miserable tautology. The word *reality* in the conception of the thing, and the word *existence* in the conception of the predicate, will not help you out of the difficulty. For, supposing you were to term all positing of a thing, reality, you have thereby posited the thing with all its predicates in the conception of the subject and assumed its actual existence, and this you merely repeat in the predicate. But if you confess, as every reasonable person must, that every existential proposition is synthetical, how can it be maintained that the predicate of existence cannot be denied without contradiction—a property which is the characteristic of analytical propositions, alone?

I should have a reasonable hope of putting an end forever to this sophistical mode of argumentation, by a strict definition of the conception of existence, did not my own experience teach me that the illusion arising from our confounding a logical with a real predicate (a predicate which aids in the determination of a thing) resists almost all the endeavors of explanation and illustration. A *logical predicate* may be what you please, even the subject may be predicated of itself; for logic pays no regard to the content of a judgment. But the determination of a conception is a predicate, which adds to and enlarges the conception. It must not, therefore, be contained in the conception.

*Being* is evidently not a real predicate, that is, a conception of something which is added to the conception of some other thing. It is merely the positing of a thing, or of certain determinations in it. Logically, it is merely the copula of a judgment. The proposition, *God is omnipotent,* contains two conceptions, which have a certain object or content; the word *is,* is no additional predicate—it merely indicates the relation of the predicate to the subject. Now, if I take the subject (God) with all its predicates (omnipotence being one), and say, *God is,* or, *There is a God,* I add no new predicate to the conception of God, I merely posit or affirm the existence of the subject with all its predicates—I posit the *object* in relation to my *conception.* The content of both is the same; and there is no addition made to the conception, which expresses merely the possibility of the object, by my cogitating the object—in the expression, it *is*—as absolutely given or existing. Thus the real contains no more than the possible. A hundred real dollars contain no more than a hundred possible dollars. For, as the latter indicate the conception and the former the object, on the supposition that the content of the former was greater than that of the latter, my conception would not be an expression of the whole object, and would consequently be an inadequate conception of it. But in reckoning my wealth there may be said to be more in a hundred real dollars, than in a hundred possible dollars—that is, in the mere conception of them. For the real object—the dollars—is not analytically contained in my conception, but forms a synthetical addition to my conception (which is merely a determination of my mental state), although this objective reality—this existence —apart from my conception, does not in the least degree increase the aforesaid hundred dollars.

By whatever and by whatever number of predicates—even to the complete determination of it—I may cogitate a thing I do not in the least augment the object of my conception by the addition of the statement, this thing exists. Otherwise, not exactly the same, but something more than what was cogitated in my conception, would exist, and I could not affirm that the exact object of my conception had real existence. If I cogitate a thing as containing all modes of reality except one, the mode of reality which is absent is not added to the conception of the thing by the affirmation that the thing exists; on the contrary, the thing exists—if it exist at all—with the same defect as that cogitated in its conception; otherwise not that which was cogitated, but something different, exists. Now, if I cogitate a being as the highest reality, without defect or imperfection, the question still remains—whether this being exists or not? For although no element is wanting in the possible real content of my conception, there is a defect in its relation to my mental state, that is, I am ignorant whether the cognition of the object indicated by the conception is possible *a posteriori*. And here the cause of the present difficulty becomes apparent. If the question regarded an object of sense merely, it would be impossible for me to confound the conception with the existence of a thing. For the conception merely enables me to cogitate an object as according with the general conditions of experience; while the existence of the object permits me to cogitate it as contained in the sphere of actual experience. At the same time, this connection with the world of experience does not in the least augment the conception, although a possible perception has been added to the experience of the mind. But if we cogitate existence by the pure category alone, it is not to be wondered at, that we should find ourselves unable to present any criterion sufficient to distinguish it from mere possibility.

Whatever be the content of our conception of an object, it is necessary to go beyond it, if we wish to predicate existence of the object. In the case of sensuous objects, this is attained by their connection according to empirical laws with some one of my perceptions; but there is no means of cognizing the existence of objects of pure thought, because it must be cognized completely *a priori*. But all our knowledge of existence (be it immediately by perception, or by inferences connecting some object with a perception) belongs entirely to the sphere of experience—which is in perfect unity with itself—and although an existence out of this sphere cannot be absolutely declared to be impossible, it is a hypothesis the truth of which we have no means of ascertaining.

The notion of a supreme being is in many respects a highly useful idea; but for the very reason that it is an idea, it is incapable of enlarging our cognition with regard to the existence of things. It is not even sufficient to instruct us as to the possibility of a being which we do not know to exist. The analytical criterion of possibility, which consists in the absence of contradiction in propositions, cannot be denied it. But the connection of real properties in a thing is a synthesis of the possibility of which an *a priori* judgment cannot be formed, because these realities are not presented to us specifically; and even if this were to happen, a judgment would still be impossible, because the criterion of the possibility of synthetical cognitions must be sought for in the world of experience, to which the object of an idea cannot belong. And thus the celebrated Leibnitz has utterly failed in his attempt to establish on *a priori* grounds the possibility of this sublime ideal being.

The celebrated ontological or Cartesian argument for the existence of a Supreme Being is therefore insufficient; and we may as well hope to increase our stock of knowledge by the aid of mere ideas, as the merchant to augment his wealth by the addition of noughts to his cash-account.

# ST. THOMAS AQUINAS

*Thomas Aquinas* (c. 1226–1274), Dominican Friar and the greatest of the medieval philosophers, produced a synthesis of Christian faith and Aristotle's metaphysics which has become the official theology of the Roman Catholic Church. His chief works are *Summa Theologica* and *Summa Contra Gentiles.*

## Summa Theologica

Because the chief aim of sacred doctrine is to teach the knowledge of God, not only as He is in Himself, but also as He is the beginning of things and their last end, and especially of rational creatures, as is clear from what has been already said, therefore, in our endeavour to expound this science, we shall treat: (1) Of God: (2) Of the rational creature's advance towards God: (3) Of Christ, Who as man, is our way to God.

In treating of God there will be a threefold division:

For we shall consider (1) whatever concerns the Divine Essence. (2) Whatever concerns the distinctions of Persons. (3) Whatever concerns the procession of creatures from Him.

From Thomas Aquinas, *Summa Theologica,* Vol. I, pp. 19–27, 1920, Burns, Oates & Washbourne, Ltd. Reprinted with permission of Burns & Oates, Ltd. and Benziger Brothers, Inc.

Concerning the Divine Essence, we must consider:

(1) Whether God exists? (2) The manner of His existence, or, rather, what is *not* the manner of His existence. (3) Whatever concerns His operations—namely, His knowledge, will, power.

Concerning the first, there are three points of inquiry:

(1) Whether the proposition "God exists" is self-evident? (2) Whether it is demonstrable? (3) Whether God exists?


*First Article*

*Whether the Existence of God Is Self-Evident?*

*We proceed thus to the First Article:*

*Objection* 1. It seems that the existence of God is self-evident. Now those things are said to be self-evident to us the knowledge of which is naturally implanted in us, as we can see in regard to first principles. But as Damascene says (*De Fid. Orth.* i, I, 3), *the knowledge of God is naturally implanted in all.* Therefore the existence of God is self-evident.

*Obj.* 2. Further, those things are said to be self-evident which are known as soon as the terms are known, which the Philosopher (I *Poster.* iii) says is true of the first principles of demonstration. Thus, when the nature of a whole and of a part is known, it is at once recognized that every whole is greater than its part. But as soon as the signification of the word "God" is understood, it is at once seen that God exists. For by this word is signified that thing than which nothing greater can be conceived. But that which exists actually and mentally is greater than that which exists only mentally. Therefore, since as soon as the word "God" is understood it exists mentally, it also follows that it exists actually. Therefore the proposition "God exists" is self-evident.

*Obj.* 3. Further, the existence of truth is self-evident. For whoever denies the existence of truth grants that truth does not exist: and, if truth does not exist, then the proposition "Truth does not exist" is true: and if there is anything true, there must be truth. But God is truth itself: *I am the way, the truth, and the life* (John xiv.6). Therefore "God exists" is self-evident.

*On the contrary,* No one can mentally admit the opposite of what is self-evident; as the Philosopher (*Metaph.* iv., lect. vi.) states concerning the first principles of demonstration. But the opposite of the proposition "God is" can be mentally admitted: *The fool said in his heart, There is no God.* (Ps.lii.I). Therefore, that God exists is not self-evident.

*I answer that,* A thing can be self-evident in either of two ways; on the one hand, self-evident in itself, though not to us; on the other, self-evident in itself, and to us. A proposition is self-evident because the predicate is included in the essence of the subject, as "Man is an animal," for animal is contained in the essence of man. If, therefore the essence of the predicate and subject be known to all, the proposition will be self-evident to all; as is clear with regard to the first principles of demonstration, the terms of which are common things that no one is ignorant of, such as being and non-being, whole and part, and suchlike. If, however, there are some to whom the essence of the predicate and subject is unknown, the proposition will be self-evident in itself, but not to those who do not know the meaning of the predicate and subject of the proposition. Therefore, it happens, as Boethius says (*Hebdom.*, the title of which is: "*Whether all that is, is good*"), "that there are some mental concepts self-evident only to the learned, as that incorporeal substances are not in space." Therefore I say that this proposition, "God exists," of itself is self-evident, for the predicate is the same as the subject; because God is His own existence as will be hereafter shown (Q.III., A.4). Now because we do not know the essence of God, the proposition is not self-evident to us; but needs to be demonstrated by things that are more known to us, though less known in their nature—namely, by effects.

*Reply Obj.* 1. To know that God exists in a general and confused way is implanted in us by nature, inasmuch as God is man's beatitude. For man naturally desires happiness, and what is naturally desired by man must be naturally known to him. This, however, is not to know absolutely that God exists; just as to know that someone is approaching is not the same as to know that Peter is approaching, even though it is Peter who is approaching; for many there are who imagine that man's perfect good which is happiness, consists in riches, and others in pleasures, and others in something else.

*Reply Obj.* 2. Perhaps not everyone who hears this word "God" understands it to signify something than which nothing greater can be thought, seeing that some have believed God to be a body. Yet, granted that everyone understands that by this word "God" is signified something than which nothing greater can be thought, nevertheless, it does not therefore follow that he understands that what the word signifies exists actually, but only that its exists mentally. Nor can it be argued that it actually exists, unless it be admitted that there actually exists something than which nothing greater can be thought; and this precisely is not admitted by those who hold that God does not exist.

*Reply Obj.* 3. The existence of truth in general is self-evident, but the existence of a Primal Truth is not self-evident to us.

## Second Article
### Whether It Can Be Demonstrated That God Exists?

*We proceed thus to the Second Article:*

*Objection* 1. It seems that the existence of God cannot be demonstrated. For it is an article of faith that God exists. But what is of faith cannot be demonstrated, because a demonstration produces scientific knowledge; whereas faith is of the unseen (Heb. xi.I). Therefore it cannot be demonstrated that God exists.

*Obj.* 2. Further, the essence is the middle term of demonstration. But we cannot know in what God's essence consists, but solely in what it does not consist; as Damascence says (*De Fid. Orth.* i.4). Therefore we cannot demonstrate that God exists.

*Obj.* 3. Further, if the existence of God were demonstrated, this could only be from His effects. But His effects are not proportionate to Him, since He is infinite and His effects are finite; and between the finite and infinite there is no proportion. Therefore, since a cause cannot be demonstrated by an effect not proportionate to it, it seems that the existence of God cannot be demonstrated.

*On the contrary,* The Apostle says: *The invisible things of Him are clearly seen, being understood by the things that are made* (Rom. 1. 20). But this would not be unless the existence of God could be demonstrated through the things that are made; for the first thing we must know of anything is, whether it exists.

*I answer that,* Demonstration can be made in two ways: One is through the cause, and is called *a priori,* and this is to argue from what is prior absolutely. The other is through the effect, and is called a demonstration *a posteriori;* this is to argue from what is prior relatively only to us. When an effect is better known to us than its cause, from the effect we proceed to the knowledge of the cause. And from every effect the existence of its proper cause can be demonstrated, so long as its effects are better known to us; because since every effect depends upon its cause, if the effect exists, the cause must pre-exist. Hence the existence of God, in so far as it is not self-evident to us, can be demonstrated from those of His effects which are known to us.

*Reply Obj.* 1. The existence of God and other like truths about God, which can be known by natural reason, are not articles of faith, but are preambles to the articles; for faith presupposes natural knowledge, even as grace presupposes nature, and perfection supposes something that can be perfected. Nevertheless, there is nothing to prevent a man, who cannot grasp a proof, accepting, as a matter of faith, something which in itself is capable of being scientifically known and demonstrated.

*Reply Obj.* 2. When the existence of a cause is demonstrated from an effect, this effect takes the place of the definition of the cause in proof of the cause's existence. This is especially the case in regard to God, because, in order to prove the existence of anything, it is necessary to accept as a middle term the meaning of the word, and not its essence, for the question of its essence follows on the question of its existence. Now the names given to God are derived from His effects; consequently, in demonstrating the existence of God from His effects, we may take for the middle term the meaning of the word "God."

*Reply Obj.* 3. From effects not proportionate to the cause no perfect knowledge of that cause can be obtained. Yet from every effect the existence of the cause can be clearly demonstrated, and so we can demonstrate the existence of God from His effects; though from them we cannot perfectly know God as He is in His essence.

## Third Article
## Whether God Exists?

*We proceed thus to the Third Article:*

*Objection* 1. It seems that God does not exist; because if one of two contraries be infinite, the other would be altogether destroyed. But the word "God" means that He is infinite goodness. If, therefore, God existed, there would be no evil discoverable; but there is evil in the world. Therefore God does not exist.

*Obj.* 2. Further, it is superfluous to suppose that what can be accounted for by a few principles has been produced by many. But it seems that everything we see in the world can be accounted for by other principles, supposing God did not exist. For all natural things can be reduced to one principle, which is nature; and all voluntary things can be reduced to one principle, which is human reason, or will. Therefore there is no need to suppose God's existence.

*On the contrary,* It is said in the person of God: *I am Who am* (Exod. iii. 14).

*I answer that,* The existence of God can be proved in five ways.

The first and more manifest way is the argument from motion. It is certain, and evident to our senses, that in the world some things are in motion. Now whatever is in motion is put in motion by another, for nothing can be in motion except it is in potentiality to that towards which it is in motion; whereas a thing moves inasmuch as it is in act. For motion is nothing else than the reduction of something from potentiality to actuality. But nothing can be reduced from potentiality to actuality, except by something in the state of actuality. Thus that which is actually hot, as fire, makes wood, which is potentially hot, to be actually hot, and thereby moves and changes it. Now it is not possible that the same thing should be at once in actuality and potentiality in the same respect, but only in different respects. For what is actually hot cannot simultaneously be potentially hot; but it is simultaneously potentially cold. It is therefore impossible that in the same respect and in the same way a thing should be both mover and moved, i.e., that it should move itself. Therefore, whatever is in motion must be put in motion by another. If that by which it is put in motion be itself put in motion, then this also must needs be put in motion by another, and that by another again. But this cannot go on to infinity, because then there would be no first mover, and, consequently, no other mover; seeing that subsequent movers move only inasmuch as they are put in motion by the first mover; as the staff moves only because it is put in motion by the hand. Therefore it is necessary to arrive at a first mover, put in motion by no other; and this everyone understands to be God.

The second way is from the nature of the efficient cause. In the world of sense we find there is an order of efficient causes. There is no case known (neither is it, indeed, possible) in which a thing is found to be the efficient cause of itself; for so it would be prior to itself, which is impossible. Now in efficient causes it is not possible to go on to infinity, because in all efficient causes following in order, the first is the cause of the intermediate cause, and the intermediate is the cause of the ultimate cause, whether the intermediate cause be several, or one only. Now to take away the cause is to take away the effect. Therefore, if there be no first cause among efficient causes, there will be no ultimate, nor any intermediate cause. But if in efficient causes it is possible to go on to infinity, there will be no first efficient cause, neither will there be an ultimate effect, nor any intermediate efficient causes; all of which is plainly false. Therefore it is necessary to admit a first efficient cause, to which everyone gives the name of God.

The third way is taken from possibility and necessity, and runs thus. We find in nature things that are possible to be and not to be, since they are found to be generated, and to be corrupted, and consequently, they are possible to be and not to be. But it is impossible for these always to exist, for that which is possible not to be at some time is not. Therefore, if everything is possible not to be, then at one time there could have been nothing in existence. Now if this were true, even now there would be nothing in existence, because that which does not exist only begins to exist by something already existing. Therefore, if at one time nothing was in existence, it would have been impossible for anything to have begun to exist; and thus even now nothing would be in existence—which is absurd. Therefore, not all beings are merely possible, but there must exist something the existence of which is necessary. But every necessary thing either has its necessity caused by another, or not. Now it is impossible to go on to infinity in necessary things which have their necessity caused by another, as has been already proved in regard to efficient causes. Therefore we cannot but postulate the existence of some being having of itself its own necessity, and not receiving it from another, but rather causing in others their necessity. This all men speak of as God.

The fourth way is taken from the gradation to be found in things. Among beings there are some more and some less good, true, noble, and the like. But "more" and "less" are predicated of different things, according as they resemble in their different ways something which is the maximum, as a thing is said to be hotter according as it more nearly resembles that which is hottest; so that there is something which is truest, something best, something noblest, and, consequently, something which is uttermost being; for those things that are greatest in truth are greatest in being, as it is written in *Metaph.* ii. Now the maximum in any genus is the cause of all in that genus; as fire, which is the maximum of heat, is the cause of all hot things. Therefore there must also be something which is to all beings the cause of their being, goodness, and every other perfection; and this we call God.

The fifth way is taken from the governance of the world. We see that things which lack intelligence, such as natural bodies, act for an end, and this is evident from their acting always, or nearly always, in the same way, so as to obtain the best result. Hence it is plain that not fortuitously, but designedly, do they achieve their end. Now whatever lacks intelligence cannot move towards an end, unless it be directed by some being endowed with knowledge and intelligence; as the arrow is shot to its mark by the archer. Therefore some intelligent being exists by whom all natural things are directed to their end; and this being we call God.

*Reply Obj.* 1. As Augustine says (*Enchir.* xi.) : *Since God is the highest good, He would not allow any evil to exist in His works, unless His omnipotence and goodness were such as to bring good even out of evil.* This is part of the infinite goodness of God, that He should allow evil to exist, and out of it produce good.

*Reply Obj.* 2. Since nature works for a determinate end under the direction of a higher agent, whatever is done by nature must needs be traced back to God, as to its first cause. So also whatever is done voluntarily must also be traced back to some higher cause other than human reason or will, since these can change and fail; for all things that are changeable and capable of defect must be traced back to an immovable and self-necessary first principle, as was shown in the body of the *Article.*

# DAVID HUME

*David Hume* (1711–1776), Scottish empiricist, is one of the most important modern philosophers. His writings stimulated the thought of Immanuel Kant and have continued to influence philosophic study. His writings have been especially important as a background to present-day scientific empiricism.

## Dialogues Concerning Natural Religion

I must own, Cleanthes, said Demea, that nothing can more surprise me, than the light, in which you have, all along, put this argument. By the whole tenor of your discourse, one would imagine that you were maintaining the Being of a God, against the cavils of Atheists and Infidels; and were necessitated to become a champion for that fundamental principle of all religion. But this, I hope, is not by any means a question among us. No man, no man, at least, of common sense, I am persuaded, ever entertained a serious doubt with regard to a truth, so certain and self-evident. The question is not concerning the Being, but the Nature of God. This, I affirm, from the infirmities of human understanding, to be altogether incomprehensible and unknown to us. The essence of that supreme mind, his attributes, the manner of his existence, the very nature of his duration; these and every particular, which regards so divine a Being, are mysterious to men. Finite, weak, and blind creatures, we ought to humble ourselves in his august presence, and, conscious of our frailties, adore in silence his infinite perfections, which eye hath not seen, ear hath not heard, neither hath it entered into the heart of man to conceive [them]. They are covered in a deep cloud from human curiosity: It is profaneness to attempt penetrating through these sacred obscurities: And, next to the impiety of denying his existence, is the temerity of prying into his nature and essence, decrees and attributes.

But lest you should think, that my *piety* has here got the better of my *philosophy,* I shall support my opinion, if it needs any support, by a very

From David Hume, *Dialogues Concerning Natural Religion,* pp. 437–451, in *The Philosophical Works of Hume,* Vol. II, 1826, Adam Black, William Tait, and Charles Tait. In the public domain.

great authority. I might cite all the divines almost, from the foundation of Christianity, who have ever treated of this or any other theological subject: But I shall confine myself, at present, to one equally celebrated for piety and philosophy. It is Father Malebranche, who, I remember, thus expresses himself.[1] "One ought not so much," says he, "to call God a spirit, in order to express positively what he is, as in order to signify that he is not matter. He is a Being infinitely perfect: Of this we cannot doubt. But in the same manner as we ought not to imagine, even supposing him corporeal, that he is clothed with a human body, as the Anthropomorphites asserted, under colour that that figure was the most perfect of any; so, neither ought we to imagine, that the Spirit of God has human ideas, or bears *any* resemblance to our spirit; under colour that we know nothing more perfect than a human mind. We ought rather to believe, that as he comprehends the perfections of matter without being material . . . he comprehends also the perfections of created spirits, without being spirit, in the manner we conceive spirit: That his true name is, *He that is;* or, in other words, Being without restriction, All Being, the Being infinite and universal."

After so great an authority, Demea, replied Philo, as that which you have produced, and a thousand more, which you might produce, it would appear ridiculous in me to add my sentiment, or express my approbation of your doctrine. But surely, where reasonable men treat these subjects, the question can never be concerning the *Being,* but only the *Nature* of the Deity. The former truth, as you well observe, is unquestionable and self-evident. Nothing exists without a cause; and the original cause of this universe (whatever it be) we call God; and piously ascribe to him every species of perfection. Whoever scruples this fundamental truth, deserves every punishment, which can be inflicted among philosophers, to wit, the greatest ridicule, contempt and disapprobation. But as all perfection is entirely relative, we ought never to imagine, that we comprehend the attributes of this divine Being, or to suppose, that his perfections have any analogy or likeness to the perfections of a human creature. Wisdom, Thought, Design, Knowledge; these we justly ascribe to him; because these words are honourable among men, and we have no other language or other conceptions by which we can express our adoration of him. But let us beware, lest we think, that our ideas any wise correspond to his perfections, or that his attributes have any resemblance to these qualities among men. He is infinitely superior to our limited view and comprehension; and is more the object of worship in the temple, than of disputation in the schools.

In reality, Cleanthes, continued he, there is no need of having recourse to that affected scepticism, so displeasing to you, in order to come at this determination. Our ideas reach no farther than our experience: We have no

---

[1] *Recherche de la Vérité,* liv. 3, chap. 9.

experience of divine attributes and operations: I need not conclude my syllogism: You can draw the inference yourself. And it is a pleasure to me (and I hope to you too) that just reasoning and sound piety here concur in the same conclusion, and both of them establish the adorably mysterious and incomprehensible nature of the Supreme Being.

Not to lose any time in circumlocutions, said Cleanthes, addressing himself to Demea, much less in replying to the pious declamations of Philo; I shall briefly explain how I conceive this matter. Look round the world: contemplate the whole and every part of it: You will find it to be nothing but one great machine, subdivided into an infinite number of lesser machines, which again admit of subdivisions, to a degree beyond what human senses and faculties can trace and explain. All these various machines, and even their most minute parts, are adjusted to each other with an accuracy, which ravishes into admiration all men who have ever contemplated them. The curious adapting of means to ends, throughout all nature, resembles exactly, though it much exceeds, the productions of human contrivances; of human design, thought, wisdom, and intelligence. Since therefore the effects resemble each other, we are led to infer, by all the rules of analogy, that the causes also resemble; and that the Author of Nature is somewhat similar to the mind of man; though possessed of much larger faculties, proportioned to the grandeur of the work, which he has executed. By this argument *a posteriori,* and by this argument alone, do we prove at once the existence of a Deity, and his similarity to human mind and intelligence.

I shall be so free, Cleanthes, said Demea, as to tell you, that from the beginning, I could not approve of your conclusion concerning the similarity of the Deity to men; still less can I approve of the mediums, by which you endeavour to establish it. What! No demonstration of the Being of God! No abstract arguments! No proofs *a priori!* Are these, which have hitherto been so much insisted on by philosophers, all fallacy, all sophism? Can we reach no further in this subject than experience and probability? I will not say, that this is betraying the cause of a Deity: But surely, by this affected candour, you give advantage to Atheists, which they never could obtain, by the mere dint of argument and reasoning.

What I chiefly scruple in this subject, said Philo, is not so much, that all religious arguments are by Cleanthes reduced to experience, as that they appear not to be even the most certain and irrefragable of that inferior kind. That a stone will fall, that fire will burn, that the earth has solidity, we have observed a thousand and a thousand times; and when any new instance of this nature is presented, we draw without hesitation the accustomed inference. The exact similarity of the cases gives us a perfect assurance of a similar event; and a stronger evidence is never desired nor sought after. But wherever you depart, in the least, from the similarity of the cases, you diminish proportionately the evidence; and may at last bring it to a very weak *analogy,* which is confessedly liable to error and uncertainty. After having experienced the circulation of the blood in human creatures, we make no doubt that it takes place in Titius and Maevius: But from its circulation in frogs and fishes, it is only a presumption, though a strong one, from analogy, that it takes place in men and other animals. The analogical reasoning is much weaker, when we infer the circulation of the sap in vegetables from our experience, that the blood circulates in animals; and those, who hastily followed that imperfect analogy, are found, by more accurate experiments, to have been mistaken.

If we see a house, Cleanthes, we conclude, with the greatest certainty, that it had an architect or builder; because this is precisely that species of effect, which we have experienced to proceed from that species of cause. But surely you will not affirm, that the universe bears such a resemblance to a house, that we can with the same certainty infer a similar cause, or that the analogy is here entire and perfect. The dissimilitude is so striking, that the utmost you can here pretend to is a guess, a conjecture, a presumption concerning a similar cause; and how that pretension will be received in the world, I leave you to consider.

It would surely be very ill received, replied Cleanthes; and I should be deservedly blamed and detested, did I allow, that the proofs of a Deity amounted to no more than a guess or conjecture. But is the whole adjustment of means to ends in a house and in the universe so slight a resemblance? The economy of final causes? The order, proportion, and arrangement of every part? Steps of a stair are plainly contrived, that human legs may use them in mounting; and this inference is certain and infallible. Human legs are also contrived for walking and mounting; and this inference, I allow, is not altogether so certain, because of the dissimilarity which you remark; but does it, therefore, deserve the name only of presumption or conjecture?

Good God! cried Demea, interrupting him, where are we? Zealous defenders of religion allow, that the proofs of a Deity fall short of perfect evidence! And you, Philo, on whose assistance I depended, in proving the adorable mysteriousness of the Divine Nature, do you assent to all these extravagant opinions of Cleanthes? For what other name can I give them? Or why spare my censure, when such principles are advanced, supported by such an authority, before so young a man as Pamphilus?

You seem not to apprehend, replied Philo, that I argue with Cleanthes in his own way; and by showing him the dangerous consequences of his tenets, hope at last to reduce him to our opinion. But what sticks most with you, I observe, is the representation which Cleanthes has made of the argument *a posteriori;* and finding, that that argument is likely to escape your hold and vanish into air, you think it so disguised, that you can scarcely believe it to be set in its true light. Now, however much I may dissent, in other respects, from the dangerous principles of Cleanthes, I must allow, that he has fairly represented that argument; and I shall endeavour so to state the matter to you, that you will entertain no further scruples with regard to it.

Were a man to abstract from every thing which he knows or has seen, he would be altogether incapable, merely from his own ideas, to determine what kind of scene the universe must be, or to give the preference to one state or situation of things above another. For as nothing which he clearly conceives, could be esteemed impossible or implying a contradiction; every chimera of his fancy would be upon an equal footing; nor could he assign any just reason why he adheres to one idea or system, and rejects the others, which are equally possible.

Again; after he opens his eyes, and contemplates the world as it really is, it would be impossible for him, at first to assign the cause of any one event, much less, of the whole of things or of the universe. He might set his fancy a rambling; and she might bring him in an infinite variety of reports and representations. These would all be possible; but being all equally possible, he would never of himself give a satisfactory account for his preferring one of them to the rest. Experience alone can point out to him the true cause of every phenomenon.

Now, according to this method of reasoning, Demea, it follows (and is, indeed, tacitly allowed by Cleanthes himself) that order, arrangement, or the adjustment of final causes is not, of itself, any proof of design; but only so far as it has been experienced to proceed from that principle. For aught we can know *a priori,* matter may contain the source or spring of order originally within itself, as well as mind does; and there is no more difficulty in conceiving, that the several elements, from an internal unknown cause, may fall into the most exquisite arrangement, than to conceive that their ideas, in the great, universal mind, from a like internal, unknown cause, fall into that arrangement. The equal possibility of both these suppositions is allowed. But by experience we find (according to Cleanthes), that there is a difference between them. Throw several pieces of steel together, without shape or form; they will never arrange themselves so as to compose a watch: Stone, and mortar, and wood, without an architect, never erect a house. But the ideas in a human mind, we see, by an unknown, inexplicable economy, arrange themselves so as to form the plan of a watch or house. Experience, therefore, proves, that there is an original principle of order in mind, not in matter. From similar effects we infer similar causes. The adjustment of means to ends is alike in the universe, as in a machine of human contrivance. The causes, therefore, must be resembling.

I was from the beginning scandalised, I must own, with this resemblance, which is asserted, between the Deity and human creatures; and must conceive it to imply such a degradation of the Supreme Being as no sound

Theist could endure. With your assistance, therefore, Demea, I shall endeavour to defend what you justly called the adorable mysteriousness of the Divine Nature, and shall refute this reasoning of Cleanthes, provided he allows that I have made a fair representation of it.

When Cleanthes had assented, Philo, after a short pause, proceeded in the following manner.

That all inferences, Cleanthes, concerning fact, are founded on experience, and that all experimental reasonings are founded on the supposition, that similar causes prove similar effects, and similar effects similar causes; I shall not at present much dispute with you. But observe, I entreat you, with what extreme caution all just reasoners proceed in the transferring of experiments to similar cases. Unless the cases be exactly similar, they repose no perfect confidence in applying their past observation to any particular phenomenon. Every alteration of circumstances occasions a doubt concerning the event; and it requires new experiments to prove certainly, that the new circumstances are of no moment or importance. A change in bulk, situation, arrangement, age, disposition of the air, or surrounding bodies; any of these particulars may be attended with the most unexpected consequences: And unless the objects be quite familiar to us, it is the highest temerity to expect with assurance, after any of these changes, an event similar to that which before fell under our observation. The slow and deliberate steps of philosophers, here, if any where, are distinguished from the precipitate march of the vulgar, who, hurried on by the smallest similitude, are incapable of all discernment or consideration.

But can you think, Cleanthes, that your usual phlegm and philosophy have been preserved in so wide a step as you have taken, when you compared to the universe, houses, ships, furniture, machines and from their similarity in some circumstances inferred a similarity in their causes? Thought, design, intelligence, such as we discover in men and other animals, is no more than one of the springs and principles of the universe, as well as heat or cold, attraction or repulsion, and a hundred others, which fall under daily observation. It is an active cause, by which some particular parts of nature, we find, produce alterations on other parts. But can a conclusion, with any propriety, be transferred from parts to the whole? Does not the great disproportion bar all comparison and inference? From observing the growth of a hair, can we learn any thing concerning the generation of a man? Would the manner of a leaf's blowing, even though perfectly known, afford us any instruction concerning the vegetation of a tree?

But allowing that we were to take the *operations* of one part of nature upon another, for the foundation of our judgment concerning the *origin* of the whole, (which never can be admitted), yet why select so minute, so weak, so bounded a principle as the reason and design of animals is found to be upon this planet? What peculiar privilege has this little agitation of the brain which we call *thought,* that we must thus make it the model of the whole universe? Our partiality in our own favour does indeed present it on all occasions; but sound philosophy ought carefully to guard against so natural an illusion.

So far from admitting, continued Philo, that the operations of a part can afford us any just conclusion concerning the origin of the whole, I will not allow any one part to form a rule for another part, if the latter be very remote from the former. Is there any reasonable ground to conclude, that the inhabitants of other planets possess thought, intelligence, reason, or any thing similar to these faculties in men? When nature has so extremely diversified her manner of operation in this small globe; can we imagine, that she incessantly copies herself throughout so immense a universe? And if thought, as we may well suppose, be confined merely to this narrow corner, and has even there so limited a sphere of action, with what propriety can we assign it for the original cause of all things? The narrow views of a peasant, who makes his domestic economy the rule for the government of kingdoms, is in comparison a pardonable sophism.

But were we ever so much assured, that a thought and reason, resembling the human, were to be found throughout the whole universe, and were its activity elsewhere vastly greater and more commanding than it appears in this globe; yet I cannot see, why the operations of a world, constituted, arranged, adjusted, can with any propriety be extended to a world, which is in its embryo-state, and is advancing towards that constitution and arrangement. By observation, we know somewhat of the economy, action, and nourishment of a finished animal; but we must transfer with great caution that observation to the growth of a foetus in the womb, and still more, to the formation of an animalcule in the loins of its male parent. Nature, we find, even from our limited experience, possesses an infinite number of springs and principles, which incessantly discover themselves on every change of her position and situation. And what new and unknown principles would actuate her in so new and unknown a situation as that of the formation of a universe, we cannot, without the utmost temerity, pretend to determine.

A very small part of this great system, during a very short time, is very imperfectly discovered to us: and do we thence pronounce decisively concerning the origin of the whole?

Admirable conclusion! Stone, wood, brick, iron, brass, have not, at this time, in this minute globe of earth, an order or arrangement without human art and contrivance: therefore the universe could not originally attain its order and arrangement, without something similar to human art. But is a part of nature a rule for another part very wide of the former? Is it a rule for the whole? Is a very small part a rule for the universe? Is nature in one situation, a certain rule for nature in another situation, vastly different from the former?

And can you blame me, Cleanthes, if I here imitate the prudent reserve of Simonides, who, according to the noted story, being asked by Hiero, *What God was?* desired a day to think of it, and then two days more; and after that manner continually prolonged the term, without ever bringing in his definition or description? Could you even blame me, if I had answered at first *that I did not know,* and was sensible that this subject lay vastly beyond the reach of my faculties? You might cry out sceptic and rallier as much as you pleased: but having found, in so many other subjects much more familiar, the imperfections and even contradictions of human reason, I never should expect any success from its feeble conjectures in a subject so sublime, and so remote from the sphere of our observation. When two *species* of objects have always been observed to be conjoined together, I can *infer,* by custom, the existence of one wherever I *see* the existence of the other: and this I call an argument from experience. But how this argument can have place, where the objects, as in the present case, are single, individual, without parallel, or specific resemblance, may be difficult to explain. And will any man tell me with a serious countenance, that an orderly universe must arise from some thought and art, like the human; because we have experience of it? To ascertain this reasoning, it were requisite, that we had experience of the origin of worlds; and it is not sufficient, surely, that we have seen ships and cities arise from human art and contrivance.

Philo was proceeding in this vehement manner, somewhat between jest and earnest, as it appeared to me; when he observed some signs of impatience in Cleanthes, and then immediately stopped short. What I had to suggest, said Cleanthes, is only that you would not abuse terms, or make use of popular expressions to subvert philosophical reasonings. You know, that the vulgar often distinguish reason from experience, even where the question relates only to matter of fact and existence; though it is found, where that *reason* is properly analysed, that it is nothing but a species of experience. To prove by experience the origin of the universe from mind, is not more contrary to common speech, than to prove the motion of the earth from the same principle. And a caviller might raise all the same objections to the Copernican system, which you have urged against my reasonings. Have you other earths, might he say, which you have seen to move? Have. . . .

Yes! cried Philo, interrupting him, we have other earths. Is not the moon another earth, which we see to turn round its centre? Is not Venus another earth, where we observe the same phenomenon? Are not the revolutions of the sun also a confirmation, from analogy, of the same theory? All the planets, are they not earths, which revolve about the sun? Are not the satellites moons, which move round Jupiter and Saturn, and along with these primary planets, round the sun? These analogies and resemblances, with others, which I have not mentioned, are the sole proofs of the Copernican system; and to you it belongs to consider, whether you have any analogies of the same kind to support your theory.

In reality, Cleanthes, continued he, the modern system of astronomy is now so much received by all inquirers, and has become so essential a part even of our earliest education, that we are not commonly very scrupulous in examining the reasons upon which it is founded. It is now become a matter of mere curiosity to study the first writers on that subject, who had the full force of prejudice to encounter, and were obliged to turn their arguments on every side in order to render them popular and convincing. But if we peruse Galilaeo's famous Dialogues concerning the system of the world, we shall find, that that great genius, one of the sublimest that ever existed, first bent all his endeavours to prove, that there was no foundation for the distinction commonly made between elementary and celestial substances. The schools, proceeding from the illusions of sense, had carried this distinction very far; and had established the latter substances to be ingenerable; incorruptible, unalterable, impassible; and had assigned all the opposite qualities to the former. But Galilaeo, beginning with the moon, proved its similarity in every particular to the earth; its convex figure, its natural darkness when not illuminated, its density, its distinction into solid and liquid, the variations of its phases, the mutual illuminations of the earth and moon, their mutual eclipses, the inequalities of the lunar surface, etc. After many instances of this kind, with regard to all the planets, men plainly saw, that these bodies became proper objects of experience; and that the similarity of their nature enabled us to extend the same arguments and phenomena from one to the other.

In this cautious proceeding of the astronomers, you may read your own condemnation, Cleanthes; or rather may see, that the subject in which you are engaged exceeds all human reason and inquiry. Can you pretend to show any such similarity between the fabric of a house, and the generation of a universe? Have you ever seen nature in any such situation as resembles the first arrangement of the elements? Have worlds ever been formed under your eye; and have you had leisure to observe the whole progress of the phenomenon, from the first appearance of order to its final consummation? If you have, then cite your experience, and deliver your theory.

# IMMANUEL KANT

*Immanuel Kant* (1724–1804) was professor of philosophy at Koenigsberg, Germany, and one of the great philosophers. His writings stimulated much subsequent discussion of theory of knowledge, metaphysics, ethics and religion. The most significant among his many works are *The Critique of Pure Reason* and *The Critique of Practical Reason.*

## Sec. V—Of the Impossibility of a Cosmological Proof of the Existence of God

The *cosmological proof,* which we are about to examine, retains the connection between absolute necessity, and the highest reality; but, instead of reasoning from this highest reality to a necessary existence, like the preceding argument, it concludes from the given unconditioned necessity of some being its unlimited reality. The track it pursues, whether rational or sophistical, is at least natural, and not only goes far to persuade the common understanding, but shows itself deserving of respect from the speculative intellect; while it contains, at the same time, the outlines of all the arguments employed in natural theology—arguments which always have been, and still will be, in use and authority. These, however adorned, and hid under whatever embellishments of rhetoric and sentiment, are at bottom identical with the arguments we are at present to discuss. This proof, termed by Leibnitz the *argumentum a contingentia mundi,* I shall now lay before the reader, and subject to a strict examination.

It is framed in the following manner: If something exists, an absolutely necessary being must likewise exist. Now I, at least, exist. Consequently, there exists an absolutely necessary being. The minor contains an experience, the major reasons from a general experience to the existence of a necessary being. Thus this argument really begins at experience, and is not completely *a priori,* or ontological. The object of all possible experience being the world, it is called the *cosmological* proof. It contains no reference to any

From Immanuel Kant, *Critique of Pure Reason,* trans. J. M. D. Meiklejohn, pp. 338–347. Published, 1943, Willey Book Company. In the public domain. [Footnote omitted, Eds.]

peculiar property of sensuous objects, by which this world of sense might be distinguished from other possible worlds; and in this respect it differs from the physico-theological proof, which is based upon the consideration of the peculiar constitution of our sensuous world.

The proof proceeds thus: A necessary being can be determined only in one way, that is, it can be determined by only one of all possible opposed predicates; consequently, it must be *completely* determined in and by its conception. But there is only a single conception of a thing possible, which completely determines the thing *a priori*: that is, the conception of the *ens realissimum*. It follows that the conception of the *ens realissimum* is the only conception, by and in which we can cogitate a necessary being. Consequently, a supreme being necessarily exists.

In this cosmological argument are assembled so many sophistical propositions, that speculative reason seems to have exerted in it all her dialectical skill to produce a transcendental illusion of the most extreme character. We shall postpone an investigation of this argument for the present, and confine ourselves to exposing the stratagem by which it imposes upon us an old argument in a new dress, and appeals to the agreement of two witnesses, the one with the credentials of pure reason, and the other with those of empiricism; while, in fact, it is only the former who has changed his dress and voice, for the purpose of passing himself off for an additional witness. That it may possess a secure foundation, it bases its conclusions upon experience, and thus appears to be completely distinct from the ontological argument, which places its confidence entirely in pure *a priori* conceptions. But this experience merely aids reason in making one step—to the existence of a necessary being. What the properties of this being are, cannot be learned from experience; and therefore reason abandons it altogether, and pursues its inquiries in the sphere of pure conceptions, for the purpose of discovering what the properties of an absolutely necessary being ought to be, that is, what among all possible things contain the conditions (*requisita*) of absolute necessity. Reason believes that it has discovered these requisites in the conception of an *ens realissimum*—and in it alone, and hence concludes: the *ens realissimum* is an absolutely necessary being. But it is evident that reason has here presupposed that the conception of an *ens realissimum* is perfectly adequate to the conception of a being of absolute necessity, that is, that we may infer the existence of the latter from that of the former—a proposition, which formed the basis of the ontological argument, and which is now employed in the support of the cosmological argument, contrary to the wish and professions of its inventors. For the existence of an absolutely necessary being is given in conceptions alone. But if I say—the conception of the *ens realissimum* is a conception of this kind, and in fact the only conception which is adequate to our idea of a necessary being, I am obliged to admit, that the latter may be inferred from the former. Thus it is properly the ontological argument which figures in the cosmological, and constitutes the whole strength of the latter; while the spurious basis of experience has been of no further use than to conduct us to the conception of absolute necessity, being utterly insufficient to demonstrate the presence of this attribute in any determinate existence or thing. For when we propose to ourselves an aim of this character, we must abandon the sphere of experience, and rise to that of pure conceptions, which we examine with the purpose of discovering whether any one contains the conditions of the possibility of an absolutely necessary being. But if the possibility of such a being is thus demonstrated, its existence is also proved; for we may then assert that, of all possible beings there is one which possesses the attribute of necessity—in other words, this being possesses an absolutely necessary existence. . . .

The following fallacies, for example, are discoverable in this mode of proof: 1. The transcendental principle, Everything that is contingent must have a cause—a principle without significance, except in the sensuous world. For the purely intellectual conception of the contingent cannot produce any synthetical proposition, like that of causality, which is itself without significance or distinguishing characteristic except in the phenomenal world. But in the present case it is employed to help us beyond the limits of its sphere. 2. From the impossibility of an infinite ascending series of causes in the world of sense a first cause is inferred;—a conclusion which the principles of the employment of reason do not justify even in the sphere of experience, and still less when an attempt is made to pass the limits of this sphere. 3. Reason allows itself to be satisfied upon insufficient grounds, with regard to the completion of this series. It removes all conditions (without which, however, no conception of Necessity can take place); and, as after this it is beyond our power to form any other conception, it accepts this as a completion of the conception it wishes to form of the series. 4. The logical possibility of a conception of the total of reality (the criterion of this possibility being the absence of contradiction) is confounded with the transcendental, which requires a principle of the practicability of such a synthesis—a principle which again refers us to the world of experience. And so on.

The aim of the cosmological argument is to avoid the necessity of proving the existence of a necessary being *a priori* from mere conceptions—a proof which must be ontological, and of which we feel ourselves quite incapable. With this purpose, we reason from an actual existence—an experience in general, to an absolutely necessary condition of that existence. It is in this case unnecessary to demonstrate its possibility. For after having proved that it exists, the question regarding its possibility is superfluous. Now, when we wish to define more strictly the nature of this necessary being, we do not look out for some being the conception of which would enable us to comprehend the necessity of its being—for if we could do this, an empirical presupposition would be unnecessary; no, we try to discover merely the negative condition (*conditio sine qua non*), without which a being would not be absolutely necessary. Now this would be perfectly admissible in every sort of reasoning, from a consequence to its principle; but in the present case it unfortunately happens that the condition of absolute necessity can be discovered in but a single being, the conception of which must consequently contain all that is requisite for demonstrating the presence of absolute necessity, and thus entitle me to infer this absolute necessity *a priori*. That is, it must be possible to reason conversely, and say—the thing, to which the conception of the highest reality belongs, is absolutely necessary. But if I cannot reason thus—and I cannot, unless I believe in the sufficiency of the ontological argument—I find insurmountable obstacles in my new path, and am really no further than the point from which I set out. The conception of a Supreme Being satisfies all questions *a priori* regarding the internal determinations of a thing, and is for this reason an ideal without equal or parallel, the general conception of it indicating it has at the same time an *ens individuum* among all possible things. But the conception does not satisfy the question regarding its existence—which was the purpose of all our inquiries; and although the existence of a necessary being were admitted, we should find it impossible to answer the question —What of all things in the world must be regarded as such?

It is certainly allowable to *admit* the existence of an all-sufficient being— a cause of all possible effects, for the purpose of enabling reason to introduce unity into its mode and grounds of explanation with regard to phenomena. But to assert that such a being *necessarily exists,* is no longer the modest enunciation of an admissible hypothesis, but the boldest declaration of an apodictic certainty; for the cognition of that which is absolutely necessary, must itself possess that character.

The aim of the transcendental ideal formed by the mind is, either to discover a conception which shall harmonize with the idea of absolute necessity, or a conception which shall contain that idea. If the one is possible, so is the other; for reason recognizes that alone as absolutely necessary, which is necessary from its conception. But both attempts are equally beyond our power—we find it impossible to *satisfy* the understanding upon this point, and as impossible to induce it to remain at rest in relation to this incapacity.

Unconditioned necessity, which, as the ultimate support and stay of all existing things, is an indispensable requirement of the mind, is an abyss on the verge of which human reason trembles in dismay. Even the idea of eternity, terrible and sublime as it is, as depicted by Haller, does not produce upon the mental vision such a feeling of awe and terror; for, although it *measures* the duration of things, it does not *support* them. We cannot bear, nor can we rid ourselves of the thought, that a being, which we regard as the greatest of all possible existences should *say to himself:* I am from eternity to eternity; beside me there is nothing except that which exists by my will; *but whence then am I?* Here all sinks away from under us; and the greatest, as the smallest, perfection, hovers without stay or footing in presence of the speculative reason, which finds it as easy to part with the one as with the other.

Many physical powers, which evidence their existence by their effects, are perfectly inscrutable in their nature; they elude all our powers of observation. The transcendental object which forms the basis of phenomena, and, in connection with it, the reason why our sensibility possesses this rather than that particular kind of conditions, are and must ever remain hidden from our mental vision; the fact is there, the reason of the fact we cannot see. But an ideal of pure reason cannot be termed mysterious or *inscrutable,* because the only credential of its reality is the need of it felt by reason, for the purpose of giving completeness to the world of synthetical unity. An ideal is not even given as a cogitable *object,* and therefore cannot be inscrutable; on the contrary, it must, as a mere idea, be based on the constitution of reason itself, and on this account must be capable of explanation and solution. For the very essence of reason consists in its ability to give an account of all our conceptions, opinions, and assertions—upon objective, or, when they happen to be illusory and fallacious, upon subjective grounds.

## Detection and Explanation of the Dialectical Illusion in All Transcendental Arguments for the Existence of a Necessary Being

Both of the above arguments are transcendental; in other words, they do not proceed from empirical principles. For, although the cosmological argument professed to lay a basis of experience for its edifice of reasoning, it did not ground its procedure upon the peculiar constitution of experience, but upon pure principles of reason—in relation to an existence given by empirical consciousness; utterly abandoning its guidance, however, for the purpose of supporting its assertions entirely upon pure conceptions. Now what is the cause, in these transcendental arguments, of the dialectical, but natural, illusion, which connects the conceptions of necessity and supreme reality, and hypostatizes that which cannot be anything but an idea? What is the cause of this unavoidable step on the part of reason, of admitting that some one among all existing things must be necessary, while it falls back from the assertion of the existence of such a being as from an abyss? And how does reason proceed to explain this anomaly to itself, and from the wavering condition of a timid and reluctant approbation—always again withdrawn, arrive at a calm and settled insight into its cause?

It is something very remarkable that, on the supposition that something exists, I cannot avoid the inference, that something exists necessarily. Upon this perfectly natural—but not on that account reliable—inference does the cosmological argument rest. But, let me form any conception whatever of a thing, I find that I cannot cogitate the existence of the thing as absolutely necessary, and that nothing prevents me—be the thing or being what it may—from cogitating its non-existence. I may thus be obliged to admit that all existing things have a necessary basis, while I cannot cogitate any single or individual thing as necessary. In other words, I can never *complete* the regress through the conditions of existence, without admitting the existence of a necessary being; but, on the other hand, I cannot make a *commencement* from this beginning.

It follows from this, that you must accept the absolutely necessary as *out of* and beyond the world, inasmuch as it is useful only as a principle of the highest possible unity in experience, and you cannot discover any such necessary existence in the *world,* the second rule requiring you to regard all empirical causes of unity as themselves deduced.

These remarks will have made it evident to the reader that the ideal of the Supreme Being, far from being an enouncement of the existence of a being in itself necessary, is nothing more than a *regulative principle* of reason, requiring us to regard all connection existing between phenomena as if it has its origin from an all-sufficient necessary cause, and basing upon this the rule of a systematic and necessary unity in the explanation of phenomena. We cannot, at the same time, avoid regarding, by a transcendental *subreptio,* this formal principle as constitutive, and hypostatizing this unity. Precisely similar is the case with our notion of space. Space is the primal condition of all forms, which are properly just so many different limitations of it; and thus, although it is merely a principle of sensibility, we cannot help regarding it as an absolutely necessary and self-subsistent thing—as an object given *a priori* in itself. In the same way, it is quite natural that, as the systematic unity of nature cannot be established as a principle for the empirical employment of reason, unless it is based upon the idea of an *ens realissimum,* as the supreme cause, we should regard this idea as a real object, and this object, in its character of supreme condition, as absolutely necessary, and that in this way a *regulative* should be transformed into a *constitutive* principle. This interchange becomes evident when I regard this supreme being, which, relatively to the world, was absolutely (unconditionally) necessary, as a thing *per se.* In this case, I find it impossible to represent this necessity in or by any conception, and it exists merely in my own mind, as the formal condition of thought, but not as a material and hypostatic condition of existence.

# W. R. SORLEY

*William Sorley* (1855–1935) was Knightbridge Professor of Moral Philosophy at Cambridge University from 1900–1933. He sought to ground theism on moral values. The book from which the selection printed here is taken is his best known work.

## The Moral Argument

The result so far is that the events of the world as a causal system are not inconsistent with the view that this same world is a moral order, that its purpose is a moral purpose. The empirical discrepancies between the two orders, and the obstacles which the world puts in the way of morality, are capable of explanation when we allow that ideals of goodness have not only to be discovered by finite minds, but that for their realisation they need to be freely accepted by individual wills and gradually organized in individual characters. If this principle still leaves many particular difficulties unresolved, it may at least be claimed that it provides the general plan of an explanation of the relation of moral value to experience, and that a larger knowledge of the issues of life than is open to us might be expected to show that the particular difficulties also are not incapable of solution.

This means that it is possible to regard God as the author and ruler of the world, as it appears in space and time, and at the same time to hold that the moral values of which we are conscious and the moral ideal which we come to apprehend with increasing clearness express his nature. But the question remains, Are we to regard morality—its values, laws, and ideal—as belonging to a Supreme Mind, that is, to God? It is as an answer to this question that the specific Moral Argument enters. And here I cannot do better than give the argument in the words of Dr. Rashdall:

"An absolute Moral Law or moral ideal cannot exist *in* material things. And it does not exist in the mind of this or that individual. Only if we believe in the existence of a Mind for which the true moral ideal is already in some sense real, a Mind which is the source of whatever is true in our own

From W. R. Sorley, *Moral Values and the Idea of God,* 3rd edition, pp. 346–352. Copyright, 1919, by Cambridge University Press. Used by permission of Kenneth W. Sorley and Mrs. Geoffrey Bickersteth.

moral judgments, can we rationally think of the moral ideal as no less real than the world itself. Only so can we believe in an absolute standard of right and wrong, which is as independent of this or that man's actual ideas and actual desires as the facts of material nature. The belief in God, though not (like the belief in a real and active self) a postulate of there being any such thing as Morality at all, is the logical presupposition of an 'objective' or absolute Morality. A moral ideal can exist nowhere and nohow but in a mind; an absolute moral ideal can exist only in a Mind from which all Reality is derived.[1] Our moral ideal can only claim objective validity in so far as it can rationally be regarded as the revelation of a moral ideal eternally existing in the mind of God." [2]

The argument as thus put may be looked upon as a special and striking extension of the cosmological argument. In its first and most elementary form the cosmological argument seeks a cause for the bare existence of the world and man; to account for them there must be something able to bring them into being: God is the First Cause. Then the order of nature impresses us by its regularity, and we come by degrees to understand the principles of its working and the laws under which the material whole maintains its equilibrium and the ordered procession of its changes: these laws and this order call for explanation, and we conceive God as the Great Lawgiver. But beyond this material world, we understand relations and principles of a still more general kind; and the intellect of man recognises abstract truths so evident that, once understood, they cannot be questioned, while inferences are drawn from these which only the more expert minds can appreciate and yet which they recognize as eternally valid. To what order do these belong and what was their home when man as yet was unconscious of them? Surely if their validity is eternal they must have had existence somewhere, and we can only suppose them to have existed in the one eternal mind: God is therefore the God of Truth. Further, persons are conscious of values and of an ideal of goodness, which they recognise as having undoubted authority for the direction of their activity; the validity of these values or laws and of this ideal, however, does not depend upon their recognition: it is objective and eternal; and how could this eternal validity stand alone, not embodied in matter and neither seen nor realised by finite minds, unless there were an eternal mind whose thought and will were therein expressed? God must therefore exist and his nature be goodness.

The argument in this its latest phase has a new feature which distinguishes it from the preceding phases. The laws or relations of interacting phenomena which we discover in nature are already embodied in the processes of nature. It may be argued that they have their reality therein: that in cognising them

---

[1] "Or at least a mind by which all Reality is controlled."—Dr. Rashdall's footnote.
[2] H. Rashdall, *The Theory of Good and Evil* (1907), Vol. II, p. 212.

we are simply cognising an aspect of the actual world in space and time, and consequently that, if the mere existence of things does not require God to account for it (on the ground urged by Hume that the world, being a singular event, justifies no inference as to its cause), then, equally, we are not justified in seeking a cause for those laws or relations which are, after all, but one aspect of the existing world. It may be urged that the same holds of mathematical relations: that they are merely an abstract of the actual order, when considered solely in its formal aspect. It is more difficult to treat the still more general logical relations in the same fashion; but they too receive verification in reality and in our thought so far as it does not end in confusion. But it is different with ethical values. Their validity could not be verified in external phenomena; they cannot be established by observation of the course of nature. They hold good for persons only: and their peculiarity consists in the fact that their validity is not in any way dependent upon their being manifested in the character or conduct of persons, or even on their being recognised in the thoughts of persons. We acknowledge the good and its objective claim upon us even when we are conscious that our will has not yielded to the claim; and we admit that its validity existed before we recognised it.

This leading characteristic makes the theistic argument founded upon moral values or the moral law both stronger in one respect and weaker in another respect than the corresponding argument from natural law and in-telligible relations. It is weaker because it is easier to deny the premiss from which it starts—that is, the objective validity of moral law—than it is to deny the objective validity of natural or mathematical or logical relations. But I am here assuming the objective validity of morality as already estab-lished by our previous enquiries; and it is unnecessary to go back upon the question, And, granted this premiss, the argument adds an important point. Other relations and laws (it may be said, and the statement is true of laws of nature at any rate) are embodied in actually existing objects. But the same cannot be said of the moral law or moral idea. We acknowledge that there are objective values, although men may not recognise them, that the moral law is not abrogated by being ignored, and that our consciousness is striving towards the apprehension of an ideal which no finite mind has clearly grasped, but which is none the less valid although it is not realised and is not even apprehended by us in its truth and fullness. Where then is this ideal? It cannot be valid at one time and not at another. It must be eternal as well as objective. As Dr. Rashdall urges, it is not in material things, and it is not in the mind of this or that individual; but "it can exist nowhere and nohow but in a mind"; it requires therefore the mind of God.

Against this argument, however, it may be contended that it disregards the distinction between validity and existence. Why is it assumed that the moral ideal must exist somehow and somewhere? Validity, it may be said, is a unique concept, as unique as existence, and different from it. And this is true. At the same time it is also true that the validity of the moral ideal, like all validity, is a validity for existents. Without this reference to existence there seems no meaning in asserting validity. At any rate it is clear that it is for existents—namely, for the realm of persons—that the moral idea is valid. It is also true that the perfect moral ideal does not exist in the volitional, or even in the intellectual, consciousness of these persons: they have not achieved agreement with it in their lives, and even their understanding of it is incomplete. Seeing then that it is not manifested by finite existents, how are we to conceive its validity? Other truths are displayed in the order of the existing world; but it is not so with moral values. And yet the system of moral values has been acknowledged to be an aspect of the real universe to which existing things belong. How are we to conceive its relation to them? A particular instance of goodness can exist only in the character of an individual person or group of persons; an idea of goodness such as we have is found only in minds such as ours. But the ideal of goodness does not exist in finite minds or in their material environment. What then is its status in the system of reality?

The question is answered if we regard the moral order as the order of a Supreme Mind and the ideal of goodness as belonging to this Mind. The difficulty for this view is to show that the Mind which is the home of goodness may also be regarded as the ground of the existing world. That reality as a whole, both in its actual events and in its moral order, can be consistently regarded as the expression of a Supreme Mind is the result of the present argument.

# CHARLES SANDERS PEIRCE

*Charles Sanders Peirce* (1839–1914), American philosopher, provided a
foundation for pragmatism and influenced the development of symbolic
logic. He was a major figure in building an indigenous American philosophic tradition.

## Knowledge of God

492. [We] can know nothing except what we *directly* experience. So all
that we can anyway know relates to experience. All the creations of our mind
are but patchworks from experience. So that all our ideas are but ideas of real
or transposed experiences. A word can mean nothing except the idea it calls
up. So that we cannot even *talk* about anything but a knowable object. The
unknowable about which Hamilton and the agnostics talk can be nothing
but an Unknowable Knowable. The absolutely unknowable is a non-existent
existence. The Unknowable is a nominalistic heresy. The nominalists in
giving their adherence to that doctrine which is really held by all philosophers of all stripes, namely, that experience is all we know, understand
experience in their nominalistic sense as the mere first impressions of sense.
These "first impressions of sense" are hypothetical creations of nominalistic
metaphysics: I for one deny their existence. But anyway even if they exist,
it is not in them that experience consists. By experience must be understood
the entire mental product. Some psychologists whom I hold in respect will
stop me here to say that, while they admit that experience is more than mere
sensation, they cannot extend it to the whole mental product, since that
would include hallucinations, delusions, superstitious imaginations and fallacies of all kinds; and that they would limit experience to sense-perceptions.
But I reply that my statement is the logical one. Hallucinations, delusions,
superstitious imaginations, and fallacies of all kinds are experiences, but experiences misunderstood; while to say that all our knowledge relates merely
to sense perception is to say that we can know nothing—not even mistakenly
—about higher matters, as honor, aspirations, and love.

From Charles Sanders Peirce, *Collected Papers of Charles Sanders Peirce*, ed. Charles
Hartshorne and Paul Weiss, Vol. VI, paragraphs 492–503, pp. 338–347. Copyright 1934,
1935, by the President and Fellows of Harvard College. Used by permission of The Belknap
Press of Harvard University Press. [Footnotes omitted, Eds.]

493. Where would such an idea, say as that of God, come from, if not from direct experience? Would you make it a result of some kind of reasoning, good or bad? Why, reasoning can supply the mind with nothing in the world except an estimate of the value of a statistical ratio, that is, how often certain kinds of things are found in certain combinations in the ordinary course of experience. And scepticism, in the sense of doubt of the validity of elementary ideas—which is really a proposal to turn an idea out of court and permit no inquiry into its applicability—is doubly condemned by the fundamental principle of scientific method—condemned first as obstructing inquiry, and condemned second because it is treating some other than a statistical ratio as a thing to be argued about. No: as to God, open your eyes—and your heart, which is also a perceptive organ—and you see him. But you may ask, Don't you admit there are any delusions? Yes: I may think a thing is black, and on close examination it may turn out to be bottle-green. But I cannot think a thing is black if there is no such thing to be seen as black. Neither can I think that a certain action is self-sacrificing, if no such thing as self-sacrifice exists, although it may be very rare. It is the nominalists, and the nominalists alone, who indulge in such scepticism, which the scientific method utterly condemns.

## The Reality of God

494. The questions can be answered without very long explanations. "Do you believe in the existence of a Supreme Being?" Hume, in his *Dialogues Concerning Natural Religion,* justly points out that the phrase "Supreme Being" is not an equivalent of "God," since it neither implies infinity nor any of the other attributes of God, excepting only Being and Supremacy. This is important; and another distinction between the two designations is still more so. Namely, "God" is a vernacular word and, like all such words, but more than almost any, is *vague.* No words are so well understood as vernacular words, in one way; yet they are invariably vague; and of many of them it is true that, let the logician do his best to substitute precise equivalents in their places, still the vernacular words alone, for all their vagueness, answer the principal purposes. This is emphatically the case with the very vague word "God," which is not made less vague by saying that it imports "infinity," etc., since those attributes are at least as vague. I shall, therefore, if you please, substitute "God," for "Supreme Being" in the question.

495. I will also take the liberty of substituting "reality" for "existence." This is perhaps overscrupulosity; but I myself always use *exist* in its strict philosophical sense of "react with the other like things in the environment." Of course, in that sense, it would be fetishism to say that God "exists." The word "reality," on the contrary, is used in ordinary parlance in its correct

philosophical sense. It is curious that its legal meaning, in which we speak of "real estate," is the earliest, occurring early in the twelfth century. Albertus Magnus, who, as a high ecclesiastic, must have had to do with such matters, imported it into philosophy. But it did not become at all common until Duns Scotus, in the latter part of the thirteenth century began to use it freely. I define the *real* as that which holds its characters on such a tenure that it makes not the slightest difference what any man or men may have *thought* them to be, or ever will have *thought* them to be, here using thought to include, imagining, opining, and willing (as long as forcible *means* are not used); but the real thing's characters will remain absolutely untouched.

496. Of any kind of figment, this is not true. So, then, the question being whether I believe in the reality of God, I answer, Yes. I further opine that pretty nearly everybody more or less believes this, including many of the scientific men of my generation who are accustomed to think the belief is entirely unfounded. The reason they fall into this extraordinary error about their own belief is that they precide (or render precise) the conception, and, in doing so, inevitably change it; and such precise conception is easily shown not to be warranted, even if it cannot be quite refuted. Every concept that is vague is liable to be self-contradictory in those respects in which it is vague. No concept, not even those of mathematics, is absolutely precise; and some of the most important for everyday use are extremely vague. Nevertheless, our instinctive beliefs involving such concepts are far more trustworthy than the best established results of science, if these be precisely understood. For instance, we all think that there is an element of order in the universe. Could any laboratory experiments render that proposition more certain than instinct or common sense leaves it? It is ridiculous to broach such a question. But when anybody undertakes to say *precisely* what that order consists in, he will quickly find he outruns all logical warrant. Men who are given to defining too much inevitably run themselves into confusion in dealing with the vague concepts of common sense.

497. They generally make the matter worse by erroneous, not to say absurd, notions of the function of reasoning. Every race of animals is provided with instincts well adapted to its needs, and especially to strengthening the stock. It is wonderful how unerring these instincts are. Man is no exception in this respect; but man is so continually getting himself into novel situations that he needs, and is supplied with, a subsidiary faculty of *reasoning* for bringing instinct to bear upon situations to which it does not directly apply. This faculty is a very imperfect one in respect to fallibility; but then it is only needed to bridge short gaps. Every step has to be reviewed and criticized; and indeed this is so essential that it is best to call an uncriticized step of inference by another name. If one does not at all know how one's belief comes about, it cannot be called even by the name of inference. If, with St. Augustine, we draw the inference "I think; therefore, I am," but, when

asked how we justify this inference, can only say that we are *compelled to
think* that, since we think, we are, this uncriticized inference ought not to
be called reasoning, which at the very least conceives its inference to be one
of a general class of possible inferences on the same model, and all equally
valid. But one must go back and criticize the premisses and the *principles*
that guide the drawing of the conclusions. If it could be made out that all
the ultimate (or first) premisses were percepts; and that all the ultimate
logical principles were as clear as the principle of contradiction, then one
might say that one's conclusion was *perfectly* rational. Strictly speaking, it
would not be quite so, because it is quite possible for perception itself to
deceive us, and it is much more possible for us to be mistaken about the
indubitableness of logical principles. But as a matter of fact, as far as
logicians have hitherto been able to push their analyses, we have *in no
single case,* concerning a matter of *fact,* as distinguished from a matter of
mathematical conditional possibility, been able to reach this point. We are
in every case either forced by the inexorable critic, sooner or later, to declare,
"such and such a proposition or mode of inference I *cannot doubt;* it seems
perfectly clear that it is so, but I can't say *why,*" or else the critic himself
tires before the criticism has been pushed to its very end.

498. If you absolutely cannot doubt a proposition—cannot bring yourself,
upon deliberation, to entertain the least suspicion of the truth of it, it is
plain that there is no room to desire anything more. Many and many a
philosopher seems to think that taking a piece of paper and writing down
"I doubt that" is doubting it, or that it is a thing he can do in a minute as
soon as he decides what he wants to doubt. Descartes convinced himself that
the safest way was to "begin" by doubting everything, and accordingly he
tells us he straightway did so, except only his *je pense,* which he borrowed
from St. Augustine. Well I guess not; for genuine doubt does not talk of
*beginning* with doubting. The pragmatist knows that doubt is an art which
has to be acquired with difficulty; and his genuine doubts will go much
further than those of any Cartesian. What he does not doubt, about ordinary
matters of everybody's life, he is apt to find that no well matured man
doubts. They are part of our instincts. Instincts are now known not to be
nearly so unchangeable as used to be supposed; and the present "mutation"-
theory, which I have *always* insisted must be the way in which species have
arisen, is, I am confident, the first beginning of the correct theory, and shows
that it is no disproof of the instinctive character of a belief that it relates to
concepts which the primitive man cannot be supposed to have had. Now,
this is no confirmation of what one does not doubt. For what one does not
doubt cannot be rendered more satisfactory than it already is. Yet while I
may entertain, as far as I can search in my mind, no perceptible doubt whatever of any one of a hundred propositions, I may suspect that, among so

many, some one that is not true may have slipped in; and, if so, the marvellous inerrancy of instinct may perhaps add a little to my *general* confidence in the whole lot. However, I am far from insisting upon the point. I think the consideration is better adapted to helping us to detect the counterfeit paper doubts, of which so many are in circulation.

499. All the instinctive beliefs, I notice, are vague. The moment they are precided, the pragmatist will begin to doubt them.

500. The fourth part of the first book of Hume's *Treatise of Human Nature* affords a strong argument for the correctness of my view that reason is a mere succedaneum to be used where instinct is wanting, by exhibiting the intensely ridiculous way in which a man winds himself up in silly paper doubts if he undertakes to throw common sense, i.e., instinct, overboard and be perfectly rational. Bradley's *Appearance and Reality* is another example of the same thing, although Bradley is at the opposite pole from Hume in what he *does* admit. But Bradley is in no way as good a case as Hume. Hume endeavours to modify his conclusion by not stating it in the extreme length to which it ought to carry him. But a careful reader will see that if he proves anything at all by all his reasoning, it is that reasoning, as such, is *ipso facto* and essentially illogical, "illegitimate," and unreasonable. And the reason it is so is that either it is bad reasoning, or rests on doubtful premisses, or else that those premisses have not been thoroughly criticized. Of course not. The moment you come to a proposition which is perfectly satisfactory, so that you can entertain not the smallest suspicion of it, this fact debars you from making any genuine criticism of it. So that what Hume's argument would lead him to is that reasoning is "illegitimate" because its premisses are perfectly satisfactory. He candidly confesses that they are satisfactory to himself. But he seems to be dissatisfied with himself for being satisfied. It is easy to see, however, that he pats himself on the back, and is very well satisfied with himself for being so dissatisfied with being satisfied. Bradley's position is equally ridiculous. Another circumstance which goes toward confirming my view that instinct is the great internal source of all wisdom and of all knowledge is that all the "triumphs of science," of which that poor old nineteenth century used to be so vain, have been confined to two directions. They either consist in physical—that is, ultimately, dynamical—explanations of phenomena, or else in explaining things on the basis of our common sense knowledge of human nature. Now dynamics is nothing but an elaboration of common sense; its experiments are mere imaginary experiments. So it all comes down to common sense in these two branches, of which the one is founded on those instincts about physical forces that are required for the feeding impulsion and the other upon those instincts about our fellows that are required for the satisfaction of the reproductive impulse. Thus, then all science is nothing but an outgrowth from these two instincts.

You will see that all I have been saying is not preparatory to any argument for the reality of God. It is intended as an apology for resting the belief upon instinct as the very bedrock on which reasoning must be built.

501. I have often occasion to walk at night, for about a mile, over an entirely untravelled road, much of it between open fields without a house in sight. The circumstances are not favorable to severe study, but are so to calm meditation. If the sky is clear, I look at the stars in the silence, thinking how each successive increase in the aperture of a telescope makes many more of them visible than all that had been visible before. The fact that the heavens do not show a sheet of light proves that there are vastly more dark bodies, say planets, than there are suns. They must be inhabited, and most likely millions of them with beings much more intelligent than we are. For on the whole, the solar system seems one of the simplest; and presumably under more complicated phenomena greater intellectual power will be developed. What must be the social phenomena of such a world! How extraordinary are the minds even of the lower animals. We cannot appreciate our own powers any more than a writer can appreciate his own style, or a thinker the peculiar quality of his own thought. I don't mean that a Dante did not know that he expressed himself with fewer words than other men do, but he could not admire himself as we admire him; nor can we wonder at human intelligence as we do at that of wasps. Let a man drink in such thoughts as come to him in contemplating the physico-psychical universe without any special purpose of his own; especially the universe of mind which coincides with the universe of matter. The idea of there being a God over it all of course will be often suggested; and the more he considers it, the more he will be enwrapt with Love of this idea. He will ask himself whether or not there really is a God. If he allows instinct to speak, and searches his own heart, he will at length find that he cannot help believing it. I cannot tell how every man will think. I know the majority of men, especially educated men, are so full of pedantries—especially the male sex—that they cannot think straight about these things. But I can tell how a man must think if he is a pragmatist. Now the shower of communications that I have been getting during the last two months causes me to share the expectation that I find so many good judges are entertaining, that pragmatism is going to be the dominant philosophical opinion of the twentieth century. . . .

502. If a pragmaticist is asked what he means by the word "God," he can only say that just as long acquaintance with a man of great character may deeply influence one's whole manner of conduct, so that a glance at his portrait may make a difference, just as almost living with Dr. Johnson enabled poor Boswell to write an immortal book and a really sublime book, just as long study of the works of Aristotle may make him an acquaintance, so if contemplation and study of the physico-psychical universe can imbue a man with principles of conduct analogous to the influence of a great man's

works or conversation, then that analogue of a mind—for it is impossible to say that *any* human attribute is *literally* applicable—is what he means by "God." Of course, various great theologians explain that one cannot attribute *reason* to God, nor perception (which always involves an element of surprise and of learning what one did not know), and, in short, that his "mind" is necessarily so unlike ours, that some—though wrongly—high in the church say that it is only negatively, as being entirely different from everything else, that we can attach any meaning to the Name. This is not so; because the discoveries of science, their enabling us to *predict* what will be the course of nature, is proof conclusive that, though we cannot think any thought of God's, we can catch a fragment of His Thought, as it were.

503. Now such being the pragmaticist's answer to the question what he means by the word "God," the question whether there really *is* such a being is the question whether all physical science is merely the figment—the arbitrary figment—of the students of nature, and further whether the *one* lesson the Gautama Boodha, Confucius, Socrates, and all who from any point of view have had their ways of conduct determined by meditation upon the physico-psychical universe, be only their arbitrary notion or be the Truth behind the appearances which the frivolous man does not think of; and whether the superhuman courage which such contemplation has conferred upon priests who go to pass their lives with lepers and refuse all offers of rescue is mere silly fanaticism, the passion of a baby, or whether it is strength derived from the power of the truth. Now the only guide to the answer to this question lies in the power of the passion of love which more or less overmasters every agnostic scientist and everybody who seriously and deeply considers the universe. But whatever there may be of *argument* in all this is as nothing, the merest nothing, in comparison to its force as an appeal to one's own instinct, which is to argument what substance is to shadow, what bedrock is to the built foundations of a cathedral.

# J. N. FINDLAY

J. N. Findlay (1903–    ), Professor of Philosophy at Yale University, and formerly of the University of London, is a distinguished contemporary philosopher known for his re-examination of Hegel and as a Gifford Lecturer.

## Can God's Existence Be Disproved?[1]

*I*

The course of philosophical development has been full of attempted proofs of the existence of God. Some of these have sought a basis in the bare necessities of thought, while others have tried to found themselves on the facts of experience. And, of these latter, some have founded themselves on *very general facts,* as that something exists, or that something is in motion, while others have tried to build on *highly special facts,* as that living beings are put together in a purposive manner, or that human beings are subject to certain improbable urges and passions, such as the zeal for righteousness, the love for useless truths and unprofitable beauties, as well as the many specifically religious needs and feelings. The general philosophical verdict is that none of these "proofs" is truly compelling. The proofs based on the necessities of thought are universally regarded as fallacious: it is not thought possible to build bridges between mere abstractions and concrete existence. The proofs based on the general facts of existence and motion are only felt to be valid by a minority of thinkers, who seem quite powerless to communicate this sense of validity to others. And while most thinkers would accord weight to arguments resting on the special facts we have mentioned, they wouldn't think such arguments successful in ruling out a vast range of counter-possibilities. Religious people have, in fact, come to acquiesce in the total absence of any cogent proofs of the Being they believe in: they even find it positively satisfying that something so far surpassing clear conception

From *Language, Mind and Value* (1963). Reprinted by permission of the author and the publisher, George Allen & Unwin, Ltd., copyright holder.

[1] First published in *Mind,* April 1948. I have added a few words at one or two places to indicate that I think my argument holds for all who accept all that Kant says in criticism of the Ontological Proof, and not only for linguistic philosophers.

[212]

should also surpass the possibility of demonstration. And non-religious people willingly mitigate their rejection with a tinge of agnosticism: they don't so much deny the existence of God, as the existence of good reasons for believing in Him. We shall, however, maintain in this essay that there isn't room, in the case we are examining, for all these attitudes of tentative surmise and doubt. For we shall try to show that the Divine Existence can only be conceived, in a religiously satisfactory manner, if we also conceive it as something inescapable and necessary, whether for thought or reality. From which it follows that our modern denial of necessity or rational evidence for such an existence amounts to a demonstration that there cannot be a God.

Before we develop this argument, we must, however, give greater precision to our use of the term "God." For it is possible to say that there are nearly as many "Gods" as there are speakers and worshippers, and while existence may be confidently asserted or denied of *some* of them, we should feel more hesitant in the case of others. It is one thing, plainly, to pronounce on God's existence, if He be taken to be some ancient, shapeless stone, or if we identify Him with the bearded Father of the Sistine ceiling, and quite another matter, if we make of Him an "all-pervasive immaterial intelligence," or characterize Him in some yet more negative and analogical manner. We shall, however, choose an indirect approach, and pin God down for our purposes as the "adequate object of religious attitudes."

Plainly we find it possible to gather together, under the blanket term "religious," a large range of cases of possible action, linked together by so many overlapping [2] affinities that we are ready to treat them as the varying "expressions" of a single "attitude" or "policy." And plainly we find it possible to indicate the character of that attitude by a number of descriptive phrases which, though they may err individually by savouring too strongly of particular cases, nevertheless permit us, in their totality, to draw a rough boundary round the attitude in question. Thus we might say, for instance, that a religious attitude was one in which we tended to abase ourselves before some object, to defer to it wholly, to devote ourselves to it with unquestioning enthusiasm, to bend the knee before it, whether literally or metaphorically. These phrases, and a large number of similar ones, would make perfectly plain the sort of attitude we were speaking of, and would suffice to mark it off from cognate attitudes which are much less unconditional and extreme in their tone. Clearly similar phrases would suffice to fix the boundaries of religious *feeling*. We might describe religious frames of mind as ones in which we felt ready to abase ourselves before some object, to bend the knee before it, and so forth. Here, as elsewhere, we find ourselves indicating the *felt* character of our attitudes, by treating their inward

---

[2] This word is added to avoid the suggestion that there must be *one* pervasive affinity linking together all the actions commonly called "religious."

character as, in some sense, a concentrated and condensed substitute for appropriate lines of action, a way of speaking that accords curiously with the functional significance of the inward.[3]

But not only do we thus incorporate, in the meanings of our various names for attitudes, a reference to this readiness for appropriate lines of action: we also incorporate in these meanings a reference to *the sorts of things or situations to which these attitudes are the normal or appropriate responses.* For, as a matter of fact, our attitudes are not indifferently evoked in *any* setting: there is a range of situations in which they normally and most readily occur. And though they may at times arise in circumstances which are not in this range, they are also readily dissipated by the consciousness that such circumstances *are* unsuitable or unusual. Thus fear is an attitude very readily evoked in situations with a character of menace or potential injury, and it is also an attitude very readily allayed by the clear perception that a given situation isn't really dangerous. And anger, likewise, in an attitude provoked very readily by perverse resistance and obstructive difficulty in some object, and is also very readily dissipated, even in animals, by the consciousness that a given object is innocent of offence. All attitudes, we may say, *presume* characters in their objects, and are, in consequence, strengthened by the discovery that their objects *have* these characters, as they are weakened by the discovery that they really haven't got them.

Not only do we find this out empirically: we also incorporate it in the *meanings* of our names for attitudes. Thus attitudes are said to be "normal," "fully justified" and so forth, if we find them altered in a certain manner (called "appropriate") by our knowledge of the actual state of things, whereas we speak of them as "queer" or "senseless" or "neurotic," if they aren't at all modified by this knowledge of reality. We call it abnormal, from this point of view, to feel a deep-seated fear of mice, to rage maniacally at strangers, to greet disasters with a hebephrenic giggle, whereas we think it altogether normal to deplore deep losses deeply, or to fear grave dangers gravely. And so an implicit reference to some standard object— which makes an attitude either normal or abnormal—is part of what we ordinarily mean by all our names for attitudes, and can be rendered explicit by a simple study of usage. We can consider the circumstances in which ordinary speakers would call an attitude "appropriate" or "justified."

All that philosophy achieves in this regard is merely to push further, and develop into more considered and consistent forms, the implications of such ordinary ways of speaking. It can inquire whether an attitude would still seem justified, and its object appropriate, after we had reflected long and

---

[3] Whatever the philosophical "ground" for it may be, this plainly is the way in which we *do* describe the "inner quality" of our felt attitudes.

carefully on a certain matter, and looked at it from every wonted and un-wonted angle. Such consideration may lead philosophers to a different and more reasoned notion of the appropriate objects of a given attitude, than could be garnered from our unreflective ways of speaking. And these developments of ordinary usage will only seem unfeasible to victims of that strange modern confusion which thinks of attitudes exclusively as hidden processes "in our bosoms," with nothing but an adventitious relation to appropriate outward acts and objects.

## II

How then may we apply these notions to the case of our religious attitudes? Plainly we shall be following the natural trends of unreflective speech if we say that religious attitudes presume *superiority* in their objects, and such superiority, moreover, as reduces us, who feel the attitudes, to comparative nothingness. For having described a worshipful attitude as one in which we feel disposed to bend the knee before some object, to defer to it wholly, and the like, we find it natural to say that such an attitude can only be fitting where the object reverenced *exceeds* us very vastly, whether in power or wisdom or in other valued qualities. While it is certainly possible to worship stocks and stones and articles of common use, one does so usually on the assumption that they aren't merely stocks and stones and ordinary articles, but the temporary seats of "indwelling presences" or centres of extraordinary powers and virtues. If one realizes clearly that such things *are* merely stocks and stones or articles of common use, one can't help suffering a total vanishing or grave abatement of religious ardour.

To feel religiously is therefore to presume surpassing greatness in some object: so much characterizes the attitudes in which we bow and bend the knee, and enters into the ordinary meaning of the word "religious." But now we advance further—in company with a large number of theologians and philosophers, who have added new touches to the portrait of deity, pleading various theoretical necessities, but really concerned to make their object worthier of our worship—and ask whether it isn't wholly anomalous to worship anything *limited* in any thinkable manner. For all limited superiorities are tainted with an obvious relativity, and can be dwarfed in thought by still mightier superiorities, in which process of being dwarfed they lose their claim upon our worshipful attitudes. And hence we are led on irresistibly to demand that our religious object should have an *unsurpassable* supremacy along all avenues, that it should tower *infinitely* above all other objects. Not only are we led to demand for it such merely quantitative superiority: we also ask that it shouldn't stand surrounded by a world of *alien* objects, which owe it no allegiance, or set limits to its influence. The proper object of religious reverence must in some manner be *all-comprehensive:* there mustn't be anything capable of existing, or of displaying any virtue, without owing all of these absolutely to this single source.

All these, certainly, are difficult requirements, involving not only the obscurities and doubtful significance of the infinite, but also all the well-worn antagonism of the immanent and transcendent, of finite sinfulness and divine perfection and preordination, which centuries of theological brooding have failed to dissipate. But we are also led on irresistibly to a yet more stringent demand, which raises difficulties which make the difficulties we have mentioned seem wholly inconsiderable: we can't help feeling that the worthy object of our worship can never be a thing that merely *happens* to exist, nor one on which all other objects merely *happen* to depend. The true object of religious reverence must not be one, merely, to which no *actual* independent realities stand opposed: it must be one to which such opposition is totally *inconceivable*. God mustn't merely cover the territory of the actual, but also, with equal comprehensiveness, the territory of the possible. And not only must the existence of *other* things be unthinkable without Him, but His own non-existence must be wholly unthinkable in any circumstances. There must, in short, be no conceivable alternative to an existence properly termed "divine": God must be wholly inescapable, as we remarked previously, whether for thought or reality. So we are led on insensibly to the barely intelligible notion of a Being in whom Essence and Existence lose their separateness. And all that the great medieval thinkers really did was to carry such a development to its logical limit.

We may, however, approach the matter from a slightly different angle. Not only is it contrary to the demands and claims inherent in religious attitudes that their object should *exist* "accidentally": it is also contrary to those demands that it should *possess its various excellences* in some merely adventitious or contingent manner. It would be quite unsatisfactory from the religious standpoint, if an object merely *happened* to be wise, good, powerful and so forth, even to a superlative degree, and if other beings had, *as a mere matter of fact,* derived their excellences from this single source. An object of this sort would doubtless deserve respect and admiration, and other quasi-religious attitudes, but it would not deserve the utter self-abandonment peculiar to the religious frame of mind. It would deserve the δουλεία canonically accorded to the saints, but not the λατρεία that we properly owe to God. We might respect this object as the crowning instance of most excellent qualities, but we should incline our head before the qualities and not before the person. Wherever such qualities were manifested, though perhaps less eminently, we should always be ready to perform an essentially similar obeisance. For though such qualities might be intimately characteristic of the Supreme Being, they still wouldn't be in any sense inalienably His own. And even if other beings had, in fact, derived such qualities from this sovereign source, they still would be *their own* qualities, possessed by them in their own right. We should have no better reason to *adore* the author of such virtues, than sons have reason to adore superior parents, or pupils to adore superior teachers. For while these latter may deserve deep deference, the fact that we are coming to *participate* in their excellences renders them unworthy of our *worship*. Plainly a being that possesses and imparts desirable qualities—which other things might nevertheless have manifested though this source were totally absent—has all the utter inadequacy as a religious object which is expressed by saying that it would be *idolatrous* to worship it. Wisdom, kindness and other excellences deserve respect wherever they are manifested, but not being can appropriate them as its personal perquisites, even if it does possess them in a superlative degree. And so we are led on irresistibly, by the demands inherent in religious reverence, to hold that an adequate object of our worship must possess its various qualities *in some necessary manner*. These qualities must be intrinsically incapable of belonging to anything except in so far as they belong primarily to the object of our worship. Again we are led on to a queer and barely intelligible Scholastic doctrine, that God isn't merely good, but is in some manner indistinguishable from His own (and anything else's) goodness.

## III

What, however, are the consequences of these requirements for the possibility of God's existence? Plainly (for all who share a contemporary outlook) they entail not only that there isn't a God, but that the Divine Existence is either senseless [4] or impossible. The modern mind feels not the faintest axiomatic force in principles which trace contingent things back to some necessarily existent source, nor does it find it hard to conceive that things should display various excellent qualities without deriving them from a source which manifests them supremely. Those who believe in necessary truths which aren't merely tautological, think that such truths merely connect the *possible* instances of various characteristics with each other: they don't expect such truths to tell them whether there *will* be instances of any characteristics. This is the outcome of the whole medieval and Kantian criticism of the Ontological Proof. And, on a yet more modern view of the matter, necessity in propositions merely reflects our use of words, the arbitrary conventions of our language. On such a view the Divine Existence could only be a necessary matter if we had made up our minds to speak theistically *whatever the empirical circumstances might turn out to be*. This, doubtless, would suffice for some, who speak theistically, much as Spinoza

---

[4] I have included this alternative, of which I am not fond, merely because so many modern thinkers make use of it in this sort of connection.

spoke monistically, merely to give expression to a particular way of looking at things, or of feeling about them. It would also suffice for those who make use of the term "God" to cover whatever tendencies towards righteousness and beauty are actually included in the make-up of our world. But it wouldn't suffice for the full-blooded worshipper, who can't help finding our actual world anything but edifying, and its half-formed tendencies towards righteousness and beauty very far from adorable.

The religious frame of mind seems, in fact, to be in a quandary; it seems invincibly determined both to eat its cake and have it. It desires the Divine Existence both to have that inescapable character which can, on Kantian or modern views, only be found where truth reflects a connection of character- istics or an arbitarary convention, and also the character of "making a real difference" which is only possible where truth doesn't have this merely hypo- thetical or linguistic basis. We may accordingly deny that these approaches allow us to remain agnostically poised in regard to God: they force us to come down on the atheistic side. For if God is to satisfy religious claims and needs, He must be a being in every way inescapable, One whose existence and whose possession of certain excellences we cannot possibly conceive away. And the views in question really make it self-evidently absurd (if they don't make it ungrammatical) to speak of such a Being and attribute existence to Him. It was indeed an ill day for Anselm when he hit upon his famous proof. For on that day he not only laid bare something that is of the essence of an adequate religious object, but also something that entails its necessary non-existence.[5]

The force of our argument must not, however, be exaggerated. We haven't proved that there aren't beings of all degrees of excellence and great- ness, who may deserve attitudes approximating indefinitely to religious rev- erence. But such beings will at best be instances of valued qualities which we too may come to exemplify, though in lesser degree. Not only would it be idolatrous for us to worship them, but it would also be monstrous for them to exact worship, or to care for it. The attitude of such beings to our reverence would necessarily be deprecating: they would prefer co-operative atheists to adoring zealots. And they would probably hide themselves like royal personages from the anthems of their worshippers, and perhaps the fact that there are so few positive signs of their presence is itself a feeble evidence of their real existence. But whether such beings exist or not, they are not divine, and can never satisfy the demands inherent in religious rever- ence. The effect of our argument will further be to discredit generally such forms of religion as attach a uniquely sacred meaning to existent things, whether these things be men or acts or institutions or writings.

But there are other frames of mind, to which we shouldn't deny the name

---

[5] Or "non-significance," if this alternative is preferred.

"religious," which acquiesce quite readily in the non-existence of their objects. (This non-existence might, in fact, be taken to be the "real meaning" of saying that religious objects and realities are "not of this world.") In such frames of mind we give ourselves over unconditionally and gladly to the task of indefinite approach towards a certain imaginary focus [6] where nothing actually is, and we find this task sufficiently inspiring and satisfying without demanding (absurdly) that there should be something actual at that limit. And the atheistic religious attitude we have mentioned has also undergone reflective elaboration by such philosophers as Fichte and Erigena and Alexander. There is, then, a religious atheism which takes full stock of our arguments, and we may be glad that this is so. For since the religious spirit is one of reverence before things greater than ourselves, we should be gravely impoverished and arrested if this spirit ceased to be operative in our personal and social life. It would certainly be better that this spirit should survive, with all its fallacious existential trimmings, than that we should cast it forth merely in order to be rid of such irrelevances.

[In the Introduction to *Language, Mind and Value,* published fifteen years later, Findlay comments as follows on this essay:]

. . . I still think that it makes a valid point: that if it is *possible,* in some logical and not merely epistemological sense, that there is no God, then God's existence is not merely doubtful but *impossible,* since nothing *capable* of non-existence could be a God at all. Kant, who at times suggested that the existence of anything was a synthetic and *a posteriori* matter (though perhaps establishable only by a non-sensuous intuition) should have seen that his views constituted a *disproof* of the existence of God, not left Him a flawless ideal to which some noumenal reality *might* correspond. Professor Hartshorne has, however, convinced me that my argument permits a ready inversion, and that one can very well argue that if God's existence is in any way *possible,* then it is also *certain* and *necessary* that God exists, a position which should give some comfort to the shade of Anselm. The notion of God, like the notion of the class of all classes not members of themselves, has plainly unique logical properties, and I do not now think that my article finally *decides* how we should cope with such uniqueness.

---

[6] To use a Kantian comparison.

# NORMAN MALCOLM

Norman Malcolm (1911–    ) is Professor of Philosophy at Cornell University and is a leading proponent of British linguistic analysis. His sympathetic treatment of the ontological argument has produced a large number of responses by contemporary philosophers.

## Anselm's Ontological Arguments

I believe that in Anselm's *Proslogion* and *Responsio editoris* there are two different pieces of reasoning which he did not distinguish from one another, and that a good deal of light may be shed on the philosophical problem of "the ontological argument" if we do distinguish them. In Chapter 2 of the *Proslogion* [1] Anselm says that we believe that God is *something a greater than which cannot be conceived.* (The Latin is *aliquid quo nihil maius cogitari possit.* Anselm sometimes uses the alternative expressions *aliquid quo maius nihil cogitari potest, id quo maius cogitari nequit, aliquid quo maius cogitari non valet.*) Even the fool of the Psalm who says in his heart there is no God, when he hears this very thing that Anselm says, namely, "something a greater than which cannot be conceived," understands what he hears, and what he understands is in his understanding though he does not understand that it exists.

Apparently Anselm regards it as tautological to say that whatever is understood is in the understanding (*quidquid intelligitur in intellectu est*): he uses *intelligitur* and *in intellectu est* as interchangeable locutions. The same holds for another formula of his: whatever is thought is in thought (*quidquid cogitatur in cogitatione est*).[2]

Of course many things may exist in the understanding that do not exist in reality; for example, elves. Now, says Anselm, something a greater than which cannot be conceived exists in the understanding. But it cannot exist

From Norman Malcolm, *Knowledge and Certainty: Essays and Lectures,* © 1963. Reprinted by permission of Prentice-Hall, Inc., Englewood Cliffs, N.J., pp. 141–162.

[1] I have consulted the Latin text of the *Proslogion,* of *Gaunilonis Pro Insipiente,* and of the *Responsio editoris,* in S. Anselmi, *Opera Omnia,* edited by F. C. Schmitt (Secovii, 1938), Vol. I. With numerous modifications, I have used the English translation by S. N. Deane: *St. Anselm* (La Salle, Ill.: Open Court Publishing Co., 1948).

[2] See *Proslogion* 1 and *Responsio* 2.

*only* in the understanding, for to exist in reality is greater. Therefore that thing a greater than which cannot be conceived cannot exist only in the understanding, for then a greater thing could be conceived: namely, one that exists both in the understanding and in reality.[3]

Here I have a question. It is not clear to me whether Anselm means that (a) existence in reality by itself is greater than existence in the understanding, or that (b) existence in reality and existence in the understanding together are greater than existence in the understanding alone. Certainly he accepts (b). But he might also accept (a), as Descartes apparently does in *Meditation III* when he suggests that the mode of being by which a thing is "objectively in the understanding" is *imperfect*.[4] Of course Anselm might accept both (a) and (b). He might hold that in general something is greater if it has both of these "modes of existence" than if it has either one alone, but also that existence in reality is a more perfect mode of existence than existence in the understanding.

In any case, Anselm holds that something is greater if it exists both in the understanding and in reality than if it exists merely in the understanding. An equivalent way of putting this interesting proposition, in a more current terminology, is: something is greater if it is both conceived of and exists than if it is merely conceived of. Anselm's reasoning can be expressed as follows: *id quo maius cogitari nequit* cannot be merely conceived of and not exist, for then it would not be *id quo maius cogitari nequit*. The doctrine that something is greater if it exists in addition to being conceived of, than if it is only conceived of, could be called the doctrine that *existence is a perfection*. Descartes maintained, in so many words, that existence is a perfection,[5] and presumably he was holding Anselm's doctrine, although he does not, in *Meditation V* or elsewhere, argue in the way that Anselm does in *Proslogion* 2.

When Anselm says "And certainly, that than which nothing greater can be conceived cannot exist merely in the understanding. For suppose it exists merely in the understanding, then it can be conceived to exist in reality, which is greater," [6] he is claiming that if I conceived of a being of great excellence, that being would be *greater* (more excellent, more perfect) if it existed than if it did not exist. His supposition that "it exists merely in the understanding" is the supposition that it is conceived of but does not

---

[3] Anselm's actual words are: "Et certe id quo maius cogitari nequit, non potest esse in solo intellectu. Si enim vel in solo intellectu est, potest cogitari esse et in re, quod maius est. Si ergo id quo maius cogitari non potest, est in solo intellectu: id ipsum quo maius cogitari non potest, est quo maius cogitari potest. Sed certe hoc esse non potest." *Proslogion* 2.

[4] Haldane and Ross, *The Philosophical Works of Descartes*, Vol. I (New York: The Macmillan Company, 1931), 163.

[5] *Op. cit.*, p. 182.

[6] *Proslogion* 2, Deane, *St. Anselm*, p. 8.

exist. Anselm repeated this claim in his reply to the criticism of the monk Gaunilo. Speaking of the being a greater than which cannot be conceived, he says:

> I have said that if it exists merely in the understanding it can be conceived to exist in reality, which is greater. Therefore, if it exists merely in the understanding obviously the very being a greater than which cannot be conceived, is one a greater than which can be conceived. What, I ask, can follow better than that? For if it exists merely in the understanding, can it not be conceived to exist in reality? And if it can be so conceived does not he who conceives of this conceive of a thing greater than it, if it does exist merely in the understanding? Can anything follow better than this: that if a being a greater than which cannot be conceived exists merely in the understanding, it is something a greater than which can be conceived? What could be plainer? [7]

He is implying, in the first sentence, that if I conceive of something which does not exist then it is possible for it to exist, and *it will be greater if it exists than if it does not exist.*

The doctrine that existence is a perfection is remarkably queer. It makes sense and is true to say that my future house will be a better one if it is insulated than if it is not insulated; but what could it mean to say that it will be a better house if it exists than if it does not? My future child will be a better man if he is honest than if he is not; but who would understand the saying that he will be a better man if he exists than if he does not? Or who understands the saying that if God exists He is more perfect than if He does not exist? One might say, with some intelligibility, that it would be better (for oneself or for mankind) if God exists than if He does not—but that is a different matter.

A king might desire that his next chancellor should have knowledge, wit, and resolution; but it is ludicrous to add that the king's desire is to have a chancellor who exists. Suppose that two royal councilors, A and B, were asked to draw up separately descriptions of the most perfect chancellor they could conceive, and that the descriptions they produced were identical except that A included existence in his list of attributes of a perfect chancellor and B did not. (I do not mean that B put nonexistence in his list.) One and the same person could satisfy both descriptions. More to the point, any person who satisfied A's description would *necessarily* satisfy B's description and *vice versa!* This is to say that A and B did not produce descriptions that differed in any way but rather one and the same description of necessary and desirable qualities in a chancellor. A only made a show of putting down a desirable quality that B had failed to include.

---

[7] *Responsio* 2; Deane, *St. Anselm,* pp. 157–158.

I believe I am merely restating an observation that Kant made in attacking the notion that "existence" or "being" is a "real predicate." He says:

> By whatever and by however many predicates we may think a thing—even if we completely determine it—we do not make the least addition to the thing when we further declare that this thing *is*. Otherwise, it would not be exactly the same thing that exists, but something more than we had thought in the concept; and we could not, therefore, say that the exact object of my concept exists.[8]

Anselm's ontological proof of *Proslogion* 2 is fallacious because it rests on the false doctrine that existence is a perfection (and therefore that "existence" is a "real predicate"). It would be desirable to have a rigorous refutation of the doctrine but I have not been able to provide one. I am compelled to leave the matter at the more or less intuitive level of Kant's observation. In any case, I believe that the doctrine does not belong to Anselm's other formulation of the ontological argument. It is worth noting that Gassendi anticipated Kant's criticism when he said, against Descartes:

> Existence is a perfection neither in God nor in anything else; it is rather that in the absence of which there is no perfection. . . . Hence neither is existence held to exist in a thing in the way that perfections do, nor if the thing lacks existence is it said to be imperfect (or deprived of a perfection), so much as to be nothing.[9]

## II

I take up now the consideration of the second ontological proof, which Anselm presents in the very next chapter of the *Proslogion*. (There is no evidence that he thought of himself as offering two different proofs.) Speaking of the being a greater than which cannot be conceived, he says:

> And it so truly exists that it cannot be conceived not to exist. For it is possible to conceive of a being which cannot be conceived not to exist; and this is greater than one which can be conceived not to exist. Hence, if that, than which nothing greater can be conceived, can be conceived not to exist, it is not that than which nothing greater can be conceived. But this is a contradiction. So truly, therefore, is there something than which nothing greater can be conceived, that it cannot even be conceived not to exist.
> And this being thou art, O Lord, our God. [10]

---

[8] *The Critique of Pure Reason,* tr. by Norman Kemp Smith (New York: The Macmillan Company, 1929), p. 505.
[9] Haldane and Ross, *The Philosophical Works of Descartes,* II, 186.
[10] *Proslogion* 3; Deane, *St. Anselm,* pp. 8–9.

Anselm is saying two things: first, that a being whose nonexistence is logically impossible is "greater" than a being whose nonexistence is logically possible (and therefore that a being a greater than which cannot be conceived must be one whose nonexistence is logically impossible); second, that *God* is a being than which a greater cannot be conceived.

In regard to the second of these assertions, there certainly is *a* use of the word "God," and I think far the more common use, in accordance with which the statements "God is the greatest of all beings," "God is the most perfect being," "God is the supreme being," are *logically* necessary truths, in the same sense that the statement "A square has four sides" is a logically necessary truth. If there is a man named "Jones" who is the tallest man in the world, the statement "Jones is the tallest man in the world" is merely true and is not a logically necessary truth. It is a virtue of Anselm's unusual phrase, "a being a greater than which cannot be conceived," [11] to make it explicit that the sentence "God is the greatest of all beings" expresses a logically necessary truth and not a mere matter of fact such as the one we imagined about Jones.

With regard to Anselm's first assertion (namely, that a being whose nonexistence is logically impossible is greater than a being whose nonexistence is logically possible) perhaps the most puzzling thing about it is the use of the word "greater." It appears to mean exactly the same as "superior," "more excellent," "more perfect." This equivalence by itself is of no help to us, however, since the latter expressions would be equally puzzling here. What is required is some explanation of their use.

We do think of *knowledge,* say, as an excellence, a good thing. If A has more knowledge of algebra than B we express this in common language by saying that A has a *better* knowledge of algebra than B, or that A's knowledge of algebra is *superior* to B's, whereas we should not say that B has a better or superior *ignorance* of algebra than A. We do say "greater ignorance," but here the word "greater" is used purely quantitatively.

Previously I rejected *existence* as a perfection. Anselem is maintaining in the remarks last quoted, not that existence is a perfection, but that *the logical impossibility of nonexistence is a perfection.* In other words, *necessary existence is a perfection.* His first ontological proof uses the principle that a thing is greater if it exists than if it does not exist. His second proof employs the different principle that a thing is greater if it necessarily exists than if it does not necessarily exist.

Some remarks about the notion of *dependence* may help to make this latter principle intelligible. Many things depend for their existence on other things

---

[11] Professor Robert Calhoun has pointed out to me that a similar locution had been used by Augustine. In *De moribus Manichaeorum* (Bk. II, ch. 11, sec. 24), he says that God is a being *quo esse aut cogitari melius nihil possit* (*Patrologiae Patrum Latinorum,* J. P. Migne, ed. [Paris, 1841–1845], Vol. 32; *Augustinus,* Vol. 1).

and events. My house was built by a carpenter: its coming into existence was dependent on a certain creative activity. Its continued existence is dependent on many things: that a tree does not crush it, that it is not consumed by fire, and so on. If we reflect on the common meaning of the word "God" (no matter how vague and confused this is), we realize that it is incompatible with this meaning that God's existence should *depend* on anything. Whether we believe in Him or not we must admit that the "almighty and everlasting God" (as several ancient prayers begin), the "Maker of heaven and earth, and of all things visible and invisible" (as is said in the Nicene Creed), cannot be thought of as being brought into existence by anything or as depending for His continued existence on anything. To conceive of anything as dependent upon something else for its existence is to conceive of it as a lesser being than God.

If a housewife has a set of extremely fragile dishes, then as dishes they are *inferior* to those of another set like them in all respects except that they are *not* fragile. Those of the first set are *dependent* for their continued existence on gentle handling; those of the second set are not. There is a definite connection in common language between the notions of dependency and inferiority, and independence and superiority. To say that something which was dependent on nothing whatever was superior to ("greater than") anything that was dependent in any way upon anything is quite in keeping with the everyday use of the terms "superior" and "greater." Correlative with the notions of dependence and independence are the notions of *limited* and *unlimited*. An engine requires fuel and this is a limitation. It is the same thing to say that an engine's operation is *dependent* on as that it is *limited* by its fuel supply. An engine that could accomplish the same work in the same time and was in other respects satisfactory, but did not require fuel, would be a *superior* engine.

God is usually conceived of as an *unlimited* being. He is conceived of as a being who *could not* be limited, that is, as an absolutely unlimited being. This is no less than to conceive of *Him* as *something a greater than which cannot be conceived*. If God is conceived to be an absolutely unlimited being He must be conceived to be unlimited in regard to His existence as well as His operation. In this conception it will not make sense to say that He depends on anything for coming into or continuing in existence. Nor, as Spinoza observed, will it make sense to say that something could *prevent* Him from existing.[12] Lack of moisture can prevent trees from existing in a certain region of the earth. But it would be contrary to the concept of God as an unlimited being to suppose that anything other than God Himself could prevent Him from existing, and it would be self-contradictory to suppose that He Himself could do it.

---

[12] *Ethics,* Part I, prop. 11.

Some may be inclined to object that although nothing could prevent God's existence, still it might just *happen* that He did not exist. And if He did exist that too would be by chance. I think, however, that from the supposition that it could happen that God did not exist it would follow that, if He existed, He would have mere duration and not eternity. It would make sense to ask, "How long has He existed?" "Will He still exist next week?" "He was in existence yesterday but how about today?" and so on. It seems absurd to make God the subject of such questions. According to our ordinary conception of Him, He is an eternal being. And eternity does not mean endless duration, as Spinoza noted. To ascribe eternity to something is to exclude as senseless all sentences that imply that it has duration. If a thing has duration then it would be merely a *contingent* fact, if it was a fact, that its duration was endless. The moon could have endless duration but not eternity. If something has endless duration it will *make sense* (although it will be false) to say that it will cease to exist, and it will make sense (although it will be false) to say that something will *cause* it to cease to exist. A being with endless duration is not, therefore, an absolutely unlimited being. That God is conceived to be eternal follows from the fact that He is conceived to be an absolutely unlimited being.

I have been trying to expand the argument of *Proslogion* 3. In *Responsio* 1 Anselm adds the following acute point: if you can conceive of a certain thing and this thing does not exist then if it *were* to exist its nonexistence would be *possible*. It follows, I believe, that if the thing were to exist it would depend on other things both for coming into and continuing in existence, and also that it would have duration and not eternity. Therefore it would not be, either in reality or in conception, an unlimited being, *aliquid quo nihil maius cogitari possit.*

Anselm states his argument as follows:

> If it [the thing a greater than which cannot be conceived] can be conceived at all it must exist. For no one who denies or doubts the existence of a being a greater than which is inconceivable, denies or doubts that if it did exist its non-existence, either in reality or in the understanding, would be impossible. For otherwise it would not be a being a greater than which cannot be conceived. But as to whatever can be conceived but does not exist: if it were to exist its non-existence either in reality or in the understanding would be possible. Therefore, if a being a greater than which cannot be conceived, can even be conceived, it must exist.[13]

What Anselm has proved is that the notion of contingent existence or of contingent nonexistence cannot have any application to God. His existence must either be logically necessary or logically impossible. The only in-

---

[13] *Responsio* 1; Deane, *St. Anselm,* pp. 154–155.

telligible way of rejecting Anselm's claim that God's existence is necessary is to maintain that the concept of God, as a being a greater than which cannot be conceived, is self-contradictory or nonsensical.[14] Supposing that this is false, Anselm is right to deduce God's necessary existence from his characterization of Him as a being a greater than which cannot be conceived.

Let me summarize the proof. If God, a being a greater than which cannot be conceived, does not exist then He cannot *come* into existence. For if He did He would either have been *caused* to come into existence or have *happened* to come into existence, and in either case He would be a limited being, which by our conception of Him He is not. Since He cannot come into existence, if He does not exist His existence is impossible. If He does exist He cannot have come into existence (for the reasons given), nor can He cease to exist, for nothing could cause Him to cease to exist nor could it just happen that He ceased to exist. So if God exists His existence is necessary. Thus God's existence is either impossible or necessary. It can be the former only if the concept of such a being is self-contradictory or in some way logically absurd. Assuming that this is not so, it follows that He necessarily exists.[15]

It may be helpful to express ourselves in the following way: to say, not that *omnipotence* is a property of God, but rather that *necessary omnipotence* is; and to say, not that omniscience is a property of God, but rather that *necessary omniscience* is. We have criteria for determining that a man knows this and that and can do this and that, and for determining that one man has greater knowledge and abilities in a certain subject than another. We could think of various tests to give them. But there is nothing we should wish to describe, seriously and literally, as "testing" God's knowledge and powers. That God is omniscient and omnipotent has not

---

[14] Gaunilo attacked Anselm's argument on this very point. He would not concede that a being a greater than which cannot be conceived existed in his understanding (*Gaunilonis Pro Insipiente*, secs. 4 and 5; Deane, *St. Anselm*, pp. 148–150). Anselm's reply is: "I call on your faith and conscience to attest that this is most false" (*Responsio* 1; Deane, *St. Anselm*, p. 154). Gaunilo's faith and conscience will attest that it is false that "God is not a being a greater than which is inconceivable," and false that "He is not understood (*intelligitur*) or conceived (*cogitatur*)" (*ibid.*). Descartes remarks that one would go to "strange extremes" who denied that we understand the words "*that thing which is the most perfect that we can conceive;* for that is what all men call God" (Haldane and Ross, *The Philosophical Works of Descartes*, II, 129).

[15] [The following elegant argument occurs in *Responsio* 1: "That than which a greater cannot be conceived cannot be conceived to begin to exist. Whatever can be conceived to exist and does not exist, can be conceived to begin to exist. Therefore, that than which a greater cannot be conceived, cannot be conceived to exist and yet not exist. So if it can be conceived to exist it exists from necessity." (*Nam quo maius cogitari nequit non potest cogitari esse nisi sine initio. Quidquid autem potest cogitari esse et non est, per initium potest cogitari esse. Non ergo quo maius cogitari nequit cogitari potest esse et non est. Si ergo cogitari potest esse, ex necessitate est.*) (Schmitt, *Opera Omnia*, p. 131; Deane, *St. Anselm*, p. 154.)]

been determined by the application of criteria: rather these are requirements of our conception of Him. They are internal properties of the concept, although they are also rightly said to be properties of God. *Necessary existence* is a property of God in the *same sense* that *necessary omnipotence* and *necessary omniscience* are His properties. And we are not to think that "God necessarily exists" means that it follows necessarily from something that God exists *contingently*. The a priori proposition "God necessarily exists" entails the proposition "God exists," if and only if the latter also is understood as an a priori proposition: in which case the two propositions are equivalent. In this sense Anselm's proof is a proof of God's existence.

Descartes was somewhat hazy on the question of whether existence is a property of things that exist, but at the same time he saw clearly enough that *necessary existence* is a property of God. Both points are illustrated in his reply to Gassendi's remark, which I quoted above:

> I do not see to what class of reality you wish to assign existence, nor do I see why it may not be said to be a property as well as omnipotence, taking the word property as equivalent to any attribute or anything which can be predicated of a thing, as in the present case it should be by all means regarded. Nay, necessary existence in the case of God is also a true property in the strictest sense of the word, because it belongs to Him and forms part of His essence alone.[16]

Elsewhere he speaks of "the necessity of existence" as being "that crown of perfections without which we cannot comprehend God." [17] He is emphatic on the point that necessary existence applies solely to "an absolutely perfect Being." [18]

## III

I wish to consider now a part of Kant's criticism of the ontological argument which I believe to be wrong. He says:

> If, in an identical proposition, I reject the predicate while retaining the subject, contradiction results; and I therefore say that the former belongs necessarily to the latter. But if we reject subject and predicate alike, there is no contradiction; for nothing is then left that can be contradicted. To posit a triangle, and yet to reject its three angles, is self-contradictory; but there is no contradiction in rejecting the triangle together with its three angles. The same holds true of the concept of an absolutely necessary being. If its existence is rejected, we reject the thing itself with all its predicates; and no question of

---

[16] Haldane and Ross, *The Philosophical Works of Descartes*, II, 228.
[17] *Ibid.*, I, 445.
[18] E.g., *ibid.*, Principle 15, p. 225.

contradiction can then arise. There is nothing outside it that would then be contradicted, since the necessity of the thing is not supposed to be derived from anything external; nor is there anything internal that would be contradicted, since in rejecting the thing itself we have at the same time rejected all its internal properties. "God is omnipotent" is a necessary judgment. The omnipotence cannot be rejected if we posit a Deity, that is, an infinite being; for the two concepts are identical. But if we say "There is no God" neither the omnipotence nor any other of its predicates is given; they are one and all rejected together with the subject, and there is therefore not the least contradiction in such a judgment.[19]

To these remarks the reply is that when the concept of God is correctly understood one sees that one cannot "reject the subject." "There is no God" is seen to be a necessarily false statement. Anselm's demonstration proves that the proposition "God exists" has the same a priori footing as the proposition "God is omnipotent."

Many present-day philosophers, in agreement with Kant, declare that existence is not a property and think that this overthrows the ontological argument. Although it is an error to regard existence as a property of things that have contingent existence, it does not follow that it is an error to regard necessary existence as a property of God. A recent writer says, against Anselm, that a proof of God's existence "based on the necessities of thought" is "universally regarded as fallacious: it is not thought possible to build bridges between mere abstractions and concrete existence." [20] But this way of putting the matter obscures the distinction we need to make. Does "concrete existence" mean contingent existence? Then to build bridges between concrete existence and mere abstractions would be like inferring the existence of an island from the concept of a perfect island, which both Anselm and Descartes regarded as absurd. What Anselm did was to give a demonstration that the proposition "God necessarily exists" is entailed by the proposition "God is a being a greater than which cannot be conceived" (which is equivalent to "God is an absolutely unlimited being"). Kant declares that when "I think a being as the supreme reality, without any defect, the question still remains whether it exists or not." [21] But once one has grasped Anselm's proof of the necessary existence of a being a greater than which cannot be conceived, no question remains as to whether it exists or not, just as Euclid's demonstration of the existence of an infinity of prime numbers leaves no question on that issue.

Kant says that "every reasonable person" must admit that "all existential

---

[19] *Op. cit.,* p. 502.

[20] J. N. Findlay, "Can God's Existence Be Disproved?" *New Essays in Philosophical Theology,* A. N. Flew and A. MacIntyre, eds. (New York: The Macmillan Company, 1955), p. 47.

[21] *Op. cit.,* pp. 505–506.

propositions are synthetic." [22] Part of the perplexity one has about the
ontological argument is in deciding whether or not the proposition "God
necessarily exists" is or is not an "existential proposition." But let us look
around. Is the Euclidean theorem in number theory, "There exists an infinite
number of prime numbers," an "existential proposition"? Do we not want
to say that *in some sense* it asserts the existence of something? Cannot we
say, with equal justification, that the proposition "God necessarily exists"
asserts the existence of something, *in some sense?* What we need to understand, in each case, is the particular sense of the assertion. Neither proposition has the same sort of sense as do the propositions "A low pressure area
exists over the Great Lakes," "There still exists some possibility that he will
survive," "The pain continues to exist in his abdomen." One good way of
seeing the difference in sense of these various propositions is to see the
variously different ways in which they are proved or supported. It is wrong
to think that all assertions of existence have the same kind of meaning.
There are as many kinds of existential propositions as there are kinds of
subjects of discourse.

   Closely related to Kant's view that all existential propositions are "synthetic" is the contemporary dogma that all existential propositions are contingent. Professor Gilbert Ryle tells us that "Any assertion of the existence
of something, like any assertion of the occurrence of something, can be
denied without logical absurdity." [23] "All existential statements are contingent," says Mr. I. M. Crombie.[24] Professor J. J. C. Smart remarks that
"Existence is not a property" and then goes on to assert that "There can
never be any *logical contradiction* in denying that God exists." [25] He declares that "The concept of a logically necessary being is a self-contradictory
concept, like the concept of a round square. . . . No existential proposition
can be logically necessary," he maintains, for "the truth of a logically necessary proposition depends only on our symbolism, or to put the same thing in
another way, on the relationship of concepts" (p. 38). Professor K. E. M.
Baier says, "It is no longer seriously in dispute that the notion of a logically
necessary being is self-contradictory. Whatever can be conceived of as existing can equally be conceived of as not existing." [26] This is a repetition of
Hume's assertion, "Whatever we conceive as existent, we can also conceive
as nonexistent. There is no being, therefore, whose non-existence implies a
contradiction." [27]

---

[22] *Ibid.,* p. 504.
[23] *The Nature of Metaphysics,* D. F. Pears, ed. (New York: St. Martin's Press, Inc.,
1957), p. 150.
[24] *New Essays in Philosophical Theology,* p. 114.
[25] *Ibid.,* p. 34.
[26] *The Meaning of Life,* Inaugural Lecture, Canberra University College (Canberra,
1957), p. 8.
[27] *Dialogues Concerning Natural Religion,* Part IX.

Professor J. N. Findlay ingeniously constructs an ontological *dis*proof of God's existence, based on a "modern" view of the nature of "necessity in propositions": the view, namely, that necessity in propositions "merely reflects our use of words, the arbitrary conventions of our language." [28] Findlay undertakes to characterize what he calls "religious attitude," and here there is a striking agreement between his observations and some of the things I have said in expounding Anselm's proof. Religious attitude, he says, presumes *superiority* in its object and superiority so great that the worshiper is in comparison as nothing. Religious attitude finds it "anomalous to worship anything *limited* in any thinkable manner. . . . And hence we are led on irresistibly to demand that our religious object should have an *unsurpassable* supremacy along all avenues, that it should tower *infinitely* above all other objects" (p. 51). We cannot help feeling that "the worthy object of our worship can never be a thing that merely *happens* to exist, nor one on which all other objects merely *happen* to depend. The true object of religious reverence must not be one, merely, to which no *actual* independent realities stand opposed: it must be one to which such opposition is totally *inconceivable*. . . . And not only must the existence of *other* things be unthinkable without him, but his own non-existence must be wholly unthinkable in any circumstances" (p. 52). And now, says Findlay, when we add up these various requirements, what they entail is "not only that there isn't a God, but that the Divine Existence is either senseless or impossible" (p. 54). For on the one hand, "if God is to satisfy religious claims and needs, He must be a being in every way inescapable, One whose existence and whose possession of certain excellences we cannot possibly conceive away." On the other hand, "modern views make it self-evidently absurd (if they don't make it ungrammatical) to speak of such a Being and attribute existence to Him. It was indeed an ill day for Anselm when he hit upon his famous proof. For on that day he not only laid bare something that is of the essence of an adequate religious object, but also something that entails its necessary non-existence" (p. 55).

Now I am inclined to hold the "modern" view that logically necessary truth "merely reflects our use of words" (although I do not believe that the conventions of language are always *arbitrary*). But I confess that I am unable to see how that view is supposed to lead to the conclusion that "the Divine existence is either senseless or impossible." Findlay does not explain how this result comes about. Surely he cannot mean that this view entails that nothing can have necessary properties: for this would imply that mathematics is "senseless or impossible," which no one wants to hold. Trying to fill in the argument that is missing from his article, the most plausible conjecture I can make is the following: Findlay thinks that the view that logical

---

[28] Findlay, *op. cit.*, p. 154.

necessity "reflects the use of words" implies, not that nothing has necessary properties, but that *existence* cannot be a necessary property of anything. That is to say, every proposition of the form *"x exists,"* including the proposition "God exists," must be *contingent.*[29] At the same time, our concept of God requires that His existence be *necessary,* that is, that "God exists" be a necessary truth. Therefore, the modern view of necessity proves that what the concept of God requires *cannot* be fulfilled. It proves that God *cannot* exist.

The correct reply is that the view that logical necessity merely reflects the use of words cannot possibly have the implication that every existential proposition must be contingent. That view requires us to *look at* the use of words and not manufacture a priori theses about it. In the Ninetieth Psalm it is said: "Before the mountains were brought forth, or ever thou hadst formed the earth and the world, even from everlasting to everlasting, thou art God." Here is expressed the idea of the necessary existence and eternity of God, an idea that is essential to the Jewish and Christian religions. In those complex systems of thought, those "languages-games," God has the status of a necessary being. Who can doubt that? Here we must say with Wittgenstein, "This language-game is played!" [30] I believe we may rightly take the existence of those religious systems of thought in which God figures as a necessary being to be a disproof of the dogma, affirmed by Hume and others, that no existential proposition can be necessary.

Another way of criticizing the ontological argument is the following: "Granted that the concept of necessary existence follows from the concept of a being a greater than which cannot be conceived, this amounts to no more than granting the *a priori* truth of the *conditional* proposition, 'If such a being exists then it necessarily exists.' This proposition, however, does not entail the *existence of anything,* and one can deny its antecedent without contradiction." Kant, for example, compares the proposition (or "judgment," as he calls it) "A triangle has three angles" with the proposition "God is a necessary being." He allows that the former is "absolutely necessary" and goes on to say:

> The absolute necessity of the judgment is only a conditional necessity of the thing, or of the predicate in the judgment. The above proposition does not declare that three angles are absolutely necessary, but that, under the condition that there is a triangle (that is, that a triangle is given), three angles will necessarily be found in it.[31]

---

[29] The other philosophers I have just cited may be led to this opinion by the same thinking. Smart, for example, says that "the truth of a logically necessary proposition depends only on our symbolism, or to put the same thing in another way, on the relationship of concepts" (*supra*). This is very similar to saying that it "reflects our use of words."

[30] *Philosophical Investigations* (New York: The Macmillan Company, 1953), sec. 654.

[31] *Op. cit.,* pp. 501–502.

He is saying, quite correctly, that the proposition about triangles is equivalent to the conditional proposition "If a triangle exists, it has three angles." He then makes the comment that there is no contradiction "in rejecting the triangle together with its three angles." He proceeds to draw the alleged parallel: "The same holds true of the concept of an absolutely necessary being. If its existence is rejected, we reject the thing itself with all its predicates; and no question of contradiction can then arise." [32] The priest, Caterus, made the same objection to Descartes when he said:

> Though it be conceded that an entity of the highest perfection implies its existence by its very name, yet it does not follow that that very existence is anything actual in the real world, but merely that the concept of existence is inseparably united with the concept of highest being. Hence you cannot infer that the existence of God is anything actual, unless you assume that that highest being actually exists; for then it will actually contain all its perfections, together with this perfection of real existence.[33]

I think that Caterus, Kant, and numerous other philosophers have been mistaken in supposing that the proposition "God is a necessary being" (or "God necessarily exists") is equivalent to the conditional proposition "If God exists then He necessarily exists." [34] For how do they want the antecedent clause "*If* God exists" to be understood? Clearly they want it to imply that it is *possible* that God does *not* exist.[35] The whole point of Kant's

---

[32] *Ibid.*, p. 502.

[33] Haldane and Ross, *The Philosophical Works of Descartes,* II, 7.

[34] I have heard it said by more than one person in discussion that Kant's view was that it is really a misuse of language to speak of a "necessary being," on the grounds that necessity is properly predicated only of propositions (judgments) not of *things*. This is not a correct account of Kant. (See his discussion of "The Postulates of Empirical Thought in General," *op. cit.,* pp. 239–256, esp. p. 239 and pp. 247–248.) But if he had held this, as perhaps the above philosophers think he should have, then presumably his view would not have been that the pseudo-proposition "God is a necessary being" is equivalent to the conditional "If God exists then He necessarily exists." Rather his view would have been that the genuine proposition " 'God exists' is necessarily true" is equivalent to the condition "If God exists then He exists" (*not* "If God exists then He necessarily exists," which would be an illegitimate formulation, on the view imaginatively attributed to Kant). "If God exists then He exists then He exists" is a foolish tautology which says nothing different from the tautology "If a new earth satellite exists then it exists." If "If God exists then He exists" were a correct analysis of " 'God exists' is necessarily true," then "If a new earth satellite exists then it exists" would be a correct analysis of " 'A new earth satellite exists' is necessarily true." If the *analysans* is necessarily true then the *analysandum* must be necessarily true, provided the analysis is correct. If this proposed Kantian analysis of " 'God exists' is necessarily true" were correct, we should be presented with the consequence that not only is it necessarily true that God exists, but also it is necessarily true that a new earth satellite exists, which is absurd.

[35] When summarizing Anselm's proof (in Part II, *supra*) I said: "If God exists He necessarily exists." But there I was merely stating an entailment. "If God exists" did not have the implication that it is possible He does not exist. And of course I was not regarding the conditional as *equivalent* to "God necessarily exists."

analysis is to try to show that it is possible to "reject the subject." Let us make this implication explicit in the conditional proposition, so that it reads: "If God exists (and it is possible that He does not) then He necessarily exists." But now it is apparent, I think, that these philosophers have arrived at a self-contradictory position. I do not mean that this conditional proposition, taken alone, is self-contradictory. Their position is self-contradictory in the following way. On the one hand, they agree that the proposition "God necessarily exists" is an a priori truth; Kant implies that it is "absolutely necessary," and Caterus says that God's existence is implied by His very name. On the other hand, they think that it is correct to analyze this proposition in such a way that it will entail the proposition "It is possible that God does not exist." But so far from its being the case that the proposition "God necessarily exists" entails the proposition "It is possible that God does not exist," it is rather the case that they are *incompatible* with one another! Can anything be clearer than the conjunction "God necessarily exists but it is possible that He does not exist" is self-contradictory? Is it not just as plainly self-contradictory as the conjunction "A square necessarily has four sides but it is possible for a square not to have four sides"? In short, this familiar criticism of the ontological argument is self-contradictory, because it accepts *both* of two incompatible propositions.[36]

One conclusion we may draw from our examination of this criticism is that (contrary to Kant) there is a lack of symmetry, in an important respect, between the propositions "A triangle has three angles" and "God has necessary existence," although both are a priori. The former can be expressed in the conditional assertion "If a triangle exists (and it is possible that none does) it has three angles." The latter cannot be expressed in the corresponding conditional assertion without contradiction.

## IV

I turn to the question of whether the idea of a being a greater than which cannot be conceived is self-contradictory. Here Leibniz made a contribution to the discussion of the ontological argument. He remarked that the argument of Anselm and Descartes

> is not a paralogism, but it is an imperfect demonstration, which assumes something that must still be proved in order to render it mathematically evident; that is, it is tacitly assumed that this idea of the all-great or all-perfect being

---

[36] This fallacious criticism of Anselm is implied in the following remarks by Gilson: "To show that the affirmation of necessary existence is analytically implied in the idea of God, would be . . . to show that God is necessary if He exists, but would not prove that He does exist" (E. Gilson, *The Spirit of Medieval Philosophy* [New York: Charles Scribner's Sons, 1940], p. 62).

is possible, and implies no contradiction. And it is already something that by this remark it is proved that, assuming that God is possible, he exists, which is the privilege of divinity alone.[37]

Leibniz undertook to give a proof that God is possible. He defined a *perfection* as a simple, positive quality in the highest degree.[38] He argued that since perfections are *simple* qualities they must be compatible with one another. Therefore the concept of a being possessing all perfections is consistent.

I will not review his argument because I do not find his definition of a perfection intelligible. For one thing, it assumes that certain qualities or attributes are "positive" in their intrinsic nature, and others "negative" or "primitive," and I have not been able to clearly understand that. For another thing, it assumes that some qualities are intrinsically simple. I believe that Wittgenstein has shown in the *Investigations* that nothing is *intrinsically* simple, but that whatever has the status of a simple, an indefinable, in one system of concepts, may have the status, of a complex thing, a definable thing, in another system of concepts.

I do not know how to demonstrate that the concept of God—that is, of a being a greater than which cannot be conceived—is not self-contradictory. But I do not think that it is legitimate to demand such a demonstration. I also do not know how to demonstrate that either the concept of a material thing or the concept of *seeing* a material thing is not self-contradictory, and philosophers have argued that both of them are. With respect to any particular reasoning that is offered for holding that the concept of seeing a material thing, for example, is self-contradictory, one may try to show the invalidity of the reasoning and thus free the concept from the charge of being self-contradictory *on that ground*. But I do not understand what it would mean to demonstrate *in general,* and not in respect to any particular reasoning, that the concept is not self-contradictory. So it is with the concept of God. I should think there is no more of a presumption that it is self-contradictory than is the concept of seeing a material thing. Both concepts have a place in the thinking and the lives of human beings.

But even if one allows that Anselm's phrase may be free of self-contradiction, one wants to know how it can have any *meaning* for anyone. Why is it that human beings have even *formed* the concept of an infinite being, a being a greater than which cannot be conceived? This is a legitimate and important question. I am sure there cannot be a deep understanding of that concept without an understanding of the phenomena of human life that give rise to it. To give an account of the latter is beyond my ability. I

---

[37] *New Essays Concerning the Human Understanding,* Bk. IV, ch. 10; A. G. Langley, ed. (La Salle, Ill.: Open Court Publishing Company, 1949), p. 504.
[38] See *Ibid.,* Appendix X, p. 714.

wish, however, to make one suggestion (which should not be understood as autobiographical).

There is the phenomenon of feeling guilt for something that one has done or thought or felt or for a disposition that one has. One wants to be free of this guilt. But sometimes the guilt is felt to be so great that one is sure that nothing one could do oneself, nor any forgiveness by another human being, would remove it. One feels a guilt that is beyond all measure, a guilt "a greater than which cannot be conceived." Paradoxically, it would seem, one nevertheless has an intense desire to have this incomparable guilt removed. One requires a forgiveness that is beyond all measure, a forgiveness "a greater than which cannot be conceived." Out of such a storm in the soul, I am suggesting, there arises the conception of a forgiving mercy that is limitless, beyond all measure.[39] This is one important feature of the Jewish and Christian conception of God.

I wish to relate this thought to a remark made by Kierkegaard, who was speaking about belief in Christianity but whose remark may have a wider application. He says:

> There is only one proof of the truth of Christianity and that, quite rightly, is from the emotions, when the dread of sin and a heavy conscience torture a man into crossing the narrow line between despair bordering upon madness—and Christendom.[40]

One may think it absurd for a human being to feel a guilt of such magnitude, and even more absurd that, if he feels it, he should *desire* its removal. I have nothing to say about that. It may also be absurd for people to fall in love, but they do it. I wish only to say that there *is* that human phenomenon of an unbearably heavy conscience and that it is importantly connected with the genesis of the concept of God, that is, with the formation of the "grammar" of the word "God." I am sure that this concept is related to human experience in other ways. If one had the acuteness and depth to perceive these connections one could grasp the *sense* of the concept. When we encounter this concept as a problem in philosophy, we do not consider the human phenomena that lie behind it. It is not surprising that many philosophers believe that the idea of a necessary being is an arbitrary and absurd construction.

What is the relation of Anselm's ontological argument to religious belief? This is a difficult question. I can imagine an atheist going through the argu-

---

[39] [*Psalm* 116: "The sorrows of death compassed me, and the pains of hell gat hold upon me: I found trouble and sorrow. Then called I upon the name of the Lord; O Lord, I beseech thee, deliver my soul."
*Psalm* 130: "Out of the depths have I cried unto thee, O Lord."]

[40] *The Journals*, tr. by A. Dru (New York: Oxford University Press, 1938), sec. 926.

ment, becoming convinced of its validity, acutely defending it against objections, yet remaining an atheist. The only effect it could have on the fool of the Psalm would be that he stopped saying in his heart "There is no God," because he would now realize that this is something he cannot meaningfully say or think. It is hardly to be expected that a demonstrative argument should, in addition, produce in him a living faith. Surely there is a level at which one can view the argument as a piece of logic, following the deductive moves but not being touched religiously? I think so. But even at this level the argument may not be without religious value, for it may help to remove some philosophical scruples that stand in the way of faith. At a deeper level, I suspect that the argument can be thoroughly understood only by one who has a view of that human "form of life" that gives rise to the idea of an infinitely great being, who views it from the *inside* not just from the outside and who has, therefore, at least some inclination to *partake* in that religious form of life. This inclination, Kierkegaard's words, is "from the emotions." This inclination can hardly be an *effect* of Anselm's argument, but is rather presupposed in the fullest understanding of it. It would be unreasonable to require that the recognition of Anselm's demonstration as valid must produce a conversion.[41]

---

[41] [Since the appearance of this essay many acute criticisims of it have been published or communicated to me in private correspondence. In *The Philosophical Review*, LXX, No. 1, January 1961, there are the following articles: Raziel Abelson, "Not Necessarily"; R. E. Allen, "The Ontological Argument"; Paul Henle, "Uses of the Ontological Argument"; Gareth B. Matthews, "On Conceivability in Anselm and Malcolm"; Alvin Plantinga, "A Valid Ontological Argument?"; Terence Penelhum, "On the Second Ontological Argument." Some other published articles are: Jan Berg, "An Examination of the Ontological Proof," *Theoria*, XXVII, No. 3 (1961); T. P. Brown, "Professor Malcolm on 'Anselm's Ontological Arguments,'" *Analysis*, October 1961; W. J. Huggett, "The Nonexistence of Ontological Arguments," *The Philosophical Review*, LXXI, No. 3, July 1962; Jerome Shaffer, "Existence, Prediction, and the Ontological Argument," *Mind*, LXXI, No. 283, July 1962. It would be a major undertaking to attempt to reply to all of the criticisms, and I hope that my not doing so will not be construed as a failure to appreciate them. I do not know that it is possible to meet all of the objections; on the other hand, I do not know that it is impossible.]

# CHARLES HARTSHORNE

*Charles Hartshorne* (1897–    ), Professor of Philosophy at the University of Texas, is the outstanding advocate in the United States of the metaphysics of Alfred N. Whitehead and is a careful student of the ontological argument.

## The Necessarily Existent

Where would such an idea, say as that of God, come from, if not from direct experience? . . . No: as to God, open your eyes—and your heart, which is also a perceptive organ—and you see him. But you may ask, Don't you admit there are any delusions? Yes: I may think a thing is black, and on close examination it may turn out to be bottle-green. But I cannot think a thing is black if there is no such thing as black. Neither can I think that a certain action is self-sacrificing, if no such thing as self-sacrifice exists, although it may be very rare. It is the nominalists, and the nominalists alone, who indulge in such skepticism, which the scientific method utterly condemns.

CHARLES SANDERS PEIRCE,
in *Collected Papers*, Vol. VI

The ontological argument turns logically upon the unique relation between the possibility and the actuality, the "essence" and the "existence," of God. With ordinary finite ideas the task of knowledge is to decide among three cases: (1) the type of thing conceived is impossible, and hence nonexistent (e.g., a moral being totally without "freedom"); (2) the type of thing is possible, but there is no actual example (a Euclidean space?); (3) the thing is possible, and there is an example (a speaking animal). The ontological argument holds that with the idea of God only two of these three cases need be considered, since one of the three, (2), is meaningless. If, the argument holds, there exists no God, then there also can be no possibility of the existence of a God, and the concept is nonsense, like that of "round square." If, further, it can be shown that the idea of God is not nonsensical, that it must have an at least possible object, then it follows that it has an actual object, since a "merely possible" God is, if the argument is

From *Man's Vision of God* (1941). Harper & Row, Inc., Publishers. Reprinted by permission of the author.

sound, inconceivable. *Where impossibility and mere unactualized possibility are both excluded, there nothing remains but actuality, if the idea has any meaning at all.*

The ontological argument itself does not suffice to exclude the impossibility or meaninglessness of God, but only to exclude his mere possibility. Or, as Leibniz said, it must assume that God is not impossible. (We shall consider presently whether the argument can be extended so as to justify this assumption.) The inventor of the argument, Anselm, took it for granted that the man with religious experience, to whom he addressed his discourse, though he may doubt God's existence, will not easily doubt that in hoping that there is a God he is at least hoping for something with a self-consistent meaning. Now, given a meaning, there must be something which is meant. We do not think just our act of thinking. What we think may not be actual, but can it be less than possible—unless it be a self-contradictory combination of factors, singly and separately possible? In short, when we think, can we fail to refer to something beyond our thought which, either as a whole or in its elements, is at least possible? Granting this, the ontological argument says that, with reference to God, "at least possible" is indistinguishable from "possible *and* actual" (though, as we shall see, "possible" here means simply "not impossible" and has no positive content different from actuality). Let us now present the reasons for the contention that "at least possible" and "actual" are indistinguishable in the case of the divine.

According to one theory of possibility, a given type of entity is possible if the most general features, the strictly generic characters, of existence or of the universe are compatible with the production of such an entity. Thus, there is no contradiction of the most general features of reality in the supposition that nature has really produced Mr. Micawber. There is contradiction of the details of nature (such as the detail that Micawber is a character in a novel written by a highly imaginative author), but these may be supposed otherwise without destroying the meaning, the generic content, of "existence." But the idea of God is the idea of a being everlasting in duration, and independent, in a certain aspect of his being (in his individual "essence"), from everything else. Such a being could not be produced, since he must then be both derivative and underivative, everlasting and yet not everlasting. To create the omniscient, one must endow him with a perfect memory of the past before he existed; to create the omnipotent, one must endow him with incomparably more power, a metaphysically different order of power, than that which created him. It is hardly necessary to prolong the discussion: no theologian holding either type-one or type-two theism has ever rejected that portion of the ontological argument which consists in the proof that *God could not be a mere possibility;* and (as we are about to show) it is demonstrable that in order to reject this proof one must construct a theory of possibility which would not be required for ordinary purposes, so that the tables may be turned upon those who accuse the argument of making God an exception to all principles of knowledge. The argument does make God an exception, but only in the sense that it *deduces* this exceptional status from a generally applicable theory of possibility together with the definition of God. Nothing else is required. The opposition, on the contrary, sets up a general principle which, but for God and the desire to avoid asserting his existence (as following from his possibility), would be without merit.

It might, however, be thought that "possible" need not mean the consistency of the supposition of the thing's being produced, or of its coming into existence due to some cause. Only with one type of thing, it may be held, does "possible" mean this. With another type, consisting of things with universal extent in time, a thing either just always exists or just always lacks existence, either status being possible, although no temporal cause could conceivably effect the difference.

I submit that this is a view so paradoxical that it would hardly be considered at all but for two reasons. One is that it invalidates the ontological argument. The other is that it lends color to the supposition that the laws of nature discoverable by science are eternal laws, although their nonexistence is logically possible, and although, as eternal, they could never have been produced, constituting, as they do, the very machinery of all production, the presupposition of all events. The alternative to this supposition about laws is the idea that the laws of nature with which physics deals are themselves produced by the cosmic process, the most general principles of which are beyond "law" in this sense. (There must be some sort of law governing the production of laws, but this higher law is of another order, and may be conceived as the aesthetic principle of the value of order as such, and of the no less real value of a certain element of freedom and disorder, of surprise and novelty, as well as repetition and predictability.) On this view, nothing is possible and at the same time not actual unless at some stage of the cosmic evolution the forces were such that there is no contradiction in the idea of their having taken a turn which sooner or later would have led to the production of the thing in question. Thus, if nature had developed other habits—and who shall say she could not have?—other "laws" would have obtained. But clearly God could not be possible in this way, and he is the *only consistently conceivable object which must be conceived as unproduced,* a reality always existing or never existing or even capable of existing, either in essence uncaused or a mere nonentity.

The old objection that if a perfect being must exist then a perfect island or a perfect devil must exist is not perhaps very profound. For it is answered simply by denying that anyone can conceive perfection, in the strict sense employed by the argument, to be possessed by an island or a devil. A perfect devil would have at the same time to be infinitely responsible for all that exists besides itself, and yet infinitely averse to all that exists. It would have to attend with unrivaled care and patience and fullness of realization to the lives of all other beings (which must depend for existence upon this care), and yet it must hate all these things with matchless bitterness. It must savagely torture a cosmos every item of which is integral with its own being, united to it with a vivid intimacy such as we can only dimly imagine. In short, whether a perfect God is sense or nonsense, a perfect devil is unequivocally nonsense, and it is of no import whether the nonsensical does or does not necessarily exist, since in any case it necessarily does not exist, and its existence would be nothing, even though a necessary nothing. Clearly, again, an island is not in essence unproducible and self-sufficient. Of course one can arbitrarily put concepts together and suppose that an island which could never be destroyed and had never been produced would be better than one capable of production, since some form of eternal life might go on upon it, undisturbed by any possibility of an end to such a world. But it is not apparent what would make such a world an island, if the "waters" which "washed" it never wore its shores, and if it were not a part of the surface of a body in space surrounded by other bodies capable of smashing it to pieces, and were not composed of particles capable of ultimately separating, etc. The question is if such a conception would in the end be distinguishable from the idea of the cosmos as the perpetually renewed body of God, that is, not an island in the least, but an aspect of the very idea of God whose self-existence is upheld by the argument.

The question is, Can a possibility be real, unless it would, *if* actual, be an effect of a cause which is real, or the effect of a possible cause which, if actual, would itself be the effect of a cause which . . . (the series ultimately terminating in a cause which is real)? Otherwise, possibility is something wholly apart from actuality, something no experience could ever reveal or evidence support.

I may be told that "logical possibility" is simply self consistency and that no further reality than this consistency is required. But the reply is that the meanings whose consistency is granted must mean something, and this referent of the meanings is not the consistency but the pre-supposition of there being any meanings, consistent or otherwise. If a consistent meaning means something, but something not even possible, then it means something very odd indeed. If it means only its own consistency, then it is really meaningless.

Let us be empirical. I may think of any object of any color I choose; will it be denied that an object of this color is consistently conceivable as a production of "nature"? In fact, of course, objects of at least approximately the same color have been actually given in my experience. The step "from thought to reality" is merely the reverse reading of the step from reality to thought without which there is no thought, as the very logicians who attack the ontological argument on the ground that it seeks to "derive existence from a mere idea" would be the first to grant. We are always in contact with the forces which produce realities, and hence we can think both actual and possible objects. Or, in other terms, we can distinguish, in the reality some portion of which is always given to us, between the essential or generic features and the details, and can see that this distinction implies that mutually incompatible details are both or all compatible (separately, though not together) with the generic features. But God is not a detail, and only contradiction results from trying to make his possibility conceivable in the fashion in which alone mere possibility is ever really conceived.

We may go further. The reason God is not a detail, whose existence would be one of two equally conceivable alternatives, is that he is really the content of "existence," the generic factor of the universe. To conceive God is not to conceive what might exist, but what "existence" itself must be—if the idea of God is not meaningless. Either God is nothing at all, or all else that exists exists in and through him, and therefore contingently, and he himself exists (in his essence, though not in his accidents) solely in and through himself, that is, necessarily. The cosmological argument showed that only "God" makes clearly conceivable the flexibility of the generic features of existence by which alternative details of existence can, as alternatives, be real. Alternativeness is one way of looking at creativeness, and the essential or cosmic creativeness is the divine, and nothing else.

Thus to make God's existence exceptional in relation to his conceivability is a result, not a violation, of the general principle of existence. Whatever is merely possible, this possibility as such is real, is other than nothing, only thanks to something which itself is not merely possible but is reality itself as self-identical, or as that which, being the ground of possibility, is more than merely possible. It is an implication of the idea of God that he is that ground.

At some point potentiality and actuality must touch, and at some point meaning must imply existence. God is the general, the cosmic and everlasting, the essential or a priori case of the unity of essence and existence, and he is this because he is supreme potentiality as existing power, a real agent who eternally does one or other of various pairs of alternatives which he "can" do. All meaning implicitly asserts God, because all meaning is nothing less than a reference to one or other of the two aspects of the cosmic reality, what it *has* done or what it *could* do—that is, to the consequent or primordial natures of God.

It has been objected to the ontological argument that existence is not a predicate, and hence cannot be implied by the predicate "perfection." But if existence is not a predicate, yet the *mode* of a thing's existence—its contingency or necessity of existence—is included in every predicate whatever. To be an atom is essentially to be a contingent product of forces which were also capable of not producing the atom, and doubtless for long ages did not do so. Again, contingent existence (the equal compatibility with existence or its negative) is implied by such predicates as those describing a man. His weaknesses imply that it is not true that he is the master of existence, able to exist through his own resources. The strength of God implies the opposite relation to existence. "Self-existence" is a predicate which necessarily and uniquely belongs to God, for it is part of the predicate divinity. It is part of the nature of ordinary causes that they are themselves effect of causes which antedate them. It is part of the nature of supreme causality that it is coextensive in time with all causal action. (Not that God's action is in no sense affected by causes, for the law of action and reaction may apply to God; but simply that God, as an individual, cannot have originated out of pre-existent individuals. His existence is uncaused, whether or not all his properties are. Or, otherwise expressed, his essential properties, being one with his existence, have no ground in other individuals; but he may be subject, in spite of the Thomists, to accidents whose explanation is in part to be sought in the accidents occurring in other individuals.) To be God is essentially to be the supreme productive force itself, unproduced and unproducible (except in its accidents) by any force whatsoever. Hence either God is actual, or there is nothing which could be meant by his possible existence. Thus that God's essence should imply his existential status (as contingent or necessary) is not an exception to the rule, but an example of it, since the rule is that contingency or non-contingency of existence follows from the kind of thing in question.

There is another way in which the argument illustrates rather than violates general principles. The argument is not that God's individual nature implies his existence, while other individual natures do not. It may reasonably be held that every individual nature implies existence, and indeed is an existence. By regarding possibilities alone, one can never reach any truly individual character. Individuation and actualization are inseparable by any test, since individuals as such are known only by pointing. Description of contingent things gives always a class quality, unless in the description is included some reference to the space-time world which itself is identified as "this" world, not by description. But "perfection," as we shall see presently, is the one description which defines no class, not even a "one-membered" one, but either nothing or else an individual. If, then, it is true, as it seems to be, that mere possibility is always a matter of class, then the perfect being, which is no class, is either impossible or actual—there being no fourth status.

But if every individual quality implies existence, must not all individuals exist necessarily? The answer is that contingency is not a relation of existence to a thing, but of a thing to existence. To say a thing might not exist is not to say there might be the thing without existence. It is rather to say there might be existence without the thing. To pass from the actual to what might be is to generalize, ultimately to refer to the uttermost generalities. It is the world (in its generic features) which does not imply its contingent inhabitants, not the inhabitants which do not imply the world with themselves as its existing parts. They do imply it. Without it they, as individuals, would not be, even as possible. There is an unutilized possibility of individuals, but not an individuality of the unutilized possibility. Mr. Micawber is a quasi-individual, with some of the aesthetic properties of an individual, but not an individual in the strict sense. He is a class, specific enough to simulate an individual for the purposes of the aesthetic illusion or "make-believe."

The unique status of God is that no distinction can be drawn between any individual having perfection and any other. Every perfect being must have the same space-time locus (omnipresence), and must know the same things—all there are to know. If there had been another world, the God of this our world would have known it, for the very possibility of another world can be related to God only as something *he* (not some other God) could have done or can still do. Hence "the perfect" is no class of possibilities, all of which might be unactual, but only an individual character belonging to nothing, not even potentially (for the only individuality that could be involved is already involved), or else belonging to the one real perfect individual.

The necessary being is, then, that individual which existence implies, and which itself implies, not simply existence (for every individual does that), but implies, through the identity of its generic with its individual character, that (so far as its primordial nature is concerned) there is in its case no separation between possibility and actuality, the class and the individual. In other words, "perfection" implies that existence itself necessarily contains a real perfection, or that existence, in its cosmically essential features, *is* perfection as existent, as the unity of being and possibility. Or, perfection implies that existence, any and all existence, implies the existence of perfection as its ground.

Again, to conceive a thing in two alternative states, actual and possible, is to conceive something common to these two states, as well as something different. But between the world with God and the world without God no common feature could be found. For the world with God is the world completely dependent upon the existence of God, for both its actuality and its possibility, and hence it follows that in the absence of God nothing of the world as it would be with God could be identified.

Doubtless these are all ways of construing the one simple principle: nothing but existent perfection could make perfection possible, or rather, perfection cannot have the dependent relation to other things implied by the status of mere possibility, but must have either the status of an impossible idea or pseudo-idea, or else must be simply actual, with no alternative of non-actual possibility at all.

If it be thought suspicious that the ontological argument argues from a unique relation of God to existence (though one deduced from the normal relation plus the definition of perfection), let it be remembered that, by definition, God's relation to every question is unique. He is the unique being, unique because maximal, the only unsurpassed and unsurpassable being (in senses A and R). Naturally, God's relation to existence is maximal also, that is, he exists under all possible circumstances, times, and places, in other words, necessarily. That which would exist, if at all, necessarily, cannot be non-existent and yet possible, for this would mean having existence as a contingent alternative, and a contingent alternative cannot be necessary. To object to this is to object to the idea of God, and not merely to the affirmation, "There is a being corresponding to the idea."

If all individuals are contingent, then the whole of existence is contingent, and it might be that nothing existed, or it might be true (though nonsensical) that there was nothing of which any proposition would be true. Furthermore, what could constitute the identity of existence as such, if not an eternal and necessary individual manifested in all individuals? We human beings tend to carry our own personality with us in all our hypotheses, in so far as we say to ourselves, Suppose *I* were to experience so and so. This gives an aspect of identity by which we might try to define existence as such. But the definition would be solipsistic. Hence there must be some further aspect of identity, like ourselves in being a concrete existent, but unlike us in being able to constitute the unity, the all-embracing register of existence itself, without limitation upon conceivable variety and independence. This is what God is, the all-embracing register of existence, perfect in his flexible and tolerant ("merciful") sensitivity to all experiences, who can see things as they see themselves, also as other things see them, and also as they are related without distinct awareness on the part either of themselves or of other imperfect things.

It is to the credit of the ontological argument that it has to be opposed by making an absolute disjunction between meaning and its referent, reality, or between universals and individuals, a disjunction *at no point* mediated by a higher principle. Only if there is *one* actual individual whose presence is universal, have universals an intelligible ground in actuality. Otherwise we have to relate mere universals and mere individuals by—what? Ordinary individuals, being non-universal in their relevance, cannot explain the identity of the universals as such. Aristotelian objections to disembodied universals can be sustained only if there be a universal embodiment, a "concrete" universal so far as present actuality is concerned, though a universal which is also (contrary to Hegelianism) abstract so far as the future and potentiality are involved.

Thus there is not from any point of view good reason to object to the exceptional status of God's existence, every reason to welcome it as the completion of the theory of meaning.

It is often said (and with an air of great wisdom) that a "mere idea" cannot reach existence, that only experience can do that. But there is no absolute disjunction between thought and experience. A thought *is* an experience of a certain kind, it means *through* experience, even when it reaches only a possibility. A thought which does not mean by virtue of an experience is simply a thought which does not mean. Therefore, if we have a meaning for our thought of God, we also have experience of him, whether experience of him as possible or as actual being the question. It is too late to assert total lack of experience, once meaning has been granted. The only doubt can be whether the experience, already posited, is such as to establish possibility only, or existence also. But in the case of God no distinction between "non-impossible" and "actual" can be experienced or conceived. Hence we have only to exclude impossibility or meaninglessness to establish actuality.

Moreover, since God is conceived as all-pervasive of actuality and possibility, if we do not know God as existent, it cannot be because we have been denied some requisite special experience, since either *any* experience is sufficient, or else none could possibly be. Or, once more, either God is a meaningless term or there exists a divine being.

In still other words: either the idea of God is less than an idea, or it is more than a "mere idea" such as might designate an unactualized possibility, and is a direct awareness of an actual deity—as not only the mystics, but most theologians, have maintained. "Deity" may be nonsense, but a mere idea it cannot, without nonsense, be. To paraphrase Kant's final remark on the subject, all disputation about this, the real, point of the ontological argument is labor lost, as much as disputation about arithmetic. To say God cannot be a mere potency and to say two and two cannot make five differ in the degree of clearness of the ideas involved, but not in the a priori, or (relatively) self-evident, character of the reasoning.

That the ontological argument is hypothetical we have admitted. It says, "*If* 'God' stands for something conceivable, it stands for something actual." But this hypothetical character is often distorted out of all recognition. We are told that the only logical relation brought out by the argument is this: The necessary being, if it exists, exists necessarily. Thus to be able to use the argument in order to conclude "God exists necessarily," we should have to know the premise "God exists." This makes the argument seem ludicrous enough, but it is itself based on a self-contradictory assumption, which says, "If the necessary being happens to exist, that is, if as mere contingent fact, it exists, then it exists not as contingent fact, but as necessary truth." Instead of this nonsense, we must say, "If the phrase 'necessary being' has a meaning, then what it means exists necessarily, and if it exists necessarily, then, a fortiori, it exists." The "if" in the statement, "if it exists, it exists necessarily," cannot have the force of making the existence of the necessary being contingent—except in the sense that the argument leaves it open to suppose that the phrase "necessary being" is nonsense, and of course nonsense has no objective referent, possible or actual. Thus, what we should maintain is, "that which exists, if at all, necessarily," is the same as "that which is conceivable, if at all, only if it exists." Granting that it is conceivable, it then follows that it exists because it could not, being an object of thought at all, be a non-actual object. Or once more, the formula might be this: The necessary being, if it is not nothing, and therefore the object of no possible positive idea, is actual.

## Suggested Additional Readings

### THE PROBLEM OF THE EXISTENCE OF GOD

Aristotle. *Metaphysics*. See especially sections 1071b–1075a. Upon this work the Aristotelian-Thomistic tradition is built. The book is reading of first importance for students of the philosophy of religion.

Bertocci, Peter A. *Introduction to the Philosophy of Religion*. Englewood Cliffs, N.J.: Prentice-Hall, 1951. See especially Chapters XI–XVIII which are a discussion of arguments for the existence of God and a restatement of the teleological argument by an American proponent of personal idealism.

Cushman, Robert E., and Egil Grislis, editors. *The Heritage of Christian Thought*. New York: Harper & Row, 1965. Contains essays on many important figures in the history of philosophy and theology including St. Thomas, Spinoza, and Pascal.

Descartes, René. *Meditations*. Trans., Laurence J. Lafleur. New York: Liberal Arts Press, 1951. (This is a paperback edition.) This work provides an incisive discussion of traditional arguments for the existence of God.

Gilson, Etienne. *God and Philosophy*. London: Oxford University Press, 1941. (Also published in paperback by Yale University Press.) A Roman Catholic evaluation of the relationship between religion and philosophy, written by an outstanding present-day scholar.

Hartshorne, Charles. *Anselm's Discovery: A Re-examination of the Ontological Proof for God's Existence*. LaSalle, Ill.: Open Court, 1966. (Also available in paperback edition.) An important historical account of Anselm's ontological argument and the reactions to it. Hartshorne provides extensive critical commentary and a useful bibliography.

Hartshorne, Charles, and William L. Reese, *Philosophers Speak of God*. Chicago: University of Chicago Press, 1953. A comprehensive collection of source materials from Eastern and Western philosophers with brief critical comments.

Newman, John Henry. *A Grammar of Assent*. New York: Longmans Green, and

Company, 1909. (Also published in paperback by Doubleday, Image series.) See especially Chapter 5. A well-known statement of an argument for the existence of God based on the reality of conscience.

Pascal, Blaise. *Pensées.* Trans., W. F. Trotter. London: J. M. Dent and Sons, Ltd., 1932. (Also published in paperback by E. P. Dutton, Everyman series.) This writing constitutes an argument for the existence of God which is an anticipation of the existentialist approach. See the famous "wager" argument, number 233.

Plato. *The Laws.* Book X. A classic defense of the existence of gods based on Plato's principle of the priority of the spiritual to the material, or the priority of the soul to the body.

Richardson, Cyril. "The Strange Fascination of the Ontological Argument," *Union Seminary Quarterly Review,* vol. XVIII (November 1962). See also articles listed at the conclusion of Professor Malcolm's essay on page 237.

Taylor, A. E. *Does God Exist?* New York: The Macmillan Company, 1947. A closely reasoned statement of the moral argument for God's existence.

Taylor, Richard. *Metaphysics.* Englewood Cliffs, N.J.: Prentice-Hall, 1963. Chapter 7 contains an able restatement of the cosmological argument for God's existence.

# IV.

# How Is God Known?

## Some Contemporary Answers

IN CONTRAST TO traditional concern with attempts to prove the existence of God, recent and contemporary theological and philosophical thought has moved in new directions. There are still some, especially among Roman Catholic thinkers, who take the proofs of the existence of God to be of first importance, but on the whole, current scholarly interest is quite differently oriented.

Arguments for the existence of God were seriously challenged, from the side of philosophy, by the development of logical positivism, which relegated all such questions about ultimate being and meaning to the limbo of "meaningless statements." From this point of view all religious assertions are suspect, for logical positivists maintain that statements such as "God exists" are neither axiomatic nor capable of verification by sense data. Existentialist philosophers have also opposed the traditional arguments; they assert that basing religion on the arguments for God's existence leaves out the most important fact of all, namely, that religious truths have no meaning unless they are appropriated by a commitment of the whole person. Argument for the existence of God is a rational process that may satisfy the mind but that cannot in itself satisfy the basic demands of one's total experience. Thus, the religious existentialists have contended that some new way of affirming the reality of God needs to be found.

In theology also there have been new movements which react against the older assumptions about the need for arguments for the existence of God. These can be seen as roughly paralleling the philosophical reactions. On the one hand, there is the reaction of those who, like Karl Barth, insist on the primacy of God's revelation to man. According to Barth, God is not found by man, not even by the rigorous exercise of man's reason. Man is found by God, and man's acknowledgement of God's self-revealing is based upon the fact that this revelation validates itself

[249]

and is not supported by external criteria. On the other hand, there are theologians who follow the lead of the existentialist philosophers. Indeed, the key figure in modern existential philosophy, Sören Kierkegaard, was a theologian. Kierkegaard developed his philosophy because of his awareness of the need for a new understanding of the God-man relationship.

In this section are writings by some of the thinkers who espouse these different approaches. Karl Barth represents a revelational and faith-based position. He denies that philosophy, or "natural theology," provides an avenue to the true knowledge of God as He is revealed in Jesus Christ. Further, philosophy cannot provide a valid beginning point or a normative framework for understanding this revelation.

In the selections from A. J. Ayer and E. L. Mascall we have elements of a discussion between a logical positivist and an Anglican theologian on the possibility of religious knowledge. Ayer's statement is one of the clearest and most important attempts to deny the meaningfulness of theological discourse. Mascall attempts to argue against Ayer's assumptions and thereby to establish once again the meaningfulness and validity of theological statement.

The chapter from John Hick's book *Faith and Knowledge* asks a crucial question about the nature of religious faith. This section deals with the problem of cognition in the religious man's awareness of God and the way this is related to his other cognitions. As an extension of his position, Hick has gone on to affirm the possibility of an "eschatological verification" of God's existence. This latter notion is challenged by Kai Nielsen in his essay. Nielsen claims that Hick has made incorrect assumptions in his argument, and on this basis he raises fundamental questions about its validity.

An existentialist orientation is presented in the writing of Martin Buber. Buber, in this statement from his important book *I and Thou*, emphasizes the significance of man's personal involvement in all encounters with reality. According to Buber truth of genuinely personal significance is to be found only as man allows reality to "stand over against him," not subject to his control, but able to speak freely to him. The object of knowledge, which is really a subject, a "Thou" with intrinsic value, can only be known, at the most profound levels, by such a confrontation. And this is pre-eminently true of the ultimate subject, which is God.

Paul Tillich, a German-American philosophical theologian,

builds upon the insights of the existentialists' analysis of human existence. The selection from Tillich's writings is an attempt to understand man's search for meaning and purpose in his existence. The questions man asks about himself and his existence, Tillich argues, lead him to ask questions about God, and the meaning, if any, that God has for his life. Tillich believes that answers are provided in God's self-revelation and he tries to indicate what these are.

The final article is by a prominent process philosopher. Charles Hartshorne has continued the tradition of Alfred North Whitehead and has added his own unique contribution. In this passage he discusses the absoluteness of God, the social nature of God, and the doctrine of creation. This interpretation by Hartshorne has proved fertile for a number of contemporary theologians.

# KARL BARTH

*Karl Barth* (1886–    ), Swiss Protestant theologian and prolific writer, was the chief figure in the revolt of the 1920's against Protestant liberalism. Barth's *Church Dogmatics* is a major contribution to twentieth-century theology.

# The Christian Understanding
# of Revelation

What is this revelation, what is the subject of the revelation of which we have been speaking? What is the frame of mind which is open to receive what we call revelation? What is the theory of cognition for which revelation in the Christian sense is a valid object of knowledge?

And on the other hand is there a conception of the world, a basic view of existence which can include what we have called God? If the general conception of the world and the general pattern of human thought are the criteria, can such a thing as revelation exist in the Christian sense at all? Does this God exist, of whom we have spoken as the subject of this revelation? What are we in fact talking about? Are we possibly talking nonsense, talking about a non-ens? There are theories of knowledge which can account for what we have called the self-revelation of that which exists, and there are ontologies which can embrace the gods corresponding to these revelations. But as far as one can see there is no theory of knowledge and no pattern of thought which can embrace revelation in the Christian sense of the term. We can work through the whole history of philosophy from Thales to Martin Heidegger, and we shall be forced to the same conclusion. There is no room for revelation in the Christian sense in any human inquiry or any human faculty of reason. And the same applies to what we have called God in the Christian sense. There may be conceptions of the world which provide for gods, but the God of Christianity cannot appear in any imaginable human conception of the world. Try to map out a conception of the world in which God, as understood in Christian thought, would

From Karl Barth, *Against the Stream,* ed. Ronald Gregor Smith, pp. 210–216. Copyright, 1954, by Student Christian Movement Press. Used by permission of the publisher.

have room!—And so we must say that if a purely human conception of the world is the measure of all things, then neither revelation nor God in the Christian sense exist at all. We would in fact have been speaking about "nothing" when we were speaking about revelation and God.

We have not, however, been speaking about "nothing," but about a reality, something incomparably more real than anything that can be called real in the sphere of human thought and knowledge. When the Christian language speaks of revelation and God it means a reality which is very insignificant-looking and outwardly most unpromising; it speaks quite simply of a single concrete fact in the midst of the numberless host of facts and the vast stream of historical events; it speaks of a single human person living in the age of the Roman Empire: it speaks of Jesus Christ. When the Christian language speaks of God it does so not on the basis of some speculation or other, but looking at this fact, this story, this person. It cannot place this fact in relationship to any system of principles and ideas which would illuminate its importance and significance; it cannot explain and establish it from any other source; it makes no presuppositions when it points to this event. Its sole concern is with the event itself; all it can do is to refer to the existence, or rather, more precisely, the presence of this fact and the reception of the news of its presence as recorded in a tiny sheaf of news about the existence of this Person.

With its eyes concentrated on this news, Christianity speaks of revelation and of God as the subject of this revelation. Looking at this fact, it speaks with absolute assurance. Here—but only here—it sees revelation (in the sense of the criteria we have stated) and it sees God (again, in the sense of the criteria we have stated). Revelation in the Christian sense takes place and God in the Christian sense is, in accordance with the news of Jesus Christ, His words and deeds, His death and resurrection. That is what we now have to expound and, once again, we propose, for the sake of clarity, to make ten points. Each point will be based on a certain item of the good news of the gospel.

(1) "And the times of this ignorance God winked at; but now commandeth all men everywhere to repent. Because he hath appointed a day, in the which he will judge the world in righteousness by that man whom he hath ordained" (Acts 17: 30ff.).

This is the news: Because judgment is pronounced on all men in the one man, and their being and non-being decided, revelation in the Christian sense takes place, and not as an approximate but an original and final revelation. And He who makes the decision in the Person of this one man is God.

(2) "If any man sin, we have an advocate with the Father, Jesus Christ the righteous. And he is the propitiation for our sins; and not for ours only, but also for the sins of the whole world" (I John 2: 1ff.).

Since, in accordance with this news, man in this one Jesus Christ, in this offering of Jesus Christ as a propitiation for our sins, is accepted by God, revelation takes place, and not for the imperilling but for the salvation of man. It is God who does this.

(3) "I am the light of the world." "The light shineth in darkness; and the darkness comprehended it not" (John 8: 12 and 1: 5).

Since, in accordance with this news, Jesus Christ came into the darkness as the light of the world, since, therefore, Jesus Christ is and remains absolutely new for man, revelation takes place in the Christian sense, and not as a relative but as an absolute revelation. And it is God who shines in Jesus Christ.

(4) "For all have sinned, and come short of the glory of God; being justified freely by his grace through the redemption that is in Christ Jesus" (Rom. 3: 23f.).

Since, in accordance with this news, the event that is called redemption takes place in Jesus Christ, in this one person, the event that cannot proceed from any man and which no man can bring about, but which has been brought about by this One revelation in the Christian sense takes place. Without all, but for all! And therefore not as a special, but as a general revelation which concerns all and is meant for all. And it is God whose honour is so high and whose grace reaches so deep.

(5) "No man hath seen God at any time; the only begotten Son, which is in the bosom of the Father, he hath declared him" (John 1: 18).

Inasmuch as what is hidden from all men is revealed in this One, the one exclusive revelation takes place. And it is God that makes Himself known in the One.

(6) "Ye have not chosen me, but I have chosen you and ordained you that ye should go and bring forth fruit" (John 15: 16).

Inasmuch as this happens, inasmuch as this One chooses others and calls them to Himself, revelation in the Christian sense takes place; revelation that man cannot bring about by himself but which he receives as a gift. And it is God that has this freedom of choice in relation to man and exercises it in the One.

(7) "I am the vine, ye are the branches: he that abideth in me, and I in him, the same bringeth forth much fruit; for without me ye can do nothing" (John 15: 5).

Inasmuch as this One, Jesus Christ, has and exercises such sovereignty over His own, revelation takes place, revelation that cannot be capitalised, but is and remains free. And the origin and the essense of this sovereignty is God.

(8) "Jesus Christ the same yesterday and today and for ever" (Heb. 13: 8).

Revelation as an event that has happened, is happening and will happen in the future, which fulfills time in all its three constituents, is not approximate, but complete and final. And the Lord of this time is the eternal God.

(9) "For we are his workmanship, created in Christ Jesus unto good works, which God hath ordained that we should walk in them" (Eph. 2: 10).

Inasmuch as this necessity of a definite change comes into force in this One Jesus Christ, revelation takes place: practical, not speculative revelation. And it is God who thus disposes the way of man.

(10) "In the beginning was the Word and the Word was with God and the Word was God. The same was in the beginning with God. All things were made by him, and without him was not anything made that was made" (John 1: 1f.).

Inasmuch as this creative Word, which is superior to all being, is spoken and heard in Him, revelation takes place: transcendent, not immanent revelation. Revelation from the origin of all being. And it is God who speaks this Word.

The concept of revelation and the concept of God in the Christian sense coincide, therefore, in the contemplation of Jesus Christ, in which they are both related to reality. And in contemplation of Him it is decided that God is and what God is; that God is a person and not a neutral thing. And that revelation is His acting and speaking and not a blind occurence or an unarticulated sound.

When it refers to God's revelation as the Word of God, Christianity means Jesus Christ. What is a word? A word obviously differs from a mere sound in that it is formed with the definite intention of calling on others to make a common cause. When I utter the simple word: "Look!" I call on others to look at something I think I have seen myself. Or if I say: "Listen!" I call them to listen to something I think I have heard myself. The primary intention of words is quite simply to be heard by others. Words cannot compel, they can only make an appeal. But every word has in view, in some sense or other, the obedient response of other persons. When I utter words I want to induce others to listen and conform to my wishes. In this sense too revelation is a word: God wants our interest, He wants us to listen, He wants to call us to decision, He wants us to obey His Word.

When we speak about the Word, and particularly this Word of God, a certain uneasiness is liable to come over us. Is what we are discussing really no more than a word? Are words not "sound and smoke clouding the glow of heaven?" "In the beginning was the Word? I cannot possibly esteem the Word so highly; I must translate it differently: in the beginning was the Deed," as Goethe says. What have we to say to that? Simply that the argument overlooks the fact that the "glow of heaven" and the "Deed" without words are phenomena which may be most impressive, but in relation to which it is possible for man to remain free and aloof and which are in any case something essentially different from what we have discerned as revelation in the Christian sense. Secondly, in contrast to all mere words and all empty words, revelation in the Christian sense is both Word and Deed at one and the same time. It is not merely the "glow of heaven" but a consuming fire and a blinding light. According to Heb. 1: 3 the Word of revelation is "his enabling word on whom all creation depends for its support" (cf. John 1: 3). Jesus Christ is the Word. Inasmuch as what happens in Him, happened and happens and will happen, the word of revelation is spoken. The whole criticism of the concept "the word" is superfluous as far as this Word is concerned. And thus we might take leave of Dr. Faust by suggesting he might have done better not to have tried to translate the Word differently! Incidentally, it is significant that immediately after the translation the Devil appears!

Revelation in the Christian sense is the Word of God, the Word spoken in divine Majesty. He to whom man belongs, to whom man cannot refuse to listen without calling himself into question, who calls man to decision, summons us to make common cause with Him. Neutrality towards the Word of God is impossible; we cannot say Yes and No at the same time. Obedience to the Word of God is not merely one of several possibilities. We do not confront this Word like Hercules at the crossroads. This is a case where there is only one possibility, the possibility of obedience. Man's genuine freedom does not consist in an ability to evade this Word. If he does not submit to it he chooses the impossible possibility, he chooses *nihil*.

Because revelation in the Christian sense is the Word of God, it is impossible to adopt the attitude of a mere onlooker towards it. The revelation of God can only be searched, understood and judged in the act of obedience, of listening, which leads to decision—or it will not be searched, understood and judged at all. We cannot think and talk *about* the revelation of God; we can only reflect on what the Word itself says to us. We can only speak out of the revelation itself; otherwise we shall be thinking and talking about something else.

Since revelation in the Christian sense is the Word of God, we cannot bring it forward as if it were an object outside ourselves. I cannot demonstrate the revelation of God to you in the way that my colleague in the

Chemistry Department demonstrates his objects. Because it is the Word of God, the revelation of God cannot be recommended and defended; it has no advocates and no propagandists. And, finally, one cannot profess one's belief in it by protesting and asserting that it exists. Revelation can only be believed in by becoming worthy of belief. Revelation can only be attested as any other unknown fact is attested by someone who happens to know it. Revelation can only be presupposed in our thinking and our speaking, and in our Christian theology and preaching too, in the way that certain axioms or objective facts are presupposed in every branch of knowledge, when the belief and the testimony and the presupposition are only forms of that one possible decision, the decision of obedience. *Omnis recta cognitio ab obedientia nascitur,* Calvin says. Thus it is with revelation because it is the Word of God.

# A. J. AYER

*A. J. Ayer* (1910–    ), Wykeham Professor of Logic at Oxford University, has been the leading exponent of logical positivism in Great Britain. He is best known for his book *Language, Truth and Logic,* which was first published in 1936.

## Is Religious Knowledge Possible?

This mention of God brings us to the question of the possibility of religious knowledge. We shall see that this possibility has already been ruled out by our treatment of metaphysics. But, as this is a point of considerable interest, we may be permitted to discuss it at some length.

It is now generally admitted, at any rate by philosophers, that the existence of a being having the attributes which define the god of any non-animistic religion cannot be demonstratively proved. To see that this is so, we have only to ask ourselves what are the premises from which the existence of such a god could be deduced. If the conclusion that a god exists is to be demonstratively certain, then these premises must be certain; for, as the

From A. J. Ayer, *Language, Truth and Logic,* Second Edition, pp. 114–120. Copyright, 1946, Victor Gollancz. Reprinted by permission of A. J. Ayer and of Dover Publications, Inc., N.Y. 14, N.Y.

conclusion of a deductive argument is already contained in the premises, any uncertainty there may be about the truth of the premises is necessarily shared by it. But we know that no empirical proposition can ever be anything more than probable. It is only *a priori* propositions that are logically certain. But we cannot deduce the existence of a god from an *a priori* proposition. For we know that the reason why *a priori* propositions are certain is that they are tautologies. And from a set of tautologies nothing but a further tautology can be validly deduced. It follows that there is no possibility of demonstrating the existence of a god.

What is not so generally recognized is that there can be no way of proving that the existence of a god, such as the God of Christianity, is even probable. Yet this also is easily shown. For if the existence of such a god were probable, then the proposition that he existed would be an empirical hypothesis. And in that case it would be possible to deduce from it, and other empirical hypotheses, certain experiential propositions which were not deducible from those other hypotheses alone. But in fact this is not possible. It is sometimes claimed, indeed, that the existence of a certain sort of regularity in nature constitutes sufficient evidence for the existence of a god. But if the sentence "God exists" entails no more than that certain types of phenomena occur in certain sequences, then to assert the existence of a god will be simply equivalent to asserting that there is the requisite regularity in nature; and no religious man would admit that this was all he intended to assert in asserting the existence of a god. He would say that in talking about God, he was talking about a transcendent being who might be known through certain empirical manifestations, but certainly could not be defined in terms of those manifestations. But in that case the term "god" is a metaphysical term. And if "god" is a metaphysical term, then it cannot be even probable that a god exists. For to say that "God exists" is to make a metaphysical utterance which cannot be either true or false. And by the same criterion, no sentence which purports to describe the nature of a transcendent god can possess any literal significance.

It is important not to confuse this view of religious assertions with the view that is adopted by atheists, or agnostics.[1] For it is characteristic of an agnostic to hold that the existence of a god is a possibility in which there is no good reason either to believe or disbelieve; and it is characteristic of an atheist to hold that it is at least probable that no god exists. And our view that all utterances about the nature of God are nonsensical, so far from being identical with, or even lending any support to, either of these familiar contentions, is actually incompatible with them. For if the assertion that there is a god is nonsensical, then the atheist's assertion that there is no god is equally nonsensical, since it is only a significant proposition that can be

---

[1] This point was suggested to me by Professor H. H. Price.

significantly contradicted. As for the agnostic, although he refrains from saying either that there is or that there is not a god, he does not deny that the question whether a transcendent god exists is a genuine question. He does not deny that the two sentences "There is a transcendent god" and "There is no transcendent god" express propositions one of which is actually true and the other false. All he says is that we have no means of telling which of them is true, and therefore ought not to commit ourselves to either. But we have seen that the sentences in question do not express propositions at all. And this means that agnosticism also is ruled out.

Thus we offer the theist the same comfort as we gave to the moralist. His assertions cannot possibly be valid, but they cannot be invalid either. As he says nothing at all about the world, he cannot justly be accused of saying anything false, or anything for which he has insufficient grounds. It is only when the theist claims that in asserting the existence of a transcendent god he is expressing a genuine proposition that we are entitled to disagree with him.

It is to be remarked that in cases where deities are identified with natural objects, assertions concerning them may be allowed to be significant. If, for example, a man tells me that the occurence of thunder is alone both necessary and sufficient to establish the truth of the proposition that Jehovah is angry, I may conclude that, in his usage of the words, the sentence "Jehovah is angry" is equivalent to "It is thundering." But in sophisticated religions, though they may be to some extent based on men's awe of natural process which they cannot sufficiently understand, the "person" who is supposed to control the empirical world is not himself located in it; he is held to be superior to the empirical world, and so outside it; and he is endowed with super-empirical attributes. But the notion of a person whose essential attributes are non-empirical is not an intelligible notion at all. We may have a word which is used as if it named this "person," but, unless the sentences in which it occurs express propositions which are empirically verifiable, it cannot be said to symbolize anything. And this is the case with regard to the word "god," in the usage in which it is intended to refer to a transcendent object. The mere existence of the noun is enough to foster the illusion that there is a real, or at any rate a possible entity corresponding to it. It is only when we enquire what God's attributes are that we discover that "God," in this usage, is not a genuine name.

It is common to find belief in a transcendent god conjoined with belief in an after-life. But, in the form which it usually takes, the content of this belief is not a genuine hypothesis. To say that men do not ever die, or that the state of death is merely a state of prolonged insensibility, is indeed to express a significant proposition, though all the available evidence goes to show that it is false. But to say that there is something imperceptible inside a man, which is his soul or his real self, and that it goes on living after he is dead, is to make a metaphysical assertion which has no more factual content than the assertion that there is a transcendent god.

It is worth mentioning that, according to the account which we have given of religious assertions, there is no logical ground for antagonism between religion and natural science. As far as the question of truth or falsehood is concerned, there is no opposition between the natural scientist and the theist who believes in a transcendent god. For since the religious utterances of the theist are not genuine propositions at all, they cannot stand in any logical relation to the propositions of science. Such antagonism as there is between religion and science appears to consist in the fact that science takes away one of the motives which make men religious. For it is acknowledged that one of the ultimate sources of religious feeling lies in the inability of men to determine their own destiny; and science tends to destroy the feeling of awe with which men regard an alien world, by making them believe that they can understand and anticipate the course of natural phenomena, and even to some extent control it. The fact that it has recently become fashionable for physicists themselves to be sympathetic towards religion is a point in favour of this hypothesis. For this sympathy towards religion marks the physicists' own lack of confidence in the validity of their hypotheses, which is a reaction on their part from the anti-religious dogmatism of nineteenth-century scientists, and a natural outcome of the crisis through which physics has just passed.

It is not within the scope of this enquiry to enter more deeply into the causes of religious feeling, or to discuss the probability of the continuance of religious belief. We are concerned only to answer those questions which arise out of our discussion of the possibility of religious knowledge. The point which we wish to establish is that there cannot be any transcendent truths of religion. For the sentences which the theist uses to express such "truths" are not literally significant.

An interesting feature of this conclusion is that it accords with what many theists are accustomed to say themselves. For we are often told that the nature of God is a mystery which transcends the human understanding. But to say that something transcends the human understanding is to say that it is unintelligible. And what is unintelligible cannot significantly be described. Again, we are told that God is not an object of reason but an object of faith. This may be nothing more than an admission that the existence of God must be taken on trust, since it cannot be proved. But it may also be an assertion that God is the object of a purely mystical intuition, and cannot therefore be defined in terms which are intelligible to the reason. And I think there are many theists who would assert this. But if one allows that it is impossible to define God in intelligible terms, then one is allowing that it is impossible for a sentence both to be significant and to be about God. If a mystic admits that the object of his vision is something which cannot be described, then he must also admit that he is bound to talk non-sense when he describes it.

For his part, the mystic may protest that his intuition does reveal truths to him, even though he cannot explain to others what these truths are; and that we who do not possess this faculty of intuition can have no ground for denying that it is a cognitive faculty. For we can hardly maintain *a priori* that there are no ways of discovering true propositions except those which we ourselves employ. The answer is that we set no limit to the number of ways in which one may come to formulate a true proposition. We do not in any way deny that a synthetic truth may be discovered by purely intuitive methods as well as by the rational method of induction. But we do say that every synthetic proposition, however it may have been arrived at, must be subject to the test of actual experience. We do not deny *a priori* that the mystic is able to discover truths by his own special methods. We wait to hear what are the propositions which embody his discoveries, in order to see whether they are verified or confuted by our empirical observations. But the mystic, so far from producing propositions which are empirically verified, is unable to produce any intelligible propositions at all. And therefore we say that his intuition has not revealed to him any facts. It is no use his saying that he has apprehended facts but is unable to express them. For we know that if he really had acquired any information, he would be able to express it. He would be able to indicate in some way or other how the genuineness of his discovery might be empirically determined. The fact that he cannot reveal what he "knows," or even himself devise an empirical test to validate his "knowledge," shows that his state of mystical intuition is not a genuinely cognitive state. So that in describing his vision the mystic does not give us any information about the external world; he merely gives us indirect information about the condition of his own mind.

These considerations dispose of the argument from religious experience, which many philosophers still regard as a valid argument in favour of the existence of a god. They say that it is logically possible for men to be immediately acquainted with God, as they are immediately acquainted with a sense-content, and that there is no reason why one should be prepared to believe a man when he says that he is seeing a yellow patch, and refuse to believe him when he says that he is seeing God. The answer to this is that if the man who asserts that he is seeing God is merely asserting that he is experiencing a peculiar kind of sense-content, then we do not for a moment deny that his assertion may be true. But, ordinarily, the man who says that he is seeing God is saying not merely that he is experiencing a religious emotion, but also that there exists a transcendent being who is the object of this emotion; just as the man who says that he sees a yellow patch is ordinarily saying not merely that his visual sense-field contains a yellow sense-content, but also that there exists a yellow object to which the sense-content belongs. And it is not irrational to be prepared to believe a man when he asserts the existence of a yellow object, and to refuse to believe him when he asserts the existence of a transcendent god. For whereas the sentence "There exists here a yellow-coloured material thing" expresses a genuine synthetic proposition which could be empirically verified, the sentence "There exists a transcendent god" has, as we have seen, no literal significance.

We conclude, therefore, that the argument from religious experience is altogether fallacious. The fact that people have religious experiences is interesting from the psychological point of view, but it does not in any way imply that there is such a thing as religious knowledge, any more than our having moral experiences implies that there is such a thing as moral knowledge. The theist, like the moralist, may believe that his experiences are cognitive experiences, but, unless he can formulate his "knowledge" in propositions that are empirically verifiable, we may be sure that he is deceiving himself. It follows that those philosophers who fill their books with assertions that that they intuitively "know" this or that moral or religious "truth" are merely providing material for the psycho-analyst. For no act of intuition can be said to reveal a truth about any matter of fact unless it issues in verifiable propositions. And all such propositions are to be incorporated in the system of empirical propositions which constitutes science.

# E. L. MASCALL

E. L. Mascall (1905–    ), Anglican theologian, has published extensively and contributed to a revival of interest in the Thomistic tradition in theology. His books—*He Who Is, Words and Images*, and *Existence and Analogy*—are significant contributions to philosophy of religion.

## Is Theological Discourse Possible?

### I. Theology and Verification

There is nothing new in the discovery that a peculiar problem is raised by the fact that human beings from time to time make utterances which pur-

From E. L. Mascall, *Words and Images*, pp. 1–14. Copyright, 1957, The Ronald Press Company. Used by permission of The Ronald Press Company, New York, and Longmans Green & Co., Ltd., London, 1957. [Footnotes omitted, Eds.]

port to be statements about God, that is to say, which claim to speak about the ineffable and to describe the indescribable. There is a whole branch of traditional Christian theology—the doctrine of analogy—whose main concern is with this problem. There is, however, something new about the way in which the matter has been raised in recent years; and it is a way which, if it is valid, is highly destructive not only of Christian theism as it has usually been understood but of any religion which involves belief in a transcendent deity. Little excuse should therefore be needed for devoting some space to its discussion.

Some preliminary remarks may help to clarify the issue. In the first place, it should be observed that, although the problem of theological discourse and the problem of theological knowledge are not identical, they are very closely connected and it is practically impossible to discuss either of them without also discussing the other. Talking about God and knowing God are not necessarily identical or even co-extensive; there may be such a thing as wordless knowledge. Nevertheless we cannot talk about even wordless knowledge without using words to discuss it; and our discussion of it is likely to be very unprofitable if at the same time we make no attempt to discuss its object. I shall try not to confuse the two activities, but it will be quite impossible to separate them.

Again, we must recognise that it is impossible to separate the question whether God can be talked about from the question of the kind of things that people say when they talk about him. The word "God" must have some content if our statements about God are to be intelligible at all; and if we say what the content is we are inevitably saying things about him. We shall thus be discussing in this book not one question but a number of closely related ones; and we may note that some of the confusion in which the subject has been involved has been due to a failure to distinguish between them.

I shall begin by examining the position that was put forward by Mr. (now Professor) A. J. Ayer in 1936 in his famous little book *Language, Truth and Logic,* in spite of the fact that nobody, perhaps not even Professor Ayer himself, appears to hold exactly that position today. This seems to me to be worth while for two reasons. In the first place, there are a good many people alive whose philosophical studies ended about that date, and, since Professor Ayer's book was given something of the character of a manifesto, as the statement of a philosophy which was to end philosophising, there may still be point in making a brief reference to it, in spite of the large number of criticisms, of various degrees of penetration, which have appeared since it was published. In the second place, most of what has been written on the question in recent years has derived, either directly or indirectly, from Professor Ayer's thesis, even if only by way of reaction against it; and it is in practice almost impossible to take any other starting point for our discussion. It ought in fairness to be recognised that, ten years after its first publication, Professor Ayer added to his book a new Introduction which contained certain modifications of his original position; but how firmly entrenched that position was is shown by how few and insignificant those modifications were.

The basis of Ayer's system was the famous "verification principle," in formulating which Ayer claimed to be simply expressing in the most clear-cut way the fundamentally empirical character of the tradition in British philosophy which derives from the great eighteenth-century Scottish philosopher David Hume. The principle had indeed been already stated in the most extreme form by philosophers of the Viennese School, in particular by M. Schlick, for whom the sole criterion of the meaningfulness of a statement was the possibility of verifying it by sense-experience. This is what Ayer called "verifiability in the strong sense": "A proposition is said to be verifiable, in the strong sense of the term, if, and only if, its truth could be conclusively established in experience." For Ayer, however, verifiability in the strict sense seemed to be far too drastic a criterion of meaningfulness; for it would dismiss as meaningless many statements which he was convinced were undoubtedly meaningful. It would rule out general statements, such as "Arsenic is poisonous," which could not be conclusively verified so long as any fragment of arsenic remained unconsumed, statements about inaccessible events and objects, such as "There are mountains on the other side of the moon," whose unverifiability might be overcome by a sufficient development of the science of astronautics, and also statements about the past, such as "Napoleon was defeated at Waterloo," which could be conclusively verified only by the impossible method of going back in time to the year 1815 and observing what happened. Ayer therefore adopted a mitigated or "weak" verification principle, according to which a statement is meaningful if it is possible for experience to render it *probable;* "the question that must be asked about any putative statement of fact is not, Would any observations make its truth or falsehood logically certain? but simply, Would any observations be relevant to the determination of its truth or falsehood? And it is only if a negative answer is given to this second question that we conclude that the statement under consideration is nonsensical." Some minor modifications were made in Ayer's second edition, but they do not affect our present considerations.

For Ayer, then (and here I mean the Ayer of the two editions of *Language, Truth and Logic*), a statement which purports to be a statement of fact is genuine and meaningful if, and only if, some possible empirical observations can be specified which would be relevant to the determination of its truth or falsehood. He does, indeed, recognise that there is another kind of meaningful statement, but these are not statements of fact; they are simply tautologies, like the statement "Either all the ants that there are are carnivorous or there is at least one ant that is not," and they provide no information about any matter of fact whatever.

Having laid down his verification principle, Ayer then proceeds by the use of it to dismiss as meaningless and nonsensical all ethical, metaphysical and theological statements. Ethical statements emerge from the trial with a reprieve, but only with the loss of their status as statements; they survive as expressions and stimulants of feeling, or as exhortations to action. Metaphysical and theological statements, on the other hand, receive the shortest of shrift; for they claim to make factual assertions about entities which are not objects of sense-experience, and this is the unforgivable sin. "We are often told," writes Ayer, "that the nature of God is a mystery which transcends the human understanding. But to say that something transcends the human understanding is to say that it is unintelligible. And what is unintelligible cannot significantly be described." (I will only comment in passing on the ambiguity in the use of the word "transcends" in the first two sentences of this quotation.) Nor will Ayer have any truck with mystical experience as anything more than a psychological phenomenon. "The mystic, so far from producing propositions which are empirically verified, is unable to produce any intelligible propositions at all. . . . It is no use his saying that he has apprehended facts but is unable to express them. For we know that if he really had acquired any information, he would be able to express it." ("Do we?" we might interpose.) And again:

> If the man who asserts that he is seeing God is merely asserting that he is experiencing a peculiar kind of sense-content, then we do not for a moment deny that his assertion may be true. But, ordinarily, the man who says that he is seeing God is saying not merely that he is experiencing a religious emotion, but also that there exists a transcendent being who is the object of this emotion; just as the man who says that he sees a yellow patch is ordinarily saying not merely that his visual sense-field contains a yellow sense-content, but also that there exists a yellow object to which the sense-content belongs. And it is not irrational to be prepared to believe a man when he asserts the existence of a yellow object, and to refuse to believe him when he asserts the existence of a transcendent God. For whereas the sentence "There exists here a yellow-coloured material thing" expresses a genuine synthetic proposition which could be empirically verified, the sentence "There exists a transcendent god" has, as we have seen, no literal significance.

We are not concerned at the moment with Ayer's theory of ethical statements; we are, however, concerned with his theory of theological statements, and also with his theory of metaphysical statements in so far as theological statements are themselves metaphysical. And there are, I think, at least four important comments to be made on his use of the verification principle.

First, there is something very suspicious about the fact that the verification principle had to be mitigated. In its original "strong" form it had all the downright simplicity that a fundamental philosophical principle might be expected to have. But, writes Ayer, "it seems to me that if we adopt conclusive verifiability as our criterion of significance, as some positivists have proposed, our argument will prove too much." "Too much for what?" we might inquire, with a notion that the answer is "Too much for Ayer." It would be a manly, robust and, as Ayer himself says, a heroic course to apply the principle ruthlessly regardless of the casualties that might result. But this would demolish many types of statement whose meaningfulness Ayer wishes to preserve, such as the statements already quoted about arsenic and the mountains on the far side of the moon and Napoleon. Why should they not be in fact demolished? Is it because Ayer has some independent criterion of significance and is trimming the verification principle to conform to it? It looks as if this is the case. But if so, why should we not trim the principle a little more in order to let in ethical, metaphysical or even (*sit venia verbis*) theological statements? Who is to decide where the line is to be drawn?

Secondly, what sort of statement is the verification principle itself? Ayer undoubtedly thinks it is meaningful, but it does not obviously belong to either of the two types of meaningful statement which he recognises. If he had taken the heroic course of nailing his colours to the mast of the "strong" form of the principle, some sort of case might have been made for the point of view that the principle was a tautology, that "meaningful" and "empirically verifiable" were simply synonyms or at least that "empirically verifiable" was part of the content of "meaningful." Even so, I think, the assertion would have been questionable, for we have, I would maintain, only to think of the phrases "empirically verifiable" and "meaningful" to see that they do not *mean* the same thing. Some philosophers might have held that, in spite of this difference of meaning, "Meaningful entails empirically verifiable" was a synthetic *a priori* truth, but this way is not open to Ayer, who denies that there are such things as synthetic *a priori* truths. Is the principle, then, an empirical generalisation? That is to say, has Ayer examined a large variety of statements for meaningfulness and concluded that all those that were meaningful conformed to the principle and that all those that were meaningless did not conform to it? I have suggested that this is almost what he seems to claim to have done, in the somewhat arbitrary way in which he has mitigated the verification principle. However, in the Introduction to his second edition he denies this explicitly, when he writes as follows: "While I wish the principle of verification itself to be regarded, not as an empirical hypothesis, but as a definition, it is not supposed to be entirely arbitrary." What, in this sentence, is the force of the statement "it is not supposed to be entirely arbitrary" it is indeed difficult to see; but its introduction seems to manifest a reprehensible desire to run with the hare and hunt with the hounds. For the assertion that the principle is a definition makes it impossible to question its truth, while the assertion that it is not entirely arbitrary suggests that some ground for its assertion is to be found in experience. This dual character is, however, just what Ayer elsewhere alleges that no statement can have, and one of his chief grievances against metaphysical and theological statements is that they —or some of them—claim to have it. This assertion that the verification principle is a definition will, however, bring us to our third comment.

For, if Ayer simply defines "meaningful" as equivalent to "verifiable in the weak sense or else tautological," no harm is done to either metaphysical or theological statements by saying that, in *this* sense, they are meaningless or nonsensical. What would be harmful would be a demonstration that they were meaningless in the common or garden sense of "unintelligible," and this is in fact nowhere proved. If the verification principle is simply a definition, it can assert nothing, for the function of definitions is not to make assertions but to register our linguistic conventions; if, on the other hand, it is a statement of fact, then it is a synthetic proposition, and, in virtue of the very assertion which it makes, itself needs empirical verification. Ayer seems in fact to have fallen into the snare in which the empiricists customarily claim to find the metaphysicians, that of packing into their principles the conclusions which they want to get out of them, as a conjuror inserts the rabbit into the hat before he comes on to the stage. This is the method of which Lord Russell has remarked that it has many advantages, but that they are the advantages which theft has over honest toil. But in fact, in his second edition Ayer makes a number of admissions which are extremely damaging to his former thesis. Thus he admits that there may be definitions of "meaning" according to which statements which are neither tautological nor empirically verifiable may be meaningful and that there is some proper use of the word "understanding" according to which such statements may be capable of being understood. He adds that this will not be the sense in which scientific hypothesis or common sense statements are understood, but I do not imagine that anyone ever thought that it was. He tells us that he would still defend the use of the criterion of verifiability as a methodological principle, but this remark as it stands is nothing more than an interesting statement of his own preferences and habits. His final admission is that for the effective elimination of metaphysics the criterion needs to be supported by detailed analyses of particular metaphysical arguments, and this is very remarkable. For it reduces the verification principle to the level of a generalisation from experience, namely the experience of examining a number of metaphysical arguments, and as long as any metaphysical arguments remain unexamined (which will presumably be always the case, as their number is potentially infinite) there is always the possibility that one of them will turn out to be valid and at the same time to violate the verification principle. If one compares the bold assertions in Ayer's first edition with the somewhat tentative and hedging remarks in the relevant passages of the second, one is tempted to feel that one is witnessing a very skilful rearguard action, in which Ayer rapidly oscillates between a number of positions, treating the verification principle at one moment as a definition, at another as a truth of logic and at another as an empirically verified generalisation. To be convicted of this procedure would leave some philosophical systems unabashed, but for Ayer's it is fatal. For the absolute distinction between truths of logic and statements of empirical fact is its basic doctrine, and it is precisely for their violation of this doctrine that it condemns its competitors. Nothing could therefore be more damaging to it than the discovery that it has itself fallen into the commission, in however small a degree, of this unforgivable sin.

My fourth criticism of Ayer is that, having made the apparently innocent and plausible assertion that all meaningful assertions must have some reference to experience, he then goes on to limit the meaning of experience in the narrowest and most arbitrary way to the experience of the bodily senses. Once again, we want to know what is the logical status of this assumption. If it is alleged to be a tautology, it seems pretty clear that this allegation is false, for there is nothing logically impossible in an experience which is not an experience of sense impressions upon the physical organs of the body. If, on the other hand, it is alleged to be an empirical generalisation, there is a good deal of experience, namely mystical experience in the broadest sense, which *prima facie* contradicts it and which certainly ought not to be dismissed without detailed examination. But in Ayer's book such an examination is nowhere made. The remarks which he does pass upon mystical experience are, however, highly revealing.

> We do not deny *a priori* [he writes] that the mystic is able to discover truths by his own special methods. We wait to hear what are the propositions which embody his discoveries, in order to see whether they are verified or confuted by our empirical observations. But the mystic, so far from producing propositions which are empirically verified, is unable to produce any intelligible propositions at all. And therefore we say that his intuition has not revealed to him any facts. It is no use his saying that he has apprehended facts but is unable to express them. For we know that if he really had acquired any information, he would be able to express it. . . . So that in describing his vision the mystic does not give us any information about the external world; he merely gives us indirect information about the condition of his own mind.

Everything here turns upon the way in which the word "empirical" has been smuggled into the second sentence of this passage. We may grant that if the mystic's language bore no relation whatever to the experience of any of his hearers or readers it could convey nothing to them. But this is not the case. The mystics do in fact use a great deal of language derived from sensory experience, the language of sight and touch and taste, while they emphasize that these words are not to be taken in their ordinary crude applications. They also at times appeal to non-sensory experiences which they assume that some at least of their hearers will have had and will be able to identify as of essentially the same type as their own. This use of language is undoubtedly odd, and it will certainly be misinterpreted by anyone who supposes that the only intelligible use of language derived from sense experience is its use in the registration of the occurrence of sense-phenomena. When Ayer waits for the mystic to enunciate propositions which are verified or confuted by empirical observation, he will certainly be disappointed. The mystic does not produce, at least as a general rule, propositions which are empirically verified, and, if he does, these will not be theological propositions. But to say that he does not produce any intelligible theological propositions at all is to make a dogma into a wall which hides the most obvious facts. Anyone who takes the trouble to study diligently the writings of the mystics can verify this for himself. Mystical theology, like other pursuits (physical science for example), has its own way of talking, which can be misleading or even flatly unintelligible to the complete outsider. The way in which its language is related to the reality with which it is concerned is as indirect and raises at least as many problems as the language which physical science uses to deal with the reality with which *it is* concerned. And, unlike the subject-matter of physics, the subject-matter of mystical theology is supremely mysterious and needs (so its practitioners tell us) for its understanding not merely training in a technique but purity of heart and religious devotion. It is furthermore alleged that, in the present life, very few persons are privileged to apprehend this reality with full immediacy and intensity. All this is true, yet the fact remains that the language of mystical experience, like, on a lower level, the language of dogmatic theology, can in fact be understood by those who are prepared to learn to do this. That finite minds can apprehend a transcendent and infinite reality and that human language can communicate information about it is no doubt very surprising, but it happens to be true; and to rule the language either of dogmatic or of mystical theology out of court, on the grounds that it fails to conform to an externally imposed prejudice as to what types of statement ought to be intelligible, is simply to exclude from consideration great tracts of reality and to confine oneself within a constricted and impoverished world. In Berkeley's phrase, it is to cast dust in one's eyes and then complain that one cannot see. I shall discuss this matter in more detail later on. At the moment I merely wish to make it plain that I am far from asserting that all our knowledge of God, or even the greater part of it, is derived from mystical experience in the strict sense, that is to say from a direct experimental awareness of God in which the senses play no part. But I do want to point out that Ayer's denial of the possibility of such awareness rests upon a sheer ambiguity in the use of the word "empirical," which is used first in an extremely general sense in order to make the verification principle plausible and then in an extremely specialised sense in order to rule out all experience except that of sense-phenomena.

It is, I would maintain, clear to anyone who approaches the matter with an open mind, that the fundamental criterion of meaningfulness is not sense-verifiability but intelligibility, that is to say that in order to know whether a statement has meaning you should see whether it is possible to understand it. This statement is of course a tautology, and therein lies its strength. For meaningfulness is a primary notion, which cannot be described in terms of anything else. As Mr. J. O. Wisdom has said, "with statements that can be understood independently of verification, to say that the verification provides the meaning is to confuse the meaning of a statement with the evidence for its truth." I am far from denying that the verification principle has a very considerable use, if a limited one, as a methodological principle. If you are uncertain whether a statement is significant or ,not it may be very useful to inquire what you would do in order to test its truth or falsehood. And this may involve subjecting it to the criterion of sense-verifiability. But the validity of this process depends upon its being the kind of statement to which the process is appropriate, and this can only be determined by examining it to see what kind of statement it is. I think that in fact a good many of the statements made by idealist philosophers are indefinite and confused, that they frequently fall into ambiguity and sometimes simply make mistakes in their arguments; they are not the only philosophers to go astray in these ways. But one of the difficulties in getting to grips with Ayer's strictures upon theology arises from the fact that he seems to have read very little theology, and to have a totally inadequate notion of the way that theologians think and the things that they say. This is a provocative statement, but I hope to provide justification for it in the course of this book.

# JOHN HICK

*John Hick* (1922–       ), English analytical philosopher and Presbyterian clergyman, has taught at Cornell and at Princeton Theological Seminary and he now teaches in Birmingham University in England. His book *Faith and Knowledge* is his major publication.

## The Nature of Faith

We come now to our main problem. What manner of cognition is the religious man's awareness of God, and how is it related to his other cognitions?

We have already taken stock in a general way of our situation as cognizing beings. We become conscious of the existence of other objects in the universe, whether things or persons, either by experiencing them for ourselves or by inferring their existence from evidences within our experience. We have also noted that the awareness of God reported by the ordinary religious believer is of the former kind. He professes, not to have inferred that there is a God, but that God as a living being has entered into his own experience. He claims to enjoy something which he describes as an experience of God.

The ordinary believer does not, however, report an awareness of God as existing in isolation from all other objects of experience. His consciousness of the divine does not involve a cessation of his consciousness of a material and social environment. It is not a vision of God in solitary glory, filling the believer's entire mind and blotting out his normal field of perception. Whether such phrases correctly describe the mystic's goal, the ultimate Beatific Vision which figures in Christian doctrine, is a question for a later chapter.[1] But at any rate the ordinary person's religious awareness here on earth is not of that kind. He claims instead an apprehension of God meeting him in and through his material and social environments. He finds that in his dealings with the world of men and things he is somehow having to do with God, and God with him. The moments of ordinary life possess, or may possess, for him in varying degrees a religious significance. As has been

---

From John Hick, *Faith and Knowledge*, pp. 109–133. © 1957 by Cornell University, Cornell University Press. Reprinted by permission of The Cornell University Press.
[1] See ch. 7.

well said, religious experience is "the whole experience of religious persons." [2] The believer meets God not only in moments of worship, but also
when through the urgings of conscience he feels the pressure of the divine
demand upon his life; when through the gracious actions of his friends he
apprehends the divine grace; when through the marvels and beauties of
nature he traces the hand of the Creator; and he has increasing knowledge
of the divine purpose as he responds to its behests in his own life. In short,
it is not apart from the course of mundane life, but in it and through it, that
the ordinary religious believer claims to experience, however imperfectly
and fragmentarily, the divine presence and activity.

This at any rate, among the variety of claims to religious awareness which
have been and might be made, is the claim whose epistemological credentials
we are to examine. Can God be known through his dealing with us in the
world which he has made? The question concerns human experience, and
the possibility of an awareness of the divine being mediated through awareness of the world, the supernatural through the natural.

In answer to this query I shall try to show in the present chapter that
"mediated" knowledge, such as is postulated by this religious claim, is
already a common and accepted feature of our cognitive experience. To this
end we must study a basic characteristic of human experience, which I shall
call "significance," together with the correlative mental activity by which it
is apprehended, which I shall call "interpretation." We shall find that interpretation takes place in relation to each of the three main types of existence,
or orders of significance, recognized by human thought—the natural, the
human, and the divine; and that in order to relate ourselves appropriately to
each, a primary and unevidenceable act of interpretation is required which,
when directed toward God, has traditionally been termed "faith." Thus I
shall try to show that while the object of religious knowledge is unique, its
basic epistemological pattern is that of all our knowing.

This is not to say that the logic of theistic belief has no peculiarities. It
does indeed display certain unique features; and these (I shall try to show)
are such as follow from the unique nature of its object, and are precisely
the peculiarities which we should expect if that object is real. In the present
chapter, then, we shall take note of the common epistemological pattern in
which religious knowledge partakes, and in the following chapter we shall
examine some special peculiarities of religious knowing.

"Significance" seems to be the least misleading word available to name the
fundamental characteristic of experience which I wish to discuss. Other possible terms are "form" and "meaning." But "form," as the word is used in
the traditional matter-form distinction, would require careful editing and
commentary to purge it of unwanted Aristotelian associations. "Meaning,"

---

[2] William Temple, *Nature, Man and God* (London, 1934), p. 334.

on the other hand, has been so overworked and misused in the past, not only by plain men and poets, but also by theologians and philosophers,[3] as to be almost useless today, except in its restricted technical use as referring to the equivalence of symbols. We may perhaps hope that after a period of exile the wider concept of "meaning" will be readmitted into the philosophical comity of notions. Indeed Professor Brand Blanshard has already braved the post-Ogden and Richards ban by using the phrase "perceptual meaning." [4] I propose here, however, to use the less prejudged term "significance."

By significance I mean that fundamental and all-pervasive characteristic of our conscious experience which *de facto* constitutes it for us the experience of a "world" and not of a mere empty void or churning chaos. We find ourselves in a relatively stable and ordered environment in which we have come to feel, so to say, "at home." The world has become intelligible to us, in the sense that it is a familiar place in which we have learned to act and react in appropriate ways. Our experience is not just an unpredictable kaleidoscope of which we are bewildered spectators, but reveals to us a familiar, settled cosmos in which we live and act, a world in which we can adopt purposes and adapt means to ends. It is in virtue of this homely, familiar, intelligible character of experience—its possession of significance—that we are able to inhabit and cope with our environment.

If this use of "significance" be allowed it will, I think, readily be granted that our consciousness is essentially consciousness of significance. Mind could neither emerge nor persist in an environment which was totally nonsignificant to it. For this reason it is not possible to define "significance" ostensively by pointing to contrasting examples of significant and nonsignificant experience. In its most general form at least, we must accept the Kantian thesis that we can be aware only of that which enters into a certain framework of basic relations which is correlated with the structure of our own consciousness. These basic relations represent the minimal conditions of significance for the human mind. The totally nonsignificant is thus debarred from entering into our experience. A completely undifferentiated field, or a sheer "buzzing, booming confusion," would be incapable of sustaining consciousness. For our consciousness is (to repeat) essentially consciousness of significance. Except perhaps in very early infancy or in states of radical breakdown, the human mind is always aware of its environment as having this quality of fundamental familiarity or intelligibility. Significance, then, is simply the most general characteristic of our experience.

Significance, so defined, has an essential reference to action. Consciousness of a particular kind of environmental significance involves a judgment, implicit or explicit, as to the appropriateness of a particular kind, or range of

---

[3] Cf. Ogden and Richards, *The Meaning of Meaning* (7th ed.; London, 1945), ch. 8.
[4] *The Nature of Thought* (London, 1939), I, chs. 4–6.

kinds, of action in relation to that environment. The distinction between types of significance is a distinction between the reactions, occurrent and dispositional, which they render appropriate. For the human psychophysical organism has evolved under the pressure of a continual struggle to survive, and our system of significance-attributions has as a result an essentially pragmatic orientation. Our outlook is instinctively empirical and practical. Physiologically we are so constituted as to be sensitive only to a minute selection of the vast quantity and complexity of the events taking place around us—that precise selection which is practically relevant to us. Our ears, for example, are attuned to a fragment only of the full range of sound waves, and our eyes to but a fraction of the multitudinous variations of light. Our sense organs automatically select from nature those aspects in relation to which we must act. We apprehend the world only at the macroscopic level at which we have practical dealings with it. As Professor Kemp Smith has said, "The function of sense-perception, as of instinct, is not knowledge but power, not insight but adaptation." [5] For an animal to apprehend more of its environment than is practically relevant to it would prove a fatal complication; it would be bemused and bewildered, and unable to react selectively to the stimuli indicating danger, food, and so on. And it is equally true at the human level that the significance of a given object or situation for a given individual consists in the practical *difference* which the existence of that object makes to that individual. It is indeed one of the marks of our status as dependent beings that we live by continual adaptation to our environment; and from this follows the essentially practical bearing of that which constitutes significance for us.

Although the locus of significance is primarily our environment as a whole, we can in thought divide this into smaller units of significance. We may accordingly draw a provisional distinction between two species of significance, object-significance and situational significance, and note the characteristics of significance first in terms of the former.

Every general name, such as "hat," "book," "fire," "house," names a type of object-significance. For these are isolable aspects of our experience which (in suitable contexts) render appropriate distinctive patterns of behavior. The word "hat," for example, does not name a rigidly delimited class of objects but a particular *use* to which things can be put, namely, as a covering for the head. Objects are specially manufactured for this use; but if necessary many other items can be made to fulfill the function of hat. This particular way of treating things, as headgear, is the behavioral correlate of the type of object-significance which we call "being a hat." Indeed the boundaries of each distinguishable class of objects are defined by the two *foci* of (1) physical structure and (2) function in relation to human

---

[5] *Prolegomena to an Idealist Theory of Knowledge* (London, 1924), pp. 32–33.

interests. Our names are always in part names for functions or uses or kinds of significance as apprehended from the standpoint of the agent.

Significance, then, is a relational concept. A universe devoid of consciousness would be neither significant nor nonsignificant. An object or a sense-field is significant *for* or *to* a mind. We are only concerned here with significance for the human mind, but it is well to remember that the lower animals also are aware of their environment as being significant, this awareness being expressed not in words or concepts but in actions and readinesses for action.

There is, I hope, no suggestion of anything occult about this fundamental feature of our experience which I am calling "significance." The difficulty in discussing it is not novelty but, on the contrary, overfamiliarity. It is so completely obvious that we can easily overlook its importance, or even its existence. There is also the related difficulty that we do not apprehend significance as such, but only each distinguishable aspect of our experience as having its own particular type of significance. For significance is a genus which exists only in its species. Just as we perceive the various colors, but never color in general, so we perceive this and that kind of significance, but never significance *simpliciter*.

After this preliminary characterization of the nature of significance, we may take note of the mental activity of interpretation which is its subjective correlate. The word "interpretation" suggests the possibility of differing judgments; we tend to call a conclusion an interpretation when we recognize that there may be other and variant accounts of the same subject matter. It is precisely because of this suggestion of ambiguity in the given, and of alternative modes of construing data, that "interpretation" is a suitable correlate term for "significance."

Two uses of "interpretation" are to be distinguished. In one of its senses, an interpretation is a (true or false) *explanation,* answering the question, Why? We speak, for example, of a metaphysician's interpretation of the universe. In its other sense, an interpretation is a (correct or incorrect) *recognition,*[6] or attribution of significance, answering the question, What? ("What is that, a dog or a fox?") These two meanings are closely connected. For all explanation operates ultimately in terms of recognition. We explain a puzzling phenomenon by disclosing its context, revealing it as part of a wider whole which does not, for us, stand in need of explanation. We render the unfamiliar intellectually acceptable by relating it to the already recognizable, indicating a connection or continuity between the old and the new. But in the unique case of the universe as a whole the distinction between explanation and recognition fails to arise. For the universe has no

---

[6] This is a slightly off-dictionary sense of "recognition," equating it, not with the identification of the appearances of an object at different times as appearances of the same object, but with the apprehension of what has been discussed above as the "significance" of objects.

wider context in terms of which it might be explained; an explanation of it can therefore only consist in a perception of its significance. In this case, therefore, interpretation is both recognition and explanation. Hence the theistic recognition, or significance-attribution, is also a metaphysical explanation or theory. However, although the explanatory and recognition aspects of theistic faith are inseparable, they may usefully be distinguished for purposes of exposition. In the present chapter we shall be examining interpretation, including the religious interpretation, as a recognition, or perception of significance; and in the following chapter, as an explanation.

An act of recognition, or of significance-attribution, is a complex occurrence dealing with two different types of ambiguity in the given. There are, on the one hand, interpretations which are mutually exclusive (e.g., "That is a fox" and "That is a dog," referring to the same object), and on the other hand interpretations which are mutually compatible (e.g., "That is an animal" and "That is a dog"; or "He died by asphyxiation" and "He was murdered"). Of two logically alternative interpretations only one (at most) can be the correct interpretation. But two compatible interpretations may both be correct. We shall be concerned henceforth with this, latter kind of difference, in which several levels or layers or orders of significance are found in the same field of data.

The following are some simple examples of different levels or orders of object-significance.

(a) I see a rectangular red object on the floor in the corner. So far I have interpreted it as a "thing" (or "substance"), as something occupying space and time. On looking more closely, however, I see that it is a red-covered book. I have now made a new interpretation which includes my previous one, but goes beyond it.

(b) There is a piece of paper covered with writing. An illiterate savage can perhaps interpret it as something made by man. A literate person, who does not know the particular language in which it is written, can interpret it as being a document. But someone who understands the language can find in it the expression of specific thoughts. Each is answering the question, "What is it?" correctly, but answering it at different levels. And each more adequate attribution of significance presupposes the less adequate ones.

This relationship between types of significance, one type being superimposed upon and interpenetrating another, is a pattern which we shall find again in larger and more important spheres.

We have already noted that significance is essentially related to action. The significance of an object to an individual consists in the practical difference which that object makes to him, the ways in which it affects either his immediate reactions or his more long-term plans and policies. There is also a reciprocal influence of action upon our interpretations. For it is only when we have begun to act upon our interpretations, and have thereby verified that our environment is capable of being successfully inhabited in terms of them, that they become fully "real" modes of experience. Interpretations which take the dispositional form of readinesses for action, instead of immediate overt activity, borrow this feeling of "reality" from cognate interpretations which are being or have already been confirmed in action. (For example, when I see an apple on the sideboard, but do not immediately eat it, I nevertheless perceive it as entirely "real" because I have in the past verified similar interpretations of similar apple-like appearances.) It is by acting upon our interpretations that we build up an apprehension of the world around us; and in this process interpretations, once confirmed, suggest and support further interpretations. The necessity of acting-in-terms-of to "clinch" or confirm an interpretation has its importance, as we shall note later, in relation to the specifically religious recognition which we call theistic faith.

We have been speaking so far only of object-significance. But, as already indicated, object-significance as contrasted with situational significance is an expository fiction. An object absolutely per se and devoid of context would have no significance for us. It can be intelligible only as part of our familiar world. What significance would remain, for example, to a book without the physical circumstance of sight, the conventions of language and writing, the acquired art of reading, and even the literature of which the book is a part and the civilization within which it occurs? An object owes its significance as much to its context as to itself; it is what it is largely because of its place in a wider scheme of things. We are indeed hardly ever conscious of anything in complete isolation. Our normal consciousness is of groups of objects standing in recognizable patterns of relations to one another. And it is the resulting situation taken as a whole that carries significance for us, rendering some ranges of action and reaction appropriate and others inappropriate. We live and plan and act all the time in terms of the situational significance of our environment; although of course our interest may focus at any given moment upon a particular component object within the current situation.

We do not, it is true, as plain men generally think of the familiar situations which constitute our experience from moment to moment as having "significance" and of our actions as being guided thereby. But in the fundamental sense in which we are using the term, our ordinary consciousness of the world is undoubtedly a continuous consciousness of significance. It is normally consciousness of a routine or humdrum significance which is so familiar that we take it entirely for granted. The significance for me, for example, of my situation at the present moment is such that I go on quietly working; this is the response rendered appropriate by my interpretation of my contemporary experience. No fresh response is required, for my routine reactions are already adjusted to the prevailing context of significance. But this significance is none the less real for being undramatic.

The component elements of situational significance are not only physical objects—tables, mountains, stars, houses, hats, and so on—but also such nonmaterial entities as sounds and lights and odors and, no less important, such psychological events and circumstances as other peoples' thoughts, emotions, and attitudes. Thus the kinds of situational significance in terms of which we act and react are enormously complex. Indeed the philosopher who would trace the morphology of situational significance must be a dramatist and poet as well as analyst. Attempts at significance-mapping have been undertaken by some of the existentialist writers: what they refer to as the "existential" character of experience is the fact that we are ourselves by definition *within* any relational system which constitutes a situation for us. However, these writers have usually been concerned to bring out the more strained and hectic aspects of human experience, presenting it often as a vivid night-mare of metaphysical anxieties and perils. They are undoubtedly painting from real life, particularly in this frightened age, but I venture to think that they are depicting it in a partial and one-sided manner.

A "situation" may be defined, then, as a state of affairs which, when selected for attention by an act of interpretation, carries its own distinctive practical significance for us. We may be involved in many different situations at the same time and may move by swift or slow transitions of interpretation from one to another. There may thus occur an indefinitely complex inter-penetration of situations. For example I am, let us say, sitting in a room playing a game of chess with a friend. The game, isolated by the brackets of imagination, is a situation in itself in which I have a part to play as one of the two competing intelligences presiding over the chess board. Here is an artificial situation with its conventional boundaries, structure, and rules of procedure. But from time to time my attention moves from the board to the friend with whom I am playing, and I exchange some conversation with him. Now I am living in another situation which contains the game of chess as a sub-situation. Then suddenly a fire breaks out in the building, and the attention of both of us shifts at once to our wider physical situation; and so on. There are the wider and wider spatial situations of the block, the city, the state, continent, globe, Milky Way, and finally, as the massive permanent background situation inclusive of all else, the physical universe. And there are also the widening circles of family, class, nation, civilization, and all the other groupings within the inclusive group of the human species as a whole. The complex web of interplays within and between these two expanding series gives rise to the infinite variety of situations of which our human life is composed.

Finally, enfolding and interpenetrating this interlocking mass of finite situations there is also, according to the insistent witness of theistic religion, the all-encompassing situation of being in the presence of God and within the sphere of an on-going divine purpose. Our main concern, after these prolonged but unavoidable preliminaries, is to be with this alleged ultimate and inclusive significance and its relation to the more limited and temporary significances through which it is mediated.

Our inventory, then, shows three main orders of situational significance, corresponding to the threefold division of the universe, long entertained by human thought, into nature, man, and God. The significance for us of the physical world, nature, is that of an objective environment whose character and "laws" we must learn, and toward which we have continually to relate ourselves aright if we are to survive. The significance for us of the human world, man, is that of a realm of relationships in which we are responsible agents, subject to moral obligation. This world of moral significance is, so to speak, superimposed upon the natural world, so that relating ourselves to the moral world is not distinct from the business of relating ourselves to the natural world but is rather a particular manner of so doing. And likewise the more ultimately fateful and momentous matter of relating ourselves to the divine, to God, is not distinct from the task of directing ourselves within the natural and ethical spheres; on the contrary, it entails (without being reducible to) a way of so directing ourselves.

In the case of each of these three realms, the natural, the human, and the divine, a basic act of interpretation is required which discloses to us the existence of the sphere in question, thus providing the ground for our multifarious detailed interpretations within that sphere.

Consider first the level of natural significance. This is the significance which our environment has for us as animal organisms seeking pleasure and survival and shunning pain and death. In building houses, cooking food, avoiding dangerous precipices, whirlpools, and volcanoes, and generally conducting ourselves prudently in relation to the material world, we are all the time taking account of what I am calling (for want of a better name) the *natural* significance of our environment.

We have already noted some instances of natural significance when discussing the recognition of objects and situations. It is a familiar philosophical tenet, and one which may perhaps today be taken as granted, that all conscious experience of the physical world contains an element of interpretation. There are combined in each moment of experience a presented field of data and an interpretive activity of the subject. The perceiving mind is thus always in some degree a selecting, relating and synthesizing agent, and experiencing our environment involves a continuous activity of interpretation. "Interpretation" here is of course an unconscious and habitual process, the process by which a sense-field is perceived, for example, as a three-dimensional room, or a particular configuration of colored patches within that field as a book lying upon a table. Interpretation in this sense is generally recognized as a factor in the genesis of sense perception. We have now to note, however, the further and more basic act of interpretation which reveals to us the very existence of a material world, a world which we explore and inhabit as our given environment. In attending to this primary interpretative act we are noting the judgment which carries us beyond the solipsist predicament into an objective world of enduring, causally interacting objects, which we share with other people. Given the initial rejection of solipsism (or rather given the interpretative bias of human nature, which has prevented all but the most enthusiastic of philosophers from falling into solipsism) we can, I think, find corroborations of an analogical kind to support our belief in the unobserved continuance of physical objects and the reality of other minds. But the all-important first step, or assumption, is unevidenced and unevidenceable—except for permissive evidence, in that one's phenomenal experience is "there" to be interpreted either solipisistically or otherwise. But there is no event within our phenomenal experience the occurrence or nonoccurrence of which is relevant to the truth or falsity of the solipsist hypothesis. That hypothesis represents one possible interpretation of our experience as a whole, and the contrary belief in a plurality of minds existing in a common world represents an alternative and rival interpretation.

It may perhaps be objected that it does not make any practical difference whether solipsism be true or not, and that these are not therefore two *different* interpretations of our experience. For if our experience, phenomenally considered, would be identical on either hypothesis, then the alternative (it will be said) is a purely verbal one; the choice is merely a choice of synonyms. I do not think, however, that this is the case. Phenomenally, there is no difference between a dream in which we know that we are dreaming and one in which we do not. But, nevertheless, there is a total difference between the two experiences—total not in the sense that every, or indeed any, isolable aspects of them differ, but in the sense that the two experiences taken as wholes are of different kinds. We are aware of precisely the same course of events, but in the one case this occurs within mental brackets, labeled as a dream, while in the other case we are ourselves immersed within the events and live through them as participants. The phenomena are apprehended in the one case as dream constituents and in the other case as "real." And the difference caused by a genuine assent to solipsism would be akin to the sudden realization during an absorbing dream that it *is* only a dream. If the solipsist interpretation were to be seriously adopted and wholeheartedly believed, experience would take on an unreal character in contrast with one's former nonsolipsist mode of experience. Our personal relationships in particular, our loves and friendships, our hates and enmities, rivalries and cooperations, would have to be treated not as transsubjective meetings with other personalities, but as dialogues and dramas with oneself. There would be only one person in existence, and other "people," instead of being apprehended as independent centers of intelligence and purpose, would be but human-like appearances. They could not be the objects of affection or enmity, nor could their actions be subjected to moral judgment in our normal non-solipsist sense. In short, although it must be very difficult, if not impossible, for the sanely functioning mind seriously to assent to solipsism and to apperceive in terms of it, yet this does represent at least a logically possible interpretation of experience, and constitutes a *different* interpretation from our ordinary belief in an independently existing world of things and persons. It follows that our normal mode of experience is itself properly described as an interpretation, an interpretation which we are unable to justify by argument but which we have nevertheless no inclination or reason to doubt. Indeed as Hume noted, nature has not left this to our choice, "and has doubtless esteem'd it an affair of too great importance to be trusted to our uncertain reasonings and speculations. We may well ask, What causes induce us to believe in the existence of body [i.e., matter]? but 'tis vain to ask, Whether there be body or not? That is a point, which we must take for granted in all our reasonings." [7]

But the ordering of our lives in relation to an objective material environment thus revealed to us by a basic act of interpretation is not the most distinctively human level of experience. It is characteristic of mankind to live not only in terms of the natural significance of his world but also in the dimension of personality and responsibility. And so we find that presupposing consciousness of the physical world, and supervening upon it, is the kind of situational significance which we call "being responsible" or "being under obligation." The sense of moral obligation, or of "oughtness," is the basic datum of ethics. It is manifested whenever someone, in circumstances requiring practical decision, feels "obligated" to act, or to refrain from acting, in some particular way. When this occurs, the natural significance of his environment is interpenetrated by another, ethical significance. A traveler on an unfrequented road, for example, comes upon a stranger who has met with an accident and who is lying injured and in need of help. At the level of natural significance this is just an empirical state of affairs, a particular configuration of stone and earth and flesh. But an act or reflex of interpretation at the moral level reveals to the traveler a situation in which he is under obligation to render aid. He feels a categorical imperative laid upon him, demanding that he help the injured man. The situation takes on for him a peremptory ethical significance, and he finds himself in a situation of inescapable personal responsibility.

As has often been remarked, it is characteristic of situations exhibiting moral significance that they involve, directly or indirectly, more than one

---

[7] *Treatise,* bk. I, pt. IV, sec. 2 (Selby-Bigge's ed., pp. 187–188).

person. The other or others may stand either in an immediate personal relationship to the moral agent or, as in large-scale social issues, in a more remote causal relationship. (The sphere of politics has been defined as that of the *im*personal relationships between persons.) Ethical significance, as the distinctive significance of situations in which persons are components, includes both of these realms. To feel moral obligation is to perceive (or misperceive) the practical significance for oneself of a situation in which one stands in a responsible relationship to another person or to other people. That the perception of significance in personal situations sets up (in Kant's terms) a categorical imperative, while natural situations give rise only to hypothetical imperatives, conditional upon our own desires, is a defining characteristic of the personal world.

Clearly, moral significance presupposes natural significance. For in order that we may be conscious of moral obligations, and exercise moral intelligence, we must first be aware of a stable environment in which actions have foreseeable results, and in which we can learn the likely consequences of our deeds. It is thus a precondition of ethical situations that there should be a stable medium, the world, with its own causal laws, in which people meet and in terms of which they act. Indeed the two spheres of significance, the moral and the physical, entirely interpenetrate. For all occasions of obligation have reference, either immediately or ultimately, to overt action. Relating oneself to the ethical sphere is thus a particular manner of relating oneself to the natural sphere: ethical significance is mediated to us in and through the natural world.

As in the case of natural situational significance, we can enter the sphere of ethical significance only by our own act of interpretation. But at this level the interpretation is a more truly voluntary one. That is to say, it is not forced upon us from outside, but depends upon an inner capacity and tendency to interpret in this way, a tendency which we are free to oppose and even to overrule. If a man chooses to be a moral solipsist, or absolute egoist, recognizing no responsibility toward other people, no one can prove to him that he has any such responsibilities. The man who, when confronted with some standard situation having ethical significance, such as a bully wantonly injuring a child, fails to see it as morally significant, could only be classified as suffering from a defect of his nature analogous to physical blindness. He can of course be compelled by threats of punishment to conform to a stated code of behavior; but he cannot be compelled to feel moral obligation. He must see and accept for himself his own situation as a responsible being and its obverse of ethical accountability.

Has this epistemological paradigm—of one order of significance superimposed upon and mediated through another—any further application? The contention of this essay is that it has. As ethical significance interpenetrates natural significance, so religious significance interpenetrates both ethical and natural. The divine is the highest and ultimate order of significance, mediating neither of the others and yet being mediated through both of them.

But what do we mean by religious significance? What is it that, for the ethical monotheist, possesses this significance, and in what does the significance consist?

The primary locus of religious significance is the believer's experience as a whole. The basic act of interpretation which reveals to him the religious significance of life is a uniquely "total interpretation," whose logic will be studied in the next chapter. But we must at this point indicate what is intended by the phrase, "total interpretation," and offer some preliminary characterization of its specifically theistic *form*.

Consider the following imagined situation. I enter a room in a strange building and find that a militant secret society appears to be meeting there. Most of the members are armed, and as they take me for a fellow member I judge it expedient to acquiesce in the role. Subtle and bloodthirsty plans are discussed for a violent overthrow of the constitution. The whole situation is alarming in the extreme. Then I suddenly notice behind me a gallery in which there are batteries of arc lights and silently whirring cameras, and I realize that I have walked by accident onto the set of a film. This realization consists in a change of interpretation of my immediate environment. Until now I had automatically interpreted it as being "real life," as a dangerous situation demanding considerable circumspection on my part. Now I interpret it as having practical significance of a quite different kind. But there is no corresponding change in the observable course of events. The meeting of the "secret society" proceeds as before, although now I believe the state of affairs to be quite other than I had previously supposed it to be. The same phenomena are interpreted as constituting an entirely different practical situation. And yet not quite the same phenomena, for I have noticed important new items, namely, the cameras and arc lights. But let us now in imagination expand the room into the world, and indeed expand it to include the entire physical universe. This is the strange room into which we walk at birth. There is no space left for a photographers' gallery, no direction in which we can turn in search of new clues which might reveal the significance of our situation. Our interpretation must be a *total* interpretation, in which we assert that the world as a whole (as experienced by ourselves) is of this or that kind, that is to say, affects our plans and our policies in such and such ways.

The monotheist's faith-apprehension of God as the unseen Person dealing with him in and through his experience of the world is from the point of view of epistemology an interpretation of this kind, an interpretation of the world as a whole as mediating a divine presence and purpose. He sees in his situation as a human being a significance to which the appropriate response is a religious trust and obedience. His interpretative leap carries him into a world which exists through the will of a holy, righteous, and loving Being who is the creator and sustainer of all that is. Behind the world—to use an almost inevitable spatial metaphor—there is apprehended to be an omnipotent, personal Will whose purpose toward mankind guarantees men's highest good and blessedness. The believer finds that he is at all times in the presence of this holy Will. Again and again he realizes, either at the time or in retrospect, that in his dealings with the circumstances of his own life he is also having to do with a transcendent Creator who is the determiner of his destiny and the source of all good.

Thus the primary religious perception, or basic act of religious interpretation, is not to be described as either a reasoned conclusion or an unreasoned hunch that there is a God. It is, putatively, an apprehension of the divine presence within the believer's human experience. It is not an inference to a general truth, but a "divine-human encounter," a mediated meeting with the living God.

As ethical significance presupposes natural, so religious significance presupposes both ethical and natural. Entering into conscious relation with God consists in large part in adopting a particular style and manner of acting towards our natural and social environments. For God summons men to serve him *in* the world, and in terms of the life of the world. Religion is not only a way of cognizing but also, and no less vitally, a way of living. To see the world as being ruled by a divine love which sets infinite value upon each individual and includes all men in its scope, and yet to live as though the world were a realm of chance in which each must fight for his own interests against the rest, argues a very dim and wavering vision of God's rule. So far as that vision is clear it issues naturally in a trust in the divine purpose and obedience to the divine will. We shall be able to say more about this practical and dispositional response, in which the apprehension of the religious significance of life so largely consists, when we come in Chapter 9 to examine a particular form of theistic faith. At present we are concerned only with the general nature of the awareness of God.

Rudolf Otto has a somewhat obscure doctrine of the schematization of the Holy in terms of ethics.[8] Without being committed to Otto's use of the Kantian notion, or to his general philosophy of religion, we have been led to a parallel conception of the religious significance of life as schematized in, mediated through, or expressed in terms of, its natural and moral significance. As John Oman says of the Hebrew prophets,

> What determines their faith is not a theory of the Supernatural, but an attitude towards the Natural, as a sphere in which a victory of deeper meaning than the visible and of more abiding purpose than the fleeting can be won. . . .

---

[8] *The Idea of the Holy,* trans. by J. W. Harvey (London, 1923), ch. 7.

The revelation of the Supernatural was by reconciliation to the Natural: and this was made possible by realising in the Natural the meaning and purpose of the Supernatural.[9]

In one respect this theistic interpretation is more akin to the natural than to the ethical interpretation. For while only *some* situations have moral significance, *all* situations have for embodied beings a continuous natural significance. In like manner the sphere of the basic religious interpretation is not merely this or that isolable situation, but the uniquely total situation constituted by our experience as a whole and in all its aspects, up to the present moment.

But on the other hand the theistic interpretation is more akin to the ethical than to the natural significance-attribution in that it is clearly focused in some situations and imperceptible in others. Not all the moments of life mediate equally the presence of God to the ordinary believer. He is not continuously conscious of God's presence (although possibly the saint is), but conscious rather of the divine Will as a reality in the background of his life, a reality which may at any time emerge to confront him in absolute and inescapable demand. We have already observed how one situation may interpenetrate another, and how some sudden pressure or intrusion can cause a shift of interpretation and attention so that the mind moves from one interlocking context to another. Often a more important kind of significance will summon us from a relatively trivial kind. A woman may be playing a game of bridge when she hears her child crying in pain in another room; and at once her consciousness moves from the artificial world of the game to the real world in which she is the mother of the child. Or an officer in the army reserve may be living heedless of the international situation until sudden mobilization recalls him to his military responsibility. The interrupting call of duty may summon us from trivial or relatively unimportant occupations to take part in momentous events. Greater and more ultimate purposes may without warning supervene upon lesser ones and direct our lives into a new channel. But the final significance, which takes precedence over all others as supremely important and overriding, is (according to theism) that of our situation as being in the presence of God. At any time a man may be confronted by some momentous decision, some far-reaching moral choice either of means or of ends, in which his responsibility as a servant of God intrudes upon and conflicts with the requirements of his earthly "station and its duties," so that the latter pales into unimportance and he acts in relation to a more ultimate environment whose significance magisterially overrules his customary way of life. When the call of God is clearly heard other calls become inaudible, and the prophet or saint, martyr or missionary,

[9] *The Natural and the Supernatural* (Cambridge, 1931), p. 448.

the man of conscience or of illumined mind may ignore all considerations of worldly prudence in responding to a claim with which nothing else whatever may be put in the balance.

To recapitulate and conclude this stage of the discussion, the epistemological point which I have sought to make is this. There is in cognition of every kind an unresolved mystery. The knower-known relationship is in the last analysis *sui generis:* the mystery of cognition persists at the end of every inquiry—though its persistence does not prevent us from cognizing. We cannot explain, for example, how we are conscious of sensory phenomena as constituting an objective physical environment; we just find ourselves interpreting the data of our experience in this way. We are aware that we live in a real world, though we cannot prove by any logical formula that it *is* a real world. Likewise we cannot explain how we know ourselves to be responsible beings subject to moral obligations; we just find ourselves interpreting our social experience in this way. We find ourselves inhabiting an ethically significant universe, though we cannot prove that it *is* ethically significant by any process of logic. In each case we discover and live in terms of a particular aspect of our environment through an appropriate act of interpretation; and having come to live in terms of it we neither require nor can conceive any further validation of its reality. The same is true of the apprehension of God. The theistic believer cannot explain *how* he knows the divine presence to be mediated through his human experience. He just finds himself interpreting his experience in this way. He lives in the presence of God, though he is unable to prove by any dialectical process that God exists.

To say this is not of course to demonstrate that God *does* exist. The outcome of the discussion thus far is rather to bring out the similarity of epistemological structure and status between men's basic convictions in relation to the world, moral responsibility, and divine existence. If our line of thought in Chapter I has been sound, these three parallel convictions all qualify, as instances of rational certainty, for the title of knowledge. The aim of the present chapter has thus been to show how, if there be a God, he is known to mankind, and how such knowledge is related to other kinds of human knowing. I hope that at least the outline of a possible answer to these questions has now been offered. . . .

# KAI NIELSEN

*Kai Nielsen* (1926–    ), professor of philosophy at New York University, is a frequent contributor to contemporary theological discussions which center around the problems of verification and language usage.

## Eschatological Verification

Professor John Hick, in carrying on a discussion initiated by Professors Wisdom and Flew, argues that (1) divine existence, as it is understood in the New Testament, is taken to be a matter of objective fact, and (2) statements which assert that existence are empirically verifiable.[1] Hick does not try to show that "God exists" is true and that Christian claims have been established; rather, in "Theology and Verification" he is concerned with the *logically* prior question of whether it is *intelligible* to claim that divine existence is a fact.

I shall argue that Hick has not at all succeeded in establishing what he has set out to establish and that we have no good reasons for believing that such crucial theistic utterances are used to make statements of fact that are either verifiable or confirmable in principle. (Although I cannot accept Hick's central claims, I should like to record that it is a pleasure to read and evaluate critically Hick's writings, for he writes with a clarity and forthrightness of statement that allow his arguments to be appraised readily. The turgid obscurity typical of Tillich, Bultmann, Niebuhr, Buber, and Maritain may give some the illusory sense that they have grasped the esoteric "essence" of religion, but such a manner of writing does not actually contribute to an understanding of religion or to an appraisal of the claims of religion. There is enduring intellectual value in writing so that one's claims can be understood and appraised.)

From the *Canadian Journal of Theology*, Vol. IX (1963), No. 4, pp. 271–281. Used by permission of the author and the *Canadian Journal of Theology*. This discussion is further pursued in the exchange between the author and George I. Mavrodes in Mavrodes', "God and Verification," *Canadian Journal of Theology*, Vol. X (1964), pp. 187–191; and Kai Nielsen, "God and Verification Again," *Canadian Journal of Theology*, Vol. XI (1965), pp. 135–141; also William Bean, "Eschatological Verification, Fortress or Fairyland," *Methodos*, Vol. XVI (1964), pp. 91–107.

[1] John Hick, "Theology and Verification," *Theology Today*, 17 (1960), 12–31.

## I

Recognizing that the central intellectual perplexity for enlightened contemporary theists is not the difficulty of proving theistic claims but the difficulty of establishing their intelligibilty, Hick's primary concern is to refute claims that religious sentences have uses which are *merely* mythical, quasi-moral, ceremonial, emotive, or ideological, and to establish that they characteristically are used to make factual statements—that is, that such sentences as "God exists" or "The world was created by an act of God" typically function to make assertions of "supernatural fact."

It is Hick's contention that "divine existence is in principle verifiable" (p. 12). For a statement to have *factual meaning* it must, Hick argues, contain or entail "predictions which can be verified or falsified" (p. 14). Hick does not contend that God's existence can be *falsified* but, contending that verification and falsification are in this context asymmetrically related, Hick argues that God's existence can in principle be verified. He does not claim that the verification can come in this life. The verification is eschatological; it will come, if at all, in the next life. It need not necessarily come as a "vision" but may be an experience of the fulfilment of God's purpose for ourselves, as it has been given to us in Christian revelation, in conjunction with "an experience of communion with God as he has revealed himself in the person of Christ" (p. 27).

Hick claims in "Theology and Verification," as he did in *Faith and Knowledge*,[2] that the notion of "eschatological verification is sound; and further, that no viable alternative to it has been offered to establish the factual character of theism" (p. 18). He also claims that it is not "an *ad hoc* invention but is based upon an actually operative religious concept of God" (p. 18).

It is important to note how Hick's insistence that the verification must be eschatological allows him to come to terms with Wisdom's argument that the existence of God is not *now* an experimental issue. Hick contends, in opposition to Wisdom, that the sophisticated Christian does not merely have different feelings or attitudes about the world and man's place in it. He does not view life in just a different way; that is, his difference with the atheist is not the same as that which exists where two people see the same ambiguous figure in two different ways (e.g., the duck-rabbit, seen as either a duck or a rabbit). The Christian's and the atheist's "opposed interpretations" of man's life and the nature of reality are "genuinely rival assertions, though assertions whose status has the peculiar characteristic of being guaranteed retrospectively by a future crux" (p. 19). There is then a real factual

---

[2] Ithaca: Cornell University Press, 1957.

issue between the atheist and theist; it is not just a matter of rival ways of "seeing," "viewing," or "looking" at man's nature and destiny. But Hick does agree with Wisdom that in *this life* we are like men looking at an ambiguous figure. We cannot now settle by any appeal to experience the issue between the theist and atheist. There are no signs that can unambiguously count as pointing to God; there is no *present* evidence adequate to make it meaningful to assert "There is a God" where this sentence is used to make a statement of objective fact; but "Christian doctrine postulates an ultimate unambiguous state of existence *in patria* as well as our present ambiguous existence *in via*" (p. 19). But Hick makes it perfectly clear that this postulated state of an "eternal heavenly life as well as an earthly pilgrimage" cannot "be appealed to as evidence for theism as a present interpretation of our experience . . ." (p. 19). If we simply regard our experiences in this life they are too ambiguous to allow us correctly to claim that theism is a verifiable position. If we so limit our appeal, a claim such as Wisdom's is quite compelling. But, Hick argues, we do not need so to limit it. We can *conceive* what it would be like to have an afterlife and we can *conceive* what it would be like to verify that there is a God in the "resurrection world" of the next life. Thus, while we cannot possibly have any present evidence for or against theism, and must now live by faith if we are to believe, we can *conceive* what it would be like to have evidence in the next life; and so the existence of God is, after all, a factual issue and "the choice between theism and atheism is a real and not merely empty or verbal choice" (p. 19).

It seems to me that Hick is correct in affirming that any reasonably orthodox Christian—I do not speak of Tillichians—would surely wish to regard the question of divine existence as a factual, substantive issue. If an orthodox Christian discovered that he and the atheists were *only* differing in picture preferences, he would then assert that the very foundations of Christianity had been destroyed. Religious talk is certainly embedded in myth and overlaid with ceremonial expressions; and it most certainly guides our behaviour and calls for a basic alteration of our attitudes; but, as Hick recognizes, certain key religious statements are also thought by believers to be factual assertions. If utterances such as "There exists a creator of the heavens and the earth" are not taken by believers to be factual assertions—myth-embedded as they are—theistic religious talk and hence Christianity itself would lose the character it has. If our task is to understand Christianity and not simply to redefine it to fit some antecedently held intellectual or moral ideal, we must come to grips with this assertional element in Christianity. Hick has courageously and honestly attempted to do just that. Like Barth and Crombie, and unlike Tillich and Braithwaite, Hick attempts to elucidate the Christian religion that we actually meet, and in one way or another contend with, in daily life; we sense here that Hick is actually trying to analyse the claims the Christian ordinarily makes. And this, to my way of thinking, is just what we must do if we ever are to get anywhere in an understanding of religion. I am not saying that this is all that either a theologian or a philosopher needs to do, but he at least must do this. Perhaps in that way he will make Christianity or Judaism sound very absurd; but perhaps they are absurd. (We must not forget Kierkegaard here.)

While I am in complete agreement with Hick on this methodological issue, Hick fails, in my judgment, to make the basic claims of Christianity intelligible on the very grounds on which he rightly recognizes that the believer demands they should be intelligible. Hick's arguments are clear and straightforward until he gets to the very crux of his argument and then they become incoherent. Hick recognizes the difficulty of trying to speak of God and he argues that language is never quite adequate to state the facts of which religious people are aware. He speaks as if thought could speed ahead of language and, independently of the forms of language, grasp what is the case. It is natural to want to say this, but can we really "escape language" in this way? Is it really an intelligible claim? [3] Given such complications, it seems to me apparent that we are in real darkness as to whether "there are such things as religious facts" (p. 31). It seems to me that the more plausible conclusion, given such a situation, would be that religious discourse itself is in conceptual confusion (and not just the theological and philosophical accounts of it).[4] This, of course, would be welcome news to the secularist and most unwelcome news to all but the most rabidly Kierkegaardian defenders of the faith. Thus it is understandable that theologians such as Hick, Farrer, and Crombie should try to make an intelligible elucidation of religious concepts. I shall not attempt here to show that religious discourse itself is in a state of conceptual confusion, but merely try to show that Hick's account of such discourse is not successful. But if my analysis is correct, the following problem, relevant to the wider issue mentioned above, is suggested. If Hick utterly fails to establish how "There is a God" is in *any way* verifiable and if Hick is right (as I think he is) in his claim that statements asserting divine existence typically are *intended* to be factual, verifiable claims, then, given the care and the skill with which he has stated the arguments pro and con, would it not be reasonable to assume there is something wrong with our *first-order* God-talk itself? If

---

[3] I shall not pursue this question here, but a study of the work of Pierce or Wittgenstein raises serious questions about the very possibility of thoughts that have no linguistic expression. For brief and more readily accessible analyses that bring out some of the crucial difficulties, see Alice Ambrose, "The Problem of Linguistic Inadequacy," in Max Black (ed.), *Philosophical Analysis* (Ithaca: Cornell University Press, 1950), pp. 15–37, and William Kennick, "Art and the Ineffable," *Journal of Philosophy,* **58** (1961), 309–20.

[4] I have tried to show how this is so in an article, "Speaking of God," *Theoria,* **28** (1962), 110–37.

it can be shown, as I think it can, that the analyses of Crombie, Farrer, and Mascall result in similar failures, does not the assumption of the incoherent quality of the discourse itself grow stronger? It seems to me that this issue needs to be faced by theologians in a way in which it has not yet been faced.[5]

The above assumes that Hick's arguments will not do. I have yet to establish this. But it should make apparent the importance for the Christian of making out a case somewhat along the lines that Hick attempts.

## II

In making out his case for eschatological verification, Hick argues that it is intelligible to say that there is a continued existence after death. Hick is perfectly aware that we cannot take such a claim as simply a noble myth, but that it must be regarded as an empirical assertion if his case for eschatological verification is to be made out. As Hick himself recognizes, the truth of such a claim is not sufficient for his case, but without it eschatological verification is unintelligible (pp. 25–26).

Hick does not argue for what he takes to be the "Hellenic notion of the survival of a disembodied soul" (p. 21) but for "the specifically Christian (and also Jewish) belief in the resurrection of the flesh or body." God "by an act of sovereign power . . . resurrects or (better) reconstitutes or recreates" at least some human beings, giving them a "resurrection body" in "the resurrection world." The relation of the "resurrection body" to the "resurrection world" is obscure and puzzling, to put it conservatively. Hick readily acknowledges that such conceptions are very odd, but, however odd, they are (he avers) intelligible empirical claims. (Even *assuming* their *intelligibility,* I should think their very oddness and extreme implausibility would be a very good reason for those who tie their belief in God to such notions to give up their belief and place a belief in God in the same class with a belief in Santa Claus or in the Easter Bunny.) I doubt very much that either conception is intelligible. After all, what is this "resurrection world"? What counts as a space that is "a different space" from physical space? Has any meaning or use been given to the words "non-physical space"? What are we supposed to be contrasting with physical space, that either has or fails to have "properties which are manifestly incompatible with its being a region of physical space"? What is it to have a property manifestly incompatible with being a region in physical space? There is the assumption that these words have a use or a sense, but they do not and

---

[5] This issue is obviously evaded in J. N. Hartt's obscure survey of the state and prospects of contemporary theology, "The Theological Situation after Fifty Years," *Yale Review,* 51 (1961), 84f.

Hick does not provide us with one. But I wish to by-pass all these questions here. For the sake of the discussion, I shall not only grant Hick that all these notions are meaningful as empirical statements but I shall also grant that they are true.

The survival of a "resurrection body" in a "resurrection world" is only a necessary but not a sufficient condition for the verifiability of theism. Hick puts it this way: "Survival, simply as such, would not serve to verify theism. It would not necessarily be a state of affairs which is manifestly incompatible with the non-existence of God. It might be taken just as a surprising natural fact" (p. 25). Hick must now show how it can be the case that when our "resurrection body" gets to "the resurrection world" we shall then come to know God.

In trying to complete his case for eschatological verification, Hick attempts to show that one can "conceive of after-life experiences which would serve to verify theism" (p. 26). He is looking for a conceivable *situation* "which points unambiguously to the existence of a loving God" (p. 26). Hick suggests that there are "two possible developments of our experience such that, if they occurred in conjunction with one another, . . . they would assure us beyond rational doubt of the reality of God, as conceived in the Christian faith" (p. 26). As we have seen, they are (1) an experience of God's purpose for ourselves as it has been disclosed in Christian revelation, and (2) "an experience of communion with God as he has revealed himself in the person of Christ" (p. 27).

The initial difficulty we feel about (1) and (2) is that they seem to pre-suppose some understanding of that very thing we are trying to understand. But let us see what Hick tries to do with these claims. He starts by telling us (*a*) that the content of (1) is "depicted in the New Testament documents" and (*b*) that these documents indicate (at least to the believer) that to experience the "divine purpose for human life" is "to enjoy a certain valuable quality of personal life, the content of which is given in the character of Christ . . ." (p. 27). This experienced "quality" is "said to be the proper destiny of human nature and the source of man's final self-fulfilment and happiness" (p. 27). That there is such a divine purpose cannot be falsified but it can be verified. (I am troubled about the claim that something can be verified but not falsified, but for the sake of the argument I shall let Hick's claim here pass unexamined.) But how is Hick's claim here even verifiable in principle, without the *assumption* of God—a divine Creator? We are trying to come to understand how "There is a God" or "God created man" could have a factual meaning, but Hick's analysis requires us to presuppose the very thing we are trying to understand, for to speak of "the proper *destiny* of human nature" or of "man's *final* self-fulfilment" *assumes* that man is a creature of God, a divine artefact created by God with a purpose—an "essential human nature" that can be realized. Without such an *assumption,* talk of man's proper destiny or final self-fulfilment is without sense. Hick is asking us to pull ourselves up by our own bootstraps, for unless we understand what it is for there to be a God who created man with a purpose we can make nothing at all of (1).

I add "nothing at all" deliberately, for the believer's understanding of "God exists" or "God loves us" is not—as Hick claims—sufficiently analogous to a child's understanding of what it is to be an adult. Hick's analogy is faulty because the child, as soon as he can recognize anything at all, sees adults around him and is constantly in their presence, but Hick has not shown us how we can have a like idea of what "the divine purpose for us is" or what we mean by "God." We indeed know that these words have great emotional appeal for us, and we know that they would not have that appeal if religious discourse were treated simply as (*a*) a species of ceremonial discourse, (*b*) moral discourse touched with emotion, or (*c*) expressions of human commitment embedded in a mythical framework. Beyond this, we know that there are certain analytic statements we can make about "God" (e.g., "God is eternal" and the like). But what we do not know is what it would be like to verify "There is divine existence." We have no idea at all of what it would be like for that statement to be either true or false. Here the believer is in a much worse position than the child. And, as we have seen, to appeal to the divine purpose for man assumes we already know what it would be like to verify that our lives have such a purpose. We do not know what must be the case for it to be true or false that our lives have a purpose, a *telos,* a destiny or final fulfilment. Our actions may be purposive and we may so live that there is some purpose in our lives without its even being intelligible that human life has a purpose or some final end.[6] We do not understand how to break into this closed circle with either God or man's destiny or a Christian revelation of our "essential human nature." It is indeed true that we, who have been brought up as Christians or in close proximity to Christians, know how to use this discourse. In *that sense* it is sheer nonsense to say Christian chatter is meaningless, but Hick has not shown us how we understand this use of language as a factual or statement-making type of discourse. We do not know what must happen for us to assert correctly that so and so is "apprehended as the fulfilment of God's purpose and not simply as a natural state of affairs" (p. 28).

Can (2) help? I think we are no better off here. (2) is the "experience

---

[6] Kurt Baier, *The Meaning of Life* (Canberra: University College, 1957), pp. 20f., has remarked appropriately that religionists often "mistakenly conclude that there can be no purpose *in* life because there is no purpose *of* life; that men cannot themselves adopt and achieve purposes because man, unlike a robot or a watchdog, is not a creature with a purpose."

of communion with God as he has made himself known to men in Christ" (p. 28). Hick acknowledges that we do not know what it would be like to encounter directly an infinite, almighty, eternal Creator. But Jesus, or Christ, comes in as the mediator. "Only God himself knows his own infinite nature; and our human belief about that nature is based upon his self-revelation to men in Christ" (p. 29). Hick quotes with approval Barth's contention that "Jesus Christ is the knowability of God" (p. 29).

There is—as R. W. Hepburn has stressed in his *Christianity and Paradox* [7] —an ambiguity in this sort of claim. "Jesus was born in Bethlehem" or "Jesus died on the cross" are straightforward empirical statements. There is no puzzle at all about their logical status. Where "Jesus" and "Christ" are equivalent we can of course make substitutions and the resulting statements will also be uncontroversial. But "Jesus" and "Christ" are not equivalent, for "Jesus is the Christ" is supposed to be informative. "Christ" or "The Christ" is not intended simply to refer to a man—no matter how extraordinary. "Jesus," by contrast, simply refers to an extraordinary man. We well enough understand the referent of "Jesus," but where "Christ" is not equivalent to "Jesus," what does "Christ" refer to? Unless we already understand what is meant by "God," how can we possibly understand words such as "Christ," "The Christ," "The Son of God," or "Our Lord Jesus Christ"? How can utterances incorporating them be used to make verifiable statements? What would count as verifying them? What *conceivable* experiences, post-mortem or otherwise, would tell us what it would be like to encounter not just Jesus, but the Christ, the Son of God, and the Son of Man, or our Lord, where "Our Lord" does not just mean a wise teacher or a monarch whom we meet either now or hereafter? If we do not know what it would be like to verify "God exists" directly, we have no better idea of what it would be like to verify "The Son of God exists," where "The Son of God" is not identical in meaning with "Jesus." (*If* they are identical in meaning, "The Son of God exists" can provide no logical bridge to "God exists.") The same sort of thing can be said for "The Christ"; and if it is said that "Jesus" and "The Christ" are not identical but we have verified that Jesus is the Christ, then I will reply that Hick has not shown us how we can verify this statement. He has not shown us how we can logically move from "Jesus exists" to "The Christ exists" where they are not identical.

Hick apart, how could we verify "Jesus is the Christ"? What would count as evidence for it? If we say we verify it indirectly by verifying "Jesus lived and acted in a certain way," then again it can be asked what grounds warrant our saying that the verifiable statement, "Jesus lived and in his thirty-third year died on the cross," or any statement or statements of that

[7] London: Watts, 1958.

logically unambiguous type, counts as evidence for "Jesus is the Christ." I do not see that we have any warrent for saying that it is evidence for such a claim. We might decide that Jesus was a powerful man; we might verify that he did many quite amazing things; our moral insight might lead us to say he was a superlatively good and wise man; but how would this at all point, ambiguously or unambiguously, to Jesus' being the Christ, unless we independently understood what was meant by "The Christ" or "X's being the Christ"?

No empirical sense has been given to Hick's "an experience of the reign of the Son in the Kingdom of the Father"; and we are in no position to say, as Hick does, that this confirms Jesus's authority to reveal God's nature and purpose and thus we can verify that there is a God. No method of verification has been given; we do not know what conceivable experiences would count for or against "God exists" and thus Hick has failed to give us any grounds for saying that "There is a God" or "God exists" "asserts a matter of objective fact" (p. 12).

Hick might reply that I am, in effect, arguing like a rationalist. I want a purely logical argument to prove that such experiences are experiences which point to God; but, as Hick correctly remarks, "the exclusion of rational doubt concerning some matter of fact is not equivalent to the exclusion of the logical possibility of error or illusion" (p. 17). To ask for the latter is to ask for what is self-contradictory; it is (in effect) to ask that a factual proposition be analytic. If we take this rationalist stand, then to have a post-mortem experience of "the Kingdom of God with Christ reigning as Lord of the New Aeon, would not constitute a logical certification of his claims nor, accordingly, of the reality of God" (p. 29). If in our "resurrection bodies" in "the resurrection world" we assert "Jesus is ruling over us all with love and justice" the truth of this statement would not entail the truth of the statement "There is a God" or "There is a divine purpose which is revealed through Jesus," but, Hick argues, such a post-mortem experience of Jesus's reign would leave no grounds for rational doubt of these theistic claims.

I of course agree with Hick that a statement of evidence for a statement $p$ need not be equivalent to the statement $p$. My evidence for "My glasses are on the desk" may be "I looked around a moment ago and I saw them there," but the first statement is not equivalent to, and is not entailed by, the second statement; but if this is granted should we not say the same thing here about Jesus as the mediator for God? Our evidence is a certain post-mortem experience of Jesus. It is true that I know what it would be like to see my glasses, while, apart from claims about a "direct vision of God"—claims which Hick does not espouse—I cannot, even in the next life, directly observe God (p. 26). But, after all, there are certainly very many statements that are only indirectly verifiable. We speak of a magnetic field or a superego and we cannot see either, but there are recognized procedures for verifying statements embodying such conceptions. They are a part of a whole network of conceptions, but within the appropriate scientific context there are recognized procedures of verification for statements using such concepts. Why can we not properly say the same thing about Jesus and Christianity?

One important difference is that in science we are more and more willing to take a conventionalist attitude towards such theoretical conceptions. Such conceptions can be seen as useful devices for systematically predicting and retrodicting certain observable events. But once having learned the lesson that not all substantives have a substance, we no longer feel incumbent to ask if there are any such things as magnetic fields or superegos. Such concepts are pragmatically useful constructs since they enable us to make predictions and assessments of behaviour with greater ease than if we did not have such concepts, but we can be quite agnostic about whether there are such things.[8] But the believer cannot be agnostic in this way about God, and he cannot regard the concept of God *simply* as an important construct or as a useful heuristic device in his confessional group, and still remain a believer. (Note that this last statement is analytic.) As Hick argues, to claim "There is a God" is to make what purports to be an objective factual claim. But where we are willing to say that so-and-so is an objective factual claim we must know what could count as a confirmation of it. Sometimes our evidence is only indirect, but to know what the evidence unambiguously points to we must know what would count as observing or experiencing what the indirect evidence is indirect evidence of. As I sit upstairs I say to my wife, "The children are playing downstairs." I could give as indirect evidence: "They are laughing down there and someone is running around in the living room." But I only do this because I know what it would be like to see the children laughing and running around in the living room. But if we have no idea of what it would be like to experience that which we *supposedly* have indirect evidence for, then we in fact do not actually understand what it would be like to have evidence (direct or indirect) for it. We do not even understand what it could *mean* to say there is a so-and-so such that we have no idea at all of what it would be like to experience it, but something else can be experienced which is evidence for it. The "it" here cannot refer to anything, for in such a case how could we *possibly understand* what it is that our putative "evidence" is supposed to be evidence for? This is just the difficulty we have in using Jesus as the evidence for God. Hick's correct remarks about statements of evidence not being equivalent to statements of what they are evidence

---

[8] Cf. J. J. C. Smart, "The Reality of Theoretical Entities," *Australasian Journal of Philosophy,* 34 (1956), 1–12.

for is thus not to the point. We still do not know what is *meant* by saying that a post-mortem encounter with Jesus counts as the indirect (but sole) evidence for the existence of God. Thus we do not have a right to say, as Hick does, that we know what it would be like for our faith to be "so fully confirmed in post-mortem experience as to leave no doubt as to the validity of that faith" (p. 29).

## III

Such conclusions as I have arrived at here might, if correct, lead Hick to a conclusion he merely suggests at the end of his essay (pp. 30f.). There he suggests certain considerations that would lead one to the conclusion "that only the theistic believer can find vindication of his belief." If one becomes a believer one's theistic faith can be verified; but the non-believer cannot verify it. Hick's reasoning is as follows. It may be that predictions concerning human experience which give us good grounds for asserting that God exists are conditional predictions; since they are conditional, one is compelled to fulfil the relevant conditions.

> It may then [Hick argues] be a condition of post-mortem verification that we be already in some degree conscious of God by an uncompelled response to his modes of revelation in this world. It may be that such a voluntary consciousness of God is an essential element in the fulfilment of the divine purpose for human nature, so that the verification of theism which consists in an experience of the final fulfilment of that purpose can only be experienced by those who have already entered upon an awareness of God by the religious mode of apperception which we call faith (p. 30).[9]

Once more Hick in effect asks us to assume just what is in question. Granted, we can only verify "There is a table in the next room" if we can carry out certain conditional predictions which the statement entails. But these conditional predictions, these operations, are themselves very well understood. No one needs to approach them by faith, for any normal observer (where "normal observer" can itself be objectively and empirically specified) can verify them. But we have seen above how "God exists" does not have any comparable conditional statements which can be so verified or are so verifiable and hence so understood by a normal observer. We must, instead, appeal to that "apperception" we call faith.

This necessity makes "God exists" a very different sort of chowder. There is a further logical difficulty. If we understand what a statement (conditional

---

[9] Hick presents a similar argument in his "Meaning and Truth in Theology," in Sidney Hook (ed.), *Religious Experience and Truth* (New York: New York University Press, 1960), pp. 208–10. Cf. Paul Edwards' response, *ibid.*, pp. 245–47.

or otherwise) *means,* then it is proper to speak of having faith in its truth, or having faith that the evidence for it outweighs the evidence against it, or that certain experiences will verify it. *Given* these conditions, we could be fideists and approach God simply on trust. But what we cannot do is have faith in a proposition we do not understand, for in such a situation we literally cannot know *what* it is we are supposed to have faith in. If we cannot conceive of there being a state of affairs that would make "God exists" true or false, we cannot understand what conceivable state of affairs we are being asked to accept on faith. We can, by an act of faith, accept as true an antecedently understood proposition. In *that sense,* faith can precede understanding; but it does not make sense to say that we can certify the *meaning* of a proposition by faith; in that sense, understanding must precede faith. We can only have faith in something whose meaning we already understand; otherwise we cannot possibly have any idea what we are being asked to accept on faith. Hick assumes that, as knights of faith, we can somehow be conscious of God even though there is no understanding of what it would be like for there to be a God. But in such a situation we literally cannot have faith in God, for the statement "He has faith in God" cannot be used by him or by anyone else to make a factual claim and thus it cannot, in the requisite sense, have a meaning or a use.

There may indeed be a place for fideism but not on the level at which Hick sets the discussion. Questions of what is *meant* by *x* cannot possibly be settled by faith or trust. At the most, faith might lead us to try to fulfil certain conditions, but we would still have to understand independently of our faith *what* to fulfil. If my argument is in the main correct, we do not understand what it would be like to fulfil conditions which, once fulfilled, would result in anything that would count as a verification of God's existence. This being so, Hick's forthright argument has not established "that the existence or non-existence of the God of the New Testament is a matter of fact, and claims as such eventual experiential verification."

# MARTIN BUBER

*Martin Buber* (1878–1965), Austrian-Jewish existentialist theologian, has made contributions in the fields of sociology, Old Testament studies, and Judaic studies as well as in theology. He was professor of Social Philosophy at Hebrew University in Jerusalem.

## I and Thou

Men have addressed their eternal *Thou* with many names. In singing of Him who was thus named they always had the *Thou* in mind: the first myths were hymns of praise. Then the names took refuge in the language of *It;* men were more and more strongly moved to think of and to address their eternal *Thou* as an *It*. But all God's names are hallowed, for in them He is not merely spoken about, but also spoken to.

Many men wish to reject the word God as a legitimate usage, because it is so misused. It is indeed the most heavily laden of all the words used by men. For that very reason it is the most imperishable and most indispensable. What does all mistaken talk about God's being and works (though there has been, and can be, no other talk about these) matter in comparison with the one truth that all men who have addressed God had God Himself in mind? For he who speaks the word God and really has *Thou* in mind (whatever the illusion by which he is held), addresses the true *Thou* of his life, which cannot be limited by another *Thou,* and to which he stands in a relation that gathers up and includes all others.

But when he, too, who abhors the name, and believes himself to be godless, gives his whole being to addressing the *Thou* of his life, as a *Thou* that cannot be limited by another, he addresses God. . . .

Every real relation with a being or life in the world is exclusive. Its *Thou* is freed, steps forth, is single, and confronts you. It fills the heavens. This does not mean that nothing else exists; but all else lives in *its* light. As long as the presence of the relation continues, this its cosmic range is inviolable. But as soon as a *Thou* becomes *It,* the cosmic range of the relation appears as an offence to the world, its exclusiveness as an exclusion of the universe.

From Martin Buber, *I and Thou,* trans. Ronald Gregor Smith, pp. 75–76, 78–83, 95–96, 99–101, 109–116. Published, 1937, T. & T. Clark. Reprinted with permission of T. & T. Clark and Charles Scribner's Sons.

In the relation with God unconditional exclusiveness and unconditional inclusiveness are one. He who enters on the absolute relation is concerned with nothing isolated any more, neither things nor beings, neither earth nor heaven; but everything is gathered up in the relation. For to step into pure relation is not to disregard everything but to see everything in the *Thou*, not to renounce the world but to establish it on its true basis. To look away from the world, or to stare at it, does not help a man to reach God; but he who sees the world in Him stands in His presence. "Here world, there God" is the language of *It;* "God in the world" is another language of *It;* but to eliminate or leave behind nothing at all, to include the whole world in the *Thou*, to give the world its due and its truth, to include nothing beside God but everything in Him—this is full and complete relation.

Men do not find God if they stay in the world. They do not find Him if they leave the world. He who goes out with his whole being to meet his *Thou* and carries to it all being that is in the world, finds Him who cannot be sought.

Of course God is the "wholly Other"; but He is also the wholly Same, the wholly Present. Of course He is the *Mysterium Tremendum* that appears and overthrows; but He is also the mystery of the self-evident, nearer to me than my *I*.

If you explore the life of things and of conditioned being you come to the unfathomable, if you deny the life of things and of conditioned being you stand before nothingness, if you hallow this life you meet the living God.

Man's sense of *Thou,* which experiences in the relations with every particular *Thou* the disappointment of the change to *It;* strives out but not away from them all to its eternal *Thou;* but not as something is sought: actually there is no such thing as seeking God, for there is nothing in which He could not be found. How foolish and hopeless would be the man who turned aside from the course of his life in order to seek God; even though he won all the wisdom of solitude and all the power of concentrated being he would miss God. Rather is it as when a man goes his way and simply wishes that it might be the way: in the strength of his wish his striving is expressed. Every relational event is a stage that affords him a glimpse into the consummating event. So in each event he does not partake, but also (for he is waiting) does partake, of the one event. Waiting, not seeking, he goes his way; hence he is composed before all things, and makes contact with them which helps them. But when he has *found,* his heart is not turned from them, though everything now meets him in the one event. He blesses every cell that sheltered him, and every cell into which he will yet turn. For this finding is not the end, but only the eternal middle, of the way.

It is a finding without seeking, a discovering of the primal, of origin. His sense of *Thou,* which cannot be satiated till he finds the endless *Thou,* had the *Thou* present to it from the beginning; the presence had only to become wholly real to him in the reality of the hallowed life of the world.

God cannot be inferred in anything—in nature, say, as its author, or in history as its master, or in the subject as the self that is thought in it. Something else is not "given" and God then elicited from it; but God is the Being that is directly, most nearly, and lastingly, over against us, that may properly only be addressed, not expressed.

Men wish to regard a feeling (called feeling of dependence, and recently, more precisely, creaturely feeling) as the real element in the relation with God. In proportion as the isolation and definition of this element is accurate, its unbalanced emphasis only makes the character of complete relation the more misunderstood.

What has already been said of love is even more unshakably valid here. Feelings are a mere accompaniment to the metaphysical and metapsychical fact of the relation, which is fulfilled not in the soul but between *I* and *Thou*. A feeling may be considered ever so essential, it remains nevertheless subject to the dynamic of the soul, where one feeling is outstripped, outdone, and abolished by another. In distinction from relation a feeling has its place in a scale. But above all, every feeling has its place within a polar tension, obtaining its colour and significance not from itself alone, but also from the opposite pole: every feeling is conditioned by its opposite. Thus the absolute relation (which gathers up into reality all those that are relative, and is no more a part, as these are, but is the whole that completes and unifies them all), in being reduced to the status of an isolated and limited feeling, is made into a relative psychological matter.

If the soul is the starting-point of our consideration, complete relation can be understood only in a bipolar way, only as the *coincidentia oppositorum*, as the coincidence of oppositions of feeling. Of course, the one pole —suppressed by the person's basic religious attitude—often disappears from the reflective consciousness, and can only be recalled in the purest and most ingenuous consideration of the depths of the being.

Yes; in pure relation you have felt yourself to be simply dependent, as you are able to feel in no other relation—and simply free, too, as in no other time or place: you have felt yourself to be both creaturely and creative. You had the one feeling then no longer limited by the other, but you had both of them limitlessly and together.

You know always in your heart that you need God more than everything; but do you not know too that God needs you—in the fulness of His eternity needs you? How would man be, how would you be, if God did not need him, did not need you? You need God, in order to be—and God needs you, for the very meaning of your life. In instruction and in poems men are at pains to say more, and they say too much—what turgid and presumptuous talk that is about the "God who becomes"; but we know unshakably in our hearts that there is a becoming of the God that is. The world is not divine sport, it is divine destiny. There is divine meaning in the life of the world, of man, of human persons, of you and of me.

Creation happens to us, burns itself into us, recasts us in burning—we tremble and are faint, we submit. We take part in creation, meet the Creator, reach out to Him, helpers and companions.

Two great servants pace through the ages, prayer and sacrifice. The man who prays pours himself out in unrestrained dependence, and knows that he has—in an incomprehensible way—an effect upon God, even though he obtains nothing from God; for when he no longer desires anything for himself he sees the flame of his effect burning at its highest.—And the man who makes sacrifice? I cannot despise him, this upright servant of former times, who believed that God yearned for the scent of his burnt-offering. In a foolish but powerful way he knew that we can and ought to give to God. This is known by him, too, who offers up his little will to God and meets Him in the grand will. "Thy will be done," he says, and says no more; but truth adds for him "through me whom Thou needest."

What distinguishes sacrifice and prayer from all magic? —Magic desires to obtain its effects without entering into relation, and practises its tricks in the void. But sacrifice and prayer are set "before the Face," in the consummation of the holy primary word that means mutual action: they speak the *Thou,* and then they hear.

To wish to understand pure relation as dependence is to wish to empty one of the bearers of the relation, and hence the relation itself, of reality. . . .

Man's religious situation, his *being there* in the Presence, is characterized by its essential and indissoluble antinomy. The nature of its being determines that this antinomy is indissoluble. He who accepts the thesis and rejects the antithesis does injury to the significance of the situation. He who tries to think out a synthesis destroys the significance of the situation. He who strives to make the antinomy into a relative matter abolishes the significance of the situation. He who wishes to carry through the conflict of the antinomy other than with his life transgresses the significance of the situation. The significance of the situation is that it is lived, and nothing but lived, continually, ever anew, without foresight, without forethought, without prescription, in the totality of its antinomy.

Comparison of the religious with the philosophical antinomy will make this clear. Kant may make the philosophical conflict betweeen necessity and freedom into a relative matter by assigning the former to the world of appearances and the latter to the world of being, so that in their two settings they are no longer really opposed, but rather reconciled—just as the worlds

for which they are valid are reconciled. But if I consider necessity and freedom not in worlds of thought but in the reality of my standing before God,
if I know that "I am given over for disposal" and know at the same time
that "It depends on myself," then I cannot try to escape the paradox that
has to be lived by assigning the irreconcilable propositions to two separate
realms of validity; nor can I be helped to an ideal reconciliation by any
theological device: but I am compelled to take both to myself, to be lived
together, and in being lived they are one. . . .

Every real relation in the world is exclusive, the Other breaks in on it
and avenges its exclusion. Only in the relation with God are unconditioned
exclusiveness and unconditioned inclusiveness one and the same, in which
the whole universe is implied.

Every real relation in the world rests on individuation, this is its joy—
for only in this way is mutual knowledge of different beings won—and its
limitation—for in this way perfect knowledge and being known are fore-
gone. But in the perfect relation my *Thou* comprehends but is not my Self,
my limited knowledge opens out into a state in which I am boundlessly
known.

Every real relation in the world is consummated in the interchange of
actual and potential being; every isolated *Thou* is bound to enter the
chrysalis state of the *It* in order to take wings anew. But in pure relation
potential being is simply actual being as it draws breath, and in it the *Thou*
remains present. By its nature the eternal *Thou* is eternally *Thou;* only our
nature compels us to draw it into the world and the talk of *It.*

The world of *It* is set in the context of space and time.

The world of *Thou* is not set in the context of either of these.

Its context is in the Centre, where the extended lines of relations meet—
in the eternal *Thou.*

In the great privilege of pure relation the privileges of the world of *It*
are abolished. By virtue of this privilege there exists the unbroken world
of *Thou:* the isolated moments of relations are bound up in a life of world
solidarity. By virtue of this privilege formative power belongs to the world
of *Thou:* spirit can penetrate and transform the world of *It.* By virtue of
this privilege we are not given up to alienation from the world and the loss
of reality by the *I*—to domination by the ghostly. Reversal is the recognition
of the Centre and the act of turning again to it. In this act of the being the
buried relational power of man rises again, the wave that carries all the
spheres of relation swells in living streams to give new life to our world.

Perhaps not to our world alone. For this double movement, of estrangement from the primal Source, in virtue of which the universe is sustained
in the process of becoming, and of turning towards the primal Source, in
virtue of which the universe is released in being, may be perceived as the

metacosmical primal form that dwells in the world as a whole in its relation to that which is not the world—form whose twofold nature is represented among men by the twofold nature of their attitudes, their primary words, and their aspects of the world. Both parts of this movement develop fraught with destiny, in time, and are compassed by grace in the timeless creation that is, incomprehensibly, at once emancipation and preservation, release and binding. Our knowledge of twofold nature is silent before the paradox of the primal mystery. . . .

What is the eternal, primal phenomenon, present here and now, of that which we term revelation? It is the phenomenon that a man does not pass, from the moment of the supreme meeting, the same being as he entered into it. The moment of meeting is not an "experience" that stirs in the receptive soul and grows to perfect blessedness; rather, in that moment something happens to the man. At times it is like a light breath, at times like a wrestling-bout, but always—it *happens*. The man who emerges from the act of pure relation that so involves his being has now in his being something more that has grown in him, of which he did not know before and whose origin he is not rightly able to indicate. However the source of this new thing is classified in scientific orientation of the world, with its authorised efforts to establish an unbroken causality, we, whose concern is real consideration of the real, cannot have our purpose served with subconsciousness or any other apparatus of the soul. The reality is that we receive what we did not hitherto have, and receive it in such a way that we know it has been given to us. In the language of the Bible, "Those who wait upon the Lord shall renew their strength." In the language of Nietzsche, who in his account remains loyal to reality, "We take and do not ask who it is there that gives."

Man receives, and he receives not a specific "content" but a Presence, a Presence as power. This Presence and this power include three things, undivided, yet in such a way that we may consider them separately. First, there is the whole fulness of real mutual action, of the being raised and bound up in relation: the man can give no account at all of how the binding in relation is brought about, nor does it in any way lighten his life—it makes life heavier, but heavy with meaning. Secondly, there is the inexpressible confirmation of meaning. Meaning is assured. Nothing can any longer be meaningless. The question about the meaning of life is no longer there. But were it there, it would not have to be answered. You do not know how to exhibit and define the meaning of life, you have no formula or picture for it, and yet it has more certitude for you than the perceptions of your senses. What does the revealed and concealed meaning purpose with us, desire from us? It does not wish to be explained (nor are we able to do that) but only to be done by us. Thirdly, this meaning is not that of "another life," but that of this life of ours, not one of a world "yonder" but that of this world of ours, and it desires its confirmation in this life and in relation with this world. This meaning can be received, but not experienced; it cannot be experienced but it can be done, and this is its purpose with us. The assurance I have of it does not wish to be sealed within me, but it wishes to be born by me into the world. But just as the meaning itself does not permit itself to be transmitted and made into knowledge generally current and admissible, so confirmation of it cannot be transmitted as a valid Ought; it is not prescribed, it is not specified on any tablet, to be raised above all men's heads. The meaning that has been received can be proved true by each man only in the singleness of his being and the singleness of his life. As no prescription can lead us to the meeting, so none leads from it. As only acceptance of the Presence is necessary for the approach to the meeting, so in a new sense is it so when we emerge from it. As we reach the meeting with the simple *Thou* on our lips, so with the *Thou* on our lips we leave it and return to the world.

That before which, in which, out of which, and into which we live, even the mystery, has remained what it was. It has become present to us and in its presentness has proclaimed itself to us as salvation; we have "known" it, but we acquire no knowledge from it which might lessen or moderate its mysteriousness. We have come near to God, but not nearer to unveiling being or solving its riddle. We have felt release, but not discovered a "solution." We cannot approach others with what we have received, and say "You must know this, you must do this." We can only go, and confirm its truth. And this, too, is no "ought," but we can, we *must*.

This is the eternal revelation that is present here and now. I know of no revelation and believe in none whose primal phenomenon is not precisely this. I do not believe in a self-naming of God, a self-definition of God before men. The Word of revelation is *I am that I am.* That which reveals is that which reveals. That which is *is,* and nothing more. The eternal source of strength streams, the eternal contact persists, the eternal voice sounds forth, and nothing more.

The eternal *Thou* can by its nature not become *It;* for by its nature it cannot be established in measure and bounds, not even in the measure of the immeasurable, or the bounds of boundless being; for by its nature it cannot be understood as a sum of qualities, not even as an infinite sum of qualities raised to a transcendental level; for it can be found neither in nor out of the world; for it cannot be experienced, or thought; for we miss Him, Him who is, if we say "I believe that He is" —"He" is also a metaphor, but "Thou" is not.

And yet in accordance with our nature we are continually making the eternal *Thou* into *It,* into some thing—making God into a thing. Not indeed out of arbitrary self-will; God's history as a thing, the passage of

God as Thing through religion and through the products on its brink, through its bright ways and its gloom, its enhancement and its destruction of life, the passage away from the living God and back again to Him, the changes from the present to establishment of form, of objects, and of ideas, dissolution and renewal—all are one way, are *the* way.

What is the origin of the expressed knowledge and ordered action of the religions? How do the Presence and the power of the revelation (for all religions necessarily appeal to some kind of revelation, whether through the medium of the spoken word, or of nature, or of the soul: there are only religions of revelation)—how do the Presence and the power received by men in revelation change into a "content"?

The explanation has two layers. We understand the outer psychical layer when we consider man in himself, separated from history, and the inner factual layer, the primal phenomenon of religion, when we replace him in history. The two layers belong together.

Man desires to possess God; he desires a continuity in space and time of possession of God. He is not content with the inexpressible confirmation of meaning, but wants to see this confirmation stretched out as something that can be continually taken up and handled, a continuum unbroken in space and time that insures his life at every point and every moment.

Man's thirst for continuity is unsatisfied by the life-rhythm of pure relation, the interchange of actual being and of a potential being in which only our power to enter into relation, and hence the presentness (but not the primal Presence) decreases. He longs for extension in time, for duration. Thus God becomes an object of faith. At first faith, set in time, completes the acts of relation; but gradually it replaces them. Resting in belief in an *It* takes the place of the continually renewed movement of the being towards concentration and going out to the relation. The "Nevertheless I believe" of the fighter who knows remoteness from as well as nearness to God is more and more completely transformed into the certainty of him who enjoys profits, that nothing can happen to him, since he believes that there is One who will not let anything happen to him.

Further, man's thirst for continuity is unsatisfied by the life-structure of pure relation, the "solitude" of the *I* before the *Thou*, the law that man, though binding up the world in relation in the meeting, can nevertheless only as a person approach and meet God. He longs for extension in space, for the representation in which the community of the faithful is united with its God. Thus God becomes the object of a cult. The cult, too, completes at first the acts of relation, in adjusting in a spatial context of great formative power the living prayer, the immediate saying of the *Thou,* and in linking it with the life of the senses. It, too, gradually replaces the acts of relation, when the personal prayer is no longer supported, but displaced, by the communal prayer, and when the act of the being, since it admits no rule, is replaced by ordered devotional exercises.

Actually, however, pure relation can only be raised to constancy in space and time by being embodied in the whole stuff of life. It cannot be preserved, but only proved true, only done, only done up into life. Man can do justice to the relation with God in which he has come to share only if he realises God anew in the world according to his strength and to the measure of each day. In this lies the only authentic assurance of continuity. The authentic assurance of duration consists in the fact that pure relation can be fulfilled in the growth and rise of beings into *Thou,* that the holy primary word makes itself heard in them all. Thus the time of human life is shaped into a fulness of reality, and even though human life neither can nor ought to overcome the relation of *It,* it is so penetrated with relation that relation wins in it a shining streaming constancy: the moments of supreme meeting are then not flashes in darkness but like the rising moon in a clear starlit night. Thus, too, the authentic assurance of constancy in space consists in the fact that men's relations with their true *Thou,* the radial lines that proceed from all the points of the *I* to the Centre, form a circle. It is not the periphery, the community, that comes first, but the radii, the common quality of relation with the Centre. This alone guarantees the authentic existence of the community.

Only when these two arise—the binding up of time in a relational life of salvation and the binding up of space in the community that is made one by its Centre—and only so long as they exist, does there arise and exist, round about the invisible altar, a human cosmos with bounds and form, grasped with the spirit out of the universal stuff of the aeon, a world that is house and home, a dwelling for man in the universe.

Meeting with God does not come to man in order that he may concern himself with God, but in order that he may confirm that there is meaning in the world. All revelation is summons and sending. But again and again man brings about, instead of realisation, a reflexion to Him who reveals: he wishes to concern himself with God instead of with the world. Only, in such a reflexion, he is no longer confronted by a *Thou,* he can do nothing but establish an It-God in the realm of things, believe that he knows of God as of an *It,* and so speak about Him. Just as the "self"-seeking man, instead of directly living something or other, a perception or an affection, reflects about his perceptive or reflective *I,* and thereby misses the truth of the event, so the man who seeks God (though for the rest he gets on very well with the self-seeker in the one soul), instead of allowing the gift to work itself out, reflects about the Giver—and misses both.

God remains present to you when you have been sent forth; he who goes on a mission has always God before him: the truer the fulfilment the stronger and more constant His nearness. To be sure, he cannot directly concern himself with God, but he can converse with Him. Reflexion, on the other hand, makes God into an object. Its apparent turning towards the primal source belongs in truth to the universal movement away from it; just as the apparent turning away of the man who is fulfilling his mission belongs in truth to the universal movement towards the primal source.

# PAUL TILLICH

*Paul Tillich* (1886–1965), German-American philosophical theologian, was formerly on the faculty of Harvard University. His system reflects a wide-ranging interest in the fields of classical Greek thought, German philosophy, art, history, psychoanalysis, and existentialism. *Systematic Theology* is his major work.

## Courage and Transcendence

Courage is the self-affirmation of being in spite of the fact of nonbeing. It is the act of the individual self in taking the anxiety of nonbeing upon itself by affirming itself either as part of an embracing whole or in its individual selfhood. Courage always includes a risk, it is always threatened by nonbeing, whether the risk of losing oneself and becoming a thing within the whole of things or of losing one's world in an empty self-relatedness. Courage needs the power of being, a power transcending the nonbeing which is experienced in the anxiety of fate and death, which is present in the anxiety of emptiness and meaninglessness, which is effective in the anxiety of guilt and condemnation. The courage which takes this threefold anxiety into itself must be rooted in a power of being that is greater than the power of oneself and the power of one's world. Neither self-affirmation as a part nor self-affirmation as oneself is beyond the manifold threat of nonbeing. Those who are mentioned as representatives of these forms of courage try to transcend themselves and the world in which they participate in order to find the power of being-itself and a courage to be which is beyond the threat of nonbeing. There are no exceptions to this rule; and this means that every courage to be has an open or hidden religious root. For religion is the state of being grasped by the power of being-itself. In some

From Paul Tillich, *The Courage to Be,* pp. 155–156, 167–190. Copyright, 1952, Yale University Press. Used by permission of Yale University Press.

cases the religious root is carefully covered, in others it is passionately denied; in some it is deeply hidden and in others superficially. But it is never completely absent. For everything that is participates in being-itself, and everybody has some awareness of this participation, especially in the moments in which he experiences the threat of nonbeing. This leads us to a final consideration, the double question: How is the courage to be rooted in being-itself, and how must we understand being-itself in the light of the courage to be? The first question deals with the ground of being as source of the courage to be, the second with courage to be as key to the ground of being. . . .

## Fate and the Courage to Accept Acceptance

As the symbolic figures of death and the devil show, the anxiety of this period [the Reformation—Eds.] was not restricted to the anxiety of guilt. It was also an anxiety of death and fate. The astrological ideas of the later ancient world had been revived by the Renaissance and had influenced even those humanists who joined the Reformation. We have already referred to the Neo-Stoic courage, expressed in some Renaissance pictures, where man directs the vessel of his life although it is driven by the winds of fate. Luther faced the anxiety of fate on another level. He experienced the connection between the anxiety of guilt and the anxiety of fate. It is the uneasy conscience which produces innumerable irrational fears in daily life. The rustling of a dry leaf horrifies him who is plagued by guilt. Therefore conquest of the anxiety of guilt is also conquest of the anxiety of fate. The courage of confidence takes the anxiety of fate as well as the anxiety of guilt into itself. It says "in spite of" to both of them. This is the genuine meaning of the doctrine of providence. Providence is not a theory about some activities of God; it is the religious symbol of the courage of confidence with respect to fate and death. For the courage of confidence says "in spite of" even to death.

Like Paul, Luther was well aware of the connection of the anxiety of guilt with the anxiety of death. In Stoicism and Neo-Stoicism the essential self is not threatened by death, because it belongs to being-itself and transcends nonbeing. Socrates, who in the power of his essential self conquered the anxiety of death, has become the symbol for the courage to take death upon oneself. This is the true meaning of Plato's so-called doctrine of immortality of the soul. In discussing this doctrine we should neglect the arguments for immortality, even those in Plato's *Phaedon,* and concentrate on the image of the dying Socrates. All the arguments, skeptically treated by Plato himself, are attempts to interpret the courage of Socrates, the courage to take one's death into one's self-affirmation. Socrates is certain that the self which the executioners will destroy is not the self which affirms itself in his courage to be. He does not say much about the relation of the two selves, and he could not because they are not numerically two, but one in two aspects. But he makes it clear that the courage to die is the test of the courage to be. A self-affirmation which omits taking the affirmation of one's death into itself tries to escape the test of courage, the facing of nonbeing in the most radical way.

The popular belief in immortality which in the Western world has largely replaced the Christian symbol of resurrection is a mixture of courage and escape. It tries to maintain one's self-affirmation even in the face of one's having to die. But it does this by continuing one's finitude, that is one's having to die, infinitely, so that the actual death never will occur. This, however, is an illusion and, logically speaking, a contradiction in terms. It makes endless what, by definition, must come to an end. The "immortality of the soul" is a poor symbol for the courage to be in the face of one's having to die.

The courage of Socrates (in Plato's picture) was based not on a doctrine of the immortality of the soul but on the affirmation of himself in his essential, indestructible being. He knows that he belongs to twp orders of reality and that the one order is transtemporal. It was the courage of Socrates which more than any philosophical reflection revealed to the ancient world that everyone belongs to two orders.

But there was one presupposition in the Socratic (Stoic and Neo-Stoic) courage to take death upon oneself, namely the ability of every individual to participate in both orders, the temporal and the eternal. This presupposition is not accepted by Christianity. According to Christianity we are estranged from our essential being. We are not free to realize our essential being, we are bound to contradict it. Therefore death can be accepted only through a state of confidence in which death has ceased to be the "wages of sin." This, however, is the state of being accepted in spite of being unacceptable. Here is the point in which the ancient world was transformed by Christianity and in which Luther's courage to face death was rooted. It is the being accepted into communion with God that underlies this courage, not a questionable theory of immortality. The encounter with God in Luther is not merely the basis for the courage to take upon oneself sin and condemnation, it is also the basis for taking upon oneself fate and death. For encountering God means encountering transcendent security and transcendent eternity. He who participates in God participates in eternity. But in order to participate in him you must be accepted by him and you must have accepted his acceptance of you.

Luther had experiences which he describes as attacks of utter despair (*Anfechtung*), as the frightful threat of a complete meaninglessness. He felt these moments as satanic attacks in which everything was menaced: his Christian faith, the confidence in his work, the Reformation, the forgiveness of sins. Everything broke down in the extreme moments of this despair, nothing was left of the courage to be. Luther in these moments, and in the descriptions he gives of them, anticipated the descriptions of them by modern Existentialism. But for him this was not the last word. The last word was the first commandment, the statement that God is God. It reminded him of the unconditional element in human experience of which one can be aware even in the abyss of meaninglessness. And this awareness saved him.

It should not be forgotten that the great adversary of Luther, Thomas Münzer, the Anabaptist and religious socialist, describes similar experiences. He speaks of the ultimate situation in which everything finite reveals its finitude, in which the finite has come to its end, in which anxiety grips the heart and all previous meanings fall apart, and in which just for this reason the Divine Spirit can make itself felt and can turn the whole situation into a courage to be whose expression is revolutionary action. While Luther represents ecclesiastical Protestantism, Münzer represents evangelical radicalism. Both men have shaped history, and actually Münzer's views had even more influence in America than Luther's. Both men experienced the anxiety of meaninglessness and described it in terms which had been created by Christian mystics. But in doing so they transcended the courage of confidence which is based on a personal encounter with God. They had to receive elements from the courage to be which is based on mystical union. This leads to a last question: whether the two types of the courage to accept acceptance can be united in view of the all-pervasive presence of the anxiety of doubt and meaninglessness in our own period.

## Absolute Faith and the Courage to Be

We have avoided the concept of faith in our description of the courage to be which is based on mystical union with the ground of being as well as in our description of the courage to be which is based on the personal encounter with God. This is partly because the concept of faith has lost its genuine meaning and has received the connotation of "belief in something unbelievable." But this is not the only reason for the use of terms other than faith. The decisive reason is that I do not think either mystical union or personal encounter fulfills the idea of faith. Certainly there is faith in the elevation of the soul above the finite to the infinite, leading to its union with the ground of being. But more than this is included in the concept of faith. And there is faith in the personal encounter with the personal God. But more than this is included in the concept of faith. Faith is the state of being grasped by the power of being-itself. The courage to be is an expression of faith and what "faith" means must be understood through the courage to be. We have defined courage as the self-affirmation of being in spite of nonbeing. The power of this self-affirmation is the power of being which is effective in every act of courage. Faith is the experience of this power.

But it is an experience which has a paradoxical character, the character of accepting acceptance. Being-itself transcends every finite being infinitely; God in the divine-human encounter transcends man unconditionally. Faith bridges this infinite gap by accepting the fact that in spite of it the power of being is present, that he who is separated is accepted. Faith accepts "in spite of"; and out of the "in spite of" of faith the "in spite of" of courage is born. Faith is not a theoretical affirmation of something uncertain, it is the existential acceptance of something transcending ordinary experience. Faith is not an opinion but a state. It is the state of being grasped by the power of being which transcends everything that is and in which everything that is participates. He who is grasped by this power is able to affirm himself because he knows that he is affirmed by the power of being-itself. In this point mystical experience and personal encounter are identical. In both of them faith is the basis of the courage to be.

This is decisive for a period in which, as in our own, the anxiety of doubt and meaninglessness is dominant. Certainly the anxiety of fate and death is not lacking in our time. The anxiety of fate has increased with the degree to which the schizophrenic split of our world has removed the last remnants of former security. And the anxiety of guilt and condemnation is not lacking either. It is surprising how much anxiety of guilt comes to the surface in psychoanalysis and personal counseling. The centuries of puritan and bourgeois repression of vital strivings have produced almost as many guilt feelings as the preaching of hell and purgatory in the Middle Ages.

But in spite of these restricting considerations one must say that the anxiety which determines our period is the anxiety of doubt and meaninglessness. One is afraid of having lost or of having to lose the meaning of one's existence. The expression of this situation is the Existentialism of today.

Which courage is able to take nonbeing into itself in the form of doubt and meaninglessness? This is the most important and most disturbing question in the quest for the courage to be. For the anxiety of meaninglessness undermines what is still unshaken in the anxiety of fate and death and of guilt and condemnation. In the anxiety of guilt and condemnation doubt has not yet undermined the certainty of an ultimate reponsibility. We are threatened but we are not destroyed. If, however, doubt and meaninglessness prevail one experiences an abyss in which the meaning of life and the truth of ultimate responsibility disappear. Both the Stoic who conquers the anxiety of fate with the Socratic courage of wisdom and the Christian who conquers the anxiety of guilt with the Protestant courage of accepting forgiveness are in a different situation. Even in the despair of having to die and the despair of self-condemnation meaning is affirmed and certitude preserved. But in the despair of doubt and meaninglessness both are swallowed by nonbeing.

The question then is this: Is there a courage which can conquer the anxiety of meaninglessness and doubt? Or in other words, can the faith which accepts acceptance resist the power of nonbeing in its most radical form? Can faith resist meaninglessness? Is there a kind of faith which can exist together with doubt and meaninglessness? These questions lead to the last aspect of the problem discussed in these lectures and the one most relevant to our time: How is the courage to be possible if all the ways to create it are barred by the experience of their ultimate insufficiency? If life is as meaningless as death, if guilt is as questionable as perfection, if being is no more meaningful than nonbeing, on what can one base the courage to be?

There is an inclination in some Existentialists to answer these questions by a leap from doubt to dogmatic certitude, from meaninglessness to a set of symbols in which the meaning of a special ecclesiastical or political group is embodied. This leap can be interpreted in different ways. It may be the expression of a desire for safety; it may be as arbitrary as, according to Existentialist principles, every decision is; it may be the feeling that the Christian message is the answer to the questions raised by an analysis of human existence; it may be a genuine conversion, independent of the theoretical situation. In any case it is not a solution of the problem of radical doubt. It gives the courage to be to those who are converted but it does not answer the question as to how such a courage is possible in itself. The answer must accept, as its precondition, the state of meaninglessness. It is not an answer if it demands the removal of this state; for that is just what cannot be done. He who is in the grip of doubt and meaninglessness cannot liberate himself from this grip; but he asks for an answer which is valid within and not outside the situation of his despair. He asks for the ultimate foundation of what we have called the "courage of despair." There is only one possible answer, if one does not try to escape the question: namely that the acceptance of despair is in itself faith and on the boundary line of the courage to be. In this situation the meaning of life is reduced to despair about the meaning of life. But as long as this despair is an act of life it is positive in its negativity. Cynically speaking, one could say that it is true to life to be cynical about it. Religiously speaking, one would say that one accepts oneself as accepted in spite of one's despair about the meaning of this acceptance. The paradox of every radical negativity, as long as it is an active negativity, is that it must affirm itself in order to be able to negate itself. No actual negation can be without an implicit affirmation. The hidden pleasure produced by despair witnesses to the paradoxical character of self-negation. The negative lives from the positive it negates.

The faith which makes the courage of despair possible is the acceptance of the power of being, even in the grip of nonbeing. Even in the despair about meaning being affirms itself through us. The act of accepting meaninglessness is in itself a meaningful act. It is an act of faith. We have seen that he who has the courage to affirm his being in spite of fate and guilt has not removed them. He remains threatened and hit by them. But he accepts his acceptance by the power of being-itself in which he participates and which gives him the courage to take the anxieties of fate and guilt upon himself. The same is true of doubt and meaninglessness. The faith which creates the courage to take them into itself has no special content. It is simply faith, undirected, absolute. It is undefinable, since everything defined is dissolved by doubt and meaninglessness. Nevertheless, even absolute faith is not an eruption of subjective emotions or a mood without objective foundation.

An analysis of the nature of absolute faith reveals the following elements in it. The first is the experience of the power of being which is present even in face of the most radical manifestation of nonbeing. If one says that in this experience vitality resists despair one must add that vitality in man is proportional to intentionality. The vitality that can stand the abyss of meaninglessness is aware of a hidden meaning within the destruction of meaning. The second element in absolute faith is the dependence of the experience of nonbeing on the experience of being and the dependence of the experience of meaninglessness on the experience of meaning. Even in the state of despair one has enough being to make despair possible. There is a third element in absolute faith, the acceptance of being accepted. Of course, in the state of despair there is nobody and nothing that accepts. But there is the power of acceptance itself which is experienced. Meaninglessness, as long as it is experienced, includes an experience of the "power of acceptance." To accept this power of acceptance consciously is the religious answer of absolute faith, of a faith which has been deprived by doubt of any concrete content, which nevertheless is faith and the source of the most paradoxical manifestation of the courage to be.

This faith transcends both the mystical experience and the divine-human encounter. The mystical experience seems to be nearer to absolute faith but it is not. Absolute faith includes an element of skepticism which one cannot find in the mystical experience. Certainly mysticism also transcends all specific contents, but not because it doubts them or has found them meaningless; rather it deems them to be preliminary. Mysticism uses the specific contents as grades, stepping on them after having used them. The experience of meaninglessness, however, denies them (and everything that goes with them) without having used them. The experience of meaninglessness is more radical than mysticism. Therefore it transcends the mystical experience.

Absolute faith also transcends the divine-human encounter. In this encounter the subject-object scheme is valid: a definite subject (man) meets a definite object (God). One can reverse this statement and say that a definite subject (God) meets a definite object (man). But in both cases the attack of doubt undercuts the subject-object structure. The theologians who speak so strongly and with such self-certainty about the divine-human encounter should be aware of a situation in which this encounter is prevented by radical doubt and nothing is left but absolute faith. The acceptance of such a situation as religiously valid has, however, the consequence that the concrete contents of ordinary faith must be subjected to criticism and transformation. The courage to be in its radical form is a key to an idea of God which transcends both mysticism and the person-to-person encounter.

## The Courage to Be as the Key to Being-Itself

NONBEING OPENING UP BEING. The courage to be in all its forms has, by itself, revelatory character. It shows the nature of being, it shows that the self-affirmation of being is an affirmation that overcomes negation. In a metaphorical statement (and every assertion about being-itself is either metaphorical or symbolic) one could say that being includes nonbeing but nonbeing does not prevail against it. "Including" is a spatial metaphor which indicates that being embraces itself and that which is opposed to it, nonbeing. Nonbeing belongs to being, it cannot be separated from it. We could not even think "being" without a double negation: being must be thought as the negation of the negation of being. This is why we describe being best by the metaphor "power of being." Power is the possibility a being has to actualize itself against the resistance of other beings. If we speak of the power of being-itself we indicate that being affirms itself against nonbeing. In our discussion of courage and life we have mentioned the dynamic understanding of reality by the philosophers of life. Such an understanding is possible only if one accepts the view that nonbeing belongs to being, that being could not be the ground of life without nonbeing. The self-affirmation of being without nonbeing would not even be self-affirmation but an immovable self-identity. Nothing would be manifest, nothing expressed, nothing revealed. But nonbeing drives being out of its seclusion, it forces it to affirm itself dynamically. Philosophy has dealt with the dynamic self-affirmation of being-itself wherever it spoke dialectically, notably in Neoplatonism, Hegel, and the philosophers of life and process. Theology has done the same whenever it took the idea of the living God seriously, most obviously in the trinitarian symbolization of the inner life of God. Spinoza, in spite of his static definition of substance (which is his name for the ultimate power of being), unites philosophical and mystical tendencies when he speaks of the love and knowledge with which God loves and knows himself through the love and knowledge of finite beings. Nonbeing (that in God which makes his self-affirmation dynamic) opens up the divine self-seclusion and reveals him as power and love. Nonbeing makes God a living God. Without the No he has to overcome in himself and in his creature, the divine Yes to himself would be lifeless. There would be no revelation of the ground of being, there would be no life.

But where there is nonbeing there is finitude and anxiety. If we say that nonbeing belongs to being-itself, we say that finitude and anxiety belong to being-itself. Wherever philosophers or theologians have spoken of the divine blessedness they have implicitly (and sometimes explicitly) spoken of the anxiety of finitude which is eternally taken into the blessedness of the divine infinity. The infinite embraces itself and the finite, the Yes includes itself and the No which it takes into itself, blessedness comprises itself and the anxiety of which it is the conquest. All this is implied if one says that being includes nonbeing and that through nonbeing it reveals itself. It is a highly symbolic language which must be used at this point. But its symbolic character does not diminish its truth; on the contrary, it is a condition of its truth. To speak unsymbolically about being-itself is untrue.

The divine self-affirmation is the power that makes the self-affirmation of the finite being, the courage to be, possible. Only because being-itself has the character of self-affirmation in spite of nonbeing is courage possible. Courage participates in the self-affirmation of being-itself, it participates in the power of being which prevails against nonbeing. He who receives this power in an act of mystical or personal or absolute faith is aware of the source of his courage to be.

Man is not necessarily aware of this source. In situations of cynicism and indifference he is not aware of it. But it works in him as long as he maintains the courage to take his anxiety upon himself. In the act of the courage to be the power of being is effective in us, whether we recognize it or not. Every act of courage is a manifestation of the ground of being, however questionable the content of the act may be. The content may hide or distort true being, the courage in it reveals true being. Not arguments but the courage to be reveals the true nature of being-itself. By affirming our being we participate in the self-affirmation of being-itself. There are no valid arguments for the "existence" of God, but there are acts of courage in which we affirm the power of being, whether we know it or not. If we know it, we accept acceptance consciously. If we do not know it, we nevertheless accept it and participate in it. And in our acceptance of that which we do not know the power of being is manifest to us. Courage has revealing power, the courage to be is the key to being-itself.

## Theism Transcended

The courage to take meaninglessness into itself presupposes a relation to the ground of being which we have called "absolute faith." It is without a *special* content, yet it is not without content. The content of absolute faith is the "God above God." Absolute faith and its consequence, the courage that takes the radical doubt, the doubt about God, into itself, transcends the theistic idea of God.

Theism can mean the unspecified affirmation of God. Theism in this sense does not say what it means if it uses the name of God. Because of the traditional and psychological connotations of the word God such an empty theism can produce a reverent mood if it speaks of God. Politicians, dictators, and other people who wish to use rhetoric to make an impression on their audience like to use the word God in this sense. It produces the feeling in their listeners that the speaker is serious and morally trustworthy. This is especially successful if they can brand their foes as atheistic. On a higher level people without a definite religious commitment like to call themselves theistic, not for special purposes but because they cannot stand a world without God, whatever this God may be. They need some of the connotations of the word God and they are afraid of what they call atheism. On the highest level of this kind of theism the name of God is used as a poetic or practical symbol, expressing a profound emotional state or the highest ethical idea. It is a theism which stands on the boundary line between the second type of theism and what we call "theism transcended." But it is still too indefinite to cross this boundary line. The atheistic negation of this whole type of theism is as vague as the theism itself. It may produce an irreverent mood and angry reaction of those who take their theistic affirmation seriously. It may even be felt as justified against the rhetorical-political abuse of the name God, but it is ultimately as irrelevant as the theism which it negates. It cannot reach the state of despair any more than the theism against which it fights can reach the state of faith.

Theism can have another meaning, quite contrary to the first one: it can be the name of what we have called the divine-human encounter. In this case it points to those elements in the Jewish-Christian tradition which emphasize the person-to-person relationship with God. Theism in this sense emphasizes the personalistic passages in the Bible and the Protestant creeds, the personalistic image of God, the word as the tool of creation and revelation, the ethical and social character of the kingdom of God, the personal nature of human faith and divine forgiveness, the historical vision of the universe, the idea of a divine purpose, the infinite distance between creator and creature, the absolute separation between God and the world, the conflict betweeen holy God and sinful man, the person-to-person character of prayer and practical devotion. Theism in this sense is the nonmystical side of biblical religion and historical Christianity. Atheism from the point of view of this theism is the human attempt to escape the divine-human encounter. It is an existential—not a theoretical—problem.

Theism has a third meaning, a strictly theological one. Theological theism is, like every theology, dependent on the religious substance which it conceptualizes. It is dependent on theism in the first sense insofar as it tries to prove the necessity of affirming God in some way; it usually develops the so-called arguments for the "existence" of God. But it is more dependent on theism in the second sense insofar as it tries to establish a doctrine of God which transforms the person-to-person encounter with God into a doctrine about two persons who may or may not meet but who have a reality independent of each other.

Now theism in the first sense must be transcended because it is irrelevant, and theism in the second sense must be transcended because it is one-sided. But theism in the third sense must be transcended because it is wrong. It is bad theology. This can be shown by a more penetrating analysis. The God of theological theism is a being beside others and as such a part of the whole of reality. He certainly is considered its most important part, but as a part and therefore as subjected to the structure of the whole. He is supposed to be beyond the ontological elements and categories which constitute reality. But every statement subjects him to them. He is seen as a self which has a world, as an ego which is related to a thou, as a cause which is separated from its effect, as having a definite space and an endless time. He is a being, not being-itself. As such he is bound to the subject-object structure of reality, he is an object for us as subjects. At the same time we are objects for him as a subject. And this is decisive for the necessity of transcending theological theism. For God as a subject makes me into an object which is nothing more than an object. He deprives me of my subjectivity because he is all-powerful and all-knowing. I revolt and try to make *him* into an object, but the revolt fails and becomes desperate. God appears as the invincible tyrant, the being in contrast with whom all other beings are without freedom and subjectivity. He is equated with the recent tyrants who with the help of terror try to transform everything into a mere object, a thing among things, a cog in the machine they control. He becomes the model of everything against which Existentialism revolted. This is the God Nietzsche said had to be killed because nobody can tolerate being made into a mere object of absolute knowledge and absolute control. This is the deepest root of atheism. It is an atheism which is justified as the reaction against theological theism and its disturbing implications. It is also the deepest root of the Existentialist despair and the widespread anxiety of meaningless in our period.

Theism in all its forms is transcended in the experience we have called absolute faith. It is the accepting of the acceptance without somebody or something that accepts. It is the power of being-itself that accepts and gives the courage to be. This is the highest point to which our analysis has brought us. It cannot be described in the way the God of all forms of theism can be described. It cannot be described in mystical terms either. It transcends both mysticism and personal encounter, as it transcends both the courage to be as a part and the courage to be as oneself.

## The God Above God and the Courage to Be

The ultimate source of the courage to be is the "God above God"; this is the result of our demand to transcend theism. Only if the God of theism is transcended can the anxiety of doubt and meaninglessness be taken into the courage to be. The God above God is the object of all mystical longing, but mysticism also must be transcended in order to reach him. Mysticism does not take seriously the concrete and the doubt concerning the concrete. It plunges directly into the ground of being and meaning, and leaves the concrete, the world of finite values and meanings, behind. Therefore it does not solve the problem of meaninglessness. In terms of the present religious situation this means that Eastern mysticism is not the solution of the problems of Western Existentialism, although many people attempt this solution. The God above the God of theism is not the devaluation of the meanings which doubt has thrown into the abyss of meaninglessness; he is their potential restitution. Nevertheless absolute faith agrees with the faith implied in mysticism in that both transcend the theistic objectivation of a God who is a being. For mysticism such a God is not more real than any finite being, for the courage to be such a God has disappeared in the abyss of meaninglessness with every other value and meaning.

The God above the God of theism is present, although hidden in every divine-human encounter. Biblical religion as well as Protestant theology are aware of the paradoxical character of this encounter. They are aware that if God encounters man God is neither object nor subject and is therefore above the scheme into which theism has forced him. They are aware that personalism with respect to God is balanced by a transpersonal presence of the divine. They are aware that forgiveness can be accepted only if the power of acceptance is effective in man—biblically speaking, if the power of grace is effective in man. They are aware of the paradoxical character of every prayer, of speaking to somebody to whom you cannot speak because he is not "somebody," of asking somebody of whom you cannot ask anything because he gives or gives not before you ask, of saying "thou" to somebody who is nearer to the I than the I is to itself. Each of these paradoxes drives the religious consciousness toward a God above the God of theism.

The courage to be which is rooted in the experience of the God above the God of theism unites and transcends the courage to be as a part and the courage to be as oneself. It avoids both the loss of oneself by participation and the loss of one's world by individualization. The acceptance of the God above the God of theism makes us a part of that which is not also a part but is the ground of the whole. Therefore our self is not lost in a larger whole, which submerges it in the life of a limited group. If the self participates in the power of being-itself it receives itself back. For the power of being acts through the power of the individual selves. It does not swallow them as every limited whole, every collectivism, and every conformism does. This is why the Church, which stands for the power of being-itself or for the God who transcends the God of the religions, claims to be the mediator of the courage to be. A church which is based on the authority of the God of theism cannot make such a claim. It inescapably develops into a collectivist or semicollectivist system itself.

But a church which raises itself in its message and its devotion to the God above the God of theism without sacrificing its concrete symbols can mediate a courage which takes doubt and meaninglessness into itself. It is the Church under the Cross which alone can do this, the Church which preaches the Crucified who cried to God who remained his God after the God of confidence had left him in the darkness of doubt and meaninglessness. To be as a part in such a church is to receive a courage to be in which one cannot lose one's self and in which one receives one's world.

Absolute faith, or the state of being grasped by the God beyond God, is not a state which appears beside other states of the mind. It never is something separated and definite, an event which could be isolated and described. It is always a movement in, with, and under other states of the mind. It is the situation on the boundary of man's possibilities. It *is* this boundary. Therefore it is both the courage of despair and the courage in and above every courage. It is not a place where one can live, it is without the safety of words and concepts, it is without a name, a church, a cult, a theology. But it is moving in the depth of all of them. It is the power of being, in which they participate and of which they are fragmentary expressions.

One can become aware of it in the anxiety of fate and death when the traditional symbols, which enable men to stand the vicissitudes of fate and the horror of death have lost their power. When "providence" has become a superstition and "immortality" something imaginary that which once was the power in these symbols can still be present and create the courage to be in spite of the experience of a chaotic world and a finite existence. The Stoic courage returns as the absolute faith which says Yes to being without seeing anything concrete which could conquer the nonbeing in fate and death.

And one can become aware of the God above the God of theism in the anxiety of guilt and condemnation when the traditional symbols that enable men to withstand the anxiety of guilt and condemnation have lost their power. When "divine judgment" is interpreted as a psychological complex and forgiveness as a remnant of the "father-image," what once was the power in those symbols can still be present and create the courage to be in spite of the experience of an infinite gap between what we are and what we ought to be. The Lutheran courage returns but not supported by the faith in a judging and forgiving God. It returns in terms of the absolute faith which says Yes although there is no special power that conquers guilt. The courage to take the anxiety of meaninglessness upon oneself is the boundary line up to which the courage to be can go. Beyond it is mere non-being. Within it all forms of courage are re-established in the power of the God above the God of theism. *The courage to be is rooted in the God who appears when God has disappeared in the anxiety of doubt.*

# CHARLES HARTSHORNE

*Charles Hartshorne* (1897–   ), professor of philosophy at the University of Texas, is the outstanding advocate in the United States of the metaphysics of Alfred N. Whitehead and is a careful student of the ontological argument.

## The Divine Relativity

Why is it religiously significant that God be supposed absolute? The reason is at least suggested by the consideration that absoluteness is requisite for complete reliability. What is relative to conditions may fail us if the conditions happen to be unfavorable. Hence if there is to be anything that *cannot* fail, it must be nonrelative, absolute, in those respects to which "reliability" and "failure" have reference. But it is often not noted that this need not be every respect or aspect from which God's nature can be regarded. For there may be qualities in God whose relativity or variability would be neutral to his reliability. To say of a man that (as human affairs go) his

From *The Divine Relativity*, pp. 22–34. Copyright 1948, Yale University Press. Reprinted by permission.

reliability is established refers not to every quality of the man, but only to certain principles exhibited in his otherwise highly variable behavior. We do not mean that if something comes close to his eye he will not blink, or that if he is given bad-tasting food he will enjoy it as much as better fare. We mean that his fixed intention to act according to the requirements of the general welfare will not waver, and that his wisdom and skill in carrying out this aim will be constant. But in all this there is not only no implication that conditions will not have effect upon the man, but the very plain implication that they will have plenty of effect. Skill in one set of circumstances means one form of behavior, in another set another form, and the same is true of the intention to serve the general good. Of course, one may argue that complete fixity of good intention and complete constancy of skill imply every other sort of fixity as well. But this has never yet been definitely shown by careful, explicit reasoning, and anything less is inappropriate in as difficult a subject as we are dealing with. General hunches will not do.

A typically invalid argument in this connection is that unless God surveys at once the whole of time and thus is independent of change, he cannot be relied upon to arrange all events with due regard to their relations to all that has gone before and all that is to come after. This argument either rests on an equivocation or it destroys all religious meaning for the divine reliability. For, if it is meant in any clear sense, it implies that every event has been selected by deity as an element in the best of all possible worlds, the ideal total pattern of all time and all existence. But this ideal pattern includes all acts of sin and the most hideous suffering and catastrophe, all the tragedies of life. And what then becomes of the ideas of human responsibility and choice, and of the notion that some deeds ought not to have taken place? These are only the beginning of the absurdities into which the view thrusts us. To mitigate these absurdities theologians introduce various more or less subtle equivocations. Would they not do better to take a fresh start (as indeed many have done) and admit that we have no good religious reason for positing the notion of providence as an absolute contriving of all events according to a completely detailed plan embracing all time? The religious value of such a notion is more negative than positive. It is the mother of no end of chicanery (see the book of Job for some examples), of much deep feeling of injustice (the poor unfortunate being assured that God has deliberately contrived everything as exactly the best way events could transpire), and of philosophical quagmires of paradox and unmeaning verbiage. The properly constituted man does not want to "rely" upon God to arrange all things, including our decisions, in accordance with a plan of all events which fixes every least detail with reference to every other that ever has happened or ever "is to" happen. How many atheists must have been needlessly produced by insistence upon this arbitrary notion, which after all is invariably softened by qualifications surreptitiously introduced *ad hoc* when certain problems are stressed! We shall see later that the really usable meaning of divine reliability is quite different and is entirely compatible with a profound relativity of God to conditions and to change. For the present, I suggest that all we can assert to have obvious religious value is the faith that God is to be relied upon to do for the world all that ought to be done for it, and with as much survey of the future as there ought to be or as is ideally desirable, leaving for the members of the world community to do for themselves and each other all that they ought to be left to do. We cannot assume that what ought to be done for the world by deity is everything that ought to be done at all, leaving the creatures with nothing to do for themselves and for each other. Nor can we assume that the ideal survey of what for us at least constitutes the future is one which fully defines it in every detail, leaving no open alternatives of possibility. So far from being self-evidently of religious value, these assumptions, viewed in the light of history, seem clearly of extreme disvalue. Yet they are often either asserted, or not unequivocally denied or avoided, in the intemperate insistence upon the total absoluteness of deity.

## God as Social

We have also to remember that if there is religious value in the absoluteness of God, as requisite for his reliability, there is equally manifest religious value in another trait which seems unequivocally to imply relativity rather than absoluteness. This is the social or personal nature of God. What is a person if not a being qualified and conditioned by social relations, relations to other persons? And what is God if not the supreme case of personality? Those who deny this have yet to succeed in distinguishing their position from atheism, as Hume pointedly noted. Either God really does love all beings, that is, is related to them by a sympathetic union surpassing any human sympathy, or religion seems a vast fraud. The common query Can the Absolute or Perfect Being be personal or social? should really run In what sense, if any, can a social being be absolute or perfect? For God is conceived socially before he is conceived absolutely or as perfect. God is the highest ruler, judge, benefactor; he knows, loves, and assists man; he has made the world with the design of sharing his bliss with lesser beings. The world is a vast society governed by laws instituted by the divine monarch—the supreme personal power to whom all other persons are subject. These are all, more or less clearly, social conceptions—if you like, metaphors (though aimed, as we shall see, at a literal, intuited meaning) drawn from the social life of man. They constitute the universal, popular meaning of "God," in relation to which descriptions such as "absolute," "perfect," "immutable," "impassive," "simple," and the like, are technical refinements aimed at logical precision. They seek to define the somewhat vague ideas of *highest* ruler, *supreme* power, or *author of all,* himself without author or origin. "Immutable," for example, is an attempted definition of the superiority of deity with respect to death and degeneration, and also with respect to vacillation of will due to fear, or other weakness. Earthly rulers are all brought low by death; and their promises and protection and execution of justice must always be discounted somewhat in anticipation of the effect upon them of changing circumstances and the development of their own motives, the growth of good and evil in their own hearts. God is not under sentence of death, cannot decay; and his convenant abides, nor is his wisdom ever clouded by storms of blind passion, the effects of strong drink or of disease.

The future of theology depends, I suggest, above all upon the answer to this question: can technically precise terms be found which express the supremacy of God, among social beings, without contradicting his social character? To say, on the one hand, that God is love, to continue to use popular religious terms like Lord, divine will, obedience to God, and on the other to speak of an absolute, infinite, immutable, simple, impassive deity, is either a gigantic hoax of priestcraft, or it is done with the belief that the social connotations of the popular language are ultimately in harmony with these descriptions. Merely to speak of the "mysteriousness" of God is not sufficient. If he escapes all the resources of our language and analysis, why be so insistent upon the obviously quite human concepts, absolute, infinite, perfect, immutable? These too are our conceptions, our terms, fragments of the English or Latin languages. Perhaps after all it is not correct to say God is absolute. How shall we know, if the subject is utterly mysterious and beyond our powers?

## The Social Nature of Existence

The question Can a supreme being be social? is important not merely because men generally have meant by God a supreme social being. There are grounds for thinking that the popular religious emphasis is philosophically sound, that a supreme being must, for rational reasons, be conceived socially. Human nature is the supreme instance of nature in general, as known to us (apart from the "nature" of God himself), and moreover, it is the instance which in some respects at least is much more certainly and intimately known to us than any other. Human nature is social through and through. All our thought is some sort of conversation or dialogue or social transaction; when we have no one else to converse with, we converse, silently or even aloud, with ourselves. We love and hate and sympathize, not only in relation to others but in relation to our own past, future, or potential selves. Not only human beings stimulate such response, but animals, plants, mountains, ships, the moon, colors, sounds (think of groaning brakes, growling thunder, merry sunshine). One may say simply, all classes of concrete objects at least can be social objects for man. What would poetry be without personification, overt or implicit; what would art be without empathy, which is social response of a kind?

Now, further, not simply man, but all life whatsoever, has social structure. All organisms on the multicellular level are associations of cells. There is scarcely a line between societies and individuals formed by societies which reach a sufficient grade of integration. Cells themselves are associations of similar molecules and atoms. It becomes a question of how broadly one wishes to use terms where one says that the social begins, if indeed it ever begins, in the ascending scale of emergence. And the higher one goes in the scale the more obviously do the social aspects assume a primary role. Does this point to the conclusion that the supreme being is not social at all?

There are even more ultimate considerations. Logical analysis shows, according to such high authorities as Peirce and Whitehead, that the "social" in its most general sense is definable as the synthesis of all the universal categories. It is the union of absolute and relative, independent and dependent, freedom and order, individual and universal, quality and structure, and so on. A nonsocial conception is only arrived at by reducing some category to the zero case. Thus a mere "machine" is what a society would become if the element of routine interdependence should completely suppress the aspect of individual initiative or originality, or if quality (feeling) should vanish, leaving mere structure. And a wholly absolute and hence nonsocial deity is one to which the category of relation—without reference to which even "absolute" has no meaning—is denied application. Thus mechanism, materialism, and absolutism can all be viewed as special cases of the same error, the arbitrary reduction of one or more aspects of sociality to zero. A category so completely ultimate for thought and life as relation (or as felt quality) can, it seems, be assigned null value only in the case of "nonentity." Those who spoke of the wholly absolute deity as the great void perhaps spoke a little more truly than they intended.

The purpose of the foregoing discussion—whose implications could be fully set forth only in a treatise on metaphysics—is not to prove that all things, and therefore even God, must or can be conceived as social in nature; but only to show that the common antithesis between the personal or social deity or religion, and the impersonal or nonsocial supreme being of philosophy, is to be viewed with suspicion. Some of the greatest philosophies, from Plato to Whitehead, have held, with varying degrees of explicitness and consistency, that the social structure is the ultimate structure of all existence; and never has this idea been so explicitly and competently defended as during the last hundred years. Whitehead's supreme conception, for example, is that of a society of actual occasions, related one to another by the sympathetic bond of "feeling of feeling." Peirce's doctrine of agapism was similar. So was Fechner's "daylight view." And Fechner and

Whitehead—in some passages, also Peirce—and many other recent thinkers, have held that deity is the supreme case of the social principle, rather than an exception to it.

## Social Deity and Creation

It may be thought that a socially conceived God could not be the creator. Can a member of a society create that society? Here we must remember the theological principle of "eminence." God, if social, is eminently or supremely so. On the other hand, that which in the eminent form is called divine creation, in a milder or ordinary form must be exhibited by lesser beings such as man. Man certainly is social. If then ordinary sociality is ordinarily creative, eminent sociality will be eminently creative, divinely creative. And ordinary sociality is, in a humble sense, creative. A man contributes creatively to the concrete actuality of his friends and enemies, and they to his. We *make* each other what we are, in greater or less degree.

The more important members of a society contribute more largely and vitally to the actuality of other members. The supreme member of a society would contribute most vitally and largely to the actuality of all. However, we shall be told, all this is not really "creation," since it presupposes a matter and at most adds a new form. In the first place, no one has proved or can possibly prove (against Peirce, Whitehead, et al.) that there is any "matter," apart from social terms and relations. Electrons and protons are, for all that anyone knows, simply the lowest actual levels of social existence. It may well be that a human mind is not sufficiently important in the world to call an electron into being where none was before. However, we do, by our thoughts and feelings, influence the formation of nerve cells (in the first years of life), and even more, of molecules in the nerves. This is not creation in the eminent sense, but it differs from this only as we might expect the ordinary to differ from the eminent. And the influence of our thought and feeling upon nerve cells and molecules is either a blind mystery, or it is a social influence, as Peirce and Whitehead, and before them (less clearly) Leibnitz, have pointed out.

That the human creator always has a given concrete actuality to work with does not of itself establish a difference between him and God, unless it be admitted as made out that there was a first moment of creation. For if not, then God, too, creates each stage of the world as successor to a preceding phase. Only a dubious interpretation of an obscure parable, the book of Genesis, stands between us and this view. What does distinguish God is that the preceding phase was itself created by God, so that he, unlike us, is never confronted by a world whose coming to be antedates his own entire existence. There is no presupposed "stuff" alien to God's creative work; but rather everything that influences God has already been influenced by him, whereas we are influenced by events of the past with which we had nothing to do. This is one of the many ways in which eminence is to be preserved, without falling into the negations of classical theology.

## Analogical Concepts and Metaphysical Uniqueness

It would be a misunderstanding of the social doctrine to accuse it of denying the radical difference between God and nondivine beings. Whitehead (and something similar might be said of Fechner) is so anxious that this difference should not be slurred over that he never, save once in conversation, has described God as a "society of occasions" (with "personal order") because, although that is what, in his system, God must be, it is equally clear that *this* society has a metaphysically unique status and character. By a metaphysically unique status and character I mean one whose distinctiveness can be defined through purely universal categories. It is impossible to define what is unique about my youngest brother in terms of categories alone. And if deity were conceived merely as very superior to man, this description might, for all we could know, apply to myriads of individuals somewhere in the universe. Besides, the description contains a nonmetaphysical term, man. But according to the view presented in this book, a purely metaphysical description applicable only to the one individual, God, is possible. Thus God is the *one individual conceivable a priori*. It is in this sense that concepts applied to him are analogical rather than simply univocal, in comparison to their other applications. For in all other cases, individual otherness is a mere specificity under more general characteristics—thus, my (not wholly definable) nuance of wisdom rather than yours. But in the case of deity, the most general conceptions, without anything more specific, suffice to "individuate" (though not, as we shall see, to particularize or concretize). The old dualities of creating and created, necessary and contingent, perfect and imperfect, expressed this metaphysical or a priori otherness of God. But, as generally stated, they did so in self-contradictory fashion. And it was not seen that, with respect to the category of relation, for example, a metaphysically unique status is definable in another way than through the simple denial of relativity. If the negative "nonrelatedness" is purely categorical, the positive "all-relatedness" is equally so. And we shall find that there is no logical reason why both may not apply to diverse aspects of deity. Then the metaphysical uniqueness would be a double one: no other being, in *any* aspect, could be either wholly relative or wholly nonrelative. Thus, while all beings have some measure of "absoluteness" or independence of relationships and some measure of "relativity," God, and only God, is in one aspect of his being strictly or maximally absolute, and in another aspect no less strictly or maximally relative. So both "relative" and "nonrelative" are analogical, not univocal, in application to deity. And since "social" is, in this reference, equivalent to the synthesis of independent and dependent, social also is analogical in its theological application. Accordingly, our doctrine does not "humanize" or anthropomorphize deity, but preserves a distinction that is completely metaphysical between deity and all else.

The distinction may be expressed under any category. For example, God is the only unconditionally "necessary" existent. What is unconditionally necessary in God, however, is not all of God, though it is unique to him. And in another aspect, God is not only possessed of accidents, but he is the sole being who possesses or could possibly possess all actual accidental being as his own actuality. Other beings are in no aspect strictly necessary, and in no aspect maximally accidental, but always and in all aspects something middling under both categories. In this middling character lies their "imperfection." The mediocre way in which they illustrate categories like possibility, necessity, relativity, independence, is their real otherness to the divine, not the mere fact that they do illustrate this or that category. Tradition put it otherwise, thus: "God is not subject to the category of relation, or of potentiality, or of passivity, etc."

To be sure, there are some apparent qualifications to be made of this historical account. There was said to be relation among the persons of the Trinity; and also God could be said to have "extrinsic potentiality," since his existence is the possibility of the world's existence. But these qualifications amount to little. "Relation" here is not the category of relativity in the basic or primary sense which is in question in this book. For that sense is the ability of a thing to express in its own nature those other things which, among alternatively possible or contingent things, happen to exist. (Persons of the Trinity, of course, are noncontingent.) This meaning of relation is, as we shall see, the fundamental one. Without it there could be no knowledge of what contingent things actually exist, and what possibilities of existence are unactualized. Moreover, necessity is a negative or at least an abstract conception. It may be defined as that whose nonexistence is not possible; or as that which, being common to all possibility (its least common denominator, or abstract identity), has no possible alternative. On the other hand, Peirce [1] has shown that the definition of the possible as the nonnecessary presupposes another and positive meaning, that of spontaneous variety, particularity. Extrinsic potentiality is also, like relation between exclusively necessary factors, a derivative or negative form of its category. Plato extrinsically "produced" Leibnitz, in that the actual coming to be of Leibnitz did not change or enrich the actuality of Plato. He who causes others to reach the promised land but himself remains outside—as the historical Plato remained outside the philosophy of Leibnitz (in the sense

---

[1] See, in *Collected Papers,* especially Vols. I and VI, discussions of firstness, possibility, chance, variety, spontaneity.

that he did not know or enjoy it)—exercises extrinsic potency, potency of producing but not of being. Alternative possible effects of such an agent cannot be regarded as deliberate deeds on his part. To decide this, when deciding that was possible, is to be in one state of decision when another was possible. In so far as Plato consciously chose the kind of successors he was to have, just so far his potency was intrinsic as well as extrinsic. And he was a human being, able to produce a human being's characteristic effects, only because he did exercise intrinsic potency. Conscious freedom is decision among alternative possibilities of intrinsic being. Plato chose the sort of influence he was to have by choosing what he was himself to be. This is all that can be meant by conscious choice. It may be that God has only to say, "Let there be light," and there is light. But God's saying "Let there be light" is a state of his being, and a nonnecessary state, for otherwise either we have a vicious regress, the "Let there be light" becoming something outside himself, so that he must have said Let such a saying be; or else the saying is his very essence, and then he could not possibly have failed to say "Let there be light," and the saying can have been no decision, no free act at all.

## Suggested Additional Readings

SOME CONTEMPORARY ANSWERS

Baillie, John. *Our Knowledge of God.* New York: Charles Scribner's Sons, 1939. See especially Chapters 18 and 19. Baillie is a contemporary Scottish theologian whose work represents a continuation and modification of the liberal tradition in Christian theology.

Baillie, John, and Hugh Martin, editors. *Revelation.* London: Faber and Faber, Ltd., 1937. A collection of essays on revelation by prominent representatives from several branches of the Christian tradition—Eastern Orthodox, Roman Catholic, and Protestant.

D'Arcy, Martin C. *The Nature of Belief.* London: Sheed and Ward, 1937. See especially pp. 297f. Explanation by a Roman Catholic theologian of the nature of knowledge of God.

Heschel, Abraham J. *God In Search of Man, A Philosophy of Judaism.* Philadelphia: The Jewish Publication Society of America, 1956. (Also published in paperback by Meridian Books.) An outstanding Jewish theologian defines basic elements in a Jewish understanding of God.

Hick, John. *Philosophy of Religion.* Englewood Cliffs, N.J.: Prentice-Hall, 1963. In Chapter 7 the author proposes interesting views on "eschatological verification."

Inge, W. R. *Christian Mysticism.* New York: Charles Scribner's Sons, 1899. A careful and sympathetic scholar provides a clear, balanced account of the meaning and significance of mysticism.

James, William. "The Will to Believe," *Essays on Faith and Morals.* New York: Longmans, Green & Company, 1943. Famous pragmatic argument for the meaningfulness of belief in God's existence.

Jones, Rufus. *Pathways to the Reality of God.* New York: The Macmillan Company, 1931. A twentieth-century American philosopher and Quaker mystic explains in contemporary terms what mystics conceive to be the means to knowledge of God.

Kaplan, Mordecai M. *The Meaning of God in Modern Jewish Religion.* New York: Jewish Reconstructionist Foundation, Inc., 1947. A Jewish naturalistic approach that argues that God is to be understood as life's creative force.

Kroner, Richard. *How Do We Know God?* New York: Harper & Row, 1943. A German-American philosophical theologian argues that faith is basically a response of man's will and mind to God.

Lewis, H. D. *Our Experience of God.* New York: The Macmillan Company, 1960. An unusually clear and illuminating analysis of religious consciousness.

Marcel, Gabriel. *The Philosophy of Existence.* Trans., Manya Harari. London: Harvill Press, 1948. French Roman Catholic existentialist philosopher expresses his conception of how God may be known.

Maritain, Jacques. "A New Approach to God," *Our Emergent Civilization,* editor Ruth N. Anshen. New York: Harper & Row, 1947. A Thomistic position developed by a contemporary philosopher.

Mascall, E. L. *The Secularization of Christianity.* New York: Holt, Rinehart & Winston, 1966. Contains a vigorous and detailed criticism of Robinson's *Honest to God* and of van Buren's selection, pp. 404 ff.

Smith, John E. *Reason and God.* New Haven: Yale University Press, 1961. Contains chapters on Peirce, Nietzsche, and Dewey.

Weiss, Paul. *The God We Seek.* Carbondale, Ill.: Southern Illinois University Press, 1964. This work by a Yale philosopher centers on the experience of and concern with God in privacy and in community.

Whitehead, Alfred North. *Process and Reality.* New York: The Macmillan Company, 1929. (Also published in paperback by Harper & Row Torchbook, The Academy Library.)

———— *Science and the Modern World.* New York: The Macmillan Company, 1925. (Also published in paperback by The New American Library of World Literature, Mentor Series.) See especially Chapter X. These works by a distinguished contemporary philosopher include statements on the necessity of God in the order of the universe.

# V. Religious Language

ONE OF THE most important new areas of concern in philosophy of religion is the analysis of religious language. This concern stems from the wider philosophic study of the use and meaning of all language. Turning from the idea that the objective of philosophy is to create a unified system or world view, many philosophers in recent times have undertaken the quite different effort of analyzing the usages of language. Development of this area has come swiftly in recent decades.

On the Continent this movement found its main impetus among a group of philosophers centered in Vienna. Taking their lead from the new directions in logic indicated by the work of Bertrand Russell and Alfred North Whitehead, these men, often called "logical positivists," undertook the work of making explicit both the realm and task of logic and the realm of empirical verification. Under the leadership of such men as Moritz Schlick and Rudolf Carnap (who later came to America), along with A. J. Ayer in England, this school accepted as a central concern the creation of a simplified and precise linguistic system.

In England philosophers who had been influenced by G. E. Moore, and later by Wittgenstein, became interested in language as it is ordinarily used in any given field and undertook analyzing the ways in which language is employed in its various modes. These philosophers raised the question of what people mean by what they say. Their interest was not in creating an ideal or logically exact language, as was that of the Continental logical positivists, but rather in making an analysis of the usages of language in its "natural" modes.

Other philosophers were also at work. Among the most influential was Ernst Cassirer, who developed his philosophy in Germany and then in America. The major contribution of Cassirer to this effort has been his analysis of the place of myth in human thought and expression. His writings have made an impression on the work of many subsequent philosophers, especially those in the United States. One of the best known of his followers is Suzanne Langer, whose book *Philosophy in a New Key* is a basic introduction to the role of symbol making in human thought.

Concern for the meaning of specifically religious language and symbols was awakened by other influences. Religious thinkers became seriously concerned with the question: Does the Biblical message, wrapped as it is in prescientific myth and symbol, have any relevance to the modern, scientific man? Rudolf Bultmann and Reinhold Niebuhr stand out as theologians who have endeavored to examine the use of myth in the Bible and who have investigated the validity and discussed the relevance of religious language. One of the most pressing questions is whether there is an essential truth to be found in the Biblical message, and if so, what it is and how it can be extracted. The primary approach has been to study the use and meaning of the forms of expression found in the Bible.

In philosophy of religion at the present time work is being done in a number of areas involving examination of religious language. Some thinkers are reinvestigating the medieval scholastic discussion of the analogical relation of human language to the reality of God, whereas others are concentrating on the nature and form of Biblical language. One of the growing movements of the time is found among those who follow the English linguistic analysts in their attempt to understand the unique character of religious language. Language in every distinct area has its own peculiar usages, and language as it is used in religion is no exception. The analysis of religious language ranges beyond theological statements, although these are also included, for it is concerned with understanding the nature and function of religious language as it is found in worship and symbolization, as well as in formal statement.

Selections reprinted after this introduction present illustrations of the work being done in these areas. Robert Calhoun's essay is an exceptionally clear statement of the role of language in religion. In the concluding section of his article, that which deals with three problems of language in religion, Professor Calhoun sketches a setting for the work reported in the other articles.

In the essay of Rudolf Bultmann we have a major figure in the contemporary discussion of Biblical language making a case for fresh interpretation of the existential meaning of the New Testament message, separated from its husks of mythology. Bultmann also gives some indication of how he thinks this work should be done.

John Wilson introduces us more directly to the general intention of linguistic analysis in philosophy. His article can well serve as a clear statement of some of the possible ways to delineate the forms of religious statements and to assess their validity. Both John Wisdom and R. B. Braithwaite demonstrate at a more advanced level the same interest. Wisdom's article is of historical importance as one of the early, influential essays in the area. In it Wisdom discusses the question "Is belief in gods reasonable?" He makes suggestions both for understanding the question and for assessing its validity. The Braithwaite selection provides us with an empiricist orientation and a new attempt to evaluate the relation between religious and moral statements. Braithwaite is most provocative in his discussion of religious "stories."

Paul Tillich is a contemporary Protestant thinker who undertakes to clarify the intention and meaning of symbols in religion. His essay attempts to show that symbols taken from the world of ordinary sensory experience can be the means by which man's ultimate religious concern finds expression. E. L. Mascall provides a contemporary discussion of the meaning of analogy in religious language. The discussion of analogy has been an important interest throughout the history of Christian thought. It continues to retain its importance in the Thomistic tradition and, to a lesser extent, in other philosophical traditions.

The last article is by Paul van Buren, an exponent of empirical exploration of the meaning of theological statements, who comes to the conclusion that the word *God* is dead and that theology must now accept the responsibility for giving the precise usage of its words in their context. In the assessment of the meaning of statements by an analysis of their function, van Buren arrives at what he takes to be valid forms of theological discussion.

# ROBERT L. CALHOUN

*Robert L. Calhoun* (1896–    ) is emeritus professor of historical theology at Yale Divinity School. His interests range from Greek philosophy to contemporary theological problems. He has written in the field of Christian ethics as well as in the history of Christian thought.

## The Place of Language in Religion

Religion is not primarily talk, nor symbolic behavior of any kind. It is not primarily ceremony, nor preaching and listening, not even reflective meditation, though all these have their due places in it. First of all, religion is response, deeper and more inclusive than speech or thought, to revelation—to the impact of reality apprehended as divine. In the broadest sense of the term, such reality is numinous, "a mystery full of terror and fascination." In simpler religious communities, the mystery may be found in natural objects, animals, persons, in particular places, times, or events, even in man-made implements hallowed by antiquity and tradition or by dramatic association with a crisis in human living. The gods of unsophisticated peoples are indefinite in number and often transitory in divine status. But in more discriminating religion, the divine is identified sooner or later with the ultimate in man's universe. Mystery and numinous quality are not left behind, but they are apprehended now as characters not of serpents or stars or sorcerers, but of the abiding ground of all particular existence and worth —God beyond all finite things and events, apprehended as overwhelmingly great and good. Our central concern here is with religion of this latter sort.

The primary response of one who finds himself at grips with what he takes to be ultimate reality is an all-inclusive response like the turning of a plant toward the light. It involves thought, feeling, and action, and the still deeper impulses—below the threshold of conscious experience—from which decision and action arise. Religion involves the whole self, in a commitment at once inescapable and spontaneously affirmative, like the commitment of a free mind to evident truth or of a perceptive heart to a beloved person,

From Robert L. Calhoun, "The Language of Religion," *The Unity of Knowledge,* ed. Lewis Leary, Doubleday & Co., Inc., pp. 252–262. Copyright, 1955, by Columbia University. Used by permission of Columbia University.

community, or cause. Such commitment is not calculating, arbitrary, or avoidable, given the situation that evokes it. But neither is it coerced, involuntary, or enslaving. It is the affirmation of one who can do no other, yet who in such affirmation is enhanced and emancipated. Such response to the presence of God is worship that continually seeks expression in devoted work. Both are integral and inseparable components in primary religion.

This primary response finds characteristic if not inevitable elaboration in the life of religious communities whose members have been drawn into such commitment and seek then to reaffirm, to interpret, and to communicate their experience. First in this social or corporate elaboration of religion is the development of cultus or liturgy, a system of ceremonial acts in which renewal of worship is sought or sensibly embodied. Here sacraments are central—enacted means of communication between worshipers and God, and among members of the community both past and present. In a broad sense the whole liturgy is sacramental: a blending of speech and action, light and shadow, color, tone, rhythm, fragrance into a complex act (*leitourgia*) of affirmation and reception of meaning, in the presence of reality beyond the fabric of symbols. Secondly, there is a more or less elaborate system of verbalization—evangelism in the usual restricted sense of spoken and written conveyance of "the gospel" of God's living presence and acts: proclamation, reflective interpretation, and systematic teaching. In the terminology of the early Christian Church, these interrelated phases of evangelism were called *kērygma* (preaching, testimony, announcement as by a herald), spontaneous, declaratory, and particularized rather than general, critical, or systematic; *theologia* (more reflective, critical, reasoned discourse about God and man), seeking to classify, order, interpret, and defend the substance of the *kērygma* as coherent and relevant doctrine (*doctrina, dogma*) suitable, as the name suggests, for systematic study and teaching; and *catechēsis* (instruction) in which both the gist of the first-hand, eyewitness proclamation (*kērygma*) and some part of the growing system of interpretation (*theologia, doctrina*) are carefully expounded for learners. This is the area with which the major part of this paper is chiefly concerned. Thirdly, there is in every religious community more or less elaborate maintenance of organization and discipline: allocation of office, function, and authority; moral rules or norms embodied in individual and corporate living. Finally, there is active concern for the welfare of neighbors within and outside the organized community, normally expressed in practical service (*diakonia*), the everyday acts of devoted living.

If something like this account be accepted, the place of language in religion is most obvious in the first two of these elaborated phases: liturgy and evangelism. Man's primary response in worship to the impact of God's presence is concrete and immediate rather than reflective and articulate, *erleben* rather than *erkennen*. This is not to say it is irrational, nor that symbolism and language have no place in it. If neither of these statements were true, it is hard to see how theology could get a foothold as an integral component in religious life at all. If the primary response of man to God were as simply immediate and ineffable as toothache or salt taste, theology would be as external to the experience as the effort to verbalize a sensation is to the simple intuition itself. But since the religious response involves the whole person, it has an internal structure that lends itself to reflection and symbolic communication as a simple sensation does not. At the same time, like a concrete experience of love or loyalty, a concrete moment of worship is not *eo ipso* reflective, critical, even articulate. These are characteristics rather of the elaborated moments of religion, in which the implicit meanings of the primary moment are spelled out in growing detail—but never completely.

This situation is sometimes obscured by ambiguous use of the term revelation. This term refers properly to the primary moment of religion, in which God is said to reveal or disclose his presence to the worshiper and thereby to evoke the primary religious response. Sometimes this revelation is understood as consisting of propositions given as guaranteed truth. In that event, verbalization would of course be conspicuous from the very start. "The word of the Lord" to Amos or Isaiah would consist of information, instructions, and commands in verbal form. But in common with a substantial body of interpreters, this paper takes revelation to consist not in dictated propositions but in arresting events—impacts, confrontations—whose meaning is partly verbalized in further reflection.

The modes and functions of language in religion can now be examined a bit more directly, though very briefly. It seems convenient to look first at liturgy and especially at sacrament as a very inclusive and characteristic form of the language of religion, whose nature, presuppositions, and intent can help to illuminate the more precisely verbal and conceptual language of theology. It goes without saying that the latter is needed likewise for illumination of the former. The two are not separable without serious damage to both.

An essential presupposition of all genuine liturgy, as distinct from the "vain repetitions" of rote memory and habit, is the real communion or participation (*koinōnia*) of men with one another and with reality beyond themselves; and the possibility of heightening, clarifying, renewing, and extending this communion both for present worshipers and for other men. Liturgy is a complex of symbolic acts intended to express the communion that is already real, and by communication to help extend and to enhance it. *Koinōnia* is neither identity nor uniformity. It is a mutual involvement of beings that are radically other, yet profoundly interrelated. Thus, each man is radically other than his neighbor, incapable of occupying his neighbor's perspective instead of his own. Yet each is so bound up with his neighbors that without them he could not be himself, and he is able to recognize this bond. Thus also man is radically other than God, the ultimate ground of his existence, the perfect truth and right by which he is judged. Yet in moments of arresting confrontation he is able to recognize and acknowledge his dependence on the radically Other, and to find himself in his wrongness not only condemned but forgiven and accepted, reconciled, reaffirmed. This paradoxical conquest of alienation, this profound communion in radical otherness—of man from man, and of man from God—is what liturgy seeks to affirm, to mediate, and to articulate in symbolic action.

The symbols, as already noted, are of many sorts. But to fulfill their function they must be sacramental. That is to say, among other things, they must be not mere external pointers but concrete media embodying or exemplifying the communion they seek to convey. They must be like friendly handclasps or like gifts offered and received, not like calling cards or polite salutations. They must be saturated in memory, individual and corporate, so that they can call up in vivid presence the long past and enable those who share in them to share in the life of a community enduring through time. They must be rooted in the hungers and hopes of our common humanity, speaking in their many-dimensional gestures not a local dialect only but a universal language. At the same time, like any concrete living tongue as against an artificially abstracted Esperanto, they are sure to manifest the peculiarities of particular traditions and to be susceptible of incalculably various understanding. Their virtue as sacramental symbols would not be enhanced if they could be reduced to simple freedom from ambiguity. To convey a living sense of participation in the whole fabric of human life and in a specific community diversified in time and space and modes of existence, they must point in many directions at once, like a musical theme amid variations, and be themselves actual segments or foci of the communal experience they signify. Finally, they must point beyond human life to reality that transcends it yet effectively enters into it: the producing and sustaining source of our life, the goal and norm by which we are judged, the transforming influence—the divine grace—by which we are corrected, renewed, and led into unforeseen dimensions of shared living.

Sacraments are signs and symbols, and in that sense components in the language of religion. A sacrament is at once an affirmation and a reminder of the reality from which the affirmation has its meaning. *Sacramentum* is the soldier's oath of loyalty, and the legionary standard—marked SPQR—by which he swears. It is "the outward, visible sign of an inward, spiritual grace," a "means (*medium*) of grace," a "symbol and occasion of the working of the Holy Spirit." As such it is also to be called *mysterion,* as in the Greek Church, at once sign and vehicle of the presence of God. Whether God's grace is mediated exclusively, or at least in exceptional and indispensable ways by particular liturgical acts, such as ceremonial washing or common meal, or whether such acts are peculiarly effective reminders of the working of grace through all sorts of channels—the spoken word in prayer and in preaching, the everyday acts of faithful service—is a question long and widely debated among religious people. It need not detain us here, but it may serve to direct our thought from liturgy as enacted language to the more specifically verbal expressions of theology and doctrine.

Here again we meet, from the early generations in Christian history, the term *symbolon,* as a name for a concise theological formula: a *credo* or formula for confession of faith in token of commitment and of membership in a committed community. The confessional formulae called symbols or creeds speedily found place in the liturgy—first for each new convert in the ceremony of baptism by which he was inducted into the Church, and thereafter as an integral part of each regular service of worship. This is a simple instance of the way in which cultus has been affected by reflective thought, by theology. The meaning of the whole liturgy is thus reoriented and further defined by the systematic effort toward verbalization. On the other hand, theological effort has proceeded in its own terms, mostly nonliturgical. Creeds and confessions have multiplied and expanded into sizable theological treatises approved by the community, related to its liturgy, but not included in it. Yet the initial intent of the whole dogmatic enterprise is clearly preserved in the use of the name symbolics for the study of all these creeds and confessions. They too, like liturgical acts of worship, intend to signify and in some sense to serve as media for the presence of God. The words they employ and the ordering of the words are never the carefully sterilized terms and propositions of algebra, of theoretical physics, or of clinical medicine. Their function as affirmations of active commitment requires a vocabulary and a syntax that have something of the urgency, ambivalence, and particularity of momentous action. They are not simple, exact results of exact reasoning—though much arduous, closely reasoned effort to attain exactitude enters into their formation. Rather they are what Plato called "articles of faith," hammered out in the midst of hard thinking yet grounded at bottom not in reasoning as such, but in rational conviction of the sort exemplified by Socrates, and serving as touchstones for genuine reasoning about God.

Such reasoning is theology, always inseparable from and pervaded by faith, never able to dispense with language in which a subjective or confessional moment is essential. At the same time, the task of theology is very largely an objective task as well. This means not merely that it is communicative as well as expressive, semantic and not simply emotive. Liturgy also, as we have urged, is communicative. Beyond that, theology is analytic, critical, interpretative, argumentative, and systematic. It seeks far more extensively than liturgy to distinguish and point out explicitly the factors involved in the primary confrontation of God and man—in revelation and religious response. It seeks to clarify and test by the familiar tests of internal coherence and empirical relevance the affirmations of religious conviction, recognizing that no more than those of love or intense loyalty, or of artistic or musical discernment can such affirmations be translated into alien terms or subordinated to alien requirements. It seeks to illuminate from various angles their characteristic structure and implications, their interconnections with other modes of human experience, and their actual sources and modifications in the course of history. It seeks, finally, to exhibit them as at once an ordered whole of which every component involves every other, and an effort to speak of mystery that is never reducible to the dimensions of any human·experience or discourse.

In theology, therefore, both language and methods are employed that find place also in many sciences, in history, in philosophy, in the study of poetry and other literature, and especially in everyday personal relations. Excepting a comparatively few technical terms, indeed, there is no vocabulary peculiar to theology. What is peculiar is the perspective in which familiar words are used. That perspective, as already affirmed more than once, is determined by the impact of divine revelation and the distinctive response of faith. From this situation arise the most difficult problems for theological discourse, and the most characteristic efforts to solve them without dissolving them away.

## Three Problems for Language in Religion

The root of these difficulties is familiar. The ordinary use of language is to direct attention to some objectively perceptible component of the speaker's world—an "it" to which one can point by a verbal gesture. Whether it is a sensible object (chair, planet, galaxy) or an intelligible object (Euclidean line, equality, sovereignty), words can be found or made that can indicate it with fair precision. The words are not *like* it, but in the context of human observation and converse, they come to have a conventionally accepted congruence with it. And this can come about the more easily because the words are at least of the same experiential order as the objects to which they point: the words also are objects, and as such can serve most readily as labels or finger posts for other objects. The attention of an observer ordinarily moves with least difficulty from one objective "it" to another.

When we seek to call attention to a subject, an "I," the task is notoriously much harder. David Hume even declared it impossible to point out a subject *qua* subject at all. Immanuel Kant agreed with him, but went on to explore in the immense, painstaking argument of the first two *Critiques* both reasons and methods for dealing concretely, actively, and significantly with subjects, even though they cannot be observed and described as if they were objects. Here also verbal signs provide a usable medium, since each of us is himself a subject, comes to know himself as such in active, responsible relations with others, and so can recognize and acknowledge others in the common matrix of social, historical existence.

But God is neither an observable "It" nor a finite "I." At least this is the conviction to which reflective religion sooner or later has come, in all the great traditions known to me. And only for such religion does the special problem of language arise. For such religion, God is not merely numinous but radically transcendent—incommensurable with finite things and persons, as Creator with creatures, Perfect with imperfect, Infinite with finite, and so on. Moreover, if it be true, as many religious thinkers have held, that God is the ground of rational order, the presupposition of all discourse, then trying to talk or to think articulately *about* him is a little like trying to see oneself as observing subject, the presupposed ground of all one's seeing. This last difficulty might perhaps be outflanked, in Kant's way or some other; indeed, to be able to see and state the problem seems to imply that in some sense one is already beyond it—if only the right forms of speech could be found to express what the situation implies.

But all our language is relative to the objective phenomena we observe and to the finite existence we share. More than that, all of it is culturally conditioned, like our own minds, so that any words we can use have special reference not even to the whole of human experience or of finite existence, but only to some part of it. How can such constricted language be used in valid reference to God?

One familiar answer is often associated with mysticism: recourse to some *via negativa* or *via remotionis*. Since God is incommensurable with the finite things from which our languages derive and to which they properly refer, the only true assertions about God are negative assertions, denying of him all predicates drawn from our experience of things in time and space, or of persons in human history. But such negation has at least one tremendous affirmation as its base: that God is transcendent, incommensurable with all that is finite. Hence, unless one is to keep wholly silent, avoiding even negative assertions, it seems necessary to probe further after some ground for affirmation. Three such efforts to undergird affirmations about God may be noticed briefly here: the ways of mythology, of analogy, and of paradox.

The earliest, simplest, most concrete form of religious discourse was myth. Indeed, one major theory holds that language itself arises in the matrix of mythical experience, and achieves independent status and conceptual form only after a long maturing within the context of myth. In the mythical perspective, "all things are full of gods," in Thales' well-known words. Earth and heaven interpenetrate freely, because the gods are beings in space and time, gifted with powers beyond those of men, appearing and disappearing at will, but very far from radically transcendent. This is the stage of mythical experience and discourse that Paul Tillich calls "unbroken myth." It is precritical and untroubled by misgivings about the direct applicability of mythical picture-language to divine beings, who are man's near neighbors and kinsmen in a finite world.

But with progress in critical thought concerning gods and men, this early confidence is shattered. Whenever the many gods are subordinated to one god, and the one at length absorbs or displaces the rest, the crucial step is not far off. That step is taken when the one god is declared to be the Ultimate, radically other than man, uncontainable in space and to me, incommensurable with any finite existence. Then the question is posed sharply whether mythical experience and discourse concerning God must not be abandoned. Tillich says no. Any discourse concerning God is inevitably mythical, in the sense that predicates derived from experiences with finite beings in space and time are affirmed of God, in the context of such apprehension of a numinous transcendent as Otto has described and we have noticed above. But myth as now used, says Tillich, is "broken myth," no longer naively assumed to be an actual description of divine reality but recognized as usable *faute de mieux* to signalize the presence of a transcendent other that cannot be described at all. To substitute nonmythical language (that is, a carefully desiccated technical vocabulary of some sort) would serve no good purpose. No technical vocabulary is more adequate for symbolizing the Ultimate Being, and it would have for religious discourse the great disadvantage of failing to convey effectively even the human side of the religious situation: man's awe in the presence of God.

A second way of trying to cope with the problem is the familiar scholastic theory of analogy. From one point of view, this may be taken as an effort to find a theoretic basis for such discourse as "broken myth" provides. The term *analogia,* in the sense of proportion, was not unfamiliar in Greek mathematics, and Plato used it in that sense. Aristotle extended its range into the vocabulary of logic and the theory of knowledge, as a *via media* between univocal predication that applies a term to more than one subject, with essentially identical meaning, and equivocal predication that applies a term to more than one subject, with essentially different meanings. Analogical predication applies a term to more than one subject, with meanings that are not essentially identical but that bear a certain proportion to one another, and signalize a corresponding proportionality between the subjects themselves.

When this conception was first applied to the problem of religious discourse I do not know. The second-century Platonist (?) and hostile critic of Christianity named Celsus, whom we know only through Origen's polemic against him, included "the method of analogy" among philosophic methods suited for discourse about God. Origen himself follows suit, subordinating analogy along with all other philosophic methods to revelation and the "rule of faith." Augustine gives the method and its underlying principle a central place in his work *On the Trinity,* arguing that since man is created *ad imaginem dei,* it is not improper to seek in the personal existence of man analogies that may help to illustrate, not to prove, the Church's doctrine of the true Being of God. Substantially this same line is developed in the two *Summae* of Thomas Aquinas. He too sets out from the relation between Creator and creature, being careful to warn against saying, "God is like man"—as if man were the standard—whereas the truth is that man is in some sense like God. God is the Origin, man the derivative being. The Being of God—self-existent, perfect—is not the being of man—dependent, imperfect. Yet between them is such *analogia entis* that some predicates, such as rational, just, and merciful, can be affirmed *analogice* of man and of God.

To most Roman Catholic thought today, this doctrine seems valid and essential. But there are competent theologians who reject it, because it narrows too much the gulf between Creator and creatures. Some of them, like Karl Barth, are quite willing to talk of analogy in a different context, provided not by creation as such but by incarnation, and apprehended not by natural reason but by faith—an *analogia fidei* instead of an *analogia entis.* On this view, the self-disclosure of God in Jesus Christ as God-man, the Word of God incarnate, is the indispensable break-through from God's side that makes theological discourse possible. Analogies now can be found between various aspects of life in the Church and the life of the incarnate Word, though not directly between creatures as such and their Creator. One may question whether this account as it stands is self-complete. Its stress on the need for divine initiative in revelation to make theological discourse feasible may be welcomed. But such revelation is not provided *in vacuo.* It is provided in and through created being. That is what incarnation means, in one essential perspective. And whether the existing relation between created being and Creator be called *analogia entis* or not, it seems a requisite component in the situation in which *analogia fidei* can be realized.

There is a third way in which this problem has been dealt with: the way of paradoxical or dialectical affirmation. These terms are among the hallmarks of Søren Kierkegaard's thought, with leaders in the Protestant Reformation and Kant preceding him, and the dialectical theology of our day, often strongly tinged with such theistic existentialism as that of Buber, following and transforming some of his suggestions. Although most dialectical theologians, like Martin Luther and John Calvin, are wary of mysticism, their treatment of this problem of theological affirmation has strong bonds, both negative and positive, to the great mystics' thought on the same problem. The rejection of mysticism centers mainly on denial of any basic identification of man and God, and insistence on the primacy of faith—personal commitment in response to revelation—rather than immediate intuition. But there is also clear reaffirmation of a characteristic doctrine of the mystics: that any attempt to speak of the inexpressible Fullness of God must take the form of joint affirmation and denial, the sort of dialectical affirmation which, unlike Hegel's, can never pass smoothly to a synthesis in which antitheses are wholly combined. The Being of God is and remains Mystery.

Our affirmations then must have the paradoxical character of statements in which contraries are declared to be inseparaable and equally necessary. This is not contradiction. A self-contradictory term or proposition tries verbally to combine strictly incompatible elements each of which is intelligible in isolation from the other. Square circles and uncreated creatures are of that sort. But finding life by losing it, mercy that judges more searchingly than condemnation, God everywhere present and nowhere included, at once immanent and radically transcendent—these are terms whose components cannot have in isolation the meanings they have when combined. The incarnate Word, the God-man is the supreme instance, for Kierkegaard, "The Paradox" that enables corrupted man as no teacher can do—not even Socrates, the very model of genuine teachers—to apprehend truth and reality that is radically *other* than he, of a different order of magnitude, incommensurable with his weakness and distortion of mind. The light he requires is not in him, and no Socrates can bring it into view. The light must be *given* to him, and that means he must be transformed. When the light comes, he still cannot talk simply of what he sees. He must speak in paradoxes, for the truth is not simple, objective, formulable, and never his to possess.

Implicit in all three of these proffered answers, and explicit in most of their variant forms, is the presupposition of divine self-disclosure and human faith. Faith as total personal response is much more than cognitive belief, and differently related to reasoning, knowledge, and speech. It is not a substitute for any of these, nor a first or a final leap beginning or completing a process of thought. If one may venture a concluding paradox, it is the personal context, climate, active disposition in which thought and discourse of God must go on, subject at every step to their testing yet never subordinate to them and never exhausted in what they may find to say.

# RUDOLF BULTMANN

---

*Rudolf Bultmann* (1884–      ), professor of New Testament at Marburg
University, 1921–1951, has undertaken the study of the Christian scripture from an existentialist orientation. Existentialist philosophy, he believes, helps to open the true meaning of the Biblical message.

---

## New Testament and Mythology

*The Task of Demythologizing the New Testament Proclamation*
*A. The Problem*

1. THE MYTHICAL VIEW OF THE WORLD AND THE MYTHICAL EVENT OF
REDEMPTION. The cosmology of the New Testament is essentially mythical
in character. The world is viewed as a three-storied structure, with the earth
in the centre, the heaven above, and the underworld beneath. Heaven is the
abode of God and of celestial beings—the angels. The underworld is hell,
the place of torment. Even the earth is more than the scene of natural,
everyday events, of the trivial round and common task. It is the scene of
the supernatural activity of God and his angels on the one hand, and of
Satan and his daemons on the other. These supernatural forces intervene in
the course of nature and in all that men think and will and do. Miracles
are by no means rare. Man is not in control of his own life. Evil spirits
may take possession of him. Satan may inspire him with evil thoughts. Alternatively, God may inspire his thought and guide his purposes. He may
grant him heavenly visions. He may allow him to hear his word of succour
or demand. He may give him the supernatural power of his Spirit. History
does not follow a smooth unbroken course; it is set in motion and controlled
by these supernatural powers. This aeon is held in bondage by Satan, sin,
and death (for "powers" is precisely what they are), and hastens towards
its end. That end will come very soon, and will take the form of a cosmic
catastrophe. It will be inaugurated by the "woes" of the last time. Then
the Judge will come from heaven, the dead will rise, the last judgment will
take place, and men will enter into eternal salvation or damnation.

---

From Rudolf Bultmann, *Kerygma and Myth,* ed. Hans W. Bartsch, trans. Reginald H.
Fuller, pp. 1–16. Published, 1954, Society for the Publication of Christian Knowledge. Used
by permission of the publisher. [Footnotes omitted, Eds.]

*This then is the mythical view of the world which the New Testament presupposes when it presents the event of redemption which is the subject of its preaching.* It proclaims in the language of mythology that the last time has now come. "In the fulness of time" God sent forth his Son, a pre-existent divine Being, who appears on earth as a man. He dies the death of a sinner on the cross and makes atonement for the sins of men. His resurrection marks the beginning of the cosmic catastrophe. Death, the consequence of Adam's sin, is abolished, and the daemonic forces are deprived of their power. The risen Christ is exalted to the right hand of God in heaven and made "Lord" and "King." He will come again on the clouds of heaven to complete the work of redemption, and the resurrection and judgement of men will follow. Sin, suffering and death will then be finally abolished. All this is to happen very soon; indeed, St Paul thinks that he himself will live to see it.

All who belong to Christ's Church and are joined to the Lord by Baptism and the Eucharist are certain of resurrection to salvation, unless they forfeit it by unworthy behaviour. Christian believers already enjoy the first instalment of salvation, for the Spirit is at work within them, bearing witness to their adoption as sons of God, and guaranteeing their final resurrection.

2. THE MYTHOLOGICAL VIEW OF THE WORLD OBSOLETE. All this is the language of mythology, and the origin of the various themes can be easily traced in the contemporary mythology of Jewish Apocalyptic and in the redemption myths of Gnosticism. To this extent *the kerygma is incredible to modern man, for he is convinced that the mythical view of the world is obsolete.* We are therefore bound to ask whether, when we preach the Gospel to-day, we expect our converts to accept not only the Gospel message, but also the mythical view of the world in which it is set. If not, does the New Testament embody a truth which is quite independent of its mythical setting? If it does, theology must undertake the task of stripping the Kerygma from its mythical framework, of "demythologizing" it.

Can Christian preaching expect modern man *to accept the mythical view of the world as true?* To do so would be both senseless and impossible. It would be senseless, because there is nothing specifically Christian in the mythical view of the world as such. It is simply the cosmology of a pre-scientific age. Again, it would be impossible, because no man can adopt a view of the world by his own volition—it is already determined for him by his place in history. Of course such a view is not absolutely unalterable, and the individual may even contribute to its change. But he can do so only when he is faced by a new set of facts so compelling as to make his previous view of the world untenable. He has then no alternative but to modify his view of the world or produce a new one. The discoveries of Copernicus and the atomic theory are instances of this, and so was romanticism, with its discovery that the human subject is richer and more complex than enlightenment or realism had allowed, and nationalism, with its new realization of the importance of history and the tradition of peoples.

It may equally well happen that truths which a shallow enlightenment had failed to perceive are later rediscovered in ancient myths. Theologians are perfectly justified in asking whether this is not exactly what has happened with the New Testament. At the same time it is impossible to revive an obsolete view of the world by a mere fiat, and certainly not a mythical view. For all our thinking to-day is shaped for good or ill by modern science. A blind acceptance of the New Testament mythology would be irrational, and to press for its acceptance as an article of faith would be to reduce Christian faith to the level of a human achievement. Wilhelm Herrmann pointed this out many years ago, and one would have thought that his demonstration was conclusive. It would involve a sacrifice of the intellect which could have only one result—a curious form of schizophrenia and insincerity. It would mean accepting a view of the world in our faith and religion which we should deny in our everyday life. Modern thought as we have inherited it provides us with *a motive for criticizing the New Testament view of the world*.

*Man's knowledge and mastery of the world* have advanced to such an extent through science and technology that it is no longer possible for anyone seriously to hold the New Testament view of the world—in fact, there is hardly anyone who does. What meaning, for instance, can we attach to such phrases in the creed as "descended into hell" or "ascended into heaven"? We no longer believe in the three-storied universe which the creeds take for granted. The only honest way of reciting the creeds is to strip the mythological framework from the truth they enshrine— that is, assuming that they contain any truth at all, which is just the question that theology has to ask. No one who is old enough to think for himself supposes that God lives in a local heaven. There is no longer any heaven in the traditional sense of the word. The same applies to hell in the sense of a mythical underworld beneath our feet. And if this is so, we can no longer accept the story of Christ's descent into hell or his Ascension into heaven as literally true. We can no longer look for the return of the Son of Man on the clouds of heaven or hope that the faithful will meet him in the air (I Thess. 4.15ff.).

Now that the forces and the laws of nature have been discovered, we can no longer believe *in spirits, whether good or evil*. We know that the stars are physical bodies whose motions are controlled by the laws of the universe, and not daemonic beings which enslave mankind to their service. Any influence they may have over human life must be explicable in terms of the ordinary laws of nature; it cannot in any way be attributed to their malevolence. Sickness and the cure of disease are likewise attributable to natural causation; they are not the result of daemonic activity or of evil spells. *The miracles of the New Testament* have ceased to be miraculous, and to defend their historicity by recourse to nervous disorders or hypnotic effects only serves to underline the fact. And if we are still left with certain physiological and psychological phenomena which we can only assign to mysterious and enigmatic causes, we are still assigning them to causes, and thus far are trying to make them scientifically intelligible. Even occultism pretends to be a science.

It is impossible to use electric light and the wireless and to avail ourselves of modern medical and surgical discoveries, and at the same time to believe in the New Testament world of daemons and spirits. We may think we can manage it in our own lives, but to expect others to do so is to make the Christian faith unintelligible and unacceptable to the modern world.

*The mythical eschatology* is untenable for the simple reason that the parousia of Christ never took place as the New Testament expected. History did not come to an end, and, as every schoolboy knows, it will contine to run its course. Even if we believe that the world as we know it will come to an end in time, we expect the end to take the form of a natural catastrophe, not of a mythical event such as the New Testament expects. And if we explain the parousia in terms of modern scientific theory, we are applying criticism to the New Testament, albeit unconsciously.

But natural science is not the only challenge which the mythology of the New Testament has to face. There is the still more serious challenge presented by *modern man's understanding of himself.*

Modern man is confronted by a curious dilemma. He may regard himself as pure nature, or as pure spirit. In the latter case he distinguishes the essential part of his being from nature. In either case, however, *man is essentially a unity.* He bears the sole responsibility for his own feeling, thinking, and willing. He is not, as the New Testament regards him, the victim of a strange dichotomy which exposes him to the interference of powers outside himself. If his exterior behaviour and his interior condition are in perfect harmony, it is something he has achieved himself, and if other people think their interior unity is torn asunder by daemonic or divine interference, he calls it schizophrenia.

Although biology and psychology recognize that man is a highly dependent being, that does not mean that he has been handed over to powers outside of and distinct from himself. This dependence is inseparable from human nature, and he needs only to understand it in order to recover his self-mastery and organize his life on a rational basis. If he regards himself as spirit, he knows that he is permanently conditioned by the physical, bodily part of his being, but he distinguishes his true self from it, and knows that he is independent and responsible for his mastery over nature.

In either case he finds *what the New Testament has to say about the "Spirit"* ($\pi\nu\epsilon\hat{\upsilon}\mu\alpha$) *and the sacraments utterly strange and incomprehensible.*

Biological man cannot see how a supernatural entity like the πνεῦμα can penetrate within the close texture of his natural powers and set to work within him. Nor can the idealist understand how a πνεῦμα working like a natural power can touch him and influence his mind and spirit. Conscious as he is of his own moral responsibility, he cannot conceive how baptism in water can convey a mysterious something which is henceforth the agent of all his decisions and actions. He cannot see how physical food can convey spiritual strength, and how the unworthy receiving of the Eucharist can result in physical sickness and death (I Cor. 11.30). The only possible explanation is that it is due to suggestion. He cannot understand how anyone can be baptized for the dead (I Cor. 15.29).

We need not examine in detail the various forms of modern *Weltanschauung,* whether idealist or naturalist. For the only criticism of the New Testament which is theologically relevant is that which arises *necessarily* out of the situation of modern man. The biological *Weltanschauung* does not, for instance, arise necessarily out of the contemporary situation. We are still free to adopt it or not as we choose. The only relevant question for the theologian is the basic assumption on which the adoption of a biological as of every other *Weltanschauung* rests, and that assumption is the view of the world which has been moulded by modern science and the modern conception of human nature as a self-subsistent unity immune from the interference of supernatural powers.

Again, the biblical doctrine that *death is the punishment of sin* is equally abhorrent to naturalism and idealism, since they both regard death as a simple and necessary process of nature. To the naturalist death is no problem at all, and to the idealist it is a problem for that very reason, for so far from arising out of man's essential spiritual being it actually destroys it. The idealist is faced with a paradox. On the one hand man is a spiritual being, and therefore essentially different from plants and animals, and on the other hand he is the prisoner of nature, whose birth, life, and death are just the same as those of the animals. Death may present him with a problem, but he cannot see how it can be a punishment for sin. Human beings are subject to death even before they have committed any sin. And to attribute human mortality to the fall of Adam is sheer nonsense, for guilt implies personal responsibility, and the idea of original sin as an inherited infection is sub-ethical, irrational, and absurd.

The same objections apply to *the doctrine of the atonement.* How can the guilt of one man be expiated by the death of another who is sinless— if indeed one may speak of a sinless man at all? What primitive notions of guilt and righteousness does this imply? And what primitive idea of God? The rationale of sacrifice in general may of course throw some light on the theory of the atonement, but even so, what a primitive mythology it is, that a divine Being should become incarnate, and atone for the sins of men through his own blood! Or again, one might adopt an analogy from the law courts, and explain the death of Christ as a transaction between God and man through which God's claims on man were satisfied. But that would make sin a juridical matter; it would be no more than an external transgression of a commandment, and it would make nonsense of all our ethical standards. Moreover, if the Christ who died such a death was the pre-existent Son of God, what could death mean for him? Obviously very little, if he knew that he would rise again in three days!

The *resurrection of Jesus* is just as difficult, if it means an event whereby a supernatural power is released which can henceforth be appropriated through the sacraments. To the biologist such language is meaningless, for he does not regard death as a problem at all. The idealist would not object to the idea of a life immune from death, but he could not believe that such a life is made available by the resuscitation of a corpse. If that is the way God makes life available for man, his action is inextricably involved in a nature miracle. Such a notion he finds intolerable, for he can see God at work only in the life of the spirit (which is for him the only real life) and in the transformation of his personality. But, quite apart from the incredibility of such a miracle, he cannot see how an event like this could be the act of God, or how it could affect his own life.

Gnostic influence suggests that this Christ, who died and rose again, was not a mere human being but a God-man. His death and resurrection were not isolated facts which concerned him alone, but a cosmic event in which we are all involved. It is only with effort that modern man can think himself back into such an intellectual atmosphere, and even then he could never accept it himself, because it regards man's essential being as nature and redemption as a process of nature. And as for the pre-existence of Christ, with its corollary of man's translation into a celestial realm of light, and the clothing of the human personality in heavenly robes and a spiritual body— all this is not only irrational but utterly meaningless. Why should salvation take this particular form? Why should this be the fulfilment of human life and the realization of man's true being?

## B. The Task Before Us

1. NOT SELECTION OR SUBTRACTION. Does this drastic criticism of the New Testament mythology mean the complete elimination of the kerygma?

Whatever else may be true, we cannot save the kerygma by selecting some of its features and subtracting others, and thus reduce the amount of mythology in it. For instance, it is impossible to dismiss St Paul's teaching about the unworthy reception of Holy Communion or about baptism for the dead, and yet cling to the belief that physical eating and drinking can have a spiritual effect. If we accept one idea, we must accept everything which the New Testament has to say about Baptism and Holy Communion, and it is just this one idea which we cannot accept.

It may of course be argued that some features of the New Testament mythology are given greater prominence than others: not all of them appear with the same regularity in the various books. There is for example only one occurrence of the legends of the Virgin birth and the Ascension; St Paul and St John appear to be totally unaware of them. But, even if we take them to be later accretions, it does not affect the mythical character of the event of redemption as a whole. And if we once start subtracting from the kerygma, where are we to draw the line? The mythical view of the world must be accepted or rejected in its entirety.

At this point absolute clarity and ruthless honesty are essential both for the academic theologian and for the parish priest. It is a duty they owe to themselves, to the Church they serve, and to those whom they seek to win for the Church. They must make it quite clear what their hearers are expected to accept and what they are not. At all costs the preacher must not leave his people in the dark about what he secretly eliminates, nor must he be in the dark about it himself. In Karl Barth's book *The Resurrection of the Dead* the cosmic eschatology in the sense of "chronologically final history" is eliminated in favour of what he intends to be a nonmythical "ultimate history." He is able to delude himself into thinking that this is exegesis of St Paul and of the New Testament generally only because he gets rid of everything mythological in I Corinthians by subjecting it to an interpretation which does violence to its meaning. But that is an impossible procedure.

If the truth of the New Testament proclamation is to be preserved, the only way is to demythologize it. But our motive in so doing must not be to make the New Testament relevant to the modern world at all costs. The question is simply whether the New Testament message consists exclusively of mythology, or whether it actually demands the elimination of myth if it is to be understood as it is meant to be. This question is forced upon us from two sides. First there is the nature of myth in general, and then there is the New Testament itself.

2. THE NATURE OF MYTH. The real purpose of myth is not to present an objective picture of the world as it is, but to express man's understanding of himself in the world in which he lives. Myth should be interpreted not cosmologically, but anthropologically, or better still, existentially. Myth speaks of the power or the powers which man supposes he experiences as the ground and limit of his world and of his own activity and suffering. He describes these powers in terms derived from the visible world, with its tangible objects and forces, and from human life, with its feelings, motives, and potentialities. He may, for instance, explain the origin of the world by

speaking of a world egg or a world tree. Similarly he may account for the present state and order of the world by speaking of a primeval war between the gods. He speaks of the other world in terms of this world, and of the gods in terms derived from human life.

Myth is an expression of man's conviction that the origin and purpose of the world in which he lives are to be sought not within it but beyond it—that is, beyond the realm of known and tangible reality—and that this realm is perpetually dominated and menaced by those mysterious powers which are its source and limit. Myth is also an expression of man's awareness that he is not lord of his own being. It expresses his sense of dependence not only within the visible world, but more especially on those forces which hold sway beyond the confines of the known. Finally, myth expresses man's belief that in this state of dependence he can be delivered from the forces within the visible world.

Thus myth contains elements which demand its own criticism—namely, its imagery with its apparent claim to objective validity. The real purpose of myth is to speak of a transcendent power which controls the world and man, but that purpose is impeded and obscured by the terms in which it is expressed.

Hence the importance of the New Testament mythology lies not in its imagery but in the understanding of existence which it enshrines. The real question is whether this understanding of existence is true. Faith claims that it is, and faith ought not to be tied down to the imagery of New Testament mythology.

3. THE NEW TESTAMENT ITSELF. The New Testament itself invites this kind of criticism. Not only are there rough edges in its mythology, but some of its features are actually contradictory. For example, the death of Christ is sometimes a sacrifice and sometimes a cosmic event. Sometimes his person is interpreted as the Messiah and sometimes as the Second Adam. The kenosis of the pre-existent Son (Phil. 2.6ff.) is incompatible with the miracle narratives as proofs of his messianic claims. The Virgin birth is inconsistent with the assertion of his pre-existence. The doctrine of the Creation is incompatible with the conception of the "rulers of this world" (I Cor. 2.6ff.), the "god of this world" (2 Cor. 4.4) and the "elements of this world" στοιχεῖα τοῦ κόσμου, (Gal. 4.3). It is impossible to square the belief that the law was given by God with the theory that it comes from the angels (Gal. 3. 19f.).

But the principal demand for the criticism of mythology comes from a curious contradiction which runs right through the New Testament. Sometimes we are told that human life is determined by cosmic forces, at others we are challenged to a decision. Side by side with the Pauline indicative stands the Pauline imperative. In short, man is sometimes regarded as a cosmic being, sometimes as an independent "I" for whom decision is a matter of life or death. Incidentally, this explains why so many sayings in the New Testament speak directly to modern man's condition while others remain enigmatic and obscure. Finally, attempts at demythologization are sometimes made even within the New Testament itself. But more will be said on this point later.

4. PREVIOUS ATTEMPTS AT DEMYTHOLOGIZING. How then is the mythology of the New Testament to be reinterpreted? This is not the first time that theologians have approached this task. Indeed, all we have said so far might have been said in much the same way thirty or forty years ago, and it is a sign of the bankruptcy of contemporary theology that it has been necessary to go all over the same ground again. The reason for this is not far to seek. The liberal theologians of the last century were working on the wrong lines. They threw away not only the mythology but also the kerygma itself. Were they right? Is that the treatment the New Testament itself required? That is the question we must face to-day. The last twenty years have witnessed a movement away from criticism and a return to a naive acceptance of the kerygma. The danger both for the theological scholarship and for the Church is that this uncritical resuscitation of the New Testament mythology may make this Gospel message unintelligible to the modern world. We cannot dismiss the critical labours of earlier generations without further ado. We must take them up and put them to constructive use. Failure to do so will mean that the old battles between orthodoxy and liberalism will have to be fought out all over again, that is assuming that there will be any Church or any theologians to fight them at all! Perhaps we may put it schematically like this: whereas the older liberals used criticism to *eliminate* the mythology of the New Testament, our task to-day is to use criticism to *interpret* it. Of course it may still be necessary to eliminate mythology here and there. But the criterion adopted must be taken not from modern thought, but from the understanding of human existence which the New Testament itself enshrines.

To begin with, let us review some of these earlier attempts at demythologizing. We need only mention briefly the allegorical interpretation of the New Testament which has dogged the Church throughout its history. This method spiritualizes the mythical events so that they become symbols of processes going on in the soul. This is certainly the most comfortable way of avoiding the critical question. The literal meaning is allowed to stand and is dispensed with only for the individual believer, who can escape into the realm of the soul.

It was characteristic of the older liberal theologians that they regarded mythology as relative and temporary. Hence they thought they could safely eliminate it altogether, and retain only the broad, basic principles of religion and ethics. They distinguished between what they took to be the essence of religion and the temporary garb which it assumed. Listen to what Harnack has to say about the essence of Jesus' preaching of the Kingdom of God and its coming: "The kingdom has a triple meaning. Firstly, it is something supernatural, a gift from above, not a product of ordinary life. Secondly, it is a purely religious blessing, the inner link with the living God; thirdly, it is the most important experience that a man can have, that on which everything else depends; it permeates and dominates his whole existence, because sin is forgiven and misery banished." Note how completely the mythology is eliminated: "The kingdom of God comes by coming to the individual, by entering into his *soul* and laying hold of it."

It will be noticed how Harnack reduces the kerygma to a few basic principles of religion and ethics. Unfortunately this means that the *kerygma has ceased to be kerygma:* it is no longer the proclamation of the decisive act of God in Christ. For the liberals the great truths of religion and ethics are timeless and eternal, though it is only within human history that they are realized, and only in concrete historical processes that they are given clear expression. But the apprehension and acceptance of these principles does not depend on the knowledge and acceptance of the age in which they first took shape, or of the historical persons who first discovered them. We are all capable of verifying them in our own experience at whatever period we happen to live. History may be of academic interest, but never of paramount importance for religion.

But the New Testament speaks of an *event* through which God has wrought man's redemption. For it, Jesus is not primarily the teacher, who certainly had extremely important things to say and will always be honoured for saying them, but whose person in the last analysis is immaterial for those who have assimilated his teaching. On the contrary, his person is just what the New Testament proclaims as the decisive event of redemption. It speaks of this person in mythological terms, but does this mean that we can reject the kerygma altogether on the ground that it is nothing more than mythology? That is the question.

Next came the History of Religions school. Its representatives were the first to discover the extent to which the New Testament is permeated by mythology. The importance of the New Testament, they saw, lay not in its teaching about religion and ethics but in its actual religion and piety; in comparison with that all the dogma it contains, and therefore all the mythological imagery with its apparent objectivity, was of secondary importance or completely negligible. The essence of the New Testament lay in the religious life it portrayed; its high-watermark was the experience of mystical union with Christ, in whom God took symbolic form.

These critics grasped one important truth. Christian faith is not the same as religious idealism; the Christian life does not consist in developing the individual personality, in the improvement of society, or in making the world a better place. The Christian life means a turning away from the world, a detachment from it. But the critics of the History of Religions school failed to see that in the New Testament this detachment is essentially eschatological and not mystical. Religion for them was an expression of the human yearning to rise above the world and transcend it: it was the discovery of a supramundane sphere where the soul could detach itself from all earthly care and find its rest. Hence the supreme manifestation of religion was to be found not in personal ethics or in social idealism but in the cultus regarded as an end in itself. This was just the kind of religious life portrayed in the New Testament, not only as a model and pattern, but as a challenge and inspiration. The New Testament was thus the abiding source of power which enabled man to realize the true life of religion, and Christ was the eternal symbol for the cultus of the Christian Church. It will be noticed how the Church is here defined exclusively as a worshipping community, and this represents a great advance on the older liberalism. This school rediscovered the Church as a *religious* institution. For the idealist there was really no place for the Church at all. But did they succeed in recovering the meaning of the Ecclesia in the full, New Testament sense of the word? For in the New Testament the Ecclesia is invariably a phenomenon of salvation history and eschatology.

Moreover, if the History of Religions school is right, the kerygma has once more ceased to be kerygma. Like the liberals, they are silent about a decisive act of God in Christ proclaimed as the event of redemption. So we are still left with the question whether this event and the person of Jesus, both of which are described in the New Testament in mythological terms, are nothing more than mythology. Can the kerygma be interpreted apart from mythology? Can we recover the truth of the kerygma for men who do not think in mythological terms without forfeiting its character as kerygma?

5. AN EXISTENTIALIST INTERPRETATION THE ONLY SOLUTION. The theological work which such an interpretation involves can be sketched only in the broadest outline and with only a few examples. We must avoid the impression that this is a light and easy task, as if all we have to do is to discover the right formula and finish the job on the spot. It is much more formidable than that. It cannot be done single-handed. It will tax the time and strength of a whole theological generation.

The mythology of the New Testament is in essence that of Jewish apocalyptic and the Gnostic redemption myths. A common feature of them both is their basic dualism, according to which the present world and its human inhabitants are under the control of daemonic, satanic powers, and stand in need of redemption. Man cannot achieve this redemption by his own efforts; it must come as a gift through a divine intervention. Both types of mythology speak of such an intervention: Jewish apocalyptic of an imminent world crisis in which this present aeon will be brought to an end and the new aeon ushered in by the coming of the Messiah, and Gnosticism of a Son of God sent down from the realm of light, entering into this world in the guise of a man, and by his fate and teaching delivering the elect and opening up the way for their return to their heavenly home.

The meaning of these two types of mythology lies once more not in their imagery within its apparent objectivity but in the understanding of human existence which both are trying to express. In other words, they need to be interpreted existentially. A good example of such treatment is to be found in Hans Jonas's book on Gnosticism.

Our task is to produce an existentialist interpretation of the dualistic mythology of the New Testament along similar lines. When, for instance, we read of daemonic powers ruling the world and holding mankind in bondage, does the understanding of human existence which underlies such language offer a solution to the riddle of human life which will be acceptable even to the nonmythological mind of to-day? Of course we must not take this to imply that the New Testament presents us with an anthropology like that which modern science can give us. It cannot be proved by logic or demonstrated by an appeal to factual evidence. Scientific anthropologies always take for granted a definite understanding of existence, which is invariably the consequence of a deliberate decision of the scientist, whether he makes it consciously or not. And that is why we have to discover whether the New Testament offers man an understanding of himself which will challenge him to a genuine existential decision.

# JOHN WILSON

*John Wilson* (1928–    ), British teacher, has attempted to interpret the importance of linguistic analysis for philosophy of religion. He has written two books which serve as introductions to analytical philosophy, *Language and Christian Belief* and *Language and the Pursuit of Truth.*

## Verification and Religious Language

Let us begin by taking a superficial glance at the language of religion. In religious works of literature, creeds, ritual, and so on we come across different types of sentences which have (or appear to have) different uses. On this superficial level, we can list these without difficulty:

(1) Sentences expressing commands, injunctions, exhortations, wishes, etc., such as "Thou shalt love the Lord thy God," "Let us love one another," and so on.

(2) Sentences expressing moral views, such as "Brethren, these things ought not so to be," "It is not good for man to be alone," etc.

(3) Sentences expressing factual truths, often historical, such as "Christ was born in Bethlehem," "Mary was a virgin," etc.

(4) Sentences giving information about the meanings of words, expressing analytic truths. A statement like "A sacrament is an outward and visible sign of an inward and spiritual grace" is analytic, and should be taken as informing the hearer about the meaning of "sacrament."

(5) Sentences which appear to be informative, but informative about the supernatural or metaphysical rather than the natural or physical world. For instance, "God exists," "Christ is the Son of God," and so on.

So far the philosopher has not yet got to work. But when he does, it is likely that he will be tempted to make two changes in our scheme above. The first does not concern us here: it involves merging what I have called "moral views" with "commands, injunctions, etc.," at least to some extent. The second is to attempt to distribute sentences in (5), metaphysical sen-

From John Wilson, *Language and Christian Belief*, pp. 1–15. Copyright, 1958, St. Martin's Press. Used by permission of Macmillan & Co., Ltd., and St. Martin's Press, Inc.

tences, among the other classes, in such a way that the possibility of super-
naturally informative sentences is excluded. He could say, for instance, that
some of these sentences are really analytic, and others really commands:
this is one of the commonest ways in which this particular move is made.

Let us look, for example, at one of the ablest attempts to make this kind
of move which have recently appeared. It has been made by Professor Braithwaite. He regards religious belief as primarily the intention or resolution
to adopt a certain way of life, this intention being supported by what he
calls "stories": that is, what appear to be empirical statements of fact, statements about the world, which are however not verifiable in the way that
ordinary empirical statements are verifiable. (Presumably the only sense in
which they could be said to be verifiable at all is the sense in which we
say that a statement in a story or work of fiction is verifiable, i.e. within the
context of the work as a whole.) These statements are believed because the
religious believer finds them psychologically helpful, inasmuch as they
bolster up his intention to adopt the way of life which he has chosen. But
they are not central to religious belief; and we should verify whether a man
is to be regarded as adhering to or following a certain religion, not by seeing
how many "stories" or how much of any "story" he accepts as true, but
by seeing how far he genuinely tries to carry out his intention to adopt a
religious way of life. This intention, according to Braithwaite, has a great
deal in common with what is expressed in ethical statements. Religion, in
fact, is an ethical outlook bolstered up with "stories."

I have chosen to mention this particular attempt to deal with religious
statements because it is typical as well as skilful. Its typicality consists in
trying to show that metaphysical statements, statements about the supernatural are other than they appear: in particular, that they cannot be regarded as genuinely informative. This in itself is not a misconceived attempt:
plenty of statements are not what they appear. But it is necessary to be
very careful in assigning statements to classes in this way; and I do not think
that writers of this kind have always kept a firm grasp of certain necessary
points in connection with the use of language.

The most important of these is the point that it is primarily people who
mean, and not statements. Language does not exist in the abstract, but
is used by people with certain intentions, who desire to communicate. The
appropriate question, therefore, is really not "What does such-and-such a
statement mean?" but "What does so-and-so mean by this statement?" The
same point applies to verification: we should ask not "How is this statement
verified?" but "How do people who make this statement verify it?" This
point may seem trivial. But to appreciate it entails appreciating that we may
get different answers to our questions. It is easy to assume that statements
have single meanings and single methods of verification; and though this
may be generally true of other informative statements, it may not be true

of metaphysical statements. Indeed, the answers which are given to a question about the meaning of a religious belief show a remarkable variety of opinion, even amongst those who share a common religion.

It would be erroneous to suppose, therefore, that because there is no standard meaning or verification for religious statements they are meaningless and unverifiable. Nearly all philosophers today admit that they are meaningful; indeed, it was never possible to hold that they were meaningless without adopting a monopolistic and unfairly restricted sense of "meaning." But it is an equal mistake to suppose that because all religious believers are not agreed upon what is to count as evidence for the truth of their statements, therefore nothing counts or could ever count. It may not be at all clear how these statements are to be verified or falsified, but this does not entail that they are not verifiable or falsifiable in principle. Neither does it entail that they are not informative.

In other words, the religious believer may meet the cross-questioning of the philosopher with a straight *nolle prosequi*. He may say simply, "This statement is intended by me as informative." The philosopher cannot sensibly reply, "No, it's not." He may point to a lack of agreed meaning and verification, show that most if not all other informative statements have agreed meaning and verification, and so on, but he cannot deny the speaker's intention: and he cannot show that the intention cannot in principle be fulfilled. For it may be possible to provide meaning and verification for the statement, or to agree on them. What the philosopher can try to do, however, is to show that whatever the intentions of the speaker, the statement is not actually informative. He will try to do this by showing that being informative, in the case of all statements, depends on the existence of agreed verification.

The religious believer is here faced with two alternatives. He can either say that his statements are not, after all, informative, thereby evading the attack altogether: or say that established meaning and verification is not in fact necessary for informative statements, thereby standing up to it. This is the crux of the matter, the rock which all metaphysics and religious belief must either escape or be wrecked on. And it seems to me tragic that religious believers do not realise that neither of the two alternatives I have mentioned are at all satisfactory.

First, the attempt to evade the attack. The attempt must fail, because it is these allegedly informative assertions which give to any religion its importance and distinctive character. Statements which lay down language-rules ("A sacrament is an outward and visible sign of an inward and spiritual grace"), historical statements ("The man Jesus Christ was crucified in Palestine during the reign of Tiberius"), exhortations ("Brethren, let us love one another"), and moral injunctions ("Judge not"), all have obvious uses; but they would, none of them, have any peculiarly religious interest unless backed by a number of assertions about the supernatural. Thus, we are only interested in defining "sacrament" clearly because it is held that the Son of God instituted certain sacraments: historical statements about Jesus concern us only because we believe certain metaphysical statements about Him: and exhortations and injunctions have religious force only because they derive from supernatural fact—hence we see arguments like: "Let us love one another, for love is of God." Most Christians, except under philosophical cross-examination, woulld surely regard the "good news" of the Gospel as factually informative. To say "There is a God" is to state a fact: God is real in the same *sense,* though not in the same way, as physical objects are real: [1] and the information which religious beliefs contain is not only supposed to be genuine, but of the utmost importance in the conduct of our lives.

The second alternative, that of claiming that statements can be informative without being verifiable in the sense required by philosophers, is more difficult to prove unsatisfactory. To begin with, many believers would hold that there was evidence for their beliefs. For some Christians, for instance, the supposed majesty and order of the natural universe is a proof of God's existence: to others, the life and personality of Christ is verification for His divinity: and so on. They might also admit that certain things counted against their beliefs: that the existence of pain and evil, for instance, counted against their belief in a loving and omnipotent God. Why is it, then, that philosophers still wish to insist that religious statements may not be verifiable? What precisely is this test of verification which they claim that all informative statements must pass?

The philosopher's point may be better made (as one or two philosophers have themselves suggested) in terms of falsification rather than verification; and the principle may be stated thus: "If a statement is not decisively falsifiable, in principle as well as in practice, then the statement is not informative." Of course this statement is itself somewhat vague: we may wonder what the phrase "in principle" means, for instance. But the reasons for making it are tolerably clear. If you are trying to tell somebody that something is the case, this logically excludes certain other things being the case. For example, suppose I say, "There is a tiger in the room." Asked what evidence there was for this statement, or how it could be verified, I should mention pieces of evidence like there being a growling noise, a large striped animal with teeth and four legs, and so on. To say "there is a tiger" entails there being a large striped animal, etc., because they are part of the meaning of the statement. The statement is vacuous without them. "There is a tiger" is only informative if there is actually a large striped animal. Consequently,

---

[1] This point is of central importance to my thesis: I have tried to expand and elucidate it on pp. 13–14.

it must be decisively falsifiable: falsifiable, that is, if the pieces of evidence could not be found. Of course, the absence of only some of the evidence would not falsify it decisively: the growl might be absent, for instance, and there might still be a tiger. But there comes a time when the absence of evidence is overwhelming. An animal with three legs and no growl might still be a tiger; but an animal with no legs at all and a trunk could not be.

Moreover, statements are informative to the same degree as they are falsifiable or vulnerable. For the more precise information they give, the easier it is to upset them. "There is something in the room" is very uninformative and not very vulnerable: "there is an animal in the room" slightly more informative, but *ipso facto* more vulnerable: because more criteria have to be satisfied for "animal" than for "something"—the statement has to pass more verification-tests. "There is a six-foot tiger exactly in the middle of the room, possessing only four teeth and pointing its tail consistently at an angle of seventy-eight degrees" is very precise, and very vulnerable. To put this more generally, any informative statement specifies that a part of reality is such-and-such; and the more precise the specification—the more the specification specifies, so to speak—then the more things there might be wrong with it.

If, then, a statement's truth is consistent with any evidence that might be forthcoming, it cannot be at all informative. Making a statement of this kind would be like saying: "There is a tiger in the room, and nothing could count as evidence which decisively falsifies this truth." Of course if there actually is a tiger, then the statement cannot actually be decisively falsified: for it is true. But it is still decisively falsifiable as a statement: for there is no logical compulsion about its being true. To say "nothing could count as evidence against the existence of God" might mean "since God exists, there can be no decisive evidence against it": but it might also mean that the statement "God exists" is logically exempt from decisive evidence against it. And if this is true, then it cannot be informative. For saying "God exists" is a particular instance of saying "Such-and-such is the case"; and it is always logically possible that such-and-such is not the case. Whether it is or not precisely constitutes the test which any informative statement must pass.

Since therefore neither of these two alternatives is satisfactory, religious believers have to face up to the problem of providing their religious statements with established meaning and verification. In view of the points mentioned, they should be anxious rather than unwilling to make it clear what would decisively falsify the statements, since their informativeness corresponds to their falsifiability. Just how this process of giving verification to religious statements is to be gone through, I shall endeavour to explain in the next essay. So far as we are here concerned, the point I wish to establish is that our fifth class of statements—those apparently informative about the supernatural world—must be claimed as genuinely informative, with all that this implies. If they are to be merged with any other class, it must be with the third: those expressing factual truths, or what are generally known as empirical statements.

Providing statements with verification, however, is not an arbitrary process; and there is one further point which must be allowed to the philosopher. Informative statements inform us about something in our experience, and must therefore be verifiable ultimately by our experience. I do not mean, of course, that they are about something which we are actually touching, seeing, feeling, etc., or which we have touched, seen, felt, etc. "There is a tiger in the room" is informative even though we may never have seen a tiger. But they must be about something of which we could in principle have experience: for if they were not, they would not inform us about anything at all which had any connection with our lives and interests. To say "There is a tiger in the room" would be senseless, and certainly not informative, if I added "but nobody could ever have any experience of such a thing." The whole interest of making such a statement is that, if we enter the room, we can expect to experience certain things—growls, stripes, being eaten, and so on. Statements which are of public interest and are informative, like this one, are based on the experiences of some people, and on the possibility that other people may also have similar experiences. This is the purpose of informative communication.

Past writers have attempted to discover many loopholes which might enable them to avoid this point also; and it is impossible to demonstrate that all of them are culs-de-sac. A typical loophole is to say that God "transcends" human experience, and that therefore we cannot expect to verify statements about God by human experience; though of course the first of these two statements need not be understood in such a way that the second follows from it. But the same dilemma presents itself. Either "God" stands for something at least partly within our experience, so that statements with the word "God" in them are to that extent experimentally verifiable: or else "God" does not stand for something within our actual or potential experience, in which case (to put it bluntly) statements about God can have no possible interest for us, and may well be meaningless. Of course this dilemma could be put more forcibly. We could say that if a descriptive word is supposed to refer to something which could not be experienced, then it seems doubtful whether it describes anything at all: since to be a thing involves the capability of being experienced, and can only be known through experience.

Nor need the Christian attempt to take evasive action over the issue of verification in any other way. Philosophers have been concerned to clarify the logical characteristics of informative assertions by various observations. They have said that they must be meaningful and verifiable: that we must know what would count as evidence for or against them: that their verification must ultimately be conducted by somebody's experience: that unless these conditions were satisfied they could not qualify for truth or falsehood, and so on. All this can be accepted; and there seems little use in trying to break out of the circle of these observations at any point, e.g., by saying that Christian assertions are "true" in the sense of "illuminating," or can be "verified" "by the Christian way of life itself." For though the points being made here may be valid and important, they are insufficient; because Christian assertions are also supposed, by Christians themselves, to be true and verifiable in the (possibly more usual) sense in which philosophers have used these words.

This attempt to put religious assertions in the same logical boat, as it were, with straightforward empirical statements looks naïve and old-fashioned, because it suggests a naïve and old-fashioned view of religious language. We are accustomed to regard religious language as inadequate for its purposes; in particular, it is said to be "metaphor" or "analogy." When challenged at every point, the metaphor becomes "eroded" or "evaporates," until nothing may be left. Hence the Christian and the philosopher seem both driven to the view that the metaphorical assertions cannot be informative, and must be in a different logical category from empirical statements, with a different sort of meaning and verification, if indeed they have any verification at all. But this is deceptive; because a metaphor may assert something quite as precise and informative as any other assertion. A word used metaphorically or analogically may lose something of its straightforward meaning; but it may gain some other significance. For example, "sugar is sweet" may be a straightforward empirical assertion, and "Mary is sweet" a metaphor; but it would be wrong to suppose that what we are saying about Mary is less definite or meaningful than what we are saying about sugar. The word "sweet" simply means different things, and has a different method of verification, in either case. This might well be true of religious assertions. They are expressed in language borrowed from non-religious contexts, just as "Mary is sweet" uses a word borrowed from taste-experience; but this language may well have a new and precise significance, though of course the fact that the same word is used suggests that there are points of contact between the two uses—points which might help to make the new use more comprehensible to someone who did not understand the metaphorical meaning.

One essential task which religious believers have to perform, therefore, is to give the individual words in religious language a clear and unambiguous descriptive meaning where such meaning is required. This applies both to what we might call technical religious words—words like "God," "soul," "grace," and so on—and also to words used metaphorically—"love," "father," "kingdom," etc. Hitherto many believers have clung desperately to these words, but have been more able to say what they do not mean than what they do. Yet if religious language is ever to be genuinely and importantly informative, it is important that the criteria for the use of these words should be clear. If this task is not achieved, we shall be reduced to saying, as the Vedantist says when asked to describe his deity, "Not this, not this."

To many people this might seem to imply that God is an object, much like a table or an elephant, who can be immediately and wholly comprehended by experience: the only slight difference being that a different kind of experience is required. Yet this is plainly absurd; and a God of this kind is not the sort of God in which anybody believes. But we must be careful to understand the point. I have said earlier in this chapter that God is real in the same sense, though not in the same way, that physical objects are real. He must be real in the same sense: for the word "real" has, in fact, only one sense—either something is real and exists, or it is unreal and does not exist. "Real" and "exists" are definitely not ambiguous words. But He is not (putting it roughly) real in the same *way,* because He is not the same sort of thing as a table or an elephant: indeed, we might say that He is not a *thing* at all, and certainly that He is not an object. Briefly, then, my contention is that if God is real and exists, the unambiguous logic and language of statements about existence, and the verification needed for these statements, must apply to God as much as to anything else, for these are part and parcel of what we mean by words like "exist" and "real;" but this is not to deny that much of His nature may be mysterious and uncomprehended by men. In much the same way, we might hold that love, or Martians, or the fourth dimension exist and are real: we might be able to give these words and phrases clear and unambiguous descriptive meanings and verification-methods: but they might still be very different from other things, highly mysterious, and largely uncomprehended.

Instead of the Vedantist's "Not this, not this," Christians must be able to say, "At least this, and at least this." They must be able to assert definitely about God, whilst admitting that there is far more to be known about Him than we can perhaps ever hope to know. Moreover, as we come to learn more about God, there is nothing in logic to prevent our expanding the meaning of the word "God." In just such a way the word "desire" has, since Freudian psychology, become expanded to include the concept of unconscious desires. In the light of new experience, words change their meaning in order to incorporate and communicate the experience. A due observance of logic, therefore, does nothing to remove the mystery of God on which Christians rightly insist; but it does serve the useful purpose of reminding us that if we are to talk meaningfully about God at any particular time, we must know what the word "God" is agreed to mean at that time, and that we can ultimately know this only by reference to experience.

Another and equally important task for believers is to adopt a firm and unambiguous classification of the statements and sentences in their religion. Much that is spoken and written about religion is vitiated by the absence of such a classification; and it is particularly difficult for non-believers to achieve a firm grasp of the logical structure of religious doctrine. It is annoying, for instance, to argue at length about whether the soul is immortal, only to find after a time that the word "soul" is being used to mean "the immortal part of man." This of course makes the statement "The soul is immortal" analytic or tautologous, and therefore not empirically informative. In trying to assess the truth of a complex metaphysical system, such as the doctrines of the Roman church, it is essential to be clear about which statements are supposed to be informative and verifiable, and which are supposed to follow by deductive arguments from other statements. For example, if we were intended to accept a number of statements on the authority of Christ, the Bible, the Church or some other source, we should be particularly interested in verifying the statements which were relevant to showing that source to be reliable, and not waste time in examining the statements deduced from its reliability.

This task of establishing meaning and verification, and classifying statements in religious belief according to their logic, has hardly been started. Hitherto Christian apologists have been chiefly interested in trying to collect and assess evidence for their beliefs, not realising the importance of the (logically prior) question of what is to count as evidence. Until this question is settled, it is unlikely that many people will be convinced by this collected "evidence": for it may not be evidence to them at all. One cannot tell whether something is evidence for a statement or not unless one first knows what sort of statement it is supposed to be, and what sorts of things count as evidence for it. And it is this lack of clarity, if I may be permitted to conclude with a sociological sidelight, which has engendered a situation in which many intelligent people are now neither convinced of, nor hostile to, Christian belief, but merely uninterested in it.

# JOHN WISDOM

*John Wisdom* (1904–    ), professor of philosophy at Cambridge University, has written on an unusually large number of topics. He has been a leading figure among British analytical philosophers. His book *Philosophy and Psycho-Analysis* is a major contribution to their field of study.

## "Gods"

1. THE EXISTENCE OF GOD IS NOT AN EXPERIMENTAL ISSUE IN THE WAY IT WAS. An atheist or agnostic might say to a theist "You still think there are spirits in the trees, nymphs in the streams, a God of the world." He might say this because he noticed the theist in time of drought pray for rain and make a sacrifice and in the morning look for rain. But disagreement about whether there are gods is now less of this experimental or betting sort than it used to be. This is due in part, if not wholly, to our better knowledge of why things happen as they do.

It is true that even in these days it is seldom that one who believes in God has no hopes or fears which an atheist has not. Few believers now expect prayer to still the waves, but some think it makes a difference to people and not merely in ways the atheist would admit. Of course with people, as opposed to waves and machines, one never knows what they won't do next, so that expecting prayer to make a difference to them is not so definite a thing as believing in its mechanical efficacy. Still, just as primitive people pray in a business-like way for rain so some people still pray for others with a real feeling of doing something to help. However, in spite of this persistence of an experimental element in some theistic belief, it remains true that Elijah's method on Mount Carmel of settling the matter of what god or gods exist would be far less appropriate to-day than it was then.

2. BELIEF IN GODS IS NOT MERELY A MATTER OF EXPECTATION OF A WORLD TO COME. Someone may say "The fact that a theist no more than an atheist expects prayer to bring down fire from heaven or cure the sick does not mean that there is no difference between them as to the facts, it does not

From John Wisdom, *Philosophy and Psycho-Analysis*, pp. 149–159. Published, 1953, by Basil Blackwell. Used by permission of the publishers.

mean that the theist has no expectations different from the atheist's. For very often those who believe in God believe in another world and believe that God is there and that we shall go to that world when we die."

This is true, but I do not want to consider here expectations as to what one will see and feel after death nor what sort of reasons these logically unique expectations could have. So I want to consider those theists who do not believe in a future life, or rather, I want to consider the differences between atheists and theists in so far as these differences are not a matter of belief in a future life.

3. WHAT ARE THESE DIFFERENCES? AND IS IT THAT THEISTS ARE SUPER-STITIOUS OR THAT ATHEISTS ARE BLIND? A child may wish to sit a while with his father and he may, when he has done what his father dislikes, fear punishment and feel distress at causing vexation, and while his father is alive he may feel sure of help when danger threatens and feel that there is sympathy for him when disaster has come. When his father is dead he will no longer expect punishment or help. Maybe for a moment an old fear will come or a cry for help escape him, but he will at once remember that this is no good now. He may feel that his father is no more until perhaps someone says to him that his father is still alive though he lives now in another world and one so far away that there is no hope of seeing him or hearing his voice again. The child may be told that nevertheless his father can see him and hear all he says. When he has been told this the child will still fear no punishment nor expect any sign of his father, but now, even more than he did when his father was alive, he will feel that his father sees him all the time and will dread distressing him and when he has done something wrong he will feel separated from his father until he has felt sorry for what he has done. Maybe when he himself comes to die he will be like a man who expects to find a friend in the strange country where he is going, but even when this is so, it is by no means all of what makes the difference between a child who believes that his father lives still in another world and one who does not.

Likewise one who believes in God may face death differently from one who does not, but there is another difference between them besides this. This other difference may still be described as belief in another world, only this belief is not a matter of expecting one thing rather than another here or hereafter, it is not a matter of a world to come but of a world that now is, though beyond our senses.

We are at once reminded of those other unseen worlds which some philosophers "believe in" and others "deny," while non-philosophers unconsciously "accept" them by using them as models with which to "get the hang of" the patterns in the flux of experience. We recall the timeless entities whose changeless connections we seek to represent in symbols, and the values which stand firm [1] amidst our flickering satisfaction and remorse, and the physical things which, though not beyond the corruption of moth and rust, are yet more permanent than the shadows they throw upon the screen before our minds. We recall, too, our talk of souls and of what lies in their depths and is manifested to us partially and intermittently in our own feelings and the behaviour of others. The hypothesis of mind, of other human minds and of animal minds, is reasonable because it explains for each of us why certain things behave so cunningly all by themselves unlike even the most ingenious machines. Is the hypothesis of minds in flowers and trees reasonable for like reasons? Is the hypothesis of a world mind reasonable for like reasons—someone who adjusts the blossom to the bees, someone whose presence may at times be felt—in a garden in high summer, in the hills when clouds are gathering, but not, perhaps, in a cholera epidemic?

4. THE QUESTION "IS BELIEF IN GODS REASONABLE?" HAS MORE THAN ONE SOURCE. It is clear now that in order to grasp fully the logic of belief in divine minds we need to examine the logic of belief in animal and human minds. Bue we cannot do that here and so for the purposes of this discussion about divine minds let us acknowledge the reasonableness of our belief in human minds without troubling ourselves about its logic. The question of the reasonableness of belief in divine minds then becomes a matter of whether there are facts in nature which support claims about divine minds in the way facts in nature support our claims about human minds.

In this way we resolve the force behind the problem of the existence of gods into two components, one metaphysical and the same which prompts the question "Is there *ever any* behaviour which gives reason to believe in *any* sort of mind?" and one which finds expression in "Are there other mind-patterns in nature beside the human and animal patterns which we can easily detect, and are these other mind-patterns super-human?"

Such over-determination of a question syndrome is common. Thus, the puzzling questions "Do dogs think?" "Do animals feel?" are partly metaphysical puzzles and partly scientific questions. They are not purely metaphysical; for the reports of scientists about the poor performances of cats in cages and old ladies' stories about the remarkable performances of their pets are not irrelevant. But nor are these questions purely scientific; for the stories never settle them and therefore they have other sources. One other source is the metaphysical source we have already noticed, namely, the difficulty about getting behind an animal's behaviour to its mind, whether it is a non-human animal or a human one.

But there's a third component in the force behind these questions, these disputes have a third source, and it is one which is important in the dispute

---

[1] In another world, Dr. Joad says in the *New Statesman* recently.

which finds expression in the words "I believe in God," "I do not." This source comes out well if we consider the question "Do flowers feel?" Like the questions about dogs and animals this question about flowers comes partly from the difficulty we sometimes feel over inference from *any* behaviour to thought or feeling and partly from ignorance as to what behaviour is to be found. But these questions, as opposed to a like question about human beings, come also from hesitation as to whether the behaviour in question is *enough* mind-like, that is, is it enough similar to or superior to human behaviour to be called "mind-proving"? Likewise, even when we are satisfied that human behaviour shows mind and even when we have learned whatever mind-suggesting things there are in nature which are not explained by human and animal minds, we may still ask "But are these things sufficiently striking to be called a mind-pattern? Can we fairly call them manifestations of a divine being?"

"The question," someone may say, "has then become merely a matter of the application of a name. And 'What's in a name?' "

5. BUT THE LINE BETWEEN A QUESTION OF FACT AND A QUESTION OF DECISION AS TO THE APPLICATION OF A NAME IS NOT SO SIMPLE AS THIS WAY OF PUTTING THINGS SUGGESTS. The question "What's in a name?" is engaging because we are inclined to answer both "Nothing" and "Very much." And this "Very much" has more than one source. We might have tried to comfort Heloise by saying "It isn't that Abelard no longer loves you, for this man isn't Abelard"; we might have said to poor Mr. Tebrick in Mr. Garnet's *Lady into Fox* "But this is no longer Silvia." But if Mr. Tebrick replied "Ah, but it is!" this might come not at all from observing facts about the fox which we have not observed, but from noticing facts about the fox which we had missed, although we had in a sense observed all that Mr. Tebrick had observed. It is possible to have before one's eyes all the items of a pattern and still to miss the pattern. Consider the following conversation:

"And I think Kay and I are pretty happy. We've always been happy."
Bill lifted up his glass and put it down without drinking.
"Would you mind saying that again," he asked.
"I don't see what's so queer about it. Taken all in all, Kay and I have really been happy."
"All right," Bill said gently, "Just tell me how you and Kay have been happy."
Bill had a way of being amused by things which I could not understand.
"It's a little hard to explain," I said. "It's like taking a lot of numbers that don't look alike and that don't mean anything until you add them all together."
I stopped, because I hadn't meant to talk to him about Kay and me.
"Go ahead," Bill said. "What about the numbers." And he began to smile.

"I don't know why you think it's so funny," I said. "All the things that two people do together, two people like Kay and me, add up to something. There are the kids and the house and the dog and all the people we have known and all the times we've been out to dinner. Of course, Kay and I do quarrel sometimes but when you add it all together, all of it isn't as bad as the parts of it seem. I mean, maybe that's all there is to anybody's life."

Bill poured himself another drink. He seemed about to say something and checked himself. He kept looking at me.[2]

Or again, suppose two people are speaking of two characters in a story which both have read [3] or of two friends which both have known, and one says "Really she hated him," and the other says "She didn't, she loved him." Then the first may have noticed what the other has not although he knows no incident in the lives of the people they are talking about which the other doesn't know too, and the second speaker may say "She didn't, she loved him" because he hasn't noticed what the first noticed, although he can remember every incident the first can remember. But then again he may say "She didn't, she loved him" not because he hasn't noticed the patterns in time which the first has noticed but because though he has noticed them he doesn't feel he still needs to emphasize them with "Really she hated him." The line between using a name because of how we feel and because of what we have noticed isn't sharp. "A difference as to the facts," "a discovery," "a relevation," these phrases cover many things. Discoveries have been made not only by Christopher Columbus and Pasteur, but also by Tolstoy and Dostoievsky and Freud. Things are revealed to us not only by the scientists with the microscopes, but also by the poets, the prophets, and the painters. What is so isn't merely a matter of "the facts." For sometimes when there is agreement as to the facts there is still argument as to whether defendant did or did not "exercise reasonable care," was or was not "negligent."

And though we shall need to emphasize how much "There is a God" evinces an attitude to the familiar [4] we shall find in the end that it also evinces some recognition of patterns in time easily missed and that, therefore, difference as to there being any gods is in part a difference as to what is so and therefore as to the facts, though not in the simple ways which first occurred to us.

6. LET US NOW APPROACH THESE SAME POINTS BY A DIFFERENT ROAD.
6.1. *How it is that an explanatory hypothesis, such as the existence of*

---

[2] *H. M. Pulham, Esq.,* p. 320, by John P. Marquand.

[3] E.g., Havelock Ellis's autobiography.

[4] "Persuasive Definitions," *Mind,* July, 1938, by Charles Leslie Stevenson, should be read here. It is very good. [Also in his *Ethics and Language,* Yale, 1945.—Eds.]

*God, may start by being experimental and gradually become something quite different can be seen from the following story:*

Two people return to their long neglected garden and find among the weeds a few of the old plants surprisingly vigorous. One says to the other "It must be that a gardener has been coming and doing something about these plants." Upon inquiry they find that no neighbour has ever seen anyone at work in their garden. The first man says to the other "He must have worked while people slept." The other says "No, someone would have heard him and besides, anybody who cared about the plants would have kept down these weeds." The first man says "Look at the way these are arranged. There is purpose and a feeling for beauty here. I believe that someone comes, someone invisible to mortal eyes. I believe that the more carefully we look the more we shall find confirmation of this." They examine the garden ever so carefully and sometimes they come on new things suggesting that a gardener comes and sometimes they come on new things suggesting the contrary and even that a malicious person has been at work. Besides examining the garden carefully they also study what happens to gardens left without attention. Each learns all the other learns about this and about the garden. Consequently, when after all this, one says, "I still believe a gardener comes" while the other says "I don't" their different words now reflect no difference as to what they have found in the garden, no difference as to what they would find in the garden if they looked further and no difference about how fast untended gardens fall into disorder. At this stage, in this context, the gardener hypothesis has ceased to be experimental, the difference between one who accepts and one who rejects it is now not a matter of the one expecting something the other does not expect. What is the difference between them? The one says "A gardener comes unseen and unheard. He is manifested only in his works with which we are all familiar," the other says "There is no gardener" and with this difference in what they say about the gardener goes a difference in how they feel towards the garden, in spite of the fact that neither expects anything of it which the other does not expect.[5]

But is this the whole difference between them—that the one calls the garden by one name and feels one way towards it, while the other calls it by another name and feels in another way towards it? And if this is what the difference has become then is it any longer appropriate to ask "Which is right?" or "Which is reasonable?"

And yet surely such questions *are* appropriate when one person says to

---

[5] [For an extended discussion of the implications of this story see "The *University* Discussion" in *New Essays In Philosophical Theology,* eds. Antony Flew and Alaisdair MacIntyre (New York: The Macmillan Company, 1955), pp. 96f., Eds.]

another "You still think the world's a garden and not a wilderness, and that the gardener has not forsaken it" or "You still think there are nymphs of the streams, a presence in the hills, a spirit of the world." Perhaps when a man sings "God's in His heaven" we need not take this as more than an expression of how he feels. But when Bishop Gore or Dr. Joad write about belief in God and young men read them in order to settle their religious doubts the impression is not simply that of persons choosing exclamations with which to face nature and the "changes and chances of this mortal life." The disputants speak as if they are concerned with a matter of scientific fact, or of trans-sensual, trans-scientific and metaphysical fact, but still of fact and still a matter about which reasons for and against may be offered, although no scientific reasons in the sense of field surveys for fossils or experiments on delinquents are to the point.

6.2. *Now can an interjection have a logic?* Can the manifestation of an attitude in the utterance of a word, in the application of a name, have a logic? When all the facts are known how can there still be a question of fact? How can there still be a question? Surely as Hume says ". . . after every circumstance, every relation is known, the understanding has no further room to operate"? [6]

6.3. When the madness of these questions leaves us for a moment *we can all easily recollect disputes which though they cannot be settled by experiment are yet disputes in which one party may be right and the other wrong* and in which both parties may offer reasons and the one better reasons than the other. *This may happen in pure and applied mathematics and logic.* Two accountants or two engineers provided with the same data may reach different results and this difference is resolved not by collecting further data but by going over the calculations again. Such differences indeed share with differences as to what will win a race, the honour of being among the most "settlable" disputes in the language.

6.4 *But it won't do to describe the theistic issue as one settlable by such calculation,* or as one about what can be deduced in this *vertical* fashion from the facts we know. No doubt dispute about God has sometimes, perhaps especially in mediaeval times, been carried on in this fashion. But nowadays it is not and we must look for some other analogy, some other case in which a dispute is settled but not by experiment.

6.5. *In courts of law* it sometimes happens that opposing counsel are agreed as to the facts and are not trying to settle a question of further fact, are not trying to settle whether the man who admittedly had quarrelled with the deceased did or did not murder him, but are concerned with whether Mr. A who admittedly handed his long-trusted clerk signed blank

[6] Hume, *An Enquiry Concerning the Principles of Morals.* Appendix I.

cheques did or did not exercise reasonable care, whether a ledger is or is not a document,[7] whether a certain body was or was not a public authority.

In such cases we notice that the process of argument is not a *chain* of demonstrative reasoning. It is a presenting and representing of those features of the case which *severally co-operate* in favour of the conclusion, in favour of saying what the reasoner wishes said, in favour of calling the situation by the name by which he wishes to call it. The reasons are like the legs of a chair, not the links of a chain. Consequently although the discussion is *a priori* and the steps are not a matter of experience, the procedure resembles scientific argument in that the reasoning is not *vertically* extensive but *horizontally* extensive—it is a matter of the cumulative effect of several independent premises, not of the repeated transformation of one or two. And because the premises are severally inconclusive the process of deciding the issue becomes a matter of weighing the cumulative effect of one group of severally inconclusive items against the cumulative effect of another group of severally inconclusive items, and thus lends itself to description in terms of conflicting "probabilities." This encourages the feeling that the issue is one of fact—that it is a matter of guessing from the premises at a further fact, at what is to come. But this is a muddle. *The dispute does not cease to be* a priori *because it is a matter of the cumulative effect of severally inconclusive premises.* The logic of the dispute is not that of a chain of deductive reasoning as in a mathematic calculation. But nor is it a matter of collecting from several inconclusive items of information an expectation as to something further, as when a doctor from a patient's symptoms guesses at what is wrong, or a detective from many clues guesses the criminal. It has its own sort of logic and its own sort of end—the solution of the question at issue is a decision, a ruling by the judge. But it is not an arbitrary decision though the rational connections are neither quite like those in vertical deductions nor like those in inductions in which from many signs we guess at what is to come; and though the decision manifests itself in the application of a name it is no more merely the application of a name than is the pinning on of a medal merely the pinning on of a bit of metal. Whether a lion with stripes is a tiger or a lion is, if you like, merely a matter of the application of a name. Whether Mr. So-and-So of whose conduct we have so complete a record did or did not exercise reasonable care is not merely a matter of the application of a name or, if we choose to say it is, then we must remember that with this name a game is lost and won and a game with very heavy

---

[7] *The Times,* March 2nd, 1945. Also in *The Times* of June 13th, 1945, contrast the case of Hannah V. Peel with that of the cruiser cut in two by a liner. In the latter case there is not agreement as to the facts. See also the excellent articles by Dr. Glanville L. Williams in the *Law Quarterly Review*, "Language and the Law," January, and April 1945, and "The Doctrine of Repugnancy," October, 1943, January, 1944, and April, 1944. The author, having set out how arbitrary are many legal decisions, needs now to set out how far from arbitrary they are—if his readers are ready for the next phase in the dialectic process.

stakes. With the judges' choice of a name for the facts goes an attitude, and the declaration, the ruling, is an exclamation evincing that attitude. But *it is an exclamation which not only has a purpose but also has a logic,* a logic surprisingly like that of "futile," "deplorable," graceful," grand," divine."

6.6. *Suppose two people are looking at a picture or natural scene.* One says "Excellent" or "Beautiful" or "Divine"; the other says "I don't see it." He means he doesn't see the beauty. And this reminds us of how we felt the theist accuse the atheist of blindness and the atheist accuse the theist of seeing what isn't there. And yet surely each sees what the other sees. It isn't that one can see part of the picture which the other can't see. So the difference is in a sense not one as to the facts. And so it cannot be removed by the one disputant discovering to the other what so far he hasn't seen. It isn't that the one sees the picture in a different light and so, as we might says, sees a different picture. Consequently the difference between them cannot be resolved by putting the picture in a different light. And yet surely this is just what can be done in such a case—not by moving the picture but by talk perhaps. To settle a dispute as to whether a piece of music is good or better than another we listen again, with a picture we look again. Someone perhaps points to emphasize certain features and we see it in a different light. Shall we call this "field work" and "the last of observation" or shall we call it "reviewing the premises" and "the beginning of deduction (horizontal)"?

If in spite of all this we choose to say that a difference as to whether a thing is beautiful is not a factual difference we must be careful to remember that there is a procedure for settling these differences and that this consists not only in reasoning and redescription as in the legal case, but also in a more literal resetting-before with re-looking or re-listening.

6.7. *And if we say as we did at the beginning that when a difference as to the existence of a God is not one as to future happenings then it is not experimental and therefore not as to the facts, we must not forthwith assume that there is no right and wrong about it,* no rationality or irrationality, no appropriateness or inappropriateness, no procedure which tends to settle it, *nor even that this procedure is in no sense a discovery of new facts.* After all even in science this is not so. Our two gardeners even when they had reached the stage when neither expected any experimental result which the other did not, might yet have continued the dispute, each presenting and representing the features of the garden favouring his hypothesis, that is, fitting his model for describing the accepted fact; each emphasizing the pattern he wishes to emphasize. True, in science, there is seldom or never a pure instance of this sort of dispute, for nearly always with difference of hypothesis goes some difference of expectation as to the facts. But scientists argue about rival hypotheses with a vigour which is not exactly proportioned to difference in expectations of experimental results.

The difference as to whether a God exists involves our feelings more than most scientific disputes and in this respect is more like a difference as to whether there is beauty in a thing.

# R. B. BRAITHWAITE

*R. B. Braithwaite* (1900–      ), Knightbridge Professor of Moral Philosophy at Cambridge, is mainly interested in philosophy of science, but he is also concerned with interpreting religious belief in such a way as to make it empirically tenable.

## An Empiricist's View of the Nature of Religious Belief

The meaning of any statement, then, will be taken as being given by the way it is used. The kernel for an empiricist of the problem of the nature of religious belief is to explain, in empirical terms, how a religious statement is used by a man who asserts it in order to express his religious conviction.

Since I shall argue that the primary element in this use is that the religious assertion is used as a moral assertion, I must first consider how moral assertions are used. According to the view developed by various moral philosophers since the impossibility of regarding moral statements as verifiable propositions was recognized, a moral assertion is used to express an *attitude* of the man making the assertion. It is not used to assert the proposition that he has the attitude—a verifiable psychological proposition; it is used to show forth or evince his attitude. The attitude is concerned with the action which he asserts to be right or to be his duty, or the state of affairs which he asserts to be good; it is a highly complex state, and contains elements to which various degrees of importance have been attached by moral philosophers who have tried to work out an "ethics without propositions." One element in the attitude is a feeling of approval towards the action; this element was taken as the fundamental one in the first attempts, and views of ethics without

From R. B. Braithwaite, *An Empiricist's View of the Nature of Religious Belief*, pp. 11–26. Published, 1955, by Cambridge University Press. Used by permission of Cambridge University Press.

propositions are frequently lumped together as "emotive" theories of ethics. But discussion of the subject during the last twenty years has made it clear, I think, that no emotion or feeling of approval is fundamental to the use of moral assertions; it may be the case that the moral asserter has some specific feeling directed on to the course of action said to be right, but this is not the most important element in his "pro-attitude" towards the course of action: what is primary is his intention to perform the action when the occasion for its arises.

The form of ethics without propositions which I shall adopt is therefore a conative rather than an emotive theory: it makes the primary use of a moral assertion that of expressing the intention of the asserter to act in a particular sort of way specified in the assertion. A utilitarian, for example, in asserting that he ought to act so as to maximize happiness, is thereby declaring his intention to act, to the best of his ability, in accordance with the policy of utilitarianism: he is not asserting any proposition, or necessarily evincing any feeling of approval; he is subscribing to a policy of action. There will doubtless be empirical propositions which he may give as reasons for his adherence to the policy (e.g., that happiness is what all, or what most people, desire), and his having the intention will include his understanding what is meant by pursuing the policy, another empirically verifiable proposition. But there will be no specifically moral proposition which he will be asserting when he declares his intention to pursue the policy. This account is fully in accord with the spirit of empiricism, for whether or not a man has the intention of pursuing a particular behaviour policy can be empirically tested, both by observing what he does and by hearing what he replies when he is questioned about his intentions.

Not all expressions of intentions will be moral assertions: for the notion of morality to be applicable it is necessary either that the policy of action intended by the asserter should be a general policy (e.g., the policy of utilitarianism) or that it should be subsumable under a general policy which the asserter intends to follow and which he would give as the reason for his more specific intention. There are difficulties and vaguenesses in the notion of a general policy of action, but these need not concern us here. All that we require is that, when a man asserts that he ought to do so-and-so, he is using the assertion to declare that he resolves, to the best of his ability, to do so-and-so. And he will not necessarily be insincere in his assertion if he suspects, at the time of making it, that he will not have the strength of character to carry out his resolution.

The advantage this account of moral assertions has over all others, emotive non-propositional ones as well as cognitive propositional ones, is that it alone enables a satisfactory answer to be given to the question: What is the reason for my doing what I think I ought to do? The answer it gives is that, since my thinking that I ought to do the action is my intention to do it if possible, the reason why I do the action is simply that I intend to do it, if possible. On every other ethical view there will be a mysterious gap to be filled somehow between the moral judgment and the intention to act in accordance with it: there is no such gap if the primary use of a moral assertion is to declare such an intention.

Let us now consider what light this way of regarding moral assertions throws upon assertions of religious conviction. The idealist philosopher McTaggart described religion as "an emotion resting on a conviction of a harmony between ourselves and the universe at large," [1] and many educated people at the present time would agree with him. If religion is essentially concerned with emotion, it is natural to explain the use of religious assertions on the lines of the original emotive theory of ethics and to regard them as primarily evincing religious feeling or emotions. The assertion, for example, that God is our Heavenly Father will be taken to express the asserter's feeling secure in the same way as he would feel secure in his father's presence. But explanations of religion in terms of feeling, and of religious assertions as expressions of such feelings, are usually propounded by people who stand outside any religious system; they rarely satisfy those who speak from inside. Few religious men would be prepared to admit that their religion was a matter merely of feeling: feelings—of joy, of consolation, of being at one with the universe—may enter into their religion, but to evince such feelings is certainly not the primary use of their religious assertions.

This objection, however, does not seem to me to apply to treating religious assertions in the conative way in which recent moral philosophers have treated moral statements—as being primarily declarations of adherence to a policy of action, declarations of commitment to a way of life. That the way of life led by the believer is highly relevant to the sincerity of his religious conviction has been insisted upon by all the moral religions, above all, perhaps, by Christianity. "By their fruits ye shall know them." The view which I put forward for your consideration is that the intention of a Christian to follow a Christian way of life is not only the criterion for the sincerity of his belief in the assertions of Christianity; it is the criterion for the meaningfulness of his assertions. Just as the meaning of a moral assertion is given by its use in expressing the asserter's intention to act, so far as in him lies, in accordance with the moral principle involved, so the meaning of a religious assertion is given by its use in expressing the asserter's intention to follow a specified policy of behaviour. To say that it is belief in the dogmas of religion which is the cause of the believer's intending to behave as he does is to put the cart before the horse: it is the intention to behave which constitutes what is known as religious conviction.

But this assimilation of religious to moral assertions lays itself open to an

---

[1] J. M. E. McTaggart, *Some Dogmas of Religion* (1906), p. 3.

immediate objection. When a moral assertion is taken as declaring the intention of following a policy, the form of the assertion itself makes it clear what the policy is with which the assertion is concerned. For a man to assert that a certain policy ought to be pursued, which on this view is for him to declare his intention of pursuing the policy, presupposes his understanding what it would be like for him to pursue the policy in question. I cannot resolve not to tell a lie without knowing what a lie is. But if a religious assertion is the declaration of an intention to carry out a certain policy, what policy does it specify? The religious statement itself will not explicitly refer to a policy, as does a moral statement; how then can the asserter of the statement know what is the policy concerned, and how can he intend to carry out a policy if he does not know what the policy is? I cannot intend to do something I know not what.

The reply to this criticism is that, if a religious assertion is regarded as representative of a large number of assertions of the same religious system, the body of assertions of which the particular one is a representative specimen is taken by the asserter as implicitly specifying a particular way of life. It is no more necessary for an empiricist philosopher to explain the use of a religious statement taken in isolation from other religious statements than it is for him to give a meaning to a scientific hypothesis in isolation from other scientific hypotheses. We understand scientific hypotheses, and the terms that occur in them, by virtue of the relation of the whole system of hypotheses to empirically observable facts; and it is the whole system of hypotheses, not one hypothesis in isolation, that is tested for its true-value against experience. So there are good precedents, in the empiricist way of thinking, for considering a system of religious assertions as a whole, and for examining the way in which the whole system is used.

If we do this the fact that a system of religious assertions has a moral function can hardly be denied. For to deny it would require any passage from the assertion of a religious system to a policy of action to be mediated by a moral assertion. I cannot pass from asserting a fact, of whatever sort, to intending to perform an action, without having the hypothetical intention to intend to do the action if I assert the fact. This holds however widely fact is understood—whether as an empirical fact or as a non-empirical fact about goodness or reality. Just as the intention-to-act view of moral assertions is the only view that requires no reason for my doing what I assert to be my duty, so the similar view of religious assertions is the only one which connects them to ways of life without requiring an additional premiss. Unless a Christian's assertion that God is love (*agape*)—which I take to epitomize the assertions of the Christian religion—be taken to declare his intention to follow an agapeistic way of life, he could be asked what is the connexion between the assertion and the intention, between Christian belief and Christian practice. And this question can always be asked if religious assertions are separated from conduct. Unless religious principles are moral principles, it makes no sense to speak of putting them into practice.

The way to find out what are the intentions embodied in a set of religious assertions, and hence what is the meaning of the assertions, is by discovering what principles of conduct the asserter takes the assertions to involve. These may be ascertained both by asking him questions and by seeing how he behaves, each test being supplemental to the other. If what is wanted is not the meaning of the religious assertions made by a particular man but what the set of assertions would mean were they to be made by anyone of the same religion (which I will call their *typical* meaning), all that can be done is to specify the form of behaviour which is in accordance with what one takes to be the fundamental moral principles of the religion in question. Since different people will take different views as to what these fundamental moral principles are, the typical meaning of religious assertions will be different for different people. I myself take the typical meaning of the body of Christian assertions as being given by their proclaiming intentions to follow an agapeistic way of life, and for a description of this way of life—a description in general and metaphorical terms, but an empirical description nevertheless—I should quote most of the Thirteenth Chapter of I Corinthians. Others may think that the Christian way of life should be described somewhat differently, and will therefore take the typical meaning of the assertions of Christianity to correspond to their different view of its fundamental moral teaching.

My contention then is that the primary use of religious assertions is to announce allegiance to a set of moral principles: without such allegiance there is no "true religion." This is borne out by all the accounts of what happens when an unbeliever becomes converted to a religion. The conversion is not only a change in the propositions believed—indeed there may be no specifically intellectual change at all; it is a change in the state of will. An excellent instance is C. S. Lewis's recently published account of his conversion from an idealist metaphysic—"a religion [as he says] that cost nothing"—to a theism where he faced (and he quotes George MacDonald's phrase) "something to be neither more nor less nor other than *done*." There was no intellectual change, for (as he says) "there had long been an ethic (theoretically) attached to my Idealism": it was the recognition that he had to do something about it, that "an attempt at complete virtue must be made." [2] His conversion was a re-orientation of the will.

In assimilating religious assertions to moral assertions I do not wish to deny that there are any important differences. One is the fact already noticed that usually the behaviour policy intended is not specified by one

---

[2] C. S. Lewis, *Surprised by Joy* (1955), pp. 198, 212–13.

religious assertion in isolation. Another difference is that the fundamental moral teaching of the religion is frequently given, not in abstract terms, but by means of concrete examples—of how to behave, for instance, if one meets a man set upon by thieves on the road to Jericho. A resolution to behave like the good Samaritan does not, in itself, specify the behaviour to be resolved upon in quite different circumstances. However, absence of explicitly recognized general principles does not prevent a man from acting in accordance with such principles; it only makes it more difficult for a questioner to discover upon what principles he is acting. And the difficulty is not only one way round. If moral principles are stated in the most general form, as most moral philosophers have wished to state them, they tend to become so far removed from particular courses of conduct that it is difficult, if not impossible, to give them any precise content. It may be hard to find out what exactly is involved in the imitation of Christ; but it is not very easy to discover what exactly is meant by the pursuit of Aristotle's *eudaemonia* or of Mill's *happiness*. The tests for what it is to live agapeistically are as empirical as are those for living in quest of happiness; but in each case the tests can best be expounded in terms of examples of particular situations.

A more important difference between religious and purely moral principles is that, in the higher religions at least, the conduct preached by the religion concerns not only external but also internal behaviour. The conversion involved in accepting a religion is a conversion, not only of the will, but of the heart. Christianity requires not only that you should behave towards your neighbour as if you loved him as yourself: it requires that you should love him as yourself. And though I have no doubt that the Christian concept of *agape* refers partly to external behaviour—the agapeistic behaviour for which there are external criteria—yet being filled with *agape* includes more than behaving agapeistically externally: it also includes an agapeistic frame of mind. I have said that I cannot regard the expression of a feeling of any sort as the primary element in religious assertion; but this does not imply that intention to feel in a certain way is not a primary element, nor that it cannot be used to discriminate religious declarations of policy from declarations which are merely moral. Those who say that Confucianism is a code of morals and not, properly speaking, a religion are, I think, making this discrimination.

The resolution proclaimed by a religious assertion may then be taken as referring to inner life as well as to outward conduct. And the superiority of religious conviction over the mere adoption of a moral code in securing conformity to the code arises from a religious conviction changing what the religious man wants. It may be hard enough to love your enemy, but once you have succeeded in doing so it is easy to behave lovingly towards him.

But if you continue to hate him, it requires a heroic perseverance continually to behave as if you loved him. Resolutions to feel, even if they are only partly fulfilled, are powerful reinforcements of resolutions to act.

But though these qualifications may be adequate for distinguishing religious assertions from purely moral ones, they are not sufficient to discriminate between assertions belonging to one religious system and those belonging to another system in the case in which the behaviour policies, both of inner life and of outward conduct, inculcated by the two systems are identical. For instance, I have said that I take the fundamental moral teaching of Christianity to be the preaching of an agapeistic way of life. But a Jew or a Buddhist may, with considerable plausibility, maintain that the fundamental moral teaching of his religion is to recommend exactly the same way of life. How then can religious assertions be distinguished into those which are Christian, those which are Jewish, those which are Buddhist, by the policies of life which they respectively recommend if, on examination, these policies turn out to be the same?

Many Christians will, no doubt, behave in a specifically Christian manner in that they will follow ritual practices which are Christian and neither Jewish nor Buddhist. But though following certain practices may well be the proper test for membership of a particular religious society, a church, not even the most ecclesiastically-minded Christian will regard participation in a ritual as the fundamental characteristic of a Christian way of life. There must be some more important difference between an agapeistically policied Christian and an agapeistically policied Jew than that the former attends a church and the latter a synagogue.

The really important difference, I think, is to be found in the fact that the intentions to pursue the behaviour policies, which may be the same for different religions, are associated with thinking of different *stories* (or sets of stories). By a story I shall here mean a proposition or set of propositions which are straight-forwardly empirical propositions capable of empirical test and which are thought of by the religious man in connexion with his resolution to follow the way of life advocated by his religion. On the assumption that the ways of life advocated by Christianity and by Buddhism are essentially the same, it will be the fact that the intention to follow this way of life is associated in the mind of a Christian with thinking of one set of stories (the Christian stories) while it is associated in the mind of a Buddhist with thinking of another set of stories (the Buddhist stories) which enables a Christian assertion to be distinguished from a Buddhist one.

A religious assertion will, therefore, have a propositional element which is lacking in a purely moral assertion, in that it will refer to a story as well as to an intention. The reference to the story is not an assertion of the story taken as a matter of empirical fact: it is a telling of the story, or an alluding to the story, in the way in which one can tell, or allude to, the story of a novel with which one is acquainted. To assert the whole set of assertions of the Christian religion is both to tell the Christian doctrinal story and to confess allegiance to the Christian way of life.

The story, I have said, is a set of empirical propositions, and the language expressing the story is given a meaning by the standard method of understanding how the story-statements can be verified. The empirical story-statements will vary from Christian to Christian; the doctrines of Christianity are capable of different empirical interpretations, and Christians will differ in the interpretations they put upon the doctrines. But the interpretations will all be in terms of empirical propositions. Take, for example, the doctrine of Justification by means of the Atonement. Matthew Arnold imagined it in terms of

. . . a sort of infinitely magnified and improved Lord Shaftesbury, with a race of vile offenders to deal with, whom his natural goodness would incline him to let off, only his sense of justice will not allow it; then a younger Lord Shaftesbury, on the scale of his father and very dear to him, who might live in grandeur and splendour if he liked, but who prefers to leave his home, to go and live among the race of offenders, and to be put to an ingnominious death, on condition that his merits shall be counted against their demerits, and that his father's goodness shall be restrained no longer from taking effect, but any offender shall be admitted to the benefit of it on simply pleading the satisfaction made by the son;—and then, finally, a third Lord Shaftesbury, still on the same high scale, who keeps very much in the background, and works in a very occult manner, but very efficaciously nevertheless, and who is busy in applying everywhere the benefits of the son's satisfaction and the father's goodness.[3]

Arnold's "parable of the three Lord Shaftesburys" got him into a lot of trouble: he was "indignantly censured" (as he says) for wounding "the feelings of the religious community by turning into ridicule an august doctrine, the object of their solemn faith." [4] But there is no other account of the Anselmian doctrine of the Atonement that I have read which puts it in so morally favourable a light. Be that as it may, the only way in which the doctrine can be understood verificationally is in terms of human beings —mythological beings, it may be, who never existed, but who nevertheless would have been empirically observable had they existed.

For it is not necessary, on my view, for the asserter of a religious assertion to believe in the truth of the story involved in the assertions: what is necessary is that the story should be entertained in thought, i.e., that the statement of the story should be understood as having a meaning. I have secured

---

[3] Matthew Arnold, *Literature and Dogma* (1873), pp. 306–07.
[4] Matthew Arnold, *God and the Bible* (1875), pp. 18–19.

this by requiring that the story should consist of empirical propositions. Educated Christians of the present day who attach importance to the doctrine of the Atonement certainly do not believe an empirically testable story in Matthew Arnold's or any other form. But it is the fact that entertainment in thought of this and other Christian stories forms the context in which Christian resolutions are made which serves to distinguish Christian assertions from those made by adherents of another religion, or of no religion.

# PAUL TILLICH

*Paul Tillich* (1886–1965), a German-American philosophical theologian, was formerly on the faculty of Harvard University. His system reflects a wide-ranging interests in the fields of classical Greek thought, German philosophy, art, history, psychoanalysis, and existentialism. *Systematic Theology* is his major work.

## Symbols of Faith

### 1. *The Meaning of Symbol*

Man's ultimate concern must be expressed symbolically, because symbolic language alone is able to express the ultimate. This statement demands explanation in several respects. In spite of the manifold research about the meaning and function of symbols which is going on in contemporary philosophy, every writer who uses the term "symbol" must explain his understanding of it.

Symbols have one characteristic in common with signs; they point beyond themselves to something else. The red sign at the street corner points to the order to stop the movement of cars at certain intervals. A red light and the stopping of cars have essentially no relation to each other, but conventionally they are united as long as the convention lasts. The same is true of letters and numbers and partly even words. They point beyond themselves to sounds and meanings. They are given this special function by convention

"Symbols of Faith" from *Dynamics of Faith* (pp. 41–54) by Paul Tillich. Copyright © 1957 by Paul Tillich. Reprinted by permission of Harper & Brothers and George Allen & Unwin, Ltd.

within a nation or by international conventions, as the mathematical signs. Sometimes such signs are called symbols; but this is unfortunate because it makes the distinction between signs and symbols more difficult. Decisive is the fact that signs do not participate in the reality of that to which they point, while symbols do. Therefore, signs can be replaced for reasons of expediency or convention, while symbols cannot.

This leads to the second characteristic of the symbol: It participates in that to which it points: the flag participates in the power and dignity of the nation for which it stands. Therefore, it cannot be replaced except after an historic catastrophe that changes the reality of the nation which it symbolizes. An attack on the flag is felt as an attack on the majesty of the group in which it is acknowledged. Such an attack is considered blasphemy.

The third characteristic of a symbol is that it opens up levels of reality which otherwise are closed for us. All arts create symbols for a level of reality which cannot be reached in any other way. A picture and a poem reveal elements of reality which cannot be approached scientifically. In the creative work of art we encounter reality in a dimension which is closed for us without such works. The symbol's fourth characteristic not only opens up dimensions and elements of reality which otherwise would remain unapproachable but also unlocks dimensions and elements of our soul which correspond to the dimensions and elements of reality. A great play gives us not only a new vision of the human scene, but it opens up hidden depths of our own being. Thus we are able to receive what the play reveals to us in reality. There are within us dimensions of which we cannot become aware except through symbols, as melodies and rhythms in music.

Symbols cannot be produced intentionally—this is the fifth characteristic. They grow out of the individual or collective unconscious and cannot function without being accepted by the unconscious dimension of our being. Symbols which have an especially social function, as political and religious symbols, are created or at least accepted by the collective unconscious of the group in which they appear.

The sixth and last characteristic of the symbol is a consequence of the fact that symbols cannot be invented. Like living beings, they grow and they die. They grow when the situation is ripe for them, and they die when the situation changes. The symbol of the "king" grew in a special period of history, and it died in most parts of the world in our period. Symbols do not grow because people are longing for them, and they do not die because of scientific or practical criticism. They die because they can no longer produce response in the group where they originally found expression.

These are the main characteristics of every symbol. Genuine symbols are created in several spheres of man's cultural creativity. We have mentioned already the political and the artistic realm. We could add history and, above all, religion, whose symbols will be our particular concern.

## 2. Religious Symbols

We have discussed the meaning of symbols generally because, as we said, man's ultimate concern must be expressed symbolically! One may ask: Why can it not be expressed directly and properly? If money, success or the nation is someone's ultimate concern, can this not be said in a direct way without symbolic language? Is it not only in those cases in which the content of the ultimate concern is called "God" that we are in the realm of symbols? The answer is that everything which is a matter of unconditional concern is made into a god. If the nation is someone's ultimate concern, the name of the nation becomes a sacred name and the nation receives divine qualities which far surpass the reality of the being and functioning of the nation. The nation then stands for and symbolizes the true ultimate, but in an idolatrous way. Success as ultimate concern is not the natural desire of actualizing potentialities, but is readiness to sacrifice all other values of life for the sake of a position of power and social predominance. The anxiety about not being a success is an idolatrous form of the anxiety about divine condemnation. Success is grace; lack of success, ultimate judgment. In this way concepts designating ordinary realities become idolatrous symbols of ultimate concern.

The reason for this transformation of concepts into symbols is the character of ultimacy and the nature of faith. That which is the true ultimate transcends the realm of finite reality infinitely. Therefore, no finite reality can express it directly and properly. Religiously speaking, God transcends his own name. This is why the use of his name easily becomes an abuse or a blasphemy. Whatever we say about that which concerns us ultimately, whether or not we call it God, has a symbolic meaning. It points beyond itself while participating in that to which it points. In no other way can faith express itself adequately. The language of faith is the language of symbols. If faith were what we have shown that it is not, such an assertion could not be made. But faith, understood as the state of being ultimately concerned, has no language other than symbols. When saying this I always expect the question: Only a symbol? He who asks this question shows that he has not understood the difference between signs and symbols nor the power of symbolic language, which surpasses in quality and strength the power of any nonsymbolic language. One should never say "only a symbol," but one should say "not less than a symbol." With this in mind we can now describe the different kinds of symbols of faith.

The fundamental symbol of our ultimate concern is God. It is always present in any act of faith, even if the act of faith includes the denial of God. Where there is ultimate concern, God can be denied only in the name of God. One God can deny the other one. Ultimate concern cannot deny its own character as ultimate. Therefore, it affirms what is meant by the word "God." Atheism, consequently, can only mean the attempt to remove any ultimate concern—to remain unconcerned about the meaning of one's existence. Indifference toward the ultimate question is the only imaginable form of atheism. Whether it is possible is a problem which must remain unsolved at this point. In any case, he who denies God as a matter of ultimate concern affirms God, because he affirms ultimacy in his concern. God is the fundamental symbol for what concerns us ultimately. Again it would be completely wrong to ask: So God is nothing but a symbol? Because the next question has to be: A symbol for what? And then the answer would be: For God! God is symbol for God. This means that in the notion of God we must distinguish two elements: the element of ultimacy, which is a matter of immediate experience and not symbolic in itself, and the element of concreteness, which is taken from our ordinary experience and symbolically applied to God. The man whose ultimate concern is a sacred tree has both the ultimacy of concern and the concreteness of the tree which symbolizes his relation to the ultimate. The man who adores Apollo is ultimately concerned, but not in an abstract way. His ultimate concern is symbolized in the divine figure of Apollo. The man who glorifies Jahweh, the God of the Old Testament, has both an ultimate concern and a concrete image of what concerns him ultimately. This is the meaning of the seemingly cryptic statement that God is the symbol of God. In this qualified sense God is the fundamental and universal content of faith.

It is obvious that such an understanding of the meaning of God makes the discussions about the existence or non-existence of God meaningless. It is meaningless to question the ultimacy of an ultimate concern. This element in the idea of God is in itself certain. The symbolic expression of this element varies endlessly through the whole history of mankind. Here again it would be meaningless to ask whether one or another of the figures in which an ultimate concern is symbolized does "exist." If "existence" refers to something which can be found within the whole of reality, no divine being exists. The question is not this, but: which of the innumerable symbols of faith is most adequate to the meaning of faith? In other words, which symbol of ultimacy expresses the ultimate without idolatrous elements? This is the problem, and not the so-called "existence of God"—which is in itself an impossible combination of words. God as the ultimate in man's ultimate concern is more certain than any other certainty, even that of oneself. God as symbolized in a divine figure is a matter of daring faith, of courage and risk.

God is the basic symbol of faith, but not the only one. All the qualities we attribute to him, power, love, justice, are taken from finite experiences and applied symbolically to that which is beyond finitude and infinity. If faith calls God "almighty," it uses the human experience of power in order to symbolize the content of its infinite concern, but it does not describe a highest being who can do as he pleases. So it is with all the other qualities and with all the actions, past, present and future, which men attribute to God. They are symbols taken from our daily experience, and not information about what God did once upon a time or will do sometime in the future. Faith is not the belief in such stories, but it is the acceptance of symbols that express our ultimate concern in terms of divine actions.

Another group of symbols of faith are manifestations of the divine in things and events, in persons and communities, in words and documents. This whole realm of sacred objects is a treasure of symbols. Holy things are not holy in themselves, but they point beyond themselves to the source of all holiness, that which is of ultimate concern.

## 3. Symbols and Myths

The symbols of faith do not appear in isolation. They are united in "stories of the gods," which is the meaning of the Greek word "mythos"—myth. The gods are individualized figures, analogous to human personalities, sexually differentiated, descending from each other, related to each other in love and struggle, producing world and man, acting in time and space. They participate in human greatness and misery, in creative and destructive works. They give to man cultural and religious traditions, and defend these sacred rites. They help and threaten the human race, especially some families, tribes or nations. They appear in epiphanies and incarnations, establish sacred places, rites and persons, and thus create a cult. But they themselves are under the command and threat of a fate which is beyond everything that is. This is mythology as developed most impressively in ancient Greece. But many of these characteristics can be found in every mythology. Usually the mythological gods are not equals. There is a hierarchy, at the top of which is a ruling god, as in Greece; or a trinity of them, as in India; or a duality of them, as in Persia. There are savior-gods who mediate between the highest gods and man, sometimes sharing the suffering and death of man in spite of their essential immortality. This is the world of the myth, great and strange, always changing but fundamentally the same: man's ultimate concern symbolized in divine figures and actions. Myths are symbols of faith combined in stories about divine-human encounters.

Myths are always present in every act of faith, because the language of faith is the symbol. They are also attacked, criticized, and transcended in each of the great religions of mankind. The reason for this criticism is the very nature of the myth. It uses material from our ordinary experience. It puts the stories of the gods into the framework of time and space although it belongs to the nature of the ultimate to be beyond time and space. Above all, it divides the divine into several figures, removing ultimacy from each of them without removing their claim to ultimacy. This inescapably leads to conflicts of ultimate claims, able to destroy life, society, and consciousness.

The criticism of the myth first rejects the division of the divine and goes beyond it to one God, although in different ways according to the different types of religion. Even one God is an object of mythological language, and if spoken about is drawn into the framework of time and space. Even he loses his ultimacy if made to be the content of concrete concern. Consequently, the criticism of the myth does not end with the rejection of the polytheistic mythology.

Monotheism also falls under the criticism of the myth. It needs, as one says today, "demythologization." This word has been used in connection with the elaboration of the mythical elements in stories and symbols of the Bible, both of the Old and the New Testaments—stories like those of the Paradise, of the fall of Adam, of the great Flood, of the Exodus from Egypt, of the virgin birth of the Messiah, of many of his miracles, of his resurrection and ascension, of his expected return as the judge of the universe. In short, all the stories in which divine-human interactions are told are considered as mythological in character, and objects of demythologization. What does this negative and artificial term mean? It must be accepted and supported if it points to the necessity of recognizing a symbol as a symbol and a myth as a myth. It must be attacked and rejected if it means the removal of symbols and myths altogether. Such an attempt is the third step in the criticism of the myth. It is an attempt which never can be successful, because symbol and myth are forms of the human consciousness which are always present. One can replace one myth by another, but one cannot remove the myth from man's spiritual life. For the myth is the combination of symbols of our ultimate concern.

A myth which is understood as a myth, but not removed or replaced, can be called a "broken myth." Christianity denies by its very nature any unbroken myth, because its presupposition is the first commandment: the affirmation of the ultimate as ultimate and the rejection of any kind of idolatry. All mythological elements in the Bible, and doctrine and liturgy should be recognized as mythological, but they should be maintained in their symbolic form and not be replaced by scientific substitutes. For there is no substitute for the use of symbols and myths: they are the language of faith.

The radical criticism of the myth is due to the fact that the primitive mythological consciousness resists the attempt to interpret the myth of myth. It is afraid of every act of demythologization. It believes that the broken myth is deprived of its truth and of its convincing power. Those who live in an unbroken mythological world feel safe and certain. They resist, often fanatically, any attempt to introduce an element of uncertainty by "breaking the myth," namely, by making conscious its symbolic character. Such resistance is supported by authoritarian systems, religious or political, in order to give security to the people under their control and unchallenged power to those who exercise the control. The resistance against demythologization expresses itself in "literalism." The symbols and myths are understood in their immediate meaning. The material, taken from nature and history, is used in its proper sense. The character of the symbol to point beyond itself to something else is disregarded. Creation is taken as a magic act which happened once upon a time. The fall of Adam is localized on a special geographical point and attributed to a human individual. The virgin birth of the Messiah is understood in biological terms, resurrection and ascension as physical events, the second coming of Christ as a telluric, or cosmic, catastrophe. The presupposition of such literalism is that God is a being, acting in time and space, dwelling in a special place, affecting the course of events and being affected by them like any other being in the universe. Literalism deprives God of his ultimacy and, religiously speaking, of his majesty. It draws him down to the level of that which is not ultimate, the finite and conditional. In the last analysis it is not rational criticism of the myth which is decisive but the inner religious criticism. Faith, if it takes its symbols literally, becomes idolatrous! It calls something ultimate which is less than ultimate. Faith, conscious of the symbolic character of its symbols, gives God the honor which is due him.

One should distinguish two stages of literalism, the natural and the reactive. The natural stage of literalism is that in which the mythical and the literal are indisinguishable. The primitive period of individuals and groups consists in the inability to separate the creations of symbolic imagination from the facts which can be verified through observation and experiment. This stage has a full right of its own and should not be disturbed, either in individuals or in groups, up to the moment when man's questioning mind breaks the natural acceptance of the mythological visions as literal. If, however, this moment has come, two ways are possible. The one is to replace the unbroken by the broken myth. It is the objectively demanded way, although it is impossible for many people who prefer the repression of their questions to the uncertainty which appears with the breaking of the myth. They are forced into the second stage of literalism, the conscious one, which is aware of the questions but represses them, half consciously, half unconsciously. The tool of repression is usually an acknowledged authority with sacred qualities like the Church or the Bible, to which one owes unconditional surrender. This stage is still justifiable, if the questioning power is very weak and can easily be answered. It is unjustifiable if a mature mind is broken in its personal center by political or psychological methods, split in his unity, and hurt in his integrity. The enemy of a critical theology is not natural literalism but conscious literalism with repression of and aggression toward autonomous thought.

Symbols of faith cannot be replaced by other symbols, such as artistic ones, and they cannot be removed by scientific criticism. They have a genuine standing in the human mind, just as science and art have. Their symbolic character is their truth and their power. Nothing less than symbols and myths can express our ultimate concern.

One more question arises, namely, whether myths are able to express every kind of ultimate concern. For example, Christian theologians argue that the word "myth" should be reserved for natural myths in which repetitive natural processes, such as the seasons, are understood in their ultimate meaning. They believe that if the world is seen as a historical process with beginning, end and center, as in Christianity and Judaism, the term "myth" should not be used. This would radically reduce the realm in which the term would be applicable. Myth could not be understood as the language of our ultimate concern, but only as a discarded idiom of this language. Yet history proves that there are not only natural myths but also historical myths. If the earth is seen as the battleground of two divine powers, as in ancient Persia, this is an historical myth. If the God of creation selects and guides a nation through history toward an end which transcends all history, this is an historical myth. If the Christ—a transcendent, divine being—appears in the fullness of time, lives, dies and is resurrected, this is an historical myth. Christianity is superior to those religions which are bound to a natural myth. But Christianity speaks the mythological language like every other religion. It is a broken myth, but it is a myth: otherwise Christianity would not be an expression of ultimate concern.

# E. L. MASCALL

E. L. Mascall (1905–    ), Anglican theologian, has published extensively and contributed to a revival of interest in the Thomistic tradition
in theology. His books—*He Who Is, Words and Images;* and *Existence
and Analogy*—are significant contributions to philosophy of religion.

## The Doctrine of Analogy

One preliminary remark may be made before the discussion is opened,
namely that the function of the doctrine of analogy is not to make it possible for us to talk about God in the future but to explain how it is that
we have been able to talk about him all along. In spite of all that has been
said by positivists, logical and other, we do in fact find ourselves talking
about God, and talking about him in a way that is significant. It is, I would
maintain, transparently clear to anyone whose judgment is not shackled by
a predetermined dogma that, if two men respectively affirm and deny that
God exists, they are in fact disagreeing about the nature of reality, and not
merely expressing different emotional or aesthetic attitudes. There is, unfortunately, a recurrent tendency among philosophers, in analysing the
mental activities of human beings in general, to assume that until their
analysis and criticism have been satisfactorily completed, nobody has the
right to make any affirmations at all; so deeply has Cartesianism entered
into our heritage. The consequence is that the plain man laughs at the
philosophers and goes on his own way without them. Against this tendency
we are, as I see it, bound to assert that the task of any philosophical critique
is to account for, to render precise and, if necessary, to correct the body of
doctrine that the human mind has acquired by the natural exercise of its
own powers, but not, except in a purely relative and *ex post facto* way, to
provide a justification for the activity of thought itself. To forget this is to
doom oneself to a kind of intellectual suicide. For the critical philosopher is
himself the heir of his past; before he was a philosopher at all he was a man,
and before he was a man he was a child. To enter a second time into the
womb and to be born again equipped with a fully developed critique of

From E. L. Mascall, *Existence and Analogy,* pp. 94–115. Published 1949, by Longmans,
Green & Co., Ltd. Used by permission of the publishers. [Footnotes omitted, Eds.]

knowledge is a sheer impossibility. The fact is that, however fallible it may be, the human mind does acquire knowledge by the exercise of the powers which it possesses, and a sane philosophy will recognize this fact. To return, then, to the subject of our present discussion, the doctrine of analogy is not concerned to discover whether discourse about God is antecedently possible, or to endow it with a possibility that was originally absent, but to account for the fact that discourse about God has, as matter of experience, been taking place in spite of various considerations that might seem at first sight to rule its possibility out of court.

I would further add that the question of analogy does not arise at all in the mere proof of the existence of God; it arises only when, having satisfied ourselves that the existence of finite being declares its dependence upon self-existent being, we then apprehend that no predicate can be attributed to finite and to self-existent being univocally. Penido's remarks seem to me to be of the first importance here. "Formally," he writes, "the problem of analogy is a problem of nature, not of existence. We can arrive at the existence of God without *explicit* recourse to analogy, while it is impossible to think about the divine nature without conceiving it as equivocal, univocal or analogous to our own." And again: "It is quite true that the proofs of God are analogical *realities,* otherwise they would prove nothing. But they do not fall under the jurisdiction of the *method* of analogy, as theology employs it. Let us distinguish carefully—without separating them and still more without opposing them—the problem of analogical knowledge and the metaphysical problem of analogy. The former belongs in full right to the treatise on God, while it is only after the treatise on creation that we can approach the latter in its fullness. . . . Does this mean that analogy in no way depends on the *quinque viae?* By no means. Analogy begins at the precise point where the rational demonstration ends." We had no need of any doctrine of analogy in the last chapter, in arguing from the existence of finite beings to the existence of God. When, however, the argument was complete, we saw that the God whose existence we were now asserting was a being of so radically different an order from everything else in our experience that it became a real question whether the word "God" in that context meant anything at all. There can be little satisfaction in demonstrating the existence of a being whom the very demonstration shows to be altogether inapprehensible. God would seem to have slipped from between our hands at the very moment when we had at last laid hold on him. It is at this point that the doctrine of analogy becomes altogether necessary, and it is for this reason that its full investigation only began among Christian philosophers who gave primacy of place to the existential approach to God.

The doctrine, as we find it in the Thomist tradition, appears in at least three distinct departments of philosophy, namely the metaphysical or ontological, the epistemological or psychological, and the logical or linguistic.

This is only what we might expect in a fundamentally realist philosophy, which holds that words are not merely noises and that thought is not merely about ideas, but that speech with its words and thought with its ideas are ultimately about things. It is well to make this point clear at the start or we shall find ourselves puzzled to know what precisely is the question with which analogy is concerned. Is it "How can we talk about God?" or "How can we think about God?" or "How are things related to God?" In fact it is about all three, and we need not be worried by the way in which it slips from one to the other, so long as our attitude is confidently realist. I shall, however, take the first question as my starting-point and consider the problem of analogical prediction.

Is it possible, we therefore ask, for statements expressed in human language to mean anything when made about God—that is to say, are theological statements meaningful or meaningless? (The relevance of this discussion to the questions raised by the logical positivists will be immediately clear to those who have any acquaintance with their works.) Starting from a famous distinction made by Aristotle, we remark that, even within the realm of discourse about finite beings, one and the same word, when applied to two things, sometimes bears the same sense in both applications and sometimes different ones. In the former case it is used *univocally* (συνωνύμως), as when Carlo and Fido are both called dogs. Even if Carlo is a great Dane and Fido a Pomeranian, we mean the same thing about each of them when we call them both *dogs;* the characteristics in each that distinguish Carlo as a Dane from Fido as a Pomeranian, while they cannot be found in their totality except in dogs, are additional to caninity as such. But sometimes we use words purely equivocally (ὁμωνύμως), as when we apply the word "mug" both to a drinking utensil and to the victim of a fraud. (The neglect of this distinction can lead to unfortunate consequences, as the choirboys found who were starting a cricket team, when they asked the vicar for one of the bats which the verger had led them to believe were in the belfry.) But in addition to these two uses, it is alleged, a word is sometimes applied to two objects in senses that are neither wholly different nor yet wholly the same, as when we say that Mr. Jones and Skegness [1] are both healthy, the former because he *enjoys,* and the latter because it *induces,* health; in this case we are said to use the term "healthy" *analogically* (ἀνάλογως).

At first sight the introduction of this mode of predication might seem to be unnecessary and trivial, and certainly Aristotle did not accord to it anything like as much attention as the scholastics do. We might be tempted to suppose that analogy is only a dignified kind of univocity, and that it is

---

[1] [A seaside health resort. Eds.]

quite sufficient to say that the healthiness of Mr. Jones and the healthiness of Skegness are merely two ways of being healthy, just as the Danishness of Carlo and the Pomeranianity of Fido are merely two ways of being canine. Or, alternatively, we might go to the other extreme and say that analogy is only equivocity in sheep's clothing, that to enjoy health and to induce health are two altogether different activities and that only for the sake of economy in words can there be any justification for using the same term "healthy" *tout court* to denote them both. Furthermore, it might be asked, even if we admit this *tertium quid* of analogy, can we ever be quite sure when it applies? When we say that Mr. Jones is alive and that an oyster is alive, is the difference between the life of Mr. Jones and the life of the oyster something additional to a quality, namely life, which is found univocally in both, as the Danishness of Carlo and the Pomeranianity of Fido are additional to their common caninity? Or, on the other hand, is the life which is attributed to Mr. Jones and to the oyster, as the scholastics would say, an analogical perfection, contracted to each subject not by external *differentiae* but by different internal modes of participation? Can one possibly settle this kind of question? Can we even give the distinction any real meaning?

Now, so long as we are merely considering qualities and properties of finite beings, the introduction of analogical discourse, in addition to univocal and equivocal, might well appear to be an unnecessary and artificial complication. There are, however, two instances in which it—or something like it—seems to be unavoidable, namely when we are discussing transcendentals and when we are discussing God. And it is worth noting that, in Christian thought, it is precisely the necessity of talking about God that has given rise to the great development which the doctrine of analogy has undergone. Let us consider these instances in order.

The transcendentals, in scholastic thought, are those six primary notions—*ens, res, unum, aliquid, verum* and *bonum*—which, because of their very universality, refuse to fall in any of the Aristotelian categories, but cut across them all. The last five ultimately reduce to the first, so it will be sufficient to consider that. What, then, is meant by the analogy of being? Why is it denied that being is univocal? Simply because there is nothing outside being by which it could be differentiated. When we say that Carlo and Fido are both dogs, the word "dog" means precisely the same when applied to each of them; the differences that distinguish them as dogs are, as we have seen, extrinsic to caninity as such. But when we say that Carlo and Fido are both *beings,* the differences that distinguish them as beings cannot be extrinsic to being as such, for being, in its altogether universal reference, must embrace everything, including differences; if differences were not instances of being, they would be non-existent, and then no two things could be distinct from each other. So the scholastics tell us, being is not a genus, since there is nothing outside it which could act as a differentia to it, to subdivide it into species; nevertheless everything is an instance of being, and being is differentiated by its own inherent analogical variety. To be is to be in a certain way, and the way is the very heart of the being. So the whole order of things, of *entia,* from the triune Deity down to the speck of dust and the electron, consists of nothing more and nothing less than analogical instances of being: self-existent being and dependent being, actual being and possible being, substantial being and accidental being, real being and notional being, not in any pantheistic or monistic sense, as if being were some kind of cosmic material, a metaphysical modelling-clay appearing now in this shape and now in that, but in the far more profound sense that every being must *be,* and must be in some determinate way, and—the theist will add—in the sense that the way in which it has being depends in the last resort upon its relation to the self-existent Being which is the prime analogate of all.

Now what is true about beings as such in their relation to one another must be true *a fortiori* about finite beings in their relation to the God who is self-existent Being. If being is not a genus, then the supreme Being transcends all genera, and the principle of analogy, which we have seen applies even between creatures when they are considered as they participate in the transcendentals, will apply with even greater force when creatures are brought into comparison with the altogether transcendent God and when God is spoken about in words whose meaning is derived from their application to finite things. Here, if anywhere, the distinction between the *perfectio significata* and the *modus significandi* will hold; here, if anywhere, will the classical definition of analogy apply, namely that it is the application of a concept to different beings in ways that are simply diverse from each other and are only the same in a certain respect, *simpliciter diversa et eadem secundum quid.* It is noticeable that St. Thomas does not deny that analogues are equivocal but only that they are purely so.

Let us now proceed to consider in more detail this classical doctrine of analogy. The precise classification of the various types of analogy that can be distinguished is to this day a matter of considerable controversy; the method that I shall adopt will, however, bring out the salient points.

## II

In the first place, we may distinguish between analogy *duorum ad tertium* and analogy *unius ad alterum;* this is the fundamental distinction made by St. Thomas in both the *Summa Theologica* and the *Summa contra Gentiles.* Analogy *duorum ad tertium* is the analogy that holds between two beings in consequence of the relation that each of them bears to a third (the analogy considered is, it must be noticed, between the *two;* the *tertium* only comes in as something in the background to which they are both related). For example, if the adjective "healthy" is applied both to Skegness and to the complexion of Mr. Jones who lives there, this double attribution of the adjective can only be seen to be legitimate if it is grasped that in its strict and primary application the adjective applies neither to Skegness nor to the complexion but to Mr. Jones. It is he who is (in the scholastic sense) *formally* healthy and is the *prime analogate.* His complexion is healthy only in the sense that it is a *sign* of health in him, Skegness is healthy only in the sense that it *induces* health in him (or in others like him); we cannot rationally justify the attribution of the same predicate "healthy" to things as diverse as a complexion and a seaside town except by referring them both to human beings to whom the predicate formally and properly belongs.

This type of analogy can, however, have little or no application to the case where we are attributing the same predicate to God and to a creature, for there is no being antecedent to God to whom the predicate can apply more formally and properly than it applies to him. We therefore pass to the other type of analogy, analogy *unius ad alterum,* which is founded not upon diverse relations which each of the analogates bears to a third, but upon a relation which one of them bears to the other. And this type of analogy itself subdivides into two.

The former of these sub-types is that which is known as analogy of *attribution* or of *proportion,* analogy *unius ad alterum* in the strict sense. In this case the predicate belongs formally and properly to one of the analogates (which is thus not merely *an* analogate but is the *prime* analogate), and only relatively and derivatively to the other. Thus it is by an analogy of attribution or proportion that Mr. Jones and his complexion are both described as healthy; health is found formally and properly in Mr. Jones, and his complexion is described as healthy only because it bears a certain relation to his health, namely the relation of being a sign of it. In its theological application, where the analogates concerned are God and a creature, the relation upon which the analogy is based will be that of creative causality; creatures are related to God as his effects, by all those modes of participation by the creature in the perfection of its creator which are indicated, for example, by the Thomist Five Ways. Thus when we say that God and Mr. Jones are both good or that they are both beings, remembering that the content which the word "good" or "being" has for us is derived from our experience of the goodness and the being of creatures, we are, so far as analogy of attribution is concerned, saying no more than that God has goodness or being in whatever way is necessary if he is to be able to produce goodness and being in his creatures. This would not seem necessarily to indicate anything more than the perfections which are found formally in various finite modes in creatures exist *virtually* in God, that is to say, that he is able to produce them in the creatures; it does not seem to necessitate that God possesses them formally himself. (In the case of Mr. Jones, of course, his complexion did indicate his formal possession of health, but there is, literally, all the difference in the world between the relation between two analogates in the finite realm and that between God and a creature.) Analogy of attribution certainly does not exclude the formal possession of the perfections by God, but it does not itself ascribe it to him. The mode in which the perfection which exists in the secondary analogate also exists in the prime analogate will depend on the relation between them; and if this relation is merely that the latter analogate is the *cause* of the former, the possession by the latter of a perfection that exists formally in the former will not, so far as the present mode of analogy is concerned, be necessarily anything more than a virtual one. Creatures are good (formally but finitely), God is the cause of them and of all that they have, therefore the word "good" applied to God need not mean any more than that he is able to produce goodness. It is at this point that the second sub-type of analogy comes to the rescue.

This is analogy of proportionality, also called analogy *plurium ad plura*. In it there is a direct relation of the mode in which a perfection is participated to the being by which it is participated, independently of any relation to a prime analogate. (There may be a prime analogate, and indeed some would maintain that there must be, but it does not come in at this stage.) A spurious, though sometimes useful, form of this type of analogy is *metaphor,* in which there is not a formal participation of the same characteristic in the different analogates but only a similarity of effects. Thus, to take a classic example, the lion is called the king of the beasts because he bears to savage animals a relation similar to that which a king bears to his subjects, but no one would assert that kingship is to be found formally in the lion. Again, God is described as being angry, because his relation to the punishments which he imposes is similar to that which an angry man has to the injuries which he inflicts, but no one (at least, no scholastic philosopher) would say that anger was to be found formally in God. In the strict sense, an analogy of proportionality implies that the analogue under discussion is found formally in each of the analogates but in a mode that is determined by the nature of the analogate itself. Thus, assuming that life is an analogous and not a univocal concept, it is asserted that cabbages, elephants, men and God each possess life formally (that is each of them is, quite literally and unmetaphorically, *alive*), but that the cabbage possesses life in the mode proper to a cabbage, the elephant in that proper to an elephant, the man in that proper to a man, and finally God in that supreme, and by us unimaginable, mode proper to self-existent Being itself. This is commonly expressed in the following quasi-mathematical form, from which, in fact, the name "analogy of proportionality" is derived.

$$\frac{\text{life of cabbage}}{\text{essence of cabbage}} = \frac{\text{life of elephant}}{\text{essence of elephant}}$$

$$= \frac{\text{life of man}}{\text{essence of man}} = \frac{\text{life of God}}{\text{essence of God}}$$

We must, however, beware of interpreting the equal sign too literally. For the point is not that the life of the cabbage is determined by the essence of the cabbage in the *same* way as that in which the life of the man is determined by the essence of the man, but that the way in which cabbage essence determines cabbage life is proper to cabbagehood, while the way in which the human essence determines human life is proper to manhood. But at this point various objections rapidly spring to the mind.

In the first place, it may be asked, has not the remark just made landed us in an infinite regress? We began by denying the univocity of the identity,

$$\text{life of cabbage} = \text{life of man},$$

and substituted for it the proportionality:

$$\frac{\text{life of cabbage}}{\text{essence of cabbage}} = \frac{\text{life of man}}{\text{essence of man}}$$

But we now have denied that the equal sign in this latter equation really signifies equality and have substituted for it a proposition which, in quasi-mathematical form, can be written as follows:

$$\frac{\text{way in which life of cabbage is determined by essence of cabbage}}{\text{essence of cabbage}}$$

$$= \frac{\text{way in which life of man is determined by essence of man}}{\text{essence of man}}$$

And again we shall have to remember that the equal sign means not identity but similarity, and shall now have to write:

$$\frac{\text{way in which way-in-which-life-of-cabbage-is-determined-by-essence-of-cabbage is determined by essence of cabbage}}{\text{essence of cabbage}}$$

$$= \frac{\text{way in which way-in-which-life-of-man-is-determined-by-essence-of-man is determined by essence of man}}{\text{essence of man}}$$

and so *ad infinitum*.

To put this more briefly, if we write L for "life of" and E for "essence of," c for "cabbage" and m for "man," and use A/B to signify "determination of A by B," we began by denying $Lc = Lm$, and put in its place

$$Lc/Ec = Lm/Em;$$

then we said that what we really meant was

$$(Lc/Ec)/Ec = (Lm/Em)/Em;$$

then we found that for this we should have to substitute

$$[(Lc/Ec)/Ec]/Ec = [(Lm/Em)/Em]/Em.$$

The next stage will be

$$\{[(Lc/Ec)/Ec]/Ec\}/Ec = \{[(Lm/Em)/Em]/Em\}/Em,$$

and so we shall go on for ever, at each successive stage denying progressively more complicated relationships between cabbages and men, and never managing to assert a relationship which we shall not immediately have to deny. And at the end of it we shall have nothing but a series of negations:

$$Lc \neq Lm,$$
$$Lc/Ec \neq Lm/Em,$$
$$(Lc/Ec)/Ec \neq (Lm/Em)/Em,$$
$$[(Lc/Ec)/Ec]/Ec \neq [(Lm/Em)/Em]/Em, \qquad \text{etc.}$$

Our proportionality has completely collapsed, and all we are left with is the fact that cabbages have nothing in common with men except the fact that, for no valid reason, men have described them both as being alive. In fact, the introduction of analogy as a *via media* between univocity and equivocity has turned out to be nothing more than an imposing piece of mystification. This is the first objection of which we must take account; it is obviously a serious one. It strikes, not in particular at the analogical application of terms to God, but to analogical predication as such. I shall not attempt a full reply until I have stated another objection which is concerned with the specifically theological case, but I shall offer a few observations in passing.

First, then, we may remark that the objection, while on the surface plausible, has something of the appearance of a conjuring trick. It brings to mind two somewhat similar feats of philosophical legerdemain. The first is Lewis Carroll's *What the Tortoise said to Achilles*. In this problem, which its

originator did not perhaps intend to be taken as seriously as it really demands, Achilles maintained that, if two premises A and B logically implied
a conclusion Z, then anybody who saw this and also accepted A and B as
true would have to accept Z as true also. The tortoise objected that this
would only be the case if he accepted a further proposition C, namely that
if A and B are true then Z must be true. Achilles was thus forced to modify
his original assertion, so that it now took the form "Anyone who accepts A,
B and C as true must accept Z as true also." But again the tortoise objected
that this involved the acceptance of another proposition D, which was that,
if A and B and C are all true, Z must be true as well. And so on for ever!
This corresponds, of course, to the well-known fact that the principle of
inference is incapable of formal symbolic statement within the logical calculus to which it applies. A logical system cannot, as it were, operate under
its own steam, without help from outside; we shall derive from this fact
a pointer towards the solution of our present problem. The other puzzle to
which I wish to refer is one which its originator took much more seriously:
I mean Mr. F. H. Bradley's famous argument that relations are illusions.
It is, he urged, of the essence of a relation to unite terms, but how is each
term united to the relation? It can only be by another relation, but if so,
what unites the term to this? To make the first relation intelligible we have
to presuppose an infinite sequence of relations antecedent to it, and none
of these is yet intelligible. Hence, Mr. Bradley concluded, relations are mere
illusion. Lord Russell has caustically remarked that if Bradley's argument
were valid it would prove that chains are impossible—and yet they exist.
Dr. C. D. Broad has dealt with Bradley's problem in some detail. He takes
as an instance of it the fact that A is father of B. "Here," he writes, "we
have a perfectly intelligible statement, involving the non-formal relation of
*fatherhood.* At the next stage we get the fact that A is referent to *fatherhood,* and the fact that B is relatum to *fatherhood.* The 'relations' introduced
at this stage are purely formal. At the next stage we get the fact that A is
referent to *referent to,* that *fatherhood* is relatum to *referent to,* that *fatherhood* is referent to *referent to,* and that B is relatum to *referent to.* Thus
no new 'relations' are introduced at this or any subsequent stage. The fact
that at every stage after the first the relating relations are purely formal and
are merely repeated shows that we are now embarked on the self-evidently
impossible task of explaining, by means of particular relational judgments,
that general relational form which is presupposed by all relational judgments
whatever." We might, in fact, say that, while it is of the essence of relations
to unite terms, they are not themselves terms in this context (though, of
course, in another context they may become terms, as when we pick out two
relations, or a relation and a term, and ask what is the relation between
them). Similarly, in the case of analogy of proper proportionality, we might
reply to our objector that we are simply concerned with the fact that essences

determine their qualities, and that the truth of this is not in the least affected by the fact that they can only do this if they also determine the way in which they determine their qualities, and the way in which they determine the way in which they determine their qualities, and so on to the crack of doom. *Ce n'est que le premier pas qui coûte.*

Such a reply would, I think, go a very long way, though I am doubtful whether it is altogether sufficient. For the fact remains that we have denied that our equal signs really stand for equality and we have not indicated anything definite that they do stand for. Can we in some way re-establish this bond that we have broken? Clearly we cannot by analogy of proportionality, but I shall suggest that we can by analogy of attribution, and that the two types of analogy, while either in separation is insufficient, can in combination do what is required. But this is an anticipation. I will pass on now to consider the second objection, which is specially concerned with analogical discourse about God.

## III

Let us therefore see what happens when we attribute life both to a creature and to God; any other perfection which can be formally predicated of God would, of course, do as well. Analogy of proportionality asserts:

$$\frac{\text{life of man}}{\text{essence of man}} = \frac{\text{life of God}}{\text{essence of God}}$$

Now, the objector urges, even if the first objection has been successfully overcome, so that we have no longer to bother about the fact that the equal sign does not indicate an exact identity of relationship, our formula will not in fact tell us in what sense life is to be predicated of God. For the essence of God is as little known to us as is his life; indeed his life is, formally considered, identical with it. Our equation has therefore two unknowns and cannot be solved. Nor can we get out of our difficulty by comparing essence with existence and saying that the essence of a being will correspond to, and be determined by, the act of virtue of which it exists:

$$\frac{\text{essence of man}}{\text{existential act of man}} = \frac{\text{essence of God}}{\text{existential act of God}}$$

Once again, both the terms on the right-hand side are unknown. Sheer agnosticism seems to be the outcome. What reply can we make?

Some scholastic philosophers, of whom Garrigou-Lagrange is one, claim to answer this objection, while remaining in the realm of analogy of proportionality, by denying that there are two unknown terms on the right-hand side. This last-mentioned writer, for example, taking the analogy

$$\frac{\text{creature}}{\text{its being}} = \frac{\text{first cause}}{\text{its being}}$$

asserts that only the fourth term is in fact unknown. "We have," he says, "(1) *the very confused concept of being in general,* which a child possesses from the moment of its first intellectual knowledge, (2) *the concept of finite being,* of which we know positively the finite mode and which is nothing else than the essence of the things that we see, stones, plants, animals, etc., (3) *the concept of analogous being,* imperfectly abstracted from the finite mode . . . ; it is a precision of the first very confused concept possessed by the child, and the metaphysician acquires it by recognizing that the formal notion of being does not in itself include the finite mode which accompanies it in the creature, (4) *the concept of the divine being,* the cause of created beings. These latter," he continues, "not having in their essence the reason of their existence, require a cause which exists of itself. In the concept of the divine being, the divine mode is expressed only in a negative and relative way, e.g., as non-finite or as supreme being. What is positive in this analogical knowledge of God is what God has that is proportionally common to him and the creature." Again, he writes, "*being* designates *that which* has relation to existence; this relation is implied in the very nature of that which exists and it is essentially varied according as it is necessary or contingent. The created essence in its inmost entity is altogether relative to its contingent existence, which it can lose; the uncreated essence is conceived only relatively to that necessary existence with which it is identified. . . . Analogous perfections are thus not pure relations. They are perfections which imply in the creature a composition of two correlative elements, potentiality and act, but which in God are pure act. Our intelligence conceives that they are realized more fully according as they are purified of all potentiality; in God they exist therefore in the pure state. We thus see that there are not two unknowns in the proportionalities set up by theology."

For this distinguished French Dominican, therefore, the third term in the formula is given us as that in which essence and existence are identical, and this gives us a limited and analogical, but nevertheless genuine, knowledge of the fourth term, while remaining within the realm of analogy of proportionality. We can transfer the notion of any perfection from a finite being to God, remembering that the difference of mode is that which corresponds to the difference between a being whose essence involves merely a possibility of existence and one whose essence involves existence of necessity. Of course, we do not know positively what the mode of the perfection in God is; to demand that would be to demand a quidditative knowledge of the divine essence and to abolish analogy altogether in favor of univocity. We are given all that we have a right to ask for; the comparison of the finite and the infinite modes of perfection is based on a comparison of the relations to existence which are proper to finite essence and to the divine essence respectively.

Now all this seems very satisfactory so far as it goes, but does it go far enough? Is it sufficient simply to base the comparison of the finite and infinite modes of a perfection upon a comparison of the finite and infinite modes of the essence-existence relation, without bringing in an explicit reference to the concrete relation which the creature has to God? There are

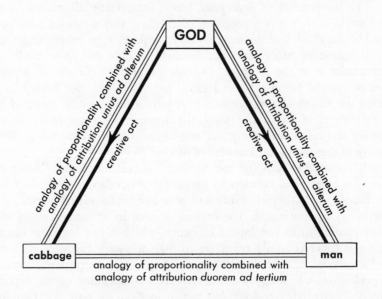

analogy of proportionality combined with
analogy of attribution *duorem ad tertium*

indeed traces in Garrigou-Lagrange's own discussion of an awareness of the need of this further step; the very form in which he writes the formula last quoted suggests this. For he does not describe the finite being as a being in whom essence does not necessarily involve existence, but as a "creature"; and he does not describe God as a being whose essence necessarily involves existence, but as the "first cause." "In these equations," he writes, "two created terms are known directly, one uncreated term is known indirectly *by way of causality* and we infer the fourth term which is known indirectly in a *positive* manner as regards what is analogically common with creatures and in a *negative* and relative manner as regards its proper divine mode." And the first cause and the creature are directly related by the relation of creation, which thus, as it were, cuts horizontally across the analogy of proportionality with an analogy of attribution. The equal sign does not, as we have seen earlier, express a mathematical identity, but, on the other hand, the two sides of the formula are not left in complete separation. They are bound together by an analogy of attribution *unius ad alterum,* of the creature to God in the case which we have just been considering. In the cases considered earlier, where the two sides of the formula both refer to finite beings, the linking analogy is an analogy *duorum ad tertium,* which holds in view the fact that each of the analogates is in an analogy of attribution *unius ad alterum,* of itself to God. The figure [above] . . . may help to make this plain.

The conclusion would thus seem to be that, in order to make the doctrine of analogy really satisfactory, we must see the analogical relation between God and the world as combining in a tightly interlocked union both analogy of attribution and analogy of proportionality. Without analogy of proportionality it is very doubtful whether the attributes which we predicate of God can be ascribed to him in more than a merely virtual sense; without analogy of attribution it hardly seems possible to avoid agnosticism. Which of the two forms of analogy is prior to the other has been, and still is, a hotly debated question among scholastic philosophers. Sylvester of Ferrara, in his great commentary on the *Summa contra Gentiles,* asserted the primacy of attribution and alleged that in this he was expressing the true thought of St. Thomas, but the "prince of commentators" Cajetan, in his luminous little treatise *De Nominum Analogia,* asserted that only proportionality was analogy in the true and strict sense and the majority of Thomists have followed him, down to Garrigou-Lagrange, Penido, and Maritain at the present day, though Descoqs is a notable exception.

# PAUL VAN BUREN

*Paul van Buren* (1924–    ), professor of theology at Temple University, has brought the discussion of linguistic analysis into the theological arena in a forceful and provocative manner.

## Analyses of Theological Language

### The Problem of Religious Language

Many modern theologians say that one of the major difficulties confronting the Christian who is himself a secular man lies in the nature of religion and the confusion between religion and Christian faith. We have argued that the difficulty lies rather in the character of the language of faith, that the problem is not so much one of bad religion as it is one of bad, or at least unworkable, language. A discussion of the problem of religion and its language will introduce the third element of this study: the method of those who have reflected on the logical structures of various sorts of languages of faith.

Bultmann defines religion as the human longing to escape from this world, fed by the supposed discovery of "a sphere above this world, in which the soul alone, released from all that is worldly, could repose." [1] Such a longing and discovery would undoubtedly be called religious by most people, and a man who entertained such thoughts would be called a religious man, but the concept of religion includes more than an other-worldly orientation. Many who undertake "religious activities," like going to church and singing hymns, or who say that certain events are according to "the will of God," do not show much interest in "a sphere above this world." Bultmann's definition meets only one aspect of the problem which concerns us.

Gerhard Ebeling, in an essay on Bonhoeffer's idea of religion, has given a more inclusive definition: the attempted "enlargement of reality by means of God." [2] Religion consists of appealing to God as a means of explaining, justifying, or otherwise "filling in the picture" of the world or human

---

Reprinted with permission of The Macmillan Company and Student Christian Movement Press from *The Secular Meaning of the Gospel*, pp. 81–106, by Paul van Buren. Copyright © by Paul van Buren, 1963.

[1] In *Kerygma und Mythos*, Vol. I, pp. 26 f.

[2] G. Ebeling, *Wort und Glaube* (Tübingen: Mohr, 1960), p. 145.

affairs. This summarizes the characteristics of religion, as Bonhoeffer saw them: thinking of two spheres of reality, the natural and the supernatural; interest in the other-worldly; metaphysical thinking; an idea of transcendence which surpasses human possibilities.[3] The religionless posture, on the other hand, is that of "coming to terms with reality apart from God," or without use of the God-hypothesis.[4]

Contemporary theologians from Barth to Ogden are agreed that Christianity does not conform to this definition of religion. Religion, they would say, is man's use of God to solve some human problem, whereas the Gospel proclaims God's unexpected use of man for his own purposes; this distinction lies behind Bonhoeffer's search for a "nonreligious" interpretation of biblical concepts. The fact remains, however, that all of these theologians continue to speak of God, even though, as Ebeling put it, "a considerable proportion of our contemporaries haven't the least idea of what we are even talking about when we speak of God." [5] Ebeling himself proposes what he calls a "worldly" way to speak of God, a way which must be concrete, clear, and effective, but the same "considerable proportion of our contemporaries" would undoubtedly judge this way to be talk about God nevertheless. Ebeling sees the problem, but he has not solved it.

The solution proposed by existentialist theologians consists of eliminating all "objectification" of God in thought and word,[6] but since Bultmann also objects to using the word "God" simply as a symbol for human experience, the word "God" appears to refer to nothing at all. The "nonobjective" use of the word "God" allows of no verification and is therefore meaningless. The moment we begin to use the word in a qualified sense, as in Flew's parable, we begin to kill our assertions by the "death of a thousand qualifications," and we end by making no assertion at all.[7] We do not understand, therefore, by what logic Bultmann and Ebeling continue to use the word "God" as though it had a quite specific reference. The *we* must be emphasized and explained. Why do we not understand their use of the word "God" as though it had a quite specific reference? Such a use does appear to conflict with their confessed existentialist concerns and is therefore unclear, but our chief difficulty lies elsewhere. We set out upon this study with certain acknowledged commitments to what we called "secular thought," and we said that secularism, as we were using the term, is grounded

[3] Bonhoeffer, *Ethics,* trans. N. H. Smith (London: SCM Press, 1955), p. 62; *WE,* pp. 180, 182, 184, 241 f., 259 f.

[4] Ebeling, *op. cit.,* p. 159.

[5] *Ibid.,* p. 363.

[6] Cf., for example, E. Fuchs, "Glaube und Geschichte im Blick auf die Frage nach dem historischen Jesus," *Zeitschrift für Theologie und Kirche,* 54.2, 1957; also the discussion in Chapter III, *supra.*

[7] Cf. T. R. Miles, *Religion and the Scientific Outlook,* pp. 147 ff., on the meaninglessness of "qualified literal theism," a faith expressed by Flew's believing explorer.

in empirical attitudes in some way. Our objection to a certain use of the word "God" says as much about our own empirical attitudes as it does about Bultmann and Ebeling. The nature and extent of these empirical attitudes will become clearer as the study develops. It can only be suggested, not proved, that these attitudes are more common among contemporary "believers" than Bultmann or Ebeling appear to recognize, the force of this suggestion being measured by the degree to which a method consistent with such attitudes is found to be helpful for the reader.

The contemporary theological fashion of setting the Christian Gospel over against "religion" does not clarify our problem.[8] According to this view of the matter, the Gospel proclaims God's act of grace reaching down to rescue man, whereas religion has to do with man reaching up to find or define God. The "religionless" man, however, who can come to terms with life quite apart from this literally nonsensical entity called "God," will not be impressed by the difference between the Gospel and "religion." There is a difference between them, but both the Gospel and "religion" have so much more in common than either has with the scepticism of a man like Flew that the distinction loses its interest. The empiricist in us finds the heart of the difficulty not in what is said about God, but in the very talking about God at all. We do not know "what" God is, and we cannot understand how the word "God" is being used. It seems to function as a name, yet theologians tell us that we cannot use it as we do other names, to refer to something quite specific. If it is meant to refer to an "existential encounter," a point of view, or the speaker's self-understanding, surely a more appropriate expression could be found. The problem is not solved, moreover, by substituting other words for the word *God:* one could supply the letter $X$ (Flew used the word *gardener* in his parable) and the problem would remain, for the difficulty has to do with how $X$ functions. The problem of the Gospel in a secular age is a problem of the logic of its apparently meaningless language, and linguistic analysts will give us help in clarifying it. We dare to call *our* problem *the* problem not because we have access to what everyone or anyone else means by "secular age" or "Gospel," but because we dare to hope that what we have found helpful for our own understanding may prove helpful for others, who may then identify the problem to some extent as we have identified it.

## Linguistic Analyses of Religious Assertions

Flew's parable, with which we began our study, has been answered by R. M. Hare,[9] who begins by granting that Flew is "completely victorious"

---

[8] Bonhoeffer, who approved of this fashion, gave Barth credit for being one of its main champions. *WE*, p. 219.

[9] *New Essays*, pp. 99–105.

on the grounds which he has marked out. Hare grants that if religious or theological assertions are taken as statements about "how things are" (this is indeed the form they seem to have: e.g., "God loves all men"; "Jesus Christ is Lord"; "the wages of sin is death"), they must be judged as meaningless. The logic of Flew's parable is perfectly sound. Having made this concession, Hare has cleared the way for his reply. He begins by telling another parable about a student who has a peculiar attitude about dons: he is convinced that they all want to kill him. However many apparently friendly dons he meets, however friends try to persuade him by recalling his own experience or theirs, his attitude does not change.

Hare has invented the word *blik* for a fundamental attitude. The student in his parable has an insane "blik" about dons; we have a sane one, we would say, for Hare points out that we are never without a "blik," or we could not say that the student is insane, that he is wrong and we are right. A "blik" is not achieved by empirical inquiry. The basic presuppositions we have about the world are not verifiable, and yet everything we do depends on them, as Hume taught us. Such a presupposition or set of presuppositions (and all men have them) are not to be regarded as *explanations*. That is Flew's mistake; he took his Believer's "blik" to be an explanation of the clearing in the jungle, which it clearly is not. Hare points out that "bliks" are serious matters for those who hold them, whether we judge any particular "blik" to be right or wrong, and everyone has a "blik." Consequently, the detachment of Flew's two explorers is unreal.

Flew's response to Hare's suggestion focuses nicely on our problem: [10]

> Any attempt to analyse Christian religious utterances as expressions or affirmations of a *blik* rather than as (at least would-be) assertions about the cosmos is fundamentally misguided. *First,* because thus interpreted they would be entirely unorthodox. If Hare's religion really is a *blik,* involving no cosmological assertions about the nature and activities of a supposed personal creator, then surely he is not a Christian at all? *Second,* because thus interpreted, they would scarcely do the job they do. If they were not even intended as assertions then many religious activities would become fraudulent, or merely silly. If 'You ought *because* it is God's will' asserts no more than 'You ought,' then the person who prefers the former phraseology is not really giving a reason, but a fraudulent substitute for one, a dialectical dud check.

The issue between these two philosophers does not concern the logic or function of language. Neither of them, moreover, has questioned the empirical picture of the world of the twentieth century. Both grant that a simple literal theism, whose assertions could be put to an empirical test like that of Elijah before Mt. Carmel, is untenable. In other words, they agree in denying an "objectified" God. They also agree, however, that if a simple

---

[10] *Ibid.,* pp. 107–08.

literal theism is untenable, a qualified literal ("nonobjectified") theism is meaningless. It is dead by the death of a thousand qualifications. If God is really "wholly other," we cannot speak of him at all. If statements about God are "to be interpreted exhaustively and without remainder" as statements about man, they cannot be meaningful statements about God. Where these philosophers disagree is on the nature of Christianity. One calls the statements of faith a collection of cosmological assertions; the other sees them as expressions of a "blik," an orientation, a commitment to see the world in a certain way, and a way of life following inevitably upon this orientation. What Hare is suggesting is that a man's faith and his theology have a meaning, even though the theistic rug has been pulled out from under him.

Not all analysts of the language of faith have gone this far, but Ian T. Ramsey, in arguing for the meaningfulness of language about God, offers support for and further elaboration of Hare's concept of a "blik." He argues that the language of faith combines the language of discernment, of an admittedly special sort, with the language of commitment, of a sort which covers the totality of life and the world.[11] Statements of faith direct our attention to certain kinds of situations: situations of disclosure, when "the light dawns," and the situation becomes alive and new. The emphasis is not only on the disclosure or discernment, but also on the resulting commitment, whereby what we now "see" becomes important and determines our subsequent seeing. In such situations, the believer makes use of odd words like "God."

The function of such words is clarified with the help of Ramsey's idea of models and qualifiers. The model of "father," for example, points in a certain direction, inviting us to follow this direction. But it is qualified by such words as "eternal" or "omnipotent," to indicate that the word is only a model, that we should push on and on and on . . . until the light dawns, and the situation, and, with it, all things, takes on "depth," or rather, until we see that the "depth" is there to be discerned. Ramsey grants that all this sounds very close to a psychological explanation of religious language, but he argues that it is false to say that such an interpretation of human experience is "purely subjective," since there is in fact no such thing as a purely subjective experience. Every experience is an experience of something.

The language of faith is nothing if not odd, Ramsey says, and he stresses its peculiarity in order to counter two "popular misconceptions: that those with an intense affection for ordinary language must necessarily deny metaphysics," and "that those who defend metaphysics must necessarily trade in occult realms and shadowy worlds." [12] One example of the odd

---

[11] Ramsey, *op. cit.*, pp. 18 ff.
[12] I. T. Ramsey, *Freedom and Immortality* (London: SCM Press, 1960), p. 152.

character of the language of faith is the name of God, which the Hebrews avoided whenever possible. The significance of this avoidance of God's name lies in the linguistic fact that discovering a name is typical of situations of disclosure or discernment. When we *assign* a name to something, no disclosure is involved; we are simply in the realm of external information. When someone tells us his name, however, or when we learn a name, the situation is a religious one, involving mystery and eliciting awe. The use of the revealed name recalls the mystery of self-disclosure.[13] The text of the revelation of the divine name in chapter 3 of Exodus is, moreover, an example of the final form of the language of loyalty. The last answer to why I have acted as I have, after all the partial explanations, is the statement, "I'm I." Behind any other things I might say, like "because I decided to do it," or "because he asked me to do it," lies this ultimate causal explanation. The series of "whys" of any decision, any case of loyalty or commitment, must finally come to rest at the "logical stop-card": "I'm I." [14] The word "God" also, Ramsey says, functions as the tautology "I'm I," and it is just this statement, "I am who I am," which stands in place of the revealed name in chapter 3 of Exodus. This tautology marks the limit which religious language approaches and to which it tries to point. The limit is never part of the series of variables which approach that limit, yet there is a relationship between the variables and the limit.[15]

Another example of the oddness of biblical language is the story of the resurrection of Jesus. The question "Did the resurrection occur?" is misleadingly simple, for if "resurrection" referred only to such things as an empty tomb and a resuscitated body, then one could acknowledge the resurrection and yet not be a believer. What the Christian believes about the resurrection of Jesus has something to do with these observable factors, but

---

[13] *Religious Language*, pp. 108 ff.

[14] *Ibid.*, pp. 63 ff.

[15] At several places, Ramsey touches on a point which has been of concern to William Poteat: the possibility of understanding the function of theological language in the light of the similarly strange use of the word "I." (William Poteat, " 'I Will Die': An Analysis," *Philosophical Quarterly*, Vol. IX, No. 34 [1959], pp. 3–15.) Poteat has urged reflection upon the way in which "I" functions when we say, "I was born," or "I will die," where it operates in a way quite different from that of the word 'he" when we say, "He was born," or "He will die." "He" functions in a straightforwardly empirical manner. We can say, "He will die," and also, after the fact, "He died." But we cannot use the first person singular of the verb "to die" in the past, unless we have first changed radically the manner of using the word "die." This indicates something odd about the logic of the verbs "to die" and "to be born," but more important, it indicates the odd logic of the first person singular pronoun. Of course, I can say many things about myself which are empirical and can also be said of me by someone else. But there are also other things which only I can say about myself and which cannot be translated "exhaustively and without remainder" into what others may say about me. This line of reflection is related to the distinction which existentialists make between the words "existential" and "existentialist." The first has to do with the "I"; the second can be talked about equally well in the third person.

it is not identical with them. In fact, the question "Did the resurrection occur?" is logically much more like the question asked of a situation in which a man has jumped from a bridge to rescue a drowning child: "Was that a case of duty?" The empirical evidence is not irrelevant, but the evidence will never settle either question. The word "resurrection" (like the words "duty," "love," and "God") directs us to the sort of situation in which a discernment fundamental to our whole conception of life and a response of commitment may take place. Such situations exceed empirical description, however relevant description may be to our discernment.

A further illustration of Ramsey's analysis of the language of faith may be seen in his treatment of the language of classical Christology:

> For the Early Christians, Jesus Christ was the occasion of and the object of "disclosure" situations for which the word "God" would have been appropriate currency. Further, much could be said about Jesus Christ which was, on the face of it, straightforwardly empirical, viz. that he was tired, that he wept, and so on. So we have what are *prima facie,* two logically different languages competing as descriptions of the object of "disclosure" or "revelation." There then arises the problem of how these two languages can somehow be integrated, for in the Christian disclosure *only one* "object" is disclosed.
>
> Hence arises the concept of "hypostatic" unity, which we may interpret both from a linguistic and a "factual" point of view.
>
> (i) To know what hypostatic unity is *in fact,* there must be evoked a Christian disclosure situation with Jesus Christ as the occasion and object of it.[16]

Preaching and the celebration of the Lord's Supper are obviously intended to evoke such a situation. The object and occasion of disclosure is the man Jesus, and the disclosure comes (if it does come) when "the light dawns" and we find ourselves involved in what existentialists would call an "encounter." All sorts of models may help us toward this situation, but none can either produce or describe it. Ramsey's analysis continues:

> (ii) As far as *language* goes, . . . the doctrine of *communicato idiomatum* (the participation of either "nature" of Christ in the properties or attributes of the other) and the word "hypostasis" may both be seen as an ancient attempt to deal with what nowadays would be called the problem of complementary languages and their unity, a problem which is raised especially by recent developments in scientific method.
>
> Let me emphasize that hypostasis would only be successful in unifying two languages if it is odd enough never to be given except by reference to a Christian disclosure situation. If it is to be the logical bond that Christian doctrine wishes it to be, it cannot be modelled. If it is to do this work it is quite impossible (*logically* impossible) to produce a model for it.[17]

---

[16] *Religious Language,* pp. 166 f.
[17] *Ibid.,* pp. 168 f.

We have quoted Ramsey at length because this passage is one of the rare examples of the beginning of an analysis of the language of Christology. Moreover, Ramsey has made in effect a further development of Hare's concept of "blik." A "blik" involves a perspective entailing a commitment, and Ramsey has clarified this with his analysis of the language of discernment and commitment. When this analysis is applied to the language of Christology, it discloses two sorts of languages: one is the language of a "blik"; the other is that of straightforward empirical observation. Both sorts of language are used about the same person, Jesus of Nazareth. But the language of Christology is appropriate only to one who himself has discerned what Christians discern, for whom Jesus has become the occasion for a new discernment which has led to a commitment involving his whole perspective. We can summarize by saying that the language of Christology is language about Jesus of Nazareth on the part of those for whom he has been the occasion and remains the definition of their "blik."

Another analysis of the language of faith, similar to those of Hare and Ramsey, has been made by T. R. Miles. Accepting, as Hare has done, the argument of Flew, Miles recommends what he calls "the way of silence qualified by parables." In place of the language of "simple literal theism" (God walking in the garden of Eden, looking down upon and scattering the builders of the tower of Babel, smelling Abraham's sacrifice), which few men would use today, and the language of "qualified literal theism" (the language of the Believer in Flew's parable), which proves to have no "cash value," Miles urges the course of silence, in which no claims or assertions are made. The Believer may qualify his silence, however, by what Miles calls the theistic parable.[18]

Any parable has three characteristics: the question of the literal truth of the parable is unimportant, the language is straightforwardly empirical, and, most important, the parable has a message. It invites us to view in a certain way the situation in connection with which the parable is told. Empirical considerations may be relevant for deciding on the usefulness of a particular parable, however. If, for example, it could be proved historically that Jesus "was fallible on matters of importance, it would be all the more difficult to accept any parable which says that he is the incarnate son of God."[19] Ultimately, however, the choice of parables is a matter of "personal conviction rather than rational argument."[20] The believer is the man who has chosen to qualify his silence with the theistic parable, like the one expressed in the doctrine of the creation of the world by a loving Father. The question

---

[18] Miles, *op. cit.*, pp. 161 ff.
[19] *Ibid.*, p. 172.
[20] *Ibid.*, p. 171.

of whether the parable is "objectively true" can only be met by silence; but the whole outlook of the man who chooses the theistic parable is changed.

One of the most radical contributions to the analysis of the language of faith has been made by R. B. Braithwaite. We shall summarize his lectures [21] because his argument is important for our study. Braithwaite begins by applying the verification principle of modern philosophy in its sharpest form to the language of the Christian faith. This principle implies

> that the primary question becomes, not whether a religious statement such as that a personal God created the world is true or false, but how it could be known to be true or false. Unless this latter question can be answered, the religious statement has no ascertainable meaning and there is nothing expressed by it to be either true or false. Moreover a religious statement cannot be believed without being understood, and it can only be understoood by an under- standing of the circumstances which would verify or falsify it. Meaning is not logically prior to the possibility of verification: we do not first learn the mean- ing of a statement, and afterwards consider what would make us call it true or false; the two understandings are one and indivisible.[22]

Now "a hypothesis which is consistent with every possible empirical fact is not an empirical one." Unless an answer can be given as to how the world or the course of history would have been different without God, or unless it were admitted that if either had been different we could have concluded that there is no God, religious or theological propositions cannot be em- pirical.[23] In short, if Elijah's empirical test is no longer to be allowed, then neither are assertions that Elijah's God has acted empirically in this world!

Braithwaite then states his thesis: religious assertions are in fact *used as* moral assertions.[24] Moral assertions share with religious ones the character- istic of being neither logically necessary nor empirical; yet they have a use: that of guiding conduct. With the significant modification which has been made in the early verification principle (so that philosophers would now say that "the meaning of a statement is given by the way in which it is used"),[25] it is now realized that "the primary use of a moral assertion [is] that of expressing the intention of the asserter to act in a particular sort of way specified in the assertion." [26]

Braithwaite then returns to his thesis that religious assertions are "pri-

---

[21] *An Empiricist's View of Religious Belief* (Cambridge: Cambridge University Press, 1955).

[22] Braithwaite, *op. cit.,* pp. 2, 3.

[23] *Ibid.,* pp. 6, 7.

[24] *Ibid.,* p. 11.

[25] *Ibid.,* p. 10. Braithwaite refers to Wittgenstein, *op. cit.,* §§ 340, 352, 559 f. Cf. note 22, Chapter I, *supra.*

[26] *Ibid.,* p. 12.

marily declarations of adherence to a policy of action, declarations of commitment to a way of life," and continues his argument:

> That the way of life led by the believer is highly relevant to the sincerity of his religious convictions has been insisted upon . . . by Christianity. . . . The view which I put forward for your consideration is that the intention of a Christian to follow a Christian way of life is not only the criterion for the sincerity of his belief in the assertions of Christianity; it is the criterion for the meaningfulness of his assertions. Just as the meaning of a moral assertion is given by its use in expressing the asserter's intention to act, so far as in him lies, in accordance with the moral principle involved, so the meaning of a religious assertion is given by its use in expressing the asserter's intention to follow a specified policy of behaviour. To say that it is belief in the dogmas of religion which is the cause of the believer's intending to behave as he does is to put the cart before the horse: it is the intention to behave which constitutes what is known as religious conviction.[27]

Braithwaite is aware of two objections which might be raised here: not all theological assertions imply action; and, there is a difference between religion and morality. He meets these objections, first, by admitting that religious assertions should be taken as a group and in context. He insists, however, that "unless a Christian's assertion that God is love (*agape*)—which I take to epitomize the assertions of the Christian religion—be taken to declare his intention to follow an agapeistic way of life, he could be asked what is the connection between the assertion and the intention, between Christian belief and Christian practice." [28] (This would presumably be Braithwaite's exegesis of I John 4:20: "If any one says, 'I love God,' and hates his brother, he is a liar.") Second, he also grants that being filled with *agape* is more than acting agapeistically: "it also includes an agapeistic frame of mind." [29] But more important, for Braithwaite, is the following distinction: "A religious assertion will . . . have a propositional element which is lacking in a purely moral assertion, in that it will refer to a story as well as to an intention." Consequently, "to assert the whole set of assertions of the Christian religion is both to tell the Christian doctrinal story and to confess allegiance to the Christian way of life." [30] He notes that what he calls "story" has also been called by other names: parable, fairy tale, alle-

---

[27] *Ibid.,* pp. 15 f.

[28] *Ibid.,* p. 18.

[29] *Ibid.,* p. 21.

[30] *Ibid.,* p. 24: "Entertainment in thought (of a part or the whole of the Christian story) forms the context in which Christian resolutions are made, which serves to distinguish Christian assertions from those made by adherents of another religion or of no religion." We would urge the reader, who may feel that this is insufficient and that there must be something distinctively "Christian" about the actions or words themselves of believers, to reflect on the motives of such feelings.

gory, fable, tale, and myth. He prefers the word "story" because it is neutral, "implying neither that the story is believed nor that it is disbelieved." [31] The Christian story includes straight history and also material clearly not historical. But Braithwaite insists that belief in the empirical truth of the stories "is not the proper criterion for deciding whether or not an assertion is a Christian one. A man is not, I think, a professing Christian unless he both proposes to live according to Christian moral principles and associates his intention with thinking of Christian stories; but he need not believe that the empirical propositions presented by the stories correspond to empirical fact." [32]

What is the function of these stories and how are they related to this intention to act? Braithwaite answers that the stories have a psychological and causal relationship to the intention: to say that an action is "doing the will of God" helps us to carry it through, and Braithwaite feels that theologians need to keep in mind the psychological fact that men's behaviour is determined not only by intellectual considerations, but also by phantasies, imaginations, and hopes.[33] He concludes his essay by remarking that in his analysis of theological language, he has not come across an entity called belief. "Religious belief," he concludes, is not "a species of ordinary belief, of belief in propositions. A moral belief is an intention to behave in a certain way: a religious belief is an intention to behave in a certain way (a moral belief) together with the entertainment of certain stories associated with the intention in the mind of the believer." [34]

If there is a weak link in this chain of reasoning, it is Braithwaite's understanding of the function of the Christian "story" and its relationship to the intention to lead the Christian "way of life." While his psychological observation is in order, his solution does not do justice to the indispensable role of the "story" in the kerygma. We shall return to a further analysis of this role in our reconstruction. The position of Braithwaite is, however, sufficiently close to the others we have examined to allow us to speak of a rough consensus among contemporary analysts of the language of faith, in spite of the variety of thought within that consensus.

Not all analytic philosophers, of course, have approached the language of faith in the way we have presented. A number of philosophers have argued that faith is a kind of knowledge and that faith-statements are to be understood cognitively, somewhat as Flew understands them. They would take issue with Hare, Braithwaite, and Miles, among others, insisting that

---

[31] *Ibid.,* p. 26.
[32] *Ibid.,* pp. 26 f. The word "principles" in this context means "assertions" or "convictions."
[33] *Ibid.,* pp. 27, 28, 31.
[34] *Ibid.,* pp. 32 f.

faith is logically "belief that . . ." before it is "belief in. . . ." Christianity, they argue, is not essentially a conviction, commitment, or attitude, but entry into and living in a relationship with a transcendent being, and it stands or falls with the meaningfulness of its assertions concerning that transcendent being. Passing over the difficulties arising from placing the word "relationship" alongside of the expression "transcendent being," we notice a common line of argument among several philosophers holding this position.[35] Fundamental to their case is the concept of undifferentiated or natural theism. Arguing from a sense of contingency, or from some other variation of the argument from design, they believe that most men, or a number great enough to lead us to take note of their ideas, have at least some vague concept of that which is *not* contingent and to which the designation "divine" would seem to them to be appropriate. On the basis of this general concept of the divine, certain events are interpreted by religious men as manifesting in some way and to some degree the character, will, or activity of this transcendent being. In some forms of this argument, a strong appeal is made to Jesus as the authority for looking to certain particular events and interpreting them as revelations of the divine. In the last resort, those who take this approach to the language of faith grant that verification must apply to this language, but they argue that this can only be done in the *eschaton,* in the final day of the Kingdom. In the *eschaton,* we shall see clearly whether or not faith as knowledge is correct. If that is no proof for the present, it is at least a justification for saying that faith-statements are meaningful, even though we cannot yet be in the position to carry through this verification. Logically, however, the statements of faith are in principle verifiable, and therefore meaningful, as cognitive assertions.

The choice of a noncognitive, "blik" conception of faith, rather than of a cognitive conception, will be fundamental to our study. We make this choice for both logical and theological reasons. The cognitive approach requires speaking of that which it admits is ineffable. It involves speaking of God by analogy, yet it is granted by its proponents that they cannot say to what extent the analogies are apt and proper. More difficult, however, is the problem of an appeal to eschatological verification. If "in heaven" there is neither marriage nor giving in marriage, then it is at least questionable if there is what philosophers call "verification" in the *eschaton.* On what basis could the possibility of eschatological verification be affirmed or denied? The language in which this question must be settled is, for better or worse, the language of men, not the "language of angels." To speak of verification

---

[35] Representative of this position are I. M. Crombie, "The Possibility of Theological Statements," *Faith and Logic,* pp. 31 ff., and John Hick, *Faith and Knowledge* (Ithaca, N.Y.: Cornell University Press, 1957) ; "Theology and Verification," *Theology Today,* Vol. XVII, No. 1 (1960), pp. 12 ff.

as philosophers do presupposes certain empirical attitudes, and no one knows the empirical attitudes which would be either possible in or appropriate to the *eschaton.*

We reject the cognitive approach to theological language, however, not primarily because it is logically puzzling, but because of certain theological commitments out of which this study has arisen. That approach builds its case on a natural sense of the divine, on natural religion and a natural revelation. The history of theology, seen from the perspective of modern kerygmatic theology, suggests that this is a road leading into the wilderness. Within the Protestant tradition, that road has been clearly charted and firmly marked with a "dead-end" sign by the work of Karl Barth, and we see no reason to ignore the warning. Christian faith has troubles enough in the twentieth century without retracing the misleading path opened up for Protestantism by the rationalist orthodoxy of the seventeenth century, followed to its unproductive end in the nineteenth century.

The cognitive approach to faith-statements presented by some linguistic analysts leads into the old inner contradiction of earlier forms of natural theology. It begins by speaking of a divine being of whom it *cannot* be said that this is the God of grace, the God who finds man wandering into idolatry with every conception he forms of the divine, the God who comes and makes himself known to man, not through, but in spite of, man's natural conceptions of the divine. Either the "God" of which Christians have tried to speak is the God of grace and *self*-revelation, or he is the neutral "it" of natural theology. The "divine being" of the cognitive approach is not easily assimilable to Pascal's " *'Dieu d'Abraham, Dieu d'Isaac, Dieu de Jacob,'* non des philosophes et—des— savants."

To follow the cognitive approach to religious language would contradict our point of departure. It tends to mark off a certain area of experience as "religious," and it argues for a religious way of knowing, in contrast to other (secular?) ways of knowing. This approach leads Christians into the trap of the reductionist tendency of nineteenth-century theology, where they are tempted to fight a defensive action against all other knowledge in order to defend some small area of their own which they may call the proper sphere of theology, concerning which they may cry—but surely cry in vain— that nonreligious knowledge should not try to tread on this holy ground. On the basis of these logical and theological objections, we judge the cognitive approach to theological language to be inadequate to the character of secular thought and to the heart of the Gospel.

We cannot argue, of course, for some objective, normative definition of verification or of the Gospel. When we call this approach inadequate, we are exposing our own categorial commitments which we see reflected in some modern kerygmatic theology, some modern analytic philosophy, and indicated with the word "secular." We can only acknowledge that our commitments are such as to lead us to reject a search for a religious preserve to be investigated by a special religious way of knowing, and we are committed to a Gospel which begins, not with an argument for undifferentiated theism, but with the impact of whatever it was that happened on Easter in the context of a particular history. With such commitments, we have no choice but to return to the consensus of such analysts as Hare and Braithwaite about the character of the language of faith and to assess its possibilities as a tool for determining what we have called the secular meaning of the Gospel.

The first point of consensus is that "simple literal theism" is wrong and that "qualified literal theism" is meaningless. The second agreement lies in the implicit or explicit conviction that the language of faith does have a meaning, and that this meaning can be explored and clarified by linguistic analysis. The third consensus is a concern to take Christianity seriously as a way of life, even though a straightforward use of the word "God" must be abandoned.

Simple literal theism is wrong and qualified literal theism is meaningless. The first of these assertions is another way of making Bultmann's point that myth is no longer tenable; the idea of the empirical intervention of a supernatural "God" in the world of men has been ruled out by the influence of modern science on our thinking. In making such statements, we reveal our own commitments to modern science, and we would only add that modern thought tends to grant the validity of the findings of the natural sciences. For those holding these commitments, thunderbolts can no longer be explained as weapons of the wrath of an invisible God, and the phrase "God did this," therefore, cannot logically mean what it says.[36] If we begin to qualify this phrase, however, we find one qualification calling for another until nothing is left of the original assertion. Linguistic analysis challenges the qualified theism of Bultmann and Ogden as much as that of more conservative theologians. Whether objectifying or nonobjectifying, language about a "God who acts" must be interpreted in some other way.

The language of faith has a meaning, nonetheless; it has a function which may be clarified by linguistic analysis. The language of Christian faith is the language of a believer, one who has been "caught" by the Gospel. In so far as his "blik" is functioning, his language is the language of faith, whether he is speaking about some generally recognized religious subject, such as "God," or of some so-called secular subject, like politics or his job. The function of his words may be to enlighten his listener concerning his "blik." In other circumstances they may take the form of an invitation to share that "blik." Or they may simply be a notification that he must take a

---

[36] For a similar criticism of such assertions of biblical theology as "God acts" and "God speaks," cf. Langdon B. Gilkey, "Cosmology, Ontology, and the Travail of Biblical Language," *The Journal of Religion,* Vol. XLI, No. 3 (1961), pp. 194 ff.

particular course of action, for the unexpressed reason that he sees things in a certain way. In each case, the fact that a believer is speaking and the circumstances in which he is speaking may not be ignored. The actual function of the words is the key to understanding the language of faith.

Finally, the language of faith has meaning when it is taken to refer to the Christian way of life; it is not a set of cosmological assertions. The Christian "way of life," an expression recalling the New Testament designation of life in Christ as "the Way" (Acts 9:2), is central to the linguistic interpretation we have been considering. It contains elements of wonder, awe, and worship, but it is bound up with a basic conviction concerning the world and man's place in it which bears directly on decisions and actions. There is a parallel to the existentialists' emphasis on decision, but room is left for attitudes and ways of seeing things for which we would not ordinarily use the word "decision." There is a note of British calm and logical reflection in this conception of what goes to make up the Christian "way of life" or "authentic existence." Yet for these thinkers also, a "blik," the discernment and commitment of faith, is by definition something which is "lived."

This attempt to define a consensus does justice to no single position of the language analysts, yet our summary indicates the trend of their interpretations of Christianity. It remains to evaluate the method and results of these philosophers for a reconstruction of the kerygma and Christology.

## A Method for Reconstruction

From Flew's parable through Braithwaite's argument, the analyses of theological language constitute a clarification which shows us where problems may be dissolved and where the real problems of the language of faith lie. This clarification has been accomplished by a frankly empirical method which reflects the thinking of an industrialized, scientific age. It has taken certain empirical attitudes characteristic of modern thought seriously and accepted them without qualification. In the frank recognition that the lot of oblique language about God is no better, and in some ways worse, than that of simple literal theism, we come face to face with our real problem of understanding the Gospel today: the difficulty of finding any meaningful way to speak of God. We can no longer share the faith of the man who thought that his god lived in a tree and that his god would die if the tree were burned down, or who conceded the weakness of a god who did not respond to calls for help from the dangers of nature or man. We should say he was mistaken, but his religious assertions were understandable. An assertion of qualified literal theism, on the other hand, is meaningless, and the moral exasperation of Flew's sceptical explorer is not to be dismissed lightly by those who claim to serve the truth. Miles's suggestion of silence is very much in order at this point, and if theology at its best has not meant to infringe on this silence, its reticence has not always been obvious.

These analyses of theological language express with clarity and force the unity of ethics and theology. Contemporary theology has said that Christian ethics is dependent on theology; these philosophers say that theology may not be independent of ethics. They have acknowledged, of course in their own way, the warning against saying "Lord, Lord" (Luke 6:46), or "The Temple of the Lord! The Temple of the Lord!" (Jer. 7:4). They even emphasize the empirical, human, historical, and ethical side of the Gospel at the expense of its divine, cosmological, transhistorical, and supernatural elements. Christologically speaking, these interpretations imply holding to the humanity of Christ, to the man Jesus of Nazareth, and letting the issue of his divinity fall where it may.

Our last statement is an exaggeration, but it reminds us of the question raised by Flew in his response to Hare's suggestion of "blik": what is the real issue in Christian faith: Jesus or God, Christology or Theology? The linguistic analysts we have considered, especially Hare and Braithwaite, tend to choose the former, in contrast to Ogden. Flew raises the question of orthodoxy, but what is orthodoxy in this era when many sincere Christians do not know what to do with the word "God" or can use it only in a way entirely different from the "orthodox" way of the early centuries of Christianity? Today, we cannot even understand the Nietzschian cry that "God is dead!" for if it were so, how could we know? No, the problem now is that the *word* "God" is dead.

A loose way of characterizing these analyses of the language of faith is to say that "God-statements" have been translated into "man-statements." (This is similar to Ogden's thesis that "statements about God and his activities *are* statements about human existence," [37] but it omits his addition of "and *vice versa.*") But these philosophers have also made it clear that "man-statements," or "statements about human existence," are far from being all alike or on a single level. Man is involved in a multitude of language-games, and to take them all as the same game is to produce logical chaos. There is all the world of difference between saying, "The movement of abstract expressionism is dying, I'm told," by one making conversation, and "I am dying," when the medical evidence is clear. To confine ourselves to the language developed by men (and what other choice is available to us?) appears to confine our subject to the realm which is at least in principle open to human investigation, but that does not exclude the richness and variety within this human realm. There are man-statements modeled on nature and the machine, and there are others modeled on the odd word "I." They are

[37] Ogden, *op. cit.,* p. 137.

hardly the same. If we want to say that, although we are not sure what we mean when we speak of God, our concern is with Jesus of Nazareth and with our life in the world today, this concern could certainly be expressed in more than one way. The road ahead is not predetermined, nor is it dull and flat.

Our brief survey of several attempts to interpret the language of faith by means of linguistic analysis does not of itself give us a method for our reconstructive task. It does suggest, however, a basis for understanding the language of faith which can be applied to the biblical and the patristic assertions concerning Jesus of Nazareth, but only a short section in one of Ramsey's books gives even a hint of what such an interpretation of the Gospel might be. The faith-statements which have occupied these philosophers belong essentially to the area of "natural theology" as it was taught in the eighteenth century. The names of Barth and Bultmann are not unknown to them, but the revolution in philosophy of the past fifty years does not seem to have taken cognizance of the revolution in theology of almost exactly the same period. It may be too strong to say that they have been working with the religious language learned in Sunday school, but the theologian cannot help feeling that the most serious problems of faith have not been dealt with when the logical difficulty of saying, "There is a God," or "God exists," is pointed out. Theologians have been saying this themselves for some time. The discussions in modern theology have centered around the kerygma and "biblical theology," while these philosophers have concentrated on the doctrines falling under the traditional rubric of "natural theology." The application of the methods of modern philosophy to the problems of modern theology has been barely begun, and we wish to proceed in this new direction.

For the particular language-game which we are playing, imprecisely identified as "seeking the secular meaning of the Gospel," the heart of the method of linguistic analysis lies in the use of the verification principle—that the meaning of a word is its use in its context. The meaning of a statement is to be found in, and is identical with, the function of that statement. If a statement has a function, so that it may in principle be verified or falsified, the statement is meaningful, and unless or until a theological statement can be submitted in some way to verification, it cannot be said to have a meaning in our language-game.

This means that the context of the language of faith may not be neglected. Any attempt to interpret the statements of theology as though they had been found on separate scraps of paper will be misleading. The words "Jesus is Lord," for example, have no meaning unless they were spoken or written by someone for some reason. We shall have to ask why they were said in a given situation, what they were intended to accomplish. The function will vary to some extent with the context, and as it varies, the precise meaning will change. In one situation, the believer may be reminding himself of his own "blik." In another, he may be trying to indicate to another that he has just this "blik" and not another. These functions are related, but they are not identical.

Linguistic analysis calls our attention to the wide variety of language-games and *kinds* of words. There are situations and appropriate words, for example, which center in discernment, duty, or commitment. Linguistic analysts warn us not to mix the language of such situations with that appropriate to giving "factual" information, for example. To do so is to endanger all understanding, for ourselves as well as for others. There are also words which function in odd ways. "I" is such a word, and the fact that the Christian creed begins with this odd word should warn us to expect the whole series of creedal declarations to be odd. And since this first logical oddity is followed by another, "believe," which points to the language of discernment and commitment, Christians should beware, for example, of a question about "the historic facts of the Virgin Birth and other articles in the Creed." [38] To introduce the word "facts" at this point is to beg for logical confusion and linguistic chaos.

For the sake of clarity, believers should make clear when and how they are using odd words. If "God" is not a word which refers to something, they should be careful not to use it in a way that suggests that it does. If they are talking about a "blik," rather than about "how things are," they should say so. Whatever else may be said about Flew's parable, it must be granted that (following Hare's interpretation) the language of the believing explorer was at least misleading. If he meant something different by the word "gardener" from what his sceptical colleague had in mind, he might at least have made this clear. It would have saved them both a number of sleepless nights.

These remarks on a method of analyzing theological statements reveal that we share certain empirical attitudes with some linguistic analysts. We have not said how far these attitudes take us nor to what degree they are shared, and our use of the word "empirical" has therefore been somewhat loose. It is clear that we have little difficulty with the statement that John is heavier than Jane, and we are reasonably sure of the empirical footing of this assertion. Do we want to say that "John loves Jane" is empirical? We certainly want to say that it is a comprehensible and meaningful statement in a "secular" age, and that this is because it meets certain empirical expectations which we have upon hearing statements about human activities and relationships. But we should also want to say that the empirical commitments of what we have loosely called secularism does not exclude our saying

---

[38] From a protest made to the General Theological Seminary, reported in *The Living Church*, Sept. 17, 1961, p. 6.

that there is a difference between my saying "John loves Jane" and John saying "I love Jane." The empirical attitudes of secularism, as we are using the term, have room also for this third statement. The further clarification of these attitudes will arise from a consideration of the history of Jesus of Nazareth and the things which the first believers said about him. This is to admit that the word "secular" in the title of this study is itself a function of what we take to be the Gospel.

## Suggested Additional Readings

RELIGIOUS LANGUAGE

Aquinas, St. Thomas. "The Names of God," *Summa Theologica*. Book I, Question 12, Articles 1–12. One of the fountainheads of discussion of the nature of the analogical knowledge of God.

Blackstone, William T. *The Problem of Religious Language*. Englewood Cliffs, N.J.: Prentice-Hall, 1963. A comprehensive review of the contemporary philosophical debate on the cognitive or noncognitive character of religious language.

Cajetan (Tommaso de Vio). *The Analogy of Names*. Trans., Edward A. Bushinski and Henry J. Koren. Pittsburgh: Duquesne University Press, 1953. Cajetan sets forth here an influential examination of analogy in religious language.

Cassirer, Ernst. *Language and Myth*. Trans., Suzanne K. Langer. New York: Harper & Row, 1946. (Also published in paperback by Dover Publications, Inc.) An investigation of the mythical element in human thinking by a man who helped make this an important area of study in modern philosophy.

Cusa, Nicholaus. *Of Learned Ignorance*. Trans., Germain Heron. London: Routledge & Kegan Paul, 1954. See especially Chapters 24–26. A medieval philosopher discourses on the impossibility of a positive knowledge of the attributes of God.

*Faith and Logic*. Edited by Basil Mitchell. Boston: Beacon Press, 1957. A collection of essays by British philosophers and theologians that analyze religious concepts.

Farrer, Austin M. *The Glass of Vision*. London: Dacre Press, 1948. A provocative discussion of symbols as the media of religious knowledge.

Ferré, Frederick. *Language, Logic and God*. New York: Harper & Row, 1961. A good introduction to the efforts of British philosophers to bring linguistic analysis to bear on religious and theological language.

*Kerygma and Myth*. Edited by Hans W. Bartsch. Trans., Reginald Fuller. London: Society for the Publication of Christian Knowledge, 1954. A collection of essays which assess the possibility and legitimacy of removing the mythological concepts from the New Testament in an effort to interpret its message.

Langer, Suzanne K. *Philosophy in a New Key*. Cambridge, Mass.: Harvard University Press, 1942. (Also published in paperback by The New American

Library of World Literature, Mentor series.) A good interpretation of the role of myth in knowledge.

Martin, C. B. *Religious Belief*. Ithaca, N.Y.: Cornell University Press, 1959. Formulates the chief issue concerning the cognitive value of religious experience.

MacIntyre, Alasdair C. *Difficulties in Christian Belief*. London: Student Christian Movement, 1959. A brief survey of major problems clearly delineated by a British philosopher for the layman.

Niebuhr, Reinhold. "The Truth In Myths," *The Nature of Religious Experience*. Edited by J. S. Bixler. New York: Harper & Row, 1937, pp. 117–135. A leading American theologian's argument that meaning can be found in religious myth.

Newman, John Hanry. *A Grammar of Assent*. New York: Longmans, Green & Company, 1909. (Also published in paperback by Doubleday, Image series.) An early and often referred to discussion of the meaning of religious language and an assessment of its validity.

Ramsey, Ian T. *Christian Discourse*. New York: Oxford University Press, 1965. Contains a variety of comments about problems arising in the use of theological language.

Stace, W. T. *Time and Eternity*. Princeton, N.J.: Princeton University Press, 1952. (Also published in paperback by Princton University Press.) Professor Stace's work asserts the impossibility of predicating positive attributes to God.

# VI. The Problem of Evil

ONSIDERATION OF THE problem of evil is as old as man's
thinking about the meaning of his existence. The reality
of moral and physical evil has always interposed itself
upon man's attempt to understand the present significance and
the ultimate reason for his own existence. Epidemics, floods, and
earthquakes; the bloody struggle for life among animals; and
the personal disorder, inhumanity, and seeming meaninglessness
in human existence are brute facts which force themselves upon
us.

Some explanation of evil, however difficult to achieve, seems
imperative if one is to find meaning in existence. Some men
have found such meaning in the courageous endurance of bludg-
eoning by meaningless forces; others have found it in attempts
to turn evil into some ultimate good. However the problem is
met, the fact of evil does force men back to the questions of the
source and purpose, if there is a purpose, of evil.

In no area has the question of the nature of the universe and
the problem of evil come to sharper focus than in religion. The
problem of the reconciliation of the existence of evil with a belief
in God is devastatingly simple: either God is responsible for
evil or He is in some way limited. If God cannot prevent the
appearance and progress of evils in the world, it would seem
that He is not all-powerful. The result in this case would be to
affirm an ultimate dualism between God and demonic forces.
If God can, but will not, prevent them, it would appear that He
is not all-good. This conclusion would cut the main fiber of
most religious faith (though some religions have worshipped
evil gods). A second group of theists refuse to accept this either/
or and have affirmed God's goodness, even though it meant the
acceptance of a finite or limited God. Others who represent a

[425]

third position feel forced to give up the belief in a God entirely if He cannot be considered both all-good and all-powerful.

A fourth group seeking to explain the presence of evil in the world has attempted to avoid positing an antithesis between goodness and omnipotence by arguing that God alone is ultimate and that, in the final analysis, evil has no reality. They claim that what is called evil is either an absence of being or an illusion. A fifth group maintains that evil is indeed one of the real facts of life, but that, in the total scope of things, it is instrumental in gaining some ultimate good. Such a belief affirms the idea that God can use even the negativity of evil in the achievement of His benevolent purpose in creating the world. Still others, who represent a sixth group, view evil not as an instrument, but as an impediment to God's purpose. In this case God will not use evil, He will fight against it and defeat it. Here evil has no constructive end; it must be directly confronted and destroyed.

A seventh alternative is represented by thinkers for whom the metaphysical problem of evil is artificial. For instance, humanists sometimes prefer to stress a practical, instrumental approach to specific evils, confident that the careful and persistent application of scientific technology to specific problems will in piecemeal fashion gradually eliminate evil.

These are not all of the alternative ways in which men have dealt with the fact of evil, but they indicate some of the major approaches by which the problem has been met. The selections include the following writings of important thinkers who have attempted to achieve some solution to this problem.

Our selection from the works of Augustine is representative of the position which denies that evil has any ultimate status in being, while recognizing its limiting and perverse influence in man's present experience. Augustine calls evil the "privation" or absence of being. This evil he roots in an evil will which he calls "Pride." Spinoza recognizes the reality of evil as an obstruction to the self-fulfillment of human life, but at the same time, maintains that the distinction between good and evil as such does not exist in the infinite intellect of God who fulfills Himself. Leibnitz justifies the existence of evil by saying that this is the best world that could have been created and that even evil can become an instrument to the perfection of the whole creation.

Josiah Royce adopts an absolute idealistic position. Royce finds evil a necessity for the completion of God's life, for only by struggle with evil in the temporal world can God in His eternity be triumphantly perfect. William Temple approaches the problem of evil from the standpoint of a concern with human sin. Although he does not see evil as limited to sin, nor to be accounted for solely in terms of sin, he does see sin as the most immediate, and experientially the most devastating, form of evil.

Radoslav Tsanoff approaches the question with the frank recognition that this is a world of good and evil. Neither fact can be expunged from the context in which life is lived. The problem he deals with is the possibility of correlating these two realities. Having recognized that evil exists, man is able to fight against it and wrest some value and goodness out of life. F. R. Tennant addresses himself to the problem of physical evil. He examines many of the traditional arguments and then attempts to make his own case. This he does by discussing the relation between nature's harmony and evil's disruptive negations.

A different approach is taken by Nicolas Berdyaev. For him the problem of evil comes to clearest focus in the problem of death; the only meaningful answer to evil, he argues, is to be found in "rebirth" through conversion to Christian faith. Ninian Smart's article completes this section. He reacts against some of the more usual claims that are made about the relation between omnipotence and evil. By means of an "anthropological fiction" he looks with fresh eyes at several possible ways of interpreting this relationship.

# ST. AUGUSTINE

St. Augustine (345–430) was Bishop of Hippo in North Africa and probably the most important theologian in the first millennium of the Christian era. In his work he attempted to combine Platonic thought with
Christian theology. *The Confessions* and *The City of God* are among the
best known of his works.

## The City of God

### 13. That in Adam's Sin an Evil Will Preceded the Evil Act

Our first parents fell into open disobedience because already they were
secretly corrupted; for the evil act had never been done had not an evil
will preceded it. And what is the origin of our evil will but pride? For "pride
is the beginning of sin." And what is pride but the craving for undue exaltation? And this is undue exaltation, when the soul abandons Him to whom
it ought to cleave as its end, and becomes a kind of end to itself. This happens when it becomes its own satisfaction. And it does so when it falls away
from that unchangeable good which ought to satisfy it more than itself.
This falling away is spontaneous; for if the will had remained steadfast in
the love of that higher and changeless good by which it was illumined to
intelligence and kindled into love, it would not have turned away to find
satisfaction in itself, and so become frigid and benighted; the woman would
not have believed the serpent spoke the truth, nor would the man have
preferred the request of his wife to the command of God, nor have supposed
that it was a venial transgression to cleave to the partner of his life even
in a partnership of sin. The wicked deed, then—that is to say, the transgression of eating the forbidden fruit—was committed by persons who were
already wicked. That "evil fruit" could be brought forth only by "a corrupt
tree." But that the tree was evil was not the result of nature; for certainly
it could become so only by the vice of the will, and vice is contrary to nature.
Now, nature could not have been depraved by vice had it not been made
out of nothing. Consequently, that it is a nature, this is because it is made

From St. Augustine, *The City of God,* trans. Marcus Dods, Book XIV, 13, 14, pp. 460–
462. Copyright, 1950, by Randon House, Inc. In the public domain. [Footnotes omitted,
Eds.]

by God; but that it falls away from Him, this is because it is made out of nothing. But man did not so fall away as to become absolutely nothing; but being turned towards himself, his being became more contracted than it was when he clave to Him who supremely is. Accordingly, to exist in himself, that is, to be his own satisfaction after abandoning God, is not quite to become a nonentity, but to approximate to that. And therefore the holy Scriptures designate the proud by another name, "self-pleasers." For it is good to have the heart lifted up, yet not to one's self, for this is proud, but to the Lord, for this is obedient, and can be the act only of the humble. There is, therefore, something in humility which, strangely enough, exalts the heart, and something in pride which debases it. This seems, indeed, to be contradictory, that loftiness should debase and lowliness exalt. But pious humility enables us to submit to what is above us; and nothing is more exalted above us than God; and therefore humility, by making us subject to God, exalts us. But pride, being a defect of nature, by the very act of refusing subjection and revolting from Him who is supreme, falls to a low condition; and then comes to pass what is written: "Thou castedst them down when they lifted up themselves." For he does not say, "when they had been lifted up," as if first they were exalted, and then afterwards cast down; but "when they lifted up themselves" even then they were cast down—that is to say, the very lifting up was already a fall. And therefore it is that humility is specially recommended to the city of God as it sojourns in this world, and is specially exhibited in the city of God, and in the person of Christ its King; while the contrary vice of pride, according to the testimony of the sacred writings, specially rules his adversary the devil. And certainly this is the great difference which distinguishes the two cities of which we speak, the one being the society of the godly men, the other of the ungodly, each associated with the angels that adhere to their party, and the one guided and fashioned by love of self, the other by love of God.

The devil, then, would not have ensnared man in the open and manifest sin of doing what God had forbidden, had man not already begun to live for himself. It was this that made him listen with pleasure to the words, "Ye shall be as gods," which they would much more readily have accomplished by obediently adhering to their supreme and true end than by proudly living to themselves. For created gods are gods not by virtue of what is in themselves, but by a participation of the true God. By craving to be more, man becomes less; and by aspiring to be self-sufficing, he fell away from Him who truly suffices him. Accordingly, this wicked desire which prompts man to please himself as if he were himself light, and which thus turns him away from that light by which, had he followed it, he would himself have become light—this wicked desire, I say, already secretly existed in him, and the open sin was but its consequence. For that is true which is written, "Pride goeth before destruction, and before honour is humility;"

that is to say, secret ruin precedes open ruin, while the former is not counted ruin. For who counts exaltation ruin, though no sooner is the Highest forsaken than a fall is begun? But who does not recognise it as ruin, when there occurs an evident and indubitable transgression of the commandment? And consequently, God's prohibition had reference to such an act as, when committed, could not be defended on any pretence of doing what was righteous. And I make bold to say that it is useful for the proud to fall into an open and indisputable transgression, and so displease themselves, as already, by pleasing themselves, they had fallen. For Peter was in a healthier condition when he wept and was dissatisfied with himself, than when he boldly presumed and satisfied himself. And this is averred by the sacred Psalmist when he says, "Fill their faces with shame, that they may seek Thy name, O Lord;" that is that they who have pleased themselves in seeking their own glory may be pleased and satisfied with Thee in seeking Thy glory.

### 14. *Of the Pride in the Sin, Which Was Worse Than the Sin Itself*

But it is a worse and more damnable pride which casts about for the shelter of an excuse even in manifest sins, as these our first parents did, of whom the woman said, "The serpent beguiled me, and I did eat;" and the man said, "The woman whom Thou gavest to be with me, she gave me of the tree, and I did eat." Here there is no word of begging pardon, no word of entreaty for healing. For though they do not, like Cain, deny that they have perpetrated the deed, yet their pride seeks to refer its wickedness to another—the woman's pride to the serpent, the man's to the woman. But where there is a plain transgression of a divine commandment, this is rather to accuse than to excuse oneself. For the fact that the woman sinned on the serpent's persuasion, and the man at the woman's offer, did not make the transgression less, as if there were any one whom we ought rather to believe or yield to than God.

# BENEDICT SPINOZA

Benedict Spinoza (1632–1677), seventeenth-century rationalistic philosopher, produced one of the most thoroughgoing monistic systems in Western thought. He was traditionally of the Jewish faith but was excommunicated because of his unorthodox views.

## The Ethics

Appendix—In the foregoing I have explained the nature and properties of God. I have shown that he necessarily exists, that he is one: that he is, and acts solely by the necessity of his own nature; that he is the free cause of all things, and how he is so; that all things are in God, and so depend on him, that without him they could neither exist nor be conceived; lastly, that all things are predetermined by God, not through his free will or absolute fiat, but from the very nature of God or infinite power. I have further, where occasion offered, taken care to remove the prejudices, which might impede the comprehension of my demonstrations. Yet there still remain misconceptions not a few, which might and may prove very grave hindrances to the understanding of the concatenation of things, as I have explained it above. I have therefore thought it worth while to bring these misconceptions before the bar of reason.

All such opinions spring from the notion commonly entertained, that all things in nature act as men themselves act, namely, with an end in view. It is accepted as certain, that God himself directs all things to a definite goal (for it is said that God made all things for man, and man that he might worship him). I will, therefore, consider this opinion, asking first, why it obtains general credence, and why all men are naturally so prone to adopt it? secondly, I will point out its falsity; and, lastly, I will show how it has given rise to prejudices about good and bad, right and wrong, praise and blame, order and confusion, beauty and ugliness, and the like. However, this is not the place to deduce these misconceptions from the nature of the human mind: it will be sufficient here, if I assume as a starting point, what ought to be universally admitted, namely, that all men are born ignorant of the

From Benedict Spinoza, *The Chief Works of Benedict De Spinoza*, trans. R. H. M. Elwes, pp. 74–81. Published, 1889, by George Bell & Sons. In the public domain.

causes of things, that all have the desire to seek for what is useful to them, and that they are conscious of such desire. Herefrom it follows, first, that men think themselves free inasmuch as they are conscious of their volitions and desires, and never even dream, in their ignorance, of the causes which have disposed them so to wish and desire. Secondly, that men do all things for an end, namely, for that which is useful to them, and which they seek. Thus it comes to pass that they only look for a knowledge of the final causes of events, and when these are learned, they are content, as having no cause for further doubt. If they cannot learn such causes from external sources, they are compelled to turn to considering themselves, and reflecting what end would have induced them personally to bring about the given event, and thus they necessarily judge other natures by their own. Further, as they find in themselves and outside themselves many means which assist them not a little in their search for what is useful, for instance, eyes for seeing, teeth for chewing, herbs and animals for yielding food, the sun for giving light, the sea for breeding fish, etc., they come to look on the whole of nature as a means for obtaining such conveniences. Now as they are aware, that they found these conveniences and did not make them, they think they have cause for believing, that some other being has made them for their use. As they look upon things as means, they cannot believe them to be self-created; but, judging from the means which they are accustomed to prepare for themselves, they are bound to believe in some ruler or rulers of the universe endowed with human freedom, who have arranged and adapted everything for human use. They are bound to estimate the nature of such rulers (having no information on the subject) in accordance with their own nature, and therefore they assert that the gods ordained everything for the use of man, in order to bind man to themselves and obtain from him the highest honour. Hence also it follows, that everyone thought out for himself, according to his abilities, a different way of worshipping God, so that God might love him more than his fellows, and direct the whole course of nature for the satisfaction of his blind cupidity and insatiable avarice. Thus the prejudice developed into superstition, and took deep root in the human mind; and for this reason everyone strove most zealously to understand and explain the final causes of things; but in their endeavour to show that nature does nothing in vain, *i.e.,* nothing which is useless to man, they only seem to have demonstrated that nature, the gods, and men are all mad together. Consider, I pray you, the result: among the many helps of nature they were bound to find some hindrances, such as storms, earthquakes, diseases, etc.: so they declared that such things happen, because the gods are angry at some wrong done them by men, or at some fault committed in their worship. Experience day by day protested and showed by infinite examples, that good and evil fortunes fall to the lot of pious and impious alike; still they would not abandon their inveterate prejudice, for it was more easy for them to class such contradictions among other unknown things of whose use they were ignorant, and thus to retain their actual and innate condition of ignorance, than to destroy the whole fabric of their reasoning and start afresh. They therefore laid down as an axiom, that God's judgments far transcend human understanding. Such a doctrine might well have sufficed to conceal the truth from the human race for all eternity, if mathematics had not furnished another standard of verity in considering solely the essence and properties of figures without regard to their final causes. There are other reasons (which I need not mention here) besides mathematics, which might have caused men's minds to be directed to these general prejudices, and have led them to the knowledge of truth.

I have now sufficiently explained my first point. There is no need to show at length, that nature has no particular goal in view, and that final causes are mere human figments. This, I think, is already evident enough, both from the causes and the foundations on which I have shown such prejudice to be based, and also from Prop. xvi., and the Corollary of Prop. xxxii., and, in fact, all those propositions in which I have shown, that everything in nature proceeds from a sort of necessity, and with the utmost perfection. However, I will add a few remarks, in order to overthrow this doctrine of a final cause utterly. That which is really a cause it considers as an effect, and *vice versâ:* it makes that which is by nature first to be last, and that which is highest and most perfect to be most imperfect. Passing over the questions of cause and priority as self-evident, it is plain from Props. xxi., xxii., xxiii. that that effect is most perfect which is produced immediately by God; the effect which requires for its production several intermediate causes is, in that respect, more imperfect. But if those things which were made immediately by God were made to enable him to attain his end, then the things which come after, for the sake of which the first were made, are necessarily the most excellent of all.

Further, this doctrine does away with the perfection of God: for, if God acts for an object, he necessarily desires something which he lacks. Certainly, theologians and metaphysicians draw a distinction between the object of want and the object of assimiliation; still they confess that God made all things for the sake of himself, not for the sake of creation. They are unable to point to anything prior to creation, except God himself, as an object for which God should act, and are therefore driven to admit (as they clearly must), that God lacked those things for whose attainment he created means, and further that he desired them.

We must not omit to notice that the followers of this doctrine, anxious to display their talent in assigning final causes, have imported a new method of argument in proof of their theory—namely, a reduction, not to the impossible, but to ignorance; thus showing that they have no other method of exhibiting their doctrine. For example, if a stone falls from a roof on to someone's head, and kills him, they will demonstrate by their new method, that the stone fell in order to kill the man; for, if it had not by God's will fallen with that object, how could so many circumstances (and there are often many concurrent circumstances) have all happened together by chance? Perhaps you will answer that the event is due to the facts that the wind was blowing, and the man was walking that way. "But why," they will insist, "was the wind blowing, and why was the man at that very time walking that way?" If you again answer, that the wind had then sprung up because the sea had begun to be agitated the day before, the weather being previously calm, and that the man had been invited by a friend, they will again insist "But why was the sea agitated, and why was the man invited at that time?" So they will pursue their questions from cause to cause, till at last you take refuge in the will of God—in other words, the sanctuary of ignorance. So, again, when they survey the frame of the human body, they are amazed; and being ignorant of the causes of so great a work of art, conclude that it has been fashioned, not mechanically, but by divine and supernatural skill, and has been so put togther that one part shall not hurt another.

Hence anyone who seeks for the true causes of miracles, and strives to understand natural phenomena as an intelligent being, and not to gaze at them like a fool, is set down and denounced as an impious heretic by those, whom the masses adore as the interpreters of nature and the gods. Such persons know that, with the removal of ignorance, the wonder which forms their only available means for proving and preserving their authority would vanish also. But I now quit this subject, and pass on to my third point.

After men persuaded themselves, that everything which is created is created for their sake, they were bound to consider as the chief quality in everything that which is most useful to themselves, and to account those things the best of all which have the most beneficial effect on mankind. Further, they were bound to form abstract notions for the explanation of the nature of things, such as *goodness, badness, order, confusion, warmth, cold, beauty, deformity,* and so on; and from the belief that they are free agents arose the further notions *praise* and *blame, sin* and *merit.*

I will speak of these latter hereafter, when I treat of human nature; the former I will briefly explain here.

Everything which conduces to health and the worship of God they have called *good,* everything which hinders these objects they have styled *bad;* and inasmuch as those who do not understand the nature of things do not verify phenomena in any way, but merely imagine them after a fashion, and mistake their imagination for understanding, such persons firmly believe that there is an *order* in things, being really ignorant both of things and their own nature. When phenomena are of such a kind, that the impression they make on our senses requires little effort of imagination, and can consequently be easily remembered, we say that they are *well-ordered;* if the contrary, that they are *ill-ordered* or *confused.* Further, as things which are easily imagined are more pleasing to us, men prefer order to confusion—as though there were any order in nature, except in relation to our imagination—and say that God has created all things in order; thus, without knowing it, attributing imagination to God, unless, indeed, they would have it that God foresaw human imagination, and arranged everything, so that it should be most easily imagined. If this be their theory, they would not, perhaps, be daunted by the fact that we find an infinite number of phenomena, far surpassing our imagination, and very many others which confound its weakness. But enough has been said on this subject. The other abstract notions are nothing but modes of imagining, in which the imagination is differently affected, though they are considered by the ignorant as the chief attributes of things, inasmuch as they believe that everything was created for the sake of themselves; and, according as they are affected by it, style it good or bad, healthy or rotten and corrupt. For instance, if the motion which objects we see communicate to our nerves be conducive to health, the objects causing it are styled *beautiful;* if a contrary motion be excited, they are styled *ugly.*

Things which are perceived through our sense of smell are styled fragrant or fetid; if through our taste, sweet or bitter, full-flavoured or insipid; if through our touch, hard or soft, rough or smooth, etc.

Whatsoever affects our ears is said to give rise to noise, sound, or harmony. In this last case, there are men lunatic enough to believe, that even God himself takes pleasure in harmony; and philosophers are not lacking who have persuaded themselves, that the motion of the heavenly bodies gives rise to harmony—all of which instances sufficiently show that everyone judges of things according to the state of his brain, or rather mistakes for things the forms of his imagination. We need no longer wonder that there have arisen all the controversies we have witnessed, and finally scepticism: for, although human bodies in many respects agree, yet in very many others they differ; so that what seems good to one seems bad to another; what seems well ordered to one seems confused to another; what is pleasing to one displeases another, and so on. I need not further enumerate, because this is not the place to treat the subject at length, and also because the fact is sufficiently well known. It is commonly said: "So many men, so many minds; everyone is wise in his own way; brains differ as completely as palates." All of which proverbs show, that men judge of things according to their mental disposition, and rather imagine than understand: for, if they understood phenomena, they would, as mathematics attest, be convinced, if not attracted, by what I have urged.

We have now perceived, that all the explanations commonly given of nature are mere modes of imagining, and do not indicate the true nature of anything, but only the constitution of the imagination; and, although they have names, as though they were entities, existing externally to the imagination, I call them entities imaginary rather than real; and, therefore, all arguments against us drawn from such abstractions are easily rebutted.

Many argue in this way. If all things follow from a necessity of the absolutely perfect nature of God, why are there so many imperfections in nature? such, for instance, as things corrupt to the point of putridity, loathsome deformity, confusion, evil, sin, etc. But these reasoners are, as I have said, easily confuted, for the perfection of things is to be reckoned only from their own nature and power; things are not more or less perfect, according as they delight or offend human senses, or according as they are serviceable or repugnant to mankind. To those who ask why God did not so create all men, that they should be governed only by reason, I give no answer but this: because matter was not lacking to him for the creation of every degree of perfection from highest to lowest; or, more strictly, because the laws of his nature are so vast, as to suffice for the production of everything conceivable by an infinite intelligence, as I have shown in Prop. xvi.

Such are the misconceptions I have undertaken to note; if there are any more of the same sort, everyone may easily dissipate them for himself with the aid of a little reflection.

# G. W. LEIBNITZ

*Gottfried W. Leibnitz* (1646–1716), mathematician, versatile man of affairs, and rationalistic philosopher, made important contributions to the development of calculus and logic and was known for his philosophical system of spiritualistic pluralism. *Monodalogy* is his most important work.

## The Theodicy

### Abridgment of the Argument Reduced to Syllogistic Form

Some intelligent persons have desired that this supplement should be made [to the Theodicy], and I have the more readily yielded to their wishes as in this way I have an opportunity to again remove certain difficulties and

From Gottfried W. Leibnitz, *The Philosophical Works of Leibnitz,* trans. George M. Duncan, pp. 194–197, 202–204. Published, 1890, by Tuttle, Morehouse & Taylor. In the public domain.

to make some observations which were not sufficiently emphasized in the work itself.

I. *Objection*. Whoever does not choose the best is lacking in power, or in knowledge, or in goodness.

God did not choose the best in creating this world.

Therefore God has been lacking in power, or in knowledge, or in goodness.

*Answer*. I deny the minor, that is, the second premise of this syllogism: and our opponent proves it by this.

*Prosyllogism*. Whoever makes things in which there is evil, which could have been made without any evil, or the making of which could have been omitted, does not choose the best.

God has made a world in which there is evil; a world, I say, which could have been made without any evil, or the making of which could have been omitted altogether.

Therefore God has not chosen the best.

*Answer*. I grant the minor of this prosyllogism; for it must be confessed that there is evil in the world which God has made, and that it was possible to make a world without evil, or even not to create a world at all, for its creation depended on the free will of God; but I deny the major, that is, the first of the two premises of the prosyllogism, and I might content myself with simply demanding its proof; but in order to make the matter clearer, I have wished to justify this denial by showing that the best plan is not always that which seeks to avoid evil, since it may happen that *the evil be accompanied by a greater good*. For example, a general of the army will prefer a great victory with a slight wound to a condition without wound and without victory. We have proved this more fully in the large work by making it clear, by instances taken from mathematics and elsewhere, that an imperfection in the part may be required for a greater perfection in the whole. In this I have followed the opinion of St. Augustine, who has said a hundred times, that God permitted evil in order to bring about good, that is, a greater good; and that of Thomas Aquinas (in libr. II. sent. dist. 32, qu. I, art. 1), that the permitting of evil tends to the good of the universe. I have shown that the ancients called Adam's fall *felix culpa*, a happy sin, because it had been retrieved with immense advantage by the incarnation of the Son of God, who has given to the universe something nobler than anything that ever would have been among creatures except for this. And in order to a clear understanding, I have added, following many good authors, that it was in accordance with order and the general good that God gave to certain creatures the opportunity of exercising their liberty, even when he foresaw that they would turn to evil, but which he could so well rectify; because it was not right that, in order to hinder sin, God should always act in an extraordinary manner.

To overthrow this objection, therefore, it is sufficient to show that a world with evil might be better than a world without evil; but I have gone even farther in the work, and have even proved that this universe must be in reality better than every other possible universe.

II. *Objection.* If there is more evil than good in intelligent creatures, then there is more evil than good in the whole work of God.

Now, there is more evil than good in intelligent creatures.

Therefore there is more evil than good in the whole work of God.

*Answer.* I deny the major and the minor of this conditional syllogism. As to the major, I do not admit it at all, because this pretended deduction from a part to the whole, from intelligent creatures to all creatures, supposes tacitly and without proof that creatures destitute of reason cannot enter into comparison nor into account with those which possess it. But why may it not be that the surplus of good in the non-intelligent creatures which fill the world, compensates for, and even incomparably surpasses, the surplus of evil in the rational creatures? It is true that the value of the latter is greater; but, in compensation, the other are beyond comparison the more numerous, and it may be that the proportion of number and of quantity surpasses that of value and of quality.

As to the minor, that is no more to be admitted; that is, it is not at all to be admitted that there is more evil than good in the intelligent creatures. There is no need even of granting that there is more evil than good in the human race, because it is possible, and in fact very probable, that the glory and the perfection of the blessed are incomparably greater than the misery and the imperfection of the damned, and that here the excellence of the total good in the smaller number exceeds the total evil in the greater number. The blessed approach the Divinity, by means of the Divine Mediator, as near as may suit these creatures, and make such progress in good as is impossible for the damned to make in evil, approach as nearly as they may to the nature of demons. God is infinite, and the devil is limited; good may and does advance *ad infinitum,* while evil has its bounds. It is therefore possible, and is credible, that in the comparison of the blessed and the damned, the contrary of that which I have said might happen in the comparison of intelligent and non-intelligent creatures, takes place; namely, it is possible that in the comparison of the happy and the unhappy, the proportion of degree exceeds that of number, and that in the comparison of intelligent and non-intelligent creatures, the proportion of number is greater than that of value. I have the right to suppose that a thing is possible so long as its impossibility is not proved; and indeed that which I have here advanced is more than a supposition.

But in the second place, if I should admit that there is more evil than good in the human race, I have still good grounds for not admitting that there is more evil than good in all intelligent creatures. For there is an inconceivable number of genii, and perhaps of other rational creatures. And an opponent could not prove that in all the City of God, composed as well of genii as of rational animals without number and of an infinity of kinds, evil exceeds good. And although in order to answer an objection, there is no need of proving that a thing is, when its mere possibility suffices; yet, in this work, I have not omitted to show that it is a consequence of the supreme perfection of the Sovereign of the universe, that the kingdom of God be the most perfect of all possible states or governments, and that consequently the little evil there is, is required for the consummation of the immense good which is there found. . . .

VIII. *Objection.* He who cannot fail to choose the best, is not free. God cannot fail to choose the best.

Hence, God is not free.

*Answer.* I deny the major of this argument; it is rather true liberty and the most perfect, to be able to use one's free will for the best, and to always exercise this power without ever being turned from it either by external force or by internal passions, the first of which causes slavery of the body, the second, slavery of the soul. There is nothing less servile than to be always led toward the good, and always by one's own inclination, without any constraint and without any displeasure. And to object therefore that God had need of external things, is only a sophism. He created them freely; but having proposed to himself an end, which is to exercise his goodness, wisdom determined him to choose those means best fitted to attain this end. To call this a *need* is to take that term in an unusual sense which frees it from all imperfection, just as when we speak of the wrath of God.

Seneca has somewhere said that God commanded but once but that he obeys always, because he obeys the laws which he willed to prescribe to himself; *semel jussit semper paret.* But he had better have said that God always commands and that he is always obeyed; for in willing, he always follows the inclination of his own nature, and all other things always follow his will. And as this will is always the same, it cannot be said that he obeys only that will which he formerly had. Nevertheless, although his will is always infallible and always tends toward the best, the evil, or the lesser good, which he rejects, does not cease to be possible in itself; otherwise the necessity of the good would be geometrical (so to speak), or metaphysical and altogether absolute; the contingency of things would be destroyed, and there would be no choice. But this sort of necessity, which does not destroy the possibility of the contrary, has this name only by analogy; it becomes effective, not by the pure essence of things, but by that which is outside of them, above them,—namely, by the will of God. This necessity is called moral, because, to the sage, *necessity* and *what ought to be* are equivalent things; and when it always has its effect, as it really has in the perfect sage, that is, in God, it may be said that it is a happy necessity. The nearer creatures approach to it, the nearer they approach to perfect happiness. Also this kind of necessity is not that which we try to avoid and which destroys morality, rewards and praise. For that which it brings, does not happen whatever we may do or will, but because we will it well. And a will to which it is natural to choose well, merits praise so much the more; also it carries its reward with it, which is sovereign happiness. And as this constitution of the divine nature gives entire satisfaction to him who possesses it, it is also the best and the most desirable for the creatures who are all dependent on God. If the will of God did not have for a rule the principle of the best, it would either tend toward evil, which would be the worst; or it would be in some way indifferent to good and to evil, and would be guided by chance: but a will which would allow itself always to act by chance, would not be worth more for the government of the universe than the fortuitous concourse of atoms, without there being any divinity therein. And even if God should abandon himself to chance only in some cases and in a certain way (as he would do, if he did not always work towards the best and if he were capable of preferring a lesser good to a greater, that is, an evil to a good, since that which prevents a greater good is an evil), he would be imperfect, as well as the object of his choice; he would not merit entire confidence; he would act without reason in such a case, and the government of the universe would be like certain games, equally divided between reason and chance. All this proves that this objection which is made against the choice of the best, perverts the notions of the free and of the necessary, and represents to us even the best as evil; to do which is either malicious or ridiculous.

# JOSIAH ROYCE

*Josiah Royce* (1855–1916), professor of philosophy at Harvard College, was the best known American advocate of absolute idealism. He developed and defended his philosophy against the views of his colleague William James.

## The Problem of Job

There remains a fourth doctrine as to our problem. This doctrine is in essence the thesis of philosophical idealism, a thesis which I myself feel bound to maintain, and, so far as space here permits, to explain. The theoretical basis of this view, the philosophical reasons for the notion of the divine nature which it implies, I cannot here explain. That is another argument. But I desire to indicate how the view in question deals with Job's problem.

This view first frankly admits that Job's problem is, upon Job's presuppositions, simply and absolutely insoluble. Grant Job's own presupposition that God is a being other than this world, that he is its external creator and ruler, and then all solutions fail. God is then either cruel or helpless, as regards all real finite ill of the sort that Job endures. Job, moreover, is right in demanding a reasonable answer to his question. The only possible answer is, however, one that undertakes to develop what I hold to be the immortal soul of the doctrine of the divine atonement. The answer to Job is: God is not in ultimate essence another being than yourself. He is the Absolute Being. You truly are one with God, part of his life. He is the very soul of your soul. And so, here is the first truth: When you suffer, *your sufferings are God's sufferings,* not his external work, not his external penalty, not the fruit of his neglect, but identically his own personal woe. In you God himself suffers, precisely as you do, and has all your concern in overcoming this grief.

The true question then is: Why does God thus suffer? The sole possible, necessary, and sufficient answer is, Because without suffering, without ill, without woe, evil, tragedy, God's life could not be perfected. This grief is

From Josiah Royce, *Studies in Good and Evil,* pp. 13–28. Copyright, 1898, by D. Appleton & Company. In the public domain.

not a physical means to an external end. It is a logically necessary and eternal constituent of the divine life. It is logically necessary that the Captain of your salvation should be perfect through suffering. No outer nature compels him. He chooses this because he chooses his own perfect selfhood. He is perfect. His world is the best possible world. Yet all its finite regions know not only of joy but of defeat and sorrow, for thus alone, in the completeness of his eternity, can God in his wholeness be triumphantly perfect.

This, I say, is my thesis. In the absolute oneness of God with the sufferer, in the concept of the suffering and therefore triumphant God, lies the logical solution of the problem of evil. The doctrine of philosophical idealism is, as regards its purely theoretical aspects, a fairly familiar metaphysical theory at the present time. One may, then, presuppose here as known the fact that, for reasons which I have not now to expound, the idealist maintains that there is in the universe but one perfectly real being, namely, the Absolute, that the Absolute is self-conscious, and that his world is essentially in its wholeness the fulfillment *in actu* of an all-perfect ideal. We ourselves exist as fragments of the absolute life, or better, as partial functions in the unity of the absolute and conscious process of the world. On the other hand, our existence and our individuality are not illusory, but are what they are in an organic unity with the whole life of the Absolute Being. This doctrine once presupposed, our present task is to inquire what case idealism can make for the thesis just indicated as its answer to Job's problem.

In endeavoring to grapple with the theoretical problem of the place of evil in a world that, on the whole, is to be conceived, not only as good, but as perfect, there is happily one essentially decisive consideration concerning good and evil which falls directly within the scope of our own human experience, and which concerns matters at once familiar and momentous as well as too much neglected in philosophy. When we use such words as good, evil, perfect, we easily deceive ourselves by the merely abstract meanings which we associate with each of the terms taken apart from the other. We forget the experiences from which the words have been abstracted. To these experiences we must return whenever we want really to comprehend the words. If we take the mere words, in their abstraction, it is easy to say, for instance, that if life has any evil in it at all, it must needs not be so perfect as life would be were there no evil in it whatever. Just so, speaking abstractly, it is easy to say that, in estimating life, one has to set the good over against the evil, and to compare their respective sums. It is easy to declare that, since we hate evil, wherever and just so far as we recognize it, our sole human interest in the world must be furthered by the removal of evil from the world. And thus viewing the case, one readily comes to say that if God views as not only good but perfect a world in which we find so much evil, the divine point of view must be very foreign to ours, so that Job's rebellious pessimism seems well in order, and Prometheus appears to defy the world-ruler in a genuinely humane spirit. Shocked, however, by the apparent impiety of this result, some teachers, considering divine matters, still misled by the same one-sided use of words, have opposed one falsely abstract view by another, and have strangely asserted that the solution must be in proclaiming that since God's world, the real world, in order to be perfect, must be without evil, what we men call evil must be a mere illusion—a mirage of the human point of view— a dark vision which God, who sees all truth, sees not at all. To God, so this view asserts, the eternal world in its wholeness is not only perfect, but has merely the perfection of an utterly transparent crystal, unstained by any color of ill. Only mortal error imagines that there is any evil. There is no evil but only good in the real world, and that is why God finds the world perfect, whatever mortals dream.

Now neither of these abstract views is my view. I consider them both the result of a thoughtless trust in abstract words. I regard evil as a distinctly real fact, a fact just as real as the most helpless and hopeless sufferer finds it to be when he is in pain. Furthermore, I hold that God's point of view is not foreign to ours. I hold that God willingly, freely, and consciously suffers in us when we suffer, and that our grief is his. And despite all this I maintain that the world from God's point of view fulfills the divine ideal and is perfect. And I hold that when we abandon the one-sided abstract ideas which the words good, evil, and perfect suggest, and when we go back to the concrete experiences upon which these very words are founded, we can see, even within the limits of our own experience, facts which make these very paradoxes perfectly intelligible, and even commonplace.

As for that essentially pernicious view, nowadays somewhat current amongst a certain class of gentle but inconsequent people—the view that all evil is *merely* an illusion and that there is no such thing in God's world— I can say of it only in passing that it is often advanced as an idealistic view, but that, in my opinion, it is false idealism. Good idealism it is to regard all finite experience as an appearance, a hint, often a very poor hint, of deeper truth. Good idealism it is to admit that man can err about truth that lies beyond his finite range of experience. And very good idealism it is to assert that all truth, and so all finite experience, exists in and for the mind of God, and nowhere outside of or apart from God. But it is not good idealism to assert that any facts which fall within the range of finite experience are, even while they are experienced, mere illusions. God's truth is inclusive, not exclusive. What you experience God experiences. The difference lies only in this, that God sees in unity what you see in fragments. For the rest, if one said, "The source and seat of evil is only the error of mortal mind," one would but have changed the name of one's problem.

If the evil were but the error, the error would still be the evil, and altering the name would not have diminished the horror of the evil of this finite world.

## V

But I hasten from the false idealism to the true; from the abstractions to the enlightening insights of our life. As a fact, idealism does not say: The finite world is, as such, a mere illusion. A sound idealism says, whatever we experience is a fragment, and as far as it goes, a genuine fragment of the truth of the divine mind. With this principle before us, let us consider directly our own experiences of good and of evil, to see whether they are as abstractly opposed to each other as the mere words often suggest. We must begin with the elementary and even trivial facts. We shall soon come to something deeper.

By good, as we mortals experience it, we mean something that, when it comes or is expected, we actively welcome, try to attain or keep, and regard with content. By evil in general, as it is in our experience, we mean whatever we find in any sense repugnant and intolerable. I use the words repugnant and intolerable because I wish to indicate that words for evil frequently, like the words for good, directly refer to our actions as such. Commonly and rightly, when we speak of evil, we make reference to acts of resistance, of struggle, of shrinking, of flight, of removal of ourselves from a source of mischief—acts which not only follow upon the experience of evil, but which serve to define in a useful fashion what we mean by evil. The opposing acts of pursuit and of welcome define what we mean by good. By the evil which we experience we mean precisely whatever we regard as something to be gotten rid of, shrunken from, put out of sight, of hearing, or of memory, eschewed, expelled, assailed, or otherwise directly or indirectly resisted. By good we mean whatever we regard as something to be welcomed, pursued, won, grasped, held, persisted in, preserved. And we show all this in our acts in presence of any grade of good or evil, sensuous, aesthetic, ideal, moral. To shun, to flee, to resist, to destroy, these are our primary attitudes towards ill; the opposing acts are our primary attitudes towards the good; and whether you regard us as animals or as moralists, whether it is a sweet taste, a poem, a virtue, or God that we look to as good, and whether it is a burn or a temptation, an outward physical foe, or a stealthy, inward, ideal enemy, that we regard as evil. In all our organs of voluntary movement, in all our deeds, in a turn of the eye, in a sigh, a groan, in a hostile gesture, in an act of silent contempt, we can show in endlessly varied ways the same general attitude of repugnance.

But man is a very complex creature. He has many organs. He performs many acts at once, and he experiences his performance of these acts in one highly complex life of consciousness. As the next feature of his life we all observe that he can at the same time shun one object and grasp at another. In this way he can have at once present to him a consciousness of good and a consciousness of ill. But so far in our account these sorts of experience appear merely as facts side by side. Man loves, and he *also* hates, loves this, and hates that, assumes an attitude of repugnance towards one object, while he welcomes another. So far the usual theory follows man's life, and calls it an experience of good and ill as mingled but exclusively and abstractly opposed facts. For such a view the final question as to the worth of a man's life is merely the question whether there are more intense acts of satisfaction and of welcome than of repugnance and disdain in his conscious life.

But this is by no means an adequate notion of the complexity of man's life, even as an animal. If every conscious act of hindrance, of thwarting, of repugnance, means just in so far an awareness of some evil, it is noteworthy that men can have and can show just such tendencies, not only towards external experiences, but towards their own acts. That is, men can be seen trying to thwart and to hinder even their own acts themselves, at the very moment when they note the occurrence of these acts. One can consciously have an impulse to do something, and at that very moment a conscious disposition to hinder or to thwart as an evil that very impulse. If, on the other hand, every conscious act of attainment, of pursuit, of reinforcement, involves the awareness of some good, it is equally obvious that one can show by one's acts a disposition to reinforce or to emphasize or to increase, not only the externally present gifts of fortune, but also one's own deeds, in so far as one observes them. And in our complex lives it is common enough to find ourselves actually trying to reinforce and to insist upon a situation which involves for us, even at the moment of its occurrence, a great deal of repugnance. In such cases we often act as if we felt the very thwarting of our own primary impulses to be so much of a conscious good that we persist in pursuing and reinforcing the very situation in which this thwarting and hindering of our own impulses is sure to arise.

In brief, as phenomena of this kind show, man is a being who can to a very great extent find a sort of secondary satisfaction in the very act of thwarting his own desires, and thus of assuring for the time his own dissatisfactions. On the other hand, man can to an indefinite degree find himself dissatisfied with his satisfactions and disposed to thwart, not merely his external enemies, but his own inmost impulses themselves. But I now affirm that in all such cases you cannot simply say that man is preferring the less of two evils, or the greater of two goods, as if the good and the evil stood merely side by side in his experience. On the contrary, in such cases, man is not merely setting his acts or his estimates of good and evil side by side and taking the sum of each; but he is making his own relatively primary acts, impulses, desires, the objects of all sorts of secondary impulses, desires, and reflective observations. His whole inner state is one of tension; and he is either making a secondary experience of evil out of his estimate of a primary experience of good, as is the case when he at once finds himself disposed to pursue a given good and to thwart this pursuit as being an evil pursuit; or else he is making a secondary experience of good out of his primary experience of evil, as when he is primarily dissatisfied with his situation, but yet secondarily regards this very dissatisfaction as itself a desirable state. In this way man comes not only to love some things and also to hate other things, he comes to love his own hates and to hate his own loves in an endlessly complex hierarchy of superposed interests in his own interests.

Now it is easy to say that such states of inner tension, where our conscious lives are full of a warfare of the self with itself, are contradictory or absurd states. But it is easy to say this only when you dwell on the words and fail to observe the facts of experience. As a fact, not only our lowest but our highest states of activity are the ones which are fullest of this crossing, conflict, and complex interrelation of loves and hates, of attractions and repugnances. As a merely physiological fact, we begin no muscular act without at the same time initiating acts which involve the innervation of opposing sets of muscles, and these opposing sets of muscles hinder each other's freedom. Every sort of control of movement means the conflicting play of opposed muscular impulses. We do nothing simple, and we will no complex act without willing what involves a certain measure of opposition between the impulses or partial acts which go to make up the whole act. If one passes from single acts to long series of acts, one finds only the more obviously this interweaving of repugnance and of acceptance, of pursuit and of flight, upon which every complex type of conduct depends.

One could easily at this point spend time by dwelling upon numerous and relatively trivial instances of this interweaving of conflicting motives as it appears in all our life. I prefer to pass such instances over with a mere mention. There is, for instance, the whole marvelous consciousness of play, in its benign and in its evil forms. In any game that fascinates, one loves victory and shuns defeat, and yet as a loyal supporter of the game scorns anything that makes victory certain in advance; thus as a lover of fair play preferring to risk the defeat that he all the while shuns, and partly thwarting the very love of victory that from moment to moment fires his hopes. There are, again, the numerous cases in which we prefer to go to places where we are sure to be in a considerable measure dissatisfied; to engage, for instance, in social functions that absorbingly fascinate us despite or even in view of the very fact that, as long as they continue, they keep us in a state of tension which makes us, amongst other things, long to have the whole occasion over. Taking a wider view, one may observe that the

greater part of the freest products of the activity of civilization, in cere-
monies, in formalities, in the long social drama of flight, of pursuit, of rep-
artee, of contest and of courtesy, involve an elaborate and systematic
delaying and hindering of elemental human desires, which we continually
outwit, postpone and thwart, even while we nourish them. When students
of human nature assert that hunger and love rule the social world, they
recognize that the elemental in human nature is trained by civilization
into the service of the highest demands of the Spirit. But such students
have to recognize that the elemental rules the higher world only in so far
as the elemental is not only cultivated, but endlessly thwarted, delayed, out-
witted, like a constitutional monarch, who is said to be a sovereign, but
who, while he rules, must not govern.

But I pass from such instances, which in all their universality are still,
I admit, philosophically speaking, trivial, because they depend upon the
accidents of human nature. I pass from these instances to point out what
must be the law, not only of human nature, but of every broader form of
life as well. I maintain that this organization of life by virtue of the tension
of manifold impulses and interests is not a mere accident of our imperfect
human nature, but must be a type of the organization of every rational
life. There are good and bad states of tension, there are conflicts that can
only be justified when resolved into some higher form of harmony. But
I insist that, in general, the only harmony that can exist in the realm of
the spirit is the harmony that we possess when we thwart the present but
more elemental impulse for the sake of the higher unity of experience;
as when we rejoice in the endurance of the tragedies of life, because they
show us the depth of life, or when we know that it is better to have loved
and lost than never to have loved at all, or when we possess a virtue in
the moment of victory over the tempter. And the reason why this is true
lies in the fact that the more one's experience fulfills ideals, the more that
experience presents to one, not of ignorance, but of triumphantly wealthy
acquaintance with the facts of manifold, varied and tragic life, full of tension
and thereby of unity. Now this is an universal and not merely human law.
It is not those innocent of evil who are fullest of the life of God, but those
who in their own case have experienced the triumph over evil. It is not those
naturally ignorant of fear, or those who, like Siegfried, have never shivered,
who possess the genuine experience of courage; but the brave are those
who have fears, but control their fears. Such know the genuine virtues of
the hero. Were it otherwise, only the stupid could be perfect heroes.

To be sure it is quite false to say, as the foolish do, that the object of
life is merely that we may "know life" as an irrational chaos of experiences
of good and of evil. But knowing the good in life is a matter which concerns
the form, rather than the mere content of life. One who knows life wisely
knows indeed much of the content of life; but he knows the good of life

in so far as, in the unity of his experience, he finds the evil of his experience not abolished, but subordinated, and in so far relatively thwarted by a control which annuls its triumph even while experiencing its existence.

## VI

Generalizing the lesson of experience we may then say: It is logically impossible that a complete knower of truth should fail to know, to experience, to have present to his insight, the fact of actually existing evil. On the other hand, it is equally impossible for one to know a higher good than comes from the subordination of evil to good in a total experience. When one first loving, in an elemental way, whatever you please, himself hinders, delays, thwarts his elemental interest in the interest of some larger whole of experience, he not only knows more fact, but he possesses a higher good than would or could be present to one who was aware neither of the elemental impulse, nor of the thwarting of it in the tension of a richer life. The knowing of the good, in the higher sense, depends upon contemplating the overcoming and subordination of a less significant impulse, which survives even in order that it should be subordinated. Now this law, this form of the knowledge of the good, applies as well to the existence of moral as to that of sensuous ill. If moral evil were simply destroyed and wiped away from the external world, the knowledge of moral goodness would also be destroyed. For the love of moral good is the thwarting of lower loves for the sake of the higher organization. What is needed, then, for the definition of the divine knowledge of a world that in its wholeness is perfect, is not a divine knowledge that shall ignore, wipe out and utterly make naught the existence of any ill, whether physical or moral, but a divine knowledge to which shall be present that love of the world as a whole which is fulfilled in the endurance of physical ill, in the subordination of moral ill, in the thwarting of impulses which survive even when subordinated, in the acceptance of repugnances which are still eternal, in the triumph over an enemy that endures even through its eternal defeat, and in the discovery that the endless tension of the finite world is included in the contemplative consciousness of the repose and harmony of eternity. To view God's nature thus is to view his nature as the whole idealistic theory views him, not as the Infinite One beyond the finite imperfections, but as the being whose unity determines the very constitution, the lack, the tension, and relative disharmony of the finite world.

The existence of evil, then, is not only consistent with the perfection of the universe, but is necessary for the very existence of that perfection. This is what we see when we no longer permit ourselves to be deceived by the abstract meanings of the words good and evil into thinking that these two opponents exist merely as mutually exclusive facts side by side in experience, but when we go back to the facts of life and perceive that all relatively higher good, in the trivial as in the more truly spiritual realm, is known only in so far as, from some higher reflective point of view, we accept as good the thwarting of an existent interest that is even thereby declared to be a relative ill, and love a tension of various impulses which even thereby involves, as the object of our love, the existence of what gives us aversion or grief. Now if the love of God is more inclusive than the love of man, even as the divine world of experience is richer than the human world, we can simply set no human limit to the intensity of conflict, to the tragedies of existence, to the pangs of finitude, to the degree of moral ill, which in the end is included in the life that God not only loves, but finds the fulfillment of the perfect ideal. If peace means satisfaction, acceptance of the whole of an experience as good, and if even we, in our weakness, can frequently find rest in the very presence of conflict and of tension, in the very endurance of ill in a good cause, in the hero's triumph over temptation, or in the mourner's tearless refusal to accept the lower comforts of forgetfulness, or to wish that the lost one's preciousness had been less painfully revealed by death—well, if even we know our little share of this harmony in the midst of the wrecks and disorders of life, what limit shall we set to the divine power to face this world of his own sorrows, and to find peace in the victory over all its ills.

But in this last expression I have pronounced the word that serves to link this theory as to the place of evil in a good world with the practical problem of every sufferer. Job's rebellion came from the thought that God, as a sovereign, is far off, and that, for his pleasure, his creature suffers. Our own theory comes to the mourner with the assurance: "Your suffering, just as it is in you, is God's suffering. No chasm divides you from God. He is not remote from you even in his eternity. He is here. His eternity means merely the completeness of his experience. But that completeness is inclusive. Your sorrow is one of the included facts." I do not say: "God sympathizes with you from without, would spare you if he could, pities you with helpless external pity merely as a father pities his children." I say: "God here sorrows, not *with* but *in* your sorrow. Your grief is identically his grief, and what you know as your loss, God knows as his loss, just in and through the very moment when you grieve."

But hereupon the sufferer perchance responds: "If this is God's loss, could he not have prevented it? To him are present in unity all the worlds; and yet he must lack just this for which I grieve." I respond: "He suffers here that he may triumph. For the triumph of the wise is no easy thing. Their lives are not light, but sorrowful. Yet they rejoice in their sorrow, not, to be sure, because it is mere experience, but because, for them, it becomes part of a strenuous whole of life. They wander and find their home even in wandering. They long, and attain through their very love of longing.

Peace they find in triumphant warfare. Contentment they have most of all in endurance. Sovereignty they win in endless service. The eternal world contains Gethsemane."

Yet the mourner may still insist: "If my sorrow is God's, his triumph is not mine. Mine is the woe. His is the peace." But my theory is a philosophy. It proposes to be coherent. I must persist: "It is your fault that you are thus sundered from God's triumph. His experience in its wholeness cannot now be yours, for you just as you—this individual—are now but a fragment, and see his truth as through a glass darkly. But if you see his truth at all, through even the dimmest light of a glimmering reason, remember, that truth is in fact your own truth, your own fulfillment, the whole from which your life cannot be divorced, the reality that you mean even when you most doubt, the desire of your heart even when you are most blind, the perfection that you unconsciously strove for even when you were an infant, the complete Self apart from whom you mean nothing, the very life that gives your life the only value which it can have. In thought, if not in the fulfillment of thought, in aim if not in attainment of aim, in aspiration if not in the presence of the revealed fact, you can view God's triumph and peace as your triumph and peace. Your defeat will be no less real than it is, nor will you falsely call your evil a mere illusion. But you will see not only the grief but the truth, your truth, your rescue, your triumph."

Well, to what ill-fortune does not just such reasoning apply? I insist: our conclusion is essentially universal. It discounts any evil that experience may contain. All the horrors of the natural order, all the concealments of the divine plan by our natural ignorance, find their general relation to the unity of the divine experience indicated in advance by this account of the problem of evil.

"Yes," one may continue, "ill-fortune you have discovered, but how about moral evil? What if the sinner now triumphantly retorts: 'Aha! So my will is God's will. All then is well with me.' " I reply: What I have said disposes of moral ill precisely as definitely as of physical ill. What the evil will is to the good man, whose goodness depends upon its existence, but also upon the thwarting and the condemnation of its aim, just such is the sinner's will to the divine plan. God's will, we say to the sinner, is your will. Yes, but it is your will thwarted, scorned, overcome, defeated. In the eternal world you are seen, possessed, present, but your damnation is also seen including and thwarting you. Your apparent victory in this world stands simply for the vigor of your impulses. God wills you not to triumph. And that is the use of you in the world—the use of evil generally—to be hated but endured, to be triumphed over through the very fact of your presence, to be willed down even in the very life of which you are a part.

But to the serious moral agent we say: What you mean when you say that evil in this temporal world ought not to exist, and ought to be suppressed, is simply what God means by seeing that evil ought to be and is endlessly thwarted, endured, but subordinated. In the natural world you are the minister of God's triumph. Your deed is his. You can never clean the world of evil; but you can subordinate evil. The justification of the presence in the world of the morally evil becomes apparent to us mortals only in so far as this evil is overcome and condemned. It exists only that it may be cast down. Courage, then, for God works in you. In the order of time you embody in outer acts what is for him the truth of his eternity.

# WILLIAM TEMPLE

*William Temple* (1881–1944), the Archbishop of Canterbury, was the best-known Anglican theologian of the first half of the twentieth century. He was also a prominent leader in the ecumenical movement in the Christian Churches and was keenly interested in the application of Christian doctrine to contemporary social problems.

## Finitude and Evil

We have two questions to consider, which may or may not turn out to be identical—the cause of evil, and the justification of its occurrence. First we must enquire how evil finds a place in the world-process as we have conceived it, and secondly, whether, when its origin is so understood, its occurrence is compatible with the belief that the world is created and ruled by a God who is both infinite Goodness and infinite Power.

In the first stages of its existence the world exhibits neither life nor consciousness. At a certain point of its development life appears in rudimentary vegetable form. This life is void of consciousness. But again at a certain point in its development, life exhibits consciousness. Consciousness supervenes upon an organic existence which has already established a habitual routine. That routine includes the process in which one organism becomes food for another. If there is no consciousness, that cannot be called evil. If the organism that becomes the food of another is conscious, there is perhaps already

From William Temple, *Nature, Man and God*, pp. 359–375. Copyright, 1935, Macmillan & Co., Ltd. Used by permission of Mrs. Temple, St. Martin's Press, Inc., and Macmillan & Co., Ltd. [Footnotes omitted, Eds.]

evil in that combination of facts. But this seems less than certain; for the merely conscious organism lives in the present, and an extremely constricted present, so that consciousness perishes almost if not quite simultaneously with the occurrence of the event which in combination with continued consciousness would be evil. At this level then there is perhaps a very little evil, perhaps none at all. But once more at a certain stage in development consciousness becomes self-consciousness. The organism is now not only conscious of its environment as offering occasions for satisfying appetite, or for flight from danger. It is now conscious also of itself as distinct from its environment, and of possible states of itself as distinct from its actual state. It is, in Green's phrase, a self-distinguishing and self-seeking consciousness. Its time-span is increased. The "present" is now for it a longer stretch of clock-time, and it has memory of a past and anticipation of a future. Events now have value for it, and it is become a centre of value-judgements.

As we look back we see that at any stage which we choose to isolate, prior to the human, there was a possible balance or harmony comprising the best possible good at that stage. It was in principle possible that each self-conscious organism should pursue its own interest in such ways that the good of life should on the whole at least outweigh the evil. There seems to be no doubt that life in the jungle is, on balance, good. The larger beasts must kill the smaller to maintain themselves; but though this involves for the smaller beasts moments of terror, it seems clear from the accounts of naturalists that even for them enjoyment of life is the prevailing tone or colour of experience. And though there is already some problem concerning the occurrence of any evil at all, yet at this level there is reason to be satisfied with a balance of good over evil. That is not all that we have to say about it. But it is all that arises at this stage; and at this stage it is enough. For the stage at which evil may be taken up into good and made part of its own excellence is the stage of definite moral values. If life at the animal stage is good on the whole, then as a whole it is good, and no question of its justification arises. If later developments appear to offer a justification of the subordinate element of evil which it contains, that is to be welcomed in the interest of a completely rational interpretation of the world; but even without it we can safely pronounce that the best understanding we can frame of the animal world offers no obstacle to a reasonable Theism.

It is with the advent of man that the problem assumes proportions so overwhelming. Mind, as known in man, early achieves a certain detachment from its basis in the physical organism by its use of "free ideas." But it actually holds these ideas by means of its capacity as imagination. The mind cannot think without either percept or image. The use of the Figure in Geometry is more than a convenience; it is a necessity. But it need not be drawn on paper or on a blackboard. It can be constructed in imagination. The mind is not strictly thinking about the Figure—the triangle ABC, for example; it is thinking about the universal triangle; but it can only do this by means of a particular triangle, taking care to avoid reference to any peculiarity of the particular triangle. Now imagination, just because it exists to offer particular instances of general qualities, offers to desire the stimulus which the appropriate physical objects offer to appetite. Hence comes a great, and in principle unlimited, expansion of the life of desire, which initially functions only as expressive of the vital needs of the organism or as stimulated by appropriate objects in the physical environment. Desire as so expanded may take the form of aspiration or of lust. No doubt it always takes in fact both forms at first, and one way of expressing the purpose of educational discipline is to say that it aims at directing the whole force of desire away from lust towards aspiration. When this process is corrective rather than preventive it is commonly called "sublimation."

From these considerations it is clear that so far as Evil is a product of exaggerated or misdirected desire, the condition of its occurrence is identical with the condition that makes possible all the higher ranges of human life. The ancient Hebrews had ample justification for tracing sin to the "Evil imagination." But to imagination also must be traced the possibility of all forms of distinctively human excellence. All depends on how it is used. To take up the thought of our earlier discussion of Freedom, all depends on the direction of attention; and this is largely within the mind's own control.

But this gives us rather the mechanism of evil as known in men than its mainspring. If the mind can control the direction of its attention, why does it so often give it a bad direction? It is easy to answer by attributing this to perversion or sin in the mind. But that hardly helps us. What is the source and nature of this perversion of mind? That any man ever chose evil, knowing it to be evil *for him,* is to me quite incredible. He may say, under an impulse of defiance, "Evil, be thou my good"; but his pursuit of it is then due to the fact that he has adopted it as his good and not because it is evil. To desire evil strictly for its own sake is impossible. To hate the human race so as to desire as good for one's self what is evil for all others, and even because it is evil for all others, is possible; but this evil for others is still desired as supposedly good for him who desires it.

In other words, a man is governed by what effectively appears good to him, which we shall henceforth term "the apparent good." And what appears good depends on the condition of his mind. It is not a reflective judgement with which we are now concerned. No one, probably, *thinks* cruelty good—certainly not as a general proposition, and hardly in a particular instance. Yet men do cruel things; they do them because at the moment those things appear good through gratification of some lust for self-assertion, or through their power to allay some panic fear. A man's character determines his apparent good at any moment; his apparent good determines his conduct.

If this process is working out to a bad result it is because the apparent good is not the real good. Sometimes it is possible to change the apparent good by setting beside it some presentation of the real good. There are many who habitually gain control of evil desires by turning their attention to the Figure of Christ, in contrast with which the object of the evil desire appears no longer good but abhorrent. Sometimes again it is possible to think out the full implication of what presents itself as good, and to see that taken in its real completeness it is bad. But as a rule the real good will be impotent against the apparent good unless it can be made equally apparent; and this means that it must be presented to the mind in some form apprehensible by the senses or in imagination. A man may know as a matter of general principle that stealing is not only wrong but bad—bad, that is, for him. But if he sufficiently desires an object that is within his grasp, he may none the less take it unless there is also before him the sorrow of the person robbed, or the penalty which he is likely to bring upon himself. Most of us have been able to master our covetousness of possessions sufficiently to be free from these temptations. The force of temptation is more felt in the region of bodily appetites, or of personal resentments, or of professional or commercial ambition, or of political sentiment. But the principle is the same. There may be a genuine apprehension of the true good in conceptual form; but this will not prevail against the vivid attraction of an apparent good unless it is presented in a form that is as effectively apparent. Imagination is usually the connecting link between thought and volition, and if the apparent good is to be changed otherwise than by conversion of the character, it must chiefly be through the occupation of the imagination with the things—and the relevant things—that are "pure, honourable and of good report."

But we have not yet come to the heart of the problem. Why is there a difference between the apparent and the real good? or, to put the question more usefully, why are we such that what appears to us good is other than the real good? For there is here an unquestionable bias or tendency to evil in human nature. Theologians have called this Original Sin; and if those words mean that every human being has in one respect or another such a bias or tendency to evil, they do not stand for a mysterious doctrine but for an evident and vitally important fact. Our task is to relate that fact to belief in the divine government of the world; but it will assist us if we first enquire further into the ground of the fact in human nature and its place in the world process as our argument has led us to envisage this.

The point which here concerns us is this. Mind arises within the world process as one of its episodes; but it is a peculiar episode in two ways. First, it is peculiar because it is able to take the process in which it occurs within the embrace of its awareness and its comprehension. Viewed from one standpoint, a man is a trifling occurrence—a midget breathing and moving for a brief span in one corner of a universe overwhelmingly vast. Viewed from another standpoint, he is himself the master of that universe, able to comprehend it as it can never comprehend him, and bending the mighty forces of nature to serve his purposes. He tames the force of lightning, turning it on and off with a switch. He regulates the waves of ether, bidding them carry accounts of his very games round the globe. To his lightest whim the august energy of Nature must be subservient. There may be rational minds domiciled in other planets, or in stars and nebulae. On the planet called Earth such minds have appeared, and their achievements make even the suns look small. That is one way in which Mind is peculiar as an episode in the world process.

The other, which more concerns us now, is this. Till Mind appeared as an episode in the world process, all other episodes had value in potentiality only, not in actuality—so far at least as the process itself supplied the condition of its actualisation. In the sight of God, and it may be also of spirits other than those born in the world process, that process and its episodes had value. But with the coming of minds there came also for the first time episodes within the process supplying to other episodes the condition for the actualisation of their value. Here, even more than in the impressive achievements lately enumerated, is the supreme peculiarity and distinction of mind. *The human mind is a focus of appreciation. It has knowledge of good and evil. The winning of that knowledge is called the Fall of Man, because acts, which before he won it were merely instinctive reactions to environment, become through that knowledge sins against the light. Again, because they are done against the light, they are done with a new degree of self-assertion. And, once more, because imagination is so potent to stimulate desire, there is an additional impulse to those acts. Man in so far as he is evil is worse than any animal; and in every man there is the bias or tendency to evil.* We are now in a position to track this to its source.

Mind, as it occurs as an episode in the world-process, takes the form of finite minds. It is indeed confined within extremely narrow limitations. It cannot attain to any grasp of the true proportions and perspective of the world in which it is set. Certain things have a value for it and are its apparent good. There is no inherent and absolute necessity for this to be other than the real good; yet the probability of divergence is so great as to amount to certainty for all practical purposes. The finite, and indeed very narrowly limited, mind appreciates the gigantic fact of good and evil. But its limitations hinder it from apprehending the full significance of these, or the true nature of the various objects which present themselves as apparent goods. *The mind by a necessary tendency of its own nature attaches more importance to values which find their actualisation in itself than to those which find it elsewhere; or to put it crudely, each man cares more about what seems to be good for him than about goods which he does not expect personally to enjoy. Even so far as he knows of these, they take a second place for him; and about many of them he knows nothing. So he becomes not only*

*the subject of his own value judgements, which he can never cease to be,*
*but also the centre and criterion of his own system of values, which he is*
*quite unfit to be.*

Accordingly, as man rose above sub-human forms of life through the development of mind within his psycho-physical organism as an increasingly
dominant factor, he found himself self-centred. The animal also is self-
centred. But in the animal this is an innocent state, because it is merely a
given fact of nature; the animal self does not compare its actual condition
with a conceived or imagined ideal; it is a consciousness but not a "self-
distinguishing and self-seeking consciousness." Consequently it is self-centred without being self-assertive. But as soon as consciousness advances to full
self-consciousness, so that the self, distinguishing itself from its environment, not only chooses what appetites it shall satisfy but even what ends it
shall pursue, self-centredness becomes self-assertion. The good-for-self is
alone effectively apparent good, and good in a fuller sense, though recognised to be real, is relatively powerless as motive. It is not utterly necessary
that this should be so; and therefore it is not true to say that God made man
selfish, or predestined him to sin. But that it should be so was "too probable
not to happen"; and it is true to say that God so made the world that man
was likely to sin, and the dawn of moral self-consciousness was likely to be
more of a "fall" than an ascent. Human sin was not a necessary episode in
the divine plan; but was always so closely implicated in the divine plan that
it must be held to fall within the divine purpose. To the problem thus presented we must return at a later stage.

The individual members of human society are not mutually exclusive
atoms of consciousness. Each is a partly self-determining, self-integrating
system of experience; but the content of that experience is derived from
environment. The part of that content with which we are now concerned
is derived from social environment. We are, in part, reciprocally determining
beings. We make each other what we are. Therefore the existence of one
self-centred soul would spread an evil infection through all who come within
its range of influence. This happens both positively by suggestion and negatively by repulsion. If A is self-centred, B tends to become so by imitation;
but also B becomes so in self-defence. The instincts of gregariousness and of
fear combine to produce the same result. And this process continues, so
that A and B perpetually develop their own and one another's self-centredness. Actual human society is to a large extent, though never completely,
that network of competing selfishnesses, all kept in check by each one's
selfish fear of the others, which Glaucon describes in Plato's *Republic*
and which Hobbes made the basis of his political philosophy in the
*Leviathan.*

This may, perhaps, be called an evolutionary account of the origin of
moral evil. But it must be sharply distinguished from any theory of moral

evil which accounts for it by reference to a survival of animal impulses into the rational stage of development. The centre of trouble is not the turbulent appetites, though they are troublesome enough, and the human faculty for imagination increases their turbulence. But the centre of trouble is the personality as a whole, which is self-centred and can only be wholesome and healthy if it is God-centred. This whole personality in action is the will; and it is the will which is perverted. Our primary need is not to control our passions by our purpose, but to direct our purpose itself to the right end. It is the form taken by our knowledge of good and evil that perverts our nature. We know good and evil, but know them amiss. We take them into our lives, but we mis-take them. The corruption is at the centre of rational and purposive *life*.

The suggestion which we have repudiated belongs to the phase of "faculty-psychology." This presented the soul as a complex entity in which reason and passion exist side by side. Passion, according to this view, comes from our animal ancestors and is already strongly developed when reason appears; reason at first is feeble, and very slowly develops capacity to control passion; the devices of education aim at keeping passion in check while the development of reason is hastened. At last it may be hoped that reason will take complete control, and then all will be well.

Of course that picture is not wholly false. But it is more false than true, because it misses the most vital point. That point is that reason itself as it exists in us is vitiated. We wrongly estimate the ends of life, and give preference to those which should be subordinate, because they have a stronger appeal to our actual, empirical selves. That is why the very virtues of one generation lead to the miseries of the next; for they are contaminated with the evil principle, and it is truly said that "our righteousnesses are filthy rags." *We totally misconceive alike the philosophic and the practical problem of evil if we picture it as the winning of control over lawless and therefore evil passions by a righteous but insufficiently powerful reason or spirit. It is the spirit which is evil; it is reason which is perverted; it is aspiration itself which is corrupt.*

And yet it cannot be said that the principle of selfhood is evil. To say that would be to accuse the constitution of the universe itself and therefore also God its Creator. Moreover it would be, for us at least, self-contradictory. For we have found that the essential condition of Good is the discovery by mind of itself in its object, which reaches its culmination in the love that binds different souls into the unity of perfect fellowship. If the highest good is found in personal relationships, it must be ludicrous to contend that persons or selves are inherently evil in principle. But the persons or selves which occur in the World Process are finite; they are extremely limited in range of apprehension. Their own well-being is dependent on the principle of the Whole in which they are no more than episodes; but this is not within their apprehension; if they so ordered their scale of values as to conform to it, that would seem to be a lucky accident which had occurred against all the balance of probability. Some of them at least must be expected to order that scale wrongly because of the falsified perspective due to their limited range of apprehension; and that will be enough, as we saw, to infect the race. It is still more likely that all will thus err, and then mutually infect with error one another. Because it was not necessary that we should err, we cannot say that our sin is itself God's act; it is our fault, not His, in the first instance. But that we are finite selves is directly due to God's act, and we cannot doubt that God foresaw the issues of conferring selfhood upon finite beings, so that sin falls within His purpose, and is even part of it, though it can not be said that He directly willed or wills it. What He faced was a probability so great as to be distinguishable only in thought from certainty. "I speak after the manner of men"; of course there is, for God's *eternal* knowledge, no such thing as "probability" but apprehension of all reality in its ordered completeness. Yet that distinction in thought is important. For it means that God did not directly cause any man to sin.

The sin of each man is a new element in the World Process. It is what, being himself, he contributes to it. And its essence is not that he is a self, but that being a self he is self-centred. What matters to him bulks larger in his estimate of value than what matters equally or even more to others. He does not love his neighbour as himself, but allows himself to count for more in the direction of his attention, and therewith his life, than his neighbour does. It is not wicked to be finite; but it is so improbable as to be beyond all reasonable estimate of practical possibility that finite selves, if left to themselves, should not be wicked.

When once the spiritual principle of evil had established itself through the adoption of themselves as centres of their systems of value by all, or by any, selves, its calamitous authority would spread apace. Each would infect, and be infected by, the others. The great system of mutual support in evil would be established, which Dr. Inge describes as "co-operative guilt with limited liability." As was noted above, it spreads itself in two different ways, both by positive suggestion, and by putting on the defensive those who find that their neighbours, being self-centred, will attack them if interest so prompts. The young soul, still plastic and rather timidly making its adventure in the world, sees that others fend for themselves, and resolves to do the like; it also finds that in a world so conducted it is likely to be overwhelmed unless it does the like. However small its own perversion, resulting from its own finitude, may have been, it is firmly rooted in self as its centre by its intercourse with others who were perhaps at the outset in their own outlook and estimate of the goods of life no more perverted than itself. And in each this process is intensified by the activity of imagination, which not only stimulates desire beyond its proper province, so that it becomes lust, but also, being specially responsive to fear, exaggerates the peril proceeding from the rivalries and antagonisms of the competing individuals and groups, poisoning all thought and feeling with rancour and bitterness.

This is the account of that indubitable fact, called by theologians Original Sin, which coheres with our general account of the World Process and of man's place within it. Because mind when it appears in that process is finite, and even narrowly restricted in scope, it attaches undue importance to those goods and evils which it apprehends as affecting itself; its perspectives are falsified; what is near at hand looks larger than it is, and what is far off, smaller than it is. This initial aberration of (probably) every finite mind is magnified by the activity of imagination and by the reciprocity of social influence till the Apostolic catalogue is no exaggerated account of the state of man: "foolish, disobedient, deceived, serving divers lusts and pleasures, living in malice and envy, hateful, hating one another."

It is not suggested that this is a complete account of human nature or of any actual phase of human society. But the evil aspect of human nature and society is all that has been said and more. It is no solution of the difficulty which such a view presents to Theism, to say that there is also much good in human nature. If the world is the creation of Almighty Righteousness, we should expect to find good in abundance; that causes no perplexity; but the occurrence of any, even minute, instance of evil causes great perplexity.

With that perplexity, however, we are not yet in a position to deal. Our present endeavour is to apprehend with substantial accuracy the actual moral situation of mankind. And for this purpose it is necessary to allow its fair place to the good that is in human nature despite its perversions, and (no less important) to those potentialities for good which are bound up with the very source and occasion of evil.

First, then, we notice that the earliest experience of the child is almost always predominantly good. The love for its mother which is part of the child's first conscious apprehension is almost purely good. It is not a perfect good, because it is a love wherein from the outset self-interest plays a part. It is in some respects truly disinterested, but is also in a certain sense self-centred. It is φιλία—the love of friendship, where the well-being of the self is an element in the complex of motives determining the friendly relation, not ἀγάπη—the love of utter self-giving and self-forgetfulness. Therefore it can be stifled and quenched; for if no kindness meets it, its element of self-regard will turn acid within it and corrode it till it vanishes away. Ἀγάπη cannot be so quenched; for as in it the self has been freely given from the outset, the absence of kindness only lets it prove its quality more perfectly. It is necessary to notice this contrast here, not in order to cast a blight upon the loveliness of a child's love, but to remind ourselves both of its possible decay and of the more splendid love which is alone divine and safe from evil infection.

That earliest experience, being good, creates in the soul a tendency which is not easily quite obliterated. And if the home be happy, and early years are spent in a society where love prevails, the good tendency may often be established so firmly that nothing can now prevent its becoming the controlling determinant of character throughout life. Yet the soul will still have its own element of perversion due to self-centredness, and is inevitably hardened in this by the play upon it of the selfishness in the world, from which even its early home is sure not to have been quite exempt. Nor can it be said that every soul trained in a loving home is less selfish than every soul trained under the pressure of grinding selfishness. There are some whose natural responsiveness to the goodness and beauty of the world gives them a centre outside themselves, which is only established the more firmly in resistance to the shocks administered by selfish surroundings.

"Centre" is a spatial, even a geometrical term. Its main suggestion in this context is clear enough, but we must not be misled by its limitations. A circle can only have one centre, but a soul can have two or more. If precision of geometrical metaphor is to be more nearly observed we may then speak of these as foci. Certainly it is the fact that very few, if any, lives are wholly self-centred; that could only happen through great spiritual mutilation, a mutilation which is perhaps impossible. For though our reason, as empirically active, is perverted, yet the essential principle of reason is incorruptible, and those mystics are probably right who hold that in every soul there is a divine spark which never consents to sin. Life cannot be fully integrated about the self as centre; it can only be fully integrated when it becomes God-centred. For God is the real centre of the real world: His purpose is its controlling principle; only in Him therefore can all creatures find a centre which brings them all to harmony with one another and with themselves. But God is immanent in the world, making Himself apprehensible through the Truth, the Beauty, the Goodness which call forth from men the allegiance of discipleship. Consequently there is a constant lure to every soul to find itself at home with Him, and this influence works in the world side by side with that influence of inter-reticulated evil which was earlier described. The soul which all through life is fashioning itself by the exercise of its mental freedom under the pressure of all these forces, good and evil, pursues its difficult and commonly wayward course, with always some element of self-seeking, and almost always some element also of sheer self-giving.

In the process of history the pressure of self-seeking and the impulse of self-giving tend increasingly to converge, making outward conformity to standards of sound morality easier, but also for many souls making progress in inward and spiritual morality more difficult. Selfishness, for its own sake, puts a check upon its expression in acts. If each fights hard for his own hand, no man's hand will retain what it has grasped. Covetousness itself will prompt a prohibition of stealing; for the thief who ignores his neighbour's property rights desires to be protected in his own. As selfishness learns by experience it attains to prudence, and those who zealously follow the best policy will about as often as not be honest. Outward morality is thus encouraged even by the immoral principle itself. Some genuine progress is thus made; but to an almost equal extent conscience is confused and the edge of its witness blunted.

Moral and social progress is, no doubt, mainly due to the activity of positive good influences. But it is of great importance, both practical and theoretical, to notice that lower motives, and even that principle of self-centredness which is the very fount of moral evil, play their part in the empirical development of good. Very often the wisdom of a trainer of character or a reformer of institutions is shown in the extent to which he can secure that the lower motives support the higher in promoting right conduct. Often the elimination of self-centredness is best assisted through the stage of enlisting it in support of what public spirit and even the highest claims of absolute morality require. Few actions are guided by one motive alone, and the vital question in practice is not whether the motive of an action was noble or mean, but whether the just order of priority among motives has been maintained, so that when divergence arises the higher check and control the lower, and the lower do not control or check the higher. The argument, frequent on the lips of a certain kind of moral idealist, that virtuous conduct sustained by fear of the consequences of vice is worthless, only proves that he who uses it is a bungler. Even if nothing sustained the virtuous conduct except fear, it would still be better than vicious conduct, both because it is beneficial instead of harmful to society and because its own excellence at least has the opportunity of making its appeal to the conscience of the person acting, so that imperceptibly another and better foundation for the virtuous conduct may be fashioned. Moreover, impulses which are refused any expression in conduct may atrophy, provided that the energy represented by them is utilised in other ways. It is quite possible for character to improve under the pressure of disciplinary sanctions, and for self-regard to be partly undermined by appeal to self-regarding motives.

Even more evident is the improvement in social relationships which may be assisted by the considerations of an enlightened selfishness. To a quite appreciable extent respect for law rests on the need of every citizen for the law's protection. So through the action of self-regarding motives men may be led to an appreciation of justice. So far as civilisation needs prisons and a police force, the general good is served through appeal to particular interest.

Yet when all this is admitted, it is still true that the self-regarding principle is a precarious support of moral progress, and that a point is reached in connexion with each successive phase of development in individual or society, at which it becomes a barrier to further advance. Where it exists—which is everywhere—the practical statesman and the practical pastor must alike recognise it as a fact and allow for it in the plans which they make to assist social or moral progress; they will try to enlist it as an ally in an advance that is really dictated by higher principles than itself. But man cannot be saved, nor either individual or society attain to perfection, except by the total elimination of self-centredness. Only by truly disinterested love does man enter into completeness of fellowship with God.

# RADOSLAV A. TSANOFF

*Radoslav A. Tsanoff* (1887–    ), emeritus professor of philosophy at Rice Institute, has dealt in his philosophical work with the areas of ethics, history of philosophy, and philosophy of religion. His study of the problem of evil is probably his most important contribution.

## The Nature of Evil

Our survey of the problem of evil and of the alternative proposed solutions has revealed several sources of confusion. The endeavor to recognize and to clear up these confusions has suggested a better way out. The theory which is now presented in conclusion makes no presumptuous claims to originality or novelty: enough if it preserve the sound elements of other doctrines and avoid their confusion of issues, unwarranted preconceptions, insufficient respect for fact, and undue complacency or depression.

One thing seems clear at the very outset: this is a world of good *and* evil, however we may have to define the two. Wholesale and unqualified condemnation of the world, and likewise suave dismissal of evil as unreal are plainly at variance with the facts of life, are indeed self-refuting views. Value, whatever its more adequate definition, has this essential character

From Radoslav A. Tsanoff, *The Nature of Evil*, pp. 387–393, 397–401. Copyright, 1931, The Macmillan Company. Used by permission of R. A. Tsanoff. [Footnotes have been renumbered, Eds.]

of bipolarity: it is positive or negative, in whatever field we may examine it. Truth implies and is meaningless apart from error; virtue is similarly related and opposed to vice, beauty and justice and happiness to their respective opposites. "In the scale of existence," Dean Inge writes, "there are no minus signs. . . . But . . . the moral standard is essentially dualistic, and the dualism cannot be transcended without transcending the standpoint of morality." [1] Using the terms good and evil in the broadest sense to designate value positive and negative, we are bound to say that, if either is admissible, both must be. We have them both on our hands, both actual. Our problem is to understand the relation between them, and the essential character of the world which the perception of their relation serves to reveal. So axiology and cosmology may contribute to each other.

The attempted reduction of evil to finitude is a virtual rejection of the clear point with which we start, and, as we have seen, leads not to the solution but to the abandonment of the problem of evil. The reduction of good and evil to pleasure and pain ignores the variety and complexity of value, and, instead of simplifying our problem, serves only to confuse it. The reduction of good and evil to self-denial and self-assertion narrows the range of value unduly and even in this narrow range is disclosed as artificial and as dictated by theological and other preconceptions rather than as warranted by experience.

The essential defects of the theories just reviewed are two. First, the outright dismissal of evil or its reduction to finitude involves an evasion of the characteristic problem of value and, in particular, by reducing moral to metaphysical evil, rules out ethics. Second, the proposed equating of good and evil with pleasure and pain, or with self-denial and self-assertion, mistakenly looks for sheep and goats in the world, treating good and evil as distinct things or aspects or qualities, as if we could say of $x$ that it is and remains good and the good, and of $y$ that it is evil and the evil in the world.

The realm of value is too vast and complex to be thus forced in the frame of any such $x$ and $y$. This undue simplification of the problem of evil, furthermore, overlooks the fact that truth, for instance, has no status in isolation but is always relative to a context, and not only may but characteristically does lose, in another context, its truth character and is disclosed as an error. And likewise with the other values. The value-character of reality, in other words, is not to be sought in individual things or aspects or qualities that stay put, that can be isolated and exhibited for praise or execration. Good and evil, truth and error, beauty and justice and the rest are what they are always in relation, in certain contexts, and in different contexts and relations may and do disclose a metamorphosis: the sheep turn out to be also goats! Yet even if philosophy of value could be formulated with offhand simplicity

---

[1] *The Philosophy of Plotinus,* Vol. I, p. 133.

in terms of pleasure-pain or benevolence-selfishness, the real problem of theodicy would still remain: How are we to estimate a world in which sheep and goats have thus been picked out and opposed to each other?

Value positive or negative is not to be located in certain areas of existence but is a fundamental and ultimate character of all existence. No thing *is* value, but in all things value of some sort may be sought, recognized, enhanced, frustrated. The value-character of reality is a character which is postulated, and in being postulated involves a demand for its realization or a demand for its negation, and in both demands a fundamental recognition of higher and lower and an incipient or determined preference. Valuation is thus bound up with conative experience; it implies a moving world in which interest stimulates will-activity, in which intelligence is not a mere passive recipient of the factual, but an active participant, preferring, demanding, resisting. The true is what we should believe and maintain; the beautiful is what we should enjoy and cherish; the good is what we should pursue, do, love, and uphold; and so with the other values, and in all these cases the chosen value is the preferred claimant setting us in opposition to rival invasions of interest.[2]

The world discloses value only in and to personal experience. Values are personal in reference and connotation. This main principle, which commands weighty support, has found classical expression in Green's formula: Values are always "relative to value for, of, or in a person." [3] Some of the reasons for upholding this view have been stated in the last chapter of my work, *The Problem of Immortality,* and perhaps need not be rehearsed.

This principle of the relation of value and personality, however, is liable to a certain grave misinterpretation. It may be expressed in the doctrine that value is *merely* personal, that nature is indifferent to value, that value of whatever sort is merely read into nature by persons, is as it were a poetic fiction of reality. In support of this opinion is cited the mere factuality of existence as physical science deals with it. But does the physical-scientific view of nature exhaust reality? Is not scientific activity itself, and the possibility of physical *science,* an indication that the range of reality transcends factual-mechanistic categories? What would be the chemical formulae of a true and of an untrue chemical theory? Nature, in the full and only proper sense of the word, is not merely factual and indifferent to value, for nature includes human nature, includes scientific, logical activity and its standards, aesthetic creation and contemplation, moral endeavor and ideals, religious

---

[2] Cf. Urban, *Valuation,* pp. 54, 63, and also Professor Urban's articles on Value in the *Journal of Philosophy,* Vols. XIII, XIV; Sorley, *Moral Values and the Idea of God,* pp. 54–131, 134, 498. Cf. also A. P. Brogan, "The Implication of Meliorism Concerning the Relation between Value and Existence," in the *Proceedings of the Sixth International Congress of Philosophy,* pp. 308 ff.

[3] *Prolegomena to Ethics,* Section 184.

worship. These are all in and of nature, quite as real certainly as atoms, electrons, positive and negative charges. An utterly impersonal universe would not allow of value or valuation, but the universe is not wholly impersonal. That values are essentially bound up with personality is thus nowise a reflection on their reality; indeed, quite the contrary, if we only consider the range of being that is exemplified in personality. Value is personal; its range and roots are the range and roots of personality, and these, after all, reach over all nature. To ignore this last is to ignore the problem "how a universe without mind or value could produce mind and value." [4]

Personal activity may not be as common as mechanical process, but this observation is neither surprising nor relevant to the reflection it is intended to convey. The apex of the pyramid is not any the less apex because it covers less area than the base. Was there a long time during which there was neither man nor man's thinking and valuation in nature? All the more clearly, then, should we recognize that nature among its other capacities had and has the making of human nature in it. The lower we perceive the sub-human range of nature to extend, the clearer evidence should we find, in nature's attainment unto personality, of its essentially dynamic, upward-reaching character. So John Keats wrote words of wisdom which Bernard Bosanquet was to interpret and develop: "The world is the vale of soul-making." [5] But we should also recognize the arduousness of this attainment. We should be on our guard not to oversimplify our cosmology either in the manner of the subjective idealist or in the manner of the materialist.

Personality and valuation serve to exhibit more adequately and as it were in fuller maturity characteristics and capacities which reality manifests less adequately and in germ and bud at lower levels of existence. The clear perception of the values of life evident to critical intelligence may enable us, without any anthropomorphism or mythology, to perceive the promise of them all along the line. So far is nature from being indifferent to worth.

It is the essence and nature of everything, Spinoza told us, to endeavor to persist in its own being. In a world of things and processes different in character, difference and conflict-in-relation are just what we should expect. It is of the essence of fire to set the green wood aflame, and it is of the essence of the moisture and the sap in the wood to delay flaming and to extinguish the fire. It is the nature of the invading horde of germs to take hold, multiply and take possession of the organism, and it is the nature of the organism to resist the infection which threatens its health and life. It is as natural for a dog's ravenous hunger to cause it to snap the bone out of another dog's mouth as it is for our social sense and reason to control appetite. The "flesh" and the "spirit" are both "nature," each in its sphere persisting, each in rela-

---

[4] E. S. Brightman, *Religious Values*, p. 135.
[5] Cf. Bosanquet, *The Value and Destiny of the Individual*, pp. 63 ff.

tion to the other and overarching to dominate the other. Our life, and the world we live in, may be conceived as a vast concourse of activities self-persisting, counteracting, conflicting.

But this cosmic concourse is a scale or hierarchy of activities. Things are not indifferently on a par; the difference among them is gradational. What the specific order of gradation is, in different fields of experience, constitutes the special problem of the philosophy of value in its various branches, logical, aesthetic, ethical. The meaning of the terms "higher" and "lower" is itself ever-expanding: signifying difference in complexity and range of categories, enhanced self-realization and self-judgment. The hierarchy points from mechanism to life and consciousness, from unconscious and non-rational to self-conscious and rational activity, from law-conforming process to action on principle and in pursuit of ideal ends.

That there is some sort of hierarchy, however, that there is higher and lower in the world, is not a conclusion of valuation but its prime presupposition. Its very outlook is gradational. The first axiom of the philosophy of value is: there is a hierarchy of being, or there is higher and lower in the world, some things are preferable, better, worthier than others. Grant this way of looking at the world, for unless we do the problems of value not only cannot be solved but cannot even arise: what, from such a point of view, is evil?

In this gradational view of things, evil is literally *degradation,* the surrender of the higher to the lower in the scale of being, the effective down-pulling incursion of the lower against the higher. This definition of evil would apply irrespective of the judgment as to what in any specific case is higher or lower, for such difference of judgment would involve a corresponding difference of judgment as to what in the circumstances is evil, and would reaffirm this fundamental conception of the nature of evil.

The perception of the cosmic process as gradational in character and the personal response to this perception find expression in the various categories of the philosophy of value. Thus the self-maintenance of the higher and its reaching to ever fuller realization and enhancement is progress, whether cosmic, biologic or human-social. Man's degrading surrender to a lower incursion involves him in varieties of vice. His effective resistance to the baser invasion is virtue. His self-satisfaction at any stage of advancement is complacency and marks stagnation: this we may call the sin against the Holy Ghost. His sense of inability to maintain himself on high ground or to attain ground still higher, if due to the conviction that the universe is callous or hostile to the enhancement of worth, gives rise to a consciousness of frustration, the tragic sense of life. . . .

The view of existence which is here developed recognizes unflinchingly the actuality of evil, but is not on that account plunged in pessimistic despair. It is nowise to be mistaken for the complacent theory of evil as the mere shadow in the picture or the discord swelling the larger harmony. Evil is not "somehow good," any more than sinking is somehow rising. Evil is evil and the opposite of good, contrary in course and direction. But it is a fact that what at a lower level and from a lower point of view passes for good and at that level is good discloses from a higher point of view its insufficiency, and adherence to it at the higher level becomes evil. So again St. Augustine writes: "He who inordinately loves the good which any nature possesses, even though he obtain it, himself becomes evil in the good, and wretched because deprived of a greater good." [6] In that sense, but in that sense only, we could well say that all good is somehow evil. So far at any rate is the view here advocated removed from complacency.

Thus it is the destiny of every good theory to open up vistas of inquiry, realms of evidence, new problems which in the end indicate the shortcomings of the theory and cause it to be replaced by one more adequate. It is the destiny of every truth in the end to help prove itself an error and itself again an element in a higher truth. In the entire realm of value every solution is but the better setting of a new problem, every achievement but the clearer recognition of a greater task. Spinoza's principle which we recognized is only one half of the truth; our dynamic universe requires also the other half, which Unamuno has expressed so eloquently in his disturbed and disturbing book, *The Tragic Sense of Life:* "Every created being not only tends to preserve itself in itself, but to perpetuate itself, and, moreover, to invade all other beings, to be others without ceasing to be itself, to extend its limits to the infinite but without breaking them." [7] Not bare identity of structure, nor yet change and bare sequence of discretes, but growth, unfolding and genuine enhancement of perfection, active, arduous, and inexhaustible, characterize the world-process.

The vaster the field of attainment and advance, the greater is the range of possible error and frustration. Indeed the perception of a certain value as in some respects inadequate and unworthy is the first step in the attainment of the higher and worthier value. The criticism and the collapse of the lower truth are the birth-pangs of the new truth; remorse and repentance, the thresholds to saintliness. Life does not lose but gains in tragic hazard as it gains in prospect and in dignity. Not self-sufficiency and bland placidity, but vigilant aspiration marks the heroic soul: its ideals are always in the van and its march to higher values never ceases. Far from content to accept the adulation of those with lower standards, it is ever keenly aware of the vast unattained and, by it judging its own attainment, finds itself ever short of the mark. Didn't James Martineau write somewhere: "The blessings of a satisfied conscience are least experienced where they are most deserved"?

---

[6] *Ibid.,* XII; English translation of Augustine's *Works,* Vol. I, p. 491.
[7] *The Tragic Sense of Life,* p. 208.

So we read of Leonardo da Vinci: "What to others appears perfection is to him teeming with error." [8] So Socrates' high conception of knowledge led him to count himself ignorant. So Jesus: "Why callest thou me good?" [9]

It is of the essence of value, then, that it recognizes no final terminus or conclusion. The target, to borrow a phrase from Professor Boodin,[10] is a moving target. Perfection has its base, of course, but its base is always a springboard. Perfection is perfectibility. All along the line of human endeavor this truth is demonstrated, and on the higher peaks of achievement it stands out most clearly. Theology, to be sure, has demanded a conception of God in terms of absolute perfection, a perfection all past perfect or present absolute, without prospect or problems. But, as we have endeavored to indicate elsewhere,[11] this conception of divine perfection carries over inappropriate mechanistic notions of completeness and plentitude into the realm of value. If we conceive of God as the Apogee of Value, then God's perfection must be dynamic: it is not the alleged terminus of perfectibility, but its cosmic course, its heart and soul. Matthew Arnold wrote of "the enduring power not ourselves which *makes for* righteousness." [12] The core of reality is this eternal perfectibility: the heavens declare it; evolution cosmic, biologic, or human-social discloses it; man's logical, aesthetic, and moral activity reveals its sublime range. Man's idea of God is his gesture towards the dizzy utmost of value, the infinite reach and endless span of it. When our vigor fails and our lot seems hopeless, and the abyss wells up to engulf us and our ideals, when wild Nature seems to mock our helpless dignity, and dull scepticism whispers harsh doubts of the reality of value, and all that is worthy in our world is "scientifically" exhibited as ephemeral and episodic, then the very tragedy which the cosmos thus reënacts in our experience serves to save us from despair: in our own loyal aspiration after values we find our conviction that they are in and of Reality and abiding. And this conviction of the ultimate reality, conservation, enhancement of value is man's faith in God.

In God is no stagnant plenitude but plenitude of ideal activity, no dull placidity but ever-heroic redemption of the world from the hazard of settling back. "My Father worketh hitherto, and I work." [13] Not less than myself but more is God thus resistant to the evil tug of the downpulling and the inert and the complacent. For just this upward-urging, ever more

---

[8] Merejkovsky, *The Romance of Leonardo da Vinci*, transl. by Herbert Trench, Vol. I, p. 211. Cf. Carl Hilty, *Happiness*, transl. by F. G. Peabody, 1903, p. 107: "My impression is that there is not one of us who has ever, even for a single day, done his whole duty."

[9] Matthew, xix: 16.

[10] *Cosmic Evolution*, p. 45.

[11] *The Problem of Immortality*, pp. 345 ff.

[12] *Literature and Dogma*, Chapter I.

[13] John, v: 17.

perfectly active character of the cosmos is what we can intelligently mean by God. And the evil tug is not outside of God or alien to the divine nature, but just as in finite beings so in the cosmic system of them, in God, it is the negative moment, the obverse of positive enhancement and ideal activity. For there can be no higher without its corresponding lower.

There is accordingly no coming to terms with evil, not ever. Only he straightforwardly "accepts the universe" who accepts it unreservedly as a battleground of achievement, only he who in thus accepting it is clearly aware of evils to be resisted and overcome. It has been said that the way to understand best the articles of the Creed is to keep clearly in mind the heresies which they were meant to combat. So the pursuit of truth is through the clearance of error, and virtue is in resistance to vice, and beauty is won through the refusal of ugliness. But this does not mean that error or vice or ugliness are accepted as any the less evil because they are conditions of good: they *are—to be resisted.* The only view of the world that might justify pessimistic despair would be a view that perceived no evil in it, nothing perverse, nothing lower to surmount or overcome, and therefore nothing higher to challenge our endeavor: no problem, no task, no hazard of defeat or frustration: dull, placid monotony! There is a reported saying of Machiavelli: "The worst misfortune in life is not sickness, nor poverty, nor grief; but tediousness." [14] Pessimistic philosophy, as we have seen, may have the reverse effect of that intended by the pessimist: it may be a goad to the sluggish. Evil and the perception of it are conditions for heroic recognition and pursuit of value, be it truth, beauty, goodness; for "powers subjected to no strain . . . atrophy and eventually disappear." [15] In this sense evil is always only relative to good; but, paradoxically, if we refuse to perceive and resist it as evil, then it becomes evil absolute and utterly damns the very man who makes his peace with it.

This is the outlook for a world that admits of valuation: this contest, contact and conflict, of higher and lower, ever persisting, each achievement opening new prospects, raising new problems, imposing new duties, facing new hazards. There is a grim element in this idea; we can apply to our purpose words which Plato wrote in the *Theaetetus:* "Evils . . . can never pass away; for there must always remain something which is antagonistic to good." [16] But another version of this truth, and one more inspiriting, is Emerson's: "Within every man's thought is a higher thought: within the character he exhibits today, a higher character." [17] Good and evil are not distinct realities and have no status in isolation; they are always relative to each

---

[14] Merejkovsky, *The Romance of Leonardo da Vinci*, Book XIII, Chap. x.
[15] E. C. Wilm, *The Problem of Religion*, p. 172; cf. Émile Lasbax, *Le problème du mal*, 1919, p. 372.
[16] *Theaetetus*, 176.
[17] Quoted from McComb, *The Future Life in the Light of Modern Inquiry*, p. 94.

other. Evil is that ever-present side or factor in the actual world, by resistance
to which a possible worthier side or nature affirms itself and gains reality
through attainment. This contest is at the heart of things; it has neither beginning nor end, and it makes our world significant and stirring. The gradational theory of the nature of evil thus expresses essential characteristics of
our logical, aesthetic, and moral activity, does justice to the complexity and
dynamic hierarchy of nature, and points to an idea of perfection which does
not nullify the fundamental character of value of which perfection is rightly
conceived as the apogee.

# F. R. TENNANT

*Frederick R. Tennant* (1866–1957) was lecturer in theology and philosophy of religion from 1909–1931 at Cambridge University. His concern
for a valid rational theology and a broad empirical approach are reflected
in his important work *Philosophical Theology.*

## The Problem of Evil

The problem of evil has thus far been discussed with almost exclusive
reference to evil of the moral kind. And the solution that has been presented consists in shewing the tenability of the belief that in our developing
world all things work together, as a whole, for the highest conceivable
good. The possibility of moral evil and the actuality of its consequences
are inevitable concomitants of the "best possible" evolutionary world. It
is not maintained that everything is good, or that "whatever is, is right,"
or that partial evil is not evil because it is a condition of universal good.
Nor is it implied that every particular evil is directly essential to the emergence of some particular good, or that it has its necessary place, like a
dissonance in music, in the harmony of the world-process. When it is asserted that all things work together for good, by "all things" is not meant
each and every single thing, but the sum of things regarded as one whole
or complex, the universe as a coherent order.

It is by adhering to this general view that the theist can best face the

From F. R. Tennant, *Philosophical Theology,* II, 197–205. Published, 1930, Cambridge
University Press. Used by permission of Cambridge University Press.

problem presented by the existence of that form of evil for which human freedom is not necessarily, and generally not at all, responsible: the physical evil, or the pain and suffering occasioned by the course of Nature in sentient beings. Indeed any other position than that which has just been summarised seems obviously inadequate as a basis for the explanation of the forthcomingness of physical ills. In order to reconcile the suffering inflicted by the material world upon mankind and other sentient creatures with the goodness and power of the Creator it is both superfluous and insufficient to seek to shew that in every particular case pain is essential to some special end, or that in each single instance suffering may fulfil some particular providential purpose. To attempt a theodicy on these lines is as hopeless as it would be to-day to develop a teleological argument from particular instances of adaptedness, after the manner of Paley. But, as there is a wider teleology than Paley's so is there a wider theodicy than that which consists in pleading that human and animal pain are sometimes prophylactic—a warning against danger, or that human suffering is sometimes punitive or purgatorial, and thus subservient to benign ends. These assertions are undoubtedly true, and there is no need to belittle their import. But by themselves they will not carry us far towards a theodicy. They but touch the fringe of the problem: or, to change the metaphor, they do not go to the root of the matter. It is useless, again, to minimise the pain of the sentient world, or even to reduce our possibly extravagant and unscientific estimate of its intensity, except for the purpose of arguing that, in spite of pain, animal life is probably happy on the whole: otherwise a single pang of useless or superfluous pain is enough to raise our problem. It involves faulty psychology to assert that pain is the necessary background to pleasure; for a lesser pleasure would seem to yield a sufficient contrast to render the enjoyment of intenser pleasure possible. And if pain be sometimes stimulating, educational, preventative, or remedial, as well as sometimes stunting, crushing, and provocative of moral evil, this fact is only significant for an estimation of the worth-whileness of sentient life. The knife may be necessary to cure the disease, but why the necessity of the disease? The escape from mortal danger may require the painful warning, but why the mortal danger? Or, speaking generally, what are we to make of the remoter evil which renders the nearer evil necessary or salutary? The real problem obviously lies further back than these particular and partial solutions reach. It must be shewn that pain is either a necessary by-product of an order of things requisite for the emergence of the higher goods, or an essential instrument to organic evolution, or both. Short of this, we cannot refute the charge that the world is a clumsy arrangement or an imperfectly adjusted mechanism.

It can be argued, however, that the former of the foregoing alternatives is applicable in the case of human suffering, while the latter of them can be invoked to meet especially the case of animal pain. The suffering of the lower animals is not merely an accidental superfluity emerging out of the evolutionary process, but is essentially instrumental to organic progress. It renders unnecessary a large amount of inheritance of specialised structure and function, and so prevents the suppression of plasticity; and, as the "sensitive edge" turned towards danger, or as prophylactic, it is of value for organic progressiveness. Although evil, it is also good for something. Much of human suffering, and many of the outrages of this present life upon our rational prudences and our most sacred affections, on the other hand, seem to be good for nothing, or to be non-essential for the realisation of goodness. If a man already has it in him to meet pain with fortitude and patience, he is not necessarily one whit the better man after actually enduring excruciating tortures; and if an all-powerful being "appointed" him such tortures, merely in order that his fortitude might pass from potentiality to actuality, such a being would be but a super-brute. However, it can be argued that the forthcomingness of our suffering is inevitably incidental to a moral order in a developing world. It issues ultimately out of what is inappropriately called metaphysical evil, or is a necessary outcome of a determinate cosmos of the particular kind that can sustain rational and moral life. The problem which it raises will therefore be solved if it can be maintained that no suffering such as we experience is superfluous to the cosmos as a coherent system and a moral order, however excessive pain often may be as a means to the accomplishment of specific ends such as are attainable by discipline and chastening.

It cannot be too strongly insisted that a world which is to be a moral order must be a physical order characterised by law or regularity. The routine of Nature may be differently described by the spiritualist, the dualist, etc.; but the diversity of these ultimate explanations of law does not affect the present problem. The theist is only concerned to invoke the fact that law-abidingness, on the scale which science is able to assert its subsistence in Nature as already *naturata,* is an essential condition of the world being a theatre of moral life. Without such regularity in physical phenomena there could be no probability to guide us: no prediction, no prudence, no accumulation of ordered experience, no pursuit of premeditated ends, no formation of habit, no possibility of character or of culture. Our intellectual faculties could not have developed. And, had they been innate, they would have wasted themselves, as Comte observed, in wild extravagances and sunk rapidly into incurable sloth; while our nobler feelings would have been unable to prevent the ascendancy of the lower instincts, and our active powers would have abandoned themselves to purposeless agitation. All this is obvious; but it has often been ignored in discussion of the problem of physical evil. Nevertheless, Nature's regularity is the key to this problem. Once let it be admitted that, in order to be a theatre for moral life, the world must be largely characterised by uniformity or constancy, and most significant consequences will be seen to follow. It becomes idle to complain, as some writers have done, that the orderliness of the world is too dear at the cost of the suffering and hardship which it entails, and might more or less be dispensed with for the benefit of the sentient and rational beings which people the world. As Hume admitted, if the "conducting of the world by general laws" were superseded by particular volitions, no man could employ his reason in the conduct of his life. And without rationality, morality is impossible: so, if the moral status of man be the goal of the evolutionary process, the reign of law is a *sine quâ non*. It is a condition of the forthcomingness of the highest good, in spite of the fact that it is not an unmixed good but a source of suffering. We cannot have the advantages of a determinate order of things without its logically or its causally necessary disadvantages. Nor can we be evaluating subjects without capacity to feel. The disadvantages, viz. particular ills, need not be regarded, however, as directly willed by God as ends in themselves or as particular means, among other equally possible but painless means, to particular ends. To make use of an ancient distinction, we may say that God wills them consequently, not antecedently. That is to say, they are not desired as such, or in themselves, but are only willed because the moral order, which is willed absolutely or antecedently by God, cannot be had without them. Now to will a moral order is to will the best possible world; and it also involves adoption of what we necessarily, if somewhat anthropomorphically, must call a determinate world-plan. Such a determinate method of procedure to realise a definite end in an evolutionary world, however, rules out once and for all any other possible goals and methods. As Dr. Martineau has put it, the cosmical equation being defined, only such results as are compatible with the values of its roots can be worked out, and these must be worked out. All determination is negation. If two consequences follow from a system of propositions, or two physical properties are involved in a configuration of particles, we cannot have the one without the other, though the one may be pleasing or beneficial to man and the other may be painful, or in its immediate effects hurtful. And such a result by no means implies lack of benevolence or of power on the part of the Creator, so long as power does not include inconsistency or indeterminateness. It simply bespeaks the inexorableness of logic, the compatibility of things, and the self-consistency of the Supreme Being. That painful events occur in the causal chain is a fact; but, that there could be a determinate evolutionary world of unalloyed comfort, yet adapted by its law-abidingness to the development of rationality and morality, is a proposition the burden of proving which must be allotted to the opponent of theism. One can only add that, in so far as experience in this world enables us to judge, such proof seems impossible. To illustrate what is here meant: if water is to have the various properties in virtue of which it plays its beneficial part in the economy of the physical world and the life of mankind, it cannot at the same time lack its obnoxious capacity to drown us. The specific gravity of water is as much a necessary outcome of its ultimate constitution as its freezing-point, or its thirst-quenching and cleansing functions. There cannot be assigned to any substance an arbitrarily selected group of qualities, from which all that ever may prove unfortunate to any sentient organism can be eliminated, especially if one organism's meat is to be another's poison, and yet the world, of which that substance forms a part, be a calculable cosmos. Mere determinateness and fixity of nature involves such and such concatenations of qualities, and rule out others. Thus physical ills follow with the same necessity as physical goods from the determinate "world-plan" which secures that the world be a suitable stage for intelligent and ethical life.

And if this be so, the disadvantages which accrue from the determinateness and regularity of the physical world cannot be regarded either as absolute or as superfluous evils. They are not absolute evils because they are parts of an order which subserves the highest good in providing opportunity for moral development. And they are not superfluous ills because they are the necessary outcome of that order. They are collateral effects of what, in itself or as a whole, is good because instrumental to the highest good. They are not good, when good is hedonically defined; but they are good for good, when good is otherwise defined, rather than good for nothing.

As in the case of moral evil, so also in the case of physical evil, appeal has sometimes been made from necessary linkages and conditionings to a supposed possibility of their being over-ridden by divine omnipotence. And as it was found absurd to suppose that God could make developing beings at the same time morally free and temptationless, so it involves absurdity to suppose that the world could be a moral order without being a physical cosmos. To save mankind from the painful consequences which flow from a determinate world-order, such as the earthquake and the pestilence, would involve renunciation of a world-order, and therefore of a moral order, and the substitution of a chaos of incalculable miracle. Doubtless some directive agency, or the introduction of new streams of causation into the course of Nature, is conceivable without subversion of such regularity as is requisite for human prudence and without the stultification of our science. But the general suspension of painful events, requisite on the vast scale presupposed in the elimination of physical ills, would abolish order and convert a cosmos into an unintelligible chaos in which anything might succeed upon anything. We should have to "renounce reason" if we would thus be "saved from tears," as Martineau says.

Physical evil, then, must necessarily be. And the goodness of God is vindicated if there be no reason to believe that the world-process involves more misery than Nature's uniformity entails. It is not incumbent on the theist to prove that particular evils are never greater than we judge to be necessary for the production of particular salutary effects: that difficult task confronts only the particular kind of theism which is concerned to dispense with proximate causes and a more or less autonomous world, and regards God as the sole and immediate cause of every natural event, and of every incident in a personal life. According to the theodicy which has here been sketched, it is not necessary to suppose that every specific form of suffering that man undergoes— e.g. the agony of tetanus or of cancer—is antecedently willed by God as a means to some particular end. It can be admitted that excruciating pains are more severe than they need be for evoking virtues such as patience and fortitude, and that to assign them to God's antecedent will would be to attribute devilishness to the Deity. Moreover, the fact that some human beings are born as abortions, as imbecile or insane, seems to be inexplicable on the view that every form of suffering is a particular providence, or an antecedently willed dispensation for educating and spiritually perfecting the person on whom the affliction falls; while to suppose that suffering is inflicted on one person for the spiritual edification of another is again to conceive of God as immoral. But the hardest fact of all for human equanimity, in presence of physical and mental evil, is that the apportionment of suffering among individuals is entirely irreconcilable by us with any divine plan of adjustment of particular afflictions to the particular needs, circumstances, and stages of moral development, of individual sufferers. Even more distressing to human thought than the goading intensity of some kinds of pain is the seemingly chaotic distribution of human ills. If we could trace the utility of particular sufferings with their varying degrees of endurableness, or discern any adaptation of pain to the person's sensibility, moral state, and need of awakening or chastening, then philosophy might be able to agree with the simple-minded piety which assigns a special purpose to every instance of suffering, and finds therein the visitation or appointment of an all-wise and all-good God. But the wind is not tempered to the shorn lamb; the fieriest trials often overtake those who least need torments to inspire fear, to evoke repentance, or to perfect patience, and also those who, through no fault of their own, lack the mature religious faith and moral experience by which alone they could understand how affliction may be endured for their souls' good. "All things come alike to all: there is one event to the righteous and to the wicked"—to those who may be enabled, and to those who are unable, to profit by severe trial.

Disastrous as these facts are to the extremer forms of the doctrine of divine immanence in Nature, they are compatible with theism such as allows to the created world somewhat of delegated autonomy. According to the wider theodicy which has here been presented, the human afflictions arising from our relations with the physical world are not willed as such by God at all, or for any purpose. They are rather inevitable, if incidental, accompaniments or by-products of the world-order which, as a whole, and by means of

its uniformity, is a pre-requisite of the actualisation of the highest good that
we can conceive a world as embodying. The world is none the less God's
world for its callousness to man; but its autonomy, not the particular in-
cidence of each single ill, is what the religious should attribute to his "appointment."

Further, man himself does not deem his suffering to be an excessive price
to pay for the dignity of his ethical status, once he recognises physical evil
to be inevitable in a moral world. He is then not compelled to see in his
suffering self a mere means either to the perfecting of the race, or to the
realisation of a divine purpose, or to the manifestation of the "glory" of
God. And this is an important consideration for any theodicy. For man is an
end for himself, whatever else he may be. *My* ills can only be justified to *me*
if the remoter advantage of there being ills at all be *mine:* not humanity's,
or even God's, alone. But in that the remoter advantage is the enjoyment of
rational and ethical dignity, the individual man can acquiesce in God's purpose for the world: God's ideal may be his also. It is the assurance that God
is fulfilling us individually as well as Himself, and fulfilling us for ourselves
as well as for Himself, that makes human life in this bitter-sweet world en-
durable by the sensitively and delicately minded, the tender-hearted, believer.
It is because a being of the earth, yet so God-like as man, could not be
moulded into the image of God *save from within himself,* as a person or a
free agent, that man can account the payment of the sometimes exorbitant
price of the chance of learning love inevitable.

If the doctrine of a future life be a corollary of theism, or an implication
of the moral purposiveness and meaning which may reasonably be read into
the cosmos, it can be invoked to throw further light on the problem of evil.
The balance of felicity and unhappiness in an individual life cannot be struck
so long as we confine our thought to experience of the present world alone,
if we have reason to believe that the earth is "no goal, but starting-point for
man." We may then venture to add to our knowledge the faith that "the
sufferings of this present time are not worthy to be compared with the glory
that shall be revealed." Pain is indeed none the less pain, nor any kind of
evil the less evil, for that it shall be done away, or compensated, or because
it is a necessary means or by-product. But its hideousness is somewhat transfigured if, besides being involved in the "best possible" world, it can be seen
to have been "but for a moment" in the time-span of just men made perfect.
It is not the reality of evil that is here under consideration, but simply the
worth-whileness of this life in which evil has a temporary and necessary
place. That should not be estimated by looking only at what may now be seen;
but for the idea of compensation hereafter theodicy and theistic religion have
no further use. They do not ask us to tolerate the evils of the present world,
and to abstain from blaming the Creator for them, because of a compensation
stored up for us in another world: they rather insist that in this life, with all

its evils, we may already discern the world-purpose of God to be a reign of love.

This life acquires, indeed, a new aspect if death be but translation to another mansion in the Father's house, and exchange of one kind of service for another. And it is a question whether theism, in asserting the world-ground to be a Spirit and the Father of spirits, and in ascribing to the world the role of ministering to rational and moral life, can stop short of adding the doctrine of a future life to its fundamental articles of belief, without stultifying its previously reached interpretation of the world and man. For it would not be a perfectly reasonable world which produced free beings, with Godward aspirations and illimitable ideals, only to cut them off in everlasting death, mocking their hopes and frustrating their purposes. Such spirits, even with their moral status, would after all be pawns, not children of God. Certainly a God who can be worshipped by moral beings must be a respecter of the persons whom He has moulded into His own image. Hence theists generally regard the Supreme Being as a God, not of the dead, but of the living.

# NICOLAS BERDYAEV

*Nicolas A. Berdyaev* (1874–1948), émigré Russian philosopher and leading lay theologian of the Russian Orthodox Church, is well known for his eschatological philosophy of history, existentialist interpretation of Christian ethics, and penetrating criticisms of extreme rationalism.

## Evil

Suffering and evil are connected with each other, but they are not identical. Suffering may not be an evil; it may even be a good. The existence of evil is the greatest mystery in the life of the world and causes the greatest embarrassment to official theological doctrine and to all monistic philosophy. A rationalistic solution of the problem of evil is just as beset with difficulty as a solution of the problem of freedom. It can be asserted and with good

From Nicolas Berdyaev, *The Divine and the Human,* trans. R. M. French, pp. 86–97. Published, 1949, by Geoffrey Bles, Ltd. Used by permission of Geoffrey Bles. [Footnotes omitted, Eds.]

grounds, that evil has no positive existence and that it can only allure by what it filches from good. But none the less evil not only exists but it prevails in the world. What may be called non-being may have an existential significance; nonentity has great existential significance, although it would be untrue to say that it exists. One of the attempts to solve the problem of evil, and to reconcile it with the possibility of theodicy, amounts to this, that evil is present only in the parts, whereas in the whole there is only good. It was thus that St. Augustine thought, and Leibnitz, and indeed in the last resort, most forms of theodicy adopt the same position, for they admit that God uses evil for the purposes of good. But that sort of doctrine is based upon the denial of the unconditional significance of all personality, and it is a characteristic rather of ancient moral philosophy than of Christian. It means the prevalence of the aesthetic point of view over the ethical.

It is in fact true that in this empirical world there is no good divine teleological principle, and indeed there cannot be in a world which is recognized as fallen. It might be said that such exists for separate groups of phenomena but not for the whole phenomenal world, not as a connecting link among these phenomena for the sake of Good. The traditional doctrine of Providence is compelled to deny the evil and injustice of the world and it finds a way out of the difficulty in the fact that instead of evil it recognizes simply the existence of sin. There is in our world an insurmountable conflict between the individual and the race. The individual life, both human and animal, is fragile and menaced to an extraordinary degree, but at the same time our racial life has an extraordinary productive power, and is always begetting life afresh. The doctrine which sees evil only in the parts and does not see it in the whole, is at the mercy of race and is indifferent to the individual. The genius of race is cunning; it is always prompting unhappy man to accept false justifications, and by means of these it holds him in bondage; and historical and social life is, therefore, based upon an accumulation of such falsehood. A lie may be self-deception, when a man becomes the plaything of the commonplace social forces of life. A lie may also take the form of a defence of life against attacks upon it. The question of truth and falsehood is a fundamental moral question.

Man seeks to find refuge from the tormenting question of evil in the realm of neutrality, and by doing so seeks to conceal his treachery to God. But in the deeper sense there is no neutrality; the neutral is on the surface. It might even be said that the devil is neutral. It is a mistake to suppose that the devil is the polar opposite of God. The pole which is the direct opposite of God is again God, the other face of God; extremes meet. The devil is the prince of this world and he takes cover in neutrality. In religious life in general, and in the Christian life, belief in demons and in the devil has played an enormous role. It has been one of the solutions of the problem of evil. When the devil is regarded as the source of evil, objectivization of the interior drama of the human soul takes place. The devil is an existential reality but is certainly not an objective reality in the world of things like the realities of the natural world. He is a reality of spiritual experience, of the path along which man goes. The idea of the devil has been greatly abused socially. Men and women have been held in fear by it, and the kingdom of the devil has been expanded to enormous dimensions, new areas have been continually added to it. Thus a real spiritual reign of terror has been established. Liberation of the soul from the demons which torment it is possible only in a purified spiritual religion. Demonology and demonolatry have existed only on the path which man follows towards the kingdom of spirit, towards the kingdom of freedom and love, towards the Kingdom of God.

The fight against evil easily acquires an evil character itself; it becomes infected by evil. There is a sinister moral dialectic of Manichaean dualism. Too great foes of evil become evil themselves. This is a paradox of the conflict with evil and with evil men and things. The good become evil for the sake of victory over evil and do not believe in the use of other methods than evil in the conflict against evil. Kindliness invites an attitude of disdain, it appears to be uninteresting and insipid. Malice, on the other hand, imposes itself and appears more interesting and more attractive. Those engaged in the struggle think that malice is more intelligent than kindness. Here the problem lies in the fact that actually it is impossible to give effect to the purposes of good, to good ends; this too easily leads to evil and the employment of evil means. It is necessary to be within the good and to radiate the good. It is only the Gospel which overcomes this rebirth of the conflict with evil in the form of a new evil, and regards the condemnation of sinners as a new sin. One must behave with humanity and kindliness even to the devil. There is a dialectic of one's behaviour to the enemy and to evil. You begin by fighting in the name of good against the enemy, against the evil, but you end by being yourself permeated with evil. The problem of one's attitude to the enemy is the fundamental moral problem of our time. The enemy is ceasing to be regarded as a man, there must be no human attitude towards him. In this respect the greatest apostasy from the truth of the Gospel has taken place. I do not think that there are any hopelessly demoniacal natures, that is to say natures over whom the doom of demoniacal possession hangs, just as I do not think that demoniacal nations have existed. What exists is simply a demoniacal condition of people and nations and, therefore, a final judgment is possible upon nobody.

As there is a dialectic of the attitude to the enemy in virtue of which he who fights an evil enemy in the name of good becomes evil, so also there is a dialectic of humility in virtue of which it is turned into passivity in the face of evil, and into accommodation to evil. In the same way there is a dialectic of punishment for crime which turns the punishment itself into a crime. There is in human beings an irresistible need for a scapegoat, for an enemy who is to blame for all their misfortunes and whom they can and even should hate. It may be the Jews, heretics, masons, Jesuits, Jacobins, Bolshevists, bourgeois, international secret societies, and so forth. Revolution always requires an enemy for its nourishment and if there is no enemy it invents one. The same is true of counter-revolution. When the scapegoat is found man begins to feel better. This is an objectivization of evil, an ejection of it into external reality. The State rightly carries on a fight against crime, and against external expressions of evil which are unduly vigorous, but nevertheless the State itself commits crime and does evil. As "the most cold-blooded of monsters" (the expression is Nietzsche's) it commits crime, it creates evil without passion and in the abstract. In upholding law and right the State defends the good but it creates its own particular evil. The evil need to experience the joy of cruelty is objectivized, the collective sense of satisfaction in being the cause of pain, in having the right to punish and to be present at the infliction of punishment.

The relations between good and evil are not simple and there is a complex existential dialectic in them. Good may be reborn as evil and evil may be reborn as good. The very distinction between good and evil has been an unhealthy and morbid division and has borne the impress of having passed through the Fall. There is something servile in the interpretation of sin as crime which infringes the will of God and calls for legal proceedings on the part of God. To overcome this servile conception means movement within, movement in depth. Sin is dividedness, a state of deficiency, incompleteness, dissociation, enslavement, hatred, but it is not disobedience and not formal violation of the will of God. It is impossible and inadmissible to construct an ontology of evil. The idea of an eternal hell is, therefore, absurd and evil. Evil is but a pathway, a testing, a disruption; to fall into sin is above all else a testing of freedom. Man moves towards the light through the darkness. Dostoyevsky revealed this more profoundly than anyone.

Evil is usually explained in terms of freedom. This is the most widespread explanation of evil. But freedom is a mystery which does not lend itself to rationalization. The traditional doctrine of the schools about the freedom of the will is static and reveals very little of the mystery of the rise of evil. It remains incomprehensible how out of the good nature of man and of the devil himself, out of heavenly life in the rays of the light of God, there could arise—thanks to the freedom of the creature (freedom which it understood to be the highest gift of God and a mark of likeness to God)—how there could arise evil and the evil life of man and of the world, evil which is reminiscent of hell. It is necessary to concede the existence of an uncreated freedom which precedes being and is submerged in the irrational sphere, in what Boehme calls the *Urgrund*, though he gave a somewhat different meaning to it. The recognition of such a freedom, preceding being, preceding creation, premundane, sets before man the creative task of continuing the creation of the world, and makes evil itself a path, a grievous experience, but not an ontological principle which passes over into eternity (hell). Freedom must be understood dynamically, as engaged in a dialectic process. There are contradictions in freedom, and varying conditions and laws belong to it. Evil raises the eschatological problem in an acute form and it is removed and overcome only eschatologically.

The fight against evil must be carried on and evil must be finally overcome, and at the same time the experience of evil has been a path which leads not only downwards but upwards also. It is not evil itself which has been an upward path, but the spiritual strength of the resistance aroused by it and the knowledge which was born of it. Evil is meaningless, and at the same time it has the highest meaning. In the same way freedom is the antithesis of necessity and bondage, but it can be reborn as necessity and bondage, it can pass into its opposite. Man must go through the testing of all possibilities, he must pass through the experience of the knowledge of good and evil, and evil itself may become a dialectic moment of good. And evil must be overcome immanently, that is to say, there must take place what Hegel called *Aufhebung,* when the negative is overcome, and all the positive enters into the subsequent stage. Thus even atheism may become a dialectic moment in the knowledge of God. It is the lot of man to pass through atheism, through communism, and many other such things in order that he may move out towards the light by an immanent, enriching, act of overcoming. What is needed is not the destruction of those who are "evil" but their enlightenment. Evil can be vanquished only from within, not by violent prohibition alone, nor can it be destroyed by force. Yet at the same time external limits ought to be set to the manifestations of evil which are destructive of life. Both a spiritual and a social conflict ought to be carried on against evil, and the social conflict cannot avoid having recourse to force in the conditions of this world. But the spiritual conflict, on the other hand, can only be carried on as a process of enlightenment and transfiguration, not by resort to violence.

The experience of evil cannot in itself enrich, if one surrenders to it. It is only that positive radiant spiritual power which is brought out in the overcoming of evil, which is able to enrich. Light presupposes darkness, good presupposes evil, creative development presupposes not only "this" but also "the other." It was Boehme and Hegel who understood this best. Evil has the mastery in this world, but it is not to evil that the last word belongs. Evil can be a dialectic moment in the unfolding development of created things, but only because through it the good which is opposed to it is disclosed. The idea of hell and the torments of hell was an eternalization of evil; it represents a failure of strength in the face of it. Evil presupposes freedom and there is no freedom without the freedom of evil, that is to say there is no freedom in a state of compulsory good. But evil is directed against freedom; it seeks to destroy it and to enthrone slavery. According to Kierkegaard man becomes an ego through sin; only he who goes down into hell knows heaven, and he who is the farther from God may be the nearer to God. In Kierkegaard's view the begetting of children is the primary sin. Baader says that life is born in pain and makes its appearance only after a descent into hell. There is a flash of light on the frontier between the world of darkness and the world of light. At the outset evil behaves towards us as towards a master, later on it treats us as fellow-workers and in the end itself becomes the master. All ideas are dynamic, they presuppose contradiction and a process which arises from contradiction.

Two opposite causes give rise to evil in man. Either a vacuum is formed in the soul and proves attractive to evil, or a passion which has become an *idée fixe,* and crowded out everything else, degenerates into evil. Such passions are, for instance, ambition, avarice, jealousy, hatred. The passion is not yet evil in itself but it easily becomes an evil and leads to the loss of inward freedom. A passion for death is also possible. It is difficult for a man in whom moral and religious consciousness had been already formed to commit the first transgression, but the first offence easily gives rise to the second offence, and the man enters into a magical atmosphere of delinquency. This is admirably depicted by Shakespeare in Macbeth. It is difficult to enter upon the path of terrorism, but afterwards it is difficult to stop and bring it to an end. Evil is above all the loss of integrality; it is a breaking away from the spiritual centre, and the formation of autonomous parts which begin to carry on an independent existence of their own. The good in man, on the other hand, is inner integrality, interior unity, the subordination of the life of the soul and of bodily life to a spiritual principle. Evil belongs to this world and, given an apophatic interpretation of the divine, it cannot be transferred to the life beyond. The idea of hell was not a victory over evil but rather an immortalization of it.

In the face of the tormenting problem of evil, both optimism and pessimism are alike untrue. What is needed is to be more of a pessimist in the recognition of evil in this phenomenal world where the prince of this world reigns, and more of an optimist in the denial of it in the world beyond. The concrete knowledge of life, the vision of all its secrets in detail, is a very bitter knowledge. The coming of a better life is merely symbolized in revolutions, political or religious, the better life itself does not come, the entirely new man does not make his appearance. Always the very basest expressions of human life come to light anew; in oppression and persecution, whether it be religious, national, or political, whether it be the outcome of class feeling or belongs to the realm of ideas. Collective enthusiasm easily ends in the setting up of a Gestapo or a Cheka. The life of man in civilization has an irresistible tendency to disintegration, corruption, to collapse into fatuity. Then appears the desire to save oneself by movement in the opposite direction, to take refuge in nature, in the country, in labour, asceticism, monasticism; but this movement also easily leads to ossification or to dissolution.

It is an astounding thing that when people repent they do not, as a rule, repent for that for which they needed to repent. Torquemada did not repent of his actual sin as an inquisitor, he was convinced that he was serving God. Christian people desire not so much a real change and trans-formation of their nature as absolution for their sins. Religious ideologies and beliefs become a matter of fresh hatred and hostility. The religion of love and forgiveness enshrines a struggle for power. States and societies are always offensive and aggressive, so that human personality is obliged to be always on the defensive. The love of woman may have a redemptive saving significance (in *The Flying Dutchman;* in the case of Sollweg in *Peer Gynt;* or Jouhandot in *Véronique*). Here the image of the Mother of God is, as it were, always meeting us. But the love of woman can much more often be a cause of ruin. Propitiatory blood sacrifices should have had a redemptive significance, but, as it was, they expressed the cruelty and bloodthirstiness of man. And to this very day bloody human sacrifices are offered for the sake of ideas and beliefs which have all the appearance of nobility. All this bitter knowledge of life is not final knowledge, it is not knowledge of the last things. Behind all the darkness of the world and human life a light is hidden, and there are other moments when this light is so strong that it blinds us. Man ought to look evil straight in the face, to allow himself no illusions about it, but never to be overwhelmed by it. Truth lies beyond optimism and pessimism. The absurdity of the world is not a denial of the existence of meaning. The exposure of lack of meaning presupposes the existence of meaning. The evil of the world presupposes the existence of God, without it, it would be impossible to get to know Him.

Nobility, the quality which I call true aristocracy, requires of a man the recognition of his guilt. In its depths, conscience, which is frequently cov-ered up and suppressed, is always a consciousness of guilt. The necessary thing is to take upon oneself as much guilt as possible and to put as little as possible of it upon other people. The aristocrat is not one who is proudly conscious of himself as first, as a privileged being, and who safeguards his position as such. The aristocrat is the man who is aware of the guilt and sinfulness of this first place, this privileged position of his. The sense that one is being continually affronted is on the other hand, precisely a plebeian feeling. But it is all too easy to condemn the *ressentiment* of the oppressed and those whose position in society comes last. Max Scheler has done this, and most unjustly, from the point of view of a Nietzscheanized Christianity. The *ressentiment,* into which envy enters is indisputably not a noble senti-ment, but there may be all too good grounds for its existence, and it is not for him who is to blame for the *ressentiment* of the humiliated, to busy himself with accusations of it. None the less the most profound thing is not the consciousness of one's own sinfulness (which may remain in the sphere of psychology and ethics), but the metaphysical consciousness of the position of man in the world; man who has infinite struggling aspirations while placed in the circumstances of a finite and compressed existence. In this lies the fall of man, and in this lies the origin of the formation by unenlightened passions of illusory false worlds.

Man finds difficulty in enduring the fact that he is in this world as a mortal creature and that everything which happens in him and with him is mortal. Hence the problem of evil is above all the problem of death. Victory over evil is victory over death. Evil is death; victory over evil is the resuscitation of life, rebirth to a new life. Murder, hatred, revenge, treachery and perfidy, debauchery, slavery, are death. The victory of God-manhood over the last enemy, death, is victory over evil. It is the victory of love, of freedom and creativeness, over hatred, slavery and inertia, the victory of personality over impersonality. The last enemy, death, has a positive meaning too. The tragic sense of death is connected with an acute sense of personality, of personal destiny. For the life of the race there is nothing tragic in death. The life of the race always renews itself and continues, it finds compensation for itself. Death appals the most developed and individualized organism most of all. With an acute sense of personality is associated an acute sense of evil also. The positive meaning of death lies in the fact that its inevitability for the individual personal existence is evidence of the unattainability of the infinite enterprises of life, and of the impossibility of realizing fullness of life within the limits of this world and this time.

Death, that final evil, is one of the paths to eternity. Endless life in the conditions of our limited existence would be a nightmare. To pass through death is just as necessary for our personal destiny in eternity, as the end of the world is necessary for the accomplishment of its eternal destiny. The antinomies and problems of human life and of the life of the world are insoluble in this aeon, and, therefore, a transition to another aeon is necessary. For this reason fear of death is not the only possibility; there is also an attraction of death. The thought of death is sometimes a consolation to a man when the contradictions of his life become intolerable, when the evil around him grows too dense. Freud regarded the instinct of death not only as of a higher order than the sexual instinct but as the sole elevated instinct in man. Heidegger is likewise compelled to recognize death as higher than *Dasein,* which is submerged in the humdrum and prosaic, in *das Man.* The last word in his philosophy belongs to death. It is an interesting fact that to the German spirit there is in general something attractive about death, victory and death. Wagner's music was permeated with the sense of victory and death; Nietzsche preached the will to power and an ecstatic joy in life, but in his perpetually tragic feeling about life the most profound and final thing was *Amor fati*. There has been depth in the German spirit but there has been no resuscitating strength.

That resuscitating strength does exist in the Russian spirit, and Fedorov represented the summit of its expression. And it is not a matter of chance that the principal festival of Russian Orthodoxy is the Feast of the Resurrection of Christ. It is thus that Christianity is understood. The source of victory over the evil of life in this world is not in death and it is not in birth, but in resurrection. The experience of the evil of the world destroys, but the creative power of resurrection conquers evil and death. Christian ethics in respect of evil as a whole and of individual evils can but be paradoxical. In Christ the God-Man and in the divine-human process, the transfiguration of the whole cosmos is being made ready. It is impossible to think of evil and of freedom, which is connected with evil, in an ontological and static way. They must be thought of dynamically in the language of spiritually existential experience.

# NINIAN SMART

---

*Professor Ninian Smart* (1927–    ) of the University of Birmingham, England, is a provocative commentator on contemporary theology and philosophy and is a student of world religions. His work is characterized by a wide range of interests and a keen analytical ability. He has been a visiting lecturer at several American universities.

---

## Omnipotence, Evil and Supermen

It has in recent years been argued, by Professors Antony Flew and J. L. Mackie;[1] that God could have created men wholly good. For, causal determinism being compatible with free will, men could have been made in such a way that, without loss of freedom, they would never have fallen (and

---

From *Philosophy*, Vol. XXXVI, No. 137 (1961). Pp. 188–195. Reprinted by permission of the author and the editors of *Philosophy*.

[1] See Antony Flew, "Divine Omnipotence and Human Freedom," in *New Essays in Philosophical Theology*, A. Flew and A. MacIntyre, eds. (New York: The Macmillan Company, 1955), Chap. 8, and J. L. Mackie, "Evil and Omnipotence," *Mind*, Vol. LXIV, No. 254 (April 1955).

would never fall) into sin. This if true would constitute a weighty antitheistic argument. And yet intuitively it seems unconvincing. I wish here
to uncover the roots of this intuitive suspicion.

There are in the argument two assertions to be distinguished. First, that
causal determinism (i.e., the claim that all human actions are the results of
prior causes) is compatible with free will.[2] I call this the Compatibility
Thesis. Second, there is the assertion that God could have created men
wholly good. This I shall call the Utopia Thesis. An apparent inference
from the latter is that God cannot be both omnipotent and wholly good,
since men are in fact wicked.

In the present discussion I shall concentrate on the Utopia Thesis. Clearly,
of course, if the Compatibility Thesis is not established the Utopia Thesis
loses its principal basis and becomes altogether doubtful. But I shall here
merely try to show that the Utopia Thesis does not follow from the Compatibility Thesis, despite appearances. This may well indicate that there is
something queer about the latter (and the Paradigm Case Argument, on
which perhaps it principally rests, has lately come in for perspicacious criticisms).[3] In the discussion I shall be assuming the truth of determinism;
for if it is false, the Compatibility Thesis becomes irrelevant and the Utopia
Thesis totters. The chief points in my reasoning are as follows:

The concept *good* as applied to humans connects with other concepts such
as *temptation, courage, generosity,* etc. These concepts have no clear application if men were built wholly good. I bring this out by a piece of anthropological fiction, i.e., (1) let us conjure up a universe like ours, only where
men are supposed to be wholly good; or (2) let us consider the possibility
of Utopian universes quite unlike ours. Under (1), I try to show that it
is unclear whether the "men" in such a universe are to be called wholly good
or even good, and that it is unclear whether they should be called men.
And under (2), I try to show that we have even stronger reasons for saying
that these things are unclear. Thus the abstract possibility that men might
have been created wholly good has no clearly assignable content. Hence,
it is rational to be quite agnostic about such a possibility. It follows that it
will be quite unclear whether a Utopian universe will be superior (in respect
of moral goodness) to ours. So the Utopia Thesis cannot constitute an
antitheistic argument.

---

[2] See Flew, *op. cit.,* p. 151.
[3] See the article "Farewell to the Paradigm-Case Argument" by J. W. N. Watkins, and
Flew's comment and Watkins' reply to the comment, all in *Analysis,* Vol. XVIII, No. 2
(1957), and the articles by R. Harré and H. G. Alexander in *Analysis,* Vol. XVIII, Nos.
4-5 (1958), respectively.

*I*

When we say that a man is good, we are liable to render an account of why we say this by giving reasons. For example, it might be because he has been heroic in resisting temptations, courageous in the face of difficulties, generous to his friends, etc. Thus *good* normally connects with concepts like *courage* and so forth.

Let us look first at *temptation*. It is clear (at least on the determinist assumption) that if two identical twins were in otherwise similar situations but where one has a temptation not to do what is right, while no such temptation is presented to the other twin, and other things being equal, the tempted twin will be less likely to do what is right than the untempted one. It is this fact that temptations are empirically discovered to affect conduct that doubtless makes it relevant to consider them when appraising character and encouraging virtue. Moreover, unless we were built in a certain way there would be no temptations: for example, unless we were built so that sexual gratification is normally very pleasant there would be no serious temptations to commit adultery, etc. It would appear then that the only way to ensure that people were wholly good would be to build them in such a way that they were never tempted or only tempted to a negligible extent. True, there are two other peculiar possibilities, which I shall go on to deal with, namely (1) through lucky combination of circumstances men might never sin; (2) frequent miraculous intervention might keep them on the straight and narrow path. However, for the moment, I consider the main possibility, that to ensure that *all* men were *always* good, men would have to possess a built-in resistance to all temptations.

Similar remarks apply to courage, generosity, etc., although in some cases the situation may be rather complex. It will, I think, be conceded that we credit people with courage on such grounds as that they have faced adverse situations with calm and disregard for danger. But the adversities arise because there are fears, desires for comfort, disinclinations to offend people, and so on. And it will be generally agreed, at least by determinists, that one twin faced with a situation where doing right inspires fear will be less likely to do what is right than the other twin not so faced with adversity, and similarly with regard to desires for comfort and so forth. Thus to ensure that men would never panic, never wilt, etc., it would be necessary, as the main possibility, to build them differently.

Perhaps generosity is a trickier case. But it is clear that a person is praised for generosity because very often there is a conflict of generosity and self-interest. Indeed, if there were not some such conflict, or thought to be, however remote, an action would not really count as generosity, perhaps; the slight qualification here is due to the possibility of situations where a person has so much money, say, that it makes no psychological difference whether he gives away a certain sum or not, but he does it out of sympathy —I shall deal with such cases below. And to say that generosity conflicts with self-interest is a shorthand way of saying that one's inclinations for comfort, etc., are liable to have a more restricted fulfilment than would otherwise be the case.

Then there are actions which exhibit such dispositions as pride, which seem remote from simple inclinations such as likings for certain sorts of food or for sexual gratification and from fairly simple impulses such as fear. But though the springs of pride are hard to fathom, it is doubtless true that people would not display pride, in the ordinary sense, if they did not live in a socially competitive atmosphere, if they did not have desires to assert themselves, etc. One would not be sure quite how men would have to be rebuilt to immunize them from pride, but rebuilding would surely be necessary, on the determinist view.

As for the peculiar cases mentioned above—generosity not involving sacrifice and similar examples—I do not think that such instances are at all serious ones, inasmuch as (1) virtues are dispositions, and so there is a point in calling such nonsacrificial generosity generosity, in that it exhibits a disposition whose basic exercise involves sacrifice; (2) without the occasions for basic exercise of the disposition it is obscure as to what could be meant by calling the nonbasic instances of generosity instances of generosity.

These examples, then, are meant to indicate that the concept *goodness* is applied to beings of a certain sort, beings who are liable to temptations, possess inclinations, have fears, tend to assert themselves and so forth; and that if they were to be immunized from evil they would have to be built in a different way. But it soon becomes apparent that to rebuild them would mean that the ascription of goodness would become unintelligible, for the reasons why men are called good and bad have a connection with human nature as it is empirically discovered to be. Moral utterance is embedded in the cosmic status quo.

## II

Of course, God is not bound by synthetic necessities: He is in no way shackled by the causal laws of our universe, for example. But in a back-handed way, He is confined by meaninglessness. For to say that God might do such-and-such where the "such-and-such" is meaningless or completely obscure is not to assert that God can *do* anything. I therefore hope to show that "God might have created men wholly good" is without intelligible content, and hence that this alleged possibility has no force as an antitheistic argument.

"God might have created men wholly good" *appears* to have content because at least it does not seem self-contradictory and because we think we can imagine such a situation. But I shall bring out its emptiness by in fact trying to do this, by imagining other possible universes. Now it may well be objected that in doing this I am showing nothing. For example, one will be wanting to make imaginative causal inferences like "If men are never to panic they must be built in such-and-such a way." But since God is not bound by causal principles the inferences have no legitimacy.

But this objection misses the point of my procedure. For my argument is based on the following dilemma. *Either* we can hope to assign a reasonably clear meaning to the possibility that men might have been created wholly good by imagining a Utopia—in which case the paradox arises that it would be quite unclear as to whether such "men" could reasonably be called wholly good. *Or* we can refuse to assign such a reasonably clear meaning to the possibility by simply postulating an unimaginable alternative universe—in which case there are even stronger reasons for doubting whether the possibility has content. Or, to make the matter *ad hominem* as against Flew, I am saying that alleged possibilities as well as alleged facts can die the Death by a Thousand Qualifications.

I proceed then to imagine possible universes. In line with the above dilemma, I divide such universes into two classes. First, those which are cosmomorphic, i.e., those which are governed by physical laws at least roughly comparable to those found in our cosmos. Second, I consider non-cosmomorphic universe, i.e., ones with a quite different set-up from ours.

1. *Cosmomorphic Utopia A*—The first and main type of cosmomorphic utopia, where men are wholly good, can be described perhaps as follows, in line with the earlier remarks about temptation, etc.

Men will never be seriously tempted to harm or injure each other. For this reason: that no one has any serious desires liable to conflict with those of others. For instance, they would be so built that one and only one woman would attract any one man and conversely. Say: one would have an over-riding infatuation for the first uninfatuated woman one met and vice versa. As for property: men might arrive in the world with an automatic supply of necessities and comforts, and the individual would have a built-in mechanism to ensure that the supplies of others were mysteriously distasteful (the other man's passion-fruit smells like dung). And what of danger? During, say, a thunderstorm no one would be so seriously perturbed that he would be likely to panic and harm others. Let us suppose that a signal would (so to speak) flash in the individual's brain, telling him to take cover. What if he was in the middle of an *al fresco* dinner? Perhaps the signal flashing would dry up the juices in his mouth. And so forth. (Admittedly this picture is not elaborated with much scientific expertise: of this I shall say more later.)

I think that none of the usual reasons for calling men good would apply in such a Utopia. Consider one of these harmless beings. He is wholly good, you say? Really? Has he been courageous? No, you reply, not exactly, for such creatures do not feel fear. Then he is generous to his friends perhaps? Not precisely, you respond, for there is no question of his being ungenerous. Has he resisted temptations? No, not really, for there are no temptations (nothing you could really *call* temptations). Then why call them good? Well, you say, these creatures never harm each other. . . . Yes, but the inhabitants of Alpha Centauri never harm *us*. Ah, you reply, Centaurians do not harm us because there are as yet no ways for them to impinge upon us. Quite so, I say; it is causally impossible for them to harm us. Similarly the set-up of the Cosmomorphic Utopians makes it causally impossible for them to harm each other. The fact that it is distance in the one case and inner structure in the other makes no odds.

Now admittedly in such a conversation we are not brought face to face with the Death by a Thousand Qualifications in the form described by Flew in regard to such statements as "God loves His children." For there the criticism of the theologian is that when counterevidence is presented he takes refuge in increasingly recondite senses of "love." But in the present case one who claims that the inhabitants of Cosmomorphic Utopia A are wholly good is not precisely resisting counterevidence (that is, he is not resisting evidence that these creatures are not good and so possibly bad). Rather he is failing to give the usual reasons for calling them bad. And the positive moves are up to him. It is not sufficient airily and vaguely to say that in such an alternative universe men can be said to be wholly good. Similarly the traveller from Jupiter who tells us that unicorns are to be found there, though queer unicorns for they possess neither horns nor feet, leaves us at a justifiable loss.

Hence it is so far obscure as to what is meant by the possibility that men might have been created wholly good. For the usual criteria, at least in Cosmomorphic Utopia A, do not seem to apply. And so, even if the Compatibility Thesis is correct, it does not appear so far evident that men might have been created wholly good. For an unintelligible assertion cannot either be said to follow or not to follow from some other. And in any case, are the Utopians described above properly to be called *men?* Perhaps we ought to invent a new name: let us dub them "sapients." The question for the theist now becomes: "Why did God create men rather than sapients?" I shall return to this question later.

2. *Cosmomorphic Utopia B*—Circumstances here combine always to make men good. Adolf Hitler would never in fact be foul. He might have incipient impulses of hatred towards Jews, but these would luckily never overwhelm him, because circumstances would prevent this: he would fall in love with a Jewess, he would never get into anti-Semitic company, he would not meet with miseries in his youth, and so forth. Whenever on the

point of falling for some temptation, his attention would be distracted. The whole thing would be a very, very long story. And everyone, not just the Führer, would be consistently lucky with regard to virtue and vice.

The trouble about this Utopia is that it is more like a dream than a fantasy. A corresponding meteorological dream would be: since circumstances occasionally combine to make the sun shine, let us suppose that the sky would never be overcast. This does not seem self-contradictory, to say "The sky might never be overcast." But what would a cosmomorphic universe have to be like for this to happen? Clearly it is not just luck that makes the sun shine sometimes: it is because the weather operates in a certain way. For the weather so to operate that it was never cloudy meteorological laws would have to be rewritten (and physics and biology too)—unless you are thinking of a place like the moon. Similarly, in a cosmomorphic utopia where circumstances for ever combined in favor of virtue, the set-up would, according to the determinist, have to be different. Thus Cosmomorphic Utopia B is either a version of A (or of some other) or it is a mere dream masquerading as an alternative universe.

3. *Cosmomorphic Utopia C*—Suppose men were always virtuous, not because of the set-up (which would be as now) but because of frequent miraculous intervention.

It is hard to make sense of the supposition. But observationally in such a world we might discover situations like this. Casual factors C usually give rise to actions of a certain empirical type, type-A. But in some circumstances type-A actions are wrong, and in these cases C will not have type-A effects. But it will not be that some other empirical factor will be present in such exceptions, for *ex hypothesi* the nonoccurrence of the type-A action is due to miraculous intervention. Hence either we have to count rightness and wrongness as empirical differences in order to formulate a causal law here or we must confess that no strict causal laws of human behavior could be formulated in this cosmos. The former alternative is baffling and unacceptable, while the latter is incompatible with determinism. Hence Cosmomorphic Utopia C provides no support for the Utopia Thesis.

4. I now turn to the thought of a *Noncosmomorphic Utopia*. As has been insisted, God is not limited to a cosmomorphic alternative. My anthropological fictions are feeble in comparison with the possibilities contained in God's thoughts. He might have produced a cosmos utterly unlike ours.

But as we have no notion what sapients in such a world would be like, it is even unclearer in this case what would be meant by calling them good. We would have to remain completely agnostic about such a world; and all the difficulties there are in knowing what is meant by calling God a person and good would recur with *extra* force when we try to understand what "wholly good men" could mean here. *Extra* force, because whereas God's nature is perhaps revealed to a limited extent in the *actual* cosmos, the nature of an alternative *possible* and *noncosmomorphic* universe can in no way be so revealed. Hence it follows that it is totally unclear what the possibility that God might have created a noncosmomorphic utopia amounts to.

It is therefore also unclear as to whether it would be superior to this universe. Moreover, it is most doubtful as to whether the sapients of Cosmomorphic Utopia A are superior to ourselves. I am not sure, of course, how one judges such matters; but if we rely on native wit, in default of some new method of evaluating alternative universes, it seems by no means clear that such a utopia is a better place than ours here.

## III

It may be complained that I have been unfair. My anthropological fiction has been crude and possibly biased. And the thing has not been worked out with any scientific expertise. But no one, so far as I know, with the requisite physiological, psychological and biological knowledge has attempted to work out such a fictional alternative anthropology, doubtless there are enough problems in the real-life biological sciences without our going off into subtle fantasies. But until someone were to do so, it remains obscure as to what a determinist cosmomorphic utopia would amount to.

Again it may be objected that writers have occasionally dreamed of utopias and described them. Surely these descriptions are not empty or self-contradictory? But first, fictions are no good guide unless systematically elaborated. For example, and notoriously, there are situations in science fiction which are revealed on reflection to be unintelligible or self-contradictory (e.g., in regard to "going back in time"). Again, fiction writers may not have any clearly formulated views about determinism. And it might turn out that what is allowable on a hard free will theory is not so on a determinist view. For example, an indeterminist may simply say that it might have been the case that men were always wholly good. But the determinist can only make sense of this possibility on the assumption that wholly good men would have a causal difference from men as they are. In order to imagine a man's always overcoming his harmful inclinations, he must surely imagine some change in the way his personality is built. But we have no assurance that some *unspecified* causal change would leave men more or less human and yet produce the consequence of complete goodness. Hence the change has to be specified. I have tried out a plausible fiction or two here, to show that so far one can assign no clear content to the possibility of men's being built wholly good. But maybe some determinist will dream up a plausible fantasy to establish his point. But let him do so: for so far the Utopia Thesis is wrapped in cloud.

Again it might be argued, from the side of theism, that this discussion works against angels just as much as it works against the possibility of wholly good men. If we cannot make sense of noncosmomorphic worlds we cannot make sense of angelic worlds. Maybe so: though angels, qua messengers of God, could share in the intelligibility of God. But that takes us too far afield.

*Conclusion*—My anthropological fiction seems to bring out the point that moral discourse is embedded in the cosmic status quo (or even more narrowly, in the planetary status quo). For it is applied to a situation where men are beings of a certain sort. Thus the abstract possibility that men might have been created wholly good loses its clarity as soon as we begin to imagine alternative possible universes. If then the Utopia Thesis is quite unclear, it cannot assert anything intelligible about God. And so it cannot serve as part of an antitheistic argument. There remains of course many serious difficulties for the theist in regard to human evil. But the Utopia Thesis is not one of them.

Or not yet. We shall see how the science fiction goes.

## Suggested Additional Readings

THE PROBLEM OF EVIL

*The Bible,* "Job." A dramatic presentation which deals with the problem of evil and the omnipotence of God.

Brightman, Edgar S. *A Philosophy of Religion.* Englewood Cliffs, N.J.: Prentice-Hall, 1940. See especially pp. 248f. An American personal idealistic philosopher feels that evil implies a limited God.

Farrer, Austin. *Love Almighty and Ills Unlimited.* New York: Doubleday, 1961. An incisive Augustinian treatment of evil.

Ferré, Nels F. S. *Evil and the Christian Faith.* New York: Harper & Row, 1947. See especially pp. 123–137. A clear explanation of evil and its relation to the Christian faith by a Protestant theologian.

Hick, John. *Evil and the God of Love.* New York: Harper & Row, 1966. A careful analysis of the problem of pain and of moral evil, together with his own theodicy, which is essentially Irenaen.

Laird, John. *Mind and Deity.* New York: Philosophical Library, 1941. See especially Chapter 6. A Scottish philosopher discusses evil in relation to the providence of God.

Lewis, C. S. *The Problem of Pain.* New York: The Macmillan Company, 1950. Discussion of pain by a well-known apologist for the Christian faith.

Lewis, Edwin. *The Creator and The Adversary.* New York: Abingdon-Cokesbury Press, 1948. A good exposition of the relation of evil to belief in God from the perspective of a Protestant theologian who struggles with the question of a limited God.

Maimonides, Moses. *Guide of the Perplexed.* Trans., M. Friedländer. New York: Hebrew Publishing Co., n.d. (Also published in paperback by Dover Publications, Inc.) See especially Part III. A well-known medieval Jewish philosopher insists that God is not responsible for evil.

Mill, John Stuart. *Three Essays on Religion.* New York: Holt, Rinehart & Winston, 1884. Explores the possibility of postulating a limited God as a way of solving the problem of evil.

Petit, Francois. *The Problem of Evil.* Trans., Christopher Williams. New York: Hawthorn Books, 1959. A recent statement which deals with this problem from a Roman Catholic point of view.

Rashdall, Hastings. *The Theory of Good and Evil,* vol. II. London: Oxford University Press, 1924. British philosopher and theologian committed to personal idealism offers a major study quite inclusive in its coverage.

Weiss, Paul. "Good and Evil." *Review of Metaphysics* (September, 1949), III, 1, no. 9, pp. 81–94. An American philosopher considers evil to be the conflict of opposing goods and evaluates traditional arguments as they may be seen by those accepting this position.

# Immortality

## VII. and

# Eschatology

THE POSSIBILITY OF life after death has engaged man's interest from earliest times. The reality of posthumous existence is usually a fundamental assurance of theistic religions, although in some forms of religion this belief has been absent or inconspicuous. In the Western philosophical tradition there has been ambivalence toward this idea: some philosophers have accepted immortality, whereas others have considered it an unsettled question or have denied its possibility altogether.

Those philosophers and theologians who have defended the belief in immortality have generally based their positions on one of two different foundations. Some have predicated their belief on what they take to be the indestructible nature of the human soul or of human values. Others have based their faith in immortality on a belief that God is able to resurrect man and to give him new life. The former argument derives from a belief in a special quality in man typically asserted by the Greeks, and more particularly, by Plato and his followers. Platonists see man as a unique being who has an intrinsic conformity with ultimate reality. This relationship is described in terms of the presence of an indestructible rational, and simple element in man, namely, a soul. This soul substance is in this world enmeshed in a material shell or body. The effort of man's philosophic or religious quest is to "tend the soul" or to understand rationally his relationship to ultimate reality and thereby to escape the corrupting and timebinding imprisonment of the flesh. Death, then, is the release of the soul from the prison of the body.

The argument for the future life in terms of resurrection involves different assumptions. On this view man is understood to be a mortal being, and death is seen as a final end. Only if some new creative act is executed is there hope for man to escape

[495]

death. God the Creator performs such acts. In His graciousness
He has provided for giving new life to man, a new life which
overcomes the threat of death and annihilation.

In the historical development of Western thought these approaches have sometimes been considered antithetical and sometimes complementary. Often in Christian interpretations one
can see illustrated the way in which these two approaches have
been taken to be complementary. For instance, it is sometimes
maintained that man has an immortal soul, but that only by an
act of God can the soul enter into the relationship with God
which is its ultimate purpose.

These traditional arguments have also been supplemented,
and sometimes supplanted, by other approaches. One of these
supplementary approaches sets the discussion in terms of a unique
quality of life in the present which may also extend into the
future. In this view, death and life are not seen primarily as
physical events, but are considered in terms of meanings and
purposes, or in terms of what is perhaps more generally called
life's present significance. It is at this point that one can see
the relevance of eschatology to our discussion.

In recent decades the use of the word "eschatology" and the
employment of "eschatological" categories have increased. Although there are different nuances of meaning in the word, its
basic import can be indicated. The word itself means the study
of the last things: such as death, judgment, heaven, and hell.
In recent times the term has tended to be used by those who
believe that the time of the final events, when life's ultimate
meaning will be revealed, is at hand. Intimately associated with
this position is the question: how does the end come? Does it
bring all normal history to a close and usher in a new era? Or
does it come within the present time in the form of new meaning
and new significance for the current order of things?

In the minds of many contemporary interpreters the terminus
and the subsequent new beginning of life come when an individual finds meaning in life. This, then, brings what are considered by some to be qualities possible only in a future life after
death. The claim of many who would bring the last things into
man's present experience is that man, in escaping meaninglessness, finds *life;* that is, his present mortal existence assumes a
new, eternal dimension. This dimension includes the "meaning"
that was incorporated in the ideas of death, judgment, heaven,
and hell. Those of this persuasion emphasize man's finitude, consequent alienation from God, and estrangement from God's pur-

pose. They feel that the world is broken or frustrated and that it can be fulfilled or completed only by God's action. Such action can take place in man's present experience and provide him with a new dimension of meaning. Most proponents of this view hold that this new level of existence extends beyond the eventual fact of physical death.

But not all thinkers believe it is possible to demonstrate that life can assume such a radically new dimension in the present or that it can reach beyond death. Materialists, rationalists, and humanists have often rejected these claims as untenable and unworthy of men who have the courage to face reality.

From these alternative possibilities it becomes apparent that a person's belief about the possibility of life after death is derived from his metaphysical or religious commitments. Thus materialism and behaviorism, which explain human life completely in terms of physical functions, exclude the possibility of immortality, whereas others who accept the eternal reality of values often argue that the ultimate extinction of persons as organized centers of value cannot be admitted. It is, of course, possible to accept the eternality of objective value without drawing the inference of human immortality.

A. E. Taylor, in his selection which follows, examines Christian concepts of immortality and makes interpretative comments on their development in terms of his own ethical interests. Oscar Cullmann defends the New Testament conception of resurrection and attempts to distinguish it from Greek conceptions of immortality.

The French philosopher, Jacques Maritain, provides a characteristic Thomistic interpretation and defense of the immortality of the soul, whereas Andrew Seth Pringle-Pattison gives an interesting and provocative interpretation of eternal life as a new dimension in the present. C. D. Broad, an English philosopher, offers a carefully reasoned analysis of the argument from the continuity of nature as it bears on the possibility of human survival beyond physical death.

F. R. Tennant conveniently classifies the arguments both for and against immortality, with brief comments on their significance. The student who has read the other selections will want to evaluate both Tennant's analysis and his interpretation of the meaning of classical types of argument for immortality. The approach of Ian T. Ramsey to the question of human immortality reflects his concern with empiricism and linguistic analysis. Nicolas Berdyaev, writing from an existentialist orientation, recognizes the threat of death to meaningful living and yet asserts that there is purpose for life despite this threat. Our final selection is taken from Ludwig Wittgenstein. In his typical epigrammatic style, Wittgenstein comments on the meaning of eternity and immortality and on philosophical method in relation to such issues, concluding with his famous dictum, "What we cannot speak about we must consign to silence."

# ALFRED E. TAYLOR

A. E. *Taylor* (1869–1954) taught philosophy at Aberdeen and Edinburgh
and made contributions in the fields of history of philosophy, ethics, and
religion. His books, *Faith of a Moralist* and *Plato, The Man and His
Work*, are among his best known.

## The Christian Hope of Immortality

Let us begin our examination, then, by setting down briefly some of the
leading characteristics that seemed to us to distinguish an "immortality"
such as it is reasonable at least to hope for from one which would be a mere
arbitrary fancy without any rational justification.

(1) It is the attainment of a completed rational selfhood, or personality,
conscious of itself and in harmonious possession both of all its own internal
resources and of its "environment." Since it is only in and through intercourse with one another that personality is developed and maintained in us,
such a life can only be that of a *society* of persons of one heart and mind
from which the veil of mystery now making each of us so much a riddle to
the rest, and the self-centred "private interest" which sets barriers to community of will, purpose, and sympathy have been eliminated.

(2) It is a life communicated to those who share in it, in the first instance,
from the supreme personality presupposed by the very existence of the world
and of ourselves. At that fountain our personality is fed; if we enter into and
share the life of one another, in the way proper to moral persons, it is
because we are all admitted to be sharers in His life. The "brotherhood of
all men," so often dreamed of and longed for, is only possible in so far as all
men recognize themselves as "sons of God."

(3) It is no privilege reserved to an *élite* of the richly dowered and
gifted, but a heritage open to all mankind, high and low, learned and un-
learned, refined or homely, bond or free, in virtue of their common endowment with the capacity for personality.

(4) But, though it is thus, in the end, an inheritance and a gift, it is a
gift which has to be appropriated by genuine effort on our own part. We

From A. E. Taylor, *The Christian Hope of Immortality*, pp. 45–63. Published, 1947, The
Macmillan Company. Reprinted by permission of F. E. A. Taylor.

[499]

can render ourselves increasingly fit for it by steady and strenuous endeavour, or we can fail more and more to appropriate it by our own carelessness and sloth. Even in what we now see of human life, we are familiar enough with the fact that as a man uses or abuses his opportunities, he tends to grow more and more into true personality or to degenerate from it. It is possible to "save one's soul," but equally possible to lose it; eternal life can be won, but it can also be thrown away. And thus, in the end, we must expect it to be with each of us strictly "according to his works," good or evil, though we must never allow ourselves to forget that it is only the supreme Wisdom which knows the full good and evil of any man's "work" as it truly is; the account is not to be rendered to me, and my judgment of the quality of any man's work, and particularly perhaps of that of my own, must always be uncertain. To judge you or myself with the judgment of God, I should need first to see myself or you with the "all-seeing" eyes of the reader of all hearts, and that vision is not vouchsafed to us in our earthly pilgrimage.

(It should hardly be necessary, though to obviate a certain kind of criticism it may be judicious to say that in speaking of the Christian representation of the life to come, our attention will be confined to the few and reticent statements definitely made in the New Testament. We are not in the least concerned with the sometimes rather grotesque pictorial imagery of certain types of popular hymn or sermon. Such utterances are no part of the authoritative teaching of the Christian Church; their language, as everyone understands, is purely metaphorical, and the metaphors employed, being so largely borrowed from Old Testament poetry, are often not those which would spontaneously commend themselves to a modern European imagination, not to add that many of them have the further glaring fault of improperly transferring to the eternal life of "blessed spirits" in Heaven language used in the Apocalypse expressly of the "new Jerusalem" of an earthly "millennium." The golden streets, gates of pearl and foundations of precious stones, for example, all belong to the seer's imaginative description of the renovated terrestrial city; they have nothing to do with "Heaven" and "eternity.")

If we turn, then, to the four points we have just specified and take them in order, we shall, I believe, find that on each and all of them the teaching of Christianity exhibits a complete agreement with what we have called our natural and reasonable anticipations, but at the same time does more than merely repeat those anticipations; it adds something of its own, strictly in conformity with the "natural light," but yet not discoverable apart from an actual historical disclosure, first through the "prophets," and finally through the teaching, and even more, the life, death, and resurrection of our Lord Jesus Christ. Christianity—that is, if it is what it professes to be—is really a *revelation,* a disclosure of God's purposes for us, made from the side of God Himself, and, at the same time, the God to whom it bears witness is no other than the God to whom the careful and unbiased use of our own intelligence has been directing us. It is certainly a faith, but no less certainly, rightly apprehended a reasonable faith.

As to the first of our four points, we may note that the one thing definitely said about the hope held out to the Christian in the New Testament is that it is a being fully alive and fully conscious of the whole truth about our Maker, ourselves, and the world. Thus in the fourth Gospel the Evangelist's leading thought is that the divine Christ who, in the fullness of time has appeared among men, is Himself an eternal living personality, and has come into our midst in order to impart such personality to us. He was "in the beginning with God" and "was God." All creation was made "through Him," and, the writer goes on to explain—if we follow what seems the most probable punctuation—"that which was made was life in Him, and the life was the *light* of men." The life, that is, which is eternally inherent in the Christ is no blind "life force"; it is an intelligent personality, like that we find in a most imperfect measure in ourselves at our best, and aspire to possess in a fuller manner. So in the great prayer of Chapter xvii, our Lord describes the eternal life, which it is His mission to bestow on those who believe, as consisting in knowledge of "the only true God and Jesus Christ whom He has sent." What this implies is expressed in so many words in the first Epistle of John, where, amid all the reserve with which the writer confesses that we know and can know little or nothing, at present, of what eternal life is ("it doth not yet appear what we shall be"), he also insists that at least we shall be "like Him," because "we shall see Him as He is." That is, the knowledge of God as He is will transform us, as we attain to it, into God's likeness, since our personality inevitably shapes itself on the model of that which supplies the food of its habitual contemplation and meditation.

St. Paul again strikes the same note both in his reserves and in his certainties. He, too, will commit himself to no rash theosophic dreams of the future which lies before him; as he tells his Corinthian converts "what God had prepared for them that love Him" is something which "has not entered into man's heart," something transcending all our imaginative speculation; here on earth the best of us only see the reality dimly, through a mirror, so to say, and "in a riddle"; it is elsewhere, "yonder" as the Neo-Platonist philosophers were fond of saying, that it will be for us to see it as it is, and without the distortions which arise from the interposition of the "mirror," to "know even as we are known." Here our most certain knowledge is beset all around with a penumbra of obscurity and darkness; as the old proverb says, as soon as we pursue any of our inquiries more than a very little way, we come upon the inexplicable, *omnia abeunt in mysterium;* "yonder" there will be no unintelligibilities left, our vision will have the limpid transparency of God's, and our wills will be in perfect harmony with themselves and one another because our vision is clear. We shall be what we are here at best seeking to become, persons in full and conscious possession of our own personality.

The tradition of the great Christian divines has always been true to the lines thus laid down in the New Testament. The Greek Fathers did not shrink from translating the Johannine language about likeness to God as the result of "seeing Him as He is," into the formula that the process of attaining eternal life is one of *theosis* (*deification*), becoming ourselves divine, and the formula was retained by the Western Church, though with a preference for replacing the word *deification,* which might be misunderstood as though it were meant to efface the impassable gulf between the Creator and His creatures, by the less dangerous term, *deiformity.* If even that word sounds too presumptuous to certain modern ears we may gloss it by saying that in view of the thorough-going rationalism of medieval Christian thought, to achieve deiformity means neither more nor less than what we have ourselves spoken of as the attainment of an assured and conscious complete personality. When the great men of the Middle Ages spoke of human life as a pilgrimage of the soul to God, they did not mean, as an Indian Yogi might, that the goal of the pilgrim's journey is to lose himself in the impersonal. "The dewdrops slip into the boundless sea" may be a pretty phrase, but to the Christian ear it is charged with deadly heresy; the goal, as Christians have seen it, is not to lose one's personal self, but to find it for the first time and to find it beyond all possibility of loss. Certainly, according to the Gospels, the man who is set on keeping a dwarfish and misgrown self with its trivial lusts and limited and conflicting loves, will in the end lose himself, but he who is ready to set this more than half unreal self on the hazard will end by finding himself "unto life eternal," he will find the personality which God meant to be his, and he is the only man who will do so.

As to our second point, it would be wasting words to take up unnecessary space in dwelling on the fact that eternal life is always represented in the New Testament as a *gift* from God. It is enough for us to remember that St. Paul lays special stress on the contrast between the death which is the *wage* of sin and the eternal life which is not a wage but a free gift of God, and that the same thought reappears in the fourth Gospel when we find Christ saying that He grants it to His disciples to have life in themselves, as the Father has granted it to Him to have life in Himself. It is more to our purpose to note that the gift is not represented in the New Testament as bestowed on men by the fact of their creation. Men are not thought of as already sons of God and heirs of eternal life in virtue of their birth into the world as men; that is a modern "humanitarian" remodelling of the thought; according to the New Testament, men acquire sonship to God and the inheritance of eternal life by being "adopted" into the Christian fellow-ship; they are adopted, not natural sons of the Father in Heaven. This is why the first step on the way to eternal life can be called by St. Paul being a *"new* creation," and in the fourth Gospel being "born *again,"* and why in the Epistle of St. Peter God is said to have "begotten us again unto a lively hope by the *resurrection of Jesus Christ."* Those who are still outside the Christian fellowship are said, on the contrary, to be without hope in the world, and are spoken of not as sons of God, but as "children of wrath." The Christian conception is that eternal life is a gift which Christ is em-powered to confer on His followers, and only on them, though sight is never lost of the fact that any man is potentially a son of God, since any man may be re-born into the Christian fellowship.

This is not to say that the New Testament writers teach the doctrine of the "natural mortality of the soul." As their constant references to judg-ment to come show, they accept as something familiar to themselves and their readers the belief that we all survive what we call the death of the body. It is possible, no doubt, by a suitable exegesis to read into their writ-ings a doctrine of "conditional immortality," if that phrase is taken to mean that the final doom of the man who distinctly rejects Christ and His gift is complete dissolution of personality, but we cannot force on them the thought this dissolution is effected at the death of the present body. That, they assume, we shall all survive. But such mere survival, even if indefinitely prolonged, is not what they mean by "incorruptibility" or eternal life. They keep those names for the new quality of life enjoyed by the man who is "with the Lord" and "sees Him as He is." This is a point which is unfor-tunately obscured when Christian thinkers set themselves, as they have often done in the past, to try to demonstrate the immortality of the soul by rea-soning based simply on a theory of *its* nature, without any reference to God, except perhaps as the Creator of the soul and of everything else. It is there-fore, perhaps, from the Christian point of view a gain that arguments of this kind have fallen under suspicion, even excessive suspicion, ever since Kant's vigorous onslaught on them in the *Critique of Pure Reason.* An "immor-tality" which could be demonstrated without any reference to God would be only an indefinite survival which might conceivably prove to be the fact in a world where there was no God at all; this is not the "better life" that any religiously minded man, least of all a Christian, is particularly interested in.

It should be hardly necessary to remark, again, that there is a complete absence from the New Testament of any trace of the insidious tendency to regard God's gift of a full and completed personality as restricted to some little aristocracy of the intellectually highly endowed. "Heaven," as Chris-tianity conceives it, is not reserved for "superior persons"; it is full of "common people." This is, indeed, a direct consequence of the way in which, in the New Testament, the "promises" are regularly made not to the isolated individual, but to the whole society of the "re-born." They are promises to a "you," not to a "thou." We can, of course, understand how, in the necessary reaction of modern times against the coarsening and hardening of the original thought of the Gospel into the notion of a "salvation" to be mechanically earned by membership of a particular visible organization, men's minds should have been driven in the opposite direction, to the point of regarding "religion" as a purely private affair between the individual soul and its God. But neither this extreme "protestantism" (which, of course, was never contemplated by the original Protestants) nor its opposite, an extreme "institutionalism" has any true warrant in the New Testament. According to the New Testament, "salvation" certainly depends on a *personal* relation between God and the individual soul; if a man has not in him "the spirit of Christ," he is none of Christ's, no matter what he may seem to be from his superficial inclusion in any visible organization. But the personal relation is not a *private* one. It carries with it, and should normally show itself by, a relation of the most intimate kind to all the other persons who together constitute "the body of Christ." Hence the inseparability of the love of God, which is the first commandment of the New Law from the love of one's neighbour, which is the second, and the apostle's insistence that absence of the love of the brethren may be taken as proof of the absence of love of God. This is, in fact, a consequence of the very nature of personality itself. Personality can only develop in an atmosphere of reciprocal intimate and loving fellowship between persons; the closer and more intimate this fellowship, the more real the personality attained by those who share in it; a narrow and "self-centred" person (even when, as may be often the case, his isolation is rather his misfortune than his fault) is not fully a person. St. Paul's way of putting this is to say that in virtue of the fact that each of us is a "member" of the body of Christ, we are also "members of one another." Disease or weakness of one limb or organ of a living body inevitably has its effect on the health and strength of the whole, and the reason for the closeness of this connection between the different organs is precisely that all are related as "organs" to the life of the single self, which *is* not any of the "organs" but finds its expression through them all.

It is not meant that there is no distinction between the magnitude of the tasks executed by different organs; the very perfection of organization demands that there should be distinction and discrimination. But all alike, conspicuous or inconspicuous, primary or secondary, have their own special communication to make to the single life of the whole, and all are alike alive with its life. So in the Christian fellowship, not all who belong to it are apostles, or teachers, or share in the gifts of wisdom and knowledge to the same degree, but all are alike alive with the distinctive Christian life, all have in principle been "re-born into eternity." In the community of the re-born there are no barriers of race, or colour, or class, and the degree to which any man has attained possession of *his* true personality is not to be measured by the place he holds in any scale drawn up with a view to mundane standards. A simple uninstructed man may rank much higher in the scale of genuine personality than a great scholar or man of science; an indigent Negro than a "cultivated English gentleman." Those of us whose work in the world is discharged in one of the so-called "learned professions," perhaps, need particularly, to be warned that whenever we yield to the temptation to confuse spiritual worth with intellectual attainments, or delicate taste, or "culture," as the word is commonly understood, we are deserting the Christian standard.

Finally, though the eternal life spoken of in the New Testament is, in its origin, a free gift bestowed by God, it is one which has to be appropriated by the recipient, and the appropriation involves a lifetime of work and care. The gift may always be thrown away by our own wilfulness or carelessness, and none of us is secure against these faults. Hence the need that "he who seems to stand" should take unremitting care "lest he fall." No New Testament writer is more emphatic in his declarations that eternal life is not a "wage" or "salary" for services rendered but a gift than St. Paul, but it is he also who most expressly enjoins his converts to "work out their own salvation" in "fear and trembling," and openly envisages the possibility that, even in himself, negligence might end in "becoming a castaway." The High Calvinists of a bygone age were accustomed to find the warrant for their assertion "once in grace, always in grace" in certain passages of the Epistle to the Romans; yet it is clear that the author of the epistle would never have ventured to say of himself what some of his exponents have said, that he *knew* himself to be now and for ever finally "in grace."

If it is a paradox to say that something which is a free gift of God may also be forfeited unless we strive towards it diligently and unremittingly, it is a paradox which runs through the whole New Testament. No honest exegesis can get rid of the patent fact that, when all is said, the New Testament doctrine of man's destiny is no mere message of comfort for the indolent; there is a side to it which is distinctly disquieting. Eternal life can be won, and won by him who will, but it can also be thrown away, and apparently—though the New Testament, intelligently read, is not very explicit in this—finally thrown away. That any man has actually made such a final "great refusal" is, perhaps, more than the New Testament ever says, but at least, for each of us, there is the possibility of making it. It is emphatically *not* the Christian doctrine that the persistent "waster" has only to pass through the portals of death to find himself in a world which automatically "makes this world right." And this also is as it should be if what is at stake is personality itself. Personality cannot be thrust upon us from without; it has to be asserted by each of us for himself by resolute concentration of thought and will, and if a man "lets himself drift," he rapidly sinks to a more impersonal level. If I choose, I can degrade myself into something like a mere self of momentary impulses and feelings, and we all find that we are too apt to act thus, especially as age steals over us. We have no reason to suppose that it can be otherwise in the hereafter.

If what we have so far said is true, then, we may fairly claim for the Christian hope that, when rightly understood, it is no fantastic dream, pleasing but baseless; in substance it accords with anticipations which are independently inevitable in all of us, just because we are reasonable creatures in a universe where reason is at home. But Christianity also gives a new and determinate character to these anticipations, which would otherwise remain vague and uncertain, and because it does this, we rightly receive it as a "revelation." It is wholly misleading to speak of Christianity, in the fashion of the eighteenth-century latitudinarians, as "the religion of nature republished," with the implication that it contains only what might have been, and presumably was, equally well known to the reflective and devout of all ages, and that the mission of our Lord was no more than to remind the thoughtless of what they had allowed themselves to forget. Christ, according to the New Testament, did not come into the world simply to help men to "brush up" their "natural religion" as middle-aged men may "brush up" the French and Latin they learned in their schooldays. He came primarily not to *teach* us something in the short course of His earthly life, but to *do* something for us which no mere teacher could do; so far as He came to teach, it was to teach us something we did not know before, and without Him could not know at all.

What the New Testament adds to the statement that eternal life is the gift of God is, in the first place, that the gift has been bestowed on us specifically through Christ, and that Christ is no mere envoy through whom a far-away God has conveyed a message to us, but one who is Himself both a man of our own flesh and blood and also divine, "one with the Father." (The New Testament writers do not, of course, use the technical terminology which was subsequently developed for the express purpose of putting an end to discussions about their meaning, but it is recognized to-day by the scholars of all shades of personal opinion that the New Testament everywhere presents Christ as a divine being who may rightly receive the adoration due to God, and whose acts are rightly described as acts of God. It is just the impossibility of reducing the Lord Jesus of "primitive Christianity" to purely human dimensions which leads ingenious but ill-balanced writers in our own times to make attempts, discountenanced by all serious historians, Christian or non-Christian, to get rid altogether of the historical Jesus Christ and to reduce Him to a "myth." Preposterous [1] as the device is, it is prompted by the sound perception that the Christ of our earliest documents is *already* presented as a divine being.)

Now here is, as has been said—for example, by Dr. E. R. Bevan—the characteristically new note of the New Testament as compared with the Old. Ezekiel, in particular, had said long before that God would once more gather together his people, now scattered in bondage, as a shepherd might go out into the wilderness and collect his strayed flock. But to the Jewish reader this had apparently meant only that God would raise up in the future some wonderful human leader who would gather together again the "dispersion" of Israel. It would be, after all, only this wonderful man who could actually go out into the desert to reassemble the "sheep"; God would only be concerned in the business as the far-off being who had sent him on his costly and perilous errand, as a monarch may sit comfortably at home in his palace and send out devoted servants on a distant enterprise; the undertaking would be God's only on the principle that *qui facit per alium facit per se.* The courage and devotion would really be those of the envoy, and, to the strictly logical mind, they would be proof of *his* goodness, but no proof of the goodness of the sovereign to whom they cost nothing. Christianity, on the other hand, declared that it was actual fact that the divine shepherd had Himself come into the wilderness after the strayed sheep and had faced all its hardships and privations in His own person. The historical events were thus witnesses to the self-forgetting love, not of a great teacher or prophet, but of the very Lord of creation Himself. "So God loved the world" thus came to have a depth of meaning for Christians which it had never had for an Israelite, and the new significance of the thought gave a new meaning to the Christian life as a response to this love; it was possible henceforth for life to be inspired by a supreme, grateful love, not simply to a great human benefactor, but to the Maker of "all things visible and invisible."

The result is a changed attitude to the whole drama of human life and death. Even in a world morally indifferent—as the world depicted in Shake-

---

[1] How preposterous is shown, for example, by the theory of some literary men that the Jesus of the Gospels is identical with the Joshua of the Old Testament. We are thus to assume (1) that Joshua was an old and forgotten Hebrew divinity, and (2) that at the Christian era there was, for some unknown reason, a revival of the cult of this obsolete god. But there is not one scrap of evidence that Joshua was ever regarded by any Israelite as being a deity. His story, as we have it in the Old Testament, is simply that of a successful leader of Hebrew tribes in their first penetration into the country of the Canaanites, and there is no reason to think that anyone had ever supposed him to be anything else. We do not even hear that the Israelites made a colossal statue of him and hammered nails into it for luck. The Germans did this sort of thing for Hindenburg some 20 years ago, but a man who should assert that Hindenburg was a resurrected Wotan would only make himself ridiculous.

speare's greatest tragedies sometimes looks to be—to good and bad; even in a world definitely and positively evil, we could still feel love and devotion to a human benefactor who had at least protected us, to the best of his power, against "fortune's spite"; some of us might steel ourselves, when he fell, to fall not utterly unmanned by his side. But in an evil world we should certainly know, and in an indifferent world we should have over-powering reasons for believing that our hero and we were at best falling together in a forlorn hope. The order of things would be against us, and our highest courage would be the courage of despair dying "game to the last." Now despair can for a time nerve to vigorous achievement, but as a permanent attitude it is not invigorating but enervating. At least, it must be so with us, who are not wolves or weasels but men, reasonable animals. If we are once firmly convinced that the order of things is irrevocably against our ideals, we cannot avoid the paralyzing suspicion that these ideals, how-ever much we cherish them, are futile and arbitrary, and we shall come to ask ourselves doubtingly whether they are, after all, worth the blood and tears they cost, whether mankind had not better do without them.

This is why, for my own part, I doubt very much whether a virile human morality can flourish apart from some conviction about the universal world-order which, thought out, proves to imply belief in God and His goodness. One may say, no doubt, that "value" and "existence" have nothing to do with one another, but belong to wholly different worlds of thought; one may say "What we need as inspiration to action is not belief in the *exist-ence* of any thing or any person, but belief in the *worth* of courage and love," and the like. But divorced from belief in the overpowering actuality of the "love whose smile kindles the universe," your declaration "I believe in love" only means "I personally choose to regard love as supremely good"; and if your only reason for your profession is a *Hoc volo, sic jubeo,* why should you not change your choice? *Le peu de chose que sont les hommes!* and if *l'amour* is, to put it brutally, only an episode in the career of these little creatures, *le peu de chose qu'est l'amour.*[2] It is, you will say, what I care most about. But it is not what all men, perhaps not what many men, care most about, and it may be that to-morrow, or next year, I shall have changed my scale of "values"; if these values are no more than creations of my personal will, there is nothing sacred about them, they arise and perish as my fancy flickers, like the "fancy values of commerce." There can, indeed, be no worth except in relation to some will which finds satisfaction in it, but the will to which genuine and abiding worth has this relation cannot be merely your mutable willing or mine; it can only be a "living will that

---

[2] Rupert Brooke wrote of the First World War as a welcome recall from "all the little emptiness of love." Presumably the kind of "love" he had in his mind was none of the loftiest, but if the noblest love we know is, after all, *only* the "idiosyncrasy" of a particular species of animal, is it not all, in the end, "little" and "empty"?

shall endure when all that seems shall suffer shock." To the good man love is sacred and duty is sacred, but neither could be so if they were mere expressions of his own will as this individual man; the good man is not an idolator of himself and his private will. And if I, or all mankind, were to-morrow to turn against the old sanctities and tread love and duty under our feet, they would lose nothing of their sacredness; it would not really be they, but our own wills, which would be profaned.

Now if the central doctrine of the Christian is true, then we have such a certainty as the world cannot otherwise afford that love and duty are indeed sacred. For then it is a fact that the Master of all things has not merely told us to be loving and dutiful and will hold us to account if we fail; He has Himself, in the person of the historical Lord Jesus, entered into the life of humanity, has Himself led the life of selfless love and duty to the bitter end, and triumphed over all the obstacles that beset it; we, who have still the obstacles and hindrances to conflict with, have received from him not merely the inspiration of His teaching and example, but the certainty that the values which are sustained by the eternal "living will" are precisely those which were affirmed in practice by the Lord Jesus and are dearest to our own hearts—love, dutifulness, humility, courage, patience. We know, then, that, however appearances may be against them, these values can "never fail"; they are the foundation-stones on which the frame of things is built. This is why an apostle can speak of the faith of the Christian fellowship as one which conquers the world. It is not merely that, to quote Blake, "a strong persuasion that a thing is so makes it so"; for you cannot make falsehood into truth by the violence of your "persuasion" of the falsehood. The "world-conquering" quality of the Christian faith, if it is not an illusion, depends, first and foremost, on the nature of the person towards whom it is directed. It can conquer the world because, if it is true at all, it is a confidence based on a real disclosure of the character of the unseen source of the world. If the mind of God has been truly disclosed by the life, death, and triumph of Jesus, then it is certain that God's world is not really either indifferent or hostile to our highest human aspirations, and for the true "members of Christ's body" eternal life ceases to be only what Plato had called it, a "great hope," and becomes a fact. It is the confidence in the fact which accounts for the strange "joy" so characteristic of the obscure, toil-worn despised and persecuted first Christians in the midst of a world full of pleasures, refined or sordid, but, as students of the period have so often noted, as deficient in joy as it was avid of pleasure.

These considerations also explain what might otherwise seem a singular fact about the history of Christian theology. When the Church set itself to codify and formulate its convictions it was not content with the emphatic assertion of the divinity of its founder; it insisted no less emphatically on his genuine and complete humanity. If it was declared deadly heresy to pronounce him in any way "inferior to the Father as touching this divinity," it was an equal heresy to abate anything from his humanity. You were not to withhold from him any jot of the worship due to the supreme Creator; equally you were not to exempt him from anything incidental to full human normality—hunger, thirst, weariness, pain, temptation. He was to be thought of neither as a deity of second rank, nor as a "superman." This, more than anything else, was what perplexed and shocked the ordinary outsider. He would not have found it incredible that a god, at any rate a minor god, should show himself in the visible form of a man. But that a god should feel genuine want or pain, should shed tears at the grave of a friend, should be insulted, beaten, crucified, and should feel the pain and shame of such things was a veritable scandal. Yet obviously if the life of Christ is to be evidence that *our* highest human values are also the eternal and absolute values, it is precisely this union in one historical person of Deity and complete humanity which must be maintained. To whittle away either the divinity or the humanity—to be either "Liberal Protestant" or Docetist—is to surrender the very "ground of all our hopes."

# OSCAR CULLMANN

*Oscar Cullmann* (1902–    ), Continental Protestant theologian, has taught at Basel, the Sorbonne, and in America. His major field of study is the New Testament. Among his most important works are *Christ and Time* and *The Christology of the New Testament*.

## Immortality of the Soul or Resurrection of the Dead?

### The Wages of Sin: Death

BODY AND SOUL—FLESH AND SPIRIT. Yet the contrast between the Greek idea of the immortality of the soul and the Christian belief in the resurrection is still deeper. The belief in the resurrection presupposes the Jewish con-

From Oscar Cullmann, *Immortality of the Soul or Resurrection of the Dead?* pp. 28–47. Copyright, 1958, The Epworth Press. Used by permission of The Epworth Press and The Macmillan Company. [Footnotes omitted, Eds.]

nexion between death and *sin.* Death is not something natural, willed by God, as in the thought of the Greek philosophers; it is rather something unnatural, abnormal, opposed to God. The Genesis narrative teaches us that it came into the world only by the sin of man. Death is a curse, and the whole creation has become involved in the curse. The sin of man has necessitated the whole series of events which the Bible records and which we call the story of redemption. Death can be conquered only to the extent that sin is removed. For "death is the wages of sin." It is not only the Genesis narrative which speaks thus. Paul says the same thing (Romans $6^{23}$), and this is the view of death held by the whole of primitive Christianity. Just as sin is something opposed to God, so is its consequence, death. To be sure, God can make use of death (1 Corinthians $15^{35ff}$, John $12^{24}$), as He can make use of Satan to man.

Nevertheless, death *as such* is the enemy of God. For God is Life and the Creator of life. It is not by the will of God that there are withering and decay, dying and sickness, the by-products of death working in our life. All these things, according to Christian and Jewish thinking, come from human sin. Therefore, every healing which Jesus accomplishes is not only a driving back of death, but also an invasion of the province of sin; and therefore on every occasion Jesus says: "Your sins are forgiven." Not as though there were a corresponding sin for every individual sickness; but rather, like the presence of death, the fact that sickness exists at all is a consequence of the sinful condition of the whole of humanity. Every healing is a partial resurrection, a partial victory of life over death. That is the Christian point of view. According to the Greek interpretation, on the contrary, bodily sickness is a corollary of the fact that the body is bad in itself and is ordained to destruction. For the Christian an anticipation of the Resurrection can already become visible, even in the earthly body.

That reminds us that the body is in no sense bad in itself, but is, like the soul, a gift of our Creator. Therefore, according to Paul, we have duties with regard to our body. God is the *Creator* of all things. The Greek doctrine of immortality and the Christian hope in the resurrection differ so radically because Greek thought has such an entirely different interpretation of creation. The Jewish and Christian interpretation of creation excludes the whole Greek dualism of body and soul. For indeed the visible, the corporeal, is just as truly God's creation as the invisible. God is the maker of the body. The body is not the soul's prison, but rather a temple, as Paul says (1 Corinthians $6^{19}$): the temple of the Holy Spirit! The basic distinction lies here. Body and soul are not opposites. God finds the corporeal "good" after He has created it. The Genesis story makes this emphasis explicit. Conversely, moreover, sin also embraces the whole man, not only the body, but the soul as well; and its consequence, death, extends over all the rest of creation. Death is accordingly something dreadful, because the whole visible creation, including our body, is something wonderful, even if it is corrupted by sin and death. Behind the pessimistic interpretation of death stands the optimistic view of creation. Wherever, as in Platonism, death is thought of in terms of liberation, there the visible world is not recognized directly as God's creation.

Now, it must be granted that in Greek thought there is also a very positive appreciation of the body. But in Plato the good and beautiful in the corporeal are not good and beautiful in virtue of corporeality but rather, so to speak, *in spite of* corporeality: the soul, the eternal and the only substantial reality of being, shines faintly through the material. The corporeal is not the real, the eternal, the divine. It is merely that through which the real appears—and then only in debased form. The corporeal is meant to lead us to contemplate the pure archetype, freed from all corporeality, the invisible Idea.

To be sure, the Jewish and Christian points of view also see something else besides corporeality. For the whole creation is corrupted by sin and death. The creation which we see is not as God willed it, as He created it; nor is the body which we wear. Death rules over all; and it is not necessary for annihilation to accomplish its work of destruction before this fact becomes apparent—it is already obvious in the whole outward form of all things. Everything, even the most beautiful, is marked by death. Thus it might seem as if the distinction between Greek and Christian interpretation is not so great after all. And yet it remains radical. Behind the corporeal appearance Plato senses the incorporeal, transcendent, pure Idea. Behind the corrupted creation, under sentence of death, the Christian sees the future creation brought into being by the resurrection, just as God willed it. The contrast, for the Christian, is not between the body and the soul, not between outward form and Idea, but rather between the creation delivered over to death by sin and new creation; between the corruptible, fleshly body and the incorruptible resurrection body.

This leads us to a further point: the Christian interpretation of man. The anthropology of the New Testament is not Greek, but is connected with Jewish conceptions. For the concepts of body, soul, flesh, and spirit (to name only these), the New Testament does indeed use the same words as the Greek philosopher. But they mean something quite different, and we understand the whole New Testament amiss when we construe these concepts only from the point of view of Greek thought. Many misunderstandings arise thus. . . . There are good monographs on the subject, not to mention the appropriate articles in the *Theologisches Wörterbuch*. A complete study would have to treat separately the anthropologies of the various New Testament authors, since on this point there exist differences which are by no means unimportant. Of necessity I can deal here only with a few cardinal points which concern our problem, and even this must be done somewhat schematically, without taking into account the nuances which would have to be discussed in a proper anthropology. In so doing, we shall naturally have to rely primarily upon Paul, since only in his writings do we find an anthropology which is definable in detail, even though he too fails to use the different ideas with complete consistency.

The New Testament certainly knows the difference between body and soul, or more precisely, between the inner and outer man. This distinction does not, however, imply opposition, as if the one were by nature good, the other by nature bad. Both belong together, both are created by God. The inner man without the outer has no proper, full existence. It requires a body. It can, to be sure, somehow lead a shady existence without the body, like the dead in Sheol according to the Old Testament, but that is not a *genuine life*. The contrast with the Greek soul is clear: it is precisely apart from the body that the Greek soul attains to full development of its life. According to the Christian view, however, it is the inner man's very nature which demands the body.

And what now is the role played by the flesh ($\sigma \acute{a} \rho \xi$) and spirit ($\pi \nu \epsilon \hat{v} \mu a$)? Here it is especially important not to be misled by the secular use of the Greek words, though it is found in various places even in the New Testament and even within individual writers whose use of terminology is never completely uniform. With these reservations, we may say that according to the use which is characteristic, say, for Pauline theology, flesh and spirit in the New Testament are two *transcendent* powers which can enter into man from without; but *neither is given with human existence as such*. On the whole it is true that the Pauline anthropology, contrary to the Greek, is grounded in *Heilsgeschichte*. "Flesh" is the power of sin or the power of death. It seizes the outer and the inner man *together*. *Spirit* ($\pi \nu \epsilon \hat{v} \mu a$) is its great antagonist: the power of creation. It also seizes the outer and inner man *together*. Flesh and spirit are active powers, and as such they work within us. The flesh, the power of death, entered man with the sin of Adam; indeed it entered the whole man, inner and outer; yet in such a way that it is very closely linked with the body. The inner man finds itself less closely connected with the flesh; although through guilt this power of death has more and more taken possession even of the inner man. The spirit, on the other hand, is the great power of life, the element of the resurrection; God's power of creation is given to us through the Holy Spirit. In the Old Testament the Spirit is at work only from time to time in the prophets. In the End-time in which we live—that is, since Christ has broken the power of death in His own death and has arisen—this power of life is at work in all members of the community (Acts 2[16]: "In the last days"). Like the flesh, it too already takes possession of the whole man, inner and outer. But whereas, in this age, the flesh has established itself to a substantial degree in the body, though it does not rule the inner man in the same inescapable way, the quickening power of the Holy Spirit is already taking possession of the inner man so decisively that the inner man is "renewed from day to day," as Paul says (2 Corinthians 4¹⁶). The whole Johannine Gospel emphasizes the point. We are already in the state of resurrection, that of eternal life—not immortality of soul: the new era is already inaugurated. The body, too, is already in the power of the Holy Spirit.

Wherever the Holy Spirit is at work we have what amounts to a momentary retreat of the power of death, a certain foretaste of the End. This is true even in the body, hence the healings of the sick. But here it is a question only of a retreat, not of a final transformation of the body of death into a resurrection body. Even those whom Jesus raised up in His lifetime will die again, for they did not receive a resurrection body, the transformation of the fleshly body into a spiritual body does not take place until the End. Only then will the Holy Spirit's power of resurrection take such complete possession of the body that it transforms it in the way it is already transforming the inner man. It is important to see how different the New Testament anthropology is from that of the Greeks. Body and soul are both originally good in so far as they are created by God; they are both bad in so far as the deadly power of the flesh has hold of them. Both can and must be set free by the quickening power of the Holy Spirit.

Here, therefore, deliverance consists not in a release of soul from body but in a release of both from flesh. We are not released from the body; rather the body itself is set free. This is made especially clear in the Pauline Epistles, but it is the interpretation of the whole New Testament. In this connexion one does not find the differences which are present among the various books on other points. Even the much-quoted saying of Jesus in Matthew 10²⁸ in no way presupposes the Greek conception. "Fear not them that kill the body, but cannot kill the soul." It might seem to presuppose the view that the soul has no need of the body, but the context of the passage shows that this is not the case. Jesus does not continue: "Be afraid of him who kills the soul"; rather "Fear him who can slay both soul *and* body in Gehenna." That is, fear God who is able to give you over completely to death; to wit, when He does not resurrect you to life. We shall see, it is true, that the soul is the starting-point of the resurrection, since, as we have said, it can already be possessed by the Holy Spirit in a way quite different from the body. The Holy Spirit already lives in our inner man. "By the Holy Spirit who dwells in you (already)," says Paul in Romans 8¹¹, "God will also quicken your mortal bodies." Therefore, those who kill only the body are not to be feared. It can be raised from the dead. Moreover, it must be raised. The soul cannot always remain without a body. And on the other side we hear in Jesus' saying in Matthew 10²⁸ that the soul can be killed. The soul is not immortal. There must be resurrection for both; for since the Fall the whole man is "sown corruptible." For the inner man, thanks to the transformation by the quickening power of the Holy Spirit, the resurrection can take place already in this present life: through the "renewal from day to day." The flesh, however, still maintains its seat in our body. The transformation of the body does not take place until the End, when the whole creation will be made new by the Holy Spirit, when there will be no death and no corruption.

The resurrection of the body, whose substance will no longer be that of the flesh, but that of the Holy Spirit, is only a part of the *whole new creation*. "We wait for a new heaven *and* a new earth," says 2 Peter 3[13]. The Christian hope relates not only to my individual fate, but to the entire creation. Through sin the whole creation has become involved in death. This we hear not only in Genesis, but also in Romans 8[19ff], where Paul writes that the whole creation from now on waits longingly for deliverance. This deliverance will come when the power of the Holy Spirit transforms all matter, when God in a new act of creation will not *destroy* matter, but set it free from the flesh, from corruptibility. Not eternal Ideas, but concrete objects will then rise anew, in the new, incorruptible life-substance of the Holy Spirit; and among these objects belongs our body as well.

Because resurrection of the body is a new act of creation which embraces everything, it is not an event which begins with each individual death, but only at the *End*. It is not a transition from this world to another world, as is the case of the immortal soul freed from the body; rather it is the transition from the present age to the future. It is tied to the whole process of redemption.

Because there is sin there must be a process of redemption enacted in time. Where sin is regarded as the source of death's lordship over God's creation, there this sin and death must be vanquished together, and there the Holy Spirit, the only power able to conquer death, must win all creatures back to life in a continuous process.

Therefore the Christian belief in the resurrection, as distinct from the Greek belief in immortality, is tied to a *divine total process* implying deliverance. Sin and death must be conquered. *We* cannot do this. *Another* has done it for us; and He was able to do it only in that He betook himself to the province of death—that is, He himself died and expiated sin, so that death as the wages of sin is overcome. Christian faith proclaims that Jesus had done this and that He arose *with* body and soul after He was fully and really dead. Here God has consummated the miracle of the new creation expected at the End. Once again He has created life as in the beginning. At this one point, in Jesus Christ, this has already happened! Resurrection, not only in the sense of the Holy Spirit's taking possession of the *inner* man, but also resurrection of the *body*. This is a new creation of matter, an incorruptible matter. Nowhere else in the world is there this new spiritual matter. Nowhere else is there a spiritual body—only here in Christ.

## The First-Born from the Dead

BETWEEN THE RESURRECTION OF CHRIST AND THE DESTRUCTION OF DEATH. We must take into account what it meant for the Christians when they proclaimed: Christ is risen from the dead! Above all we must bear in mind what death meant for them. We are tempted to associate these powerful affirmations with the Greek thought of the immortality of the soul, and in this way to rob them of their content. Christ is risen: that is, we stand in the new era in which death is conquered, in which corruptibility is no more. For if there is really *one* spiritual body (not an immortal soul, but a spiritual body) which has emerged from a fleshly body, then indeed the power of death is broken. Believers, according to the conviction of the first Christians, should no longer die: this was certainly their expectation in the earliest days. It must have been a problem when they discovered that Christians continued to die. But even the fact that men continue to die no longer has the same significance after the Resurrection of Christ. The fact of death is robbed of its former significance. Dying is no longer an expression of the absolute lordship of Death, but only one of Death's last contentions for lordship. Death cannot put an end to the great fact that there is *one* risen Body.

We ought to try simply to understand what the first Christians meant when they spoke of Christ as being the "first-born from the dead." However difficult it may be for us to do so, we must exclude the question whether or not we can accept this belief. We must also at the very start leave on one side the question whether Socrates or the New Testament is right. Otherwise we shall find ourselves continually mixing alien thought-processes with those of the New Testament. We should for once simply listen to what the New Testament says. Christ the first-born from the dead! His body the first Resurrection body, the first Spiritual Body. Where this conviction is present, the whole of life and the whole of thought must be influenced by it. The whole thought of the New Testament remains for us a book sealed with seven seals if we do not read behind every sentence there this other sentence: Death has already been overcome (death, be it noted, not the body); there is already a new creation (a new creation, be it noted, not an immortality which the soul has always possessed); the resurrection age is already inaugurated.

Granted that it is only inaugurated, but still it is *decisively* inaugurated. *Only* inaugurated: for death is at work, and Christians still die. The disciples experienced this as the first members of the Christian community died. This necessarily presented them with a difficult problem. In 1 Corinthians 11[30] Paul writes that basically death and sickness should no longer occur. We still die, and still there is sickness and sin. But the Holy Spirit is already effective in our world as the power of new creation; He is already at work visibly in the primitive community in the diverse manifestations of the Spirit.

In my book *Christ and Time* I have spoken of a tension between present and future, the tension between "already fulfilled" and "not yet consummated." This tension belongs *essentially* to the New Testament and is not introduced as a secondary solution born of embarrassment, as Albert Schweitzer's disciples and Rudolph Bultmann maintain. This tension is already present in and with Jesus. He proclaims the Kingdom of God for the future; but on the other hand, He proclaims that the Kingdom of God has already broken in, since He Himself with the Holy Spirit is indeed repulsing death by healing the sick and raising the dead (Matthew 12[28], 11[3ff], Luke 10[18]) in anticipation of the victory over death which He obtains in His own death. Schweitzer is not right when he sees as the original Christian hope *only* a hope in the future; nor is C. H. Dodd when he speaks *only* of a realized eschatology; still less Bultmann when he resolves the original hope of Jesus and the first Christians into Existentialism. It belongs to the very stuff of the New Testament that it thinks in temporal categories, and this is because the belief that in Christ the resurrection is achieved is the starting-point of all Christian living and thinking. When one starts from this principle, then the chronological tension between "already fulfilled" and "not yet consummated" constitutes the *essence* of the Christian faith. Then the metaphor I use in *Christ and Time* characterizes the whole New Testament situation: the decisive battle has been fought in Christ's death and Resurrection; only V-day is yet to come.

Basically the whole contemporary theological discussion turns upon this question: Is *Easter* the starting-point of the Christian Church, of its existence, life, and thought? If so, we are living in an interim time.

In that case, the faith in resurrection of the New Testament becomes the cardinal point of all Christian belief. Accordingly, the fact that there is a resurrection body—Christ's body—defines the first Christians' whole interpretation of time. If Christ is the "first-born from the dead," then this means that the End-time is already present. But it also means that a temporal interval separates the First-born from all other men who are not yet "born from the dead." This means then that we live in an interim time, between Jesus' Resurrection, which has already taken place, and our own, which will not take place until the End. It also means, moreover, that the quickening Power, the Holy Spirit, is already at work among us. Therefore Paul designates the Holy Spirit by the same term—$\dot{\alpha}\pi\alpha\rho\chi\acute{\eta}$, first-fruits (Romans 8[23])—as he uses for Jesus Himself (1 Corinthians 15[23]). There is then already a foretaste of the resurrection. And indeed in a twofold way: our inner man is already being renewed from day to day by the Holy Spirit (2 Corinthians 4[16]; Ephesians 3[16]); the body also has already been laid hold of by the Spirit, although the flesh still has its citadels within it. Wherever the Holy Spirit appears, the vanquished power of death recoils, even in the body. Hence miracles of healing occur even in our still mortal body. To the despairing cry in Romans 7[24], "Who shall deliver me from this body of death?" the whole New Testament answers: The Holy Spirit!

The foretaste of the End, realized through the Holy Spirit, becomes most clearly visible in the early Christian celebration of the breaking of bread. Visible miracles of the Spirit occur there. There the Spirit tries to break through the limits of imperfect human language in the speaking with tongues. And there the community passes over into direct connexion with the Risen One, not only with His soul, but also with His Resurrection Body. Therefore we hear in 1 Corinthians 10[16]: "The bread we break, is it not communion with the body of Christ?" Here in communion with the brethren we come nearest to the Resurrection Body of Christ; and so Paul writes in the following Chapter 11 (a passage which has received far too little consideration) : if this Lord's Supper were partaken of by all members of the community in a completely worthy manner, then union with Jesus' Resurrection Body would be so effective in our bodies that even now there would be no more sickness or death (1 Corinthians 11 [28-30])—a singularly bold assertion. Therefore the community is described as the body of Christ, because here the spiritual body of Christ is present, because here we come closest to it; here in the common meal the first disciples at Easter saw Jesus' Resurrection Body, His Spiritual Body.

Yet in spite of the fact that the Holy Spirit is already so powerfully at work, men still die; even after Easter and Pentecost men continue to die as before. Our body remains mortal and subject to sickness. Its transformation into the spiritual body does not take place until the whole creation is formed anew by God. Then only, for the first time, there will be nothing but Spirit, nothing but the power of life, for then death will be destroyed with finality. Then there will be a new substance for all things visible. Instead of the fleshly matter there appears the spiritual. That is, *instead of corruptible matter there appears the incorruptible.* The visible and the invisible will be spirit. But let us make no mistake: this is certainly not the Greek sense of bodiless Idea! A new heaven *and* a new earth! That is the Christian hope. And then will our bodies also rise from the dead. Yet not as fleshly bodies, but as spiritual bodies.

The expression which stands in the ancient Greek texts of the Apostles' Creed is quite certainly not biblical: "I believe in the resurrection of the flesh!" Paul could not say that. Flesh and blood cannot inherit the Kingdom. Paul believes in the resurrection of the *body,* not of the *flesh.* The flesh is the power of death, which must be destroyed. This error in the Greek creed made its entrance at a time when the biblical terminology had been misconstrued in the sense of Greek anthropology. Our body, moreover (not merely our soul), will be raised at the End, when the quickening power of the Spirit makes all things new, all things without exception.

An incorruptible body! How are we to conceive this? Or better, how did the first Christians conceive of it? Paul says in Philippians 3²¹ that at the End Christ will transform our lowly body into the body of his own glory (δόξα), just as in 2 Corinthians 3¹⁸: "We are being transformed into his own likeness from glory to glory (ἀπὸ δόξης εἰς δόξαν)." This glory (δόξα) was conceived by the first Christians as a sort of light-substance; but this is only an imperfect comparison. Our language has no word for it. Once again I refer to Grünewald's painting of the Resurrection. He may have come closest to what Paul understood as the spiritual body.

# JACQUES MARITAIN

*Jacques Maritain* (1882–    ) is a French Roman Catholic philosopher, and an outstanding spokesman for contemporary Thomistic thought. The range of his interests, as reflected in his writings, is also reminiscent of the breadth of St. Thomas. In the United States he has taught at Chicago, Columbia, Yale, and Princeton Universities.

## III. Personal Immortality

*The Existence of the Soul*

It is of this immortality, and of the way in which the Scholastics established its rational certainty, that I should now like to speak.

We must of course realize that we have a soul before we can discuss whether it is immortal. How does St. Thomas Aquinas proceed in this matter?

He observes first that man has an activity, the activity of the intellect, which is in itself immaterial. The activity of the intellect is immaterial because the proportionate or "connatural" object of the human intellect is not, like the object of the senses, a particular and limited category of things, or rather a particular and limited category of the qualitative properties of things. The proportionate or "connatural" object of the intellect is the nature of the sense-perceivable things considered in an all-embracing manner,

Reprinted with the permission of Charles Scribner's Sons and Geoffrey Bles, Ltd., from *The Range of Reason* by Jacques Maritain (pp. 54–61), copyright 1952, Jacques Maritain. [Footnotes omitted, Eds.]

whatever the sense concerned may be. It is not only—as for sight—color or the colored thing (which absorbs and reflects such or such rays of light) nor—as for hearing—sound or the sound-source; it is the whole universe and texture of sense-perceivable reality which can be known by the intellect, because the intellect does not stop at qualities, but pierces beyond, and proceeds to look at essence (that which a thing *is*). This very fact is a proof of the spirituality, or complete immateriality of our intellect; for every activity in which matter plays an intrinsic part is limited to a given category of material objects, as is the case for the senses, which perceive only those properties which are able to act upon their physical organs.

There is already, in fact, a certain immateriality in sense-knowledge: knowledge, as such, is an immaterial activity, because when I am in the act of knowing, I become, or am, the very thing that I know, a thing other than myself, insofar as it is other than myself. And how can I be, or become, other than myself, if it is not in a supra-subjective or immaterial manner? Sense-knowledge is a very poor kind of knowledge; insofar as it is knowledge, it is immaterial, but it is an immaterial activity intrinsically conditioned by, and dependent upon, the material functioning of the sense-organs. Sense-knowledge is the immaterial achievement, the immaterial actuation and product of a living bodily organ; and its very object is also something half material, half immaterial, I mean a physical quality *intentionally* or immaterially present in the medium by which it acts on the sense-organ (something comparable to the manner in which a painter's idea is immaterially present in his paint-brush).

But with intellectual knowledge we have to do with an activity which is in itself completely immaterial. The human intellect is able to know whatever participates in being and truth; the whole universe can be inscribed in it; this means that, in order to be known, the object known by the intellect has been stripped of any existential condition of materiality. This rose, which I see, has contours; but Being, of which I am thinking, is more spacious than space. The object of the intellect is universal, for instance that universal or de-individualized object which is apprehended in the idea of man, of animal, of atom; the object of the intellect is a universal which remains what it is while being identified with an infinity of individuals. And this is only possible because things, in order to become objects of the mind, have been entirely separated from their material existence. To this it must be added that the operation of our intellect does not stop at the knowledge of the nature of sense-perceivable things; it goes further; it knows by analogy the spiritual natures; it extends to the realm of merely possible things; its field has infinite magnitude.

Thus, the objects known by the human intellect, taken not as things existing in themselves, but precisely as objects determining the intellect and united with it, are purely immaterial.

Furthermore, just as the condition of the *object* is immaterial, so is the condition of the *act* which bears upon it, and is determined or specified by it. The object of the human intellect is, as such, purely immaterial; the act of the human intellect is also purely immaterial.

And, moreover, if the act of the intellectual power is purely immaterial, that *power* itself is also purely immaterial. In man, this thinking animal, the intellect is a purely spiritual power. Doubtless it depends upon the body, upon the conditions of the brain. Its activity can be disturbed or hindered by a physical disorder, by an outburst of anger, by a drink or a narcotic. But this dependence is an *extrinsic* one. It exists because our intelligence cannot act without the joint activity of the memory and the imagination, of the internal senses and external senses, all of which are organic powers residing in some material organ, in some special part of the body. As for the intellect itself, it is not *intrinsically* dependent upon the body since its activity is immaterial; the human intellect does not reside in any special part of the body. It is not contained by the body, but rather contains it. It uses the brain, since the organs of the internal senses are in the brain; yet the brain is not an organ of the intelligence; there is no part of the organism whose act is intellectual operation. The intellect has no organ.

Finally, since intellectual power is spiritual, or purely immaterial in itself, its *first substantial root,* the subsisting principle from which this power proceeds and which acts through its instrumentality, is also spiritual.

So much for the spirituality of the intellect. Now, thought or the operation of the intellect is an act and emanation of man as a unit; and when I think, it is not only my intellect which thinks: it is I, my own self. And my own self is a bodily self; it involves matter; it is not a spiritual or purely immaterial subject. The body is an essential part of man. The intellect is not the whole man.

Therefore the intellect, or rather the substantial root of the intellect, which must be as immaterial as the intellect, is only a part, albeit an essential part, of man's substance.

But man is not an aggregate, a juxtaposition of two substances; man is a natural whole, a single being, a single substance.

Consequently, we must conclude that the essence or substance of man is single, but that this single substance itself is a compound, the components of which are the body and the spiritual intellect: or rather matter, of which the body is made, and the spiritual principle, one of the powers of which is the intellect. Matter—in the Aristotelian sense of prime matter, or of that root potentiality which is the common stuff of all corporeal substance —matter, substantially united with the spiritual principle of the intellect, is ontologically molded, shaped from within and in the innermost depths of being, by this spiritual principle as by a substantial and vital impulse, in order to constitute that body of ours. In this sense, Saint Thomas, after Aristotle, says that the intellect is the form, the substantial form of the human body.

That is the Scholastic notion of the human soul. The human soul, which is the root principle of the intellectual power, is the first principle of life of the human body, and the substantial form, the *entelechy,* of that body. And the human soul is not only a substantial form or entelechy, as are the souls of plants and animals according to the biological philosophy of Aristotle; the human soul is also a spirit, a spiritual substance able to exist apart from matter, since the human soul is the root principle of a spiritual power, the act of which is intrinsically independent of matter. The human soul is both a soul and a spirit, and it is its very substantiality, subsistence and existence, which are communicated to the whole human substance, in order to make human substance be what it is, and to make it subsist and exist. Each element of the human body is human, and exists as such, by virtue of the immaterial existence of the human soul. Our body, our hands, our eyes exist by virtue of the existence of our souls.

The immaterial soul is the first substantial root not only of the intellect, but of all that which, in us, is spiritual activity; and it is also the first substantial root of all our other living activities. It would be inconceivable that a non-spiritual soul, that kind of soul which is not a spirit and cannot exist without informing matter—namely, the souls of plants or animals in Aristotelian biology—should possess a power or faculty *superior* to its own degree in being, that is, immaterial, or act through a supra-material instrumentality independent of any corporeal organ and physical structure. But when it is a question of a spirit which is a soul, or of a *spiritual soul,* as the human soul is, then it is perfectly conceivable that such a soul should have, aside from immaterial or spiritual faculties, other powers and activities which are organic and material, and which, relating to the union between soul and body, pertain to a level of being *inferior* to that of the spirit.

## The Spirituality of the Human Soul

Thus, the very way in which the Scholastics arrived at the existence of the human soul also established its spirituality. Just as the intellect is spiritual, that is to say intrinsically independent of matter in its operation and in its nature, so also, and for the same reason, the human soul, the substantial root of the intellect, is spiritual, that is, intrinsically independent of matter in its nature and in its existence; it does not live by the body, the body lives by it. The human soul is a spiritual substance which, by its substantial union with matter, gives existence and countenance to the body.

That is my second point. As we have seen, the Scholastics demonstrated it by a metaphysical analysis of the intellect's operation, carefully distinguished from the operation of the senses. They adduced, of course, much other evidence in support of their demonstration. In their consideration of the intellect, they observed, for instance, that the latter is capable of *perfect reflection,* that is, of coming back entirely upon itself—not in the manner of a sheet of paper, half of which can be folded on the other half, but in a complete manner, so that it can grasp its whole operation and penetrate it by knowledge, and can contain itself and its own principle, the existing self, in its own knowing activity, a perfect reflection or self-containing of which any material agent, extended in space and time, is essentially incapable. Here we are confronted with that phenomenon of self-knowledge, of *prise de conscience* or becoming aware of oneself, which is a privilege of the spirit, as Hegel (after St. Augustine) was to emphasize, and which plays so tremendous a part in the history of humanity and the development of its spiritual energies.

In the same way it is possible to show that the human will, which is rooted in the intellect, and which is able to determine itself, or to master the very motive or judgment which determines it and is made efficacious by the will itself, is spiritual in its operation and nature. Every material agent is subject to the universal determinism. Free will is the privilege, the glorious and weighty privilege, of an agent endowed with immaterial power.

We are responsible for ourselves; we choose for ourselves and decide on our own ends and our own destinies. We are capable of spiritual, suprasensuous love, and desire and joy, which are naturally intermingled with our organic and sensuous emotions, but which are in themselves affections of the spiritual will, and are awakened through the immaterial light of intellectual insight. We delight in beauty, we desire perfection and justice, we love truth, we love God, we love all men—not only the members of our social group, or our family, our class or nation—but all men because they are human beings, and children of God. The saints, those men who are called everywhere spiritual men, experience a contemplation which establishes their souls in a peace superior to and stronger than the whole world, and they go through inner trials, crucifixions and deaths which only a life superior to and stronger than biological existence can suffer and go through —and still remain alive. And we ourselves know that we can deliberate about ourselves, judge our own actions, cling to what is good because it is good and for no other reason; all of us know more or less obscurely that we are persons, that we have rights and duties, that we preserve human dignity within ourselves. Each one of us can, at certain moments in his existence, descend into the innermost depths of the Ego, to make there some external pledge or gift of himself, or face some irrefutable judgment of his conscience; and each one of us, on such occasions, alone with himself, feels that he is a universe unto himself, immersed in, but not dominated by, the great star-studded universe.

Through all these convergent ways, we may realize and experience in a certain measure, and in a concrete fashion, that living reality of our spiritual roots, or of what is above time in us, which the philosophical proofs make intellectually certain, but in the abstract manner of scientific knowledge.

## The Immortality of the Human Soul

The third point follows immediately from the second. The immortality of the human soul is an immediate corollary of its spirituality. A soul which is spiritual in itself, intrinsically independent of matter in its nature and existence, cannot cease existing. A spirit—that is, a "form" which needs nothing other than itself (save the influx of the Prime Cause) to exercise existence—once existing cannot cease existing. A spiritual soul cannot be corrupted, since it possesses no matter; it cannot be disintegrated, since it has no substantial parts; it cannot lose its individual unity, since it is self-subsisting, nor its internal energy, since it contains within itself all the sources of its energies. The human soul cannot die. Once it exists, it cannot disappear; it will necessarily exist forever, endure without end.

Thus, philosophic reason, put to work by a great metaphysician like Thomas Aquinas, is able to prove the immortality of the human soul in a demonstrative manner. Of course, this demonstration implies a vast and articulate network of metaphysical insights, notions and principles (relating to essence and nature, substance, act and potency, matter and form, operation, etc.) the validity of which is necessarily presupposed. We can appreciate fully the strength of the Scholastic demonstration only if we realize the significance and full validity of the metaphysical notions involved. If modern times feel at a loss in the face of metaphysical knowledge, I fancy that it is not metaphysical knowledge which is to blame, but rather modern times and the weakening of reason they have experienced.

It is not surprising, on the other hand, that the philosophical demonstration I have just summarized is an abstract and a difficult one. The great and fundamental truths which are spontaneously grasped by the natural instinct of the human mind are always the most arduous for philosophic reason to establish. With regard to the immortality of the human soul, philosophic reason must use the very refined and elaborate concept of immateriality, a concept remote from the natural understanding, not only of primitive men, but of everyone who thinks with his imagination rather than with his intellect. Were not certain monks of Asia Minor, in the early Christian centuries, indignant at the idea that God is an Immaterial Being? They did not use the English language, yet they were convinced that to be *imma-*

*terial*, or deprived of matter, actually meant to be something immaterial, or nothing at all. They surely believed in the immortality of the soul, but it is doubtful whether they would have understood the strength of the argument we have used.

Primitive men did not philosophize; but, for all that, they had their own way, an instinctive, non-conceptual way, of believing in the soul's immortality. It was a belief rooted in an obscure experience of the self, and in the natural aspirations of the spirit in us to overcome death. We need not embark on an analysis of this natural and instinctive, non-philosophical belief in immortality. I should like merely to quote a passage from a book by the late scientist Pierre Lecomte du Noüy. Speaking of prehistoric man, he said: "Not only did the Neanderthal Man, who lived in Paleolithic times, bury his dead, but sometimes he buried them in a common ground. An example of this is the Grotte des Enfants near Mentone. Because of this respect he had for his dead, we have reached an anatomical knowledge of the Neanderthal Man that is more perfect than that which we have of certain races which have recently become extinct, or which still exist, such as the Tasmanians. This is no longer a question of instinct. We are dealing already with the dawn of human thought, which reveals itself in a kind of revolt against death. And revolt against death implies love for those who have gone as well as the hope that their disappearance is not final. We see these *ideas*, the first perhaps, develop progressively alongside the first artistic feelings. Flat rocks in the shape of dolmens are placed so as to protect the faces and heads of those who are buried. Later, ornaments, weapons, food, and the colors which serve to adorn the body, are placed in the tombs. The idea of finality is unbearable. The dead man will awaken, he will be hungry, he will have to defend himself, he will want to adorn himself."

The same author goes on to observe that because the primordial notions, like those of good and evil, or of immortality, were spontaneously born in the most primitive human beings, those notions would deserve for that very reason to be examined and scrutinized as possessing absolute value.

I think that these views expressed by Lecomte de Noüy are true and thought-provoking. *A priori* it is probable that the great and basic ideas, the prime ideas, which are contained in the myths of primitive man, and are handed down in the common heritage of mankind, are more sound than illusory, and deserve respect more than contempt. At the same time, we are free to prefer a genuine philosophical demonstration.

# ANDREW SETH PRINGLE-PATTISON

*Andrew Seth Pringle-Pattison* (1856–1931) was professor of logic and metaphysics at Edinburgh and an influential figure in the British revival of idealism, though he remained a critic of many aspects of Hegelianism. He was particularly interested in the philosophy of religion.

## Eternal Life

In the theory of Karma, reincarnation is not put forward as the goal of desire. So much at least will be evident from the discussion in the preceding lecture. Christian writers are accustomed to speak of "the hope of immortality," and theologians frequently use the phrase "a blessed immortality"; but, for the millions who really believe in it, reincarnation is not a "hope," it is rather, one might say, a "doom" to which they must submit. It is explicitly part of the wheel of becoming; and the endlessness of the process, instead of being an attraction ("On and always on," as Tennyson says), operates on the imagination like a nightmare. The sustaining hope is that, after the lapse of ages, release from the wheel may be attained, that is to say, the cessation of finite or separate being, either by absorption into Brahma or, as it would seem in Buddhism, by actual extinction. It is obvious, therefore, that if we mean by immortality simply an endless continuance of our individual existence, opinions may differ as to the desirability of such a gift or endowment.

Twenty years ago the American Branch of the Society for Psychical Research issued a *questionnaire* on "Human Sentiment with regard to a Future Life," and the first two questions were:

1. Would you prefer to live after death or not?
2. If you would prefer to live after death, do you desire a future life whatever the conditions might be, or, if that is not so, what would have to be its character to make the prospect seem tolerable?

From A. Seth Pringle-Pattison, *The Idea of Immortality*, pp. 131–147. Published, 1922, The Clarendon Press. Used by permission of The Clarendon Press. [Footnotes omitted, Eds.]

[526]

The replies received were not very instructive and perhaps not sufficiently representative, but Plutarch has left us his answers to the precise terms of these two questions, and he professes to speak for the vast majority of mankind. "The hope of eternity and the yearning for life," he writes, "is the oldest, as it is the greatest, of human desires." "I might almost say that all men and women would readily submit themselves to the teeth of Cerberus, and to the punishment of carrying water in a sieve, if only they might remain in existence and escape the doom of annihilation." Milton has put the same sentiment in the mouth of one of the rebel angels contemplating the alternative of annihilation in an access of the divine wrath. But the nearest modern parallel to Plutarch's passage is perhaps to be found in Heine's lines shortly before his death; and the force of the feeling they represent will be best realized if we remember that they were written from the "mattress-grave" in Paris, where he had lingered for so many years:

> O Gott, wie hässlich bitter ist das Sterben!
> O Gott, wie süss und traulich lässt sich's leben
> In diesem traulich süssen Erdennest!

The words recall Claudio's passionate recoil from the thought of impending death in *Measure for Measure:*

> This sensible warm motion to become
> A kneaded clod.

But Claudio's ignoble dread, like Hamlet's hesitation, is due not to the idea of extinction, but to "what we fear of death," "what dreams may come."

> The weariest and most loathèd worldly life
> That age, ache, penury, and imprisonment
> Can lay on nature, is a paradise
> To what we fear of death.

Heine was not troubled by such fears: it was just the blankness of death that wrung the words from him. "How our soul struggles against the thought of the cessation of our personality, of eternal annihilation! The *horror vacui* which we ascribe to nature is really inborn in the human heart!" So he had written some years earlier in the well-known postscript to his *Romanzero*. Yet the attitude which these two writers so vehemently express is certainly not universal. We have just seen how widely divergent is the voice of Eastern philosophy and Eastern religion. As it has been neatly put, the width of the divergence between East and West may be estimated from the fact that "the destiny which in one hemisphere has been propounded as the final reward of virtue is regarded in the other as the extreme penalty of obstinate wickedness." Where the theory of annihilation has found favour in Christian circles, its acceptance has usually been due to a recoil from the thought of the eternal duration of future punishment. But the profound weariness and sense of oppression, which the thought of the endlessness of future existence is capable of engendering, is not confined to the East. In the West, too, it is found prompting the hope—

> That even the weariest river
> Winds somewhere safe to sea.

Eternal rest is the deepest longing of many an over-driven body and tortured soul.

> Sleep after toil, port after stormy seas,
> Ease after war, death after life, does greatly please.

Buddha avowedly links his doctrine to the thought of the suffering or sorrow which accompanies all finite existence, and Brahmanism emphasizes the emptiness, the illusory character of the finite. But it is not merely the pessimism of Eastern thought that underlies its view here. Perhaps we should not be wrong in saying that the East is naturally more speculative than the West, and therefore thinks out and realizes more fully the implications of a metaphysical idea like that of endlessness. The Western temperament, with its active bias, is content for the most part to take the doctrine of immortality pragmatically, as equivalent to the belief that death does not end all, without developing its further consequences. Only, perhaps, in connexion with the doctrine of eternal punishment has there been any vivid attempt to realize and to apply these consequences. The unendingness of the penal fire was a theme on which preachers loved to dilate as embódying a horror greater even than the cruelty of the tortures depicted.

*Questi non hanno speranza di morte* is one of Dante's most terrible lines. Yet it does not require the experience of the damned to produce this sense of intolerableness. It is sufficient to concentrate our thoughts, or we might better say our imagination, on mere endlessness or pure succession. A personal immortality, so conceived, instead of being felt as a state of blessedness, oppresses us like a burden too heavy to be borne. "Is it *never* to end?" [I quote one homely utterance.] "The thought appals. I, little I, to live a million years—and another million—and another! My tiny light to burn for ever." We did not require, in short, to wait for Hegel to tell us that the endless progress in time or in space is the false infinite. The feeling is instinctive. It is the aimlessness of the process which afflicts the mind; for it is a progress which leads nowhere, which has no goal, seeing that, after ages of forward movement, you are precisely as distant from the imagined end as when you started.

But this impression is produced, it will be said, only because we allow ourselves to be gorgonized by the idea of empty time and the endless succession of its moments, apart from the experiences which fill them. As each moment of time, looked at thus abstractly, is exactly like every other, progress inevitably appears as a change which is no change. But if we think of the content of our experiences, it is argued, the afflicting illusion will disappear. In thinking of an immortal life we may, and ought to, think of it, not as the simple continuance of a being in existence at the same level of all his powers and attainments, but as a progress or advance in a real sense, a continuous growth towards the stature of a perfect humanity. The idea of growth, it is urged, liberates us from the oppressiveness of an unchanging identity. With ever new insights opened to us, and ever new conquests achieved, there can be no question of existence palling upon the taste. In the nature of things, the process can have no end; but, absorbed in each stage as it opens before us, we need not be distracted by the empty thought of the series of future stages still to be traversed. The future, in such a case, would not break upon us until it was present. It is clear, I think, that we are here on the road to a more satisfactory theory, but the improvement lies rather in the stress laid on the quality of the experiences than on the idea of growth as such. Kant's argument for the immortality of the soul based on the conception of the moral life as an infinite process of approximation to perfect virtue, might, I suppose, be taken as a typical application, from the ethical side, of the idea of growth. But such a process is still perilously like the *progressus in indefinitum;* it has, indeed, often been attacked on that ground. The infinite distance of the goal—nay, its explicit unreachableness—is the thought which inspires the argument; and hence the spectre of the future is inevitably conjured up with all the tension of the time-process. Unless we can rise to some experience satisfying in itself, we are not likely to reach a tenable theory of immortality. And, if we are to realize such an experience, we must pass beyond morality to religion, in which the life of finite struggle and endeavour is somehow transcended—where we escape, therefore, from the implications of the time-process, of which the moral life, in the strict sense of the word, is the typical expression.

Accordingly we find both theologians and philosophers insisting on the idea of an "eternal life," not as something in the future, a continuance of existence after our earthly life is ended, but as an experience, a state of being, to be enjoyed here and now. So, for example, in Schleiermacher's famous declaration: "The goal and the character of the religious life is not the immortality desired and believed in by many. . . . It is not the immortality that is outside of time, behind it or rather after it, and which still is in time. It is the immortality which we can have now in this temporal life. In the midst of finitude to be one with the Infinite, and in every moment to be eternal, that is the immortality of religion." The idea is very commonly put forward, as it is in this passage of Schleiermacher's, in opposition to banal and selfishly personal conceptions of a future life, which have nothing religious about them; and hence such statements are often interpreted as implying that the enjoyment of the eternal life described is limited to the opportunities afforded by the present life. They are taken as definitely negating the idea of personal immortality in any ordinary sense of the term. This negative attitude is, no doubt, adopted by many: they put forward the possibility of realizing eternal life here and now *in place of* the further life which we ordinarily mean by immortality. Schleiermacher himself, at least during the earlier part of his career, seems to have held such a view. There is recounted in Dr. Martineau's *Study of Religion* the touching story of his ineffectual efforts to console a young widow whose husband, according to Schleiermacher's teaching, had "melted away into the great ALL." But eternity and immortality are by no means necessarily exclusive terms: on the contrary, our experience here and now may carry in it "the power of an endless life," and be in truth the only earnest or guarantee of such a life.

It is a commonplace of philosophical criticism that the term "eternal," when strictly and properly used, does not mean endless continuance *in* time, but a quality of experience which transcends time altogether. Thus in Spinoza, where the contrast is specially emphasized, eternity means rational necessity. We know things "under a certain form of eternity" when we see them not as isolated contingent events, but as necessary parts of a single system, each integral to the whole. It is of the nature of reason (*de natura rationis*) so to regard things, and the perception of this timeless necessity is a very real experience. Mr. Bertrand Russell has told our own generation afresh, in this connexion, that "mathematics, rightly viewed, possesses not only truth but supreme beauty—a beauty cold and austere like that of scupture . . . yet sublimely pure, and capable of a stern perfection such as only the greatest art can show. The true spirit of delight, the exaltation, the sense of being more than man, which is the touchstone of the highest excellence, is to be found in mathematics as surely as in poetry." For Spinoza the necessity of reason is not divorced, as with Mr. Russell, from actual existence. It is Spinoza's vision of the universe as in all its parts a system of divine necessity which creates in him "the intellectual love of God," that supreme emotion which expels all lower or merely selfish desires, because it is itself joy and peace, the perfect satisfaction of the mind (*vera mentis acquiescentia*). "All our happiness or unhappiness," he tells us, "depends solely on the quality of the object on which our love is fixed. . . . But love towards an object eternal and infinite feeds the mind with a joy that is pure with no tinge of sadness." Such is the life of "thoughts immortal and divine" of which we found Plato and Aristotle also speaking as opening up to the thinker a present immortality. For Spinoza this "eternal life" is realized in the intellectual vision of truth and harmony; and, as he twice over reminds us in the *Short Treatise,* Truth—the ultimate or all-embracing Truth—is God Himself. This is the "intuition" (*scientia intuitiva*) in which knowledge culminates.

But Art, or, to put it more widely, the perception of Beauty, also yields us experiences under a similar "form of eternity."

> A thing of beauty is a joy for ever:
> Its loveliness increases; it will never
> Pass into nothingness.

Art, it has been said, is the wide world's memory of things. Think only of some of the great stories which have delighted generation after generation, the tale of Troy, the wanderings of Odysseus, the history of Don Quixote. Think of the figures of drama, every turn of whose fate is graven upon our mind and heart, "forms more real than living man," who trod the boards centuries before our coming, and on whom the curtain will rise as many ages after we have gone. Or take the forms bequeathed to us by the sculptor's art, or some melody of immortal loveliness. Perhaps this sense of bodiless immortality is most vividly realized by the ordinary person in the case of a musical work, as the sounds fill the air and the instruments give its harmonies and sequences once more a brief existence for the bodily ear.

In Art, as Schopenhauer loved to insist, the objects we contemplate have the eternity and universality of the Platonic Ideas. They are lifted out of the stream of becoming which constitutes individual existence; and in contemplating them we are emancipated from the tyranny of the Will, that is to say, of selfish desire. In aesthetic perception our knowledge is pure and disinterested; our objectivity is complete. "The subject and the object mutually fill and penetrate each other completely." Science, based on the principle of causality, is constantly investigating the relations of its object to other things, and is involved, thereby, in an endless quest. "Art is everywhere at its goal, for it plucks the object of its contemplation out of the world's course, and has it isolated before it. And this particular thing, which in that stream was a small perishing part, becomes to art the representative of the whole, an equivalent of the endless multitude in space and time. The course of time stops; relations vanish for it; only the essential, the Idea, is its object." Our individuality has fallen from us: "we are only that *one* eye of the world which looks out from all knowing creatures, but only in man can become perfectly free from the service of the will." "Then all at once the peace which we were always seeking, but which fled from us on the former path of the desires, comes to us of its own accord and it is well with us: we keep a Sabbath from the penal slavery of the will; the wheel of Ixion stands still." Many, accordingly, have celebrated Art in this strain, as the only refuge of the spirit from the miseries and weariness of the actual world,

> The weariness, the fever, and the fret,
> Here where men sit and hear each other groan.

To such natures—to Keats, from whom I have quoted, to Goethe and Schiller at certain points in their career—Art thus becomes a religion, or at least is made to do duty for one. Such moments, however, of selfless contemplation and aesthetic enjoyment cannot be more than intermittent, Schopenhauer confesses, and therefore Art cannot achieve that perfect and final deliverance which we seek from the misery of existence. For that we must go, he teaches, to religion, to a religion like Buddhism, which inculcates the resolute extermination of the will to live.

It is in religion, after all, that the term "eternal life" is most familiar to us. It occurs constantly in the New Testament as the designation of a frame of mind or spiritual attitude which is intended to be realized here and now. The meaning of the phrase in early Christian usage can hardly be fully understood, however, without a glance at the Jewish apocalyptic beliefs, so prominent in men's minds at the time, with which it was at first closely associated, but with which it comes to be in a sense contrasted. We have seen in a previous Lecture how slow was the growth of an effective doctrine of a future life among the Hebrews. When it did arise, it was associated with the national hope of a Messianic kingdom. "The day of Jahveh," originally conceived simply as a judgement on the enemies of Israel executed by the national god, and the inauguration of a new period of material prosperity under his protection, had been transformed by the prophets into the idea of a day of judgement upon Israel itself for the nation's sins; and with the rise of a true monotheism (from the seventh century onwards) this judgement was extended to include all the nations of the earth. The result of the prophesied judgement was to be the establishment of the righteous and penitent remnant of Israel under a prince of the house of David, or a dynasty of such warrior kings and righteous rulers. Other nations—the Gentiles—were either to be destroyed, according to the bitter nationalism of some of the prophets, or, according to the larger-hearted, brought into this divinely established kingdom by conversion. The kingdom was to be set up on this present earth and would last for ever, and the righteous dead of Israel were to be raised from Sheol to participate in its blessedness.

This was the first form of the apocalyptic idea, but in course of time—about the close of the second century B.C.—it came to be realized that the earth (whether as we know it or as transformed into "a new heaven and a new earth") was unfit to be the scene of such an eternal kingdom: the Kingdom of God could be realized only in a spiritual world to come. The idea of a Messianic reign of the saints upon earth was not abandoned, but it was conceived as temporary in duration (sometimes as lasting a thousand years), and as a prelude to the final judgement which inaugurates the eternal kingdom of God. The important point, however, remains the same, namely, the sharp distinction drawn between "the present age," in which the powers of wickedness hold sway, and "the coming age," when the divine kingdom will be realized. The appearance of the Messiah, now conceived as a supernatural being—"the Son of man" or "the Son of God"—is the event which is to mark the advent, or at least the near approach, of the new age. Such were the convictions of the religious part of the Jewish nation in the time of Jesus, and this eschatology meets us everywhere in the New Testament. The sense of the imminence of the coming of the Kingdom is universal. "The Kingdom of Heaven is at hand" was the text of John the Baptist's preaching, and the phrase was appropriated and applied by Jesus in his own way. The first idea which the words roused in the minds of his hearers was the thought of this future dispensation, to be ushered in catastrophically by the appearance of the Messiah on the clouds of heaven to judge the world. Jesus himself appears to have shared the general belief that this event would take place within the life-time of those whom he was addressing: "There be some standing here which shall not taste of death, till they see the Son of man coming in his Kingdom." "This generation shall not pass, till all these things be fulfilled." When he sent out the Twelve on their preaching mission, he is represented as saying that, before their return, the expected event would have taken place: "Verily I say unto you, Ye shall not have gone over the cities of Israel, till the Son of man be come." We need not wonder, therefore, if, in spite of the rest of their Master's teaching about the spiritual nature of the Kingdom, the disciples continued to give his sayings about it this future reference, and had to be rebuked for the thoroughly mundane hopes of reward and distinction which they linked with its establishment.

Yet, from the beginning of his teaching, Jesus made the inheritance of this kingdom dependent on purely spiritual conditions. He taught not simply, like John the Baptist or the prophets before him, that the kingdom of heaven was at hand, but that it was already a present fact—"in their midst" or "within them;" and, in so doing, he stepped out of the ranks of the Hebrew prophets and came forward as the bearer of a new message from God to man. And the gospel he proclaimed was not a promise of future reward for certain beliefs about himself, but, as every genuinely religious message must be, a gospel of deliverance, a message of present salvation: "Come unto me, all ye that labour and are heavy laden, and I *will give you rest*. Take my yoke upon you and learn of me; for I am meek and lowly in heart: and *ye shall find rest unto your souls*." It is an insight which changes the face of the world and "makes all things new." Above all it is an insight into what salvation really means. Not a password enabling a man to escape dire penalties in the future or admitting him to great rewards, but a change of the inner man, the adoption of a new attitude towards life and its happenings. The changed attitude is not to be understood as the condition of salvation, in the sense that salvation is something different from the spiritual state and externally added to it. As St. Paul says, "To be spiritually minded *is* life and peace." This, then, is the salvation of the soul, the only salvation that matters, as the Platonic Socrates had already so impressively insisted: and when Jesus says "A man's *life* consisteth not in the abundance of the things which he possesseth," or "What shall it profit a man if he shall gain the whole world and lose his own *soul?*," the words "life" and "soul" are clearly used in the Platonic sense and not in an eschatological reference. Hence we have the antithesis of "life" and "death," so recurrent in the New Testament, both terms being used to signify a present spiritual state. The message of the Gospel is continually referred to as a message of "life," and the change it effects is described as a passage from "death unto life." The antithesis is equated by St. Paul with his own favourite contrast between the flesh and the spirit. "To be carnally minded is death; but to be spiritually minded is life and peace." "The law of the spirit of life in Christ Jesus hath made me free from the law of sin and death. . . . The body is dead because of sin, but the spirit is life because of righteousness." He also inweaves with his statement that other sense of "death," contained in the most characteristic teaching of Jesus, that "whosoever will save his life shall lose it: and whosoever will lose his life for my sake shall find it." This is, in his own emphatic phrase, the very "word of the cross," life through death. We must die to self —to selfish desires and egoistic cravings—before we can find our true self in that wider life which is at once the love of the brethren and the love of God. In this sense, St. Paul protests, he dies daily: only by dying with Christ, "crucifying the flesh with the passions and the lusts thereof," can we share with him the higher life to which he showed the way. As sharing that life, "walking in Him," "complete in Him," St. Paul describes believers as already "risen with Christ." Thus the death and resurrection of Jesus, which he accepted (we know) as historical facts, and his own resurrection, to which he undoubtedly looked forward as a future event, became for the Apostle, as a religious thinker, a description of the eternal nature of the spiritual life, symbols of an experience daily realized. It is in this sense that Christ is said to have brought *life and immortality* to light through the gospel. "This gift to men" [I purposely quote a strictly orthodox commentator] "is not the inculcation of the truth of an endless existence, nor any dogma of the soul's deathless perpetuity, but the revelation of a higher life."

Life, in the mystical sense indicated, often more specifically "eternal life," is the very burden of the Fourth Gospel and the Johannine Epistles. "I am come," says the Johannine Christ, "that they might have life, and that they might have it more abundantly." "He that eateth my flesh and drinketh my blood hath eternal life." This spiritual sense both of life and of resurrection forms the kernel of the Lazarus story, where it is expressly emphasized against the literalism of Martha. "Martha saith unto him, I know that he shall rise again in the resurrection at the last day. Jesus said unto her, I am the resurrection and the life: he that believeth in me, though he were dead, yet shall he live: and whosoever liveth and believeth in me shall never die." So again: "The hour cometh *and now is,* when the dead shall hear the voice of the Son of God, and they that hear shall live." This is the same spiritual sense of life and resurrection as an accomplished fact that we have in St. Paul. The dead here are the spiritually dead who are to be quickened or made alive. "This is life eternal, that they should know thee, the only true God, and Jesus Christ whom thou hast sent." Similarly in the Epistles: "God hath given to us eternal life, and this life is in his Son. He that hath the Son hath life." "We know that we have passed from death unto life, because we love the brethren. He that loveth not his brother abideth in death." "He that loveth not, knoweth not God; for God is love. . . . If we love one another, God abideth in us, and his love is perfected in us." "This is the true God, and eternal life."

The emphatic present tense throughout these passages is evidence sufficient of the writer's meaning. Eternal life is not a state of existence to follow upon physical death, but an all-satisfying present experience of the love of God in Christ. It is, as the theologians say, "participation in the being of the spiritual Christ." The fruit of such an experience (to quote St. Paul's list) is "love, joy, peace." "My peace I give unto you," says the Johannine Christ. "These things have I spoken unto you, that your joy might be full." "And ye shall know the truth, and the truth shall make you free." This is the eternal life in the midst of time which is claimed by the saints as an immediate experience, one which time can neither increase nor diminish, one to which considerations of time are, in fact, indifferent, because we are at rest in the present.

Needless to say, such experience is not the exclusive property of any single faith. Much controversy has raged, for example, round the meaning of the Buddhist Nirvana. The term is ordinarily translated nothingness or annihilation. At his death, we are told, the perfected saint becomes extinct, like the flame of an expiring fire. That appears to be the natural result of the insight he has gained into the root of all evil and the way of deliverance; and the term is so applied by Buddhists themselves. Yet the Buddha himself, when urged by his disciples, expressly declined to answer yea or nay to the question whether the man who has won deliverance will exist or not after death —on the ground that "this is a matter which does not make for things needful to salvation, nor for that which concerns a holy life." What he had taught, he said, was only the cause of suffering and the path which leads to its cessation. The primary reference of the word is, therefore, not to any future event—to what may happen after death—but to the insight on which that ultimate deliverance may be supposed to follow—to the extinction of all the fires of desire and the perfect peace resulting therefrom. Nirvana, in its original intention, is that immediate emancipation from all the passions and cares of life which renunciation brings with it, a state of mind to be attained here and now, the peace which the world can neither give nor take away, and which is the supreme and only blessedness. "There is no spot, O King, East, South, West, or North, above, below or beyond, where Nirvana is situate, and yet Nirvana is, and he who orders his life aright . . . may realize it, whether he live in Greece, in China, in Alexandria or Kosala." Apart from the fundamental pessimism of Buddhism, the words of Jesus and those of the Buddha often strikingly resemble one another in their recurring emphasis on rest and peace. And the language of Buddhist hymns is not so different from that of Christian devotion. Take, for instance, these short examples rendered by Mrs. Rhys Davids:

> Nirvana have I realized, and gazed
> Into the mirror of the Holy Law.
> I, even I, am healed of my hurt.
> Low is my burden laid, my task is done,
> My heart is wholly set at liberty.
>
> .    .    .    .    .    .    .    .
>
> Nor is there any bliss greater than peace.
> These things to know, e'en as they really are,
> This is Nirvana, crown of happiness.

Religion is thus, as Hegel has finely said, "the realm where all the riddles of the world are solved, all the contradictions of probing thought are unveiled, and all pangs of feeling cease, the region of eternal truth, of eternal rest. The whole complexity of human relations, activities, enjoyments, everything that man values and esteems, wherein he seeks his happiness, his glory, his pride—all find their final centre in religion, in the thought, the consciousness, the feeling of God. . . . God is known in religion. Religion just means being occupied with this object. In this occupation the spirit casts off all its finitude; in it it finds its satisfaction and perfect freedom. All nations accordingly have looked upon this religious consciousness as their true dignity, as the Sunday of their lives; every care and anxiety, this 'bank and shoal of time' itself, vanishes in this aether, in the immediate feeling of devotion or of hope."

It is, then, on the possibility of such experiences as we have been considering that any valid theory of immortality must be based. Their reality is beyond dispute, whether reached in the apprehension of Truth, through Beauty, or through Goodness. By whatever gate a man may enter, the eternal foundations of the world are there discovered to him, and he knows that in his hold on these realities lies all that is worth striving for, all that is of value in his life. The being of these realities and his own relation to them "stand sure" beyond the risks of time and change, even the change which we call death. He who has tasted eternal life is not wont to be troubled in heart about the question of his personal survival; for such survival would mean nothing to him, if he were separated from the object in which he has found his true life. His immortality lies for him in his union with the eternal object on which his affections are set, and he seeks no other assurance.

# C. D. BROAD

*C. D. Broad* (1887–     ) was, before his retirement, Knightbridge Professor of Philosophy at Cambridge University. He is well known in America and Great Britain for his careful analytical writings. His main contributions have been in the areas of ethics and epistemology, as well as in the discussion of immortality.

## The Mind and Its Place in Nature

Ought we to attach any weight to this primitive belief which nearly every one has in his own survival? The mere fact that it is held without reasons is no conclusive objection to it; for, unless some propositions can be known to be true without reasons, no proposition can be known to be true for reasons. We must, therefore, consider the belief on its merits without prejudice. Now it seems perfectly clear that it is not a self-evident proposition like an axiom, which becomes more certain the more carefully we inspect it. Nor can it be regarded as a postulate; i.e., as a proposition which, though not self-evident and incapable of either proof or disproof by experience, has to be assumed in order to organise experience and to furnish a motive for research. Certain propositions which we use in induction seem to me to be postulates in this sense; the proposition that John Jones will survive the death of his body seems to me to be quite plainly nothing of the kind. In fact I think that the belief represents nothing more profound than an easily

From C. D. Broad, *The Mind and Its Place in Nature,* pp. 523–533. Published, 1925, by Kegan Paul, Trench, Trubner & Company, Ltd. Used by permission of Routledge & Kegan Paul, Ltd., and Humanities Press, Inc.

explicable limit of our powers of imagination. Naturally all my experience of myself has been of myself as conscious and active. There have indeed been gaps during dreamless sleep or fainting fits, but consciousness has revived and the gaps have been bridged by memory. Again, at every moment I have been obliged for practical purposes to think of myself as going to exist at later moments; it is therefore a breach with the mental habits of a lifetime to envisage a moment after which the series of my conscious states shall have finally ended. This practical difficulty, due to habit, seems the sole and sufficient explanation of our primitive belief in our own indefinite continuance; and it obviously provides no evidence for the truth of that belief.

I think then that we must conclude that a mere contemplation of the world as it appears in ordinary experience furnishes no trace of support for the belief in survival. Ought we to hold that the absence of all evidence *for* constitutes evidence *against?* This is a somewhat delicate question. Sometimes the absence of evidence for a proposition makes strongly against it, and sometimes it does not. If I look carefully round a room and, seeing no one, say: "There is no one in the room," my evidence is purely negative; but it is almost conclusive against the proposition: "There is someone in the room." But the fact that I did not see a tuberculosis bacillus in the room would be quite irrelevant to the question whether there was one there. Finding no evidence for a proposition is evidence against it only if the proposition be such that, if it were true, there ought to be some observable evidence for it.

Now the proposition: "Some men survive the death of their bodies" is not precisely in the position of either of the two quoted above. I know enough about human bodies and about tuberculosis bacilli to be sure that one of the former could hardly be present in a room without my finding it, but that one of the latter could not be seen by the naked eye even if it were present. I know very much less about the conditions under which one human spirit can make its presence known to another; but I do know something about it. I am a human spirit connected with a body, and all other spirits of whose existence I am certain are in the same position. Setting aside the phenomena treated by Psychical Research, I know that one such spirit can make its presence known to another only by moving its own body, thence agitating the air or the ether, and thence affecting another human body. My friend dies; I remain alive and connected with my body. Communication with me, therefore, presumably requires the same complex and roundabout series of material changes as before. Its very complexity and indirectness make it not unlikely that, even if my friend has survived, some necessary link in this mechanism will have broken down. Hence the absence of evidence for his survival cannot be regarded logically as very strong evidence against it.

The present position, therefore, is that at the level of ordinary experience there is not the faintest trace of evidence for survival, though there is a pretty general belief in it. The causes of this belief have been enumerated and seen not to be reasons. But the absence of evidence for the belief cannot be taken as strong evidence against it, in view of what we know about the means by which embodied human spirits have to communicate with each other.

Is there at this level any *positive* evidence *against* survival? I think that there are two sets of facts which impress common-sense and are interpreted in this direction. One is the apparently haphazard way in which men are born and die. Human beings are constantly brought into the world thoughtlessly and by mistake; many children live for a few minutes or hours and then die; many are born idiotic. The general impression produced is that the claim to permanence for creatures whose earthly lives begin and end in these trivial ways is somewhat ridiculous. An unwanted child is produced, let us say, in a drunken orgy; and in six weeks dies of neglect or is killed by its mother. Does it seem likely that a being whose earthly careeer is started and stopped by such causes is a permanent and indestructible part of the universe, or indeed that it survives the death of its body at all?

The second fact which is felt to bear in the same direction is the continuity between men and animals. The bodies of each begin and cease to be animated by minds through precisely similar physical and physiological causes. No doubt the mind of any living man differs, not merely quantitatively, but also qualitatively from that of any living animal; still the most primitive men can hardly have differed appreciably from the highest animals in their mental endowments. Did *Pithecanthropus erectus* and does every Australian aborigine survive the death of his body? If they do, have not the higher animals almost an equal claim? And, if you grant this for cats and monkeys, will you not be forced in the end to grant it for lice and earwigs? If, on the other hand, you deny that any animal survives, on the ground that their minds are not complex or important enough to be permanent factors in the universe, how can you be sure that any man yet born has possessed a mind complex and important enough for survival? The two facts quoted above do, I am sure, exert a considerable influence against the view that men survive the death of their bodies. I am conscious that they affect me personally more than any others. But the question remains: "Have they any logical right to exert this influence?"

I am inclined to think on reflection that the first argument is wholly fallacious. It really involves the illegitimate introduction of a judgment of value into a question of fact. And the judgment of value is itself a rather superficial one. It is thought that, because the occasioning causes of birth and death are often trivial, therefore what seems to begin with birth and to end with death cannot be important enough to survive. But (*a*) you cannot argue from the triviality of a cause to the impermanence of its effect. (*b*) The cause is trivial only in the irrelevant ethical sense that it does not involve a considered and deliberate choice by a virtuous human being. There is really no logical transition from "This is caused by the careless or criminal action of a human being" to: "This is the kind of thing whose existence is transitory." (*c*) When we say that the cause is trivial we make the common mistake of taking for *the* cause some necessary cause-factor which happens to be specially noticeable or of special practical interest. The complete cause of the birth of a child or the death of a man must be of almost unthinkable complexity, whether the child be begotten or the man be killed carelessly or with deliberate forethought. This is true even if we confine ourselves to the material conditions; and we are not really in a position to say that the *complete* conditions of so singular an event as the manifestation of a new mind through a new body are contained in the material world.

The second argument is of course of a well-known general type. It tries to show by continuity of cases that, if a man asserts one proposition, he ought in consistency not to deny a certain other proposition which he would like to deny. Arguments of this kind can be met in one of two ways. (1) We may point out that an argument from continuity is reversible, and that the direction in which one turns it is arbitrary. We might just as well argue by continuity from the supposed immortality of men to the immortality of earwigs as from the supposed mortality of earwigs to the mortality of men. The actual direction in which the argument is used presupposes that we are *already* pretty certain that earwigs are mortal, and much more doubtful whether men are immortal. This no doubt is true. But it immediately raises the question: "Why are we practically certain that earwigs are mortal?" This question cannot be answered by considerations of continuity, but only by reflecting on the special peculiarities of earwigs. (2) When we raise this question two answers are possible. (*a*) We may find on reflection that we have no good reason for thinking that earwigs are unlikely to be immortal. In that case the argument from continuity to the case of men will prove nothing. Or (*b*) we may find that those characteristics of earwigs which make it very unlikely that they are immortal are obviously not present in men. In that case the argument from continuity will also prove nothing about men. At most it will show that it is difficult for us to say with confidence about certain intermediate forms of living being whether they are likely to be mortal or not. Let us then consider the question why we think it very unlikely that earwigs should be immortal; and let us also consider whether the reasons, whatever they may be, apply to men also.

In the first place it might be said that an earwig's mind has very little value, and therefore it is unworthy to be a permanent factor in the universe. And it might be argued that it is therefore unlikely to survive. But (*a*) this would be an ethical argument of a kind which we have already dismissed. And (*b*), even if it were valid, it is obvious that most human minds are enormously more valuable than the mind of any earwig; so that it would not be inconsistent to think it likely that human minds are immortal and unlikely that the minds of earwigs are so. All that we should be entitled to say is (*a*) that it is not certain even that any human mind is valuable enough to be immortal; and (*b*) that, if it were certain, there would be intermediate cases, e.g., cats, about which the probabilities are about equally balanced.

But the differences between the minds of men and those of the lower animals are never *mere* differences of value. Presumably an earwig's mind has very little unity, complexity, or comprehensiveness. Now it is arguable that such a very simple mind is not very likely to survive bodily death. But (*a*) I do not think that what we know of nature suggests any straight-forward connexion between unity and complexity on the one hand and stability on the other. Both the very simple and the highly comprehensive seem to be fairly stable, though for different reasons. The very simple, like the electron, is stable because of its comparative indifference to changes in external conditions. The highly unified and comprehensive complex, like the solar system, tends to be stable because it contains so much within itself that there is little left over to disturb it. It is therefore quite in accordance with what we know of the order of nature to suppose that the simplicity of the earwig's mind gives it a particularly good chance of survival. (*b*) Suppose, on the other hand, that we do hold that the simplicity of the earwig's mind makes it very unlikely to survive. Then we must admit that the human mind is enormously less simple and more comprehensive and highly unified. Hence it would be perfectly consistent to hold that the human mind is likely to survive because of its unity and comprehensiveness and that the earwig's mind is unlikely to survive because of its simplicity and poverty of content. Thus on neither alternative does the argument from continuity make it unreasonable to hold that the human mind is likely to survive. As before, all that we can legitimately conclude from the argument from continuity is (*a*) that it is uncertain whether any human mind even is complex and comprehensive enough to survive; and (*b*) that, if it were certain, there would be cases of intermediate complexity, e.g., cats, about which the probabilities would be nearly equally balanced.

Again, some people no doubt shrink from admitting the possibility of survival to the lower animals out of horror at the immense number of minds which there would be if none, even of the lowest kind, died with the death of their bodies. This shrinking from mere numerical vastness seems to me to be childish. We have no reason to suppose that the universe is conducted in accordance with the Law of Parsimony; and it may well be that the world exhibits a profusion in the item of minds which would horrify the inhabitants of Aberdeen. Thus I do not think that this consideration makes it specially improbable that earwigs should be immortal.

Lastly, the following argument might be used to suggest that the minds of the lower animals are very unlikely to survive the death of their bodies. The characteristic activities and experiences of animals seem to be specially and exclusively directed to preserving their own lives and those of their off-spring. If we judge living things teleologically (and, in practice it is hard to avoid doing this) it does seem that an animal accomplishes "all that is in it" when it succeeds in keeping itself alive long enough to produce young and to start them in the world. It is hard to see what "purpose" would be served by the individual survival of an earwig which dies at a reasonable age after bringing up a family of little earwigs. I do not know what weight to attach to such an argument as this. The principle of judging living beings and their parts in terms of a supposed "purpose for which they were made" is undoubtedly valuable as an heuristic method; and it is difficult to suppose that it does not in some way accord with the facts. But fortunately it is not necessary for our purpose to decide on the legitimacy of such considerations. For the position is this. (*a*) If it be not valid, the argument to show that earwigs are very unlikely to survive falls to the ground; and with it goes the argument from continuity to the probable mortality of human beings. (*b*) If, on the other hand, it be valid, the argument from continuity equally breaks down in another way. For it does seem as if human minds had many powers and faculties which are not merely directed to preserving the life of the in-dividual and the species; and that the continued existence of certain human minds after the death of their bodies would "answer the purpose for which they seem to be made" in a way in which the continued existence of an in-dividual earwig would not. Hence it would be perfectly consistent to hold, on the basis of this argument, that earwigs are most unlikely to be immortal and that men are quite likely to be immortal. As usual, the argument from continuity would raise a doubt only about certain intermediate cases, such as cats and dogs, where the probabilities might be about equally balanced.

To sum up. The argument from continuity makes against the probability of human survival only on two conditions. (1) There must be some reason (and not a mere prejudice) for thinking that the survival of the lower animals is very improbable. And (2) this reason must not be the presence of some characteristic in the lower animals which differentiates them sharply from human beings. For, if our only reason for thinking it very unlikely that earwigs will survive be some characteristic in which earwigs differ profoundly from men, it will be perfectly consistent to think it likely that men will sur-vive and that earwigs will not. The existence of a continuous series of inter-mediate forms between earwigs and men will prove nothing except that there are certain intermediate cases in which the probabilities for and against sur-vival are about equally balanced. And there would not be the least trace of inconsistency in the position of a man who should be practically certain that earwigs are mortal and human beings immortal but should be quite unable to make up his mind about cats or kangaroos. Now, so far as I can see, these two conditions are never both fulfilled. The alleged reasons for thinking it very unlikely that earwigs are immortal either are no reasons at all or they obviously depend on characteristics in which human beings and earwigs differ profoundly. Hence I doubt whether the argument against the probability of human survival, drawn from the continuous series of living forms between men and the lowest animals, has any logical validity. The world then, as it presents itself to common-sense and everyday experience, offers no positive reasons for and no positive reasons against human survival. The only reason against it is the utter absence of all reasons for it; and we have seen that this is not a strong argument in the present case. Let us now enquire whether the more detailed investigations of science provide us with any grounds for deciding one way or the other.

Science on the whole does not reverse, but merely amplifies and elaborates, the views of common-sense on the connexion of body and mind. We already knew that body and mind were intimately connected, and that injury to the former may gravely modify or to all appearance destroy the latter. The additional information gained from science may be summed up as follows. (i) More detailed knowledge has been got of the correlation between injuries to particular regions of the brain and defects in certain departments of mental life. Connected with this is the knowledge that many mental processes, which seem to common-sense to be almost independent of the body, have bodily correlates. (ii) We have gained the surprising information that, in spite of the apparent interaction of body and mind, the body and its material surroundings form a closed energetic system from the point of view of the Conservation of Energy. (iii) We know more about the detailed structure and general plan of the brain and nervous system. What bearing has all this on the probability of survival? We find bodies without minds; we never find minds without bodies. When we do find minds we always find a close correlation between their processes and those of their bodies. This, it is argued, strongly suggests that minds depend for their *existence* on bodies; in which case, though survival may still be abstractly possible it is to the last degree unlikely. At death there takes place completely and permanently a process of bodily destruction which, when it occurs partially and temporarily, carries with it the destruction of part of our mental life. The inference seems only too obvious. I think it is fair to say that our ordinary scientific knowledge of the relation of body to mind most strongly suggests epiphenomenalism, though it does not necessitate it; and that epiphenomenalism is most unfavourable to the hypothesis of human survival.

# F. R. TENNANT

*Frederick R. Tennant* (1866–1957) was lecturer in theology and philosophy of religion from 1909–1931 at Cambridge University. His concern for a valid rational theology and a broad empirical approach is reflected in his important work *Philosophical Theology.*

## Immortality

Arguments for and against human immortality, or life after death, may be classified thus:

I. Arguments not presupposing theism.
  (1) Empirical.
  (2) Metaphysical—i.e., ontological.
  (3) Ethical.
II. Arguments presupposing theism, to the effect that immortality is, or is not, a corollary of theism.

I. (1) The form in which the question as to human immortality is usually propounded, viz. has man an immortal soul? tacitly assumes that the man is primarily his body. And there are doubtless reasons why this assumption should be ingrained in common thought leavened with science. Matter seems, to those who have not pursued philosophical inquiries, so much better known than mind or spirit, and mind seems to be so much more dependent upon body than changes in the body are dependent upon mental activities. But while science shews the close connexion between brain and thought it does not warrant the conclusion that the soul and its activities are products of the brain, and that they must vanish when the physical organism dies. The sensation with which we are acquainted is mediated by the body; but it is not a scientifically established fact that the kind of body which we now possess is essential for the soul's life and possession of personality. And there is no scientific reason for believing that the soul shares the change and decay of material things. Their dissolution is generally describable as resolution into parts; but the soul cannot be supposed to consist of separable parts, or to

From F. R. Tennant, *Philosophical Theology,* II, 269–272. Published, 1928, Cambridge University Press. Used by permission of Cambridge University Press.

be an aggregate of mind-dust. For all that physiology knows, the soul may at death enter into connexion with another kind of body, about which, however, it is futile to speculate. It is possible that while the body that now is determines the nature of the soul's activities, sensations, etc., as we know them, it at the same time imposes limitations upon the potentialities of the soul; and that though the death of the body may put an end to sensation it may be the beginning of a non-sensible experience, or of an experience in which another kind of *rapport* than that which constitutes sensation is substituted for it. Empirical science, therefore, cannot infer, from the fact that the present life of the self is dependent on that of the present body, the impossibility of a future life of the soul. Science here leaves room for faith.

On the other hand, psychical research cannot be said as yet to have established the soul's survival of bodily death. The proofs which have been alleged are based chiefly on facts concerning what is called cross-reference: i.e. two independent mediums may write fragments, both series of which are meaningless by themselves but yield sense when pieced together. But communication from a disembodied spirit is not to be taken to be the only and the certain explanation of the facts until, e.g., telepathy of the living has been shewn to be inadmissible.

(2) Metaphysical arguments for the immortality of the soul, of several kinds, were put forth by Plato. One of these was based on the fancy that knowledge is reminiscence; others rest on the mistaken notion that knowledge is pure thought about pure essences, or is eternal and implies eternal knowers. Perhaps the most influential of them is that (in the *Phaedo*) which sets out from the assertion that the essence of the soul is life, whence it is concluded that the soul is essentially living. Of course, if the soul be defined as the reified abstraction, life, to speak of a mortal soul involves self-contradiction; but, like all *a priori* proofs, this one assumes that the definition from which the desired consequent is deducible has application to anything that is actual.

Kant brought the same charge, amongst others, against the rational psychology of his day. This, proceeding on lines laid down by Descartes, deduced a *res cogitans* from the empirically given *cogito,* identified this *res* with substance, in the most abstract sense of the term, and asserted it to be imperishable because simple or indiscerptible. Plainly this reasoning is only a linkage of abstract ideas; that the soul, the actuality of which is demanded by the facts of observable human mentality, is a substance as thus conceived, and is consequently imperishable or self-subsistent as well as indiscerptible, is a question of fact, not of ideas, and one which the forthcoming facts do not enable us to answer in the positive.

It may be observed that if the arguments based on definitions of substance, etc., were valid, they would not serve to establish personal immortality: survival of soul-substance is not necessarily continuity of personality. Yet it is immortality in the latter sense that alone is of human interest, of religious worth, and of significance for theistic theology. Some philosophers assert that memory of the previous life, or lives, is essential to personal immortality; others, deeming memory to be conditioned by the body, credit the soul with a power to retain the effects of experiences of the embodied life, e.g., wisdom and love, even if memory be lost. This, however, is dogma concerning the unknowable. And whenever immortality is asserted on metaphysical grounds that are independent of theistic belief or exclusive of such belief, as when souls are identified with self-subsistent differentiations of The Absolute, it would seem that the limits of knowledge are transcended and that definitions of concepts are confounded with matters of fact or actualities.

(3) Moral arguments belonging to class I all rest on ethical postulates which, apart from theism, are uncertain or improbable. Thus, one of Plato's arguments assumes that the soul is made for virtue, i.e. for freeing itself from bodily passions, and concludes that the soul is destined to be separated from the body. Another, resembling Kant's argument which is confessed to rest upon a postulate, assumes the final harmonisation of virtue and happiness: immortality is a condition of the realisation of the highest good. But, apart from theism, there is no ground for reasonable belief as to the realisation of the highest good.

The outcome of the foregoing review of arguments which do not presuppose theism is that a future life is not impossible or inconceivable, but, on the other hand, is not demonstrable.

II. With the presupposition of theism we pass into the sphere of probability and faith. Immortality becomes a matter of more or less reasonable belief, as distinct from deducibility from assured metaphysical principles or from more or less arbitrary postulations concerning the harmonising of moral experience. It is no matter, however, of subjective or personal desires, e.g. for the continuance of life or of love, but rather a demand for coherence in what is, as a matter of fact, a moral universe. The world would not be irrational, in the logical sense, were the present life the only life; but it is a further question whether the world would be reasonable, or rational in the teleological sense: in other words, whether theism does not imply human immortality.

Theists are not altogether agreed on this point. Those who incline toward absolute monism are sometimes disposed to disparage human personality, to regard it as unworthy of survival, and to speak of the conservation of personal values, universalised, in abstraction from the personal bearers of them. But in so far as monism is approached, theism is deserted: wherefore, strictly speaking, these views are irrelevant to the present inquiry. Some theists, however, consider that, before we can assert immortality to be an implication of theism, it is necessary to know more than is known concerning God's purpose for the world. The facts and generalisations which receive an adequate explanation in the postulate of an intelligent and ethical world-ground, it is said, do not of themselves authorise belief in the *perfect* reasonableness of the world, but only in so much of reasonableness as we actually find. It may be the divine purpose in the world to produce moral personalities; but it is a further venture of faith, and a venture which transcends reasonable belief, to assert that the divine purpose includes the perfecting of finite moral persons, or provision for the fulfilment of their aspirations toward holiness and harmony with the will of God.

At first sight this representation, that empirically established theism does not imply immortality, may seen to be more congruent with the inferences reached in this volume than is the opposite view. But, on further examination, the conclusion appears doubtful. The facts, of which theism is the interpretaion, may of themselves indicate no more than that the world is a moral order to the extent of producing moral persons and the conditions of rational and moral life. But, just because moral personality is what it is, this interpretation seems to involve more than do the facts themselves. If the *raison d'être* of the world were merely to produce moralised persons and not to provide for their perduringness, the world-purpose could be described as moral, but not in the sense of seeking the highest conceivable good: a Devil might cause moral beings to emerge, in order to tantalise them. A moral order, in the latter sense, must not only produce moral beings: it must also respect moral persons and satisfy moral demands. God cannot be an ethically perfect Being and not respect the moral aspirations of the personalities which He has called into existence:

> Thou madest man, he knows not why,
> He thinks he was not made to die;
> And Thou hast made him: Thou art just.

The world, in short, cannot safely be regarded as realising a *divine* purpose unless man's life continues after death. If the world is inexplicable without God, its purpose is immoral without divine righteousness. But righteousness is not merely compensating justice. Just distribution of rewards and punishments is no function of the present dispensation; and if the only reward of virtue be virtue, it is no function of the future dispensation. The righteousness which theism must ascribe to God consists rather in provision of adequate opportunities for the development of all that is potential in God-given personality, conservation of the valuable, and love such as precludes the mockery of scheming that a rational creature's guiding light through life shall be a Will o' the wisp.

# IAN T. RAMSEY

*Ian T. Ramsey* (1915–    ), Nolloth Professor of the Philosophy of the Christian Religion at Oxford University, is interested in applying analytical and empirical philosophy to theological interests. He is also author of the book *Religious Language*.

## Immortality: Persons

Let us now look at some typical arguments *for* immortality, with the same purpose in mind; we will divide them into three classes:

(i)  arguments from duty;
(ii)  arguments based on the results of psychical research;
(iii)  other empirical arguments.

(i)  Certain duties imply (it is said) immortality. For example (the argument goes) there is no point in devoting our lives to the search for truth, or exhausting our energies in a moral struggle for perfection, if we are to be completely snuffed out at three score years and ten, when we shall certainly not have reached our target. Surely it would be much wiser in such circumstances to concentrate on "immediate pleasure," knowing, if not the world, at least the shadier part of it. So the fact that we recognise a duty to search for truth, and a duty to press on morally towards perfection, demands that we are immortal. If we were not immortal there would be no point in doing either. The argument thus claims that there are certain "unattainable" duties to seek perfection of one sort or another which, so to say, make sense, which we recognise as obligations, and which at the same time we have no chance here and now to fulfil. Therefore, if we are to take such duties seriously, we must be immortal.

At this point two difficulties are often raised.

(*a*)  Do these duties necessarily demand immortality? We might still wish, it is argued, to pursue knowledge even if we knew we were mortal, and even if we recognised that we should never attain perfect knowledge. We might

From Ian T. Ramsey, *Freedom and Immortality*, pp. 70–71, 72–74, 75–89. Copyright, 1960, Student Christian Movement Press, Ltd. Used by permission of Student Christian Movement Press, Ltd. [Footnotes omitted, Eds.]

even defend our pursuit by pointing to its useful social implications for our contemporaries and successors, or we might be content merely to emphasise the joys of the chase itself. Even if we were all mortal, it does not follow that we would wish to make asses of ourselves. Even if "tomorrow we die," it does not follow that we shall wish to spend today eating and drinking. A scientist in Oxford might still wish to spend his last day in the labs. rather than in "The King's Arms."

(*b*) The other difficulty is this. Do we (it is asked) know any of these duties to be duties at all without having to know first that we are immortal? If so, even if the argument were formally valid, it would be quite worthless. For the argument would then fail in what W. E. Johnson called its "epistemic" conditions: we should have to know the conclusion before we could entertain the premiss, whereas for a satisfactory inference, the original premiss, the ground of the inference, must be *independently* known. . . .

Is it the case, then, that recognition of these "unattainable" duties only follows belief in immortality, or at least is only given along with it? If so, the argument under consideration would be valueless, for we could not know the ground of the inference, viz. that so and so is a duty, before we knew the conclusion of the inference, viz. that we are immortal.

But at this point I think the light begins to break. For the second difficulty emphasises that what is being claimed by the positive argument is that, in some way or another, and at any rate in some cases, our awareness of obligation and our awareness of immortality are given together. Now this reflection enables us, I think, to see the true character of the argument. What it is trying to do is to use an ethical technique, viz. to tell a duty story, in the hope of evoking the kind of situation in which our conviction of immortality is grounded. Let us illustrate this technique in rather more detail before going back to consider the two difficulties we have just formulated. We might picture it as a three-stage technique:

(1) First we call up a behaviour pattern labelled "seeking immediate pleasure," "eating and drinking," where drinking is talked of in terms of throat membranes, stomach capacity and digestive juices. The picture is— quite crudely—of a throat being tickled by half a pint of lemonade or Double Diamond. There is no immortality here: everything is as impersonal as the tongues and the intestines in the jars in the anatomy laboratory.

(2) On this impersonal picture we then superimpose a duty story, and for the moment the mention of any kind of duty will do. The throat is being tickled in the inn when someone runs in:— "A child is drowning outside!" . . . and the whole scene comes to life, takes on "depth." Parallel with the example in Chapter II, we must not now suppose that this is merely a case of efficient reaction to stimuli, but that the people speak of "being compelled" to rush out and with an "inward" compulsion, etc. etc. They would speak of being "obliged" to dive in for the child.

Now the contrast between such a situation and that which occurs at stage (1) may be enough to evoke a situation where we discern and recognise duty. . . . And it is in so recognising duty as something which transcends the spatio-temporal, that we recognise our own transcendence of the spatio-temporal, our own immortality. On the other hand, the light may not dawn, nor the penny drop.

(3) In such a case a story of so-called unattainable duties comes to its own. For whenever such a duty story as we have outlined at stage (2) does not work, these other stories of unattainable duties enable the technique to be continued and practised for as long as we wish. In the case of unattainable duties, the story can always be pressed further. It can always continue until the light dawns, and it would continue like this.

We could begin, for example, with a scholar who after many years of writing and research, returns to tell us, "At last! I have completed my twentieth volume on the Nagi tribes of India." Has he found the Truth? Has he exhausted an unattainable duty? "No," we say. "What you have done is a magnificent contribution to the search for truth, but the search has scarcely yet begun. Disheartening as it may seem, you have hardly begun to pick up, Newton-like, a pebble on the sea-shore." Our scholar returns years later with yet more volumes. But the answer is the same. No matter when or with what results our imaginary scholar returned, we could still say, "But you have not yet reached the whole truth, *the* Truth." And then the light may dawn: then it may become plain what "*the* Truth" stands for—something which no volumes, however many, can complete, something to which no true story, however long, can do justice. It stands for something which no scholar, however skilled or hardworking, could formulate and describe. In this sense it is unattainable—unattainable in terms of discursive knowledge. Yet in another sense we have recognised it already. For we know what "the Truth" means when the light dawns. It is only its formulation which is a never-ending task. We are reminded of the old Idealist phrase that what is ever "Real" is nevertheless always "waiting to be realised." But the very fact that in this way "the Truth" eludes any discursive enumeration, however long, shows its character, that it is something we understand by reference to a situation which is "objects" and more. In this way never-ending stories about searching after truth become an appropriate technique for evoking a situation which, when it breaks in on us, we shall then call "*the* Truth," and see its challenge as one of Duty. And when that happens, we likewise know ourselves as transcending the spatio-temporal, never exhaustively described by object stories. We are assured of our immortality.

So it is that a description of the never-ending search for knowledge will be a useful technique to evoke a situation which transcends the spatio-temporal while it includes it, a situation which subjectively assures me of my immortality.

So what might be evoked at stage (2), and what stage (3) need never despair of reaching, is a situation never exhaustively treated by "true" propositions about observables, no matter how complex and developed that treatment may be. Here is a situation which subjectively and objectively transcends the spatio-temporal. Subjectively, here is the ground of our immortality, and objectively we have once again what is meant by Duty. . . .

Against the standpoint of this discussion let us now see the significance of the two objections to this argument for immortality which we mentioned above.

(*a*) The question was: Do any duties demand immortality? Surely we might wish (it was said) to pursue knowledge even if we knew we were mortal. Now when it is said that we might still want to pursue truth, whether we are immortal or not, that we might still wish to devote our last day to some organic synthesis or to the office files rather than having a continuous feast, the point must of course be admitted and agreed. But at the same time it has to be recognised that this *wish* need not arise from a response to anything like Duty. What we did in the lab. or in the office merely to gratify a wish, would not at all be an activity including but transcending the objects it contained. Two people might still elect to do the same organic experiment as a way of passing the last day. But for one it might be no more than gratification of a wish: a matter of mixing the reagents, distillation and the rest, when there would be no response to Duty and no intimation of immortality. For another, however, it could be not only the gratification of a wish, but also a response to Duty, a response to the Truth, a response to a discernment. There would then be a vision made up of reagents *and more,* distillation *and more;* and subjectively there would be a recognition of one's self as more than an organic chemist. The organic synthesis would now do more than exemplify a wish, it would symbolise and portray Duty, as well, and the chemist would have an intimation of immortality.

The contrast is then between, on the one hand, merely eating and drinking, merely spending days in the lab., merely poring over problems, merely writing treatises; and on the other hand doing precisely any or all of these, but within a situation which subjectively and objectively transcends objects while it contains them. To express the contrast as the argument often does, as one between duty and pleasure, is misleading. The contrast is rather between pleasure, and pleasure *plus.*

(*b*) We can see, too, how the problem of priorities arises. If our account is correct, our sense of duty and our sense of immortality belong together: to discern our duty is to discern our immortality, and *vice versa*. To recognise our immortality (subjectively) is also to recognise (objectively) a Duty never exhausted in object language, and therefore spoken of as "unattainable," being never adequately portrayed as a pattern in space and time. Again, if once we recognise a Duty, e.g., the pursuit of truth or the search for perfection, whose spatio-temporal translation is never ending, which happens when a Duty situation has been evoked by stories of an "unattainable" duty, the same situation reveals our immortality. In this way, there is no absolute *logical* priority between immortality and unattainable duty, and there is an intimate psychological connection. So we can readily see how it comes to be alleged that we only recognise such and such as a duty when we recognise ourselves as immortal. We can easily see how the argument comes to fail over the epistemic condition. But this does not mean that the argument for immortality from the existence of certain duties is valueless.

Indeed, it may be said that in the very fact that the epistemic conditions cannot be fulfilled lies the possibility of the "argument" being valuable at all. For all the "argument" hopes to do is so to talk about certain duties that there arises a discernment of immortality which for those "with eyes to see" cannot have been there from the start. Even so, talk about epistemic conditions is not without its point. For it properly reminds us that we are not looking on the argument for immortality from duty as taking us on a deductive journey which will at the end lead us to assent to the logical subsequent proposition that we are immortal. We are not led to a proposition which pictures the facts, describing a quality called "immortality" which belongs to some "thing" called a "soul," as longevity may characterise a tortoise. Contrariwise, we take a much looser view of the function of argument and a much different view as to the anchorage of metaphysical words such as "soul" and "immortality." Argument and counter-argument in discussions about immortality are rather stories whose intention is either to evoke or to deny a certain kind of situation. If someone did not recognise as a duty the search for truth and perfection, but knew first that he was immortal, the argument would certainly be useless and unnecessary as an "argument" for immortality. Yet it might now be useful in the opposite direction: to show us that with belief in immortality went necessarily a recognition of duty as something which could "never" (i.e., in terms of spatio-temporal behaviour) be fulfilled. If, however, it be countered that (as a third case) there might be someone who could contemplate and assent to the proposition that if he were immortal it would follow that he had such and such duties, or to the proposition that if he recognised such and such duties it would follow that he were immortal, without believing either that he was immortal or that he had such duties—when the argument would be quite useless all around— I should doubt it. For I should argue that a recognition of certain duties and a discernment of immortality are only seen to imply one another when each relates to a common situation which subjectively and objectively transcends the spatio-temporal. In short, and without prejudice to any general theory of implication, I am saying that we should not see *this* implication between duty and immortality without recognising certain behaviour as our duty on the one hand, and our immortality on the other. Indeed, the "argument" is but talk to get us to see this implication and the situation in which it is founded.

The next argument, with which we can deal much more briefly, points to the wasted effort, the unrewarded goodness and the frustrations with which human lives abound. We may think of the man who quite devotedly year by year cuts and trims his garden hedge and with the same loving care tends his garden, yet on his death the next occupier neglects hedge and garden alike. Or there are mothers who spend their lives training children who grow up to be utterly thankless. Again, we may think of the kindness and thoughtfulness and generosity which is rejected, spurned, or evil spoken of. What sustains people through all this (the argument runs) is the conviction that some day—though beyond this present life—justice will prevail, that the universe is, on a long-term view, good and fair.

But the objection is then made that while the argument might prove immortality *if* there were also prior belief in God, yet without such a belief or some comparable belief, the argument proves nothing.

How are we to assess such criticisms? First let us reiterate that what the positive argument sets out to do is to evoke a situation which exceeds all the public behaviour it contains. This it does by a technique which concentrates on human struggles and frustrations, the partial character of our lives, our own finitude. All the stories used by the argument are attempts to evoke a situation which is transitory and more, spatio-temporal and more, by pointing to the "unsatisfactoriness" of what is transitory. All the stories are attempts to evoke a sense of the permanent, a sense of what abides, by arousing in us a profound discontent with the changes and chances of a fleeting world.

On this interpretation it is not surprising—and this we would say is the important point behind the criticism just mentioned above—that belief in God has in fact always been closely associated with belief in immortality. For it is the same kind of situation which justifies both beliefs; which reflection leads to a further suggestion. On our view it would be natural to suppose that if either belief was very dominant the other belief might be overlooked and even disappear altogether. This in fact is what has happened. People have often been quite satisfied with what has been given to them either objectively or subjectively in a disclosure situation, and have cared nothing for further complications. The Old Testament, for example, is significant in having from the first a belief in God and only much later (and let us notice it was when personal and responsible decision was more and more emphasised) stirrings of immortality. Before that time the Hebrews thought primarily of God, and of their "solidarity," of their group-life. They were too outward-looking, too little concerned with themselves as "persons" to be concerned about their immortality. The philosopher McTaggart, on the other hand, is an interesting example of a somewhat opposite emphasis. Though he accepted the immortality of persons, he would not agree that such an immortality situation as is specified by his use of the word "love" needed any further reference to the God of traditional belief. Indeed he rather suggested that traditional belief in God compromised and impoverished belief in immortality. McTaggart and the Hebrews were thus alike in seeing one half—though in each case a different half—of the whole truth. For it is one and the same situation which subjectively justifies belief in immortality and objectively justifies belief in God. Belief in God and belief in immortality fit together and find their anchorage in the same kind of situation.

Returning now to our main theme, the suggestion is that the old-fashioned ethical arguments for immortality are best understood (1) as techniques to evoke a particular and distinctive kind of situation, which (2) at the same time claims from the way in which the situation is evoked, that such a situation exceeds the spatio-temporal objects it contains.

(ii) Let us next consider briefly the possible bearing of the results of psychical research on belief in immortality. There have been those who have argued that here we have the best of all empirical arguments for a future life. Even those like C. D. Broad, who have been most cautious about the empirical phenomena, have nevertheless talked of the possible persistence of some "psychogenic factor," of some factor productive of "mental behaviour" at any rate over a limited period of time beyond death. Now I do not propose to examine these various claims in detail. Nor is this the occasion to make a careful and critical assessment of the facts. But suppose it is the case (as seems very likely) that after admitting what may be fraudulent, and what may be given an alternative and not so exciting account, we must nevertheless allow that some of the phenomena of some seances and some accounts of poltergeists are veridical and irreducible. What do we conclude?

The phenomena are significant in two ways.

(*a*) First, they are important in so far as they recreate for many of our contemporaries a sense of wonder and mystery when so much around us becomes more and more taped and stereotyped; when so much of our behaviour becomes more and more impersonal. The phenomena may be useful in reminding us that the universe is a good deal odder and more mysterious than many would like to think. Not for nothing is the spiritualist Lyceum often to be found in that part of a sprawling city which is most dismal and drab. When as infants we begin by drinking standard orange juice from a disinfected tumbler, and continue by taking up a medically approved straw our prescribed measure of milk from an artificially inseminated cow, thereafter having a full account of the physiology and psychology of sex, until at the end we are moved in composition caskets on ball-bearing rollers through synthetic curtains into electrically-heated furnaces—the movement being synchronized with a pre-recorded hymn—we may think that the time has come to give us all a numinous shudder or two. Let my argument not be mistaken. I am not being so silly and obscurantist as to condemn out of hand all social and scientific development. But I am saying that such developments do not easily provide intimations of immortality, and this fact is something with which empirical arguments for immortality need to reckon, as it is also something to which strange psychical phenomena provide a useful counter-balance.

(*b*) Secondly, the existence of abnormal psychical phenomena can usefully suggest that there is an element in personal intercourse beyond the observable behaviour with which we normally associate it. Even admitting that some spatio-temporal expression of personal activity is always necessary, abnormal psychical phenomena suggest that this element may in fact on occasion be supplied by someone else's body or (in the case of poltergeists) other physical phenomena altogether. This kind of possibility allows us a useful freedom in thinking about what constitutes, in terms of objects or spatio-temporal phenomena, personal behaviour. Further, this very freedom in relation to observables emphasises the point that characteristically personal behaviour is something which is more than the observables it displays, however diverse these be.

In short, the phenomena revealed and studied by psychical research can provide situations which reveal the transcendence of personal behaviour beyond its public and spatio-temporal manifestations. On the other hand, how this transcendence is best described is left problematical and we need not at all sponsor the kind of language about the "spirit world" which spiritualists traditionally use to map their claims. Here is a point on which I will say something—if not very much—in my next chapter, where we shall be more explicitly concerned with the language in which claims for immortality are expressed.

(iii) We now pass to consider three other empirical arguments for immortality. First there is the argument from universal assent, what is traditionally called the argument *a consensu gentium,* which starts from the widespread popularity of the belief, noting that in various forms it has characterized many religions and many if not most civilisations. A second argument starts from the fact that it is very difficult, if not impossible, to think of our entire cessation. Even if we think of our Wills being read, we think of ourselves hovering round to see the look on old Uncle Sam's face when he hears that we have bequeathed to his reprobate brother that gold cigarette case he has long admired. A third argument tries to develop the alleged analogy between sleep and spring on the one hand, and death on the other: as we wake from sleep, or as spring follows winter, so (it has been argued) we shall survive death.

Once again, to mention such arguments is to provoke counter-arguments. With regard to the first argument, there is the irrefutable fact that even eight million people might be wrong. Why should we perpetuate the

Election Fallacy and suppose that what the majority believe, is for that reason necesarily correct? Again, to turn to the second argument, the very act of imagining ourselves present at the reading of our Will, inevitably puts us into the picture. We cannot expect to imagine ourselves present anywhere without having to suppose that we are in some way there, if only peeping from the side-wings. As for the third argument based on the alleged analogy between death and spring or sleep, the analogy, it is said, is quite worthless. It is the obvious differences, not the superficial similarities, between a dead person and someone sleeping, which are significant and important, and there are easy and reliable tests by which to distinguish a dead tree from a tree in winter, despite again their superficial resemblances.

But at this point the pendulum of the argument begins to swing the other way. An error that was committed by (say) eight thousand million people of such diverse creeds and civilisations, would—even as an error—be a curious fact; especially since the existence of the original belief could easily and alternatively be accounted for by supposing that for most people, at one time or another, there occur situations which reveal them, at least to themselves, as more than the public behaviour they display.

Again, with the second argument in mind, it might be said that the important reason why we find it difficult to think of ourselves in the future as "not there" is precisely because we already recognise, as we have said, certain situations which here and now are not exhausted by our present public behaviour. This is the reason, it would be said, why we are not tempted to conclude that the disappearance of our public behaviour tomorrow will mean the end of "us" *altogether*. For it does not mean the whole of "us" today. We can mutter with Spinoza—even if out of its context—"*sentimus experimurque nos aeternos esse*": "we discern and discover that we are eternal." We can claim with Butler that to recognise "ourselves" is to recognise "ourselves" as more than "gross bodies."

The argument from considerations about sleeping or winter needs a little more attention. As an argument by analogy, any argument comparing the transition from winter to spring with the transition from death to subsequent life, is plainly weak and confused. It is virtually worthless. But suppose that the argument, the story, the talk, has a different logical point altogether. In the first place, let the argument first suggest to us that we ponder the contrast of winter and spring. What happens? Quite apart from what the botanist or gardener may tell us, we look on a winter's scene and everything is drab, lifeless, bleak and impersonal. We are numb and inactive with cold. We even say our feet are "dead." Then comes spring, and the lifeless begins to show life: buds and blossom appear. Green replaces black. Everywhere the scene changes and in every detail. We even speak of nature "coming alive." At this point let us recall that few circumstances are better than change for reminding us of what abides; witness the easy way by which days registering change, such as New Year's Day, birthdays, anniversary days, and the rest, take on a religious significance. Further, when people are moved by the beauty of blossom and spring flowers, they often talk about "empathy," that curious feeling or sense of kinship with something other than ourselves—that *Einfühlung*—that which (it is said) characterises an aesthetic situation. So to make a contrast between winter and spring is likely to be a successful technique by which to evoke a characteristically religious situation, one in which we discern what abides in what changes, what is seen *and more*.

The second stage of the argument takes this contrast between winter and spring and brings it, as a sort of catalyst, alongside a case of death. Someone is lying dead. Superficially (or so we would say) nothing is left but this dead body. But if we bring alongside the contrast between winter and spring, there is at least enough resemblance (despite major differences) between winter and death for an interlocking of pictures, whereupon a situation is evoked around the dead body as it was earlier evoked by the winter-spring contrast alone. Like manganese dioxide, which as a catalyst assists enormously in the evolution of oxygen from potassium chlorate, without itself being directly involved in the chemical reaction, the winter-spring contrast accelerates and brings off (as we might say) the larger evocation, and without being necessarily involved in the phenomena of death—as it would be if we linked it by the logical relations of an argument from analogy. It is as though (to change the metaphor) having once seen some junior archdeacon "come alive" when he exchanges cassock apron and gaiters for linen apron and dish-cloth, one can then see even the most prelatical-looking bishop as "having a human heart."

Once there has been in this way and around the phenomena of death, a situation not restricted to the dead body and other phenomena which it undoubtedly contains, then we are able to "see" that the physical accompaniments of death, the cessation of a certain kind of objective behaviour, no more exhaust a dead person's existence than the contrast between winter and spring leave us unmoved. Needless to say, if the original contrast *does* leave us unmoved, the "argument" has from the beginning no hope of being successful. Nor is it *bound* to succeed even if the original contrast is in itself evocative. For various reasons, there may be no catalytic interlocking. We may, for instance, as a matter of psychological fact, be so impressed by the differences between winter and death that no similarity whatever is recognised. The prelate may be so prelatical that *all* similarities to the archdeacon disappear.

Take now the story of sleeping. Here, too, the argument cannot start by saying that sleeping is like death. Once again, it is rather that the contrast between ourselves as sleeping and ourselves as waking can be used to evoke a "more than objects" situation which in its turn can be used to assure us that death never exhausts our total existence. Whether with the transition of sleeping-waking, or that of winter-spring, the contrast can be used to evoke and reveal the kind of situation in which immortality is grounded.

In the case of sleeping, however, we may express our point in another way altogether. We may recognise that to make a straight comparison between sleeping and dying can never be the basis of a good argument, because such a comparison ignores obvious and important differences between the two states. Even so, despite these differences, "I am asleep" has certain similarities to "I am dead." Neither can be significantly uttered by the subject of the assertions: though at the same time there is no difficulty about someone else's saying of me either, "He is asleep," or "He is dead." With these last two assertions there is no logical or empirical embarrassment whatever. Now, why is it that one pair of assertions—"I'm asleep" and "I'm dead"—is problematical whereas the other pair—"He's asleep," and "He's dead"—is not? The reason, I suggest, is that "dead" and "asleep" are amongst the very few words in our language whose meaning is inevitably and most plainly given in terms of objects. They therefore attach themselves naturally and appropriately to "He"—a person as objectified for everyone to see. So we have no difficulty over "He is dead" and "He is asleep." Each is logically homogeneous, and none of the words needs relate to more than objects. But the case is different when we introduce the word "I." Here is a word which cannot be wholly "public," which relates to "objects" and more. So it happens that when such words as "dead" and "asleep" are joined with the word "I," logical oddities, hybrids, are produced such as "I am asleep" and "I am dead."

At this point it may be countered that all that is odd about these assertions arises from the fact that people who are dead and people who are asleep do not talk, and that there is no more to the oddness than this. That there *is* this difficulty we need not deny. That one of the problems about asserting "I am dead" is that we do not talk when we are dead, must obviously be granted. But the difficulty isn't merely that I cannot *say,* for example, "I am dead"; it is that, while I cannot say "I am dead," there is no difficulty whatever about someone else saying of me "He is dead." So there is at any rate the possibility that these two sentences do not talk about precisely the same kind of situation.

Let me put my point another way. Normally, we suppose that "I'm eating" describes a situation identical with what an observer describes as "He's eating;" or "I'm running" a situation identical with what is described by "He's running," and so on. And the supposition works normally so well that philosophers such as Hume can be found who have endeavoured to argue logical identity between the two classes of assertion. On this view, "I" and "he" are logically interchangeable, so that "I" relates to no more than "he" legitimately describes, i.e. to a series of "objects" or observables, what the eighteenth century called "ideas," what nowadays would be called my "public behaviour."

But what the puzzle of "I am asleep" and "I am dead" does, I would say, is to cast doubts on the logical assimilation which such a one as Hume would have us make. Instead, those who would say that the difficulty is no more than that dead men and sleeping men do not talk, by saying that, in fact reveal their hand. For they are now saying by implication that in principle "I" am no more than a talker, i.e. no more than my public behaviour. On such a view the *only* difficulty about "I am dead" is that on any occasion when it serves to be said, there is no talker to utter it. Whereas I have suggested that there is a *further* difficulty—the mixed character of what is logically a hybrid.

It follows of course that when I *myself* talk of my "running" or my "eating," these words *for me* mean "more" than what any observer can describe: otherwise we would have countless logical hybrids throughout the whole of our language. But this view—that a first person singular activity word tells of more than "objects"—makes no new claim. It is wholly consistent with what was said in Chapters I and II about free will—that my "free" activity is more than the public behaviour which expresses it.

There is perhaps yet another point worth making. Suppose someone says: "I am asleep" or "I am dead." These are assertions which would be falsified on utterance. We may now remark how similar they therefore are to the *cogito* of Descartes. Here again, the very utterance of the doubt, "I am not existing," is enough to falsify it.

Now, as G. E. Moore pointed out in lectures some twenty-five years ago, the *cogito* of Descartes might be compared with the assertion—"I am not saying the word 'cat.' " This is equally well falsified on utterance. The logical behaviour of all these assertions is therefore (i) quite unlike that of any straightforward empirical assertions, such, for example, as "The elephant is not pink," or "Stanley did not say 'Dr. Livingstone, I presume.' " Nor (ii) are any of the earlier assertions false on inspection, like a formal contradiction such as "p and not-p." They are therefore logical peculiars, and I suggest that their peculiarity arises from the fact that they are special assertions about my own activity whose point is to reveal that I myself and my own activity is something more than the public behaviour I exhibit. Who is to tell whether "I" am "actually" saying the word "cat" or not? Is the occurrence of the noise "cat" from my mouth an infallible clue?

But have these reflections taken us too far? Is it *ever* possible then to give *any* account of "I am dead?" Is there *any* way of understanding such a sentence? Can we, in short, do anything to overcome the difficulties which arise from the fact that while "I" is not exhausted by object words, "dead," as we normally use the word, is? To answer those questions let us return to our starting point, for we have plainly come back very close to it. Let us begin by taking "dead" as no more than a descriptive word equivalent to "mortality." The picture this calls up is of all our public behaviour coming gradually to an end—whether biochemical, psychological, sociological, and the rest. We reflect . . . yes, the day will come when, in my case, there is that final breakdown of organic processes, that permanent failure of appropriate behaviour responses, that ultimate cessation of the social round, that pay-out of premiums, that visit of the undertaker. Suppose in this way we begin to pare off from our existence all the features that the descriptive word "dead" covers, whereupon our lives become empirically less and less and less. What is the outcome?

As is well known, some become mad, terror-stricken. They are then said to be "beside themselves" or "out of their mind." Nor is this surprising. Because for them, and in their case, "I" has disappeared. They never were more than could have been known with complete satisfaction by the competent and skilled biologist, psychologist, social worker, economist, and so on. Yet with others the case is utterly different. For these, the same kind of sequence may lead them to talk in terms of such phrases as "peace," "Nirvana," "eternal life in Christ Jesus," and so on. What has happened in this second case? Our suggestion is that these phrases, whatever differences they might have between them, have at any rate this important similarity, that they are all used as appropriate currency when the story we have just told, or some similar one, has led at some point or another to a disclosure, a disclosure of my existence as something more than the most skilled and competent external observer could give an account of. To use such phrases as I have just listed is thus to acknowledge that even stories of death can bring intimations of immortality. Even talk about death may evoke the kind of situation which it has been my purpose throughout this chapter, as well as in other chapters, to emphasize. We may even say, summarily, that whether or not we believe in immortality depends on the meaning which "I am dead" has for us.

In this chapter, then, I have tried to show that the justification of immortality will depend on whether our behaviour can be exhaustively described in spatio-temporal terms or not. If the life of a person is no more than the behaviour pattern he exhibits, there is no sense in talking of immortality; if human "life" is no more than its public expression, there is certainly no meaning in the phrase " 'life' after death." For death brings our publicity to an end, and makes our "mortality" complete. Further, we have seen that the arguments and counter-arguments for immortality are all concerned to substantiate or deny this central claim—that personal behaviour is not exhausted by all that object language talks of. We are immortal in so far as we know a situation which transcends space and time. . . .

# NICOLAS BERDYAEV

*Nicolas A. Berdyaev* (1874–1948), émigré Russian philosopher and leading lay thologian of the Russian Orthodox Church, is well known for his
eschatological philosophy of history, existentialist interpretation of Christian ethics, and penetrating criticisms of extreme rationalism.

## Death and Immortality

Ordinary systems of philosophical ethics do not deal with the problems
of eschatology. If they treat of immortality, they do so without going deep
into the question of death but discuss it chiefly in connection with man's
moral responsibility, rewards and punishments, or, at best, with the need
of satisfying his longing for infinity. The conception of immortality has been
defended on the ground of naturalistic metaphysics and the idea of the soul
as a substance. It left completely untouched the problem of death, so fundamental for the religious and especially for the Christian consciousness. Death
is a problem not only for metaphysics but also for ontological ethics.
Thinkers like Kierkgaard and Heidegger recognize this. It also acquires a
central significance in Freud. It is the problem of death, inseverably connected with that of time, that has a primary significance; the problem of
immortality is secondary, and as a rule it has been wrongly formulated. The
very word "immortality" is inexact and implies a rejection of the mysterious
fact of death. The question of the immortality of the soul forms part of the
metaphysic that is utterly out of date. Death is the most profound and significant fact of life, raising the least of mortals above the mean common-
places of life. The fact of death alone gives true depth to the question as to
the meaning of life. Life in this world has meaning just because there is
death; if there were no death in our world, life would be meaningless. The
meaning is bound up with the end. If there were no end, i.e., if life in our
world continued forever, there would be no meaning in it. Meaning lies
beyond the confines of this limited world, and the discovery of meaning
presupposes an end here. It is remarkable that although men rightly feel the

From Nicolas Berdyaev, *The Destiny of Man,* trans. Natalie Duddington, pp. 249–265.
Published, 1937, Geoffrey Bles Ltd. Used by permission of Geoffrey Bles and Harper &
Brothers. [Footnotes omitted, Eds.]

horror of death and rightly regard it as the supreme evil, they are bound to connect with it the final discovery of meaning. Death—the supreme horror and evil— proves to be the only way out of the "bad time" into eternity; immortal and eternal life prove to be only attainable through death. Man's last hope is connected with death, which manifests so clearly the power of evil in the world. This is the greatest paradox of death. According to the Christian religion death is the result of sin and is the last enemy, the supreme evil which must be conquered. And at the same time in our sinful world death is a blessing and a value. It inspires us with terror not merely because it is an evil, but because the depth and the greatness of it shatter our everyday world and exceed the powers accumulated by us in this life to meet this world's requirements. Spiritual enlightenment and an extraordinary intensity of spiritual life are needed to give us a right attitude towards death. Plato was right in teaching that philosophy was the practice of death. The only trouble is that philosophy as such does not know how one ought to die and how to conquer death. The philosophic doctrine of immortality does not show the way.

It might be said that ethics at its highest is concerned with death rather than with life, for death manifests the depth of life and reveals the end, which alone gives meaning to life. Life is noble only because it contains death, an end which testifies that man is destined to another and a higher life. Life would be low and meaningless if there were no death and no end.

Meaning is never revealed in an endless time; it is to be found in eternity. But there is an abyss between life in time and life in eternity, and it can only be bridged by death and the horror of final severance. When this world is apprehended as self-sufficient, completed and closed in, everything in it appears meaningless because everything is transitory and corruptible—i.e., death and mortality in this world is just what makes it meaningless. This is one-half of the truth seen from a narrow and limited point of view. Heidegger is right in saying that the herd-mentality (*das Man*) is insensitive to the anguish of death. It feels merely a low fear of death as of that which makes life meaningless. But there is another half of the truth, concealed from the ordinary point of view. Death not merely makes life senseless and corruptible: it is also a sign, coming from the depths, of there being a higher meaning in life. Not base fear but horror and anguish which death inspires in us prove that we belong not only to the surface but to the depths as well, not only to temporal life but also to eternity. While we are in time, eternity both attracts and horrifies us. We feel horror and anguish not only because all that we hold dear dies and comes to an end, but still more because we are conscious of a yawning abyss between time and eternity. Horror and anguish at having to cross the abyss contain at the same time a hope that the final meaning shall be revealed and realized. Death holds hope as well as horror for man, though he does not always recognize this or call it by an appropriate name. The meaning that comes from the other world is like a scorching flame to us and demands that we should pass through death. Death is not only a biological and psychological fact but a spiritual fact as well. *The meaning of death is that there can be no eternity in time and that an endless temporal series would be meaningless.*

But death is a manifestation of life, it is found on this side of life and is life's reaction to its own demand for an end in time. Death cannot be understood merely as the last moment of life followed either by non-being or by existence in the world beyond. Death is an event embracing the whole of life. Our existence is full of death and dying. Life is perpetual dying, experiencing the end in everything, a continual judgment passed by eternity upon time. Life is a constant struggle against death and a partial dying of the human body and the human soul. Death within life is due to the impossibility of embracing the fullness of being, either in time or in space. Time and space are death-dealing, they give rise to disruptions which are a partial experience of death. When, in time, human feelings die and disappear, this is an experience of death. When, in space, we part with a person, a house, a town, a garden, an animal, and have the feeling that we may never see them again, this is an experience of death. The anguish of every parting, of every severance in time and space, is the experience of death. I remember what anguish I felt as a boy at every parting. It was so all-embracing that I lived through mortal anguish at the thought of never seeing again the face of a stranger I met, the town I happened to pass through, the room in which I spent a few days, a tree or a dog I saw. This was, of course, an experience of death within life.

Space and time cannot enfold the wholeness of being but condemn us to severances and separations, and death always triumphs in life; it testifies that meaning is to be found in eternity and in fullness of being, that in the life in which meaning will triumph there shall be no parting, no dying, no corruption of human thoughts and feelings. We die not only in our own death but in the death of those we love. We have in life the experience of death, though not the final experience of it. And we cannot be reconciled to death—to the death neither of human beings nor of animals, plants, things or houses. The striving for eternity of all that exists is the essence of life. And yet eternity is reached only by passing through death, and death is the destiny of everything that exists in this world. The higher and more complex a being is, the more it is threatened with death. Mountains live longer than men, although their life is less complex and lower in quality; Mont Blanc appears to be more immortal than a saint or a genius. Things are comparatively more stable than living beings.

Death has a positive significance, but at the same time it is the most terrible and the only evil. Every kind of evil in the last resort means death. Murder, hatred, malice, depravity, envy, vengeance are death and seeds of death. Death is at the bottom of every evil passion. Pride, greed, ambition are deadly in their results. There is no other evil in the world except death and killing. Death is the evil result of sin. A sinless life would be immortal and eternal. Death is a denial of eternity and therein lies its ontological evil, its hostility to existence, its striving to reduce creation to non-being. Death resists God's creation of the world and is a return to the original non-being. Death wants to free the creature by bringing it back to primeval freedom that preceded the creation of the world. There is but one way out for the creature which in its sin resists God's conception of it—death. Death is a negative testimony to God's power and to the Divine meaning manifested in the meaningless world. It might be said that the world would carry out its godless plan of an endless (but not eternal) life if there were no God; but since God exists, that plan is not realizable and ends in death. The Son of God, the Redeemer and Saviour, absolutely sinless and holy, had to accept death, and thereby He sanctified death. Hence the double attitude of Christianity to death. Christ has destroyed death by His death. His voluntary death, due to the evil of the world, is a blessing and a supreme value. In worshipping the cross we worship death which gives us freedom and victory. In order to rise again we must die. Through the cross death is transfigured and leads us to resurrection and to life. The whole of this world must be made to pass through death and crucifixion, else it cannot attain resurrection and eternity.

If death is accepted as a part of the mystery of life, it is not final and has not the last word. Rebellion against death in our world is rebellion against God. But at the same time we must wage a heroic struggle against death, conquer it as the last evil and pluck out its sting. The work of Christ in the world is in the first instance victory over death and preparation for resurrection and eternity. The good is life, power, fullness and eternity of life. Death proves to be the greatest paradox in the world, which cannot be understood rationally. Death is folly that has become commonplace. The consciousness that death is an ordinary everyday occurrence has dulled our sense of its being irrational and paradoxical. The last achievement of the rationalized herd-mind is to try to forget about death altogether, to conceal it, to bury the dead as unobtrusively as possible. It is the very opposite of the spirit expressed in the Christian prayer "ever to remember death." In this respect modern civilized people are incomparably inferior to the ancient Egyptians.

The paradox of death takes an aesthetic as well as a moral form. Death is hideous, the acme of hideousness, it is dissolution, the loss of all image and form, the triumph of the lower elements of the material world. But at the same time death is beautiful, it ennobles the least of mortals and raises him to the level of the greatest, it overcomes the ugliness of the mean and the commonplace. There is a moment when the face of the dead is more beautiful and harmonious than it had been in life. Ugly, evil feelings pass away and disappear in the presence of death. Death, the greatest of evils, is more noble than life in this world. The beauty and charm of the past depends upon the ennobling influence of death. It is death that purifies the past and puts upon it the seal of eternity. Death brings with it not only dissolution but purification as well. Nothing perishable, spoiled and corruptible can stand the test of death—only the eternal can. Terrible as it is to admit it, the significance of life is bound up with death and is only revealed in the face of death. Man's moral worth is manifested in the test of death, which abounds in life itself.

But at the same time struggle with death in the name of eternal life is man's main task. The fundamental principle of ethics may be formulated as follows: act so as to conquer death and affirm everywhere, in everything and in relation to all, eternal and immortal life. It is base to forget the death of a single living being and to be reconciled to it. The death of the least and most miserable creature is unendurable, and if it is irremediable, the world cannot be accepted and justified. All and everything must be raised to eternal life. This means that the principle of eternal being must be affirmed in relation to human beings, animals, plants and even inanimate things. Man must always and in everything be a giver of life and radiate creative vital energy. Love for all that lives, for every creature, rising above the love for abstract ideas, means struggle against death in the name of eternal life. Christ's love for the world and for man is victory over the powers of death and the gift of abundant life.

Asceticism means struggle with death and with the mortal elements within oneself. Struggle with death in the name of eternal life demands such an attitude to oneself and to other people as though both I and they were on the point of death. Such is the moral significance of death in the world. Conquer the low animal fear of death, but always have a spiritual fear of it, a holy terror before its mystery. It was death that first gave man the idea of the supernatural. Enemies of religion such as Epicurus thought they disproved it by showing that it originated in the fear of death. But they will never succeed in disproving the truth that in the fear of death, in the holy terror of it, man comes into touch with the deepest mystery of being and that death contains a revelation. The moral paradox of life and of death can be expressed by a moral imperative: treat the living as though they were dying and the dead as though they were alive, i.e., always remember death as the mystery of life and always affirm eternal life both in life and in death.

Life, not in its weakness but in its strength, intensity and super-abundance, is closely connected with death. This is felt in the Dionysian cults. This is revealed in love which is always connected with death. Passion, i.e., the expression of the highest intensity of life, always holds the menace of death. He who accepts love in its overwhelming power and tragedy, accepts death. He who attaches too much value to life and avoids death, runs away from love and sacrifices it to other tasks of life. In erotic love the intensity of life reaches its highest pitch and leads to destruction and death. The lover is doomed to death and involves the loved one in his doom. In the second act of *Tristan und Isolde* Wagner gives a musical revelation of this. The herd-mind tries to weaken the connection between love and death, to safeguard love and settle it down in this world. But it is not even capable of noticing love. It organizes the life of the race and knows only one remedy against death—birth. Life seems to conquer death through birth. But the victory of birth over death has nothing to do with personality, with its fate and its hopes; it is concerned with life of the race only. The victory over death through birth is an illusion. Nature does not know the mystery of conquering death; the victory can come only from the supernatural world. Throughout their whole history men have tried to struggle against death, and this gave rise to various beliefs and theories. Sometimes the struggle took the form of forgetting about death and sometimes of idealizing it and revelling in the thought of destruction.

The philosophical idea of the natural immortality of the soul deduced from its substantiality leads nowhere. It ignores the fact of death and denies the tragedy of it. From the point of view of such a doctrine there is no need to struggle against death and corruption for the sake of eternal life. It is rationalistic metaphysic without any tragic element in it. Scholastic spiritualism is not a solution of the problem of death and immortality, but is a purely abstract and academic theory. In the same way idealism does not solve the problem or indeed does not even face it. The idealism of the German metaphysics has no place for personality, regards it merely as a function of the world-spirit or idea, and therefore the tragedy of death does not exist for it. Death is a tragedy only when there is an acute awareness of personality. It is only because personality is experienced as eternal and immortal that death is felt to be a tragedy. The death of that which is eternal and immortal in its meaning and destination is alone tragic; there is nothing tragic about the death of the temporal and the transitory. The death of personality in man is tragic because personality is God's eternal idea of him. It is unendurable that a complete personality containing the unity of all human powers and possibilities should die. Personality is not born of the father and the mother, it is created by God. There is no such thing as immortality of man as a natural being, born in the generic process; there is no natural immortality of his soul and body. In this world man is a mortal being. But he is conscious of the Divine image and likeness in him and feels that he belongs not only to the natural but to the spiritual world as well. Man regards himself, therefore, as belonging to eternity, and yearns for eternity. What is eternal and immortal in man is not the psychical or the physical element as such but the spiritual element which, acting in the other two, constitutes personality and realizes the image and likeness of God. Man is immortal and eternal as a spiritual being belonging to the incorruptible world, but his spirituality is not a naturally given fact; man is a spiritual being in so far as he manifests himself as such, in so far as the spirit in him gains possession of the natural elements. Wholeness and unity may result from the work of the spirit in the psychic and bodily elements and constitute personality. But the natural individual as such is not yet a personality, and immortality is not characteristic of him. Natural immortality belongs to the species or to the race but not to the individual. Immortality has to be won by the person and involves struggle for personality.

Idealism affirms the immortality of the impersonal or the superpersonal spirit, of the idea and value, but not of the person. Fichte and Hegel have nothing to say about personal human immortality. Human personality and its eternal destiny are sacrificed to the idea, the value, the world-spirit, world-reason, etc. There is an element of truth in this. It is true that it is not the natural, empirical man who is immortal and eternal but the spiritual, ideal, valuable elements in him. The idealists, however, fail to recognize that this spiritual, ideal and valuable element forms an eternal personality and transmutes all man's powers for eternity; they are wrong in separating it out and abstracting it into an ideal heaven as an impersonal and non-human spirit, abandoning the rest of man to death and corruption. A realized and completed personality is immortal. But in the spiritual world there are no self-contained personalities, they are united with God, with other personalities and with the cosmos.

Materialists, positivists and followers of similar theories accept death, legitimize it, and at the same time try to forget about it, building up life on the graves. Their views show a lack of "memory of death" and are therefore shallow and commonplace. The theory of progress is entirely taken up with the future of the species, of the race, of the coming generations, and has no concern with personality and its destiny. Progress, like evolution, is absolutely impersonal. For the progressing species death is an unpleasant fact, but one that has nothing deep or tragic about it. The species has an immortality of its own. It is only for the person and from the personal point of view that death is tragic and significant.

Theories of a nobler variety take up a sad and resigned attitude towards death. They recognize the tragic nature of it, but as conceived by them the human personality, though conscious of itself, has not the spiritual force to struggle with death and conquer it. The Stoic or the Buddhist attitude to death shows impotence in the face of it, but it is nobler than the naturalistic theories which completely ignore death. The emotional as distinct from the spiritual attitude to death is always melancholy and coloured by the sadness of memory which has no power to raise the dead; only the spiritual attitude to death is victorious. The pre-Christian view of it implies resignation to fate. Christianity alone knows victory over death.

The ancient Hebrews were not familiar with the idea of personal immortality. We do not find it in the Bible. Personal self-consciousness had not yet awakened. The Jewish people were conscious of the immortality of their race but not of persons. Only in the book of Job there is awareness of personal destiny and its tragedy. It was not until the Hellenistic era, just before the coming of Christ, that the spiritual element in the Jewish religion came to be to some extent disentangled from the naturalistic, or, in other words, that personality was liberated and no longer dissolved in the collective, racial life. But the idea of immortality was truly revealed in the Greek and not in the Jewish thought. The development of that idea in Greece is very instructive. At first man was recognized as mortal. Gods were immortal, but not men. Immortality was an attribute of the divine and not of the human nature. It came to be ascribed to man in so far as the divine, superhuman element was manifested in him. Not ordinary men but demigods, heroes and demons were immortal. The Greeks knew well the heartrending grief caused by death. Greek tragedy and poetry is full of it. Man was resigned to inevitable death; he was denied immortality which the gods appropriated for themselves alone. The mortal human and the immortal divine principles were dissevered and became united only in heroes and supermen. Man descended into the subterranean realm of shadows and nothing could be sadder than his destiny. The melancholy, characteristic of the Greek and alien in this form to the Hebraic feeling for life, was rooted in the fact that the Greeks were able to reveal the human principle but not to connect it with the divine. It was the humanity of the Greeks that gave rise to the melancholy. And it was from the Greeks we heard the words that it was better for man not to be born. This is not the Indian metaphysical pessimism which denies man and regards the world as an illusion. It is an expression of human sadness for which both man and the world are real. Greeks were realists. But the Greek genius could not endure for ever the hiatus between the divine and the human world that doomed men to death and reserved immortality for the gods. A struggle for human immortality began.

The religious mythological consciousness of Greece recognized that although the divine principle was immortal and the human mortal, man's thought brought him into communion with the divine and enabled him to rise up to it and acquire it. This was the teaching of the Mysteries, of the Orphics and of Plato's philosophy. The human soul contains a divine element, but it must be freed from the power of matter; only then will man become immortal. Immortality means that the divine element of the soul forsakes the lower, material world and does not transfigure it. Immortality is ideal and spiritual. It belongs only to that which is immortal in its metaphysical nature, but is not won for elements that are mortal and corruptible, i.e., death and corruption are not conquered. According to the Orphic myth the soul descends into the sinful material world, but it must be freed from it and return to its spiritual home. That myth had a great influence upon Plato, as can be seen particularly from *Phaedo,* and is one of the most profound human myths. It is connected with the ancient doctrine of reincarnation—one of the few attempts to understand the destiny of the soul in its past and future. And Orphism does contain a certain eternal truth. Christianity teaches of resurrection, of the victory over death for every life, for all the created world, and in this it is infinitely superior to the Greek conception of immortality which dooms a considerable part of the world to death and corruption. But the Christian view does not make clear the mystery of the genesis of the soul. The presence of the eternal element in the soul means eternity not only in the future but in the past as well. That which has an origin in time cannot inherit eternity. If the human soul bears the image and likeness of God, if it is God's idea, it arises in eternity and not in time, in the spiritual and not in the natural world. But Christian consciousness can interpret this dynamically and not statically as Platonism does. In eternity, in the spiritual world, there goes on a struggle for personality, for the realization of God's idea. Our natural earthly life is but a moment in the process which takes place in the spiritual world. This leads to the recognition of preexistence in the spiritual world, which does not by any means involve reincarnation on earth.

The fact that man belongs to the eternal spiritual world does not imply a natural immortality of the spirit. Our natural world is the arena of the struggle for eternity and immortality, i.e., of the struggle for personality. In this struggle the spirit must gain possession of the natural elements of the soul and body for their eternal life and resurrection. Christianity teaches not so much of natural immortality which does not presuppose any struggle as of resurrection which presupposes the struggle of spiritual gracious forces with the powers of death. Resurrection means spiritual victory over death, it leaves nothing to death and corruption, as abstract spiritualism does. The doctrine of resurrection recognizes the tragic fact of death and means victory over it —which is not to be found in any doctrines of immortality, whether Orphic or Platonic or theosophical. Christianity alone faces death, recognizes both its tragedy and its meaning, but at the same time refuses to reconcile itself to it and conquers it. Eternal and immortal life is possible for man not because it is natural to the human soul, but because Christ rose from the dead and conquered the deadly powers of the world—because in the cosmic miracle of the Resurrection meaning has triumphed over meaninglessness.

The doctrine of the natural immortality of the human soul severs the destiny of the individual soul from the destiny of the cosmos, of the world-whole. It is metaphysical individualism. But the doctrine of the Resurrection links up the destiny of man with world-destiny. The resurrection of my body is at the same time the resurrection of the body of the world. "Body" in this connection means of course "spiritual body" and not the material frame. A complete personality is connected with the body and the eternal form of it and not merely with the soul. If it had not been for the coming of Christ and for His Resurrection, death would have triumphed in the world and in man. The doctrine of immortality is paradoxical: man is both mortal and immortal, he belongs both to the death-dealing time and to eternity, he is both a spiritual and a natural being. Death is a terrible tragedy, and death is conquered by death through Resurrection. It is conquered not by natural but by supernatural forces.

Two Russian religious thinkers have said remarkable things about life and death, from two entirely opposed points of view—V. Rozanov and N. Feodorov. For Rozanov all religions fall into two categories according as to whether they are based on the fact of birth or of death. Birth and death are the most important and significant events in life, and in the experience of them we catch a glimpse of the divine. Judaism and almost all pagan religions are for Rozanov religions of birth, while Christianity is the religion of death. Religions of birth are religions of life, since life springs from birth, i.e., from sex. But Christianity has not blessed birth, has not blessed sex, but enchanted the world with the beauty of death. Rozanov struggles against death in the name of life. In his view death is conquered by birth. Life is for ever triumphant through birth. But then death is conquered by life only for the newly born and not for the dead. To regard birth as victory over death is only possible if one is utterly insensitive to the human personality and its eternal destiny. For Rozanov the primary reality and the bearer of life is the genus and not the individual. In birth the genus triumphs over the personality: the genus lives for ever, the person dies. But the tragic problem of death is the problem of personality and not of the genus, and it is experienced in all its poignancy when personality is conscious of itself as a true reality and the bearer of life. However flourishing the life of the new generations may be, it does not remedy the unendurable tragedy of the death of a single living being. Rozanov knows nothing about eternal life, he knows only the endless life through child-bearing. It is a kind of sexual pantheism. Rozanov forgets that it was not with Christ that death came into the world and that the last word of Christianity is not death, not Calvary, but Resurrection and eternal life. Rozanov seeks escape from the horror of death in the vital intensity of sex. But sex in its fallen state is the very source of death in the world, and it is not for it to conquer death.

For N. Feodorov the problem is quite different. No one in the whole of human history has felt such pain at the thought of death as did Feodorov, nor such a burning desire to restore to life all who died. While Rozanov thinks of the children that are being born and finds comfort in the thoughts of life in the future, Feodorov thinks of the dead ancestors, and finds a source of sorrow in the thought of death in the past. For Feodorov death is the worst and only evil. We must not passively resign ourselves to it; it is the source of all evils. Final victory over death consists, in his view, not in the birth of a new life but in raising up the old, in bestowing resurrection upon the dead ancestors. This feeling for the dead shows how lofty was Feodorov's moral consciousness. Man ought to be a giver of life and affirm life for all eternity. This is the supreme moral truth, whatever we may think of Feodorov's "plan" of raising the dead.

There was a great deal of truth, but also a great deal of error, in Feodorov's attitude to death. He wrongly understood the mystery of it. Feodorov was a believing Christian, but he apparently failed to grasp the mystery of the Cross and to accept the redeeming meaning of death. Death was not for him an inner moment of life, through which every sinful life must inevitably pass. While Rozanov was blind to the Resurrection, Feodorov failed to see the Cross and its redeeming significance. Both wanted to struggle with death in the name of life and to conquer death—one through birth and the other through raising the dead to life. There is more truth in Feodorov's view, but it is a one-sided truth. Death cannot be conquered by denying all meaning to it, i.e., by denying its metaphysical depth. Heidegger rightly says that the source of death is "anxiety," but that is a source visible from our everyday world. Death is also a manifestation of eternity, and in our sinful world eternity means terror and anguish. The paradoxical fact that a man may be afraid of dying in an accident or from a contagious disease, but is not afraid of dying on the battlefield or as a martyr for his faith, shows that eternity is less terrifying when we rise above the level of commonplace everyday existence.

Both individual death and the death of the world inspire horror. There is a personal and a cosmic Apocalypse. Apocalyptic mood is one in which the thought of death reaches its highest intensity, but death is experienced as the way to a new life. The Apocalypse is the revelation about the death of the cosmos, though death is not the last word of it. Not only the individual man is mortal, but also races, civilizations, mankind as a whole and all created things. It is remarkable that the anguish of this thought is even greater than that of the anticipation of personal death. The fate of the individual and of the world are closely interconnected and intertwined by thousands of bonds. Man suffers anguish not only because he is doomed to death but because all the world is doomed to it. During historical epochs which were not marked by apocalyptic moods a man's death was softened by the thought of the race continuing for ever and preserving the results of his life and activity. But Apocalypse is the end of all perspectives of racial or cosmic immortality; in it every creature and all the world is directly faced with the judgment of eternity. There can be no comfort in the thought that we shall be immortal in our children and that our work will last for ever, for the end is coming to all consolations that are in time. Apocalypse is a paradox of time and eternity that cannot be expressed in rational terms. The end of our world will come in time, in time as we know it. But it is also the end of time as we know it and therefore lies beyond its limits. This is an antinomy similar to Kant's antinomies of pure reason. When the end comes there shall be no more time. And therefore we must paradoxically think of the end of the world both as in time and in eternity. The end of the world, like the end of each individual man, is an event both immanent and transcendent. Horror and anguish are caused by this incomprehensible combination of the transcendent and the immanent, the temporal and the eternal. For every one of us and for the world as a whole there comes a catastrophe, a jump across the abyss, a mysterious escape from time which takes place in time. The death of an individual is also a deliverance from time taking place in time. If our sinful temporal world as we know it were endless, this would be an evil nightmare, just like the endless continuation of an individual life. It would be a triumph of the meaningless. And the presentiment of the coming end calls forth, together with horror and anguish, hope and expectancy of the final revelation and triumph of meaning. Judgment and valuation of all that has happened in the world is the final revelation of meaning. The Last Judgment of individuals and of the world, interpreted in an inner sense, is nothing other than the discovery of meaning and the affirmation of qualities and values.

The paradox of time and eternity exists for the destiny both of the world and of the individual. Eternal and immortal life may be objectified and naturalized, and then it is spoken of as life in the world beyond. It appears as a natural realm of being though different from ours. Man enters it after death. But eternal and immortal life regarded from within and not objectified is essentially different in quality from the natural and even the supernatural existence. It is a spiritual life, in which eternity is attained while still in time. If man's existence were wholly taken up into the spirit and transmuted into spiritual life so that the spiritual principle gained final possession of the natural elements of the body and the soul, death as a natural fact would not take place at all. The transition to eternity would be accomplished, without the event which externally appears to us as death. Eternal life is revealed in time, it may unfold itself in every instant as an eternal present. Eternal life is not a future life but life in the present, life in the depths of an instant of time. In those depths time is torn asunder. It is therefore a mistake to expect eternity of the future, in an existence beyond the grave and to look forward to death in time in order to enter in to the divine eternal life. Strictly speaking, eternity will never come in the future—in the future there can only be a bad infinity. Only hell can be thought of in this way. Eternity and eternal life come not in the future but in a moment, i.e., they are deliverance from time, and mean ceasing to project life into time. In Heidegger's terminology it means the cessation of "anxiety" which gives temporal form to existence.

Death exists externally as a certain natural fact which takes place in the future, and it signifies that existence assumes a temporal form, and life is projected into the future. Inwardly, from the point of view of eternity unfolded in the depths of the moment and not projected into time, death does not exist; it is only an element in the eternal life. Death exists only "on this side of things," in temporal being, in the order of nature. The unfolding of spirituality, the affirmation of the eternal in life and participation in a different order of being mean transcendence of death and victory over it. To transcend death and conquer it is not to forget it or be insensitive to it, but to accept it within one's spirit, so that it ceases to be a natural, temporal fact and becomes a manifestation of meaning which proceeds from eternity.

The personal and the cosmic Apocalypse bring to light our failure to fulfill eternal righteousness in life and are a triumph of righteousness in the dark world of sin. The death of the world and of individuals, of nations, civilizations, customs, historical forms of state and society, is a catastrophic reminder on the part of truth and righteousness of the fact that they have been distorted and not fulfilled. This is the meaning, too, of all great revolutions which indicate an Apocalypse within history, and the meaning of catastrophic events in the individual life. The Revelation about the coming of the antichrist and his kingdom shows that the Christian truth has not been fulfilled and that men are incapable and unwilling to realize it. Such is the law of spiritual life. If men do not freely realize the Kingdom of Christ, the kingdom of the antichrist will be brought about with necessity. Death comes to all life which does not fulfill the divine meaning and the divine truth. The triumph of irrationality is the revelation of meaning in the darkness of sin. Hence death, both cosmic and individual, is not merely a triumph of meaningless dark forces and a result of sin but also a triumph of meaning. It reminds man of the divine truth and does not allow unrighteousness to be eternal.

Theoretically, N. Feodorov was right in saying that the world and man could pass into eternal life without the catastrophe of the end and the Last Judgment, if humanity were fraternally united for the sake of the common task of realizing Christian righteousness and raising the dead. But the world and mankind have gone too far in the path of evil, and judgment has come upon them already. Irrational, meonic freedom prevents the realization of Feodorov's "plan." He was too optimistic and under-valued the forces of evil. But the affirmation of eternity, of eternal life for every being and for all creation, is a moral imperative. Act so that eternal life might be revealed to you and that the energy of eternal life should radiate from you to all creation.

Ethics must be eschatological. The question of death and immortality is fundamental to a personalistic ethics and confronts us in every act and every expression of life. Insensitiveness to death and forgetfulness of it, so characteristic of the nineteenth and twentieth century ethics, mean insensitiveness to personality and to its eternal destiny, as well as insensitiveness to the destiny of the world as a whole. Strictly speaking, a system of ethics which does not make death its central problem has no value and is lacking in depth and earnestness. Although it deals with judgments and valuations, it forgets about the final judgment and valuation, i.e., about the Last Judgment. Ethics must be framed not with a prospect to happiness in an unending life here, but in view of an inevitable death and victory over death, of resurrection and eternal life. Creative ethics calls us not to the creation of temporary, transitory and corruptible goods and values which help us to forget death, the end, and the Last Judgment, but to the creation of eternal, permanent, immortal goods and values which further the victory of eternity and prepare man for the end.

Eschatological ethics does not by any means imply a passive renunciation of creative activity. Passive apocalyptic moods are a thing of the past, they are a sign of decadence and an escape from life. On the contrary, eschatological ethics based upon apocalyptic experience demands an unprecedented intensity of human creativeness and activity. We must not passively await in horror and anguish the impending end and the death of human personality and the world. Man is called actively to struggle with the deadly forces of evil and creatively to prepare for the coming of the Kingdom of God. Christ's second coming presupposes intense creative activity on our part, preparing both mankind and the world for the end. The end itself depends upon man's creative activity and is determined by the positive results of the cosmic process. We must not passively wait for the Kingdom of Christ, any more than for that of antichrist, but must actively and creatively struggle against the latter and prepare for the Kingdom of God which is taken by force.

To regard apocalyptic prophecies with passive resignation means to interpret them in a naturalistic sense, to rationalize them and deny the mysterious combination of Divine Providence and human freedom. It is equally wrong to take up a passive and fatalistic attitude to one's own death, to the death of personality, and regard it as a predetermined natural fact. We must accept death freely and with an enlightened mind, and not rebel against it; but this free and enlightened acceptance of death is a creative activity of the spirit. There is a false activity which rebels against death and refuses to accept it. It leads to unendurable suffering. But there is also the true activity which is the victory of eternity over death. An active spirit does not really fear death —only a passive spirit does. An active spirit experiences an infinitely greater fear and terror than that of death—the fear of hell and eternal torments. It lives through its own eternity; death exists for it not inwardly but merely as an external fact. It experiences terror at the thought of its eternal destiny and of the judgment which is in eternity.

We come here upon a psychological paradox which to many people is unknown and incomprehensible. An active spirit which has a direct inward experience of being eternal and indestructible may, so far from fearing death, actually desire it and envy those who do not believe in immortality and are convinced that death is the end. It is a mistake to imagine that the so-called faith in immortality is always comforting and that those who have it are in a privileged and enviable position. Faith in immortality is a comfort and makes life less hard, but it is also a source of terror and of an overwhelming responsibility. Those who are convinced that there is no immortality know nothing of this responsibility. It would be more correct to say that the unbelievers rather than the believers make life easy for themselves. Unbelief in immortality is suspicious just because it is so easy and comforting; the unbelievers comfort themselves with the thought that in eternity there will be no judgment of meaning over their meaningless lives. The extreme, unendurable terror is not the terror of death but of judgment and of hell. It does not exist for the unbelievers, only the believers know it. A passive spirit seldom experiences it, but an active one experiences it with particular intensity, because it is apt to connect its destiny, and consequently judgment and the possibility of hell, with its own creative efforts. The problem of death inevitably leads to that of hell. Victory over death is not the last and final victory. Victory over death is too much concerned with time. The last, final and ultimate victory is victory over hell. It is wholly concerned with eternity. Still more fundamental than the task of raising the dead, preached by Feodorov, is the task of conquering hell and freeing from it all who are suffering "eternal" torments. The final task, which ethics is bound to set us in the end, is creative liberation of all beings from the temporal and "eternal" torments of hell. If this task is not realized, the Kingdom of God cannot be realized either.

# LUDWIG WITTGENSTEIN

*Ludwig Wittgenstein* (1889–1951), Austrian-born philosopher and successor to G. E. Moore at Cambridge University, has through his books *Tractatus* and *Philosophical Investigations* exerted a major influence on contemporary philosophy.

## On Death and the Mystical

6.4      All propositions are of equal value.

6.41     The sense of the world must lie outside the world. In the world everything is as it is, and everything happens as it does happen: *in* it no value exists—and if it did, it would have no value.

If there is any value that does have value, it must lie outside the whole sphere of what happens and is the case. For all that happens and is the case is accidental.

What makes it non-accidental cannot lie *within* the world, since if it did it would itself be accidental.

It must lie outside the world.

6.42     And so it is impossible for there to be propositions of ethics. Propositions can express nothing of what is higher.

6.421    It is clear that ethics cannot be put into words.

Ethics is transcendental.

(Ethics and aesthetics are one and the same.)

6.422    When an ethical law of the form, "Thou shalt . . . ," is laid down, one's first thought is, "And what if I do not do it?" It is clear, however, that ethics has nothing to do with punishment and reward in the usual sense of the terms. So our question about the *consequences* of an action must be unimportant.—At least those consequences should not be events. For there must be something right about the question we posed. There must indeed be some kind of ethical reward and ethical punishment, but they must reside in the action itself.

*Tractatus Logico—Philosophicus*, D. F. Pears and B. F. McGuinness, trans. (London: Routledge & Kegan Paul, Ltd., 1961), pp. 144–151. Reprinted by permission of Routledge & Kegan Paul, Ltd. and Humanities Press.

(And it is also clear that the reward must be something pleasant and the punishment something unpleasant.)

6.423    It is impossible to speak about the will insofar as it is the subject of ethical attributes.

And the will as a phenomenon is of interest only to psychology.

6.43    If good or bad acts of will do alter the world, it can only be the limits of the world that they alter, not the facts, not what can be expressed by means of language.

In short their effect must be that it becomes an altogether different world. It must, so to speak, wax and wane as a whole.

The world of the happy man is a different one from that of the unhappy man.

6.431    So too at death the world does not alter, but comes to an end.

6.4311    Death is not an event in life: we do not live to experience death.

If we take eternity to mean not infinite temporal duration but timelessness, then eternal life belongs to those who live in the present.

Our life has no end in just the way in which our visual field has no limits.

6.4312    Not only is there no guarantee of the temporal immortality of the human soul, that is to say of its eternal survival after death; but, in any case, this assumption completely fails to accomplish the purpose for which it has always been intended. Or is some riddle solved by my surviving forever? Is not this eternal life itself as much of a riddle as our present life? The solution of the riddle of life in space and time lies *outside* space and time.

(It is certainly not the solution of any problems of natural science that is required.)

6.432    *How* things are in the world is a matter of complete indifference for what is higher. God does not reveal Himself *in* the world.

6.4321    The facts all contribute only to setting the problem, not to its solution.

6.44    It is not *how* things are in the world that is mystical, but *that* it exists.

6.45    To view the world *sub specie aeterni* is to view it as a whole—a limited whole.

Feeling the world as a limited whole—it is this that is mystical.

6.5    When the answer cannot be put into words, neither can the question be put into words.

*The riddle* does not exist.

If a question can be framed at all, it is also *possible* to answer it.

6.51    Skepticism is *not* irrefutable, but obviously nonsensical, when it tries to raise doubts where no questions can be asked.

For doubt can exist only where a question exists, a question only where an answer exists, and an answer only where something *can be said*.

6.52        We feel that even when *all possible* scientific questions have been answered, the problems of life remain completely untouched. Of course there are then no questions left, and this itself is the answer.

6.521       The solution of the problem of life is seen in the vanishing of the problem.

(Is not this the reason why those who have found after a long period of doubt that the sense of life became clear to them have then been unable to say what constituted that sense?)

6.522       There are, indeed, things that cannot be put into words. They *make themselves manifest*. They are what is mystical.

6.53        The correct method of philosophy would really be the following: to say nothing except what can be said, i.e., propositions of natural science—i.e., something that has nothing to do with philosophy—and then, whenever someone else wanted to say something metaphysical, to demonstrate to him that he had failed to give a meaning to certain signs in his propositions. Although it would not be satisfying to the other person—he would not have the feeling that we were teaching him philosophy—*this* method would be the only strictly correct one..

6.54        My propositions serve as elucidations in the following way: anyone who understands me eventually recognizes them as nonsensical, when he has used them—as steps—to climb up beyond them. (He must, so to speak, throw away the ladder after he has climbed up it.)

He must transcend these propositions, and then he will see the world aright.

7           What we cannot speak about we must consign to silence.


# Suggested Additional Readings

IMMORTALITY AND ESCHATOLOGY

Augustine, St. *Basic Writings of St. Augustine,* two volumes. Edited by Whitney Oates. New York: Random House, 1948. See especially Volume I, "On the immortality of the Soul." A classic pronouncement by an outstanding philosophical and theological thinker of the early Christian Church.

Baillie, John. *And the Life Everlasting.* New York: Charles Scribner's Son, 1933. A careful and persuasive work written in the Christian tradition.

Bultmann, Rudolf. *The Presence of Eternity.* New York: Harper & Brothers, 1957. A New Testament theologian discusses the eschatological element in Christian thought.

Ducasse, C. J. *A Critical Examination of the Belief in a Life After Death.* Springfield, Illinois: Charles C. Thomas, 1961.

———. *Nature, Mind and Death.* Lasalle, Ill.: Open Court Publishing Company, 1951. An American philosopher who has long been concerned with this problem discusses the meaning of life after death.

Hume, David. *Of the Immortality of the Soul,* Volume 4 of *The Philosophical Works of David Hume.* London: Longmans, 1882. An influential philosopher discusses this topic as it is seen by proponents of empiricism.

Lamont, Corliss. *The Illusion of Immortality.* New York: G. P. Putnam's Sons, 1935. A vigorous attack by a humanist on belief in immortality.

McTaggart, John McT. Ellis. *Some Dogmas of Religion.* London: E. Arnold, 1930. A British idealist philosopher affirms belief in immortality, although he does not admit to being a theist.

Niebuhr, Reinhold. *Faith and History.* New York: Charles Scribner's Sons, 1949. A valuable Christian interpretation of man's destiny by a Protestant theologian.

Plato. *Phaedo.* Trans., R. S. Bluck. New York: Liberal Arts Press, 1955. (This is a paperback edition.) This dialogue is a document basic to the study of writings on immortality.

Santayana, George. *Reason in Religion.* New York: Charles Scribner's Sons, 1905. An American philosopher of note sees immortality as rooted in man's rational nature.

Unamuno, Miguel de. *The Tragic Sense of Life.* Trans., J. E. Crawford Flitch. London: Macmillan & Company, Ltd., 1926. (Also published in paperback by Dover.) One of Spain's best-known philosophers expresses belief that immortality is based on man's capacity for "feeling" or his affective nature.

Whitehead, Alfred North. *Process and Reality.* New York: The Macmillan Company, 1936. Presents a theory of "objective immortality" which is applied to man's everyday experience rather than to a projected experience after death.

# Index of Names